JOZEF PILSUDSKI

JOZEF PILSUDSKI

FOUNDING FATHER OF MODERN POLAND

Joshua D. Zimmerman

Harvard University Press

CAMBRIDGE, MASSACHUSETTS & LONDON, ENGLAND   2022

Library of Congress Cataloging-in-Publication Data

Names: Zimmerman, Joshua D., author.
Title: Jozef Pilsudski : founding father of modern Poland / Joshua D Zimmerman.
Description: Cambridge, Massachusetts : Harvard University Press, 2022. |
Includes bibliographical references and index.
Identifiers: LCCN 2021047231 | ISBN 9780674984271 (cloth)
Subjects: LCSH: Piłsudski, Józef, 1867–1935. | Heads of state—Poland—Biography. |
Poland—History—1864–1918. | Poland—History—1918–1945.
Classification: LCC DK4420.P5 Z56 2022 | DDC 943.804092 [B]—dc23/eng/20220105
LC record available at https://lccn.loc.gov/2021047231

For my father, Norman A. Zimmerman,
who taught me how to think historically, and,
by example, the value of respect and kindness for others

Contents

Abbreviations

CKN	Central National Committee (Centralny Komitet Narodowy), established December 1915, Warsaw
CKR	Central Workers Committee of the Polish Socialist Party (Centralny Komitet Robotniczy PPS), established 1894
KNP	Polish National Committee (Komitet Narodowy Polski), Warsaw (1914–1915), Petrograd (1915–1917), Lausanne and Paris (1917–1919)
KPP	Polish Communist Party (*Komunistyczna Partia Polski*), established December 1918
LSDP	Lithuanian Social Democratic Party, established 1896 in Vilna
MKR	Local Worker's Committees of the PPS (Miejscowe Komitety Robotnicze)
NKN	Supreme National Committee (Naczelny Komitet Narodowy), established August 1914 in Kraków, dissolving itself in October 1917
ONR	National-Radical Camp (Obóz Narodowo-Radykalny), 1934, 1937–1939
OUN	Organization of Ukrainian Nationalists (founded in 1929)
PON	Polish National Organization (Polska Organizacja Narodowa), established September 1914
POW	Polish Military Organization (Polska Wojskowa Organizacja), established October 1914
PPS	Polish Socialist Party (Polska Partia Socjalistyczna), established 1892
PPS Left	Left wing of the PPS, established 1906
PPS Right	Right wing of the PPS, under Pilsudski, established 1906
PPSD	Polish Social Democratic Party of Galicia
PSL-Piast	Polish Peasant Party (Polskie Stronnictwo Ludowe "Piast")
SDKP	Social Democracy of the Kingdom of Poland (1893–1901)
SDKPiL	Social Democracy of the Kingdom of Poland and Lithuania (1901–1918)

SPD   German Social Democratic Party (Die Sozialdemokratische
            Partei Deutschlands)

TRS   Provisional Council of State (Tymczasowa Rada Stanu),
            December 1916–September 1917

ZWC   Union of Active Struggle (Związek Walki Czynnej), 1908–1914

ZZSP   Union of Polish Socialists Abroad, London (Związek Zagraniczny
            Socjalistów Polskich), 1892–1901

Note on Polish Pronunciation

Polish diacritics have been preserved throughout, with the sole exception of the subject of the book, whose name in Polish, Józef Piłsudski, is rendered Jozef Pilsudski, for the purpose of readability. I use the common English spelling for Vilna—rather than Vilnius—due to the book's pre-1939 chronology.

The following pronunciation guide is provided to help readers sound out Polish terms, names, and places. Note that Polish words have fixed stress on the penultimate syllable.

a	*a* as in "father"
ą	nasalized *a*
c	*ts*
ć	*ch*
cz	*ch*
ę	nasalized *e*
i	*ee* as in "meet"
j	*y* as in "yellow"
ń	*n* as in "onion"
o	*o* as in "go"
ó	*oo* as in "boot"
rz	*zh*
ś	*sh*
sz	*sh*
u	*oo* as in "boot"
w	*v*
y	*i* as in "it"
ź	*zh*
ż	*zh*

Maps

JOZEF PILSUDSKI

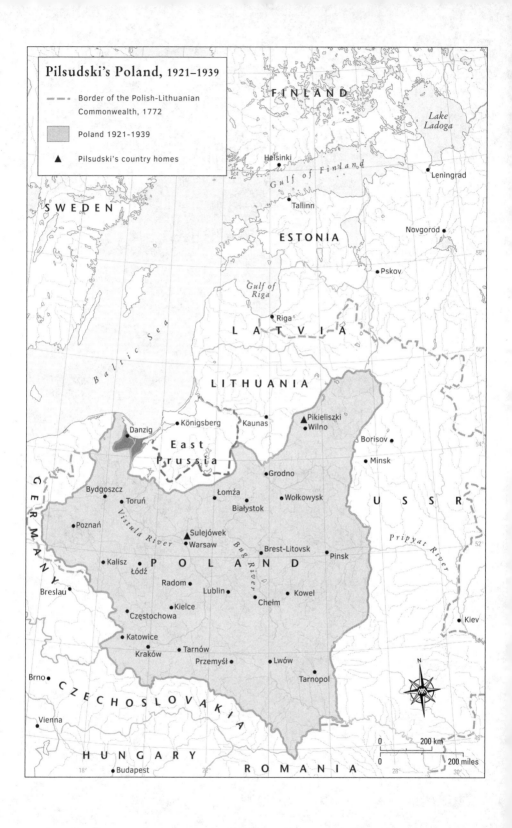

Pilsudski's Poland, 1921–1939

– – – Border of the Polish-Lithuanian
Commonwealth, 1772

Poland 1921-1939

▲ Pilsudski's country homes

FINLAND

Lake
Ladoga

Helsinki

Gulf of Finland

Leningrad

SWEDEN

Tallinn

Novgorod

ESTONIA

Pskov

Gulf of
Riga

Riga

LATVIA

Baltic Sea

LITHUANIA

Königsberg

Kaunas

▲ Pikieliszki
Wilno

Borisov

Danzig

East
Prussia

Grodno

Minsk

Bydgoszcz

Łomźa

Wołkowysk

U S S R

Toruń

Białystok

Vistula River

Poznań

▲ Sulejówek
Warsaw

Brest-Litovsk

Pinsk

Pripyat River

Bug River

Kalisz

P O L A N D

Łódź

Radom

Lublin

Kowel

Breslau

Kielce

Chełm

Częstochowa

Kiev

Katowice

Kraków

Tarnów

Przemyśł

Lwów

G E R M A N Y

Brno

C Z E C H O S L O V A K I A

Tarnopol

N

Vienna

0   200 km

0   200 miles

H U N G A R Y

Budapest

R O M A N I A

Introduction

Pilsudski saw Poland as the motherland of many nations, a
commonwealth of many cultures; he wanted it to be a state in
which not only Poles but also Lithuanians, Ukrainians, and Jews
could live in solidarity. . . . He was formed by the special climate of
the Vilna province, the common motherland of peoples from
different nations, cultures, and religions.

—ADAM MICHNIK

Pilsudski believed that he was able to shape the course of history,
that Poland's destiny was dependent on his will and that, like
other greats from the past, he should dominate over all others.

—ANDRZEJ GARLICKI

When Poland emerged from communist rule in 1989, observers noted that the country's population made a great rush to the past. "It seems sometimes that Poland is trying to take a great leap backward," observed Eva Hoffman in 1993. "There's a strengthening cult of Marshal Pilsudski."[1] Hoffman's description of a "cult of Marshal Pilsudski"—referring to Jozef Pilsudski, the dominant figure in Polish political life before World War II—aptly foreshadowed what was to come. The communist government's attempt to erase Pilsudski's memory during the Cold War was giving way to a veritable explosion of interest in him. The result was a dramatic spike in scholarly and popular publications, museum exhibitions, academic conferences, government declarations, and the renaming of streets and parks after him, as well as in the erection of Pilsudski monuments that today dot Poland's urban landscape.

The public revival of Pilsudski's memory began immediately after the fall of communism. In 1990 the largest square in Warsaw, located in the city center, was renamed Pilsudski Square. In May 1995, on the sixtieth anniversary of Pilsudski's death, the Polish parliament declared, "Jozef Pilsudski will remain in the memory of our nation as the founder of independence and as the victorious leader who fended off a foreign assault that threatened the whole of Europe and its civilization. Jozef Pilsudski served his country well, and entered our history forever."[2] In a poll taken the following year to determine the one hundred most influential figures in the country's history, Pilsudski ranked second behind Piast, Poland's first ruling monarch, from the tenth century.[3]

Following the government declaration restoring Pilsudski's place in national memory, city councils around the country erected monuments to the revered figure. In 1993 a Pilsudski monument was erected in Katowice. In August 1995 the city of Warsaw unveiled the Jozef Pilsudski Monument next to Pilsudski Square in a ceremony attended by President Lech Wałęsa; Warsaw mayor Marcin Święcicki; and Pilsudski's daughter, seventy-five-year-old Jadwiga Piłsudska, as well as his granddaughter and her husband, Joanna and Janusz Onyszkiewicz.[4] Warsaw unveiled a second Pilsudski monument outside the Belvedere Palace in November 1998 in a ceremony attended by President Alexander Kwaśniewski, Jadwiga Piłsudska, and Mayor Święcicki.[5] Other cities followed suit, with Pilsudski monuments erected in Toruń (2000), Lublin (2001), Gdańsk (2006), Kraków (2008), Białystok (2008), Sulejówek (2010), and abroad, in Brussels (2018) and Budapest (2018).

Public interest surged again in May 2015 on the eightieth anniversary of Pilsudski's death, as large posters of the familiar figure were hung all over the capital city. The country's second-largest weekly magazine devoted an entire issue to Pilsudski, with essays from leading historians, photographs, artistic portraits, and excerpts of his writings. What's more, the country's leading daily included two free photo albums in its weekend edition marking the commemorations.[6] National interest in Pilsudski culminated in the much-anticipated opening of the Jozef Pilsudski Museum in Sulejówek, outside of Warsaw, on August 16, 2020, marking the one-hundredth anniversary of the Battle of Warsaw.

The cult of Pilsudski that observers noted in the early 1990s had, in fact, been a recurring theme under communism, to the chagrin of the authorities. In 1985 an American correspondent in Warsaw reported that the fiftieth anniversary of Pilsudski's death was being commemorated "in churches all over the country. Old copies of his out-of-print books are highly coveted and his whispered image hangs over tens of thousands of sofas."[7] A writer for the *New Yorker* noted in October 1981, soon after the legalization of the trade union Solidarity, that Solidarity offices "all over the country are suddenly selling photographs of Marshal Jozef Pilsudski." When Solidarity was banned and martial law imposed shortly afterward, the same writer observed that the government was increasingly concerned by "the growing cult of Pilsudski."[8] As Jan Kubik noted in his study of the Solidarity movement, "the name and legend of Jozef Pilsudski became the focal point of many Solidarity celebrations in 1981."[9]

As the man who stood up to Bolshevik Russia and defeated its army in 1920, Pilsudski continued to be a potent symbol. In 1973, twenty-seven-year-old Adam Michnik smuggled an essay out of communist Poland and published it abroad under a pseudonym. Summarizing a letter Pilsudski had written in 1908 about humiliating oppression in tsarist Russia, Michnik commented, "Pilsudski's voice sixty years earlier was salvation for me." Through Pilsudski's writings from the period before 1914, Michnik continued, "the conquered and captive nation was regaining its real voice and dignity."[10]

The legend of Pilsudski as creator and defender of Polish statehood was evident even in his own lifetime. He was regarded by many citizens as the gallant founder of the Polish Legions in World War I, the first head of state and commander in chief of independent Poland, the brilliant military strategist who led Poland to victory over the Bolsheviks in 1920, and the "grandfather" of the people, who unwaveringly protected minority and Jewish rights. His towering stature was given permanent form upon his death in May 1935 when he was laid to rest alongside Polish royalty at Wawel Castle in Kraków.

THERE IS A STRIKING CONTRAST between the lack of knowledge about Pilsudski in today's English-speaking world and the importance attached to him during his lifetime. To a large degree this is due to the fact that Pilsudski's principal achievements—the creation and defense of an independent democratic Poland that formed a bulwark against the spread of communism and fascism—were eclipsed by events that followed his death in 1935: the country's invasion in World War II, the Soviet occupation of Eastern Europe, and the consequent obliteration of the Versailles system of sovereign democratic states lying between Soviet Russia and Germany. Sealed behind the Iron Curtain for the next forty-five years, Poland receded into the background of world affairs, and interest in its recent past correspondingly waned.

From the moment he was named head of state and commander in chief in November 1918, Pilsudski was recognized as an important figure in European affairs. In February 1920 one of the most influential British monthlies described him as having "a genius for statesmanship" and as being, "in a time when there are so many who can destroy, the greatest builder of our age." A Russian émigré writer who met Pilsudski in Warsaw in 1920 came away with the impression that Pilsudski possessed a combination of knowledge, insight, and analytical reasoning "in a higher degree than any other politician of the present time." An American professor at the University of Notre Dame who served with the American Red Cross Committee to Poland from 1919 to 1922 was granted an interview with Pilsudski, and described him as "a man of few words. Yet when he speaks you feel that he has explored your thoughts. He understands the things unsaid as well as the things unseen." An American foreign correspondent likewise referred to Pilsudski in 1928 as "one of the most remarkable figures of our times."[11]

For many, the real significance of Pilsudski was the role he played in halting a Bolshevik conquest of Europe in 1920. This sentiment was most dramatically expressed by Lord D'Abernon, the British statesman who was part of the Inter-Allied Mission to Poland in 1920, and who referred to Pilsudski's victory over Bolshevik Russia as one of the decisive battles of world history. "The history of contemporary civilization knows no event of greater importance than the Battle of Warsaw," Lord D'Abernon said in a 1930 interview marking the tenth anniversary of the battle. He added that "never had Poland's service been greater, never had the danger been more immediate. The events in 1920 also deserve attention for another reason: victory was attained above all thanks to the strategic genius of one man and thanks to the carrying through of a maneuver so dangerous as to necessitate not only genius, but heroism. . . . It should be the task of political writers to explain to European opinion that Poland saved Europe in 1920, and that it is necessary to keep Poland powerful and in harmonious relations with Western European civilization."[12]

A prominent American writer on European affairs echoed Lord D'Abernon's emphasis on the importance of Poland for international security and the preservation of the balance of power. "In all," Robert Machray wrote in 1932, "Poland may rightly be considered a bulwark of Western civilization and a powerful factor making for the equilibrium of Europe and the peace of the world." He noted that "in Marshal Pilsudski she has a great man as leader and teacher, guardian and guide. Europe, hardly less than Poland, is in his debt, for it is now perfectly clear that it was the Marshal's military genius that conceived and won the decisive battle which overthrew and put to flight the hordes of Soviets in August and September 1920."[13]

Upon Pilsudski's death in 1935, obituaries emphasized this point. The *Times* of London hailed him as having "frustrated the only serious attempt made by the USSR to carry Bolshevism across Europe by force of arms. Having established the frontiers of the new Republic, he spent the last ounce of his already overtaxed strength in consolidating its position at home and abroad." The *New York Times* stated that "in 1920, Pilsudski's defeat of an advancing Bolshevik army, in the opinion of many, spared Europe another general war." Some referred to Pilsudski as "a great soldier and capable master of statecraft." For others, Pilsudski's importance lay elsewhere. "His greatness is already looming, foreshadowing the verdict of history," wrote American biographer Grace Humphrey in 1936. "He belonged to the group, small throughout history, whom God chooses to carve out human destiny, to map roads for the nations and conduct the people along them."[14]

Alongside the praise, however, vociferous opponents at home and abroad publicly expressed opposite views. Critics regarded Pilsudski's occupation of Kiev in May 1920 as a provocative and reckless move. Although Western Europeans regarded Pilsudski's federalist plan—which ended up failing miserably—as hostile to Russia and dangerous to Europe, they anticipated accurately the future organization of European states whereby the territorial integrity of independent Ukraine was to become a chief foreign policy aim of Western European and American governments as a bulwark against Russian aggression. One observer of Polish affairs maintained that the occupation of Kiev "gave a new lease of life to the legend of Polish Imperialism and created a prejudice against the infant Republic in the minds of the Allied statesmen, and especially in England, which persists."[15] A French Army major similarly criticized Pilsudski's military thrust into Kiev as "connected with the worst escapades of recent years."[16]

At home, Pilsudski's opponents—social democrats and communists on the left and the National Democrats on the right—bitterly criticized his increasingly authoritarian style of rule and the erosion of parliamentary democracy. In 1923 an activist in the center-right Christian Democratic movement maintained that Pilsudski's ideas were murky and barren and that his style of rule was marked with megalomania and vanity.[17] An activist similarly expressed the view of many on the left after the 1926 coup d'état when he characterized Pilsudski as a dictator, an enemy of progress, and a foe of parliamentary democracy.[18]

A Dual Legacy

In this book, I portray Pilsudski's dual legacy of authoritarianism and pluralism: he was a military leader who used extralegal, strong-arm tactics to suppress his opponents while safeguarding and protecting minority rights. On the one hand, he was an exceptional figure who marched against the broader trends of totalitarianism and anti-Semitism taking root in Central and Eastern Europe between the two world wars. Pilsudski, who legally took absolute power in November 1918, believed in a pluralistic society where all law-abiding citizens received equal treatment and protection, although this principle began to erode after 1926. As one historian commented, "Pilsudski was far more respectful of cultural pluralism than most interwar European leaders."[19] The last nine years of Pilsudski's rule, on the other hand, saw the marked erosion of the parliamentary democratic system in part because Pilsudski was unable to pass through the Sejm meaningful constitutional reform that would allow the government to function smoothly.

Pilsudski linked the support for tolerance and diversity to his federalist plan, which favored the organization of European states along national—not imperial—lines. The central idea behind this project was the political sovereignty of Ukraine, either in federation with Poland or as an independent state. "Poland cannot be truly independent between two giants," Pilsudski commented in 1919. "As long as many nations are enslaved by Russia, we cannot look calmly into the future."[20]

One of Pilsudski's distinctive features as a statesman was his support for federalism, cultural pluralism, and minority rights. Nowhere is Pilsudski's positive legacy more pronounced than in his relations with Poland's Jews, the second largest Jewish community in the world before 1939. Upon his death, the outpouring of grief among Polish Jews was unmistakable. This special relationship is widely noted in the scholarly and memoir literature.[21] Dina Abramowicz, who grew up in Vilna between the two world wars, vividly recalled the day Pilsudski died. "We felt like a dark cloud was hovering over the Jews of Poland—that difficult times were ahead," she said.[22] Rafael Scharf, a Polish Jew who grew up in Kraków between the wars, recalled the same day: "I remember that my father, usually wrapped up completely in his daily cares, cried on hearing the news of the Marshal's death. I was startled by this reaction; I was not used to seeing my father moved to tears by matters of that sort." Scharf's father "shared a perception common among Jews in Poland that Pilsudski . . . would protect them . . . and that with his passing away history would take a more threatening, dangerous course. That premonition proved accurate all too soon."[23]

Another Polish Jew from Kraków, Irena Bronner, remembered frequent discussions in her home about rising anti-Semitism. She wrote that "a kind of cult of Pilsudski dominated in our home. That we, [Jewish] children, loved 'grandfather' was nothing unusual. . . . My parents simply believed in him and received the news of his death as a heavy blow."[24] Alexander Blumstein, although only five at the time, remembered the Polish leader: "Jozef Pilsudski was himself not an anti-Semite. In fact, he tried hard to control the tide of anti-Semitism, but this was a difficult task. [He] died in 1935 and I vaguely remember fear and gloom sweeping over us at the time."[25] Sixty-year-old Wiktor Chajes, a Jewish banker who had served in Pilsudski's Legions during World War I, jotted down his thoughts after Pilsudski's death. "For me," Chajes wrote on May 13, 1935, "Marshal Pilsudski was everything: he *was* the homeland. I fear what fate has in store for us. I fear that my heart belonged so entirely to him, and that my faith [in Poland] was my faith in him alone. . . . He brought us out of the country of captivity and made me a free son of Poland." He continued, "My tears are the tears of a son over his father's grave."[26]

The legend of Pilsudski as tolerant and unbiased was also based on his early years as leader of the Polish Socialist Party before 1914, where Polish Jews, like Feliks Perl and Stanisław Mendelson, were some of his closest collaborators.[27] "The Marshal in his revolutionary days," one historian noted, "had taken little account of which comrade was Jewish and which was not, and his sense of history led him to recognize the Jews as a part of Poland's heritage."[28]

Many Jews also fought in the Polish Legions during World War I. It is not surprising, then, that the vast majority of Jews were relieved when Pilsudski took power in 1926 after three years out of office, "not because they opposed democracy," Ezra Mendeslohn observed, "but rather because they regarded Pilsudski as a moderate nationalist, a federalist, . . . a bitter enemy of the [right-wing] National Democrats, and a former socialist opposed to antisemitism as a political or economic weapon. To a certain degree, Pilsudski's ten years in office as the supreme arbiter of Poland's fate justified these expectations. He was successful in holding the extreme antisemites in check and welcomed the participation of Jews in his government lists during elections to the Sejm."[29]

The legacy of Pilsudski as tolerant and benevolent is inscribed in the permanent gallery of the POLIN Museum of the History of Polish Jews in Warsaw. On May 12, 2020, the POLIN Museum marked the 85th anniversary of Pilsudski's death with a public statement on its website. "There were a number of reasons why the majority of Polish Jews held a positive opinion on Pilsudski," it read. "Pilsudski became an embodiment of Poland which welcomed Jews as equal citizens."[30] To be sure, this adoration was not confined to Poland's Jews. The famous wartime courier of the Polish government-in-exile, Jan Karski, recalled the way Pilsudski was discussed in his home as a child in Warsaw. "My mother was a fanatical admirer of Pilsudski," Karski remarked in an interview in the 1990s. "She never spoke of him as Marshal Pilsudski but only as Father of the Homeland [Ojciec Ojczyny]."[31]

The imposition of authoritarian rule after 1926, though, forms the background to a dark side of Pilsudski's legacy. This period brought abuses of power and the gradual erosion of parliamentary democracy. Pilsudski's abrupt and violent return to power in May 1926 in a military coup came after three days of fighting between government and pro-Pilsudski forces. The country was startled by the civil unrest that led to the deaths of 215 soldiers and 164 civilians, with 1,500 wounded.[32] Spilling blood on the streets of Warsaw was never Pilsudski's intention, but it was the direct result of his extralegal, military actions.[33] The needless military and civilian casualties continue to be part of family histories. One Polish woman I corresponded with, born in 1947 and raised in communist Poland, recalled that her grandfather had been a colonel in the Polish Army in 1926 and had fought during the coup on the side of government forces. Her mother, she recalled, "would reproach Pilsudski for his assault on the young democracy." What's more, her mother "was proud of my grandfather's loyalty to President Wojciechowski which actually cost him his military career."[34]

New parliamentary and presidential elections were held shortly thereafter, but Pilsudski's personal rule was now nearly absolute, even if he allowed parliamentary opposition parties and their presses to function. After 1926 the Pilsudski government repressed political opponents perceived as existential threats to the regime. The most notorious case was the so-called Brześć Trials, which followed the arrest in August 1930 of twenty former members of the parliamentary opposition interned at a prison in Brześć without formal charges for fourteen months before they were put on trial in October 1931. These included longtime and well-respected politicians such as Adam Ciołkosz, Herman Lieberman, and Adam Pragier of the Polish Socialist Party, as well as Wincenty Witos (a former prime minister) and Adolf Sawicki of the Peasant Party. The trial lasted three months, leading to convictions in January 1932.[35]

The second development that contributed to Pilsudski's dark legacy—particularly in communist Poland—was the signing of a nonaggression pact with Nazi Germany in January 1934 and the establishment of an internment camp for political prisoners at Bereza Kartuska in July of the same year. Inmates under Pilsudski's government included communists, Ukrainian nationalists, and members of the banned, fascist-leaning National Radical Camp (ONR).[36] The German-Polish Non-Aggression Pact Pilsudski signed in January 1934 was a step that Polish critics, Western democratic leaders, and Soviet Russia alike regarded as a dangerous diplomatic move.[37] Yet Pilsudski decided on a negotiated treaty with Nazi Germany only after his proposal to France for a joint military strike on Germany was rejected. To be sure, this was by no means the first time Pilsudski's foreign policy raised concerns abroad. The several border wars he initiated in 1918–1920 were regarded as dangerous and irresponsible ventures by the Western democracies—with the crucial exception of France, which generally supported Pilsudski. The third development was Pilsudski's approval, one month before he died, of a new constitution that gave permanent form to authoritarian rule by severely eroding the power of the legislature.[38]

Pilsudski Literature

It is instructive to understand how Pilsudski has been portrayed in the historical literature. As modern Poland's founding father, first commander in chief, and head of state, Pilsudski is the subject of a vast literature. His legendary stature, in fact, appeared in the earliest works published before 1918. In the first biography ever published, which appeared in 1915, the author, Wacław Sieroszewski, a fifty-seven-year-old member of the 1st Cavalry Regiment of the Polish Legions, aimed to tell the story of Pilsudski to the wider public. Discussing the fanatical loyalty of the soldiers under Pilsudski's command as well as Pilsudski's growing popularity among the masses, Sieroszewski described the national figure in the following manner: "For the broad masses of people, Pilsudski is regarded as a symbol of the unbending struggle for spiritual good, for the liberation of our homeland, for individual and national dignity, and for a better, more just . . . and brighter future."[39]

In the first biographical study of Pilsudski after 1918, one of his loyal followers portrayed him as a legend in the making. "Pilsudski is today the living symbol of Poland," wrote Janusz Jędrzejewicz in 1919, "representing her conscience and longing into the future."[40]

Pilsudski was portrayed as a gallant military hero by several foreign authors, including Alexander Bruce Boswell, an Oxford history graduate. In his study published in 1919, after Poland's resurrection as a nation, Boswell wrote that Pilsudski was acclaimed as a "national hero" and "the successor of Kościuszko."[41] Another British author, Sisley Huddleston, was similarly lavish in his praise, writing in 1920 that Poland's leader was "the man who has not only hewn out a territorial Poland, but who has given Poland a soul."[42]

A contemporaneous work noted Pilsudski's extreme popularity and charisma. "In my opinion," the author writes, "there is in the personality of the Chief of the State that vital magnetic quality which defies analysis but which all great leaders of men possess in some degree."[43] A professor at the Jagiellonian University, in a study published in 1933, wrote that "order was introduced by the Pilsudski regime after 1926, when Parliament no longer hampered . . . constructive efforts."[44] With Pilsudski in power, the professor continued, conditions for the Jews had improved. "It was only under the rule of Marshal Pilsudski since 1926," he wrote, "that the tension between Poles and Jews began visibly to diminish."[45]

In the period between Pilsudski's death in 1935 and the outbreak of war in 1939, a few scholarly and more popular biographies began evaluating Pilsudski's life and legacy. One, by Grace Humphrey, was published in the United States in 1936. The late Polish leader's importance, Humphrey wrote, was so enormous for the people of Poland and Europe that his true significance could not yet be ascertained: "Two or three generations must pass before there is perspective enough to see [Pilsudski] in relation to his era, to Poland's history, to the rest of Europe, to the world. As commander in chief in 1920, as executive, as advisor in financial matters, as initiator of plans for the Foreign Office, he gave a monumental service to the reborn state. Separately these speak of greatness. All of them together arouse our admiration." She concluded that "the merest outline of his life is a summary of the story of Poland."[46]

In another 1936 biography, Robert Machray stressed Pilsudski's singular importance in the early history of the state. "The work Pilsudski had to do in the making of the Polish Republic," Machray noted, "might well have daunted and defeated a spirit and a heart less strong and courageous than his own. Virtually a new state had to be created out of chaos."[47] In 1939, the British historian William F. Reddaway likewise argued that "the regeneration of Poland was in great measure the work of one rare man—Marshal Pilsudski."[48]

Standing out among all the studies on Pilsudski published before World War II is the pioneering work of Władysław Pobóg-Malinowski. His massive two-volume biography, published in 1935, numbered 1,022 pages and covered the subject's life only to the year 1908.[49] Although deeply partisan—the author was a Pilsudski loyalist—it was the only biography before 1939 based on extensive archival research. Pobóg-Malinowski's landmark biography was followed by various initiatives to promote the study of Pilsudski's life and thought. After Pilsudski's death, the Research Institute for the Study of Modern History in Warsaw was renamed the Jozef Pilsudski Institute for the Study of Modern Polish History, dedicated to collecting and preserving documents on the Polish leader. Its most important achievement was the publication, in 1937–1938, of Pilsudski's collected writings, totaling ten volumes and numbering 2,700 printed pages.[50]

The largely positive image of Pilsudski in studies appearing before 1939 was reinforced during World War II in *The Cambridge History of Poland,* published in 1941. In the aftermath of Poland's destruction, Pilsudski was portrayed as the founder of independent Poland who helped to establish its democratic institutions and promote minority rights. The Cambridge history attributed Pilsudski's coup in 1926 to the inflexibility of the parties in power to modify or amend the 1921 constitution that had undermined the office of the president and led to extreme fragmentation, crippling gridlock, instability, and an unstable currency, arguing that "the great majority of the nation" approved of Pilsudski's actions.[51] His support for minority rights never wavered, the Cambridge history stated, adding that "anti-Semitism in particular [Pilsudski] would not tolerate, and he encouraged the depressed Jews to look to him for protection."[52] In its final summation, the Cambridge history concluded: "[Pilsudski] had the combination of qualities which his country needed at a critical time, in action vigorous and relentless, in council resourceful and subtle. His powerful intelligence was wholly realistic.... [with] a clearness of vision which enabled him to foresee events in a manner which seemed to his followers miraculous."[53]

Oscar Halecki, a Polish historian who immigrated to the United States in 1940 and became a university professor, published an English-language history of Poland in 1943. Here, Pilsudski is portrayed in both a positive and a negative light for the first time. While recognizing the central role Pilsudski played in founding the state and preserving its frontiers, Halecki did not let the marshal off the hook for his extralegal, authoritarian actions. Describing Pilsudski's decision to arrest and imprison members of the parliamentary opposition in 1930, Halecki concluded that Pilsudski "once more took violent measures, condemning [parliament's] leaders to a cruel imprisonment at Brześć in the autumn of 1930, thereby arousing universal indignation."[54]

During the Cold War, two historiographical camps emerged. Behind the Iron Curtain in communist Poland, a dark-legend camp adhered to a government position characterizing Pilsudski as a fascist dictator, an enemy of freedom and democracy. In foreign affairs, this group portrayed Pilsudski as an imperialist who sought the annexation of Russian lands. Using arguments from Pilsudski's political opponents from the interwar period, the dark-legend camp hammered away at Pilsudski's legacy. "As a nationalist and an enemy of the Russian Revolution," we read in a 1953 scholarly work, Pilsudski "collaborated with the bourgeoisie and betrayed the working classes." During World War I, it was argued, Pilsudski was an agent of Austrian intelligence and of German imperialism.[55] In the 1926 coup d'état, he "betrayed the interests of the Polish nation" and became "the creator of a fascist state."[56]

Outside Poland, meanwhile, the dark-legend camp could be found on the opposite end of the political spectrum among Polish writers who had fled communist Poland and were living in Western Europe. Followers of the extreme right-wing National Democrats, these writers were inspired by the ideas of the movement's founder, Roman Dmowski. Their most prominent spokesperson was Jędrzej Giertych, who in the 1970s and 1980s argued that Pilsudski was a Bolshevik who imposed a foreign and hostile ideology on the country.[57]

It was Warsaw University historian Andrzej Garlicki who produced the first full-length scholarly biography, which constituted both a continuation of and a departure from the dark-legend camp. On the one hand, the work is a relentless assault on the character and personality of Pilsudski, emphasizing above all his failures and authoritarian style of rule. Written with an eye to censorship, the work is organized unevenly, with great detail and attention to certain periods such as Pilsudski's early life before 1914 and his rule in 1926–1935. In contrast, Garlicki pays much less attention to the period of Pilsudski's greatest achievements: as founder of the Polish Legions in World War I, as founder of the reborn state in 1918, and as commander in chief during Poland's victory in the 1920 Polish-Soviet war. The book's emphasis on failures is reflected in the voluminous chapters on the 1926 coup d'état and the so-called Brześć affair of 1930, when Pilsudski arrested and imprisoned twelve members of parliament whom he accused of plotting to overthrow him.[58] And yet it is precisely in Garlicki's account of these controversial actions that we observe a real departure from the dark-legend camp. Instead of characterizing Pilsudski's rule after 1926 as fascist, Garlicki pointed out that "he had no wish to flaunt his absolute power. He was quite willing to share it with . . . the parliament. This did not alter the fact that what was his to give was also his to take back."[59] What's more, Garlicki emphasized, Pilsudski "allowed the continued existence of legal opposition parties and of their presses" even after the 1930 Brześć affair. He thus qualified the dark-legend camp's characterization of Pilsudski, arguing instead that "his was a dictatorship incomparably milder than in other countries."[60]

Outside of Garlicki and the dark-legend camp, a more accurate reflection of Polish attitudes to Pilsudski was expressed in an essay smuggled out of Poland and published abroad. In 1973, twenty-seven-year-old Adam Michnik's essay on Pilsudski, written under a pseudonym, appeared in the Paris-based monthly *Kultura*.[61] "Pilsudski saw Poland," Michnik wrote, "as the motherland of many nations, a commonwealth of many cultures; he wanted it to be a state in which not only Poles but also Lithuanians, Ukrainians, and Jews could live in solidarity." Pilsudski's pluralistic concept of the state "was airtight, impermeable to the germ of chauvinistic demagoguery."[62] Michnik concluded, "If we try to rediscover a formula for tolerance and harmony, the patron of our quest will be . . . none other than Jozef Pilsudski."[63]

Michnik's perspective, never allowed to be shared inside communist Poland, mirrored the overwhelmingly positive views expressed in the white-legend camp in historical writing predominating in the West. The most influential historian of the white-legend camp during this time was Wacław Jędrzejewicz, whose 1982 popular biography was for many years the only one available in English.[64] Jędrzejewicz describes Pilsudski unabashedly as a national hero whose central achievements were forming the Polish Army during World War I, presiding over the state in 1918, and preserving Poland's boundaries in the 1920 Polish-Soviet War. "The further we are from the time of his death," Jędrzejewicz reflected, "the more strongly his image, his life and his deeds, emerge as great examples to follow, as a bedrock of strength that we can depend on." He pointed to ordinary Poles' continuing admiration for Pilsudski: "A symbol of esteem for Jozef Pilsudski are the fresh flowers always placed on his coffin, alongside the graves of the Polish kings, as well as the school emblems of the youngsters who rip them from their sleeves and lay them at the feet of the Great Master."[65] Jędrzejewicz concluded, "He gave Poland . . . freedom, boundaries, strength and respect. That is how the history of Poland will record him."[66] Prominent historians of Poland from the Cold War down to the present, including Adam Zamoyski, Piotr Wandycz, Norman Davies, and Antony Polonsky, frequently comment on Pilsudski in their works, portraying his role in the restoration of Poland in a positive light while criticizing the marshal for the 1926 coup and the erosion of democratic norms and institutions that followed.

Historians began to transcend the two mutually exclusive camps in the late 1980s. As the censors in communist Poland relaxed their hold, several prominent scholars published more balanced works on Pilsudski.[67] After 1989, scholarly circles in postcommunist Poland took up the study of Pilsudski's life and thought, a response in part to the increased interest in the subject in the country at large. Popular biographies and photo albums began to proliferate.[68]

In several key works appearing since 1989, the picture of Pilsudski has become increasingly nuanced and balanced. The most important scholarly biography is undoubtedly that of Włodzimierz Suleja.[69] Suleja, who holds a doctorate in history from Wrocław University, conducted the bulk of his research at the Pilsudski Institute in New York. He paints a complex picture of Pilsudski devoid of the sharp, partisan tone of Garlicki's work. Although sparsely documented, Suleja's biography represented a new direction in the literature on Pilsudski, highlighting both positive and negative traits.[70] Despite the emerging consensus since 1989, debates over Pilsudski's legacy continue among professional historians. While the vast majority of scholarly works on Pilsudski since 1989 are balanced, remnants of the dark-legend camp occasionally surface.[71]

HOW, THEN, ARE WE TO understand this polarizing, enigmatic statesman about whom so much has been written? Pilsudski's transformation from democratic to authoritarian ruler developed during the period between the two world wars when he became Poland's dominant figure. So much did his style of rule change that he is often portrayed as if he were two entirely different men: the Pilsudski of 1918–1922, when he presided over the creation of a parliamentary, constitutional democracy; and the Pilsudski of 1926–1935, when he returned to power through a military coup d'état, tampered with the opposition press, arrested some of his political opponents, and presided over the transition to authoritarian government.

Pilsudski, to be sure, was modern Poland's greatest champion for freedom and independence. As commander of the First Brigade during World War I, reborn Poland's first commander in chief, first head of state, and first marshal, who personally led his troops into battle in the 1920 Polish-Soviet War, history has anointed him as modern Poland's founding father. In the first years of Poland's independence, which saw the settlement of the frontiers,

the formation of a freely elected parliament, and the adoption of a liberal constitution, Pilsudski represented the democratic wing in Polish political life.
During his second period of rule between 1926 and 1935, however, Poland witnessed an abrupt transformation into an authoritarian state, beginning with
Pilsudski's coup d'état in May 1926. For the remaining nine years of his rule
before his death in 1935, Pilsudski positioned himself in foreign affairs as defender of Poland's freedom against Germany and Soviet Russia. At home,
however, he abandoned the principle of democracy as freedom bound by the
rule of law.[72]

At the very moment of the restoration of Polish independence in November 1918, Pilsudski assumed power but did not seize it. Poland's acting
authorities—the Regency Council—reached out to him. Having been released
from a German military prison only three days before, Pilsudski was asked
to serve as commander in chief on the day Poland became a state. Three days
later, on November 14, 1918, the Regency Council voluntarily disbanded and
named Pilsudski head of state, entrusting him with the task of forming a provisional government.

Having the entire authority of the state in his hands, Pilsudski ordered
a speedy transition to democracy. He announced the formation of a provisional government on November 18, 1918, and set a date for elections to a
legislative parliament for January 28, 1919. In the two-month period before
the elections, when Pilsudski ruled as a de facto dictator, he repeatedly assured the press that he had no intention whatsoever of betraying the public's trust. In December 1918, for example, he told a *New York Times* correspondent in Warsaw that he was a democrat by conviction and an admirer
of the United States.[73]

When the election took place as planned, and the freely elected parliament
held its first session on February 10, 1919, Pilsudski addressed the assembly,
stressing the need to strengthen and deepen the country's ties with Western
democracies. Poland had to adopt these policies, he said, not only to secure
its frontiers but also out of ideological affinity. "In our foreign relations," he
said, "there is one ray of hope, the tightening of the bonds of friendship which
unite us with the Entente Powers. There has long been the closest sympathy
between Poland and the democratic peoples of Europe and America," he said,
interrupted upon enunciating "America" by thunderous applause and chants
of "Long Live Wilson!"[74] He continued: "This sympathy has increased since

the victorious armies of the Allied Powers broke the last vestige of the power of our oppressors and have freed Poland from her servitude."[75]

In a dramatic moment at the speech's end, Pilsudski tendered his resignation, handing over power to parliament to choose a new head of state. Even though he was reinstated on the same day by unanimous vote, the act of resignation itself reflected Pilsudski's fidelity at the time to a democratic, legal transition of power. Two years later, in March 1921, Poland's parliament adopted the country's first constitution, granting equality before the law, civil liberties, minority rights, an independent judiciary, universal suffrage, and a free press, all of which Pilsudski wholeheartedly championed. Under his rule and guidance, therefore, Poland reborn became a liberal democratic republic in the heart of Europe, one that under his command had staved off a Bolshevik invasion and now was to form a permanent barrier against the spread of communism from the east.

The beginnings of Pilsudski's departure from fidelity to the rule of law can be traced to the assassination of Poland's first president, Gabriel Narutowicz, on December 16, 1922, after a mere five days in office. The assassination had followed a vicious smear campaign by Pilsudski's right-wing opponents, who had argued that Narutowicz had been elected not by a majority of ethnic Poles but with the help of the national minorities—the Jews in particular. The fact that they were unwilling to accept the legitimate outcome of a free and fair election changed Pilsudski. His indignation turned to extreme cynicism when, in the weeks after the execution of the assassin, right-wing opposition papers praised the assassin as a "true patriot" and "national martyr," coupled with police reports showing hundreds of cases where Poles had placed the assassin's photograph in their window as a display of veneration. Pilsudski vowed he would never allow that same right-wing opposition—whom he believed never accounted for their role in the assassination—to rule.

Profoundly disillusioned, Pilsudski withdrew from public life in 1923 and moved with his family to their country home outside of Warsaw. On May 10, 1926, a new government was named that for the first time consisted exclusively of right-wing populists and nationalists, led by the very leaders who had tried to delegitimize Narutowicz after his election. Pilsudski decided to take action. When, accompanied by loyal armed forces, he marched on Warsaw two days later to order Poland's president to dissolve the government, Pilsudski believed he was acting in Poland's best interests by restoring order to a country that was descending into chaos at a time when Germany and Soviet Russia had just signed a pact of mutual assistance (the Treaty of Berlin). When Poland's president refused to back down, Pilsudski seized power after three days of fighting in the capital between government and pro-Pilsudski soldiers. The coup revealed Pilsudski's willingness to act outside the law when he believed it was in the country's best interest.

Shortly after the coup, Pilsudski sat down in Warsaw with a foreign affairs correspondent for the Paris-based *Le Matin*. After clarifying that the constitution and parliament would remain intact, the reporter commented, "You don't speak at all, Marshal, like a dictator," to which Pilsudski replied, "No! I am not in favor of dictatorship in Poland." To the question of whether he would run for president, Pilsudski took a swipe at the constitution, saying that it had to be amended to allow for efficient government. "The president is obligated to swear that he will defend this country and the national honor, but he is given no authority to carry this out," he said. "I would prefer a list of candidates and not to be alone, for I would like, in accordance with other candidates, to take the initiative together in order to say that the Polish constitution is bad in its limitation of the powers given to the president."[76] Pilsudski emphasized that he was not advocating absolute power for the sitting president. To the contrary, he referred to the United States of America as the ultimate guide for constitutional reform:

> When I look at the history of my country, I do not believe that it can be governed by coercion. I do not like coercion. . . . I have a different conception of the head of state. He must be given the right to hasten decisions about vital issues. My country inherited the laws and regulations of three states, and still new ones have been added. All this must be simplified in restoring authority to the president. I am not saying that we must imitate exactly the United States of America, where the great power of the federal government is balanced by the autonomy of the individual states. But we must seek something of this kind and apply it to Poland.[77]

In Pilsudski's view, a generation would have to pass before Poland was ready to apply the American model. "Our generation is not perfect, but it has some right of consideration. The next generation will be still better," he reflected in the same interview. What he said in public he repeated in private. As he told a trusted advisor in the weeks after the coup, "I do not want to be Mussolini nor do I want to go around with a whip."[78]

During the last period of his rule, Pilsudski did not hesitate to suppress harshly critical views of himself and the ruling government. When Pilsudski stepped down as prime minister in June 1928, and then publicly castigated the parliament in unsavory language, the central organ of the country's powerful socialist party took offense at the marshal's tone and decided to run an editorial the following day. Before the morning edition appeared, the government confiscated the paper, allowing it to be reissued with a blank space where the article had originally appeared.[79] When, in September 1929, Pilsudski wrote a scathing critique on parliamentary gridlock, the opposition Peasant Party issued a resolution calling for the resignation of the current cabinet but also an end to Pilsudski's domination of political life. When the Peasant Party printed the resolution in its central organ, the government confiscated that issue, claiming it constituted incitement to violence.[80]

Pilsudski's willingness to periodically violate the opposition's right to freedom of the press raised concerns in foreign diplomatic circles. In December 1931, for example, Pilsudski complained about an American newspaper that had printed an interview with the chairman of the US Senate Foreign Relations Committee, who believed Poland should return territory to Germany for the cause of peace. Pilsudski had evidently expressed the opinion that the US government should have instructed the press to refrain from disseminating views that were harmful to the public good and contradictory to the long-standing American position of adherence to the terms of the Treaty of Versailles. The US chargé d'affaires in Poland, John C. Wiley, noted: "That political personages and the press in the United States should be free in their utterances from the influence of governmental pressure is doubtless not fully understood by Marshal Pilsudski."[81]

It is significant that although Pilsudski's style of rule changed from democratic to authoritarian, his foreign policy favoring strong ties with the Western democracies remained unchanged. No example is more representative than the starkly different manner in which he received two prominent foreign dignitaries in the last year of his life. In April 1934, Louis Barthou became France's first foreign minister to make an official state visit to reborn Poland.

The French ambassador to Poland described the atmosphere of the meeting: "Marshal Pilsudski gave Mr. Barthou an exceptionally friendly welcome," he wrote, adding that Mr. Beck, Poland's foreign minister, "told us that the Marshal had never shown so much friendship towards a foreign personality."[82] In contrast, Pilsudski snubbed German propaganda minister Joseph Goebbels when he came to Poland in June 1934 on a private visit. Pilsudski kept the German minister waiting before replying to a request for a meeting, then agreeing to a brief, thirty-minute exchange. "The fact that Marshal Pilsudski kept Mr. Goebbels waiting for twenty-four hours before agreeing to receive him," a British paper commented, "made this first visit of the Nazi minister to the Polish capital a very disappointing affair."[83]

Pilsudski's dual legacy continues to define Poland's enigmatic leader. To his fervent critics during his lifetime and after, including the official position of the communist government, Pilsudski was portrayed as an enemy of progress, a dictator responsible for the internment of political opponents in Brześć and at the camp for political prisoners in Bereza Kartustka. Overshadowing the dark legacy, however, are the striking statues and the naming after him of parks, streets, bridges, museums, academic institutes, sports arenas, and railroad stations all over Poland. At the moment of Poland's restoration as a state in November 1918, when all authority was placed in Pilsudski's hands, the country saw him as a symbol not only of national pride but also of a new open and free society. One day after Poland became independent, on November 12, 1918, a group of high school students in Warsaw circulated a leaflet calling on the new country to back Pilsudski not only because they considered him a strong and decisive leader but also because he was a champion for democracy: "The eyes of the entire nation are turned to Pilsudski as the only person able to unify the country under a democratic banner. [By supporting Pilsudski], we are spreading the principles of democracy by creating a homeland of freedom and equality."[84]

CHAPTER 1

Childhood and Adolescence

This brother of mine has insane luck. Everything good comes
to him and he always puts himself at the center of things.
He talks a lot (but does very little). Foolishly believed, everyone
raves about him.

—DIARY OF SIXTEEN-YEAR-OLD BRONISŁAW PILSUDSKI ABOUT
FIFTEEN-YEAR-OLD JOZEF, VILNA, FEBRUARY 8, 1883

Jozef Klemens Pilsudski was born December 5, 1867, in Zułów, a village
thirty-eight miles northeast of Vilna, to a Polish-Lithuanian landed-gentry
family. He was the fourth child and second son of Józef Wincenty Piotr
Pilsudski (1833–1902) and Maria Billewicz (1842–1884). His ancestors had
been prominent in the region for centuries. The family name first appeared in 1539 when Bartłomiej Giniatowicz, a district administrator (*starosta*),
adopted the surname after the local village, Piłsudy, northeast of Kaunas.
Pilsudski's parents were first cousins once removed, the two families having
become linked by marriage in the eighteenth century and ultimately passing
down sizable properties to their children, including Pilsudski's grandfather
Piotr Kazimierz.[1]

In the early 1830s, Piotr's grandfather met Countess Teodora Butler, of
Scottish descent, and they married in 1833. That same year Teodora gave birth
to Pilsudski's father in Rapszany, twenty miles northeast of Kowno. From an
early age, Józef Wincenty showed leadership qualities as well as intellectual
and artistic promise. By his late teens, he had become a gifted pianist and
composer. Pilsudski's older brother, Bronisław, described their father as a

man "with a broad, encyclopedic intellect but one who was unfit for practical work."[2] Pilsudski's wife, Alexandra, described her father-in-law as an elegant and handsome man "of considerable mental gifts, cultured, extremely well-read, a brilliant pianist and a talented composer."[3]

The Pilsudski and Billewicz sides of the family were different in character and disposition. An eminent sociologist who knew the Pilsudski family, Ludwik Krzywicki, commented that the Billewicz side was frugal and cautious whereas the Pilsudski branch was impulsive and reckless with money. The Pilsudskis, Krzywicki remarked, "believed in the idea that pennies in a piggybank are there to be spent."[4] Pilsudski's father in many ways embodied the family traits.

Pilsudski's mother, on the other hand, was pragmatic and well organized. She was born in 1842 to Antoni and Helena Billewicz in Adamowo, a village in Tenenie county in Kaunas province. The Billewiczes were one of the area's oldest and most distinguished noble families.[5] Wealthier than the Pilsudskis, Maria's family lived on the estate owned by her grandfather, Kacper Billewicz. She grew up as an only child after her younger brother, Adam, died in infancy. When Maria was merely four years old, in 1846, a second tragedy struck the family when her mother died of tuberculosis. Maria's father remarried and gave over care of his daughter to her kind and generous grandfather. Fearing he was unable to provide the proper care, Kacper arranged for Maria to live with a nearby family, whose daughter, Celina, provided a much-needed playmate. Celina would remain Maria's close and loyal friend for the rest of her life.[6]

Maria's grandfather had been an influential judge who retired as head of the Vilna district court. He took a great interest in Maria's upbringing, providing excellent teachers and making sure she was well cared for. But his wealth and influence could not change the poor health Maria was born with. At age six she fell ill with inflammation of the pelvic joint, a condition that led to chronic pain and caused irregular growth, resulting in one leg being shorter than the other. While treatment by a specialist in Berlin improved her condition, the disability remained with her for the rest of her life. Maria's health problems motivated Kacper to give his granddaughter the best education possible. He employed highly regarded teachers who were "as strong and as relentless as possible so as to overcome the weakness of her body."[7] Kacper's love and care "was nevertheless mixed," one historian observed, "with a certain educational method: strict, rigid, sometimes ruthless, but with the goal of developing and deepening [Maria's] will, toughness, sense of self-respect, integrity, and courage in life."[8] At the age of nine, Maria came into extraordinary wealth, inheriting several hundred thousand rubles and three estates totaling thirty thousand acres of land. The first was in Suginty (Lithuanian: Suginicai), fifty-three miles north of Vilna, the second in Adamowo, and the third in Zułów, Jozef Pilsudski's birthplace.[9]

Maria Billewicz and Józef Wincenty Pilsudski were married on April 23, 1863, in Adamowo. The wedding took place in the shadow of the Polish insurrection that had begun three months earlier. Although he did not engage in direct combat, Józef Wincenty wholeheartedly threw his support behind the rebellion, serving as commissioner in the Lithuanian county of Rapszany, his birthplace, for the Provisional National Government in Warsaw.[10] The 1863 Polish insurrection had begun when the clandestine Central National Committee in Warsaw announced the creation of a Provisional National Government on January 22, 1863, calling upon the peoples of Poland, Lithuania, and Ukraine to support its demand for territorial separation from Russia. Fighting broke out between the poorly trained and ill-equipped Polish insurgents concentrated in the Kingdom of Poland as well as in Lithuania, in an armed rebellion that lasted more than a year and spread significantly beyond the kingdom, particularly into the northwestern provinces of tsarist Russia. During the uprising, the Polish insurgent army ranged from twenty thousand to thirty thousand men, with a total of two hundred thousand fighters taking part over the course of the uprising.[11]

In December 1863 Romuald Traugutt suspended the National Government and began ruling by decree. But the uprising began to wane without hoped-for foreign intervention from France or Britain. In April 1864 Traugutt was captured and the rebellion collapsed.[12] As losses were tallied and mass arrests took place, it became clear the Poles had a national catastrophe on their hands: 10,000 insurgents fell in battle, 669 insurrectionary leaders were rounded up and summarily executed, and 26,500 Poles were sent in chains to Siberia—16,000 from the Kingdom of Poland and 10,500 from Lithuania— many of whom never returned. In Lithuania—where the Pilsudski family lived—two hundred battles took place followed by the confiscation of eighteen hundred Polish estates.[13]

Pilsudski's parents,
Maria and Józef,
ca. 1863.

Early Childhood in the Countryside

At the beginning of 1864, as the tide of insurrection turned inexorably in favor
of the Russians, Józef Wincenty and Maria fled their home under cover of
night to evade arrest. They traveled two hundred miles eastward to Maria's
country estate in Zułów, far enough away to elude notice. In the second half

of 1864, Maria gave birth to their first child, Helena, named after her late mother. Helena was followed by Zofia in 1865, Bronisław in 1866, and Jozef Klemens in 1867. During the remaining time they lived in Zułów, Maria and Józef Wincenty welcomed three more children: Adam in 1869, Kazimierz in 1871, and Maria in 1873.[14]

Meanwhile, Pilsudski's father combined family wealth with broad ambition and an advanced education. He had graduated from the Agricultural Academy of Horki in eastern Belarus and frequently contributed articles to the Warsaw-based periodical on agriculture, *Gazeta Rolnicza* (Agricultural Gazette). In Zułów he embarked on a plan to develop advanced agriculture and industries in the area. Within a few years he had established the region's first yeast, turpentine, and brick factories.[15] He lacked managerial skills and business acumen, though, and none of his investments became profitable. He "had the irresponsibility that so often accompanies the artistic temperament," Alexandra, Pilsudski's second wife, later commented.[16] The result was that a succession of ill-conceived farming projects led the family to near financial ruin. Pilsudski's great aunt Zofia Billewicz-Zubowowa, who used to teach the children mathematics, described Józef Wincenty as a "schemer" of poorly thought-out projects, unable to implement projects effectively in the rural setting of Zułów.[17]

Józef Wincenty's dream of bringing advanced agriculture and industry to the Zułów region was nonetheless genuine. Pilsudski's father was a visionary with many ideas, including the development of a breeding farm and bringing the land under cultivation. Yet he also envisioned the transformation of Zułów into an industrial center, purchasing agricultural machinery from abroad. The paucity of skilled labor in a rural county, however, meant that such equipment went practically unused. Krzywicki noted that the local worker in the Zułów region "was uncouth. He was accustomed to using a plow and a wooden harrow but was incapable of working with a metal harrow of any variety."[18] Józef Wincenty's machinery therefore fell into disuse and disrepair, gradually becoming merely rust-covered scrap iron. Pilsudski's father attempted to recover his losses by founding a distillery. But he proved equally unfit to run that business even though the soil in Zułów was ideal for potato crops. A pattern emerged whereby Pilsudski's father chased after every new idea before completing existing projects. Józef Wincenty had extraordinary plans for Zułów and was always busy with the affairs of the estate, "taking up each new project enthusiastically but soon dropping it to begin another. He made none of them pay off and little by little got deep and deeper into debt."[19] Reflecting on his father, Pilsudski remarked that he "was an extraordinarily learned agronomist . . . but for whatever reason—God only knows— he was not able to run the large Zułów estate. He [simply] was not an administrator."[20]

Despite his father's problems, Jozef Pilsudski's early childhood was by all accounts idyllic. Located along the Mera River, the Zułów estate was surrounded by forests, fields, and meadows. The manor, built of larch wood and set on the banks of a stream, consisted of twelve bedrooms that housed the Pilsudski family, domestic servants, Maria's childhood friend Celina, and relatives. Rows of tall chestnut trees and fragrant lime trees stood alongside the house. The front had a circular lawn with a glass-roofed porch flanked by lilac bushes and a Madonna over the door.[21] Pilsudski would later write, "I was born in the country in a family of the gentry whose members, both by the long line of their ancestors and by the extent of their property, belonged to the rank that was formerly called 'bene nati et possessionati.' Since my family was numerous and our parents were very considerate and affectionate with us, I could call my childhood a country idyll."[22] Pilsudski's older brother similarly recalled that their childhood in the countryside was full of happiness and cheerfulness—a loving environment with family and relatives ever present.[23] Indeed, Józef Wincenty and Maria regularly offered their hospitality to relatives and family in need of a place to stay, including two aunts and several cousins.

The idyllic life on the country estate, however, did not wholly shield the children from the collective mourning of national defeat. Pilsudski's brother Bronisław recalled the impact of 1863, including hiding a wounded rebel in their home. The children were aware not only that their father had taken part in the uprising but also that several relatives had either fallen in battle, been imprisoned or expelled, or lost property to confiscation. This included Aleksander Pilsudski, Pilsudski's first cousin once removed, who died from battle wounds at the age of twenty-nine. Pilsudski's second cousin once removed, Leon Billewicz, was deported to Siberia for participating in the rising and died there at age thirty-one; his great uncle, Tadeusz Butler, was similarly sent into Siberian exile. Several female relatives were arrested as well, including Pilsudski's grandmother, Teodora Butler Billewicz, who was

Pilsudski and his older
brother, Bronisław, ca. 1872.

charged with material aid to the rebels. Moreover, the Butler estate in Tenenie was confiscated, forcing them to temporarily move into the Pilsudski
home in Zułów. This further increased the children's awareness of the tragedy
of 1863.[24]

It is not surprising, therefore, that Pilsudski later stressed the centrality of
the 1863 uprising. In a 1903 essay he commented that his childhood would
have been ideal "were it not for one cause of bitterness, which saddened my
father's face, drew tears from my mother's eyes, and deeply impressed our

childish minds. This bitterness was due to the national disaster of 1863, the memory of which was still fresh." He continued: "Our mother, an irreconcilable patriot, did not even try to hide from us the pain and disappointments that the failure of the rising caused her, and indeed educated us with particular emphasis on the necessity of a further struggle with our country's enemies."[25] One biographer insightfully commented, "For a whole generation at least, the spirit of the Poles was broken."[26] Bronisław acknowledged that their childhood in Zułów was wondrous, but "there were no loud parties and dancing," he commented. "Life was marked by national mourning after the insurrection."[27] He also remembered stories as a child about fallen heroes of the insurrection.

Inside the serene country home, the children benefited from a gentle and loving mother. Their father often traveled, one biographer noted, "always busy with the affairs of the estate and of the community, he gave little time to his family and left the upbringing of the children to his wife."[28] Jozef and Bronisław both pointed to their mother's infectious patriotism and national pride. But perhaps more important was what Bronisław described as her strong and honest character. Their mother, Bronisław commented, "was adored by all—her neighbors, family, local officials, and servants. She took utmost care in the highest development of our character."[29] Maria also impressed upon her children the importance of independent thinking and personal sacrifice. Pilsudski later wrote:

> I must say that from our earliest years my mother tried to develop in us independence of thought, and encouraged a feeling of personal dignity which was formulated in my mind as follows: "Only he is worthy to be called a human being who has a sure conviction and succeeds in confessing it in action without regard for the consequences."[30]

Maria looked to the nation's bards for a source of patriotism and pride for her children while instilling in them a love for Polish poetry. "The national idea based on the works of our great poets," Bronisław remarked, "was for us a type of bible. Our mother read them to us out loud in the evenings during secret gathering."[31] Alexandra Pilsudska similarly described this influence: "In the evening when servants were safely in the kitchen, Maria Pilsudski would unlock a drawer in her cabinet and take out the forbidden books of Polish history and literature to read them to her children."[32] Maria also taught her children the principle of respect for all people without regard to social rank. "She molded [in us] integrity, diligence, and sibling harmony," Bronisław remarked. "She chastised mutual complaints, promoted comradeship among the children, and forbade us to look down on others." This extended to the treatment of domestic servants. "The servants were told," he continued, "to ignore the children if they did not ask for things politely enough." Maria, Bronisław concluded, possessed "a good heart and lofty ideals."

Maria took charge of her children's education. She hired two governesses—one French and one German—but took upon herself the teaching of history and literature. In these lessons, she taught the poetry of the nation's bards: Adam Mickiewicz, Zygmunt Krasiński, and Juliusz Słowacki as well as *Historical Songs* (*Śpiewy historyczne*) by Julian Niemcewicz. The result was that the Piłsudski home, according to one historian, "was imbued with deep national tradition. Polishness—without which all would be deprived of meaning—permeated the household."[33] As Piłsudski's second wife would later write, "it was from her lips that [Piłsudski] first heard the story of Poland."[34]

Madame Piłsudski also used bedtime as an opportunity to recite poetry. This included Mickiewicz's "The Pilgrim's Litany," published in Paris in 1832 as part of the poet's messianic manifesto, *The Books of the Polish Nation and Pilgrims*. Upon publication, the demand so far exceeded supply that the work was reprinted four times in two years. "Copies were distributed throughout all the partitions, where over the course of the following decades," one scholar observed, "the *Books* became required reading for patriots and conspirators."[35] Regarded as one of Mickiewicz's finest expressions of the Polish messianic idea, the poem refers to Poland's unique, universal mission to free Europe from despotism. "From the slavery of Moscow, of Austria, and of Prussia, Deliver us, O Lord," we read in "The Pilgrim's Litany," the book's concluding poem. With remembrances of past and present wrongs, the poet's words reverberated powerfully in the Piłsudski home: "For a universal war for the Freedom of the People, We beseech thee, O Lord. For the arms and the eagles of our nation, We beseech thee, O Lord. For the burial of our bones in our own land, We beseech thee, O Lord. For the independence, unity, and freedom of our Fatherland, We beseech thee, O Lord."[36]

Maria routinely concluded her clandestine bedtime readings with verses from Krasiński, her favorite poet. In particular, she read from "Psalms for the Future" ("Psalmy przyszłości," 1847). In the poem's last line, the main character's parting words constituted a kind of spirit voice of the nation: "Poland shall be in the name of the Lord."[37] She likely also read excerpts from Krasiński's 1837 play, *Irydion,* which emphasized the messianic idea whereby partitioned Poland was destined to save and regenerate the world. "Be calm before the pride and oppression and derision of the unjust," reads an almost biblical verse. "They shall pass away, but thou and My word shall not pass away. And after long martyrdom I will send My dawn upon you. I will give you what I gave my angels before the ages—happiness—and what I promised to men on the summit of Golgotha—freedom."[38] As one literary scholar noted, "These words comforted many generations of Poles in days of misfortune and humiliation."[39]

Pilsudski recalled the importance of his mother's teachings. "From our earliest childhood," he wrote, "she made us acquainted with the works of our greatest poets, especially those which were forbidden, taught us Polish history, and bought none but Polish books."[40] The influence of the three national bards was pronounced. "It was during this time," he recounted, "that my mother pulled out, sometimes from the secret hiding place, a few books from which she read out loud to us. She made us learn verses from our national poets by heart. These moments, surrounded by secrecy and emotion, left an indelible impression on our minds."[41] Indeed, as one biographer observed, "it was a continual conspiracy in their own family."[42]

The national bards were not undifferentiated. Krasiński's conservative social and political orientation—he was the son of the landed aristocracy—was expressed in a poem written in 1845 that condemned revolutionary movements and favored cooperation between the peasants and the nobles. It was the right and duty of the latter, Krasiński believed, to lead the nation, a right conferred by history and God. The democratic-minded Juliusz Słowacki responded forcefully in a poem titled "Response to the *Psalms for the Future,*" published in 1848. Here Słowacki invoked the spirit of "the eternal revolutionary," calling for the liberation of Poland not only from foreign rule but also from aristocratic privilege. Słowacki's poetic reply to Krasiński constituted, according to one scholar, "the most revolutionary poem of Polish Romanticism."[43] Another scholar characterized the poem as "a violent attack against the traditions of the aristocratic families, proclaiming the superiority of revolutionary principles over the timid conservative policy."[44] Słowacki became the young Pilsudski's favorite poet. "I was always enchanted by Słowacki," Pilsudski wrote, "who was also my first teacher of democratic principles."[45]

The Move to Vilna

The Pilsudski children were blissfully unaware of their father's failed projects and mounting debt. Their idyllic life changed abruptly in July 1874 when a fire broke out in Zułów while their father was away and their mother was in Vilna receiving medical treatment. The fire consumed the manor house and everything around it. Much was destroyed, including the furniture, library, stables, and barns as well as the factory. In short, the entire family property now lay in ruins.[46] Initially a neighbor offered the Pilsudskis a place to stay. Sometime in the following year, in 1875, the family packed their bags and moved to an apartment in Vilna. To the young Jozef's parents, the loss of the Pilsudski fortune was devastating. For the seven-year-old Jozef, it was painful to lose his home, along with the comfort and affluent environment of the country estate. Vilna nonetheless gradually became Pilsudski's cherished hometown, where he would live for the next eleven years of his life.

The move to Vilna brought the Pilsudski children into contact with the modern world. The city was characterized by a diverse population and rapid growth. In 1875, Vilna had 77,102 inhabitants, of whom 45.9 percent were Jewish by religion and 33.6 percent were Catholic. In the course of the next quarter century, the population doubled, reaching 154,532 by 1897, at which time the mother tongue of the city's inhabitants was 40 percent Yiddish, 30.8 percent Polish, 20.9 percent Russian, 4.2 percent Belarussian, 2.1 percent Lithuanian, and 1.4 percent German.[47] In Vilna, therefore, no single ethnolinguistic group constituted a majority, making it a truly multinational urban setting. Yet Vilna was also a powerful symbol of Polish culture. Vilna University was the alma mater of such Polish literary luminaries as Adam Mickiewicz and Juliusz Słowacki, who had attended in the early nineteenth century before it was closed by the Russian authorities in 1831.

Initially Pilsudski and his brother were homeschooled. That changed in the fall of 1877 when Pilsudski, two months shy of his tenth birthday, entered the first class of the Russian State Gymnasium in Vilna.[48] On the entry exam, he had shown himself to be a very capable and advanced learner, scoring a 5, the highest mark, in every subject. With superior test scores, he was placed in the same classroom as his older brother, Bronisław. For the precocious, energetic boy, gymnasium was his first encounter with representatives of the Russian state. His view of Russia and the Russian people had already been colored, however, by an anti-Russian sentiment that had enveloped the family home. Inculcated with maternal whispers of patriotic verse, the young Pilsudski was bound to clash with the Russian gymnasium. "This," Pilsudski acknowledged, "was the disposition and these were the views—so far as a child's thoughts can be called views—with which I crossed the school threshold."[49]

Pilsudski's quick and inquisitive mind, combined with his good Russian, made school relatively easy. "As a matter of fact," he modestly wrote, "I was a fairly capable boy, my work never troubled me, and I passed easily from class to class." When asked at age sixty-three about school, he remarked that he never had to study for exams. When the interviewer queried if he meant that literally, Pilsudski replied, "I never ever studied."[50] The portrait of Pilsudski as a highly gifted child who never needed to study to do well in school is consistent with the gymnasium's own assessment. "Jozef Pilsudski does not always prepare his lesson carefully," one gymnasium teacher noted in a report card. "His written work is performed satisfactorily. In class, he tries to draw attention to himself but he has not shown any particular interest for study." His classroom teacher added a note to the file, writing, "Pilsudski possesses good ability, particularly in math, but treats schoolwork somewhat frivolously."[51]

The two brothers usually sat together in class. One classmate recalled that Pilsudski stood out among the other students. Although one of the youngest, Pilsudski behaved with unusual self-confidence, calmness, and firmness, the classmate recalled. But Pilsudski also openly defied school regulations such as the ban on speaking Polish to classmates or showing disrespect for the schoolmaster. Sixty-five years later, another classmate expressed a different impression: "The [Pilsudski] brothers did not stand out among their classmates, neither in terms of their intelligence—they were not among the top students—nor in their behavior."[52] Pilsudski, in fact, was officially reprimanded on three occasions: for speaking Polish on school grounds; for failing to

salute the governor-general of Vilna during a street parade; and for disrespect shown to the school headmaster. In a diary entry from February 1883,
Bronisław remarked that their math teacher reminded students not to speak
Polish in class or anywhere on school grounds. The teacher went as far as to
say that gymnasium students should only speak Russian on the streets of
Vilna as well. When the students questioned the latter, the teacher allegedly
shouted, "You eat Russian bread, you make use of all of the rights of Russian
citizenship and yet you don't want to speak Russian!"[53]

Pilsudski and his brother shared a sense of humiliation over the way Poland and the Poles were portrayed by the Russian teachers. Pilsudski, for example, was unable to restrain himself in school one day when the history
teacher disparaged the Polish insurrection of 1863. "The Pilsudski boys sat
in the front row. Suddenly Ziuk [Jozef] stood up, crying out something,"
one biographer wrote. "Bronisław jerked him down into his seat. But the
master had caught a bit of it and reported the boy to the principal."[54] Incensed and humiliated, Pilsudski is said to have complained to his mother.
Bronisław was present and recalled the words his mother used to try to comfort Pilsudski: "There is nothing to do, my son. You must endure and will one
day avenge. But for now [your job is to] study, study and study! And don't
ever give the slightest pretext for them to taunt you."[55]

At the beginning of 1880, twelve-year-old Pilsudski began clandestinely
putting together with Bronisław a handwritten periodical, *The Zułów Dove*
(*Gołąb Zułowski*). The brothers produced forty-six issues between January 10
and February 23, 1880.[56] The periodical provides the earliest evidence of what
Pilsudski read and thought as he was entering adolescence. It confirms his
later claims about childhood influences. *The Zułów Dove* included lyrical
songs and family stories about the 1863 uprising, biographical essays of national heroes, excerpts from Niemcewicz's *Historical Songs,* and even essays
on the struggles of Native Americans for their land. The periodical, according
to one journalist, "shows that the young Pilsudski, in his early adolescence,
was already imagining himself as a rifleman. It goes without saying that [these
essays] all possessed a huge patriotic ring and love of fatherland."[57] *The Zułów
Dove* also included personal stories about a pony named Rappan, which we
learn was Pilsudski's before the family moved to Vilna, and about a beloved
dog named Karo, revealing how much the young boy missed life in the
country. There were also children's fables that Pilsudski copied down.[58]

The Zułów Dove clearly reveals that Pilsudski had already developed an interest in Napoleon by the age of twelve. Stories about Napoleon's military victories and battles appear repeatedly in his own handwriting. These tales were a reflection of a book that fell into Pilsudski's hands at the time: a biography of Napoleon in Polish translation by Émile Saint-Hilaire.[59] "I lost my heart to Napoleon," Pilsudski remarked in 1903 about his childhood, "and everything concerning my hero filled me with emotion and inflamed my imagination." The young boy concluded from the example of Napoleon that armed struggle alone could liberate Poland: "All my dreams were then concentrated around an insurrection and an armed struggle with the Muscovites."[60] In a 1931 interview, Pilsudski's favorite topic of discussion was Napoleon, whose letters he recited by heart in the original French.[61]

Within a short time Pilsudski entered a new, more serious phase in conspiratorial activity. In the fall of 1882, at age fourteen, he, with his brother, joined a clandestine self-education group called "Union" (Spójnia) founded and led by a fellow gymnasium student, Witold Przegaliński. The group, which later came under Bronisław's leadership, by February 1883 had sixteen members, two of whom—Chonan Rappaport and Leon Jogiches—were Jewish. The organization's purpose was to strengthen patriotism through exposure to Polish literature. For the first two years Pilsudski attended infrequently, preferring instead to read on his own at home where the family possessed a substantial library. This changed in his last year of gymnasium, when he became an enthusiastic member in 1884–1885. The formation of a clandestine illegal library was a key part of the union's activities. Members paid a monthly fee that gave them borrowing privileges and allowed the group leaders to acquire books from St. Petersburg and Warsaw. By the beginning of 1884 the library contained over one hundred books, including the newest publications from illegal presses, and was eventually stored at the Pilsudski home.[62] Although the group discussed British, French, and German literature, its main interest was in Polish patriotic works. "With eagerness," one biographer commented, "they devoured works on Polish history, including histories of armed insurrections against Russia."[63] These works included memoirs of Polish insurgents but also the poetry of Mickiewicz, Krasiński, and Słowacki.

The readings and discussions eventually led Pilsudski to conclude that national independence had to be accompanied by social revolution. By age sixteen, in the fall of 1884, Pilsudski began to identify as a socialist. He attributed this to his involvement in the clandestine Vilna student group.[64] Pilsudski's brother noted that "the period of childhood dreams about armed struggle for Poland changed to . . . debates on social issues and Russian persecution." They learned about socialist movements in Western Europe and discussed socialism "as a great ethical principle for a new society."[65] Pilsudski's wife later reflected on the significance of this embrace of social—not just national—revolution. "It was a step without precedent for a member of a noble family," she wrote, "for it entailed breaking down centuries-old barriers of tradition and inherited prejudice."[66] For the Pilsudski brothers, therefore, the embrace of socialism reflected dual aspirations for national sovereignty and democratic society. The two concepts became inextricably linked.

The uprising of 1863 was often a topic of discussion in the illegal study group, especially after the first systematic history of the insurrection, published in 1882 by Bolesław Limanowski, was smuggled into Russia. Limanowski's history was received enthusiastically in particular among Polish youth, as it combined the romantic tradition of struggle for independence with a progressive social orientation. Other materials on 1863 available to the reading group included insurgents' testimonies.[67] "Today we read out loud a history of the 1863 insurrection in Lithuania," Bronisław noted in December 1883.[68] The 1863 Polish uprising was a subject to which Jozef Pilsudski frequently returned. "He would remain under the spell of the legend of 1863," stated political scientist Adam Bromke, adding that "this admiration of Pilsudski's for the uprising of 1863 played a very important part in shaping his political outlook."[69] When Pilsudski spoke on the topic in 1924, he remarked that "the year 1863 gave us an unknown greatness . . . the greatness of an effort of collective will."[70] In the last year of gymnasium, Pilsudski became more active in the illegal study group.

The last year of gymnasium was also a period that began with a tragedy in the family. The health of Pilsudski's mother had been in decline for a few years. In 1882 she gave birth to twins Piotr and Teodora, her eleventh and twelfth children, both of whom died before reaching age two. A rapid deterioration of Maria's physical and mental health followed, leaving her bedridden. On September 9, 1884, Maria, mother of ten children between the ages of three and nineteen, passed away at forty-two. Her funeral was held in the family estate in Suginty, where she was laid to rest next to her mother. Pilsudski, now sixteen, mustered the strength and psychological wherewithal to enter his last year of gymnasium. The huge vacuum left by Maria's death

Pilsudski, age seventeen
(*second from right*), with
members of a clandestine
study group from the Russian
State Gymnasium, Vilna, 1885.

was partly filled by the children's beloved aunt, Stefania Lipmanówna, to whom they now gravitated and who became their main caretaker.

Pilsudski finished gymnasium in June 1885 as a strong but not straight-A student. On his final exams, he received a 5 in history, geography, and religion; a 4 in math, Latin, and Greek; and a 3 in Russian and German.[71] The gymnasium left the seventeen-year-old youth with a bitter memory. He recalled that, yes, he had learned academically,

> but the atmosphere of the gymnasium crushed me, the injustice and the politics of the schoolmasters enraged me; the way of teaching harassed

Zofia, Pilsudski's older sister, Vilna, 1883.

and bored me. A whole ox's skin would not contain a description of the unceasing humiliating provocations from our teachers and the degradation of all that I had been accustomed to respect and love. How deep the impression of this school system was on my mind may be judged by this one fact: although I have since passed through . . . Siberia, and have had to do with a variety of Russian officials, it is still one of my dear Vilna schoolmasters who plays some part in every bad dream.[72]

While his encounters with Russian teachers and administrators in gymnasium stirred up resentment, the gymnasium years were not the only cause of his bitterness. The yearning for active resistance against Russia had been developing earlier. "Sometime between the ages of seven and nine," Pilsudski stated, referring to the two years he was homeschooled in Vilna, "I decided that if I am still alive at the age of fifteen . . . then I would lead an uprising and throw out the Muscovites."[73] The yearned-for struggle and sacrifice for Poland, he continued, began at an early age. "From as early as I can remember," he recalled, "I thought about serving Poland. I dreamed of greatness."[74]

The last year of gymnasium was also a time of change in Pilsudski's personal life. In 1885, less than a year after Madame Pilsudski died, his older sister, Zofia, became the first sibling to marry, tying the knot with Dr. Bolesław Kadenacy, nineteen years her senior. That year also saw Jozef and Bronisław graduate from gymnasium and prepare to leave home for college. Pilsudski was eager to see the world. "I always count the years spent in the gymnasium amongst the most unpleasant of my life," he later commented.[75]

The Extrovert

A unique window into Pilsudski's personality as an adolescent is provided in his brother's teenage diary. Bronisław admits to envying Jozef for his high native intelligence and charm, and the adoration he received from others. As a quiet, contemplative, and introverted boy, Bronisław resented what he saw as his younger brother's lighthearted and extroverted nature. In June 1883, for example, after final exam reports had been received, Bronisław marveled with frustration that his fifteen-year-old brother had done well in all subjects without ever having studied.[76] Bronisław expressed jealousy, moreover, that Jozef easily attracted the attention of others and delighted in such attention. "This brother of mine has insane luck," Bronisław wrote in February 1883. "Everything good comes to him and he always puts himself at the center of things. He talks a lot (but does very little). Foolishly believed, everyone raves about him."[77] Bronisław's sense of inferiority came through in another entry from 1883. "Ziuk [Jozef] always rises . . . and his actions stand much higher than mine. . . . The craving for revenge burns within me. . . . I now see ever clearer that I am holding on to Ziuk's tail," he wrote, noting that others "regard me only as Ziuk's brother."[78] Jozef, Bronisław noted, was outgoing and entertaining, writing in one entry that Jozef had danced all night and everyone was amused.[79]

Bronisław maintained that Pilsudski's pronounced air of self-confidence came off as arrogance. "The character of [Jozef]," Bronisław remarked of his brother, then fifteen, "will always be the same. Always a bumpkin, he is egotistical and conceited, his good luck never ends. He is often unbearable." Bronisław also resented that their younger brothers, Adam and Kazimierz, then ages thirteen and eleven, adored Jozef. Adam, for example, "totally admires [Jozef] and follows him wherever he goes."[80] Bronisław also expressed resentment at the lectures he sometimes received from his younger brother. "Today I had a conversation with Ziuk," he wrote in October 1883. "He tried to persuade me that I am an old young person, unlike himself, who is a model youth. He said that a young person has to sow his own wild oats and to laugh, but that I think seriously and that just as down fluff disappears in the wind over the years, so too will youth. He was regretful that I had not experienced my youth. I told him I don't want to experience the foolishness of youth, which is his ideal."[81] Looking beyond the sibling rivalry, Bronisław painted a portrait of Pilsudski as charismatic, extraordinarily bright, self-assured—a person with whom others like to tag along, and who had a strong desire to achieve "greatness."

Later, in his early sixties, Jozef reflected on his own personality traits, concluding, "I inherited my intellect from my father and my character from my mother."[82] He possessed his father's sharp intellect but without any of his father's artistic talents. He inherited from his mother a passion for justice, a powerful ethical impulse, and the managerial skills his father lacked. Pilsudski became a fiercely independent thinker able to grasp every aspect of complex problems entirely on his own, resorting to counsel only rarely. "I can think about everything from different angles and from all points of view. . . . That is the mind I was born with. Most people think in terms of stereotypes. I have opposed stereotypes my whole life. From the time I was a young child, I thought differently than everyone around me."[83] Pilsudski acknowledged that his charisma and adoration from others often made life easy. "I have been beloved and pampered my whole life," he remarked, "although I never sought it out nor did I do anything to prevent it." He remarked that he rarely asked a stranger in a new town for directions. Similarly, he always figured out problems on his own. "In all important issues, either small or large, I never asked anyone for advice. I was always this way. For as long as I can remember, I figured out how to navigate problems on my own so that I would not be dependent on others."[84]

Pilsudski's critical mind and ethical impulse were evident during childhood. His seemingly innate skepticism regarding binary, black-and-white thinking made him a nuanced, precocious boy. We see the latter traits in Pilsudski's reminiscences about his childhood. For example, he recounted an exchange he had as a child with the local priest, who told the children that lying was immoral. Were there not instances, Pilsudski asked, in which it was ethical to tell a white lie? Pilsudski put forward the argument that a white lie is preferable to the truth in several instances. "I also asked," Pilsudski recalled, "why God, who is all powerful, allows people to sin. The priest was angered by this question. He had no understanding for me and did not know how to deal with someone with my psyche. He was alarmed and warned my mother that my way of thinking was dangerous." In the same interview, Pilsudski commented on the strong ethical impulse he felt as a child. "Certain things," he said, "were and are entirely foreign to me, like favoritism in any form. I also always hated gossip and slander, nor was I ever capable of deceiving or betraying anyone for personal gain."[85]

At University in Kharkov

After graduating gymnasium, Pilsudski applied to the school of medicine at the university in Kharkov in eastern Ukraine.[86] He was accepted and began university in the fall of 1885, while still seventeen. He later claimed to have never had a genuine interest in medicine. The choice was instead a show of defiance against his father, who had insisted Pilsudski study in St. Petersburg at either the Technological Institute or the School of Engineering. "An interest in medicine?" he later replied to a question about his choice to study. "None whatsoever. I chose it out of spite."[87]

Pilsudski's year in Kharkov was a crucial one. He was initially engrossed in his studies and did well, passing final exams easily in December 1885 with a 4 out of 5 in anatomy, biology, and physics.[88] But he unknowingly altered his future forever when he became active in clandestine student politics. In the 1885–1886 academic year, Pilsudski was arrested twice. In the fall of 1885 he was held for two days. In March 1886 he was detained for six days, and threatened with expulsion in the event of further misconduct, for taking part in student demonstrations commemorating the twenty-fifth anniversary of the emancipation of the Russian serfs.[89] In December 1885 two Polish students convinced him to attend a Russian socialist student circle linked to the outlawed People's Will, the Russian revolutionary organization behind the 1881 assassination of Tsar Alexander II. Finding that the readings of Russian socialists had no appeal, Pilsudski stopped attending after two meetings, but the meetings coincided with events that did spark his interest in socialist thought. During high school in Vilna, the clandestine study group had taken up the study of socialism only as a movement for social and national revolution. It was in Kharkov that Pilsudski first developed an interest in the ideology of socialism in and of itself.[90]

Events outside of Kharkov had piqued Pilsudski's interest in socialism. During the fall semester Russian authorities in Warsaw arrested 190 members of the Polish socialist organization "Proletariat." The trial lasted from November 23 to December 20, 1885, leading to twenty-nine long prison terms and four death sentences. On January 28, twenty-five-year-old Stanisław Kunicki, twenty-one-year-old Michał Ossowski, twenty-year-old Jan Petrusiński, and a forty-one-year-old Russian, Piotr Bardovsky, were hanged on the grounds of the Warsaw Citadel. They were the first political prisoners executed in Warsaw since the 1863 Polish uprising.[91] News of the dramatic events heightened Pilsudski's curiosity about the ideology these Polish socialists had so passionately embraced. To learn more about Polish approaches to socialism, he began to search for literature on the subject and stumbled upon one of the earliest and most influential Polish commentaries on Marxist theory—Szymon Dickstein's *Who Lives from What?*[92]

In his personal life, meanwhile, Pilsudski became increasingly frustrated with his living conditions. In exasperation he wrote to his aunt that he had no return address to provide "because lodging is uncertain—today I am here, tomorrow I'm in another place, such that giving one address is not possible." The only way to reach him was to address a letter in his name to the university. Whether the letter would actually get to him was another question.[93] Despite his chaotic living conditions, Pilsudski did surprisingly well on his final spring semester exams. He received the highest score of 5 in chemistry, 4 in physics and biology, and 3 in anatomy.[94]

Return to Vilna and Arrest

After the spring semester, Pilsudski made his way back to Vilna in May 1886 for summer vacation, stopping in St. Petersburg to visit his brother Bronisław. En route to Vilna he decided he had no desire to return to Kharkov. He re-called later, "I detested Kharkov and took away from my time there the most unpleasant memories. The muck of Kharkov made my life miserable and ex-posed me to trouble."[95] He wanted to study abroad but his father was op-posed. Pilsudski therefore decided to transfer to the university in Dorpat (Tartu), Estonia, where he planned to continue medical school. Unlike Kharkov at the time, where Russians made up over 60 percent of the popula-tion, Dorpat—then in northwestern tsarist Russia—was 55 percent Estonian, 35 percent German, and only 6 percent Russian. What's more, the university was allowed considerable autonomy, as German was still the language of in-struction. After the Polish universities of Vilna and Warsaw were closed in 1831, the university in Dorpat had become a popular place for Polish students in the Russian Empire due to the city's sympathetic climate and Western European cultural orientation.

In August 1886, Pilsudski sent a formal request to the university in Kharkov to transfer his transcripts to Dorpat.[96] The records were duly forwarded, but unbeknownst to Pilsudski, a police file was inserted. "As a student at the university in Kharkov," it stated, "Pilsudski took an active part in riots taking place March 2 & 3 of the present year. He was punished with six days of detention and a warning that he would be expelled from the university should any further incidences occur."[97] Needless to say, the university in Dorpat informed Pilsudski that his application to the school of medicine was denied.

The rejection letter hit Pilsudski hard. The last thing he wanted was to sit idle for twelve months between his first and second years of university. So he rushed a request to the university in Kharkov to resume studies in the spring 1887 semester, but the filing deadline had already passed.[98] The sudden turn of events was a huge blow, sending Pilsudski into a period of turmoil and uncertainty. Denied entry to Dorpat and Kharkov, he fell into a state of deep despair and depression. He dramatically recalled this moment of crisis in a 1931 interview:

> There came a time when I doubted I could do great things, and life immediately lost its charm. I told myself that since I could not do great things, I had no reason to live. It was the time after I returned [home] from the university in Kharkov. I was overcome with fatigue and decided to end my life irrevocably. I even came up with a plan of how to go about it. I ultimately decided to go on a boat onto my favorite river. Standing on the edge of the boat, I would shoot myself with a pistol. I reckoned that I would fall in the water and no one would be able to save me if the shot wasn't fatal.[99]

Piłsudski's sense of anguish gave way to a desire for action. At the end of 1886 and beginning of 1887, he founded a circle of socialist youth consisting primarily of former Vilna gymnasium classmates. He had first formulated the idea for this circle at university upon learning about the fate of Proletariat members. "News of Proletariat in Warsaw," Piłsudski recalled, "quickened me to a keener interest. . . . I only came to the conclusion that it was essential to form some organization to work out a program of socialist activity among ourselves at home."[100] With time on his hands, it was the perfect opportunity to go ahead with his plan. The focus now was on socialist theory rather than on the labor movement and national revolts. The group discussed socialist brochures in Polish translation, including recently printed ones by Karl Marx and Wilhelm Liebknecht. During this period Piłsudski read the first volume of Marx's *Das Kapital* for the first time.[101]

As it turned out, the interruption in his university education, and his psychological distress, were to become the least of Piłsudski's worries. His fate was to change forever as a result of a brief encounter with a student from St. Petersburg University connected with his brother Bronisław. At the end of 1886, students at St. Petersburg University established the terrorist faction of People's Will and devised a plot to assassinate Tsar Alexander III.[102] The organization's leaders were Vladimir Lenin's older brother, Aleksandr Ulyanov, and Józef Łukaszewicz, a Pole from Vilna who had graduated from the gymnasium there two years before the Piłsudski brothers.[103] The plot was to be carried out by separate small groups. One of these groups chose Vilna as its site of activity.

Fate would have it that the safe house in Vilna identified by the St. Petersburg conspiracy was none other than the Pilsudski residence, due only to the fact that one of its members knew Bronisław in St. Petersburg. In January 1887, while Bronisław was on winter break in Vilna, he got a knock on the door. The unexpected visitor was Michał Kanczer, a Polish student at St. Petersburg University. Kanczer had been sent by the terrorist faction of People's Will with two letters addressed to Bronisław—one from Łukaszewicz, the other from Konstanty Hamolecki (also a Pole from Vilna)—with requests for a place to stay. Bronisław contacted his aunt, Stefania Lipmanówna, who agreed to put up Kanczer for a few nights. Jozef Pilsudski lived with his aunt at the time.[104] In making this arrangement, Bronisław altered his younger brother's life forever.

For the next two days, Kanczer drew the Pilsudski brothers into the conspiracy. Kanczer's assignment had been to bring acid nitrogen, atropine, and two revolvers back to St. Petersburg. Bronisław played no role in planning the assassination, nor is there evidence that he had any knowledge of the plot, but he agreed to help Kanczer obtain various chemicals, such as atropine—a poisonous crystalline alkaloid herb extract. While Bronisław also did not help his guest obtain guns, he did loan him forty rubles.[105] The day after Kanczer arrived, Bronisław left Vilna for St. Petersburg, handing over to his brother the responsibility of hosting Kanczer. Jozef showed Kanczer around Vilna, a city Kanczer was visiting for the first time. Kanczer returned to St. Petersburg the next day. Awaiting his arrival at the St. Petersburg train station was Ulyanov, who was satisfied to learn that Kanczer had brought acid nitrogen and atropine.[106] On March 11, 1887, two days before the planned assassination, Ulyanov began composing the manifesto of his terrorist faction in Bronisław's St. Petersburg apartment.[107]

The plot to assassinate Tsar Alexander III, however, was uncovered just in time. On March 13, 1887, the Russian secret service captured five members of the terrorist faction. Kanczer broke under interrogation and divulged the names of the Pilsudski brothers. Bronisław was arrested on March 14 and Jozef on March 22. Jozef was taken to St. Petersburg on April 2, and the trial of the conspirators began on April 27. In the end, five were condemned to death, including Ulyanov, while ten were given long prison sentences. Among the latter was Bronisław, who received fifteen years' hard labor in Siberia. Jozef, who was not charged with taking part in the preparation of the crime, was presented as a witness on the third day of the trial. But instead of his being freed after the trial, his case was transferred to the minister of justice, who took the fact that Kanczer—one of the chief conspirators—knew Jozef as sufficient evidence for conviction. Jozef Pilsudski was sentenced to five years' exile in Siberia.[108]

CHAPTER 2

Exile and Romance

You asked me, beloved, about my mental state. I would not say
it was super great. . . . The thing, my love, is that this same mental
state leaves me with faith in my ability and, connected to this,
a belief that an uncommon destiny awaits me. This faith
is very deeply felt.

—TWENTY-THREE-YEAR-OLD JOSEF PILSUDSKI, LETTER FROM
SIBERIAN EXILE, MARCH 11, 1891

Exile became a period of solitude, contemplation, and inner turmoil
for the young Pilsudski. Siberia was a faraway region of tsarist Russia with
vast rivers and forests. Here, between the ages of nineteen and twenty-
four, Pilsudski forged friendships with political exiles ranging from
former leaders of the failed 1863 Polish insurrection in their mid-fifties to
pioneers of the Polish socialist movement in their thirties. Unlike the men
sentenced to hard labor, Pilsudski was among those with the status of
exile only. Not required to work, he initially received a modest monthly
stipend of ten rubles and was allowed to move about freely within the designated residence area. For the most part, therefore, he did as he pleased—
socializing with a variety of people, corresponding, reading, hunting, or
playing chess.

The journey to Siberia began in May 1887 when Pilsudski was transported
from the Peter and Paul Fortress in St. Petersburg to the Butyrki Prison in
Moscow. On May 25 he was placed, along with sixty others, on a train with
barred windows to Nizhni Novgorod, three hundred miles to the east along

Pilsudski, age nineteen, in a Russian police photo after his arrest, March 1887.

the Volga River. There the convicts were housed in a barge described as a cramped, stuffy room with tiny windows. The trip from Moscow was distinctly unpleasant, Pilsudski noted.[1] From Nizhni Novgorod, the prisoners traveled 612 miles east by a combination of boat and rail to the foot of the Ural Mountains, the border between Europe and Asia. They crossed into Asiatic Russia, continuing 437 miles east to the city of Tyumen. The prisoners then went on foot to the city of Krasnoyarsk, walking at a pace of 16.5 miles per day while resting every third day. They arrived one month later, pausing long enough for Pilsudski to write to his family. The letter home chronicled his arduous journey. He noted exasperatingly, "We still have before us about a two-month journey to Irkutsk, which is 673 miles away." They were due to depart in three days, on July 22, 1887.[2]

Pilsudski, age nineteen and eager to see the world, did not fail to appreciate the vast country and terrain he was seeing for the first time. A lover of nature, he was moved by the landscapes and mountains. "The land here is quite interesting and one can see its value. I've never seen anything like these huge mountains surrounding us," he wrote. The mostly birch forests were full of fragrant pine trees. Still, the longer he traveled eastward, the more he felt severed from home and family:

> In a word: masses of new impressions and new thoughts; if the journey was not detached from real life and I was not receiving news from all of you so infrequently, the trip would be rather pleasant. Write me about everything, my dearests, and try to understand where I am coming from—how hard the situation is for me, so very far away from home and with no news! Each morsel, each detail no matter how frivolous and which I normally would have no interest in, will now bring me great joy.[3]

Three days after Pilsudski penned that letter, he and the others began their journey to Irkutsk, arriving in October 1887. He came under the jurisdiction of the Irkutsk governor-general. Most of the prisoners were assigned to places in surrounding counties, where they were sent within a week. Pilsudski was one of a dozen assigned to remote areas hundreds of miles away. His designated place of exile was the village of Kirensk, 625 miles to the north. Travel there was to take place by sleigh on ice. Pilsudski and twelve others had to wait two months for the Lena River to freeze over, requiring them to wait in an Irkutsk jail.

Pilsudski penned a long letter during the two months he spent in Irkutsk. "It has been a long time—very long (and in my imagination, even longer)—since I last saw you," he wrote to family in Vilna. The separation and distance led him to reflect upon the unfortunate events in the family's recent past, including the death of his mother and the fifteen-year sentence for his older brother, Bronisław. "Great misfortune has fallen on our family," he wrote despondently. Bronisław "may never return to us, forced to abandon the family at a time when he was most needed." Lonely, isolated, and robbed of a university education, the future was anything but certain. "As for me," he wrote, "I live now for the future; the future for me is everything. It is as if there is no present. And when I do have to acknowledge the present, it speaks to me negatively." The past also dominated his thoughts. The past, he mused with emotion, "what can I write about it? It went like a dream; it went, without giving the possibility of spreading in me all of its power; to start to live a full life—in continuous fear, pessimism and joy. How true that life to now did not come to pass the way I had expected!"[4]

Pilsudski also discussed material life and conditions of travel. The monotony combined with the lack of physical activity was taking its toll, not to mention the frustration of being cut off from the world. "As with me, I feel sometimes bad and sometimes good due to these conditions. I feel fortunate because I am sitting in prison for only two months whereas some have been here for as much as three years and most for at least a year. I feel bad because almost everyone here knows someone from the time they were free . . . while I am alone without friends." He therefore did not fit in with the other prisoners. "I converse very little," he remarked, "only infrequently with a few people. More often I go into my own thoughts and dreams. Secretiveness, a character trait of mine that has been evident for some time, is growing ever stronger."[5]

Because of the censors who read every piece of incoming and outgoing mail, Pilsudski could not write about the prison rebellion he had taken part in. On November 1–2, 1887, the inmates in Irkutsk refused to allow a fellow prisoner to be taken for solitary confinement, a sentence that had been imposed for a minor infraction. When the prisoners refused to hand the inmate over, Pilsudski recalled, the prison chief ordered the guards to withdraw. But on the next day, armed soldiers took the prisoner by force. "The soldiers threw themselves at us like infuriated wolves, their rifles raised," Pilsudski recounted. "We were crowded in a corner between the stove and the wall. I stood in the front row. I looked up and saw the butt of a rifle above me. I warded it off with my hand, and it glanced across my forehead, but at the same time I got another blow with a butt on the other side of my head, then a second, then a third."[6] Minutes later, a second round of blows knocked out Pilsudski's two front teeth before the rebellion was suppressed. Pilsudski was charged with incitement and sentenced to six months in prison upon being stationed in his place of exile. Twenty-five years later, he vividly described the Irkutsk prison incident and its meaning. "[For a long time] I could not look at a soldier, at a uniform ever with indifference; I felt my fists clench, and often if I closed my eyes I saw the whole horrible picture of an armed crowd of soldiers wildly attacking an unarmed handful of men collected in a corner."[7]

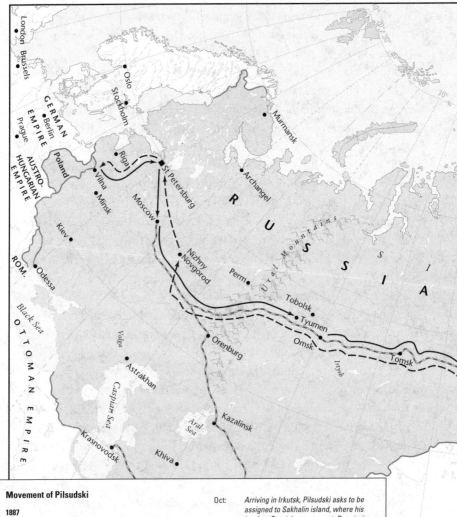

Movement of Pilsudski

1887

Mar 14–22: *Pilsudski and older brother, Bronislaw, arrested in Vilna.*

April 2:   *Taken to St. Petersberg prison, Pilsudski sentenced to 5 years exile; Bronislaw to 15 years hard labor on the Sakhalin Island in the Pacific.*

May 25:   *Pilsudski sent to Nizhny Novgorod, then east via Tyumen to Krasnoyarsk.*

July: *Arrives in Krasnoyarsk.*

Oct: *Arriving in Irkutsk, Pilsudski asks to be assigned to Sakhalin island, where his brother, Bronislaw, was sent. Permission was denied.*

Dec. 25:   *Arrives in Kirenski to where he is confined for the next two and half years.*

1890

July 1:   *Pilsudski is moved to Tunka, arriving Aug. 5.*

1892

June 1:   *Pilsudski exile comes to an end.*

June 30:   *Pilsudski arrives back in Vilna.*

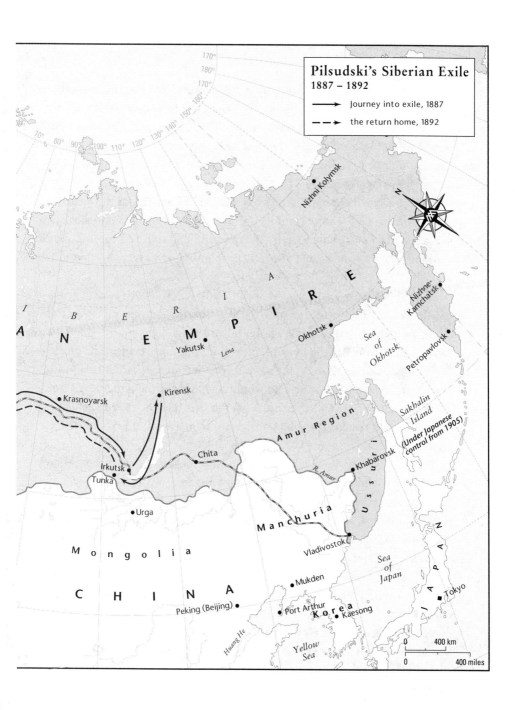

Pilsudski's Siberian Exile
1887 – 1892

→ Journey into exile, 1887

--→ the return home, 1892

Kirensk

The nightmare of Irkutsk eventually came to an end. On December 11, 1887, a week after Pilsudski turned twenty, the Lena River froze over. Two days later Pilsudski departed by sleigh on a journey of more than six hundred miles northeast. Kirensk, an island in the Lena River at the same latitude as northern Canada and the Scandinavian countries, had a bitter, subarctic climate with an average winter temperature between minus 6 and minus 26 degrees Fahrenheit. Pilsudski arrived on December 23, and would remain for the next two and a half years, in relative comfort.[8] With escape practically impossible, he was allowed to move about freely. The most difficult times in Kirensk were the long winters—sometimes lasting nine months—with very short periods of daylight.

Pilsudski came to lead an active social life in Kirensk with a small group of fellow exiles. They eventually developed a routine of conversation over tea, along with chess and card games. Yet he also longed for family. When he learned that Bronisław had been sent to the Sakhalin Island in the North Pacific Ocean, he appealed to the authorities. "Seeing how hard it is for us to live apart," Pilsudski requested, "I would like to serve the remaining three years living together with [my brother]. For this reason, Your Excellency, I would like to request that I be transferred to the island of Sakhalin."[9] The request was denied.

Realizing he was stuck in Kirensk, Pilsudski began investing more time in building friendships. His most significant bond was with Stanisław Landy, twelve years his senior, and Landy's wife, Felicja. Landy had already been in exile for nine years when Pilsudski arrived. He had been one of the founders of the first Polish socialist circles while a medical student at Warsaw University in the 1870s. He was arrested in August 1878 and detained at the Pawiak Prison in Warsaw. On July 22, 1879, twenty-five-year-old Landy was sentenced to twelve years' hard labor in Siberia, a sentence later changed to exile only.[10] En route to Siberia, Landy met fellow political exile Felicja Lewandowska, a Pole from the Ukrainian region of Podolia, and they married in January 1880 in Irkutsk. In October 1881, Felicja gave birth to their son, Aleksander, and the following year the authorities relocated the Landys to Kirensk.[11]

Felicja Landy recalled that she and her husband first met Pilsudski in February 1888, when he was twenty years old. The rapport was instant, based on a common interest in the past and future of their country as well as on shared sacrifice. Pilsudski was drawn to the Landys' cultured home, filled with books and lively conversation.[12] With customary Polish hospitality, Felicja and Stanisław took the young man under their wing. Pilsudski began visiting the Landy home often, spending whole days there. "We met Jozef Pilsudski in February 1888," Felicja recalled, "after he arrived in Kirensk. He spent entire days at our home and within a short time became like a member of our family."[13] The Landy family proved increasingly important after Pilsudski's request to live with his brother was denied. The closeness with the Landys broke the monotony of exile and provided warmth and comfort to a young man severed from his family and home.

Stanisław Landy was unique in the community of Polish exiles in Kirensk. From an acculturated Jewish family in Warsaw, he was part of a line of Jewish patriots known for their passionate support for Polish freedom. His uncle had died fighting for Poland. During an unarmed demonstration in April 1861 in Warsaw, the Russian police opened fire, killing a priest who had been marching at the head of the demonstration. Michał Landy, a sixteen-year-old Jewish gymnasium student, famously raised the priest's cross, which had fallen to the ground, and continued marching in defiance of the Russians. He was immediately shot dead, becoming one of five demonstrators killed that day.[14]

The story of Michał Landy, ripe with symbolism, had inspired poets and painters. Cyprian Kamil Norwid, one of the most distinguished poets of the time, then in exile in Paris, portrayed Landy in his 1861 poem "Polish Jews." Artist Aleksander Lesser completed a painting in 1866, *Funeral of the Five Victims of the Demonstration in Warsaw in 1861,* that depicted clergymen of different faiths, including the Roman Catholic archbishop alongside two rabbis, presiding over five coffins about to be laid to rest.[15] "We have here," Ezra Mendelsohn insightfully observed, "a striking visual representation of the idea ... that the struggle for Polish freedom bore a universal character and could unite under its flag people of different faiths and ethnic backgrounds, including ... Jews."[16] Given Pilsudski's particular interest in the 1863 uprising and how close he became with Stanisław Landy, he likely learned

Stanisław Landy, a Pole of Jewish
background who became one of
Pilsudski's mentors in Siberian exile,
ca. 1910.

about Michał Landy in Kirensk. In the Landy living room, Pilsudski may have
first read Norwid's poem or viewed a reproduction of Lesser's painting. Landy,
a Pole from a Jewish family who provided hospitality and companionship,
served as an example of sacrifice for Poland. This had to have made an impression on the young Pilsudski. Reinforcing his innate disdain for prejudice,
the twin stories of Michał and Stanisław Landy stood in sharp contrast to
widespread stereotypes of Polish Jews as unpatriotic and indifferent to Polish
affairs.

Time spent with the Landys was short-lived. In November 1888 the Landys
received permission to relocate to Irkutsk for a better school for their son. It
was something of a blow for Pilsudski, followed not long after by his having
to serve the six-month prison term for the Irkutsk revolt. Prior to his release
from prison on April 8, 1889, Felicja Landy's younger sister, Leonarda Lewan-

dowska, had arrived in Kirensk to serve a sentence for alleged antigovernment activities.[17] At the Landys' request, Leonarda knocked on Pilsudski's door to introduce herself, hoping the two would enjoy passing the time together. Leonarda, twenty-seven, and Pilsudski, twenty-one, took an immediate liking to one another. Not too long after, Leonarda became Pilsudski's first love. For the next eleven months, the only relief from the monotony of life in Kirensk for Pilsudski was the presence of Leonarda.

Pilsudski kept in touch with the Landys, asking for details about their lives in Irkutsk. One letter revealed his apprehension about the near future. Feeling sickly and weak, he requested permission to live in a warmer climate, and he informed the Landys that Leonarda was certainly planning to come to stay with them after her release from Kirensk. "As for me," he wrote on December 31, 1889, "I would like to live somewhere else other than this marshland." He noted that the authorities had discontinued his monthly stipend of ten rubles due to his aristocratic birth and his father's financial status. He had therefore become entirely dependent upon odd jobs. So even though he wanted to relocate, he wondered whether it was wise to risk moving to a new place where work was uncertain. "But I would [still] move eagerly to somewhere else," he explained, "because Kirensk is hugely dull. And it will be unpleasant here when everyone goes their separate ways."[18]

Separation anxiety set in as Pilsudski's relationship with Leonarda became more serious. They knew their time together was limited, because her sentence ended in the spring of 1890. It is not surprising, then, that Pilsudski tried desperately to devise a scheme to stay together. Whereas the Landys had provided a warm and intellectually vibrant home environment during his first year of exile, Leonarda gave Pilsudski romance and affection during his second year in Kirensk. In the course of 1889 the relationship between Lewandowska and Pilsudski became closer, and the two moved in together at the beginning of 1890.[19]

The romance between Pilsudski and Lewandowska was put to its greatest test when the two were forced to separate. In March 1890, eleven months after they met, Leonarda's sentence was completed and she was required to return home. She left for Irkutsk on March 19, to stay temporarily with her sister and brother-in-law.[20] On the same day, Pilsudski sent a letter to the Landys informing them that Leonarda had departed. She had so many things to take care of and so many people to bid farewell to, he wrote, that she asked him

Leonarda Lewandowska, Pilsudski's
first love, ca. 1890.

to write on her behalf. He apologized for not having been able to obtain permission to relocate to the Irkutsk region in time to accompany Leonarda.
"Having still hoped that permission was forthcoming and that I would be able
to leave with your sister-in-law, I asked her to wait as I thought it would be
more comfortable for her to travel with me," he wrote. But the expected permission did not come and Leonarda could no longer wait. Rest assured, he
added, she would be fine traveling alone.[21]

Pilsudski's request to relocate to the Irkutsk region was one of several
schemes he concocted in a desperate attempt to stay with his first love. The
second idea was to reunite with Leonarda in Vilna shortly after her return to
Russia, a farfetched plan that depended on the Russian authorities cutting
his sentence practically in half. On March 24, 1890—five days after Leonarda
left Kirensk—he formally asked permission to return home and live under
police surveillance, arguing that his presence was sorely needed there. The

request was denied. In his first letter to Leonarda after her departure, Pilsudski expressed regret that his plan to leave together had been thwarted. He nonetheless assured her that he would shortly relocate to Irkutsk and that she should wait for him. His longing for Leonarda was palpable: "Now, always, when I step out into the street, I think of you. If the wind blows, I am angry, because it must be bad for you. When the night has light and the moon shines brightly, I am pleased because you can travel without an accident at night."[22]

Pilsudski impatiently waited for permission to relocate to the Irkutsk region. He feared the authorities would delay and delay. Without Leonarda, life in Kirensk left much to be desired. "I come home [from work in the evening hours]," he wrote, "and drink tea, pace up and down the room, think about you, reminisce about better times, think a bit about the future, read some, and then collapse into bed and go to sleep. That's my typical day." Pilsudski yearned for news about Leonarda's life in Irkutsk. "Write me about everything— everything that is going on in your mind . . . ," he wrote her. "That would make me content because I would feel like we were together."[23]

Pilsudski shared some family news in his second letter to Leonarda. His aunt, Stefania Lipman, was having serious financial trouble and had moved back to the country. His younger brother, Kazimierz, was ill, and his older brother, Bronisław, complained that he was aging quickly.[24] Pilsudski discussed his poor health, complaining that his body quivered, he felt weak, and he got tired earlier in the day than ever before.[25] More family news followed in his third letter. His aunt's financial situation had become so dire that she could no longer afford to host guests. If he returned to Vilna today, she had no place for him to stay. This came as something of a blow to Pilsudski, who had been living with his aunt in Vilna when he was arrested in 1887. "As for me," he wrote to Leonarda, "Kirensk is boring and I no longer know if I will be able to wrench myself free from this place." He continued despondently, "When I think that my request for relocation may be denied, it makes the hair on my head stand."[26] So he tried to pass the time by socializing as much as possible when he was not at work.

Pilsudski's spirits were lifted two weeks later when he got news that his request to leave Kirensk had been approved. He only had to wait for the Lena River to thaw. With his time in Kirensk now limited, he reminisced to Leonarda about the period "when I hung out at your place for whole nights" and they talked about leaving Kirensk together down the Lena River.[27] Pilsudski was hopeful and exuberant in his last letter to Leonarda from Kirensk. "You have no idea how much joy [your letters] bring me," he began. "Each time after reading, I feel as if I was talking to you."[28] Yet he was also preoccupied with family affairs. He had received a letter from his older sister, Zofia, about the family's properties and investments. The estate and land in Suginty had been sold. Worse still, the rest of the family properties would have to be sold by the first of July. Zofia, he wrote, "appears to be in a pitiful state." He also shared news about his younger siblings. Kazimierz, nineteen, was in poor health; Jan, fourteen, was not doing well in school. His younger sisters Maria, seventeen, and Ludwika, eleven, were doing well in school, but Zofia felt they lacked any real adult supervision at home without a mother and with a father who was often away. Pilsudski expressed terrible guilt that he was not there to mentor and help care for his younger siblings.[29]

Irkutsk

Things changed for the better in July 1890. The Lena River was declared ready for transport, and Pilsudski, permission in hand, left Kirensk by ferry, traveling 660 miles south to Irkutsk. There, while waiting to go to his new place of exile, he stayed with the Landys, arriving just in time to reunite with Leonarda.[30] She left for Russia proper on July 29, 1890.[31] The two had agreed that Leonarda would go to Vilna, and Pilsudski gave her four letters addressed to family that she was to hand-deliver. Pilsudski also sent letters to Leonarda in care of his family in Vilna in the weeks after her departure. The letters to family members entrusted to Leonarda reveal Pilsudski's heartfelt wish that she would settle in Vilna permanently. Pilsudski asked his uncle to take Leonarda under his wing during her visit. She would be a great resource, Pilsudski noted, because she knew everything about his life in exile. "Perhaps, if she eventually finds work, she will make Vilna her home. In any case," Pilsudski remarked, "please show her around and introduce her to people so that she doesn't feel like a stranger among our family in Vilna."[32] The second letter Leonarda was to hand-deliver was addressed to Celina Bukont, his mother's childhood friend who had lived in the Pilsudski home and helped raise the children. Please, he asked Bukont, introduce Lewandowska to his brothers Adam and Kazimierz so she could make their acquaintance and give them letters he wrote to them.[33]

The letters, however, were intended not only to introduce Leonarda but also to share his concern about the crumbling state of his family's properties. He pleaded with his paternal uncle to make sure that Pilsudski's father did not squander the family fortune. "As you know," he wrote, revealing the low opinion he had for his father, "my dad himself is not known for his managerial skills, or what is key, for honesty in selecting investments. So after returning to the country, I want to remove Dad [from control of the family properties] and myself get to work. I don't want to have the responsibility for the outcome of our material interests to also fall on me, since Dad governs, having my authorization."[34]

Pilsudski, meanwhile, penned three letters to Leonarda in care of family she was supposed to visit. In the first, he admitted that he had never believed the two of them would part. Writing two days after Leonarda left Irkutsk, Pilsudski had been encouraged by Leonarda's sister, Felicja Landy, who believed Leonarda was going to return to Irkutsk. "This has given me some hope," he wrote, "that I will see you again soon."[35] In his next letter, Pilsudski acknowledged that Lewandowska was not going to return. "And so, my dearest," he wrote her, "you are not coming back as I had hoped. And this is probably better for you anyhow. It was egotistical of me to have been delighted at the idea that you [may] . . . remain [here] for a time in Siberia." But it was so dull without her, he admitted. "The evenings and nights are the worst," he wrote. "That is when I so strongly feel loneliness and longing for you." He had no prospects for work and little money. "Tomorrow," he wrote, "I leave for Tunka and I absolutely have no idea how things will work out."[36]

Tunka

On August 5, 1890, Pilsudski left Irkutsk and traveled 125 miles southwest to Tunka, a village in the Sayan Mountains along the border with China, where the authorities had assigned him. Tunka had a milder climate than Kirensk and was dotted with lakes and hills, and cottages scattered along the local river. In his first letter from Tunka, Pilsudski described meeting several fellow exiles who helped him get settled. The small, tight-knit community of political exiles consisted of about twenty people (including some children and spouses) ranging in age from thirty to fifty-five.[37] On the day Pilsudski arrived, Afanasy Michalewicz, a fellow exile and Ukrainian physician, invited him to his home, offering him tea and a place to stay for the night. The next morning Pilsudski was visited by Stefan Juszczyński, a political exile who had been in Tunka since December 1887. Juszczyński had joined the illegal Polish socialist organization Proletariat, was arrested in 1885, and was imprisoned before being sentenced to five years' exile in Siberia.[38] Juszczyński took a liking to Pilsudski, offering to show him around town. In the course of the day, Pilsudski met Juszczyński's roommate, Michał Mancewicz, who had joined Proletariat in Warsaw in the mid-1880s and also had been arrested and sentenced to exile.[39]

Realizing Pilsudski had no place to stay, Mancewicz and Juszczyński offered to rent out a room for two and a half rubles a month.[40] Juszczyński remembered Pilsudski at the time as sickly and frail. "He was the youngest among us, then in his early 20s," Juszczyński recalled. "He was very thin and frail, slightly stooped over, with a sunken chest and a persistent cough."[41] Juszczyński's observations corresponded with Pilsudski's own description of his health at the time. Prior to leaving Kirensk, Pilsudski believed he had contracted pulmonary tuberculosis and had no more than two years to live. But within weeks of living in Tunka, his health began to improve.[42]

Tunka itself, however, did not make a good first impression. "Tunka, my darling, is not for me," he wrote to Leonarda. "It is a hole that has this name for people able and wishing to do physical activity (hunting, chopping and floating timber, tilling the soil, etc.). For these people, Tunka could be heaven. For people are generally free here and travel is allowed in the range of 40 verst [26 miles], even for 10 days at a time." Pilsudski was nonetheless drawn to the social milieu. "As for the people here," he continued, "they have not made a bad impression, at least with a few of them." He had taken a liking to Juszczyński, whom he described as less bitter than the others. Juszczyński was an emotional guy with some warmth to his personality, and the two of them, he believed, could become friends. For entertainment, he played chess and read whatever he could get his hands on. "As for my health," he added, "I feel not bad. I walk almost every day. There is only the damn mud, something I never had to deal with in Kirensk."[43]

Some of the people Pilsudski met in Tunka became important influences with whom he kept in touch long after the period of exile. One of them was Bronisław Szwarce (1834–1904), a prominent figure. Thirty-three years Pilsudski's senior, Szwarce had been part of a clandestine organization in Warsaw founded in June 1862 and tasked with preparing a national insurrection. Captured by the Russians in December 1862, Szwarce was sent into internal exile, a sentence he was still serving twenty-seven years later when Pilsudski arrived in Tunka. Szwarce gradually became Pilsudski's mentor. The two "used to sit over the fire in Szwarce's little cabin talking for hours, the old patriot, white-haired after [more than] twenty years in exile, defeated but still unbroken in spirit, full of his dreams of another armed insurrection that should free Poland. And the young man listening to him was fired by his enthusiasm."[44] Szwarce, one historian observed, "strengthened [Pilsudski's] sense of the continuity of national tradition."[45] Pilsudski described his impressions of Szwarce two weeks after his arrival in Tunka. "Szwarce, a pleasant guy," Pilsudski wrote to Leonarda on August 20, 1890, "is a bit too old to become friends with. But I have had remarkably interesting conversations with him. He's someone who has seen and read so much, and the slightly crazy aspects of his personality [only] add to the joyfulness of our conversations."[46] Despite their difference in age, they in fact became friends during the course of the next year. Szwarce was released in August 1891 after serving a twenty-eight-year sentence, left the Russian Empire, and moved to Lwów. The two kept in touch until Szwarce's death in 1904.

The people Pilsudski met, however, could not fill the void left by Leonarda's absence. Although Pilsudski and Lewandowska had pinned their hopes on the plan to reunite in Vilna, he was beginning to be concerned. It had been twenty-two days since her departure and still no word. In his letter of August 20, 1890, he was almost frantic with worry. "I am very worried," he wrote, "because I did not receive a letter from you in the last arrival of mail. I am out of sorts not knowing how you are doing, my love. I haven't received any news from you."[47]

Pilsudski nonetheless continued to comment on his daily life. He was dining evenings with his housemates, Mancewicz and Juszczyński, who made tea with their samovar. He played a Russian card game (*wint*), played chess,

Bronisław Szwarce, Pilsudski's mentor in
Siberian exile, ca. 1900.

and had even gone hunting on two occasions. With regard to health, he assured Leonarda that she need not worry: his new friend Michalewicz was a
doctor by profession and was taking good care of him. Yet he was not feeling
well psychologically, he acknowledged. "You have to understand," he wrote,
"that I still have not gotten used to Tunka. I feel like a guest, a passerby.
I will certainly feel this way for the duration of my time here." Whether or not
she was receiving his letters was unclear. "And you, beloved, when will you
read my letter?" he asked, continuing: "I still do not cease dreaming that you
will be in Vilna; that you will find a place and settle down there. How wonderful that would be, for I love Vilna and I love you. It is no wonder that I want
us to be together there . . . ; this is why I dream about your stay in Vilna."[48]

Pilsudski had not yet found work and so he turned to a discussion of finances. The authorities had ceased paying his monthly stipend, and his father
does not appear to have ever sent money. This dire situation led Pilsudski to

rethink his decision to move to Tunka. In Kirensk, at least, he had never worried about where his next piece of bread would come from. "But enough about me," he concluded the letter to Leonarda. "My dear—be well and content. Warm kisses. I love you dearly."[49] Eventually he would find work tutoring the children of fellow exiles.

When Pilsudski finally received a letter from Leonarda, his suspicions were confirmed. The return address was not Vilna but the city of Orla, 333 miles east of Kiev, where Leonarda was staying with relatives in the area she grew up in.[50] He was nonetheless elated to hear from her. "Finally I can write you!" he began his reply on October 15, 1890. Concealing his disappointment at the change of plans, Pilsudski delved right into discussing his life in Tunka. "At this point," he wrote, "I have fully established myself in Tunka. To some degree, I have gotten used to it here." She had asked him to describe his daily life. "During the day," he replied, "I use my stove to heat my flat. Occasionally, once a week, I cook for myself something wretched. I limit myself to tea, milk and eggs. For a long time I couldn't bring myself to clean [the place]. But it got so filthy that . . . today I swept."[51]

Despite feeling more at home in Tunka, Pilsudski was in low spirits. He had begun to avoid others as his separation from Leonarda began to take a toll. He also missed the Landys' warm hospitality and companionship. "In a word," he wrote, "I now am entirely alone spiritually. While sometimes I am totally fine, other times . . . I find myself apathetic or very ill-tempered." He acknowledged experiencing mood swings, however, even before the two separated. "I often think that I did not know how to enjoy the good fortune that surrounded me when we were together," he wrote. "Many of the moments that we had been together went to waste, not having left any remembrance, any keepsake. I cannot forgive myself," he continued, "that I so often irritated and saddened you, my Love."[52] The sweet hope of reunion was becoming ever more unlikely. "It stands to reason," he continued, "that I am focused on the future, which I often dream about. I think about you and when we'll meet again in Russia."

On a positive note, Pilsudski's health continued to improve. The old symptoms in Kirensk had vanished along with feelings of weakness and fatigue. He noted that a sign of his improved health was the fact that he now spent an average of three days a week out and about. In fact, he was planning on going hunting the following day.

With contact reestablished, Pilsudski and Lewandowska correspond weekly. When Pilsudski lagged behind a week, Leonarda was incensed. He responded with humor and lightheartedness. "Your letter made me laugh a little and gladdened me at the same time," he wrote in October 1890. "You write that the only justification for my silence is that I had entirely forgotten about your existence. But your letter shows, at the same time, that you don't believe this at all." Pilsudski tried to diffuse Leonarda's emotional outburst by expressing gratitude for having watched over his health in Kirensk.[53] He concluded the letter by complaining about the lack of news from home.

Pilsudski's letters to Leonarda in the fall of 1890 reveal a new phase of optimism. The first thing he noted was that the old, lurking suspicion that the Russian authorities planned to arbitrarily extend his five-year sentence had disappeared. "The old restless feeling that I would never return home," he excitedly wrote Leonarda, "has withered away entirely." The new, more positive attitude about the future was connected to his improved health and psychological state. "From the time I left Kirensk, my health has undoubtedly much improved. And this in turn," he wrote, "has strongly affected my mental disposition here in exile."[54] He was writing late into the night, the lamp was flickering, and he was out of kerosene oil, "so I will say goodnight then, my beloved. Warm kisses and I wish you sweet dreams. I'll finish the letter tomorrow." He continued the next morning. "Good morning, my beloved. How did you sleep? As for me, I slept not badly and you even appeared in my dreams." He recalled how much pleasure it brought him that an acquaintance, glancing at a photograph of Leonarda, had commented on how beautiful she was.

Although things were looking up, the lack of a steady job was still a problem. The issue was not only the lack of income but the idleness. Winter was now approaching, and Pilsudski could no longer go hunting in the woods with his friends. Having endless time on his hands, his apprehension about the future surfaced again. "Yes, one can aspire, as I do, to a literary career, but I still have a bit to learn about its rudiments," he wrote in November 1890. "As I have said before, I generally cannot imagine, in practice, what I will do when I return to Vilna, and that frightens me somewhat. Don't get me wrong," he added, "I believe in my strengths and abilities. Yet on the other hand, I have come across many who believed in themselves but ended up as losers."[55] Pilsudski also kept Leonarda informed about his social life, writing that he enjoyed going out for tea with friends in the evening. "I come home late, at about 9 or 10 nearing the end of the evening. I spend these late evening hours reading, thinking and dreaming. That is to say, it is a time to concentrate on my spiritual well-being."

The theme of reunion appeared more frequently in their letters. "You write about how much you want to see me," he wrote in November 1890, "and that you miss the good times we had in Kirensk." The combination of homesickness and separation from Leonarda was even worse for Pilsudski because he was still in exile. "The longing for home," he wrote Leonarda, "significantly increased after you left." He continued, "Every day I think and dream about returning home, about seeing you again. Every day I count how long I have left in Siberia, making me irritable and anxious." He noted that in her letter, Leonarda had emphasized that she wanted to see Pilsudski immediately after his return. "How could it be otherwise," he wondered.[56] "By the time you receive this," he wrote in his next letter, "it will likely be 1891. I heartily, then, wish you a Happy New Year. I hope you, my beloved, have good fortune. But it makes me sad," he continued, "that I will not see you in this new year. Remember last New Year's Eve when you shortly afterward moved to a new apartment, and the life we shared there? What great times those were and what a pity they went by so quickly."[57]

As the year 1891 approached, Pilsudski recorded his plan for the months following his release. He was to be released in a mere one year and three months, he reminded Leonarda, landing him in Russia proper by April 1892. "I will go first to you and afterward to Vilna where I'll spend the whole summer," he wrote. "During the summer, I hope to visit you again." After the summer of 1892, he was to travel to Sakhalin Island to visit his brother. He would return to Vilna in November or December.[58] "See how widely I've planned ahead for the whole year of 1892," he wrote hoping to impress Leonarda. "All this will be possible when I have money in my pocket" after returning to Vilna. Responding to Leonarda's inquiry, Pilsudski turned to daily life in Tunka. "I am out all day," he replied, "as I am not accustomed to hosting people at my place." Besides, he continued, his place was "at the height of disorder."[59]

In the next letter, Pilsudski's tone suggested a change in disposition. He had not received a reply from Leonarda and expressed concern for her. At the same time, conditions in Tunka were getting him down. As he had written three months prior, Pilsudski regretted taking Leonarda's advice to leave Kirensk, where he at least had a stable job. His goal was to be together after exile and find happiness. "We will either live from hand to mouth or, together, find success," he wrote.[60] He understood that circumstances might prevent him from achieving this goal, but he refused to succumb to pessimism.

Another factor lowering Pilsudski's morale was the continued lack of news from family, no doubt increasing his sense of isolation. To date, he had been getting only snippets of family news. He was concerned about his younger brother Adam, twenty-one, who had been conscripted into the Russian Army. Pilsudski had no idea if Adam had begun his military service. He was similarly disquieted by the fact that he had not received replies from Bronisław for some time. Leonarda understood the distress this caused Pilsudski and must have asked him to let her know right away if he received more family news, because Pilsudski wrote that if letters from family were waiting for him at the post office, he would insert in the present letter a summary of the latest family news. The eagerness with which Pilsudski shared news about his family revealed the close intimacy he felt with Leonarda.

Pilsudski began relying more and more on social ties in Tunka. He described spending time with Mancewicz, chatting throughout the day and playing cards at night. For staying at home alone was not an option, he wrote Leonarda. "As I write, I am heating my apartment with the stove and thinking about where I will be going later for tea. I do not want to stay here." He felt better about prospects for work. "In a word," he wrote, "I feel better now than I did before. For at the very least I can now envision some kind of work and productive use of my time. Up to now, the thought of having to make a living made me anxious and so I simply avoided the subject." Yet the topic of money was complicated and delicate. "What a nuisance and a shame," he wrote, "but one has to recognize that money and livelihood in general have a tremendous impact in people's lives, affecting mood and disposition."[61] At the end of 1890 Pilsudski expressed joy that he had finally received a letter from Bronisław, who seemed to be doing well and was in good spirits.

Pilsudski wrote more about the people he spent time with. Two of them were Michał Mancewicz and Lidia Łojko, a woman thirteen years older than Pilsudski. "Nowadays," Pilsudski wrote, "I often visit Łojko, a gal who has been putting more and more emphasis on [our] friendship." Friendships, he continued, were essential for his psychological well-being in exile. He had become accustomed to being part of her social circle. Pilsudski assured Leonarda, however, that there was nothing to worry about: Mancewicz had fallen in love with Lidia and Lidia, anyhow, was much older than he. "I have a feeling," he added, "that [Michał] is uncomfortable with Lidia and me becoming more friendly."[62]

Leonarda suspected there was more to this story than Pilsudski was letting on. The moment there was a lag in Pilsudski's correspondence, Leonarda asked bluntly, "'Where have you [and Mancewicz] been? At Lidia's?" Leonarda admitted that she was in tears, so Pilsudski tried to reassure her by reminiscing about their time together, stressing how much she occupied his thoughts. Kirensk, he wrote, "was an optimistic time for me when we were together." He remembered becoming frail at the time. "My physical state started deteriorating and I fell into a state of apathy and pessimism."[63]

He turned his thoughts again to fears about the future. Although he was doing better in Tunka, exile was deepening his hatred for Russia. "Of course, I don't know nor can I even hint at what I will do in Europe," he wrote, "and what work I'll end up finding. Well, you know, everyone here in Tunka is waiting impatiently for the coming year because we all complete our sentence in 1892 with the exception of a few people." A letter from his older sister, Zofia, only increased the feeling of uncertainty. She expressed pessimism about the state of the family wealth and wrote that she would not be surprised if the family properties were lost by the end of the year. The combination of uncertainly about the future and financial troubles at home caused Pilsudski, who had just turned twenty-three in December 1890, extreme anxiety. "So you can see, my beloved," he concluded his letter, "that I am unable to stop worrying as you have suggested I do."[64]

As the year 1891 progressed, correspondence between Leonarda and Pilsudski became less frequent. This led to uncertainty about their relationship. For the first time since they began their correspondence, Leonarda waited nearly a month before writing. Pilsudski was worried something had happened, and was relieved when a letter arrived. "Finally, after a long period of silence, I received your letter," he wrote. "Wow. That was not nice of you to wait so long to write. I did not hear from you for four weeks, and I seriously began to worry. A thousand thoughts raced through my mind—that you had been arrested and were sitting in a prison cell or that you had fallen ill and died. And in the last week, I waited for the mail [frantically]. My love—write often and don't take such long breaks in between letters. Write more frequently so, at the very least, I won't get so worried." The long wait for a reply made him realize just how much he cared for her. "You know, my love," he wrote, "that all this time . . . when I was convinced something had happened to you, I came to realize how dear you are to me."[65]

Pilsudski's penchant for precise dates and numbers came through in his next letter. Writing to Leonarda on March 4, 1891, he recalled the date one year before. "Today is March 4, Leonarda. Do you remember? On this day last year you made pierogis stuffed with cottage cheese on the occasion of my brother Kazimierz's name day. It seems so long ago and yet like yesterday at the same time. When I think about that time last year when you were in Kirensk, I almost don't believe it was real." He continued: "How I love you so. How much I would like to see you, to hold you, and to be able to peer into your eyes to see if they are joyous and if you love me."[66]

Pilsudski began ruminating about his own abilities and potential. Leonarda had asked him about his mental state, to which he candidly replied that his morale was pronouncedly low. "You asked me, beloved, about my mental state. I would not say it was super great," he commented facetiously on March 11, 1891. He could not escape the feeling, he continued, that a dark cloud hovered above, reminding him of the discontent with his surroundings and the life he was leading in exile. Yet his self-esteem was unaffected, for he still regarded himself as a capable person with unusual potential. He was hopeful about the future after exile, even if such thoughts also aroused apprehension. "The thing is, my love," he continued, "that this same mental state leaves me with faith in my ability and, connected to this, a belief that an uncommon destiny awaits me. This faith is very deeply felt. But at the same time it has not brought with it the perseverance without which, it stands to reason, many goals go unrealized." Life in exile, he added, had given him no means to capitalize on such abilities and on the uncommon destiny he was certain awaited him. "In adapting these two aspects of my character to life [in exile], they apply as follows. I feel that I have to work very, very hard. Feeling these innate abilities, I blame myself that I'm wasting away here without being able to make use of them. . . . What's left are a deep dissatisfaction and a guilty conscience that does not give me a moment of peace."[67]

It was by comparing himself to other people that Pilsudski began to see himself as exceptionally gifted. He felt that he was quicker and sharper than his peers despite being ten years younger on average. "Often I try to tell myself to stay calm. I remind myself . . . that everywhere I count myself—and I am counted by others— . . . as intellectually more developed despite my young age. It gives me some satisfaction to know," he continued, "that, in so much as I can gather, I will be more advanced than my acquaintances are now when I reach their age."[68]

Pilsudski meanwhile wanted to address Leonarda's concerns about his low morale. Why did she not understand, he asked her, that his low morale was the outcome of circumstance alone. "No, love, don't worry unnecessarily," he wrote. "Of course, I also have very good moments and at times feel a certain contentedness. But honestly, such moments are rare." The suggestion that the lack of a positive outlook was the problem made him doubt if Leonarda really understood him. "I have described to you the main reasons for my mental state. I wish I hadn't done so," he wrote. He ended his letter on a pessimistic note about their future as a couple for the first time. "My God, it has been a year since you left Kirensk and a year since my love disappeared from my eyes, probably forever."[69]

Despite Pilsudski's admission that he often felt down during quiet moments of contemplation, his social life appeared to be full. On his name day, for example, he described lively gatherings in his honor. "I must admit that I did drink a tad bit but not to the point of getting drunk—just a bit to celebrate," he wrote. "We had a gala dinner. Lidia parched some perogies and there were a few guests over. Later, during the evening, we went for a walk. We then went to my place for tea and then [everyone went] to Lidia's to cap off the evening."[70] He recounted going hunting on horseback from 9 a.m. to 7 p.m., playing cards from 7 p.m. to 2 a.m. and then sleeping until 3 p.m. the next day. "I read and think more," he commented to Leonarda, "and feel somewhat merrier." The calendar itself helped to lift his spirits. "In one year from today," he noted on April 8, 1891, "I will be a free man."[71]

Now that Pilsudski was scheduled to return to Vilna in a year, he became somewhat apprehensive about seeing family and friends after so much time had passed. He had been receiving news infrequently and wondered what changes he would observe. "And here, as if out of spite," he wrote, "I so

rarely receive news from [home] that it is even hard to grasp how things are
going with them. Well, I'll be able to see with my own eyes soon enough."
Leonarda responded dismissively, evidently suggesting he try to be more positive. He replied that his low morale had everything to do with the unnat-
ural circumstances in which he was living. Poverty and misery, he argued,
made it difficult for individuals to seriously ponder anything beyond their
daily bread. "I am generally convinced," he wrote, "that individual happiness,
particularly in our lousy conditions (that is to say, here in exile), always influences one so that the mind does not dwell on social concerns."[72]

Separation took a harder toll as more time passed. "On Saturday," Pilsudski
wrote in April 1891, "I received a letter where you reproach me for the long
silence. You claimed," he continued, "there were changes [in my feelings]
toward you." He admitted that, at an earlier time, he had questioned his feelings toward her but those doubts had since dissipated. Thus, he wrote, there
was no need for concern. Having allayed her fears, he turned to daily life.
The coming of spring, he remarked, meant he could spend more time out-
doors. Another psychological boost was the fact that the one-year mark of
his release from captivity had passed. "I am so pleased to know," he wrote,
"that with every passing day I am closer to [freedom]. At first, when it was
still more than a year, I wasn't as thrilled as I am now. I am more joyous as I
inch closer and closer to the time I get out of here and back home to you, to
everyone." Pilsudski made sure to share family news with Leonarda on those
occasions when he received it from Vilna.

In some of his letters, he expressed concern about Leonarda's psychological well-being, including her unhealthily low self-esteem and consequent lack
of faith in her own abilities to pursue a career or success in her personal life.
In his attempt to comfort her, one could sense Pilsudski's gut feeling that
Leonarda suffered from depression. "I dreamed," he wrote, referring to their
time in Kirensk, "that I would inspire in you a hopefulness about life and the
prospects for work. But I unfortunately was not successful."[73] The contents
of Leonarda's letters, together with traits he had observed when they were
together, increased Pilsudski's concern that symptoms of depression were becoming more severe. "I know," he wrote, "that you are absolutely of the
opinion, firstly, that you are not suitable for anything and, secondly, that you
have bad fortune. [This leads you to believe] that everything you put your
hands on turns into something bad. But dear Leonarda," he asked, "is it seri-

ously possible that you believe such things?" Pilsudski tried to help Leonarda by suggesting she become part of a movement or cause. Devoting herself to an idea would diminish the feeling of insignificance. "I cannot help but want to impress upon you," he wrote, "the importance of . . . serving something higher than one's self—an idea; and that out of respect for this idea one should not fall into pessimism, but believe that the future belongs to us; only then when we will work for such a future."[74] The result, Pilsudski stressed, would be a new sense of purpose.

As more time passed, Pilsudski began to feel impatient and claustrophobic, his sense of confinement making him wonder if he could wait another eleven months. "Ach—may this exile quickly come to an end, may I soon be my own master," Pilsudski wrote, "without feeling this damn police and administrative surveillance hovering over me. Forgive me, Leonarda, for writing so fragmentarily. But it is difficult for me to do otherwise. It is enough that you know I love you as I have in the past; that I would like to see you, to heartily hold you and to restore calm in us."[75]

But the long-distance relationship between Pilsudski and Leonarda began to break down in the summer of 1891. Sometime the previous February, Pilsudski began seeing another woman. He did not have the heart to deceive Leonarda, so he sat down to write a breakup letter. The brief, three-sentence note ending the relationship was full of emotion:

> It has been so long since I wrote you because I didn't have the strength or heart to tell you that our relationship as it has been to now can no longer continue. Leosia! Forget about me. I am not worthy of you. If you are able, forgive me. I would like to . . . but no. Paper can't suffice for everything I want to tell you. So, regardless, my lovely one, my dear—be well.
>
> Goodbye, perhaps forever,
> Ziuk[76]

Pilsudski's involvement with another woman turned out to merely be a fling. By the time he received Leonarda's reply, it had already ended. Full of grief and a guilty conscience for his affair, he struggled to explain himself. "I, loving you, gave myself to someone else. I write . . . because, having convinced myself that this wasn't the case—my love for you, dear Leonarda—

[I came to realize] that this love is [still] strong. It is easy to understand that I behaved very unkindly toward you, to put it mildly." That is why it was impossible to carry on a relationship with another woman. "You ask me, Leonarda, why I wrote you such a letter without explaining the reasons I decided to end our relationship. . . . I could not have written that I fell out of love with you," he explained, "because that was not true."[77]

Pilsudski asked for Leonarda's forgiveness with the hopes of reconciling. "I ask you for one thing," he wrote in September 1891. "Consider if you can let this go and feel the same about me. Can you ever really trust me again? Please think hard and seriously whether or not this is possible or if [my affair] will, despite our love for one another, embitter our lives." Pilsudski suggested she send him a telegram with either "Write" or "Don't write," which would tell him if she had forgiven him.[78] Due to the fact that none of Leonarda's letters have been preserved, we do not know how long it took Leonarda to reply. We only know that Pilsudski's next and last letter to Leonarda from exile was written almost three months later. "Oh, Leonarda," he began in December 1891, "I sometimes simply want to cry when I think of old times and what has become of us. As for me, I will think about us only upon my return home when we shall see each other and speak about everything in person. Now I will write about everything [even if] the pen does not hear feelings or the mind, nor can it express everything that is thought and felt, particularly in a hurried letter like this one. I want to talk to you about so many things," he continued, "but not on paper. Let's postpone everything, therefore, until my return which is so close—in 120 days."[79]

He wondered how he would manage the trip back home. He was still earning money from tutoring children, but he did not have enough for a train ticket to Vilna. To pay for the trip, he would surely have to receive money before his release. To date, however, none of his family had promised him such help. All he knew was that Aunt Lipman wrote in her last letter that the state of the family properties was grim. It was likely, she reported, that all would be lost prior to his return.

The excruciatingly long year of 1891 finally came to pass. Pilsudski was twenty-four years old when his exile ended on April 20, 1892. After some delay in arranging his formal release, he got final permission on May 24, 1892. Further delaying any possibility of receiving a university education in tsarist Russia, the authorities cruelly inserted a clause into the release document, banning Pilsudski from living in any Russian city with a university for the next five years.[80] On that day, Pilsudski began his long journey back to Vilna. For reasons that have never come to light, he chose not to travel to Odessa, where Leonarda was then living. Instead, he went straight to Vilna, arriving on June 30, 1892. The two went their separate ways and never saw each other again. Little is known about Leonarda's life after this time. When she met with a friend of Pilsudski's in July 1897, she handed him the thirty letters she had received from Pilsudski while in Siberian exile, requesting they be returned to him. In or around 1900, Leonarda tragically took her own life while in her late thirties, possibly as a result of hearing the news of Pilsudski's marriage.[81]

DURING THE PERIOD OF SIBERIAN exile, the young Pilsudski became personally acquainted with two generations of Polish national and socialist leaders. These included men and women who inspired Pilsudski and set him on a path to leadership, such as Bronisław Szwarce, Stanisław Landy, and Michał Mancewicz. At the same time, Pilsudski's letters to fellow political exile and lover Leonarda Lewandowska provide a unique window into his thinking during these formative years. They reveal, among other things, the importance he attached to family ties, particularly his closeness to his older siblings Zofia and Bronisław, but also concern for the well-being of his six younger siblings. He faulted his father not only for mishandling the family properties but also for the failure to provide proper care of the six children still living at home. The absence of a reliable father figure, combined with the twin tragedies of his mother's premature death and the fifteen-year sentence of exile for his older brother, Bronisław, gnawed at Pilsudski's conscience precisely because he felt responsible for his family's well-being.

Pilsudski's letters reveal the extent to which he became estranged from his father during this period. Pilsudski diligently mentioned news he had received from home, citing by name the people with whom he corresponded. The estrangement is revealed in the fact that Pilsudski never noted receiving any letters from his father. The issue of his father was in some ways connected to the recurring theme of financial troubles after the authorities ceased providing a monthly stipend due to their assessment that Pilsudski's father could afford to provide such a sum. In his letters to Leonarda, which discussed family news and finances, there is no mention of Pilsudski's father having ever sent a single payment during this period.

From a social-intellectual point of view, the Siberian period was extraordinarily enriching for the young Pilsudski. Recollections of Pilsudski's friends in Siberia tell us how others saw him at the time. Lidia Łojko, for example, remembered Pilsudski as having a friendly, sunny disposition and a sharp intellect. Yet his lack of a university education and young age sometimes stood out. "Pilsudski lacked a serious education," she wrote, ". . . but he was undoubtedly very smart and talented. He was a person with a strong will and vivid mind who was then a convinced socialist." On the national question, Pilsudski's views were explicit and openly expressed. Pilsudski was "a passionate Polish patriot [and] a long-established nationalist," she wrote. He "loved Mickiewicz, reciting his works from memory, especially *Pan Tadeusz*. He used to say, 'I hate Russia but love Russians,'" people he regarded as comrades-in-arms in the struggle against tsardom.[82]

One of the people Pilsudski frequently dined with in Tunka was Stefan Juszczyński, who recalled that Pilsudski often showed his age. "He absolutely did not take care of his own comforts," Juszczyński observed. "For example, he never prepared meals for himself, making do with bread and milk if one of us didn't feed him." Interestingly, Juszczyński was of the opinion that Pilsudski did not stand out in any way among exiles, "neither in abilities nor in intellect." Pilsudski's closest buddy in Tunka was Mancewicz. "In the fall and spring," Juszczyński recalled, Pilsudski and Mancewicz "were often waist-deep in water hunting ducks or they went to the mountains to chop wood for fuel, which they brought back on a raft floating down the river."[83]

Pilsudski's relationship with Mancewicz was indeed influential. As a student of natural science at Warsaw University in the early 1880s, Mancewicz had become active in Polish socialist circles, eventually becoming a member of the central committee of the Proletariat party. Arrested in 1885, he was interned at the Pawiak Prison in Warsaw and sentenced to five years' exile in 1887.[84] For Pilsudski, then, Mancewicz represented the new socialist movement. Szwarce, on the other hand, symbolized the old, patriotic, national movement of his parents' generation. In gatherings where politics was discussed, socialist theory was often the topic. According to Juszczyński, Pilsudski was largely silent at these meetings. Indeed, Pilsudski himself acknowledged he was never interested in theory. "The abstract logic of Marx and the domination of goods over man," Pilsudski later wrote, "did not suit my brain."[85] Finally, one cannot discuss Pilsudski's Siberian period without reference to Stanisław Landy. A veteran leader of the Polish socialist movement, Landy became a mentor to Pilsudski. "Pilsudski, who in 1890 relocated to Tunka, was our frequent guest," Landy's wife recalled. "Under the pretext of illness he got permission to come to Irkutsk during which time he stayed with us for an entire week."[86]

There is disagreement among historians about the relative influence of these figures during Pilsudski's Siberian period. Garlicki maintained that Szwarce's influence was minimal because Pilsudski referred to him but once in his correspondence with Leonarda. Bohdan Urbankowski countered that Szwarce's impact was important. He pointed out that Pilsudski tutored Szwarce's children in Latin and French, lessons that earned him a monthly salary and led to frequent contact with Szwarce.[87] Evidence weighs more in favor of Urbankowski's thesis. For after the Siberian period, Pilsudski kept in touch not only with Mancewicz but also with Szwarce. And when Szwarce passed away in February 1904 in Lwów, Pilsudski traveled from imperial Russia to Austria-Hungary to attend the funeral. In a 1924 lecture on the 1863 Polish uprising, Pilsudski referred to Szwarce as a "dear old friend" with whom he had "a genuinely cordial friendship."[88] Szwarce and Mancewicz thus constituted the key influences on Pilsudski during the period of Siberian exile: Szwarce, a national hero of the 1863 uprising, and Mancewicz, a pioneer of the early Polish socialist movement, became the young Pilsudski's mentors and educators. Landy fulfilled a similar role while providing a model for the Jewish contribution to the Polish struggle for freedom.

Eleven years after his release from Siberia, Pilsudski attributed the following importance to his time of exile: "It was only there in Siberia, where I could peacefully think over everything I had gone through in the past and everything I wished to do in the future, that I became what I am."[89] Nearing the end of his life, Pilsudski reflected upon it again. "Even in Siberia," he said, "I did not cease meditating on greatness. I thought about what paths lead to it and what characteristics a person has to possess in order to achieve it."[90]

CHAPTER 3

Socialist Leader and Conspirator

Every opposition movement must be harnessed to our chariot. We
must be hosts not only at home but in the entire tsarist state. In a
word, "Polish intrigue" must entangle the whole colossus.

—JOZEF PILSUDSKI (1895)

After five years in Siberian exile, Pilsudski traveled for several weeks
before arriving in Vilna on June 30, 1892. Walking into town from the train
station, he bumped into his cousin Zygmunt Nagrodzki on the street. So
changed was Pilsudski's appearance that Nagrodzki did not recognize him.
The person who greeted him had a full beard, "a face the color of unclean
copper," and two missing front teeth. "Sorry sir," Nagrodzki said; "are you
sure you're not confusing me with someone else?" Pilsudski replied, "No.
There's no mistake. I see I need to introduce myself: Jozef Pilsudski here."[1]
Embarrassed, Nagrodzki embraced his old buddy. The two strolled, catching
up on the last five years. Excited and apprehensive, Pilsudski made his way
to the home of his older sister, Zofia. Hearing footsteps approaching the
house, Zofia came to the front door and, laying eyes on the man standing
before her, did not immediately recognize him. Seconds later, she burst into
tears and wrapped her arms around her beloved and cherished brother.[2]

It was immediately apparent upon stepping into Zofia's home that much
had changed in the five years Pilsudski had been away. Pilsudski set eyes on
his three nieces and nephews, aged four, two, and one, for the first time.[3] Zofia
proceeded to tell Pilsudski about the latest family news. His brothers Adam,
23, and Kazimierz, 21, were working after graduating from gymnasium, while

his father was handling various small business affairs.[4] Pilsudski was eager to see his four other younger siblings—Maria, 19; Jan, 16; Ludwika, 13; and Kacper, 11. They were doing fine, Zofia said hesitatingly, but she was concerned they lacked adult supervision. They were growing up without a mother, and their father was frequently away on business. Zofia also spoke about the dwindled family fortunes: the estates in Zułów and Suginty had been sold.[5] The only property remaining was the estate in Adamowo in the province of Kowno.[6] The Adamowo estate was not insignificant: it would provide a modest but stable income that later allowed Pilsudski to focus entirely on his antigovernment, conspiratorial activity.[7]

Freed from captivity and back in Vilna, Pilsudski's future was far from certain. Under police surveillance, he initially stayed clear of trouble. He decided to go to law school and began studying for the entrance exam. Slim, bright, with some university education, and now assuming the role of oldest male sibling, Pilsudski was seen by his family as having great promise. Zofia's husband—a prominent physician twenty-one years his senior—promised Pilsudski a job. Pilsudski's aunts, sisters, and cousins began serving as matchmakers, introducing him to marriage prospects from wealthy, aristocratic families. But he was not interested in marriage.

Politely declining his brother-in-law's offer, Pilsudski decided instead to return to conspiratorial work. This was partly due to the Russian government's restrictions whereby he could be a student but was forbidden to live in a university town for five years.[8] This draconian measure sharpened his bitterness while reinforcing his longing for historical justice and a desire to be a national leader. In Siberia, Pilsudski had believed that an unusual and great destiny awaited him. Now back in Vilna, he was more mature, better informed, and more knowledgeable. "Politically speaking," Pilsudski's first biographer notes, "he was already very sophisticated when he returned to Vilna in 1892."[9] He brought to this political-mindedness an extraordinary ability to synthesize various views and historical facts.

Pilsudski's decision to become active in clandestine antigovernment activity came in the fall of 1892 when he became aware of an underground group of socialists in Vilna. He began attending meetings and discovered they were mostly followers of the revolutionary Polish populist organization Second Proletariat. It was not a natural fit for Pilsudski, whose dreams of national independence outweighed his interest in socialist thought. "I eventually

decided to join a group of Proletariat followers after returning from exile,"
Pilsudski recalled in 1903, "and tried to persuade them to reform their ideas
in the direction that today we call the Polish Socialist Party."[10] Consisting of
a dozen people, the group included individuals not only from Vilna but also
originally from Warsaw and St. Petersburg. One of them was twenty-six-
year-old Maria Juszkiewicz, from a well-respected, well-to-do family in Vilna.
Pilsudski also met Roman Dmowski, future founder of the right-wing National Democratic Party, who appeared periodically at the meetings. Dmowski
took a liking to Maria, but she rejected his overtures. Her affection was instead directed toward Pilsudski. Divorced, with a three-year-old daughter,
Wanda, Maria became romantically involved with Pilsudski, and the two would
later marry.

Maria Juszkiewicz, Pilsudski's first
wife, ca. 1888.

The clandestine group did not engage in political work. Instead it discussed progressive, democratic and socialist ideas. Wishing to make contacts beyond Vilna, Pilsudski set out for Warsaw in December 1892. Seeing the Polish metropolis for the first time, he met individuals from diverse ideological currents, including figures from the emerging conservative, nationalist camp.[11]

Upon his return to Vilna in January 1893, Pilsudski met a visitor from London, Stanisław Mendelson, sent by the recently formed Union of Polish Socialists Abroad (ZZSP). Founded in November 1892, the new organization created the Polish Socialist Party (PPS) and issued a program of political and economic goals: universal suffrage, equality before the law regardless of religion or nationality, an eight-hour workday, a minimum wage, equal pay for women, the right to strike, and the right to form unions.[12] What made the new organization unique was its demand for the breakup of imperial Russia and the formation of an independent Polish republic. The future state's frontiers, the program specified, were to be based on historic—not ethnic—borders from the eighteenth century. Such a state would possess a unified political force with Lithuania and Ukraine against a common oppressor. By charactering Lithuania and western Ukraine as part of "our country," the new organization was calling for a large, multinational federal state whose eastern border was to correspond with that of pre-partition Poland. With regard to Russian revolutionaries, the program called for cooperation conditional upon recognition of the Polish Socialist Party as sole representatives of workers living on Polish lands (*nasz kraj*). According to one of the participants, Stanisław Wojciechowski, the resolution placing Lithuania and Ukraine inside the boundaries of a future state passed unanimously.[13]

The outline program also included remarks on the complex question of the Jews, a population that formed a significant proportion of the urban population on Polish lands. "The conference has agreed," the program stated, "that our party should distribute a proclamation as soon as possible to Russian-Jewish circles in Lithuania and Ukraine, exposing their russifying activities to be contradictory to both the political interests of liberation and the interests of freedom in Russia."[14] Pilsudski, as we shall see, would be called upon to write that proclamation.

In Vilna, Mendelson presented the outline program to the Vilna group of Polish socialists. The new program had a natural appeal for Pilsudski. As a native of the Lithuanian borderlands, he identified with the idea of a multi-national state based on historical borders. Within two weeks of his meeting with Mendelson, Pilsudski sent an article, dated February 1, 1893, to *Przedświt* (Dawn) in London, the monthly newspaper of the ZZSP. He discussed the imperial mindset and psychological climate in St. Petersburg that made the country's leaders justify the subjugation of Polish lands.[15] For the next two years Pilsudski was the London paper's correspondent in Lithuania. His literary career—an aspiration he spoke about in Siberia—had begun.

In a private letter to the editors of *Przedświt* dated February 15, 1893, Pilsudski reported that his comrades in Vilna had objected to the content of an article that had unfavorably judged several Polish socialist parties. Pilsudski was of the opinion that such polemics were counterproductive. Highlighting ideological differences among Polish socialists, he stated, deflected attention away from the wider question of socialism's purpose. In Polish lands, he argued, socialism was not an end in and of itself but a rallying point for the attainment of independence. "As for me," he wrote, "I believe it is necessary at the present time to abandon this antiquated polemic with 'patriots.' We have so many common objectives with all democratic elements that it is quite unnecessary to inflame old divisions between various currents. I do not doubt that it is necessary to highlight the principled difference between socialists and socialist parties on the one hand, and pure patriotic demands that incorporate socialism only because of the popularity of its slogan." But they need not be stated openly. The seed of Pilsudski's political mind began to emerge here—avoiding parochial, particularistic party politics and instead never losing sight of the big picture on larger, long-term goals. With regard to the paper in general, Pilsudski suggested it should provide more news about the labor movement in Polish lands, which he could deliver regularly.[16]

In his next public correspondence printed in *Przedświt,* dated February 17, Pilsudski discussed the prohibition on speaking Polish at the Russian State Gymnasiums in Vilna. He noted that in the Minsk province, where no such prohibition existed, Polish student enrollment was higher.[17] Beginning with his third correspondence, dated March 4, Pilsudski wrote under the pseudonym "Rom" (short for "Romantic"). He discussed the new governor-general of Vilna province, describing a crowd welcoming him in Vilna with cheers on March 1, 1893. What happened to this province, he wondered aloud, that had risen in open rebellion against Russia in 1863?[18]

One of the subjects Pilsudski addressed in print at this time was the Jews. Mendelson had sparked interest in the topic when he persuaded Pilsudski that winning over the Russian-speaking Jewish intelligentsia in Lithuania was a key objective. To this end, the two reached out to Arkadi Kremer and Tsemakh Kopelzon, leaders of the recently formed Vilna Group, an organization of Jewish social democrats who had attended Russian universities and were now agitating among Jewish workers in Vilna. Kremer shared Pilsudski's geographical and educational background. Born in Svencionys, a town near Pilsudski's birthplace, he moved to Vilna at the age of twelve to attend gymnasium, where, like Pilsudski, he joined an illegal study group and began to identify as a socialist. When he later attended a Russian university, he was expelled for his involvement in an illegal student circle.[19] Blocked from attaining a university degree, Kremer returned to Vilna in 1891 and joined the Vilna Group, led by Kopelzon and Leon Jogiches. Pilsudski and Jogiches had known each other since gymnasium as members of the illegal student study group Union.

At their meeting in January 1893, Pilsudski and Mendelson expressed concern to Kremer and Kopelzon about the Vilna Group's Russian orientation. Heated discussion reportedly ensued, with Pilsudski criticizing the Vilna Group for leading circles in Russian. Why not, Pilsudski asked, switch to Yiddish, the language of Lithuanian Jewry? Also, Pilsudski and Mendelson stressed, the Vilna Group should agitate under the banner of the PPS.[20] The discussions broke down over the question of Polish independence. Kremer and Kopelzon shared the opinion, then widely held in social democratic circles, that stateless peoples' demand for independence should be suspended until after the transformation of existing states into constitutional democracies with equality before the law. That is to say, the goal of socialists in tsarist Russia should be the overthrow of the tsar and the creation of a democratic country, not the separation of Poland.

Having failed to persuade the Vilna Group in private, Pilsudski decided to air their differences in the pages of the party press. In a piece from Vilna dated March 4, 1893, Pilsudski reminded readers that Jews made up not only nearly half of Vilna's inhabitants, but the majority of the urban population in the Lithuanian-Belarussian provinces as a whole. "If, since 1863, russification has made progress in our country," Pilsudski wrote, "it is precisely among the Jewish people." The russified nature of the Vilna Group made it difficult for Jewish and Christian workers to work together, he stated. "I do not take exception to the study of Russian culture and language in and of itself. This is about denationalization and russification in our country. With the current state of affairs," he declared, "no socialist for whom any manifestation of oppression is loathsome . . . has the right to hold a neutral position on this question, not to any extent." A neutral stand on the national question among the Jewish socialists, he concluded, would paralyze the building a mass movement.[21]

Formation of the Polish Socialist Party in Tsarist Russia

After meeting with Pilsudski, Mendelson traveled to Riga, Warsaw, and St. Petersburg to garner support for the establishment of a new party in tsarist Russia. The culmination of his efforts came in March 1893 in Warsaw when the Polish Socialist Party (PPS) formally came into being. The new party united loosely bound groups of socialists, including former adherents of the Second Proletariat in Warsaw and St. Petersburg, as well as Pilsudski's group in Vilna, which renamed itself the Lithuanian Section of the PPS.[22] Pilsudski now took charge as the recognized leader of the party's Lithuanian branch.

In his capacity as leader of the Lithuanian Section, Pilsudski continued to devote articles to the problem of Russian-speaking Jewish socialists. In May 1893 he penned the proclamation Mendelson had requested, titled "To Our Jewish Socialist Comrades in the Occupied Polish Territories." Pilsudski warned that a negative attitude toward Jews was forming among the local population due to what he called "some Jews' hostile attitude toward the politics of [our] country." The young generation of Russian-speaking Jews was "full of false ideas and principles" about Poland that they had learned in Russian schools. "In our country . . . the brutal violence of tsarist despotism has found expression in the politics of 'unification,' and Jewish socialists have begun working among the Jewish proletariat with the aim of imposing Russian as the path to culture." The Russian government, Pilsudski argued, was using Russian-speaking Jews as an instrument for diluting Polish cultural heritage. "It has become increasingly clear," he wrote, "that the Russian government is using . . . the russified Jews as a weapon against the political aspirations of the Poles"[23] He concluded with two demands. The first was that Jewish socialists take a "clear and unambiguous" position on the question of

Polish independence. The second was a veiled threat that Jewish socialists would be perceived as supporters of the tsarist regime if they did not harmonize their program with those of Polish and Lithuanian workers.

Pilsudski's proclamation on the Jews rested on two assumptions. The first was that the Poles and Lithuanians shared the same vision for the future of their lands (a federation with Poland). Yet no separate party among ethnic Lithuanians had yet formed and thus no Lithuanian program outlining a future state had yet been declared. The second assumption was that the platform of the Polish Socialist Party on the national question and on relations with Russian revolutionaries reflected the views of all its members. As we shall see, both proved to be wrong. Within a matter of months, a radical wing within the party openly challenged Pilsudski, arguing that the demand for independence was premature, unnecessarily divisive, and a source of discord with Russian revolutionaries.[24] These individuals feared that the party was moving too far away from class and revolutionary aims. In a visible trace of the future split in the party, the breakaway wing characterized the party's anti-Russian orientation as unhelpful and alienating. The emerging conflict led Stanisław Wojciechowski of the ZZSP to travel from London to Warsaw in June 1893 to prevent a party schism. Unable to achieve compromise, Wojciechowski set out for Vilna. There, he met the twenty-five-year-old Pilsudski in person for the first time. "I already had good feelings about him back in London," Wojciechowski recalled, due to the several letters Pilsudski had published earlier in *Przedświt*.[25]

Wojciechowski found wholehearted support in Pilsudski and the party's Lithuanian division. Vilna, he realized, was the most hospitable setting to convene the First Party Congress.[26] Held in the Belmont Forest outside Vilna in June 1893, much of the gathering was taken up by Pilsudski's proposed revision of the party's position on relations with Russian revolutionaries, which the participants accepted. His ideas on Russian revolutionaries revealed the degree to which his family's experience with autocratic Russia guided his politics. "[Pilsudski's] profound disdain for Russia," one close comrade later remarked, "was one of the principal components of his political worldview."[27]

After the party congress, Pilsudski sent three pieces to the party's London paper. The first reported on the harsh conditions of the average worker in Lithuania—fourteen-hour workdays and the scandalous persistence of child labor. A second report revolved around the death of the former director of the Russian State Gymnasium in Vilna. For decades, this headmaster had strictly enforced the prohibition on speaking Polish in the classroom. "It was under his directorship in particular," Pilsudski wrote, "that the school saw a growth in the suppression of the Polish language and of Polish cultural expression in general." That is why, according to Pilsudski, many in Vilna greeted his passing with joy and relief.[28]

Rise to Leadership

In the third article, titled "Relations with Russian Revolutionaries," printed in August 1893, Pilsudski presented the party's new position on Russian dissidents. The piece marked the beginnings of Pilsudski's rise to party leadership. Recognizing its significance, the *Przedświt* editors inserted a preface stating that the article should be regarded as the official voice of the party. Pilsudski laid out the new policy, maintaining that the party should refrain from ideological debates on socialism with Russian revolutionary groups. Instead, discussion should revolve around the common demand for political rights. "For the Polish Socialist Party," he stressed, "the struggle against the tsarist system merely constitutes a fight over one form of Russian rule in Poland and it is by no means the sum of our political demands. In our program, the Polish Socialist Party also demands an independent democratic republic." The party programs thus had to pronouncedly condemn the government's "policy of russification and oppression of [non-Russian] nationalities inhabiting the Russian Empire."[29]

Pilsudski reminded readers that Russian revolutionary groups had neither condemned the treatment of national minorities nor expressed solidarity with their aspirations. Relations with Russian revolutionaries had therefore to be based on mutual recognition precisely because the PPS demanded territorial separation. "And here," he wrote, "slander and lies are forced into the minds of school-age youth" while the censors suppressed literature at odds with the government's position. As far as Pilsudski could see, the Russian revolutionary movement was silent on this issue. "One can observe here either native ignorance of this state of affairs or, what's worse, silent support for the policy of russification." He concluded:

All of this demonstrates that at present we do not have genuine friends even in the ranks of Russian revolutionaries. The question of independence is for us too important, and the Russian government's oppression too barbaric, for us to remain passive in the face of the indifference of Russian revolutionaries. For this reason the PPS can and must require Russian revolutionary groups to abandon their passive stand. Recognition of our political aspirations shall now be the condition for entering into relations with us.[30]

According to historian Andrzej Nowak, this piece marked Piłsudski's debut as one of the founders of the political framework for the Polish independence movement.[31]

Meanwhile, ideological differences within the party led one faction to secede. The schism occurred in August 1893 at the international socialist congress in Zurich when the fiery twenty-three-year-old Rosa Luxemburg voiced opposition to the party's independence platform. Unable to exact concessions from the party leadership, Luxemburg announced the formation of a new party—Social Democracy of the Kingdom of Poland (SDKP). The SDKP spelled out a decidedly internationalist standpoint in favor of unconditional cooperation with Russian revolutionary groups. The party schism led the PPS to step up recruitment efforts. To this end, Piłsudski went to Warsaw in September 1893 to meet with Stanisław Wojciechowski. The result was that Wojciechowski formed the Workers' Committee (*Komitet Robotniczy*, KR) in October 1893, the PPS's first executive body, with Piłsudski as the Lithuanian Section's representative.[32]

Elevated to a top leadership role, Piłsudski sent off several articles to London regarding the growing worker's movement in Lithuania. In one, he reported on a strike of 160 Jewish tailors in Vilna employed by a local clothing manufacturer. The group demanded a twelve-hour workday and a 25 percent wage hike. After five weeks the owner granted a twelve-hour workday and a 10 percent raise. For Piłsudski, the strike had enormous moral significance, serving as an example of the labor movement's growing influence. What this event proved, he concluded, was that strikes were the labor movement's chief weapon. The fact that the strike took place in Vilna, where the labor movement was still in its infancy, was important. "That is why," he concluded, "we need to wholeheartedly express gratitude to our comrades—workers—who persevered . . . until their demands were met, something new here [in Lithuania]."[33]

In December 1893 Pilsudski outlined his concept of cooperation among peoples inhabiting the lands of partitioned Poland. In order to win over the peoples of the eastern borderlands belonging to the historic Polish-Lithuanian Commonwealth, he remarked in a private letter, it was important to repeatedly emphasize that this region was a part of historical Polish lands whose peoples shared the same political history. A separate piece was needed in the party press on Lithuania and Ukraine "where we should simply point out that we have common interests. And based on these common interests, we must formulate a common program."[34]

The opportunity for Pilsudski to formally present his nationalities program came in February 1894 at the Second Party Congress in Warsaw when the party formally adopted Pilsudski's position on relations with Russian revolutionaries. "Our position on relations with Russian revolutionaries," the protocols stated, "is defined in *Przedświt,* No. 8," referring to Pilsudski's article, "Relations with Russian Revolutionaries."[35] The resolution was significant, demonstrating party deference to Pilsudski.

At the gathering, the party's Workers' Committee was reorganized as the Central Workers' Committee (CKR), now consisting of twenty-six-year-old Pilsudski; twenty-four-year-old law school graduate Jan Strożecki; medic Juliusz Grabowski; and a typesetter, twenty-five-year-old Paulin Klimowicz.[36] The CKR was to organize and direct local workers' committees on Polish lands. Local committees were to organize and direct the smallest party subdivision, referred to as Circles of Agitators, whose members distributed propaganda literature. According to the protocols, the Circles of Agitators was the first organizational arm that was to bring into the party the most energetic and intelligent people for future party work.[37]

Pilsudski returned to Vilna in the spring of 1894. To raise party funds, he traveled to Riga, Dorpat, St. Petersburg, Moscow, and Kiev. In Moscow he met with Sulkiewicz, where the two recruited Napoleon Czarnocki, a Polish medical student. Czarnocki recalled his first encounter with the party leaders, noting that Pilsudski and Sulkiewicz "moved among Polish youths" during their stay in Moscow. For Czarnocki, the meetings were transformative, as he and his wife joined the PPS at this time. Regarding a visit to the Kremlin with Pilsudski, Czarnocki recalled: "While visiting the Kremlin and its museum with me, my wife, and her sister, Pilsudski broke out with a joke. Passing by a display of 'the Polish Crown,' Pilsudski turned to the ladies and said, with a characteristically frivolous expression, 'I would steal that with pleasure.'"[38]

Upon arriving back in Vilna, Pilsudski returned to the issue of relations with the city's Jewish socialist leaders, individuals with whom Pilsudski had been in contact since the previous year. After his first meeting with Kremer and Kopelzon, Pilsudski had been facilitating the transport of Yiddish socialist publications to Vilna from Galicia, New York, and London, in an effort to steer the Vilna Group away from agitation in Russian. All in all, the PPS smuggle 167 Yiddish brochures into the Russian Empire in 1893 for the Vilna Group, a quantity that increased annually, reaching 1,676 in 1896.[39] The aid reflected Pilsudski's emerging federalist strategy of supporting cultural autonomy in the borderlands while spreading the Polish state idea among its inhabitants as the only hope for attaining political rights.

Given that four out of every ten residents of Vilna were native Yiddish speakers, Pilsudski promoted active work among this community. In April 1894, moreover, he came to the conclusion that the party had to have its own literature in Yiddish.[40] In the meantime, he asked his comrades in London for more Yiddish-language propaganda literature, including the new Yiddish newspaper of the Lwów-based Social Democratic Party of Galicia, *Der arbeter*. In Pilsudski's view, winning over the Vilna Group was a key objective. If they eventually joined the party, he remarked in May 1894, "that would be the greatest triumph I could imagine."[41] His efforts regarding the Vilna Group were significant. In the course of 1894, the PPS smuggled 788 copies of Yiddish socialist brochures into the Russian Empire, including fifty copies of *Der arbeter* from Lwów. Hopeful that the Vilna Group would one day operate as a Jewish section of the PPS, Pilsudski arranged for a Hebrew mimeograph machine to be smuggled into Russia for use by the Vilna Group.[42]

In an article for *Przedświt,* he wrote on relations with Jewish workers in the Russian Empire. Discussing the distinctive features of the Jewish community in Lithuania, he commented that "Jewish artisans in Lithuania—due to their numbers—constitute a central theme for socialist propaganda." The increase in strikes by Jewish artisans was leading to more identification with the class struggle. The task, according to Pilsudski, was to increase awareness of the larger, worldwide labor movement. To this end, the party had to print its own Yiddish organ, one that should be a vehicle for impressing upon Jewish workers the importance of extending their demands from the economic to the political, including calling for an end to autocracy.[43]

The reason the Vilna Group leaders showed little interest in Polish concerns was clear, Pilsudski wrote. They were "almost exclusively under the influence of Russian revolutionary literature," which was silent on the subject of the national aspirations of the non-Russian peoples among whom the Jews lived. Such Russian publications "almost without exception are overflowing with brazen falsehoods about Poles, who are seen only as backward and clerical aristocrats." The Vilna Group leaders, educated in Russian gymnasiums and universities, appeared unaware of such Polish concerns. "Hence the logic of their argument," Pilsudski wrote, "that changes in the fate of the Jews can only follow the triumph of Russian revolutionaries. None of them believes in the independence of Poland, regarding it as a chimera . . . as merely the product of a vivid imagination inherent in their Polish comrades."[44]

Pilsudski's intention was to pressure Arkadi Kremer and his Vilna Group to restrict their agitation literature to Yiddish and Polish—to distribute a literature that took into account the language, culture, and aspirations of the local population among whom the Vilna Group and its followers lived. "Our Jewish comrades," Pilsudski wrote, "rather than derive . . . spiritual sustenance from our publications, continue to draw on Russian revolutionary writings from the '90s, '80s, and even the '70s. What's stranger is that even publications in Yiddish are looked down upon by those who see in them a turn to a 'national' viewpoint . . . and this is so despite the fact that the available quantity of socialist literature in Yiddish now equals, or perhaps exceeds, what there is in Russian."[45]

Pilsudski presented the case for Jews to support the party program. "The question here is not only whether Jewish socialists should model themselves after Poles or Russians, but instead what is the most favorable for the Jews: the separation of Lithuania and Poland or the attainment of a constitution in tsarist Russia. We, adhering to our program, have tried to persuade our Jewish comrades that the first benefits them most. Yet we often encounter stiff resistance."[46] He pointed out that Russia "above all has been a pronouncedly anti-Semitic state for centuries" due to "religious fanaticism. In a democratic Polish republic, the Jewish proletariat will have a definite, strong ally among class-conscious Polish workers who will continue the mortal struggle against injustices whether they be national, economic or political." Pilsudski concluded that "while our Jewish comrades waste their energy on sterile workers' circles [conducted in Russian], the Polish labor movement is growing in numbers and influence. . . . It would be lamentable if the Jewish proletariat stood as silent bystanders in the face of [our] growing movement." He was confident that "the class struggle will take place when the Jewish workers join our ranks. We, from our side, are doing everything to accelerate that process."[47]

Pilsudski was concerned about poor recruitment numbers, not only among Jews but for the party as a whole. Noting in May 1895 that no party leaders had been arrested, he added, "If the situation [of low recruitment] lasts much longer, then we are in great risk of being the first and the last of the PPS." The first step in rectifying the problem, he argued, was to put out a party newspaper inside the Russian Empire. "I am of the opinion," he remarked, "that a party newspaper printed in the homeland would make a great impression."[48]

Aware that some socialists were uncomfortable with the party's emphasis on statehood, Pilsudski reassured readers that support for independence did not weaken the party's commitment to class struggle. The party was fighting, he emphasized, not only against foreign-rule and autocracy but against the Polish privileged elite as well. "Like the situation everywhere," he wrote, "our privileged class is ideologically bankrupt and bogged down in the mud of selfishness." This privileged class acted not for the good of the country as a whole, Pilsudski maintained, but for financial gain alone. That is why the national leadership was in the process of falling to the "underprivileged working class." Characterizing the successful strike of Jewish cloth makers in Vilna as an example of this trend, he reported on a similar strike in progress in which female factory workers were demanding a twelve-hour workday and higher wages. "In any case," he concluded, "we can be certain that the worker's movement in Vilna, although in its early stages, will soon grow in strength like in other cities of Poland."[49]

Pilsudski reported subsequently on a large-scale strike in Białystok as evidence of a widening strike movement in western Russia. He praised the strikers, and commented that docility only perpetuated bondage. "Over 20,000 of our Białystok brothers," Pilsudski wrote, "are struggling with the government in defense of rights that are being violated." As they prepared for a showdown, "we cannot passively stand by and indifferently endure government policy. Dignity must always guide us. The yoke of captivity is not fastened to a barge, debasing our patient spirit with insults. [We must] fight off government attacks directed toward us. Always and everywhere," he concluded, "the government must experience us as a foe who does not allow insults to be hurled at us without resistance."[50]

In order to remain engaged in antigovernment work, Pilsudski had to devise elaborate tactics to evade police detection. To shield his family from harm, he limited all communication with them, rarely visiting, and refrained from any written communication. He further evaded police detection by using a multitude of pseudonyms that made it virtually impossible to trace his whereabouts. In print he used the bylines "Rom" (Romantic) or "Czasowy" (Time). In private correspondence he signed his letters "Z" (for Ziuk, the diminutive of Jozef), "Wiktor," or "Mieczysław." Never revealing his surname, Pilsudski became nameless and often homeless, changing locations frequently to elude the authorities. Only briefly did he appear in police records. In July 1894 a Vilna police department informant spotted him, describing Pilsudski as twenty-six years old, five feet eight inches tall, with a beard, fused dark-blond eyebrows, blond sideburns, and grey eyes. The police chief ordered that Pilsudski be secretly surveilled rather than arrested. But within days law enforcement lost all trace of him.[51]

Founding the First Party Paper

In cooperation with the London organization, Pilsudski stepped up preparations for a party press inside Russia. Wojciechowski traveled from London to Leipzig, where he purchased a printing press. A key figure in the plan was Aleksander Sulkiewicz, a member of the party's Central Workers' Committee, who worked for Russian customs at the town of Wierzbołów on the German-Russian frontier. Pilsudski arranged for Wojciechowski to smuggle the printing press into Russia at Wierzbołów with the help of Sulkiewicz, who ensured its safe passage across the border. It continued on to Lipniszki, a remote town thirty-four miles southeast of Vilna.[52] Pilsudski had been preparing for this for several months. His recruit from Moscow, Czarnocki, had earlier arranged for a Polish pharmacist friend to open a pharmacy in Lipniszki as a cover for the placement and operation of the printing press. After the arrival of the printing press in June 1894, Pilsudski spent two weeks learning to operate it and preparing to launch the paper. "The machine rattles a bit when in use," Pilsudski reported back to London, "but we'll work on that. In any case, I heartily thank you for this. It is entirely safe here with us."[53]

The inaugural issue of *Robotnik* (The Worker) appeared on July 12, 1894. To confuse the authorities, however, the masthead read "Warsaw, June 1894." With Sulkiewicz's help, Pilsudski acted as both editor in chief and typesetter. "The task of this paper," Pilsudski wrote in the front-page editorial, "is to defend the interests of the working classes. So as not to be cut off from life in our country, we are producing *Robotnik* here in the homeland." Produced locally, the party paper would be connected directly with the issues that mattered most to workers living on Polish lands. "Our priority," Pilsudski continued, "is to inform readers about all aspects of the labor movement here and abroad; to present facts about abnormal political and social relations; to scrutinize government decrees intended to harm workers; to expose all forms of government abuses; and to tear off the mask of hypocrisy of our own propertied class."[54] For the remainder of 1894 Pilsudski spent half of every month in Lipniszki, putting out the first six issues of the monthly paper.[55] Sulkiewicz, who assisted, described working with Pilsudski in Lipniszki, writing that "he was extremely pleasant to work with. He was never without patience. He didn't ever lose his temper, raise his voice or fall into despair."[56]

According to Feliks Perl, then active in the ZZSP, "the greatest splendor of the party was the consistent appearance of the secret publication, *Robotnik*, under the vigilant care of Pilsudski."[57] In fact, the party's growing influence at this time was due in large part to *Robotnik*. Pilsudski devoted most of his time to recruiting stories, gathering reports, and writing. He frequently traveled outside Vilna to gather firsthand news for stories, and combined these reports with labor news from Germany, England, Italy, Belgium, France, and the United States.[58] In Warsaw, meanwhile, police crackdowns struck a blow to the party when over a hundred underground activists in Warsaw were arrested on August 29 and 30, 1894. The sweep included nearly the entire membership of the SDKP as well as the editors of the clandestine conservative weekly *Głos*. The police also picked up members of the PPS, including three-fourths of the party's Central Workers' Committee—Jan Strożecki, Juliusz Grabowski, and Paulin Klimowicz. Only Pilsudski evaded arrest.[59] One of the two deputy CKR members, Kazimierz Pietkiewicz, escaped arrest and joined Pilsudski. The two functioned as the party's executive body until the middle of 1895.[60] Pilsudski appeared exasperated at the lack of manpower after the arrests, which had abruptly elevated him to the position of de facto party leader. He nevertheless filled the void with ease and capability. It was a remarkable moment in the early stages of a career: in less than two years, Pilsudski had become, at age twenty-seven, the clandestine party's leader.

Pilsudski began as leader by examining the party's weaknesses, expressing concern about its lack of internal cohesion. "Organizationally, we are very poor," he wrote to his comrades in London, "and it's necessary to use a thousand ploys and bluster to conceal the party's weakness before immodest eyes." He continued that "party work is now based on a few energetic individuals" and the party coffers were nearly empty.[61] To help build the party, he focused on recruitment, raising funds, putting out *Robotnik,* and writing. In an article from October 1894, Pilsudski highlighted the differences between the labor movement on Polish lands and in Western Europe. In the West, he wrote, class consciousness was widespread. "The first barrier, the first obstacle in the path of our labor movement," he maintained, "is, in our view, tsardom—the lack of political freedoms. Our first step, therefore, must be its demolition."[62]

In response to the death of Tsar Alexander III on November 1, 1894, Pilsudski wrote a party circular that did not mince words. "The tsar has died!" Pilsudski proclaimed. "Fourteen years of rule . . . was marked in the pages of history by continuous oppression of free thought, gradually stripping away the last scraps of liberty. A cowardly tyrant, [he was] afflicted with the madness of absolute autocracy and national chauvinism." Pilsudski concluded: "How will history judge [Tsar Alexander III]? Economic bankruptcy of the Russian people, misery from excessive taxes, a hostile disposition toward the diverse masses of peoples who have the misfortune of living inside the Russian state, the deceased tsar presided over a system of forced domination in which heroes were spies and gendarmes, baseness became a virtue, and virtue was considered treasonous."[63]

First Foreign Travels

Pilsudski traveled abroad for the first time in December 1894 to attend a conference of the Union of Polish Socialists Abroad. On the train across Europe, he commented on the dizzying array of languages. "I had problems with the various people who gabbed on and on in every language other than Polish," he wrote.[64] In London, Pilsudski for the first time met key party figures, including Feliks Perl, Stanisław Grabski, Aleksander Dębski, and Ignacy Mościcki, the future president of Poland. Like Pilsudski, Mościcki had recently turned twenty-seven. He worked as a barber and recalled that Pilsudski got rid of his beard and trimmed his eyebrows while in London.[65] Pilsudski attended to other personal health-care matters as well while in London. Alexander Dębski introduced him to his wife, Rozalia Dębska, a dentist by profession. Pilsudski was delighted to accept her offer to replace the two front teeth he had lost in Siberia with false ones.[66]

Upon returning to Vilna, Pilsudski discovered that the party's printing press had been abruptly removed from Lipniszki and was temporarily inoperative. This was a blow. During Pilsudski's trip abroad, Sulkiewicz had arranged for the relocation of the printing press when a female employee at the pharmacy got wind of what was going on and began to act suspiciously.[67] With the printing press out of commission, Pilsudski focused on maintaining correspondence while writing numerous articles for the party's London periodical. Pilsudski even mentioned his father in a letter from this time. He remarked that he had spoken to his "old man [*baćka*]," who had proposed to send cheap Polish ham to the Union Abroad that it could sell at a profit. "I am doubtful anything will come of it," Pilsudski wrote discouragingly, a reflection of his long-held lack of confidence in his father's business acumen.[68]

With production of *Robotnik* suspended, Pilsudski used the printing facilities of the ZZSP in London to put out a special, onetime edition, which appeared in April 1895. Pilsudski's cover piece was on Russia and the nationalities. "The biggest enemy of the Polish working classes," he began, "is the Russian tsarist regime." The Polish worker "now understands the need for broad political freedoms and is increasingly drawn to a party whose program, in the interests of the working classes, includes the demand for an Independent Democratic Polish Republic."[69] Pilsudski then hinted at his federalist concept, writing of the Poles, Lithuanians, Latvians, and Ukrainians who, "by sheer force are in chains and oppressed." These inhabitants of the historic Polish-Lithuanian Commonwealth "have an entirely different history and traditions." The weakest link in imperial Russia was found here in the area of national and religious subjugation, Pilsudski argued. "All of these conditions suggest that precisely from them will emerge the strength that will crush to dust the might of tsarism."[70]

The party's May Day circular for 1895, penned by Pilsudski, was a powerful call for political and national rights. He reminded readers that their socialist comrades in the constitutional states of Western and Central Europe had the right to freedom of assembly and of association. "But among us, the voices of protesters . . . are muffled. With fierce virulence, we are punished more severely than even the law allows," he wrote, adding that "the yoke of political slavery and abuse of our sovereignty . . . hovers over us." He continued, "We despise this and will not cease struggling until a new, just system arises. Only then will there be no place for exploitation and oppression." With unbending optimism he continued, "Our strength is growing and our victory is near."[71]

Pilsudski continued to express his concern that the Vilna Group was drawing support away from his own party. Wishing his party would step up its work among Jewish workers, he decided to get in touch with the editors of the Yiddish paper, *Der arbeter,* in Galicia. "Find out from them," Pilsudski wrote to London, "what kind of connection they have with our Jews [the Vilna Group]. Can they not exert influence on the publications [of the Vilna Group] that would have a desirable outcome for us?"[72]

In Pilsudski's letters, one occasionally finds comments on personal matters. In June 1895, for example, he complained that the dentures he received in London six months earlier were painful and had to be removed. "Please tell Pani Ska [Rozalia Dębska]," he wrote despondently, "that unfortunately the teeth she gave me are of no use. A few weeks ago, they had to be pulled out together with three rubles. *Que faire!* I guess my fate is to be without teeth."[73]

Meanwhile, Pilsudski went about working on restarting the party paper. He asked the London center for supplies, including six hundred sheets of mimeograph paper, a rolling pin, bottles of ink, and materials to operate a Neo-Cyclostyle duplication machine—the world's first such, invented in 1888—that he had in his possession. The printing press was housed in Stanisław Wojciechowski's apartment in Vilna—a perfect location, right

under the nose of the Russian police.[74] The seventh issue of *Robotnik* appeared
on June 7, 1895, and Pilsudski's articles filled the first five pages. "After a long
break," he wrote in the front-page editorial, "*Robotnik* returns anew." From
far and wide, he continued, "the need for a newspaper of the worker could
be felt." Occasional brochures and the spoken word "are not in a position to
satisfy all the needs of today's movement which . . . has become a first-rate
political force in our country." He asserted that *Robotnik* would "spread class
consciousness among the Polish working masses, persuade them about the
need to abolish the present political and social order, . . . and put an end to
both political oppression and the predatory government's abuses based on
economic and social exploitation."[75]

Pilsudski's historical mindedness was on full display in his second piece.
Here, he traced the revolutionary current in Europe back to the French Revolution, an event that "abolished the royal throne, put an end to aristocratic
and ecclesiastical privilege, introduced equality before the law, and declared
war with despotic governments." He emphasized Poland's role during the
French Revolutionary Wars, noting that in 1794 the Polish armed revolt under
General Tadeusz Kościuszko diverted parts of the central European armies
away from their war with France. The Kościuszko Uprising, he argued, had
preserved "the revolutionary flame in France."[76] Pilsudski discussed the writings of August Bebel, Karl Marx, Friedrich Engels, and Wilhelm Liebknecht
to bolster his argument that the Russian regime was a barrier to progress. In
Polish lands today, he wrote, the Polish Socialist Party was leading the revolutionary struggle. "The historical role of socialism in Poland," Pilsudski wrote,
"is the defense of the West against annexationist and reactionary Russia."[77]

At the Third Party Congress on June 29, 1895, Pilsudski introduced a resolution on the future of Lithuania and Ukraine. The PPS would henceforth
ally with the "subjugated nations" (*narody ujarzmione*) in Russia in order to
bring about "the separation of the nationalities subjugated by the tsarist government." The resolution concluded: "The Third Congress resolves that the
PPS should spread separatist demands among opposition groups of other nationalities. We shall emphasize the necessity of overthrowing the tsar
through joint action."[78] The resolution was adopted, becoming an integral
part of the party platform.

Emboldened by his newly passed resolution, Pilsudski wrote a flurry of
pieces on the theme of Russia as a prison house of nations. He first discussed

the debilitating effects of russification. "Nationalist oppression," he wrote, "hinders the natural development of our country" and "is a permanent phenomenon that became particularly pronounced under Tsar Alexander III." He pointed out that half of imperial Russia's subjects were non-Russian— including ethnic Poles, Lithuanians, Ukrainians, Latvians, and Georgians.[79] This fact helps people "understand how wide is the scope of russification that stands as the axis of the whole state machinery." Pilsudski concluded that Russian rule over the peoples of historic Poland was a colonial enterprise.[80]

In "Our Motto," appearing in August 1895, Pilsudski emphasized the link between national and class oppression. "Nationalistic oppression reaches into every sphere of life in our country," he wrote. He cautioned against the assumption that the adoption of a constitution in Russia would solve the problem of national subjugation. "Historical experience has taught us," he wrote, responding to critics of the party program, "that democratic constitutions, responsible to the interests of the working classes, are possible only in lands where a numerous and politically aware proletariat stands as an important force . . . in the political apparatus and thereby imprints democracy [on the society]."[81]

While the peoples in western Russia were ripe for democratic government, Pilsudski argued, the same could not be said for the inhabitants of Russia proper. The attainment of a constitution in Russia would not bring about an end to the struggle for political rights. "Responding to the needs of workers, and resulting from a careful analysis of social relations between Russia and Poland," Pilsudski wrote, "it follows that the achievement of political rights will only follow the creation of an Independent Polish Republic."[82] In a subsequent article he similarly stressed that "an Independent Democratic Polish Republic is today the motto . . . of the struggle for freedom and political rights."[83]

In private Pilsudski advocated a long-term, concerted campaign to propagate the Polish state idea among Lithuanians, Ukrainians, and Jews. He discussed relations with these borderland peoples in a letter from September 1895. Jews, spread throughout the Kingdom of Poland, Lithuania, and Ukraine, played a special role. To campaign among them, Pilsudski wrote, the party had to put out its own Yiddish paper. "I have discussed the idea of [publishing] our own party paper in Yiddish with various people here on a few occasions," he wrote from Vilna in September 1895, "but the details still have to be worked out." In the meantime, he intended to meet in person with Joachim Fraenkel, the editor of *Der arbiter* in Austrian Galicia, to discuss cooperation.[84]

The importance Pilsudski attached to the need for Jewish support was only made stronger by a group of Polish-speaking Jews who appealed in writing in December to the party leadership. The authors began by expressing disappointment with the Third Party Congress the previous June. "Neither a resolution at the last congress nor any special articles in *Robotnik* have addressed the party's relations with Polish Jewish workers." The letter suggested increasing the distribution of literature in Yiddish that advocated for the party program. What was needed most was a party paper in Yiddish, the letter stressed. "Given the ignorance of the Jewish masses," the letter concluded, "appealing to them with Polish publications is not an option."[85]

To Pilsudski, the party's weak appeal to Jews reflected a larger problem of relations with the non-Polish peoples. In a letter from September 1895 he summarized his outreach efforts among Lithuanians, Latvians, Ukrainians, and Jews. In considering how to draw these peoples into the party, Pilsudski promoted the federalist idea. "In my view," he wrote his comrades in London, "we hold two huge trump cards in our hands: the [porous] border and the printing house, which firmly gives us the advantage we want." He continued:

> Regarding relations between the nationalities in Russia, to which I seem to attach more importance than others, I hold the principle that the center of domestic policy in Russia must be decisively shifted from the Neva River [in St. Petersburg] to the Vistula River [in Warsaw] while demonstrating this to the whole world in the clearest fashion possible. Every opposition [movement] must be harnessed to our chariot. (I apologize for the florid style). We must be hosts not only at home but in the entire tsarist state. In a word, "Polish intrigue" must entangle the whole colossus.[86]

In the course of the next decade, until the 1904 Russo-Japanese War and its aftermath, Pilsudski adhered to this analysis. It was his view at this time that the separation of Poland and the formation of a democratic republic would come about as the result of a popular uprising. A tireless conspirator, Pilsudski became a perennial thorn in the side of the Russian regime, disseminating the idea through the illegal press that the separation from Russia of Poland, Lithuania, and Ukraine was a prerequisite for the realization of civil society and the attainment of democratic institutions.

CHAPTER 4

Into the International Arena

The only hope of pushing reactionary Russia back from central
Europe lies in the reconstitution of a strong Poland

—HENRY HYNDMAN, CHAIRMAN OF THE 1896 INTERNATIONAL
SOCIALIST CONGRESS

Pilsudski traveled to London in March 1896 to attend the upcoming
Fourth Congress of the Second Socialist International. During his five-
month stay in the British capital, he met many comrades in the Union of
Polish Socialists Abroad (ZZSP) in person for the first time. He stayed in the
East London neighborhood of Leytonstone at the home of Bolesław Antoni
Jędrzejowski, a member of the ZZSP's executive board.[1] Pilsudski managed
party affairs from there, as evidenced by the voluminous correspondence
he kept up with the party's Central Workers' Committee. He also used the
time to edit two brochures, to write articles for the London-based socialist
periodical *Przedświt,* and to establish important ties with British, Russian,
German, Jewish, Lithuanian, and Ukrainian socialist leaders.

Early in his stay Pilsudski prepared a brochure for the occasion of May Day
1896. His goal was both to print articles by members of the Polish Socialist
Party in all of the three partitions and to include greetings from European
socialists sympathetic to the party program. Such a brochure, he wrote, "will
be very useful for us as agitation literature for May Day and beyond."[2] By the
end of March, Pilsudski had already received contributions from Ignacy
Daszyński, the leading Polish socialist in Austrian Galicia, and from Rosa
Altenberg, a leading advocate for women's rights in the labor movement, as

well as a piece from Jędrzejowski on the Russian partition. What was needed, Pilsudski suggested in a March 23 letter, was an article on partitioned Poland as a whole. So he appealed to Witold Jodko-Narkiewicz, a founding member of the ZZSP, then residing in Switzerland. Jodko-Narkiewicz had earlier come out in support of Pilsudski's position on the national question and on relations with Russian revolutionaries, making him the ideal candidate to write such a piece.

Pilsudski's project came to fruition at the end of April 1896 when the volume of essays by Polish and European socialists appeared in time for May Day. Published in London as *Pamiątka majowa* (In Remembrance of May), it bore the subtitle "Published by the Polish Socialist Party in the Three Partitions," stressing party unity across state lines. "For the first time," Pilsudski wrote in an announcement of the publication, "Polish socialists from all of the three partitions have come together in a single publication in honor of May Day. Despite the artificially established borders, they want to share their common goals as members of one family—socialist Poland."[3] The brochure included essays from leading French, British, Belgian, German, Italian, and Russian socialists.

One of the contributors was Italian socialist theorist Antonio Labriola, a strong supporter of the party program. "When today we put forth the slogan, 'Long Live Poland!'" Labriola wrote in a letter printed in *Pamiątka majowa*, "we are clearly emphasizing the necessity of liberating Poland from the yoke of Russian, Prussian and Austrian rule, above all because only [in a free Poland] can the conditions be created for the realization of the slogan, 'Long live the proletariat! Long live socialism!'"[4] In the pages of *Robotnik*, Pilsudski referred to Labriola's words as expressing "the essential idea of the entire publication."[5] As the late Polish historian Jan Kancewicz aptly remarked, the significance of Labriola's statement was that it linked the independence of Poland with the victory of socialism.[6] Yet the fact that only two of the sixteen essays by European socialists (by Labriola and Wilhelm Liebknecht) explicitly came out in favor of Polish independence in the brochure signaled that the campaign to garner international support for the party program would be long and arduous.

Pilsudski's contribution to *Pamiątka majowa* was about the significance of the party newspaper, *Robotnik*. Emphasizing its role in the life of the Polish working class, the piece reminded readers that *Robotnik* was the first Polish socialist paper produced inside the Russian Empire since 1884, when the tsarist police in Warsaw dismantled the socialist party, Proletariat, and its clandestine printing press. Pilsudski stressed that only a clandestine paper could circumvent the oppressive and stifling censor in imperial Russia. "Here, where one careless utterance in the wrong company can result in several years in prison and exile, or where one is harshly convicted for the smallest gathering, and where the Sword of Damocles hangs over every home," Pilsudski wrote, ". . . the printed word is the simplest, easiest . . . and sometimes the only way to influence the masses."[7] Producing a party paper in oppressive conditions was risky, he acknowledged, and many discouraged him. "To be sure," he continued, "the difficulty was so great, the obstacles so numerous, that many were skeptical about such an undertaking." Some of his comrades, he added, had felt the resources needed to put out an underground periodical were too costly.

Robotnik, Pilsudski wrote, "is now essential for the party, taking its place as its adored child—its pride and joy. In fact, there is no better comparison for our attitude toward *Robotnik* than that of a mother toward her child. And even more so, of a mother with many children for whom this is her favorite and most beloved." For the paper constituted the party's link to the masses, a vehicle for the free expression of ideas the tsarist regime was intent on suppressing.[8]

While managing the party's publication projects, Pilsudski also wrote many articles of his own. For the London paper, he wrote a column on May Day, emphasizing the expanding influence of the party, which distributed May Day proclamations in Warsaw, Radom, Lublin, Kielce, Łódź, Częstochowa, Białystok, and Vilna. Taking into account the ethnic diversity of the Polish lands, the party distributed the May Day circular in other languages as well. "For the first time," Pilsudski announced in the May 1896 issue of *Przedświt,* "the party's Central Workers' Committee has issued a circular in Yiddish, distributed in workshops and factories with Jewish workers." Issuing the party's circular in Yiddish was intended not only to spread class consciousness but also to send a message that the PPS was responsive to the needs of Jewish workers. According to Pilsudski, "the whole [Jewish] district [of Warsaw] was aware, reading and commenting on it."[9] Another article likewise confirmed that "the circular made a strong impression in the Jewish quarter."[10] The May Day leaflet, readers were informed, appeared not only in

Polish (five thousand copies) and Yiddish (six hundred copies) but also in German (five hundred copies) for the large population of German factory workers in Łódź.

Pilsudski's letters from London reveal the growing number of personal contacts he was making with Europe's major socialist leaders. In June 1896 he met Wilhelm Liebknecht, co-chairman of the German Social Democratic Party (SPD) and editor in chief of its central periodical, *Vorwärts* (Forward). The two discussed the resolution Pilsudski was helping to prepare on Polish independence for the upcoming international socialist congress. Liebknecht was sympathetic, remarking to Pilsudski, "'Russia is a barbarous country where your people are powerless.'"[11]

Reaching Out to Lithuanians and Jews

After putting out the May Day brochure, Pilsudski focused his attention on forming ties with the emerging Jewish and Lithuanian socialist movements. His goal was to persuade them to embrace the federalist idea of a breakaway democratic republic. In the case of the Jews, Pilsudski took a special interest in a letter received in London by a member of the ZZSP, Bolesław Miklaszewski, who was then visiting New York. Miklaszewski had met some Jewish immigrants who would be willing to prepare literature in Yiddish for Jews in tsarist Russia under the PPS imprint. The leader of the group, Benjamin Feigenbaum, was a native of Warsaw who had immigrated to New York in 1891. "On Feigenbaum's initiative," Miklaszewski wrote from New York, "the best and most active Jewish comrades from Warsaw have established themselves here, and have taken it upon themselves to collect funds for the creation of Yiddish literature to aid our cause."[12] Miklaszewski later recalled that he and Feigenbaum had a natural rapport and the two gained each other's trust.[13]

Pilsudski read Miklaszewski's letter with great interest and responded in detail. First, he inquired if these Polish Jews in New York were in contact with Jewish socialists in Vilna. To establish formal ties, Pilsudski asked Miklaszewski to determine if the Polish Jews had a "gravitational pull to Russia" as did, in Pilsudski's opinion, the Lithuanian Jews. "In any case," he continued, "we must try, and even more so, because our work among Jews is terribly deficient. We lack the literature and the people."[14] Assured that Feigenbaum's circle was composed of Jews from Warsaw sympathetic to the party program, Pilsudski and the ZZSP favored cooperation. Under Feigenbaum's direction, the New York–based organization of Polish Jews started producing party literature in Yiddish, calling themselves the "Jewish Socialist Post from America to Poland."[15]

Pilsudski sent a set of guidelines to oversee the content of Feigenbaum's publications and excitedly informed the Central Workers' Committee about the creation of the Jewish Socialist Post from America. "Under the influence of Miklaszewski," Pilsudski wrote in May 1896, "Jewish comrades have formed an organization wishing to work in the spirit of the Polish Socialist Party. They are hugely eager to provide new publications. I have already posted a few letters, asking for details."[16] The ties with the New York–based organization proved fruitful. Within a short time, Pilsudski received two thousand copies of the first Yiddish brochure under the party imprint for distribution in the homeland.[17] "We believe," Pilsudski wrote in a spirit of optimism, "that in this way—with the help of Jewish comrades in Poland—we will learn how to win over a wide Jewish following to our movement in a short period of time."[18]

Pilsudski continued to emphasize the importance of tailoring Yiddish publications to the party program. "Remind them," Pilsudski instructed Miklaszewski, "of the necessity of having a set of unified *political* goals of the entire proletariat in Poland [*w kraju*], among which is the necessity of spreading the idea of the independence of Poland among the Jewish proletariat." If the Jewish Socialist Post produced brochures on general principles of socialism only, "then it would be no different from those publications put out by the Lithuanian Jews [the Vilna Group], and nothing new would come of it." Economic aims should not be excluded or marginalized, he continued, only that the publication project would be ineffective "without full solidarity with [our political program]."[19] In his guidelines on Yiddish party literature, Pilsudski was merely applying the resolution on the nationalities passed at the third party congress the previous year. Given that Jews made up approximately half of the urban population in the six Lithuanian-Belarussian provinces, there was no question in Pilsudski's mind that gaining Jewish support for the party program was a significant objective.

Another issue Pilsudski addressed at this time was the recent formation of a separate socialist party by ethnic Lithuanians. The Lithuanian Social

Democratic Party (LSDP) came into being in May 1896. The program, adopted in Vilna on May 1, called for "an independent democratic republic, consisting of Lithuania, Poland, and other countries, based on a loose federation."[20] The federation, the program specified, was to include Poland, Latvia, Belarus, and Ukraine: that is, a federation without Russia.

Pilsudski obtained a copy of the party's founding program in June 1896 and informed his comrades that he and the party's foreign committee regarded it as entirely acceptable. The new Lithuanian party represented "actual Lithuanians," as Pilsudski put it, rather than all the inhabitants of historic Lithuania. "Extend my congratulations to the Lithuanians on the adoption of their program," Pilsudski wrote. "In my opinion, we should be grateful to them for guiding Lithuanians down this path." Pilsudski was pleased that the new Lithuanian party's program "entirely avoids the question of the future Lithuania's borders" and stated that "we applaud this party as long as it envisions an ethnographic Lithuania."[21] The clear distinction between imperial versus ethnic Russian territory was evident when Pilsudski referred to an underground circle with whom he was in contact as being in Riga "and therefore not in Russia."[22]

Pilsudski continued to discuss the new Lithuanian socialist party in the summer of 1896. In correspondence with his comrades in Vilna, Pilsudski included a copy of a French newspaper that had printed a letter to the editor announcing the formation of the Lithuanian Social Democratic Party. The letter described the party's founding program but left out the part about supporting a breakaway federal republic. Pilsudski asked Sulkiewicz to meet with the Lithuanian party's leaders to inquire whether or not they were aware of the letter. Perhaps, Pilsudski wondered aloud, Rosa Luxemburg's party had planted the letter? Pilsudski subsequently stressed the importance of harmonizing the LSDP and the PPS programs.[23]

At the International Socialist Congress

In the months leading up to the international socialist congress, Pilsudski began preparing materials in collaboration with his London colleagues. The process began by reaching out to the congress organizers. Back in January 1896, when B. A. Jędrzejowski wrote to Henry Hyndman, founder of

Britain's Social Democratic Federation, who was to serve as chairman of the international socialist congress, he asked whether the Polish delegation could rely on Hyndman's support. "I do not generally care very much for the national . . . by itself," Hyndman replied. "But in the case of Poland, I think that the only hope of pushing reactionary Russia back from central Europe lies in the reconstitution of a strong Poland, and I see no hope of any movement in that direction except from the Socialists."[24]

Encouraged by Hyndman's support, Jędrzejowski and Pilsudski drafted a resolution in April 1896 for adoption at the upcoming congress that stated:

> At the International Socialist Congress in London, the Polish Socialist Party (in the Russian, Austrian, and Prussian partitions), considering that the subjugation of one nation by another is advantageous only to despots and capitalists while harmful to the proletariat of both nations; and considering that the Russian tsarist system . . . is a permanent threat to the progress of the international proletariat;
>
> The Congress declares that the independence and autonomy of Poland is an indispensable political demand serving the interest both of the Polish proletariat and of the international labor movement.[25]

Jędrzejowski mailed the resolution to leading European socialists in the spring of 1896. Pilsudski hoped the draft would persuade Labriola to promote the resolution among his countrymen. Labriola "understands Polish to some degree," Pilsudski commented, "and we want him to distribute all of our publications." As an Italian whose country had only recently been unified into a single democratic state, Pilsudski continued, Labriola was more likely to sympathize with the Polish case.[26] In a letter to Labriola, Jędrzejowski suggested that he remind his Italian comrades that none other than Karl Marx supported the independence of Poland. "A similar resolution, as you well know," Jędrzejowski noted, "was approved by the executive council at the Geneva Congress of the First International in 1866."[27] Jędrzejowski also sent the draft resolution to German, Belgium, British, and Bulgarian socialist leaders.

Jędrzejowski tried to counter Luxemburg in the pages of *Justice,* the paper of the British Social Democratic Federation, by promoting the resolution. "There was only one political claim ever cherished by Polish people," he wrote, "understood and felt by millions in the remote corners of our country as well as in Warsaw—it is the claim for an independent democratic Polish republic." The creation of an independent Poland would provide a space for the establishment of democratic institutions. Why not, Jędrzejowski asked, join forces with Russian revolutionaries for the transformation of Russia into a democratic, constitutional state? "To hope to get even adult suffrage . . . in the present Russian Empire with its hordes of savage Kalmucks," Jędrzejowski wrote, "would be sheer nonsense." For this reason, Jędrzejowski continued, the upcoming international socialist congress had to go on record in support of the independence of Poland. Citing Henry Hyndman, he argued that national independence was a precondition for the attainment of social democracy in Poland.[28]

The draft resolution eventually found its way into the hands of the indefatigable Rosa Luxemburg, leader of the rival Social Democracy of the Kingdom of Poland (SDKP). Some readers had remembered her from the Third Congress of the Second International in 1893, when she had filed a report against the independence of Poland and gave a fiery speech on the topic. Between April and July 1896, Luxemburg used the German and Italian socialist press to express her staunch opposition to the PPS resolution. The controversy over the question of Polish independence consequently spilled out into the international arena. Her sharply critical article appeared in *Critica Sociale,* the paper of the Italian Socialist Party, and the German Social Democratic Party's *Die Neue Zeit*, where Luxemburg presented her case by citing the PPS resolution in full, calling on all socialists to oppose it.[29]

Many renowned socialists replied to Luxemburg by coming out in favor of the PPS resolution. These included Georgi Plekhanov, who replied to Luxemburg in June 1896 in the pages of *Vorwärts,* the central periodical of the German Social Democratic Party (SPD). The renowned editor of *Die Neue Zeit,* Karl Kautsky, similarly responded to Luxemburg in print, arguing that active opposition to the fight for Polish independence was tantamount to siding with Russian autocracy.[30] Liebknecht could also be counted among the supporters of the PPS resolution, going so far as to suggest in private that Luxemburg might be an agent of the Russian secret police.[31] These same leaders also knew that Luxemburg's meticulously reasoned arguments in the pages of the German and Italian press had the potential to sway public opinion.

Luxemburg's articles caused a stir. Some prominent European socialists came down on her side, including Filippo Turati, a key figure behind the establishment of the Italian Socialist Party in 1892 and editor in chief of *Critica Sociale*. In the weeks prior to the socialist congress, Labriola conceded that his efforts to persuade Italian socialists had failed thus far. In a letter dated May 3, 1896, he agreed to circulate the resolution among his comrades in Italy but warned that leaders of the Italian Socialist Party were unlikely to support it. In response, Jędrzejowski tried to embroil Labriola further, asking him to reach out to Spanish socialists as well as to the Austrian socialist Victor Adler to request that they too circulate the resolution.[32]

Pilsudski, then staying at Jędrzejowski's home in London, kept his comrades in Poland abreast of the situation. On May 13, 1896, he sent the disappointing news that the Italian Socialist Party and its leader, Turati, were going to vote against the resolution. "I am becoming increasingly worried about the fate of our resolution. Labriola's efforts are coming to naught," he wrote.[33] Although Labriola had written an article on the topic in *Critica Sociale* "even here, Turati—damn him—added an editorial note that directed his readers to Rosa Luxemburg's article in *Die Neue Zeit*." What's more, French socialist Georges Sorel had told Labriola that most French socialists were entirely unfamiliar with the national question in Poland and planned to remain neutral. Pilsudski's earlier confidence that the resolution would pass was now waning. "I am feeling more and more disquiet about the fate of the resolution," he wrote to comrades, continuing, "How unpleasant it will be if there are either amendments imposed or if there is strong opposition to it."[34] The problem, Pilsudski argued, was not French or Italian socialists but instead that "Luxemburg's Polish social democrats are ruining [our chances] with the French. What's more, the proverbial French ignorance triumphed here."[35]

In June and July 1896, Luxemburg's influence became even more widespread. "There's a chance," Pilsudski informed his comrades in Poland on June 9, 1896, that the resolution would not pass without major amendments. He nonetheless insisted he would continue his efforts to sway opinion. "At Beaumont Square," he wrote, describing a meeting with Liebknecht at the headquarters of the Union of Polish Socialists Abroad in London, "we discussed the resolution with Liebknecht. He replied that 'with pride, I will defend your resolution at the congress.'" Liebknecht promised he would try to win over French socialists during his upcoming trip to France and to write a piece on the topic for *Vorwärts*. A key ally, Liebknecht "is for an historic—not ethnographic—Poland that extends as far east as possible," wrote Pilsudski. "[At our meeting], he raised his glass and toasted, 'Poland is not yet lost.'"[36]

In the months of June and July, Pilsudski became increasingly concerned about Luxemburg. In June he received word that Luxemburg and her comrade in the SDKP, Adolf Warski, had prepared a counterresolution for the upcoming international socialist gathering that, Pilsudski wrote, "is in opposition to us and argues that rebuilding an independent Poland prior to a social revolution is a fantasy."[37] At the same time, he was pleased that Karl Kautsky had forcefully opposed Luxemburg's views, advocating for the resolution of the Polish Socialist Party.

To Pilsudski's chagrin, Luxemburg's most forceful piece appeared in *Critica Sociale* two weeks before the international congress. Her article, "The Polish Question at the International Congress in London," characterized the Polish delegation's resolution as contrary to the interests of the international labor movement.[38] The PPS resolution, Luxemburg maintained, was flawed for two reasons. The first was its argument that Russian autocracy relied on the subjugation of Poland and, therefore, the separation of Polish lands would be its downfall. The Russian tsarist system, she maintained, "derives neither its inner strength nor its external significance from the subjugation of Poland." Consequently, she continued, "the hope of breaking the hold of Russian omnipotence through the restoration of Poland is an anachronism stemming from that bygone time when there seemed to be no hope that forces within Russia itself would ever be capable of achieving the destruction of tsardom."[39]

The second reason was the resolution's silence on the national aspirations of other stateless peoples in Europe. Why, Luxemburg asked, should congress pass a resolution on the national question limiting its demand for the separation of Poland? Why not also make mention of the Czechs, the Irish, and the inhabitants of Alsace-Lorraine? "The liberation of Alsace-Lorraine in particular would be far more important for the international proletariat, and far more likely at that," she added in a sharp rebuke to the Polish delegation. "If the Poles in the three partitioned sectors organize themselves along nationalist lines for the liberation of Poland, why should the other nationalities in Austria not also do the same, [and] why should the Alsatians not organize themselves with the French?"[40] In sum, the PPS resolution divided the laboring classes of Europe by dismissing the grievances of other stateless peoples.

Great disquiet gripped Pilsudski and his comrades upon the appearance of Luxemburg's article. "Once again, Rosa has come out against us," Pilsudski wrote on July 15, 1896. Luxemburg's piece, he well continued, was formulated. What's more, it was going to be the last word on the topic prior to the congress because it was already too late to reply in print.[41]

When the international socialist congress convened in London on July 26, 1896, Pilsudski's ten-person delegation gathered along with 755 others.[42] Among the delegates was a three-person minority Polish delegation representing the SDKP: Rosa Luxemburg, Adolf Warski, and Julian Marchlewski. The congress heard from both Polish delegations and came down remarkably even between them. At first the PPS tried to get Luxemburg's group expelled by claiming that its members were agents of the Russian secret police. The congress allowed the minority Polish delegation to defend itself and concluded the accusation was without merit. The minority delegate who spoke in their defense "thought it a great pity that one political faction should come to the congress with a majority and try to crush another party."[43]

After hearing arguments from both sides, the congress debated the PPS resolution. Congress chairman Henry Hyndman assigned the British delegate, George Lansbury, to head a commission to draft a revised resolution. The commission passed the following amended version:

> The Congress declares in favor of the full autonomy of all nationalities, and its sympathy with the workers of any country at present suffering under the yoke of military, national, or other despotisms; and calls upon the workers in all such countries to fall into line, side by side with the class-conscious workers of the world, to organize for the overthrow of international capitalism and the establishment of International Social Democracy.[44]

The resolution neither condemned Russia nor endorsed the restoration of Poland. Pilsudski was quite disappointed but not entirely surprised. "Our resolution," he wrote five days later, "did no go through. The congress . . . made it apply to all subjugated nations to whom their sympathy is expressed. But about Poland? Not a word."[45] Compared to the resolution in support of Polish independence at the First International in 1866 put forward by none other than Karl Marx, Pilsudski's delegation could only have seen the current outcome as a step backward for the Polish cause.

The subject of Poland nevertheless found its way into other discussions. A resolution on labor and education, for example, made direct reference to the subjugation of the Polish people. "The old kingdom of Poland," it stated, "is now divided into Russian, Prussian and Austrian Poland, and . . . the language taught [in the schools] is that of the dominant power, which uses the schools of the country as a means of introducing discord among the members of a nationality famous for its love of country. . . . The great grievance of the Poles," the resolution concluded, "is the fact that the language of 18,000,000 people may not be taught in the primary schools of the country."[46]

Despite the disappointing outcome of the congress, Pilsudski forged new and important ties during his five-month stay in London. They included not only such luminaries as Wilhelm Liebknecht of Germany and Georgi Plekhanov of Russia, but also French socialists Alexander Millerand and Aristide Briand, not to mention American Jewish socialists as well as Lithuanian socialists.

Travels to Kraków and Lwów

On August 20, 1896, Pilsudski began his trip back to Vilna. To elude detection, he asked Ignacy Mościcki, his friend and comrade who worked as a barber in London, to give him a makeover. Mościcki shaved Pilsudski's beard and trimmed his eyebrows and mustache. Well-groomed and with a new haircut, Pilsudski walked into a photo studio. The picture taken that day has become the iconic image of Pilsudski as a young man.[47] On his way home, Pilsudski stopped in Austrian Galicia to obtain false papers for entry into Russia. Having stayed in Kraków for several days, he continued on to Lwów, concerned that he had still not secured the necessary false passport and would have to stay put for the time being.[48]

While waiting in Lwów, Pilsudski visited his old mentor from exile, the sixty-one-year-old national hero Bronisław Szwarce. With a keen interest in the history of the 1863 Polish insurrection, Pilsudski spent much of his visit listening to firsthand accounts, as Szwarce had played a key role as a member of the illegal Provisional National Government in Warsaw established in 1862. Besides the stories, Pilsudski saw for the first time Szwarce's collection of documents and materials on the 1863 uprising published in 1894.[49] It was a subject to which Pilsudski would return frequently throughout his life, and he

Pilsudski, age twenty-eight, London, 1896.

was clearly inspired to be in the presence of such a distinguished figure in the recent history of his country.

Pilsudski also engaged in party work during his stay in Lwów. He met with Joachim Fraenkel, editor of the Social Democratic Party of Galicia's Yiddish paper, *Der arbeter*, who agreed to publish a Yiddish brochure for the PPS. The paper reflected Fraenkel's position that Jewish socialists should align their political demands with those of the dominant local social democratic party.[50]

As the days passed, Pilsudski wondered how long he would have to stay in Lwów. "As you can see," he wrote three weeks after he arrived in Austrian Galicia, "I have not been able to leave from here since I last wrote. I have had to arm myself with patience and wait."[51] Making the best of his situation, he initiated contact with the Ukrainians in Lwów. Like Poles, he wrote, Ukrainians in Galicia felt affinity for Ukrainians in tsarist Russia. One Ukrainian

socialist Pilsudski spoke with pinned his hopes for a united Ukraine on revolution in Russia and the overthrow of the tsar. "I laughed heartily," Pilsudski commented, "and told him that this will not work with help from the
Poles. The guy nodded sorrowfully and replied, 'yes—either Poles or Jews.
We don't know how to do this on our own.'" In the end, Pilsudski wrote, the
party would be able to work with both Ukrainians and Jews.[52]

In addition to contacts with Jewish and Ukrainian socialists, Pilsudski had
the opportunity to observe the party's main opponent on the right—the
nationalist National League. The league had been founded in April 1893
by Roman Dmowski, Zygmunt Balicki, and Jan Ludwik Popławski. Judging
from what he was seeing in Austria-Hungary, Pilsudski concluded that the
National League had very little influence in Austrian Galicia. Its paper,
Przegląd Wszechpolski (All-Polish Review), was nowhere to be found in the
cafes of Kraków and Lwów, Pilsudski observed.[53] Pilsudski recommended
that the party exploit the National League's weakness in Galicia by dramatically increasing its activities there. The way to begin was to send more activists to Galicia, and to increase the circulation of *Przedświt*.

Return to Vilna

Pilsudski finally received his false papers on September 15, 1896. Eager to return home, he departed for Russia the same day. After crossing the border,
he sent a note from inside Russia using a pseudonym. "Dear Uncle, at last
good fortune has smiled upon me," he wrote to the ZZSP in London, addressed to "uncle" to elude the authorities. "After a long time of sitting idly
by and waiting, I was given the possibility of departing. Fearing I would not
have enough money, I had to borrow heavily."[54] He had already met with
Aleksander Sulkiewicz and Stanisław Wojciechowski, whom he reported
were in good health. "Please do not forget about me and write often," he
concluded, informing them that he was at the moment having a cup of tea at
Wojciechowski's home.

The first subject Pilsudski addressed after returning to Vilna was Jewish
party membership. The CKR had just received a letter, signed "Jewish members of the P.P.S. in Warsaw," highlighting what the authors maintained was
the PPS's neglect of Jewish workers. "The party has not given us any aid: not

with materials, not with a sufficient amount of essential Yiddish literature, not with our people. Nor have you provided advice, suggestions or moral support," the letter continued, "by raising issues relevant to us in party newspapers."[55] The authors warned that the party was losing support among Jewish workers due to the activities of the newly formed Union of Jewish Workers in Warsaw, linked to the Vilna Group. The letter recommended the party take concrete steps to counter the influence of the Union of Jewish Workers, including providing steady supplies of Yiddish literature and creating a Jewish Section with representation in the Central Workers' Committee, as well as increasing the coverage of Jewish issues in the party press. The letter warned that the Union of Jewish Workers was spreading the message that the behavior of the PPS was demonstrating indifference toward Jewish workers.

Pilsudski agreed with the letter's assessment. Bringing it to the attention of his comrades in London, he lamented that the party had been heretofore unable to put out a Yiddish paper. Unfortunately, he wrote, the party lacked people with sufficient experience. Pilsudski consequently recommended working with the editor of *Der arbeter* in Lwów to make a joint publication with space reserved for articles by Jewish members of the PPS in the Russian Empire.[56] "The majority of our members (and I belong to the minority)," he wrote, "are of the opinion that we do not need Yiddish literature in the Kingdom of Poland. But I know we cannot win over those who only read Yiddish."[57]

Much more pressing than the problem of the Jews were the party's financial woes. Pilsudski informed London in October 1896 that he was frequently borrowing money on credit. "Adaś," he wrote, referring to Wojciechowski, "still goes around in a summer coat and I without rubber boots despite the cold and mud. We are in debt up to our ears."[58] The income for October, he explained, had been thus far minimal ("130 rubles and change"), due in part to the fact that his trip to St. Petersburg yielded pitifully little.

Pilsudski meanwhile put out monthly issues of *Robotnik*. The first after his return from London reported on the international socialist congress. It included a four-page reprint of the congress resolutions, and on the cover was Pilsudski's firsthand report. That the Polish resolution failed to pass, Pilsudski wrote, was not surprising. "First," he wrote, "socialism is divided into Western Europe, where—with the exception of Ireland—there are no countries under occupation or partition. The German, the French and the English do not demand independence for their countries. They cannot complain about the subjugation of their peoples. For this simple reason—that they have enjoyed sovereignty for so long—they do not know [national] oppression." The resolution the Polish Socialist Party proposed, he wrote, "stated that the independence of Poland is a political demand indispensable for both the international labor movement and the Polish proletariat." In the end, a committee reshaped it into a general resolution on the national question.[59]

Under Pilsudski's editorship, *Robotnik* took on a distinctly anticlerical orientation. In its edition of November 1896, an article titled "The Clergy against the People" argued that the priesthood stood squarely against "our struggle." *Robotnik* lamented what it described as changes in the Polish clergy since the time of the 1863 uprising, when the clergy supported the independence fighters. The paper equally castigated the Polish landed elite (*szlachta*). Pilsudski also wrote about Tsar Nicholas II's brief visit to Warsaw, deriding the behavior of the Polish landed aristocracy who sought close ties with the tsar. "In this short time, Polish tycoons and rich magnates managed to once again lick his feet."[60]

A letter from December 1896 revealed Pilsudski's growing concern about political forces on the Polish street that were inimical to the Polish Socialist Party. He noted that in Vilna, one frequently saw the populist, right-wing underground paper of the National League. A person affiliated with the paper was in Vilna for the purpose of fundraising and recruitment. The paper had a higher print run than *Robotnik,* and its readers, Pilsudski maintained, were "extreme reactionaries." He also came upon an underground paper from the other end of the political spectrum—*Robotnik Litewski* (The Lithuanian Worker)—published by the new Lithuanian Social Democratic Party. According to Pilsudski, this paper was of little influence and infrequently discussed. But he had a bad feeling about relations with the new Lithuanian party. The one member Pilsudski was in touch with expressed no interest in formal ties.[61] The Polish Socialist Party "has no personal ties whatsoever" with the LSDP, he warned. "They are really set against us. . . . I get the feeling that they have a whole list of accusations ready."[62] Given that its leaders were native Polish speakers, the antagonistic relations puzzled Pilsudski, who would eventually need the support of such a party to realize his plan to create a federal state with Lithuania and Ukraine.

Pilsudski's last article in 1896 focused on captive nations. He wrote of economic exploitation in the form of higher taxes, attacks on language rights, and religious persecution. But for Pilsudski the most egregious act was the attempt to suppress a people's national literature. He stressed that the exploitation of captive nations in Russia contributed to poverty and mass emigration. "In all countries," he wrote, "literature is today the most powerful mainspring of a people's social development. How impoverished and poor it is here under tsarist rule."[63]

CHAPTER 5

Party Leadership and Arrest

Any trace of anti-Semitism among our comrades will be persistently fought against, and under no conditions will we allow its manifestation in the life of our movement.

—JOZEF PILSUDSKI, *ROBOTNIK*, FEBRUARY 13, 1898

After a five-month stay in London and travels through Austrian Galicia, Pilsudski returned to Russia with renewed vigor. He now faced new challenges. In London he had failed to pass the party's resolution at the international socialist congress. During the same time, new competing forces on the Polish street appeared. These included parties both on the left (Lithuanians, Jews, Latvians, Ukrainians, and Rosa Luxemburg's SDKP) as well as on the right (Roman Dmowski's National League). In response Pilsudski crafted a series of persuasive articles intended to draw more people into the party. Back at home, Pilsudski was under constant threat of arrest, imprisonment, and exile. Unlike in the constitutional states of Central and Western Europe that guaranteed freedom of speech and freedom of the press, tsarist Russia forbade advocacy of Polish independence and barred speaking Polish in public outside of the Kingdom of Poland, including in Polish cultural centers such as Vilna and Grodno. In those areas communications with the public were confined almost solely to the written word in publications that were illegally printed and distributed. Pilsudski's distinctive and influential literary voice thus served as a powerful tool for mobilizing support. It is no surprise, as Andrzej Garlicki has commented, that Pilsudski, with no public speaking experience, was subsequently not known as a good public speaker.

He could stir thousands upon thousands to action through the written word, but he lacked the ability to captivate a live audience.[1]

Sources suggest that Pilsudski was already developing a kind of legendary status at this time. Not only was he becoming a formidable writer, he was also a gifted organizer and a leader with a distinctive ability to inspire loyalty. Evidence includes the recollections of a new recruit at the close of the year 1896. Leon Wasilewski was a new party member who traveled to St. Petersburg in the fall of 1896 to attend a gathering of the PPS division there. One of the persons he met introduced himself only as "Comrade Wiktor." The comrade made an impression with Wasilewski describing him as having "dark brown hair, a short beard, a thick moustache that covered his lips, and gentle, grey eyes under bushy eyebrows. He made a charming impression."[2]

After the meeting, Wasilewski inquired about the mysterious man and discovered, to his surprise, that Comrade Wiktor was in fact the party leader, Józef Piłsudski. Wasilewski's hosts expressed great admiration for Pilsudski. As a fugitive from the law in constant pursuit by the Russian secret police, Pilsudski led a terrible existence. Exposed to danger at all hours of the day and night, he did not live in any one place for more than a few days and never revealed his real name. Wasilewski, who was studying in Switzerland at the time, returned to his home in Zurich. One of his classmates, Bolesław Miklaszewski, who had been a member of the Polish delegation at the international socialist congress in London, "spoke of 'Wiktor' as an outstanding and influential person in the party who commands huge respect and much sympathy."[3]

Commemorating the Nation's Martyrs

Part and parcel of Pilsudski's growing legend was his ability to regularly produce the party's central paper under the most precarious conditions. Pilsudski's articles in *Robotnik* consistently touched a nerve, articulating the longings and aspirations of a subjugated people. He frequently used anniversaries as occasions to bring attention to stories of national heroes, either in the period of nineteenth-century insurrections or with Poland's first socialist party—Proletariat—whose founders had been executed. Readers opening the January 1897 issue of *Robotnik* were likely struck by the cover story about the role of socialism on Polish lands. "After the bloodbath in 1863," Pilsudski's lead story began, "Poland was overwhelmed by silence." But soon after the initial shock of defeat, "a storm of revenge spread throughout the country: brutal lawlessness became common while exceptional laws and persecution rained down. The tsarist government," he continued, "saw nowhere any obstacle in the oppression and exploitation of the disgraced peoples. The first resistance that the tsar met, the first stones he encountered on the road, connected to the blood and bodies of his victims, were socialists."[4]

Pilsudski was referring to the rise of the first Polish socialist party in the late 1870s. With its formation, the struggle against tsarist despotism continued. Soon the road to the Warsaw Citadel, where the leaders of the 1863 Polish insurrection had been taken for execution, was once again crowded, only now with the leaders of the Proletariat party. Pilsudski penned his article exactly eleven years after the four leaders of Proletariat had been hanged. By executing those four leaders of Proletariat, Pilsudski wrote, "the government wanted to extinguish the idea of struggle and liberty. On the casket of the Citadel, together with the corpses of our comrades, [the government] meant to bury hope for a better future for the exploited proletariat . . . or, in Siberia, to lock up the consciousness and feeling of injustice among workers."[5]

Pilsudski followed with excerpts from Poland's bards. Citing poetry for the first time in his writing, he discussed Zygmunt Krasiński, his late mother's favorite poet. In his 1843 poem "Dawn," Krasiński described the division of humankind into nations as part of the natural order of the world. The partitions of Poland were thus a crime against humanity, abruptly undoing the natural order of things. The evocation of national rebirth haunts the reader, as the poem communicates the ideas that Poland's misfortune had been preordained as a redeeming sacrifice. Pilsudski cited these five verses:

> [He] who dies in sacrificing self,
> Floweth into lives of others,
> Dwells in human hearts in secret:
> With each day, each little moment,
> Groweth living in that grave.[6]

As Pilsudski commented, not only were the martyrs of the 1863 Polish revolt alive in the hearts and minds of Poles everywhere, so too were the martyred leaders of the country's first socialist party. Preserving the memory of the nation's fallen heroes was an important part of the struggle for a free and sovereign Poland, Pilsudski wrote. The Proletariat party was the first serious attempt to organize Polish workers into a wider struggle for labor rights. The execution of the party's leaders in 1886 "was thus the baptism of fire of Polish socialism. We have lived through a lot since then. Our movement, hardening like steel and in the heat of battle, has grown and intensified." That is why Pilsudski informed his readers that the 1896 international socialist congress in London agreed to henceforth mark the third Sunday of January each year as the day to commemorate the execution of the leaders of Proletariat, Polish socialism's "first martyrs. This anniversary will be the holiday that unifies the Polish proletariat."[7]

In private correspondence Pilsudski discussed a variety of topics related to party matters. These letters reveal that his thoughts were never far from the party's broad federalist goals. That is why he kept London informed about his contacts with Ukrainians, Jews, Lithuanians, Latvians, and Belarussians. He reported on helping Ukrainians in Galicia print their paper. He spoke of a letter he received from the Jewish Socialist Post organization in New York. He expressed the fear that relations with Jews in Warsaw were being undercut by the Vilna-linked organization, the Union of Jewish Workers in Poland. "Until now," Pilsudski wrote, "we had relations [with Jewish workers] in Warsaw, but even there those damn Vilna Jews [*żydki wileńskie*] are making their influence felt."[8] The interest in incorporating minorities into the movement demonstrated the impact of geography on Pilsudski's outlook. Unlike his comrades in Warsaw, Pilsudski in Vilna was in daily contact with ethnic groups of the borderland region. His emerging federalist principle derived to a large degree from this geographic origin.

The late Polish scholar Jan Kancewicz noted Pilsudski's use of the derogatory forms "Żydkowie," "Żydki," and "Żydy" (the little Jews), writing that acknowledging Pilsudski's use of those terms "is not easy but necessary in the name of historical truth—[it] is the style and tone Pilsudski utilized when referring to the Jews."[9] While this is undoubtedly evident in Pilsudski's private correspondence when he referred to Jews in rival political parties—using pejorative words for Jews that were in common use by Poles of aristocratic background at the time—it should be noted that Pilsudski used more extreme derogatory language for ethnic Russians, such as "mochy" (conflation of Muscovite gendarme and thief) and "kacapy" (Russky).

Polish Socialist Progress in Austrian Galicia

Pilsudski also discussed developments in Austrian Galicia. Ignacy Daszyński had been the leader of the Social Democratic Party of Galicia and editor of its newspaper, *Naprzód* (Forward). In January 1897 Aleksander Dębski met with Daszyński. The two had attended the 1896 international socialist congress in London the previous year alongside Pilsudski.[10] In Dębski's opinion, Daszyński "behaves wretchedly," exhibiting a mentality particular to natives of Kraków. "For him," Dębski wrote to Pilsudski, "Galicia exists in Poland, there is only Kraków in Galicia, and there is only him in Kraków."[11] Pilsudski concurred, replying, "Ignaś [Daszyński] talks a lot of nonsense. . . . The guy has a few too many trifle ambitions and love for himself."[12]

Pilsudski publicly expressed only praise for Austrian Galicia's leading Polish socialist. In the Austrian parliamentary elections of March 11, 1897, Daszyński ran in the Kraków district. He received 74.6 percent of the votes cast, giving him a seat in the Austrian parliament in Vienna.[13] The historic victory made Daszyński the first Polish socialist to sit in parliament. According to historian Joshua Shanes, Daszyński's landslide victory was in part due to his large following among Kraków's Jews, "who in study houses and synagogues the previous Shabbat . . . called on everyone to vote 'for the beloved Jewish supporter' Daszyński."[14]

Emboldened by the victory, Daszyński persuaded his party that it should have a more Polish—rather than regional—character. In September 1897 the Social Democratic Party of Galicia renamed itself the Polish Social Democratic Party of Galicia and Silesia (PPSD). Daszyński's election victory and the emphasis on the party's Polish character represented a new phrase in the history of Polish socialism. Pilsudski praised Daszyński in the pages of *Robotnik,* writing that his victory in the Austrian parliamentary elections "has echoed widely and broadens the struggle" within the Polish working class. Pilsudski sent Daszyński heartfelt congratulations in the name of the Polish Socialist Party.[15] Like the PPS in the Russian sector, the PPSD included Jews and other minorities in its ranks. In his memoirs, Daszyński acknowledged his gratitude for Jewish electoral support.[16]

At home, meanwhile, Pilsudski continued to express concern about relations with Jewish socialists. The Jewish Socialist Post from America to Poland was active, and Pilsudski was content to receive Yiddish materials from them. But it was developments with the Vilna Group and its Warsaw branch, the Union of Jewish Workers in Poland, that kept him awake at night. He had heard rumors that the two were developing close ties to the Russian revolutionary movement. Its leaders "intend to enter into a Russian party," Pilsudski noted in May 1897. "Can you imagine the scandal—Warsaw Jews in a Russian party!" He characterized such Jewish socialists as "our misfortune," concluding that the PPS would have to organize its own Jewish section "because these rascals will try to oppose us."[17]

In the next issue of *Robotnik,* meanwhile, Pilsudski wrote about Russian imperial law. "The tsar rules over Poland," Pilsudski commented, "with the law of the invader. Unlike in Russia proper, tsarist rule does not have any natural foundation in our country. To maintain control of the conquered peoples, it is therefore necessary to give the government greater and greater power. It is for this reason that nowhere in the Russian Empire is there such horrific degradation and lawlessness than here in Poland." To remove the cause of this injustice, he continued, "it is necessary to return legislative rule into the hands of these people and assure them the widest control [over their own lives]." He concluded, "Accomplishing this end is possible only through a people's revolution that would topple the rule of the tsars and bring about the most favorable parliamentary form of government based on universal suffrage, complete freedom of speech and freedom of assembly. . . . We will demand the struggle for an independent Polish Republic based on democratic principles."[18]

Pilsudski's fear about the formation of an all-Russian union of Jewish workers eased up in the coming weeks. We recall that Jewish members of the PPS had complained in 1896 that the needs of Jewish workers were not being met, and in January 1897 that the group renamed itself the Union of Jewish Workers in Poland, formally withdrawing support for the PPS. But after disagreements with the Vilna Group over the future of the Polish territories, the Union of Jewish Workers in Poland broke off ties and pledged renewed loyalty to the PPS. Pilsudski was jubilant upon hearing the news. "The alliance of Warsaw [and Vilna] Jews has fully come to naught!" he wrote from Vilna in July 1897. "Now I hope we can undertake serious Jewish work." He noted that a local Jewish acquaintance was of the opinion that the antipathy between Polish and Lithuanian Jews was too great for any alliance. To Pilsudski, these developments indicated that the party was "significantly closer" to gaining a sizable Jewish following.[19]

Pilsudski also discussed relations with the Latvians at this time. There had been a crackdown on a group of Latvian socialists in Riga, with the Russian police searching the homes of 138 Latvians and arresting 87. In addition, they closed down *Dienas Lapa* (Daily Paper), the publication of the new Latvian socialist organization.[20] Pilsudski wanted to help in any way possible. Some of the Polish students at Riga Polytechnic University were active members of the PPS, and through them Pilsudski forged ties with the local Latvian socialists.[21] "I say," Pilsudski wrote in July 1897, "that [these Latvian workers] are ours even though they have not joined our party. They hugely gravitate toward us as they rely on us for many things." The Latvian-language May Day circular in Riga—printed by the PPS—"made a big impression among workers." Lastly, Pilsudski spoke about tense relations with the Lithuanian socialists. He had decided not to collaborate with the Lithuanian Social Democratic Party in the publication of its Polish-language paper, *Echo życia robotniczego* (Echo of Workers' Lives). As in the past, he expressed discomfort with the Lithuanian party's orientation. "We have no guarantee that any agreement will be fulfilled," Pilsudski wrote.[22]

The first visit of Tsar Nicholas II to Warsaw provided Pilsudski with the perfect pretext to discuss imperial rule. What enraged Pilsudski was the warm welcome the tsar received from local Polish conservatives such as Zygmunt Wielopolski, who believed he and the tsar had a common interest in suppressing radicalism.[23] The visit caught the attention of the international press. The tsar's presence in Warsaw, the *New York Times* stated, could lead to a thaw in Russo-Polish relations, for it "has sensibly diminished ill-feeling and paved the way for a reconciliation." The result was that some Poles had a "cordial feeling toward the Czar."[24] In fact, the situation in Warsaw had already improved since Prince Alexander Imeretinsky, an ethnic Georgian prince, began serving as governor-general of the Kingdom of Poland in 1897. He relaxed the more severe restrictions on the use of Polish in administration and in the schools.[25]

To Pilsudski, who regarded Imeretinsky's decrees as merely token gestures, the tsar's visit to Warsaw was scandalous. His biting circular in the name of the Polish Socialist Party did not mince words. "This is not the first time that the feet of a tsar trod on the sidewalks of Warsaw as if to demonstrate his rule over us," Pilsudski wrote. "But for the first time, Warsaw met the tsar not as a people rattling the chains of insurrection, but instead as an enslaved people lying down in humiliation at the feet of the master."[26] Do not be fooled, he warned readers, by the governor-general and conciliatory members of the Polish landed nobility who maintained that living conditions in the Kingdom of Poland were improving. "Understand, workers, that they declare in your name how good things are under the tsar's care at a time when . . . the police and gendarmerie abuse you, when snoops track your every step and monitor your every word, when thousands of your brothers & sisters are imprisoned at the [Warsaw] Citadel and taken away to Siberia." Only the socialist movement could overthrow the tsar, Pilsudski argued, adding that "in socialism, in the labor movement today, lies the power to crush the shackles of the invader and to bring liberation to our society. . . . Nothing can restrain the rising discontent of the working masses and their demands for freedom and equality. Relentless in the face of our enemies, we fight with great energy while preparing and gathering strength. And at the moment, the mighty cry of the rising people will resound on the streets of Warsaw: Death to despotism! Down with slavery! Long live a free Polish people!"[27]

In October 1897 Pilsudski visited university centers inside the empire to collect dues from student party members and meet leaders of various national groups.[28] One of the university towns he visited was Riga, where he held meetings with student party members. He also used the opportunity to meet with Latvian socialists to get feedback on the circular the PPS had distributed.[29] Upon his return to Vilna, Pilsudski expressed fear of the imminent formation of Jewish and Russian socialist parties that would merge together. "I am prepared for disappointment," he conceded. "The participation of Lithuanian Jews in a future Russian party will be a hard nut to crack." In about a year's time, he wrote, the party would be more prepared to conduct serious work on this matter. "We have done poorly so far in our work among Jews. . . . We have definite plans but we lack the people to carry them out."[30]

The Jewish Labor Bund and the Russian Social Democratic Labor Party

On October 7, 1897, leaders of the Vilna Group and the Union of Jewish Workers in Poland met in Vilna and announced the creation of a Jewish socialist party. Claiming sole representation of Jewish workers in the Russian

Empire, the General Jewish Labor Bund in Russia and Poland came into being. In his opening statement, party leader Arkadi Kremer remarked that the main impetus for the creation of the party was the anticipation of the imminent formation of an empire-wide Social Democratic Party of Russia that the Bund intended to join as official representatives of the Jewish working class.[31]

Pilsudski's reaction to the formation of a separate Jewish labor party was in part impacted by the rise of a labor movement among ethnic Lithuanians and their attitude toward the Polish Socialist Party. We recall that at its First Party Congress in May 1896, the Lithuanian Social Democratic Party (LSDP) had come out in favor of a breakaway federal republic with Poland. At the Second Party Congress, held on January 25, 1897, however, the Lithuanian party abruptly changed its platform to include Russia.[32] With only the Latvians on board, it appeared Pilsudski's federal project was beginning to fray at the seams.

There was thus a lot on their plate when leaders of the Polish Socialist Party met in Warsaw on November 7, 1897, to convene its Fourth Party Congress. The congress began with Pilsudski distributing a draft resolution on relations with Russians, Latvians, Lithuanians, and Jews. The resolution affirmed the unity of the Polish proletariat in the three partitions that acted in concert for the attainment of common goals. With regard to the Jews, the resolution recognized the importance and usefulness of the Yiddish publications of the party's sister organization in New York, Jewish Socialist Post from America to Poland, and wished them continued success in their work. Regarding other socialist organizations, Pilsudski applauded the formation of a new Latvian social democratic circle in Riga. "The congress, marking with joy the news of the rise of a socialist movement among Latvian workers, welcomes Latvian comrades in the name of the Polish proletariat as a new branch of the revolutionary proletarian army in the Russian state, and sends the Riga Workers' Committee heartfelt wishes for success in its hard work."[33]

Warm wishes were nonetheless extended only to the Latvians. With regard to the Russian, Jewish, and Lithuanian socialists, Pilsudski's resolutions were sharply worded. They first addressed the anticipated formation of a Russian Social Democratic Party, demanding that the future party "recognize entirely our aspiration for Polish Independence and to oblige itself to disseminate among its Russian comrades recognition of the necessity and legitimacy of this demand." The future Russian party "is obliged not to enter into any formal ties with revolutionary organizations in Poland or Lithuania without the express permission of the PPS." The congress "recognizes the organizational separateness of revolutionary Lithuanian groups—that is, those that exclusively employ the Lithuanian language in their agitation." But because the Lithuanian Social Democratic Party leadership agitated mostly in Polish, Pilsudski refused to recognize it as authentically Lithuanian. "The vast majority of the proletariat in Lithuania do not know the Lithuanian language," the resolution stated, "and are linked with the Polish proletariat in both speech and historical traditions. We resolve that neither political nor economic conditions require a separate party organization for the proletariat ... under the name of Lithuanian Social Democracy." The resolution concluded that the congress did not recognize the rationale for the existence of the Lithuanian Social Democratic Party.

Pilsudski's resolution included a separate statement on the newly formed Jewish Labor Bund. The congress resolved:

> Considering that the Jewish proletariat can only have a common mission with the proletariat of the nation among whom it lives; and considering that until now the activities of Jewish groups appearing under the name, General Jewish Labor Bund in Russia and Poland, whose character of organizational and programmatic separateness is harmful to the movement and whose positions are antagonistic in relation to us; the Congress deems the political direction of the Bund to be a false one that relies on the renunciation of solidarity with the Polish and Lithuanian proletariat in our struggle for liberation from the rule of the Russian invaders.[34]

To compete with the Bund, Pilsudski intensified his efforts to find a Jewish party member with competency in Yiddish and journalism experience.

In the last week of December 1897 Pilsudski left for Zurich to attend a conference of the Union of Polish Socialists Abroad (ZZSP). Prior to his departure, he put out the twenty-fifth edition of *Robotnik*. His lead editorial reflected on the paper's significance: "In the course of its three-year history, we have printed 298 pages distributed throughout the whole of Poland in 32,000 copies made from 1,700 pounds of paper." He added, "It is not enough to have kept a secret printing press secure from thousands of oppressive tsarist secret police—it has been necessary to provide the paper with sufficient numbers of collaborators from all over the country to properly manage our operation. Taking this into account, each issue of *Robotnik* attests to the number of contacts [we are reaching]." These thousands of readers, he stated, "show that in spite of its illegality, *Robotnik* is the most widely distributed paper for workers, is the undisguised mouthpiece desired by the whole working class, one that showcases the struggle for its interests and ideals." He noted, "That is why *Robotnik,* bringing with it courage and faith where there was once depression and uncertainty, has become our beloved child, our pride and joy."[35] Pilsudski represented the party's Central Workers' Committee. For Pilsudki it was exhilarating to be among major party figures, many of whom would later serve under him in interwar Poland. These included, among others, Ignacy Mościcki, Leon Wasilewski, Feliks Perl, Kazimierz Kelles-Krauz, Witold Jodko-Narkiewicz, and Bolesław Antoni Jędrzejowski. Pilsudski also met new, younger recruits, such as Max Horwitz, who would later spearhead the party's first Yiddish organ.[36]

In February 1898 Pilsudski published the first article in *Robotnik* devoted to the issue of the Jews. Presented as the party's official position, "On the Jewish Question" maintained that the socialist movement was eroding the foundations of old prejudices and hatreds. Socialism provided an environment in which Poles and Jews were struggling together for a common cause. But anti-Jewish prejudice was still a problem even among socialists: "There exists in parts of Europe—and Poland is no exception in this regard—an intellectual current inimical to the Jews called anti-Semitism." Pilsudski put forward the thesis that there were three causes. The first was racial prejudice, "a relic of the distant past when a person of a different religion or nationality is regarded as an adversary." The second and third causes were capitalism and reactionary politics. The Polish Socialist Party, he maintained, would continue to unambiguously combat anti-Semitism: "Any trace of anti-Semitism among our comrades will be persistently fought against, and under no conditions will we allow its manifestation in the life of our movement."[37]

At the same time, the article derided Jews in Lithuania for their Russian cultural orientation. "Jews in Lithuania, in spite of the interests of the whole country, do not present any resistance to russification, and even, to a certain extent, support it." What would serve the interests of Jews and non-Jews in the region was unity. Pilsudski concluded, "We are exploited as a proletariat, we are oppressed by barbarism, and persecuted as Poles and Jews. Our salvation can only be a common struggle under a single banner."[38]

Pilsudski had thought carefully about the article's tone. In a letter to the editors of *Przedświt* in London, he noted that in printing the article, he was aware of the delicate nature of the topic, wanting neither to alienate Jewish readers nor to inflame anti-Jewish sentiments. "In the article on the Jews in issue no. 26," he wrote, "we were, for understandable reason, unable to raise all the views on this issue. We thus avoided all thorny topics because they have to be precisely and broadly explained [rather than summarized]." Mere mention of all aspects of the Jewish issue could easily lead to misinterpretation. "And therefore," he commented, "the idea of 'Jewish russification in Lithuania' decidedly merits attention as well as does our discussion of 'political anti-Semitism,' which proves that the Bund is permeated with views that can only increases anti-Semitism."[39] But better, he concluded, to refrain from addressing it than to oversimplify a complex issue for the reading public.

After discussing *Robotnik,* Pilsudski commented on the situation in Austrian Galicia. As we have seen, Pilsudski did not have a high opinion of Daszyński. But he recognized that Daszyński's electoral victory was historic for Polish socialism, making the Galician Polish leader a key figure. The undeniable fact, Pilsudski commented, was that the two Polish socialists elected to the Austrian parliament—Daszyński from Kraków and Jan Kozakiewicz from Lwów—"are regarded in all of Poland as representatives of Polish socialism and, judged as such, their errors and mistakes are generally attributed to the entire movement, including our own." Pilsudski doubted their dedication to the independence platform. "Neither Daszyński nor Kozakiewicz have convincingly demonstrated that the Polish movement [i.e., the demand for Polish independence] is dear to them. Above all, they are seen primarily as representatives of the Austrian movement." Thus, according to Pilsudski, the manner in which the Polish socialist members of parliament conducted themselves was surprisingly aloof from the goals of the party. "No one," he remarked, "expected the 'Galician' MPs to be worthy representatives of 'Polish' socialism at the outset, but we did not anticipate such a lack of attention to our needs."[40]

Pilsudski's preoccupation with the Bund was part of a broader effort to widen support for the party's federalist platform in Lithuania and Ukraine.

At the same time, Pilsudski sent the London center copies of a party circular in Latvian and German for distribution in Riga. Outside of imperial Russia, he reached out to leading European social democrats. Karl Kautsky, one of Europe's leading socialist thinkers, came out in favor of the party platform in an essay translated and published by the Polish Socialist Party.[41]

Pilsudski continued to facilitate the importation of Hebrew typeface in order to produce propaganda literature in Yiddish. Yet obstacles continued to appear. In May 1898 he complained to London that the set of Hebrew type-face he received was incomplete; the remaining parts had to be sent as soon as possible.[42] The same letter, presenting the party's finances in detail, revealed Pilsudski's multifaceted leadership concerns.

Pilsudski also continued his work to bring more Jews into the party. He relied on the circle of Polish Jews in New York for Yiddish literature. The crit-ical figure in New York was Maurycy Montlak, a bilingual Polish-Yiddish activist in the Polish Socialist Party's Warsaw branch who had settled in New York. A locksmith by profession, Montlak established the Aid Alliance of the Jewish Workers' Movement in the Russian Empire, providing Yiddish literature for the PPS, but he expressed concern about PPS influence. "I don't know where [Montlak] came across the idea that Jews are distancing them-selves from us," Pilsudski wrote in March 1898, "but be assured that our work [among the Jews] is developing more and more. We will soon be in a position to mount a resolute campaign against the Bund even in its main centers."[43]

Pilsudski's sense of urgency regarding Yiddish party literature at this time was due to the increasing number of new labor parties competing for Jewish support. An important development took place on March 1, 1898, when del-egates gathered in Minsk to announce the foundation of the empire-wide So-cial Democratic Worker's Party of Russia (RSDP). Three of nine delegates at the gathering—Alexander Kremer, Avrom Mutnik, and Shmuel Katz—were Bundists, and Kremer was selected to sit on the new party's central com-mittee. The new party granted the Bund limited autonomy as "sole represen-tatives of the Jewish proletariat." The Bundist representatives, well aware of Pilsudski and the PPS, insisted on the use of "rossiiskaia" (of Russia) in the party's name instead of "russkaia" (Russian), to which the party agreed. Thus the "Rossiiskaia Sotsialno-Demokraticheskaia Robochaia Partiia" (Social Democratic Party of Russia) was born.

Pilsudski took the new party of *rossiiskaia* instead of *russkaia*—indicating its intention to represent the whole of imperial Russia—as an affront. "The union of the Bund and '*rossiiskaia*,'" he wrote to London, "makes us unsympathetic and ill-disposed toward the new party." Although it may share common political goals, its position on russification in the western provinces among the oppressed nationalities was going to be key. It had been rumored that the new party wanted the PPS to join on the same basis as the Bund. "But here there is a hindrance marked already at the beginning of the party's establishment," Pilsudski wrote in June 1898, "with its call for 'unification' under the name *rossiiskaia,* and the incorporation of the Bund, a party whose name includes the words 'in Poland.'"[44]

For Pilsudski, this historical injustice of partition had to be rectified, and the support of the minority nationalities in that endeavor—Lithuanians, Latvians, Jews, Ukrainians, and Belarusians—was key. He saw it as an alarming development that the establishment among these peoples of socialist parties—the Bund, the Russian Social Democrats, and the Lithuanian Social Democrats—affirmed instead the territorial integrity of the present borders.

Travel to London

In June 1898 Pilsudski crossed the border into Austria-Hungary en route to London. Concealed in his luggage was the reason for his trip—a secret document of the Russian government revealing its hostile attitude toward reform and the labor movement in the Polish provinces. In May a scathing memorandum from Prince Alexander Imeretinsky to the tsar had fallen into the hands of the PPS in St. Petersburg.[45] Originally submitted to the tsar in January 1898, it was accompanied by the minutes of the tsar's council of ministers commenting on the memorandum. The documents exposed the government's intention to crush the workers' movement and limit reforms. Tsar Nicholas II's views were presented in the minutes, in which he ignored Imeretinsky's suggestion to extend more freedoms to the kingdom.[46]

Upon his arrival in London in July 1898, Pilsudski promptly delivered the secret memorandum to the ZZSP. The party's foreign branch set about printing copies, together with Pilsudski's nineteen-page introduction, which presented a historical overview of the Russian government's hostile and oppressive policies. Editorial comments on the margins of most pages helped readers interpret the documents. The publication exposed Russian authorities to considerable embarrassment.[47]

Announcing the forthcoming publication to readers of *Robotnik* back home, Pilsudski warned them not to be deceived by Imeretinsky's reform proposals, which demonstrated a hostile attitude toward the workers' movement and exposed the governor-general as a foe of labor. It was not surprising, Pilsudski commented, that Imeretinsky suppressed a recent strike by the use of bayonets and bullets. "No faithful servant of the tsar can otherwise proceed," he wrote, "because—regardless of one's opinion about workers' demands—there is a germ of rebellion against the tsar himself [in every strike]. That is why," he continued, "tsarist autocracy and the assertiveness of labor are in fact contradictory and irreconcilable. That also explains the entire monstrosity of the Muscovite invader, the barbarism of the various tsarist governments toward the rising consciousness of the people."[48] Historians agree that publication of Imeretinsky's memorandum was the most successful action to date of the Polish Socialist Party, and increased its popularity.[49] Even before the memorandum appeared in print, readers of the *Times* of London had learned about the secret document. "The Minister of War agreed with his colleague, the Minister of the Interior," the article stated, "that the state of feeling in Poland was as menacing to Russia to-day as it was in 1863. . . . There is no doubt that Poland is a thorn in Russia's side, and those officials who have been allowed to study the 50 printed copies of Prince Imeretinsky's report admit this fact." The *Times* concluded that "the further fact that this secret report has fallen into the hands of a Polish revolutionary is perhaps not the least of the many symptoms that testify to the weakness of the Russian government of Poland."[50] *Le Temps* of Paris argued that the forthcoming publication was "irrefutable proof" that any hopes of a thaw in Russo-Polish relations stemming from the tsar's visit to Warsaw in September 1897 were now abandoned.[51]

While in London, Pilsudski took the opportunity to see many comrades and reach out to those in other West European cities. He coordinated meetings with Kazimierz Kelles-Krauz in Paris for his anticipated stop in France. He also reminded Feliks Perl in Lwów to finish the biography of the Polish bard Adam Mickiewicz to coincide with the upcoming centennial anniversary of his birth.[52] Meanwhile, back home, *Robotnik* celebrated its fourth anniversary. "Four years of being pursued, thousands of apartments combed from top to bottom, hundreds of people being interrogated," Pilsudski wrote in the cover-page piece, "and a new issue of *Robotnik* has again appeared."[53] He further thumbed his nose at the Russian government when he stated that the May Day celebrations of 1898 had for the first time included recitations of workers' hymns on the main avenue of Warsaw.

In the same *Robotnik* issue Pilsudski announced the coming centennial anniversary of the birth of Poland's celebrated poet, Mickiewicz. In December 1898 the first monument to Mickiewicz in the Russian partition was to be unveiled at a ceremony in Warsaw. The planning for the ceremony was a scandal, Pilsudski stated. No deputies, wreaths, or gathering would accompany the ceremony, and the only invitations were to be sent out to Mickiewicz's children, who lived abroad. What's more, the speeches would have to be preceded by the playing of the hymn "God Save the Tsar." It was not surprising that no Polish public figure agreed to appear.[54] "On the day of the unveiling," Pilsudski wrote in July 1898, "the monument will be surrounded by a thick cordon of troops and inside will be allowed only those with preassigned tickets. All of Warsaw's workers will turn out on Krakowskie Przedmieście Street and no cordon will stop us." He concluded, "We, caretakers of our bard's memory, cannot entrust it to servants of the tsar or to a monument committee hand-selected by the tsar. We shall all guard his memory because only the Polish people can properly commemorate their own poet."[55]

In London, Pilsudski socialized with many of his comrades. Leon Wasilewski and his wife, for example, hosted Pilsudski on many occasions at their London home. In one visit, the conversation became heated over a letter Wasilewski had written to a group of Polish socialists in Lwów. The content had evidently upset Pilsudski. "I had to hear a reprimand by him," Wasilewski recalled, "uttered in a harsh tone and emphasized by a repeated stomping of his foot on the floor." Wasilewski continued that "the prestige [*autorytet*] of comrade 'Wiktor,' as representative of the country for whom there was boundless devotion, was so great that I heard this reprimand as a justified 'punishment' for the error I committed." He continued that "the image of comrade Wiktor stomping his foot will forever remain in my memory, especially because I never once saw him lose his temper like that again." Every subsequent visit to the Wasilewskis, however, was warm and friendly. Sitting with Wasilewski and his wife over tea, Pilsudski "cheerfully talked about various things relating to happenings in Poland."[56]

Returning Home to Vilna

After a two-month stay in London, Pilsudski left for Vilna on August 2, 1898. The journey began with a stay in Ostend, Belgium, at the home of comrade Max Horwitz (party name: Henryk Walecki). At that time Horwitz was completing a PhD in mathematics and physics at Ghent University. In anticipation of his visit, Pilsudski had earlier asked Horwitz to prepare a column on events in the international labor movement for *Robotnik* to be completed prior to his arrival.[57] For Pilsudski's stay, Horwitz arranged a meeting of local party members, and invited his sister, Janina, who vividly recalled her first impression of Comrade Wiktor. "I . . . listened to the animated conversation of several participants," Janina recalled, "of whom one in particular caught my attention, because of his outward appearance as well as his wit. Only once we were back at home did my brother inform me secretively: 'Do you know who that was? Jozef Pilsudski, the man who escaped from exile recently.'" She remembered her first impression of Pilsudski, describing him as "young, fair and slender with a small beard, keen, bright blue eyes and an unusually calm, abstemious way of life."[58]

Pilsudski left Belgium for Lwów, where he noticed the attention the publication of Imeretinsky's report was getting both in the local Polish press and in German and British papers.[59] After nearly three months abroad, Pilsudski was relieved to be returning home. "At last," he wrote London a few days after reaching Katowice, the transfer point to Russia from Germany, "I am writing you from Russian Poland. I don't know how you are all doing there but I am hugely delighted [to be home]. I feel good here." Once home in Vilna, he noticed the buzz around the publication of the Imeretinsky report. The memorandum, he wrote, "is going like hotcakes here" and he only regretted that too few copies had been printed.[60]

Pilsudski rubbed shoulders with Lithuanian socialists in Vilna. One of the leaders of the LSDP, Alfonsas Moravskis, reached out to express his disappointment with the Polish Socialist Party's fourth congress resolution on Lithuanian socialists. Russian Social Democrats were pressuring Moravskis

and the LSDP to merge with the Russian party. But Moravskis had decided
not to join the new Social Democratic Party of Russia. "In part, this is completely natural," Pilsudski wrote. "It stems from the element of kinship between the LSDP and PPS, a kinship that cannot be dealt with by any separatist ghosts wishing to tear apart the Union of Lublin," Pilsudski reasoned,
referring to the political union between Poland and Lithuania in 1569 that
brought into being the Polish-Lithuanian Commonwealth.[61]

Pilsudski urged the Lithuanian party leaders to explicitly advocate for the
PPS program. "I have already chatted a few times with their leaders," Pilsudski
wrote in October 1898, "yet when I press them on their 'federation' program,
it's unclear with whom they want to federate. That is why I could not come
to any understanding with them. They couldn't even utter that they want a
federation with Poland," he noted discouragingly.[62] Pilsudski then drew up
a draft unification agreement for the two parties. But when he presented it to
his Lithuanian comrades, "the subject was already so acrimonious" that the
agreement fell through. Pilsudski nevertheless did not lose faith. "I have not
lost hope," he wrote, "that in due time all will be arranged according to our
wishes."[63]

At the end of 1898 Pilsudski turned his attention away from local affairs
with Lithuanians and Jews to instead focus on two monuments. The first, unveiled on November 8, 1898 in Vilna, was a monument to Mikhail Muraviev,
former governor-general of the Northwest Territories who had brutally suppressed the 1863 Polish uprising, thereby gaining the nickname "The
Hangman." At the unveiling of the monument, Muraviev was praised as a
savior of the fatherland. In a cover article in *Robotnik*, Pilsudski lashed out
at the government for erecting this monument in Vilna of all places. In "Monument to an Executioner," he wrote that "captivity under Moscow differs
from many others [despotic regimes] in that, aside from the injustice and oppression of a conquered nation, we must endure humiliation constantly. . . .
It is not enough for [the tsar] to strike the conquered people with a whip. He
wants the broken stick to be kissed. It's not enough for the tsar to knock down
his foes. It is also necessary to slap the face of the defeated."[64]

The erection of the Muraviev monument evoked genuine outrage in Pilsudski. He used the occasion to discuss the meaning and significance of the
1863 uprising. As he explained, the Russian government became gravely concerned when the Provisional National Government in Warsaw emancipated

the Polish peasants in 1864. With the freeing of the Polish peasants, Russia feared that the entire Polish people would support the secessionist government in Warsaw "and sympathy for the Poles among the people of Europe, now demanding a war with Russia, thus raising hopes for a decisive defeat of the tsar."

For a brief moment, according to Pilsudski, Russia believed that the Kingdom of Poland was going to be lost. A poorly armed force, too few weapons, and the absence of any threat of force from France or Britain proved decisive. "The governments of France, England and Austria," he wrote, "limited their protests to written statements alone. Contrary to public opinion, they did not want to back their words with force." This gave the Russian government the green light to put down the uprising. The victory of the Russian armed forces was meant "not only to defeat the captive peoples of Poland and Lithuania who wanted to secede from Russia. It was also necessary to punish them in a way that would destroy any desire for rebellion in the future. . . . In Lithuania, the man for the job was none other than Muraviev." With Muraviev's leadership in Vilna, "murder, horror and plunder engulfed Lithuania. I cannot catalog all of Muraviev's atrocities in this brief article. Suffice it to say," Pilsudski maintained, "that his governorship was so repugnant and so appalling . . . that the tsar had to dismiss him immediately after the collapse of the [1863] uprising."[65]

Pilsudski concluded with powerful words. "Now the government is erecting a monument to a man tainted with treachery and blood in the same Vilna where the soil is soaked with the blood of his victims, where the tortured bodies have not yet decayed, and where the tears are not yet dried. Such a monument . . . is an idea worthy of the tsar." He declared that "this is both the height of barbarism and abasement. The brazen taunting of human feeling rises in this system of government that tramples for so many years over the dignity of a people."[66] For the unveiling ceremony, Pilsudski wrote a one-page proclamation, signed by the Polish Socialist Party, that hit the streets of Vilna on the morning of the event. The city's residents, he wrote, will see Orthodox priests and tsarist officials, "a swarm of leeches." "For us," the proclamation declared, "this block of stone and bronze, this monument is a symbol of bondage, enforced by the tsar in Vilna." It was meant to mock the misery of the local population. "This monument of slavery will crumble to the ground," Pilsudski promised, "when Poland and Lithuania will be bathed in the sunlight of freedom."[67]

The cruel irony of the location of the two monuments—one to Poland's beloved bard Mickiewicz and the other to the Russian official who put down the 1863 uprising—was not lost on Pilsudski. As Patrice M. Dabrowski observed, "Given that the poet's connection to Vilna, a place where he had lived and studied (in contrast to Warsaw . . . which he had never visited), the choice of location for the Muraviev monument was particularly painful."[68] Pilsudski noted that "they have authorized a monument to Mickiewicz but at the same time have erected in Vilna a monument to Muraviev, a man who drowned the city in Polish blood."[69]

Pilsudski emphasized the latter point in a series of editorials that followed. *Robotnik*'s issue of December 1898 was devoted to Mickiewicz and his legacy, complete with a striking cover image of the poet. The issue was accompanied by a proclamation in the name of the Polish Socialist Party. "Mickiewicz," the proclamation stated, "has become a part of the soul of every genuine Pole." The sharply negative feelings toward the ceremony were palpable: "At a time when the shackles on Poland's feet rattle and a gloomy melody of subjugation sounds, there's the desire of the nation to properly celebrate its poet."[70]

Meanwhile, Pilsudski's longtime efforts to bring out a party newspaper in Yiddish bore fruit. Having arrived back in Vilna after the conference, Pilsudski wrote to London. The letter revealed that the London center had previously agreed to send Hebrew typeface fonts to enable the party in Vilna to print Yiddish materials. "In the near future," he wrote, "we are setting up a new small Yiddish printing house for Jewish workers."[71] In Max Horwitz, Pilsudski had found a capable candidate to edit the paper. Although Horwitz was raised in Warsaw, his father was from Vienna and Horwitz spoke German and Polish at home. He thus had to learn Yiddish for the purposes of editing the paper. With able assistants who were Yiddish-speaking Jewish party members, the first issue of *Der arbeter* (The Worker), printed in London, appeared in December 1898.

Delighted at the news, Pilsudski asked for as many copies as possible to be smuggled to Vilna.[72] But his goals for a Yiddish party paper nonetheless fell short, for he had envisioned a publication that would be produced and printed *inside* the Russian Empire. The real handicap was the dearth of party members who had been capable of putting out a Yiddish paper, a problem that soon became painfully evident. After Horwitz was arrested in 1899 in Warsaw, the Yiddish paper's second issue did not appear for another two years, in December 1900. At the same time, Pilsudski was preparing leaflets in Latvian for distribution in Riga, demonstrating his broader efforts to incorporate non-Polish borderland nationalities into the party fold (and, ultimately, into a future breakaway state).[73]

Matrimony and Relocation

The year 1899 ushered in three important changes for the thirty-one-year-old Pilsudski. The first was a change in personnel in Vilna. At the beginning of the year, Stanisław Wojciechowski was thinking about marriage and family. A member of the party's Central Workers' Committee, Wojciechowski had been Pilsudski's main collaborator on the party newspaper, housing the party's secret printing press in his Vilna apartment. So when Wojciechowski announced that he was engaged to be married and was going to emigrate to England, Pilsudski had mixed feelings. He was genuinely happy for Wojciechowski and his fiancée, Maria Kiersnowska. Pilsudski had known Kiersnowska for many years, as the two had been classmates at the Russian State Gymnasium in Vilna. At the same time, Pilsudski did not want to see his comrade and friend leave. Wojciechowski promised to stay until the next issue of the paper was completed, after which he bid farewell, handed Pilsudski the apartment keys, and left the country for good, marrying Maria in London later that year.[74]

Pilsudski also had marriage on his mind. Feeling the passing of time, he remarked in August 1898 that "more and more, I feel that I am approaching old age."[75] It is not surprising, therefore, to learn from Pilsudski's younger brother, Jan, who lived in Vilna, that the most reliable place to find Pilsudski at this time was at the home of Maria Juszkiewicz.[76] Pilsudski had known Maria for six years. They had met in Vilna at a gathering of Polish socialists in 1892. In the spring of 1899 he asked Maria for her hand in marriage. In many ways they were ideal companions. Maria was not only intelligent and cultured, with a university education, but also passionately engaged in the party's conspiratorial work. As a divorced woman, Maria could not marry in a Catholic Church, so in May 1899 the couple converted to Protestantism. On July 15, Pilsudski married Maria at the Evangelical-Augsburg Confessional Church in the village of Paproć Duża in the Łomża district, becoming stepfather to Maria's eleven-year-old daughter, Wanda. Pilsudski's younger brothers, Adam and Jan, served as witnesses. The marriage certificate listed the newlyweds as Jozef Dąbrowski and Maria Dąbrowska née Karczewska. Using their new false identities, the couple settled in Vilna, moving into Wojciechowski's old apartment.[77]

Pilsudski turned again to vigorous party work, putting out two issues of *Robotnik* in rapid succession. In the first, he spoke of tsarist Russia as a country "where one is barely free to breathe without the explicit permission of the authorities."[78] In the next issue, *Robotnik* celebrated its five-year anniversary in July 1899. "Our five-year jubilee," Pilsudski wrote in the cover-page editorial, "is an important victory, achieved inside tsarist Russia, and [the paper] owes its indefatigable strength to the growing life of a conscious Polish working class."[79] Pilsudski was also managing party affairs, writing to London and mobilizing party publicists to write more propaganda literature. To this end he leaned heavily on Feliks Perl, asking the London center to have Perl write an article on the Polish poet Juliusz Słowacki, edit a volume of national poetry, and compose a brochure on the international socialist movement. "In general," Pilsudski wrote to London, "it would be a good idea if you guys in the London organization could put out more brochures of a historical nature. It is a shame that such literature comes out so infrequently."[80] Pilsudski and his comrades felt that the movement he was heading was of historical significance. To document it, the London center began a party archive, to which Pilsudski began to frequently contribute materials. In a letter from 1899, for example, he inserted two things for the archive: a photograph of Stanisław Landy (his close friend from his Siberian exile) and a draft agreement proposed between the PPS and the Lithuanian Social Democratic Party in August 1899.[81]

In the next issue of *Robotnik,* Pilsudski hammered away at the repressive tsarist system. "Our struggle with tsarism," he wrote, "is a struggle between two entirely alien worlds. On the one hand, there is wild, barbaric Asia forcing its way on our lives with all its ruthlessness, cruelty and servility. Against this, on the other hand, has arisen a movement that is, in every sense of the word, European. It relies on breaking the shackles constraining the development of its people and on removing every last trace of captivity and control of one person upon another. Between these two forces, a life-and-death struggle is being waged."[82]

The third change in Pilsudski's life in 1899 was the decision to move to Łódź. In the fall of 1899 he decided that the Russian authorities were getting closer to discovering his whereabouts and the coveted secret printing press. In October he got word that the Russian secret police were circling in on him. Almost immediately the Pilsudskis arranged to move to Łódź, where they believed they would evade notice. After relocating the printing press, Jozef and Maria, along with their thirteen-year-old daughter, abruptly left Vilna on October 28, 1899. They moved into the apartment in Łódź that now housed the party printing press. For Jozef and Maria, relocating was an undesirable change. Maria was born and raised in Vilna, while Pilsudski had lived in Vilna since the age of seven. They had been uprooted from their beloved ancestral home.

As he began preparing the next issue of *Robotnik,* Pilsudski returned to the complex subject of the fate of the borderland nationalities in the tsarist regime. The occasion was a letter from London in which Leon Wasilewski included a proposal for a party brochure. In great detail, Pilsudski advised Wasilewski on the contents. One of the points he believed had to be emphasized was that the subjugation of the non-Russian peoples was worse than in other multinational empires "due to the political system and wildness of Russia."[83] After some general comments, Pilsudski urged Wasilewski to advocate for the union of Lithuania and the western, Catholic part of Belarus. For it was only "that part [of Byelorussia] that we can count on for support [for a federal state] in the future." He continued that "it is necessary to emphasize and put forward the idea that to a large degree Lithuania is a continuation of Poland. In Lithuania, one finds a large percentage of Poles, of Polish in the towns, and a considerable influence of Polish culture. In a word, Poles make a major contribution to the country. The result is a common historical tradition, of participation in insurrections, Polish revolutions and in the socialist movement."[84]

Pilsudski also counseled Wasilewski to emphasize that the future of Lithuania was inextricably tied to the future of Poland. While the future of Lithuanian independence was unclear, he wrote, "the best plan with Poland is to ensure the free development to the Poles, Lithuanians, Belarussians and Jews, and to do away with the great advantage of one people over another, which is necessary in the face of the huge entanglement of national relations. Socialists in Lithuania must put forth such a position and the PPS should promote this in its work in Lithuania." With an enemy as strong as imperial Russia, it was necessary that Poland and Lithuania be linked in every Polish struggle, with the strength of the PPS "and all socialists of all nationalities in Lithuania for a common struggle."[85]

Pilsudski, age thirty-two, with his first wife, Maria, and stepdaughter, Wanda. Łódź, 1900.

The proposed brochure included a section on the Jews. The subject of the Jews, he commented, was very delicate. Rather than devote a separate section, Pilsudski advised Wasilewski to write merely a few lines on the topic. "We believe that it would be best to insert [such sentences] in the section on Lithuania," he wrote, "in the following manner: The Jews are oppressed perhaps more than anyone else. But just as with other oppressed peoples, they should seek salvation in a common struggle alongside Christians for the freedom of *their* country." By the end of the lengthy letter, Pilsudski had exhausted himself. "It is now terribly late," he confided, "and I am getting tired. So forgive me if this letter is slightly chaotic. A big hug and my regards to your wife."[86] Wasilewski later commented that Pilsudski's letter became the basis for a party brochure published two years later. So significant was the letter that Wasilewski reprinted it in full in his recollections on Pilsudski.[87] Pilsudski's stamp on that publication, which appeared in 1901 under the title *We wspólnym jarzmie* (Under a Common Oppressor), was everywhere, with many ideas borrowed from his letter. "It is entirely accurate," Wasilewski wrote in the brochure, "to say that the intelligentsia in Lithuania is Polish."

He added, "It is therefore entirely fair for us to regard Lithuania as almost a part of Poland, even more so because Polish cultural influence as well as the influence of Polish political currents from the insurrections to socialism are so enormous."[88]

At the end of 1899 Pilsudski and his new assistant put out two more issues of *Robotnik*. In a powerful editorial, "A New Phase," Pilsudski discussed a demonstration among factory workers in Dąbrowa Górnicza to protest the arrest of two workers who mysteriously died in prison. "The common thread of all this revolutionary activity among the proletariat here," he wrote, "is its illegality and incompatibility with the law in tsarist Russia. Yet . . . the very thought of change in the present circumstances among this proletariat is criminal according to the autocratic regime." He added, "In history, where revolutions are directed against despotism, demonstrations play an important role. Namely, a multiplicity of such demonstrations signals a phase preceding an outbreak. In other words, we are now in a prerevolutionary period."[89]

Always conscious of historical events that had meaning in the present, Pilsudski marked the fourteenth anniversary of the execution of the leaders of Proletariat, the first Polish socialist party. A front-page piece in January 1900 included a striking photo of the former organization's leaders as well as an artist's sketches of those executed. For Pilsudski, this anniversary had a very personal connection. He had been a first-year university student in Kharkov in 1886 when lengthy prison terms and four death sentences were imposed on Proletariat leaders and followers. "The first clash of our labor movement with tsardom was the appearance of the Proletariat party. We know well that the fight will still continue with dedication. We are certain that our ranks . . . will finish with a victory over them."[90]

Six months after Wojciechowski left for England, Pilsudski was feeling overworked and trapped in Łódź. He was doing much more work to put out the party paper, and pleaded with London to send Wojciechowski back to Łódź. If that was not possible, he asked that Bolesław Jędzejowski come instead to stand in for Pilsudski as editor of *Robotnik*. Pilsudski was also frustrated that not a single article he had requested for the next issue had arrived. As a result, he would have to write twice as many pieces as usual. Please send, he continued, ink seals for the paper with the slogan "Help political prisoners."[91] Pilsudski's frustration and discontent were palpable. "In the last few weeks when I've had more free time," he wrote on February 7, 1900, "I feel exhausted and idiotically anxious. I haven't been able to sleep the past few nights. For this reason, I cannot do any work."[92]

One of the things that gave Pilsudski extreme unease was the increasing presence of government spies. He wrote on January 7, 1900, "I have never seen such a mass of spies. They are brimming everywhere."[93] To continue production of *Robotnik,* Pilsudski needed a spare part for the printing press but feared it would be difficult to replace. One month later he commented that "for the last two and half weeks I have not so much as stepped foot outside my apartment. I want to wait until the number of spies decreases."[94]

On February 20, 1900, Alexander Malinowski, a member of the party's central committee, visited Pilsudski from Warsaw. Unbeknownst to him, Malinowski was being followed by the police. As he waited for a train back to Warsaw on the night of February 21, Malinowski was arrested after the police observed him entering Pilsudski's apartment. A few hours later, at 3 a.m. on February 22, the police raided the apartment of Jozef and Maria Pilsudski in Łódź. Not only did they apprehend the long-sought-after leader of the illegal Polish Socialist Party and his wife, but they seized the party's secret printing press. In Pilsudski's own account of the arrest, smuggled out of a prison cell in April 1900, we learn that he was in the middle of preparing the thirty-sixth issue of *Robotnik.* When he went to bed the evening of the arrest, nine of the issue's twelve pages had been completed and Pilsudski had just finished writing the cover article.[95] Jozef and Maria were taken into custody in Łódź and were transferred to a prison in Warsaw on April 17.

The arrest of Pilsudski and the seizure of the printing press was a huge blow. Wasilewski, in London at the time, recalled that "the news hit us all very hard. We all wondered what the fate of the party would be in the wake of this catastrophe. The loss of the printing press, which the Russian gendarme had been pursuing unsuccessfully [for so long] a time, troubled me less than the loss from our party ranks of the most eminent leader of the PPS. No one in the party doubted that comrade 'Wiktor' was the most distinguished leader of the PPS at that time." Indeed, Pilsudski had already acquired legendary status. "Even then," Wasilewski reminisced, "a certain kind of legend was radiant, and personal devotion to him within the party thus spread and deepened the legend."[96] Everyone now feared for Pilsudski's fate. With trepidation they wondered if he would ever return from a tsarist prison.

CHAPTER 6

An Extraordinary Escape and
a New Home in Austrian Galicia

With all its energy, our socialist party shall fight against anti-
Semitism as an injurious and backward current. [Russian] policies
limiting the rights of any group are to us repugnant.

—JOZEF PILSUDSKI, PARTY RESOLUTION (1902)

After leading the party for eight years, producing and editing its central paper, expanding its membership, and raising the party's prestige at home and abroad, Pilsudski, together with his wife, was placed behind bars. Not only had the Russian secret police prevented the next issue of *Robotnik* from coming out, they also found a large stash of materials including Hebrew typeface and various other printing implements. Also discovered were a host of letters to activists like Stanisław Wojciechowski and Bolesław A. Jędrzejowski and personal letters from Pilsudski's older brother, Bronisław. The gendarmerie also found notebooks filled with Pilsudski's ideas for articles as well as newspaper clippings in Russian, Ukrainian, German, Latvian, and Yiddish.[1]

With the arrest of Pilsudski and the removal of the party's printing facilities, the tsarist government dealt a huge blow to the party. And with the arrest of Aleksander Malinowski, two of the party's three central committee members were now behind bars. Although devastated by the turn of events, party figures in tsarist Russia, like Aleksander Sulkiewicz, vowed to do everything possible to free Pilsudski while continuing the activities of the party.

Within days of the arrest, Sulkiewicz formed a new, provisional central committee. Its leadership body included, among others, Sulkiewicz, Feliks Sachs, and Kazimierz Rożnowski, Pilsudski's assistant who had fled to Vilna the night of the arrest.[2] The new central committee resolved that the way to restore morale was to have a new printing press put out the next issue of *Robotnik*. But the party took another blow on February 26, 1900, when the tsarist police raided the old Vilna apartment where the Pilsudskis had lived, taking into custody Rożnowski and Sachs. The arrest not only eliminated half of the new provisional central committee but also blew the cover of the intended site for the replacement printing press.[3]

The crisis at home, meanwhile, compelled Wojciechowski to leave London for Russia in an effort to reconstitute the party. When he crossed the border on March 20, 1900, he traveled to Białystok, where he met up with Sulkiewicz to discuss plans for rebuilding the party. Both agreed that *Robotnik* was to be produced in London until the importation of a new printing press. Wojciechowski said he would arrange for the purchase of a new press using funds from London. In the course of his first week in Russia, he and Sulkiewicz put together a new central committee consisting of the two of them and Bolesław Czarkowski.[4]

Wojciechowski returned to London with materials for the next issue of *Robotnik*. After the new issue was done, he returned to Russia and on April 20, 1900, met Sulkiewicz in the East Prussian border town of Ejtkuny (today Chernyshevskoye, Russia) to hand him copies.[5] Coming out two months after the seizure of the party printing press in Łódź, the new issue was a show of defiance, with a lead editorial informing readers about the dramatic arrests in Łódź in February. "The chance triumph of the gendarmerie over our organization," *Robotnik* stated, "did not break us. After a two-month period, readers have in their hands issue No. 36 of *Robotnik*."[6]

Pilsudski described the prison in Łódź as dreadful. "The cell was minute, without a stick of furniture in it," he recalled, "and I was forbidden to smoke tobacco—in fact there was everything to make the dirty hole detestable."[7] The Pilsudskis were transferred from Łódź to the infamous Warsaw Citadel, where Pilsudski was interned at the Tenth Pavilion for political prisoners. The transfer to Warsaw was a huge improvement, Pilsudski noted: "I was very satisfied indeed when they brought me to Warsaw. But in truth, the most serious cause of my excellent temper was the elation I felt on entering the walls of the institution which was so closely bound up with the history of our country's martyrs." He was allowed to smoke, and the cell included movable furniture. "That is why I look back with pleasant emotion upon my confinement in the Tenth Pavilion of the Warsaw Citadel," Pilsudski commented later. "In other prisons you had nothing for yourself, but here everything belonged to you, because you had the right to move it. When I was brought into the delightful cell, number 26 of the Tenth Pavilion of Warsaw Citadel, it seemed to have all the charm of a hotel room, though a very mediocre one; my suitcase was lying there, and I could move my things freely from one corner to another; when I kicked the table, it moved obediently."[8]

Party informants had for several years infiltrated the Tenth Pavilion. Through these channels Pilsudski smuggled out a secret report in April 1900 detailing his arrest. Written on scraps of red tissue paper from a cigarette box, the report made its way to party comrades first in Warsaw and then in London. Complete with a diagram of the Łódź apartment, Pilsudski provided a firsthand account of the arrest and the materials seized.[9] He subsequently smuggled out a letter to his stepdaughter, Wanda, who was likely still in Łódź at the time. "When you return to Vilna," he wrote emotionally, "please greet the whole city from me, all these marvelous things that are contained in the five-letter word—Wilno."[10]

Things started looking up for the party in May 1900 when Feliks Sachs was released on bail and the central committee found a site for its new printing press in Kiev. The new issue of *Robotnik,* the first printed inside tsarist Russia since the seizure of the printing press in February, signaled that the party was fully operational. The issue was dedicated to the memory of veteran German socialist Wilhelm Liebknecht, who had just passed away at age seventy-three, in honor of his support of the Polish Socialist Party's independence platform.

Escape from a Mental Hospital

Sulkiewicz meanwhile went about organizing Pilsudski's escape. He first reached out to Maria Paszkowska, a party sympathizer active in the secret Society for Helping Prisoners (*Kasa Pomocy Więziennej*). She vowed to arrange for Pilsudski's move out of the Warsaw Citadel because it was an impossible place from which to escape. The only way out was for Pilsudski to fake a condition for which there was no treatment there: mental illness.[11]

Paszkowska turned to an old Russian acquaintance, Alexei Sedelnikov, then serving as deputy head of the Warsaw Citadel prison. His wife was Polish, and he had consequently developed a certain sympathy for Polish concerns. He had in fact been working with Paszkowska for the past six years, and agreed to deliver a message to Pilsudski.[12] Paszkowska and Sulkiewicz turned to a Polish psychiatrist, Rafał Radziwiłłowicz, for guidelines on how to simulate mental illness. Paszkowska then made contact with Pilsudski, "owing to the goodness of Sedelnikov. And in this way, we were able to quite thoroughly keep [Pilsudski] abreast [of the plan]." She remarked that "without [Sedelnikov's] help, Pilsudski's escape would have been unimaginable." Given that Pilsudski would have received a minimum of eight years Siberian exile, "the Polish Socialist Party was not about to let this happen. There was no other option than to organize his escape," she wrote.[13]

In the course of the next few months, Pilsudski simulated symptoms of mental illness, including rejecting food from prison guards, which led to a dramatic weight loss and the deterioration of his health. Paszkowska got Pilsudski's aunt, Stefania Lipman, to write the prison urgently requesting a psychiatric evaluation. Having gained the trust of Ivan Sabashnikov, director of the Insane Asylum of St. John the Divine in Warsaw, Paszkowska told him that Pilsudski was a relative and his psychological state was of grave concern to his family. She convinced Sabashnikov that Pilsudski needed to be under the care of mental health professionals and asked that he visit the prisoner to see for himself.[14]

The meeting could not have gone better. Pilsudski evidently charmed Sabashnikov, a native of Siberia, with stories about the region from Pilsudski's years of exile. "Sabashnikov warmly thanked me," Paszkowska wrote, "for giving him the opportunity to meet such a remarkable individual whom he described as having a big heart. On more than one occasion, he told me that the one hour he spent with Pilsudski was one of the finest in his whole life."[15] Despite knowing the affair was being faked, Sabashnikov submitted a report that Pilsudski's mental state was dangerous and severe. Shortly after, the Russian gendarmerie received an order to transfer Pilsudski to the Nicholas and Miracle Maker Mental Hospital in St. Petersburg, where Pilsudski arrived on December 15, 1900, and was placed in solitary confinement.

Sulkiewicz now proceeded to the next stage of the escape plan, which involved the local PPS organization in St. Petersburg, made up of university students. He saw it as a good sign that the mental hospital director in

St. Nicholas the Miracle Worker Hospital for the Insane in St. Petersburg, where
Pilsudski was taken after faking insanity and from which he escaped in May 1901.

St. Petersburg, Otton Czeczot, was Polish. Meanwhile, Sulkiewicz reached
out to Władysław Mazurkiewicz, a party member who had just completed
his degree at the Military-Medical Academy in St. Petersburg in January 1901.
Mazurkiewicz's first assignment was to seek employment at the mental hospital where Pilsudski was being held. In March, the director of the hospital
offered him a position on the hospital staff. Walking Mazurkiewicz through
the facility on his first day, Czeczot stopped next to a room where, in a
hushed voice, he indicated that the editor of *Robotnik*, Jozef Pilsudski, was
under observation there. Czeczot revealed, however, that he knew Pilsudski
was fully healthy in all aspects.[16]

In preparation for the escape, Mazurkiewicz smuggled into his office
clothing, a coat, footwear, and a special cap worn by employees. The opportunity to act came on May 14, 1901, when Czeczot was away at a conference
and had placed Mazurkiewicz in charge. A fair was being held in the city that
evening, so Mazurkiewicz gave the majority of the staff the night off. Around
8 p.m., he ordered Pilsudski brought to his office for medical examination.
The staff member who brought Pilsudski hesitated to leave the room until he
was ordered to close the door and return in one hour. Pilsudski snapped into
action the moment the door closed, changing into the new clothes, and ten

minutes later was ready to leave.[17] The two quietly left the office, made sure the hallway was clear, and walked out the back door of the hospital. Mazurkiewicz panicked when he discovered that the hospital's outer gate was locked from the inside. But the night porter recognized the doctor, unlocked the gate, and let the two leave the premises. Mazurkiewicz hailed a horse-drawn droshky and the two sped off toward a secret apartment where Sulkiewicz was waiting.

Mazurkiewicz recalled being terribly nervous with the exceedingly slow pace of the horse. "You should transport cadavers and not living people!" Mazurkiewicz barked at the driver. But he was struck by Pilsudski's calm demeanor: "Wiktor [Pilsudski] tried to calm me down, saying, 'Look around at how green it is and how nice it smells.'" Mazurkiewicz recalled taking pity on the escaped fugitive, remarking, "I looked at him and shuddered: a big, disheveled beard, disheveled hair and this hapless cap on the back of his head."[18] Arriving finally at the meeting place, Pilsudski was warmly and emotionally greeted by Sulkiewicz, his longtime comrade and cofounder of the party. Sulkiewicz and Pilsudski, now dressed as a customs official, boarded a train to Tallinn, the Estonian city on the shores of the Gulf of Finland in tsarist Russia.

In Tallinn, Sulkiewicz coordinated a plan to reunite Pilsudski with his wife. Maria had been released from prison on January 21, 1901, and was living in Vilna with Wanda. Upon receiving the news of her husband's escape, she left Vilna—in violation of the terms of her prison release—and proceeded to a prearranged meeting place on May 24. The plan was to meet in Czysta Łuża, a village in the remote region of Polesie, on the estate of a Mr. and Mrs. Lewandowski. When Sulkiewicz and Pilsudski arrived there in the last days of May, Maria was waiting. After fifteen months of separation, the couple was reunited.

For security reasons, Pilsudski and Maria fled Russia separately. In June 1901, Sulkiewicz accompanied Pilsudski, making a brief stop in Kiev, where the latest issue of *Robotnik* was being prepared. In Kiev at the time was Feliks Perl, who had come from abroad in May 1901 to serve as the paper's new editor. With him was Ksawery Prauss, a student member of the PPS from St. Petersburg in whose name the apartment was rented. "As the door opened," Prauss recalled of the two guests' arrival, "I saw Pilsudski. Behind him was Sulkiewicz who was slyly smiling as if to say to us: 'Instead of merely the joyful

Pilsudski's Arrest and Escape, 1900–1901

- – – – Border of the Polish-Lithuanian Commonwealth, 1772
- ——— Frontiers of three partitioning powers
- ⋯⋯⋯ Boundary between the Congress Kingdom and Western Gubenias
- → Pilsudski's imprisonment and escape Feb 1900 - June 1901

⊠ Prussian partition
▨ Austrian partition
▢ Russian partition
▲ Pilsudski family estates at the time of his birth
✚ Pilsudski's birthplace

Feb. 22, 1900: Pilsudski arrested in Łódź

April 17, 1900: Pilsudski taken to Warsaw Citadel Prison

Dec. 15, 1900: Pilsudski transferred to mental hospital in St. Petersburg after faking insanity

May 14, 1901: Pilsudski escapes and travels to Tallinn

Late May, 1901: Pilsudski begins escape from Russia, first stopping in Czysta Łuża, reuniting with his wife, Maria

June, 1901: Continues path of escape, stopping in Kiev. Going through Zamość, the Pilsudskis traveled south to the Tanew River where they reached the village of Rebizanty across the border

news of Ziuk's escape, he is actually right here!'" Embraces, sturdy hand-
shakes, and excited conversations followed, "but these were merely trifle
words. Everyone felt exhilarated that Pilsudski was actually here among us—
free, healthy and even cheerful."[19] That evening, either Prauss or Perl took
notes as Pilsudski described the details of his escape. They decided to prepare a detailed article about the harrowing escape for the upcoming issue of
the paper, identifying Pilsudski by his real name.[20]

Pilsudski and Sulkiewicz left Kiev the following day for Austria. After
joining Maria in Zamość, the couple was welcomed by St. Petersburg university student Jan Miklaszewski, who had been assigned to guide the couple
across the border. He accompanied the Pilsudskis south to a bend in the
Tanew River, about two kilometers from the border, "to a footbridge on a river
hidden in the thicket of the forest" where they crossed over onto free soil in
the village of Rebizanty.[21]

To Freedom and Back

Compared to tsarist Russia, Austria-Hungary was a beacon of freedom. A
constitutional monarchy since the creation of the Dual Monarchy in 1867,
Austria-Hungary had a parliamentary system guaranteeing freedom of speech,
the press, and assembly. What's more, Vienna formally recognized Poles
as the dominant nationality in Galicia. Under the system of Galician autonomy adopted in 1868, the governorship of Galicia was reserved for ethnic
Poles, and Polish became the language of instruction in schools and universities. Austrian Galicia thus offered a fundamentally different political and
social climate for Pilsudski, who would make it his home for the next twelve
years. In the former medieval capital of Poland, Kraków, Poles made up two-
thirds of the city's population in 1900, with Jews constituting 28 percent.[22] In
contrast to Vilna, where Jews made up the largest ethno-linguistic group,
Poles comprised a solid majority in Kraków. Here, Polish culture was dominant, evidenced by the fact that an estimated 82.5 percent of Kraków Jewry
were Polish speakers.[23] East Galicia's capital, Lwów, was more diverse. By 1910,
Poles comprised 51.2 percent of the population with the rest divided between
Ukrainians (19.2 percent) and Jews (27.8 percent).[24]

In Lwów, the Pilsudskis initially stayed where they were well connected—
at the home of longtime party comrade Witold Jodko-Narkiewicz and his

wife.[25] Władysław Mazurkiewicz, who had aided in Pilsudski's escape from the hospital in St. Petersburg, was in Lwów as well, staying at the home of Jozef Uziembło, who had lived in the city since 1900 when he left tsarist Russia with his wife and children.[26] Uziembło's son, Adam, noted that Pilsudski had been a legend in their home since the early 1890s when Adam's father became an ardent PPS sympathizer. Adam vividly recalled seeing his father reading one of the first issues of *Robotnik* in 1894, when Adam was a young boy. "I saw *Robotnik* for the first time at the age of eight or nine," he wrote, when he walked into their living room and his father motioned to him. "He brought out an issue of the paper and—very slowly, in a stern voice—said that no one should know about the existence of this paper in our home. Nobody! It must remain a secret because one could get sent to Siberia merely for possession of it."[27] The way his father held the paper in such high esteem, combined with the secrecy and danger surrounding it, made a strong impression on the boy.

When, seven years later, the founder of *Robotnik* visited their home, sixteen-year-old Adam was elated to meet the legendary figure. The thirty-three-year-old Pilsudski was still in the early stages of recovery, feeling tired and noticeably depleted. "On several occasions," Uziembło recalled, "Ziuk [Pilsudski] lost his strength in the course of a long conversation. His eyes drooped, he got a long face and, suddenly despondent, walked around [the room] with an unsteady step."[28]

In a letter to Bolesław Jędrzejowski in London, Pilsudski himself referred to his poor physical state but could not hide his exhilaration at being a free man: "I will only say," he wrote on June 20, 1901, "that I am unendingly happy that I miraculously succeeded in getting here and can be among you."[29] To help his recovery, the Pilsudskis left Lwów for the nearby village of Brzuchowice, where they stayed at the villa of Adam and Olga Tołłoczko. The couple's daughter, Helena, recalled that Pilsudski "looked very sickly, although due to the thorough care he was receiving, he quickly got better." Despite his poor health, Helena continued, "he always had a sense of humor, frequently joking around. He enjoyed most reciting [the poet] Słowacki either in the house or in the gardens." His favorite activity at the time was playing chess.[30]

Pilsudski received several visitors while in Brzuchowice, mostly party activists among the university students in Lwów. One guest, Stanisław Siedlecki, had recently completed his degree in chemical engineering at the Polytechnic Institute. Like all party members, he had learned about Pilsudski's arrest and the seizure of the party's printing press. "*Robotnik*," Siedlecki wrote, "was close to our hearts for its boldness and straightforwardness in relation to the life of workers." He noted that "the joyful news spread like wildfire that Jozef Pilsudski had escaped from St. Petersburg and had found his way abroad." The press accounts in Galicia had indicated that Pilsudski was in England.[31]

In August 1901, Siedlecki, with a few party comrades, were invited to a gathering in Brzuchowice. When they entered the villa gate, Siedlecki recalled, "we were met by a slim man of medium height in a loose-fitting brown checkered suit. He had a small, dark blond goatee with a pointed end." A few dozen steps away stood the elder statesman and Pilsudski's mentor from Siberian exile, Bronisław Szwarce, "with his tall figure . . . and a stately grey beard that gave a special atmosphere to this scene." As they entered the grounds, "the unknown man politely, but solemnly, put out his hand. 'Pilsudski,' he said, introducing himself to each guest by his real name." The students looked at each other in disbelief. Everyone had been told Pilsudski was in England. "We needed a little time to catch on to what was happening," Siedlecki wrote. "After some time, however, we realized that here before us was the leader of the Polish Socialist Party who had erased all traces of himself and led Russian intelligence down a false path."[32]

Shortly after the gathering, Pilsudski returned to Lwów. He continued to feel quite weak. "Lately, I feel silly about my state of health," he wrote on July 15, 1901. "Everything torments me terribly. Even minor physical and mental efforts exhaust me." Pilsudski was preoccupied with party work, expressing eagerness to resume underground activity. Acting as a party leader in illegal conditions "accords more with my natural inclinations, to put it plainly. I have nothing against this idea and have every intention of continuing my [underground] career." He added that "one of my concerns is, in fact, that the current central committee cannot thoroughly manage its obligations and has too little authority among the rank and file."[33] But Pilsudski maintained that his time as editor of *Robotnik* was over—the future was in organizational party work in the homeland.

SINCE THEIR ARRIVAL in Austrian Galicia, the Pilsudskis had regarded Kraków as the place they would make as their permanent home. Five weeks after their stay in Lwów, the couple moved to Kraków. Within days of their arrival, Pilsudski had met with several people. "I live in such chaos and bustle that I have no time to think or write," he wrote on July 25, 1901.[34] He continued to tend to his lingering health concerns. A doctor determined that Pilsudski had high levels of exhaustion and fatigue but was not ill, so the prescription was not medicine but rest and relaxation. In August 1901 the Pilsudskis left for Zakopane, a resort town at the base of the Tatra Mountains.[35] From home, meanwhile, Pilsudski received bad news: the Russian police had searched the Pilsudski homes in Vilna and seized documents. His brother Jan had been taken into custody for questioning. Pilsudski expressed concern about one item in particular taken from Jan's home: the only photograph of Pilsudski without a beard, an image that gave away Pilsudski's disguise for entering Russia on false papers.[36]

The news of the Vilna police raid hit Pilsudski hard. He now appeared unsettled and idle. "You have no idea," he wrote to London on September 3, 1901, "how lazy I have become lately. I don't read, I don't write, nor am I in any mood to chat. I explain this by telling myself that I am undergoing treatment . . . and I console myself with the knowledge that the treatment is going well." There were some lingering health concerns. Pilsudski mentioned, for example, that he weighed a mere 142 pounds. He nonetheless received several visitors during this time in the mountains, including Sulkiewicz and Maria Paszkowska, as well as several in-laws from Vilna. The reality of being severed from family and party life in the homeland began to set in. Pilsudski's increasingly volatile disposition leaps off the page in a letter from Zakopane. "I haven't received any letters from Russian Poland," he complained, "and, for this reason, I am not at all up to date on affairs at home. Nor do I have the latest issue of *Robotnik*, No. 40."[37] Pilsudski felt somewhat better the following day when the new issue of *Robotnik* arrived in the mail. He was very impressed, commenting that the issue was an improvement over the last one. That it included a host of reports from correspondents at home and abroad was particularly effective, he wrote.[38]

In November 1901 Jozef and Maria Pilsudski left Kraków for London. Upon their arrival in the British capital on November 26, Pilsudski's closest comrades, including Bolesław Jędrzejowski and Leon Wasilewski, greeted them at Victoria Station. By 1901 the former Union of Polish Socialists Abroad had been renamed the Foreign Committee of the Polish Socialist Party. Wasilewski and Jędrzejowski, the heads of this party division, waited with great anticipation as the train pulled in, about to see Pilsudski for the first time since his arrest and harrowing escape. "When we finally set eyes on comrade 'Wiktor,'" Wasilewski recalled, "we all noticed that he looked much better than before his arrest. No longer were there traces of fatigue on his face. In a word, he returned to life in freedom in better health than he had had before his incarceration."[39]

At the time, Wojciechowski and his wife resided in Southbourne-on-Sea, 105 miles southwest of London. The Pilsudskis stayed there for Christmas. Pilsudski kept abreast of foreign affairs by reading the London-based *Daily News* thoroughly every day.[40] The Pilsudskis and Wojciechowskis got along well; as we recall, Pilsudski had known Wojciechowski's wife, Maria, since the early 1880s. "We discussed a host of issues regarding our organization in the homeland as well as future plans," Wojciechowski recalled about Pilsudski's stay.[41] The two agreed that the most urgent issue in the homeland was the lack of funds for party operatives. Because it was too early for Pilsudski to return to Russia, Wojciechowski agreed to make the trip himself to visit university towns for the purpose of collecting dues. Wojciechowski traveled to St. Petersburg, Moscow, and Kharkov before returning to England on February 14.[42]

Rethinking the Party Position on the Jews

The Pilsudskis left Southbourne-on-Sea on January 7, 1902. In London, Pilsudski received an unexpected visit from an old adversary when Leon Wasilewski stopped by, accompanied by Arkadi Kremer, head of the Jewish Labor Bund. Despite the bitter polemics that had passed between the two in the 1890s, Pilsudski reportedly greeted Kremer quite warmly. Wasilewski recalled that the two seemed to genuinely enjoy each other's company. "I was witness to a very friendly conversation between Pilsudski and the eminent leader of the Bund, [Arkadi] Kremer," Wasilewski wrote, "who asked about Pilsudski's stay in London."[43] Kremer invited Pilsudski to speak at a gathering of Bundist exiles in London, asking whether the talk could be in Russian. Pilsudski agreed, although remarking on his dislike for the language. Pilsudski spoke publicly on only one other occasion during his stay in London.

Kremer's visit, and conversations that ensued at the Bund gathering, led Pilsudski to rethink the party's position on the Jews. Kremer had informed Pilsudski about a key change in the Bund's own platform. At its Fourth Party

Congress in May 1901, the Bund resolved that Jews were a nation entitled not only to civil rights as individuals but to national rights as well.[44]

In addition to the exchange with Kremer, Pilsudski received a letter from a member of the party organization in Zurich asking what the party's official position was on the Bund's new program. Pilsudski stated that the goal was to achieve "party and program unity of the entire proletariat on our territory." The party, therefore, should grant the Bund full internal autonomy in Jewish matters in exchange for joining the PPS. In Pilsudski's view, the old polemical approach had been entirely ineffective. "Seeing that a worst-case scenario in a future Poland would be the rise of anti-Jewish politics, at least here [in Poland] we can manage this better than the Russians." Pilsudski conceded, moreover, that the party's open critique of the Bund had carried with it "a certain anti-Jewish tone" that alienated Jews.[45]

Pilsudski concluded that the party program inadequately addressed Jewish concerns. General demands of equal civil rights in a democratic republic were not enough without explicit guarantees for the Jews, he reasoned. In February 1902 Pilsudski received advice from Max Zetterbaum, former editor of the Yiddish newspaper of the Polish Social Democratic Party of Galicia (PPSD) in Lwów, on wording for a policy change on Jews that would improve ties with the Bund. "The PPS should recognize the Bund's organizational independence," Zetterbaum wrote, "as well as the right of Jews to regard themselves as a nationality (even though they are not)."[46] Pilsudski took into account these suggestions, concluding that "a point should be introduced into the program especially about the Jews—that in a future Poland they will have the right to remain Jews if they so wish, and that we would defend their rights as a nationality."[47]

Still, Pilsudski was of the opinion that merely extending recognition to the Jews as a nationality was not sufficient. It was necessary to convince the Bund that in a future Polish state "the Jews would be granted independence in their own internal affairs, for those are 'the rights of national minorities' . . . which Poland will . . . grant to the Jews." He continued that "our program lacks a guarantee for the rights of Jews as a group." It contained guarantees for Lithuanians and Ruthenians, he noted, "but on the Jews, nothing explicit is put forth, with the exception of the general phrase on equality for all nationalities and faiths."[48]

Meanwhile, Pilsudski complained that the party's central committee in tsarist Russia was far too unresponsive. He had received no reply to his queries about the party's relations with the Jews in Lithuania. "This issue is very important to us," he wrote, "on account of news we are hearing of the Bund's agreeable mood toward us." The moment had to be seized in an effort to bring the Bund into the party. Frequent and detailed updates were key.[49] Pilsudski turned to Wojciechowski, who had recently returned from Russia, for updates on the party's Yiddish paper, *Der arbeter*. He wondered aloud how it was possible to lead the party from abroad in these conditions. "In a word," he added, "we are operating here in the dark, walking blindfolded."[50]

The Return to Tsarist Russia

Pilsudski continued to express frustration at the slow and ineffective communication he was receiving from the homeland in tsarist Russia. His communication with the leadership there became sterner. "Remember," he wrote to the party's central committee of February 20, 1902, "that everything received from Poland about party activity is important not only for a future historian but is also necessary for us to be informed." The kinds of information required regularly included facts about the internal life of the party as well as its relations with local organizations like the Bund and the Lithuanian Social Democrats. These communications should also report on the party's work among Jewish workers and the state of Yiddish publications. Pilsudski also sent a series of tips to improve *Der arbeter*.[51]

The decision to return to Russia so soon after his escape came after a series of events that troubled Pilsudski. On March 16, 1902, two comrades who had helped Pilsudski escape from Russia—Jan Miklaszewski and Ksawery Prauss—were arrested. Pilsudski worried that extracted confessions could jeopardize the safety of Feliks Perl and the party printing press in Kiev.[52] On April 5 Pilsudski informed Jodko-Narkiewicz in Lwów that he and his wife would be arriving there shortly en route to Russia and asked him to draw up the necessary false papers in advance. He then informed Wojciechowski of his plans, adding, "I prefer to be present [in Russia] to organize party work and determine positions."[53]

Pilsudski and Maria set out for Austrian Galicia on April 10. During a brief stay in Kraków, Tadeusz Gołęcki, a fellow émigré from Russia and a party enthusiast, invited them to his home. Present at the gathering was Antonia Domańska, a socialist sympathizer and actress. Pilsudski, she recalled, "had classic features, steely eyes with a deep and penetrating look. He had lovely

hands with a strong grip, a spring to his step, a vaulted forehead and beautiful lips." The impressive appearance, she added, was accompanied by a certain intellectual grace with words. "But how beautifully he spoke about a
free Poland," she wrote. "God, what a crazy pipe dream, but when HE speaks,
one believes that there will not be Galicia but only a free Poland. He is simply
obsessed with the vision of casting off [his people's] chains."[54]

With his wife remaining in Kraków, Pilsudski left for Lwów, where he
stayed with Jodko-Narkiewicz while waiting for his false papers. In a letter
from Lwów, Pilsudski was full of new ideas and excitement at the prospect
of returning to Vilna, where he had last been in 1899. One idea was to restore
strong leadership in the homeland, whereupon he, Wojciechowski, and Jodko-
Narkiewicz would each travel separately to Russia twice annually. This way,
one of the three would at any given time be in the homeland. Pilsudski
also put forward a proposal to overhaul the party structure by demarcating
Polish lands into six districts (the fifth and sixth being Lithuania and
Ukraine) with each region having a district head who would sit on the
party's central committee.[55]

Pilsudski began his journey to Vilna on April 21, 1902, when he crossed
the border into Russia. "His entry into Russia within a year of his renowned
escape," William Reddaway commented in his 1939 biography, "must rank
among the bravest actions of even Pilsudski's life."[56] Indeed, Pilsudski was
well aware that the Russian authorities had circulated two photographs of him
and a description to all local officials and border crossing agents. Armed
guards were stationed day and night not only at the border but along transportation lines as well.

Pilsudski made his way unscathed to Vilna, where he received the bad news
that his sixty-nine-year-old father, at that time the director of a liqueur factory in St. Petersburg, had died on April 15 of pneumonia. Pilsudski helped
with settling his father's affairs as much as he could in his circumstances. He
also found time to reunite with old comrades and meet new ones, including
then-twenty-two-year-old Walery Sławek, who later would become one of
Pilsudski's closest aides and prime minister in the 1930s. Pilsudski was first
introduced to Sławek in May 1902 by his precocious stepdaughter, Wanda.
Sławek vividly remembered their first encounter, noting, "We greeted one
other as if we were old friends who had known each other for years and who
were now just catching up on things."[57] Wanda, living at the time with relatives in Vilna, would later become romantically involved with Sławek.

Conversations with comrades in Vilna gave Pilsudski the opportunity to discuss his new ideas for reorganizing the party. Revising his earlier plan, he now proposed five districts the party would administer: Warsaw, Lithuania, Łódź, Dąbrowa, and Radom. Each of the five regions would have a district head, and Pilsudski suggested the following candidates: Adam Buyno (Warsaw), Feliks Sachs (Lithuania), Bolesław Czarkowski (Łódź), Walery Sławek (Dąbrowa), and Jan Rutkiewicz (Radom). The party's central committee would consist of the district heads plus the editor of *Robotnik* (Feliks Perl) and the three representatives of the foreign committee (Pilsudski, Jodko-Narkiewicz, and Wojciechowski).[58]

On a personal note, Pilsudski was clear about his intention to live permanently in Galicia. He regretted having to be outside the country, but he acknowledged that living in Russia was too dangerous for him and his wife. With Maria in Kraków, Pilsudski vowed to save enough money to be able to bring Wanda with him to Galicia to reunite with her mother.[59]

The Sixth Party Congress in Lublin

Pilsudski's main task was to call a party congress at which he could breathe new life into the party and provide a new organizational structure. In June 1902 he summoned delegates to Lublin for the Sixth Congress of the PPS. The delegates accepted his proposal to restructure the party on territorial lines as well as the composition of a new central committee. Pilsudski's goal was to expand the party's influence from cities to towns and even into the countryside. The congress also agreed to the formation of an Executive Commission, with Pilsudski as a member, inside the central committee.[60]

The subject of relations with Lithuanians and Jews divided the congress. After a debate over wording, the congress approved Pilsudski's resolutions, with a minority opposed. The resolution "The Socialist Movement in Lithuania" began:

> Considering that Poles constitute an important part of the population in Lithuania, a country linked to Poland with a common history and culture; that for this reason the Polish revolutionary movement finds, both in the past as well as in the future, a common action in Lithuania.
>
> Considering that in the interest of working peoples we shall liberate Poland and Lithuania from tsarist oppression and build an independent

existence and that hence the aim of struggle with the Russian regime in both countries is one in the same.

The congress recognizes the necessity of grouping together all socialist forces in both countries into one organization with the aim of strengthening proletarian influences in Poland and Lithuania on the path to struggle and the formation of ties after the future victory.[61]

The resolution on Lithuania reflected Pilsudski's broader federalist principles. It acknowledged the possibility that Lithuania might one day be independent but expressed the view that the country's heterogeneous character made that idea less likely. The congress thus resolved:

> Considering that today's Lithuania is inhabited not by one nation but by peoples of different origins, languages, and religions; and that particular nationalities inhabiting Lithuania live not in one compact territory but instead in areas of mixed populations; and that the lack of a clear national consciousness is today a common phenomenon among the masses of the greater part of Lithuania, . . . and considering further that the PPS has no intention to Polonize other nations, . . .
>
> The congress resolves that the question of whether or not Lithuania will be linked in the future to Poland, allied with Poland in a federation, or be wholly independent, can only be resolved by liberation from tsarist oppression, which will allow Lithuanians to freely decide their own fate alongside other peoples living in Lithuania.[62]

In addition to the Lithuania resolution, Pilsudski gained enough votes to pass the resolution, "The Socialist Movement among Jews," which maintained that "Jewish workers should take part in a common struggle under a common banner with its Christian counterparts in Poland and Lithuania." The Jewish proletariat in Lithuania and Poland had to harmonize their political goals with the native inhabitants among whom they lived. Pilsudski's resolution concluded: "The demand for independence and a democratic republic serves the interest of the Jewish proletariat not only as workers, but as Jews. A democratic republic would secure equality for Jewish citizens and give them the possibility to freely develop and exert a formidable influence in public affairs."[63]

The resolutions on the Jews included a condemnation of anti-Semitism. "In our society, just as in other countries, anti-Semitism has spread among the middle and upper classes, demonstrating a hostile attitude to the Jews. With all its energy, our socialist party shall fight against anti-Semitism as an injurious and backward current." Particularly onerous was the anti-Semitism of the tsars, which imposed special laws restricting Jewish rights. "Such policies limiting the rights of any group," the resolution stated, "are to us repugnant [*wstrętny*]."[64] The resolution concluded with a section on agitation among the Jews, stating that such work had to be done in Yiddish and that a special Jewish Committee with representation in the central committee would be set up for such a purpose.

Walery Sławek remembered that "a mood of joyful fraternity was created, a moment of personal convergence of people who for many years had been working together for a common struggle." At a meal at the conclusion of the conference, Piłsudski was quoted as saying, "We are a group that cannot bear servitude and that will fight for independence because we ourselves want freedom."[65]

Back to Austrian Galicia

Piłsudski returned to Austrian Galicia on June 25, 1902, and made his way to Kraków. Shortly after, he settled in Brzuchowice, the villa outside Lwów where he would remain until October. In a detailed letter on the party congress, he discussed sharp exchanges over his resolution on Lithuania and on the Jews. Among those opposing the resolutions on Lithuania and the Jews was Feliks Sachs, who, Piłsudski commented, "sneered ironically at our 'new tactics' and our 'spirit of conquest' [*zaborczość*]."[66] Sachs subsequently clarified his position in a letter to London. "People here regard Lithuania on the same footing as Poland, and recognize the complete equality of all nationalities—Poles, Lithuanians, Belarussians and Jews," Sachs wrote from Vilna. This new assertiveness reflected "the 'spirit of the times': if you were here, you would understand and even feel this 'spirit.'" Sachs continued that "the more closely I come to know the conditions [here], the more poorly I regard the [Sixth] congress resolutions on Lithuania. We will have to unambiguously stress that we regard Lithuania as a sister, not a daughter, of Poland."[67] Sachs's view, supported by a minority at the congress, reflected an emerging division in the party between the older members and the younger members, who expressed discomfort with what they perceived as a nationalist orientation.

Pilsudski was well aware of Lithuanian concerns with the congress resolutions. He informed London that he would address those concerns in an editorial. Some Jewish socialists linked to the Bund also expressed unease with the resolution's tone. The real problem, Pilsudski argued, was that Lithuania was a region of mixed nationalities, which greatly complicated the work of socialists due to "the presence of different groups who don't know how to extricate themselves from entangled relations between the nationalities and inveterate social conditions."[68]

AUSTRIAN GALICIA WAS PART OF A FREE, constitutional state in a center of Polish culture. Yet Pilsudski lived in conditions of near poverty. During his brief stay in Vilna to chair the party's sixth congress, he complained bitterly about the problem of money. "The most urgent issue by far," he wrote in May 1902, "is finances." He had been waiting for funds from London but to no avail. "Due to the lack of money, I and Leon [Bolesław Czarkowski] have more than once waited for weeks at a time for a mere 15 rubles. And as I write, I have in my pocket—and I am not exaggerating!—a total of eight rubles and change. That is my entire source of funds." He pleaded with London to send money at once. He had only a meager, haphazard income derived from his writings, made more difficult by the poor living standards.[69] "I now have devilishly sordid conditions for any work," Pilsudski wrote from Brzuchowice. "All the time, cramped as I don't know where else, virtually no furniture—I am writing to you standing, so please forgive me that I am scribbling so horribly."[70]

CHAPTER 7

Creating a Party Platform

Our fight for the transformation of the political system is
indistinguishable from the struggle for independence.

—JOZEF PILSUDSKI (OCTOBER 1902)

While Pilsudski was residing in Kraków throughout 1902 and 1903, his
productivity gradually increased. The party's foreign committee and printing
facilities relocated from London to Kraków, including Leon Wasilewski and
the foreign committee's newspaper, *Przedświt* (Dawn). The principal center
of free expression of Polish culture, Kraków was also home to the party's
sister organization, the Polish Social Democratic Part of Galicia (PPSD),
whose main newspaper, *Naprzód* (Forward), had been appearing as a daily
since 1901. The PPSD daily competed with three other Polish dailies in
Kraków: the conservative *Czas* (The Times), the liberal democratic *Nowa
Reforma* (New Reform), and the clerical Catholic *Głos Narodu* (Voice of the
Nation).

At the beginning of 1902, when Pilsudski regained his health, he decided
to strike at the tsarist regime from exile with the power of the pen. He sent
his first essay since his prison escape to an émigré Russian publication. The
lengthy article introduced Russian readers to a Polish interpretation of the
recent past and was signed with his real name, indicative of an open, legal
phase of his life in exile. The essay began with a discussion of the partitions.
At the close of the eighteenth century, he wrote, the disappearance of Poland from the map of Europe had abruptly halted a democratic process on
European soil: "Under the influence of the French Revolution, [Poland] was

undergoing a constitutional experiment, the expansion of rights to new layers of the society to participate in government as well as a reduction in the weight of the peasants' burden. From the moment of Russia's annexation of Poland, these experiments were rudely interrupted and political life ceased in the conquered lands." Pilsudski added that "the feeling of the Poles is like that of a man whose home has been invaded by robbers."[1]

To Pilsudski, therefore, Russia had given inhabitants of the Polish lands no option other than to revolt. "In the last hundred years, the entire history of the Polish nation is the story of the wildest lawlessness and oppression on the one hand," he wrote, "and that of heroic struggle on the other. Every generation exerts its strength with the aim of liberation from a heavy and disgraceful yoke." Frequent insurrections were symptomatic of this harsh reality. "After each insurrection, suppressed with extraordinary cruelty," Pilsudski continued, "new, even more severe persecution of the Poles followed, growing stronger after 1863. The tsars did not regret utilizing all their powers merely to remove the Polish spirit from Poland and transform it into a 'Russian' one."[2]

Pilsudski described how Polish culture had been systematically suppressed. "The Polish language has been removed everywhere—all inscriptions on station buildings, in train cars, in public announcements—these are all written in a language the majority of people do not know." Pupils were taught in Russian, "a language many children hear for the first time in school. . . . Try to imagine," Pilsudski wrote to his Russian readers, "if all schools in the Moscow regions were taught in German." Russian schoolchildren would fall behind, as had Polish children. He argued that the dual forces of russification and autocracy gave inhabitants in the Polish lands no option other than to resist. He emphasized that the PPS was also waging class struggle within Polish society for the rights of workers and the socialist idea. He concluded with the following note to the Russian people: "We understand that the greatness of Russia in no way depends on conquest and subjugation of other countries and peoples."[3]

Pilsudski's work on putting out a party newspaper dedicated to Lithuania, meanwhile, finally came to fruition. He decided in July 1902 that the paper would be titled *Walka* (The Struggle), subtitled "Organ of the Polish Socialist Party in Lithuania." Because it could be published legally in Austria-Hungary,

Pilsudski edited the new organ in Kraków, writing most of the content for the first three issues.[4]

Pilsudski addressed the articles to the inhabitants of his native Lithuania, which he characterized as a neglected, underdeveloped periphery. Presented as a correspondence from Vilna, he began the inaugural issue with these powerful words:

> The current policies of the Russian government are ruining the borderlands of the tsarist state. We are speaking here of a politics of russification for which Lithuania has become the government's favorite terrain and testing ground. Here, thanks to the defenselessness of the population, it is the most ruthless. . . . Russification has extended into all aspects of life, from the schools to the church, from theaters to libraries, and from public to private life. None of the peoples living in Lithuania has escaped persecution. If the point of russification has been primarily directed at the Poles, it is also felt by Lithuanians, by Belarussians and the Jews, although the special limits imposed on the Jews have no parallel.[5]

Pilsudski attributed Lithuanian backwardness directly to Russian rule. "Industry in Lithuania," he wrote, "has been limited to small production. Education and erudition of the people is rudimentary, there are no good schools, and it is a rarity to hear of a good library, a good museum, a decent hospital or, for that matter, good roads." He used a striking metaphor, comparing the people of Lithuania to plants in a basement: "Just as plants without sun and clean air will lose their color and the strength for growth, so too the society under excessive weight tumbles. Traces of the ability for rapid progress are weakened."[6]

Against this backdrop of imperial neglect, Pilsudski argued that real progress in Lithuania depended on the ability to wrest the country from Russian rule. Achieving this end had to begin with the full unity of likeminded people in Lithuania. Thus, all socialist parties in Lithuania had to unite under a single banner. "The first step toward the creation of a formidable political power among working peoples," Pilsudski argued, "must be the union of all socialist organizations into a single body, animated with one spirit and one aim." Addressing the lack of unity among the movements in Lithuania, he continued: "The further we move forward and the closer we are to a firm showdown with the nightmare of the tsarist invaders, the more necessary joint action will be. Only such a united socialist organization can accomplish our task. Supported by the people, we shall exert the right influence on the country's fate."[7]

Pilsudski urged leaders of various socialist organizations in Lithuania to set aside their differences in the light of their common foe—the tsarist regime. The imperial regime, he stressed, "was formed not here [in Lithuania] but in Russia. It was imposed on us by sheer force and today rules over us by the laws of conquest and annexation. . . . The great fight with tsarism is, in the immediate sense, a fight with the invader. Victory over tsarism means nothing other than the expulsion of the invaders from our lands." Democratic institutions and freedoms could be established only after the removal of the Russian rulers, he added: "Our fight for the transformation of the political system is indistinguishable from the struggle for independence."[8]

Pilsudski thus maintained that the future of Lithuania depended on its ability to replace Russian with native rule. The goals were no different among socialists in the neighboring Polish provinces under Russian rule. "That same fight that lies in Lithuania's future," he wrote, "awaits Poland. The same goal that enlivens the working peoples in Lithuania is likewise the aim of Polish socialists. Lithuania and Poland share numerous common bonds of history and culture. After all," he continued, "part of the working masses in Lithuania are Polish, if not by identity or origins then by language."[9]

Pilsudski's long editorial was intended to demonstrate the need for unity among *all* socialist organizations in Poland and Lithuania. "Having before us such an overwhelming enemy as tsarism, it would be unreasonable to dilute our strength rather than act with a single purpose." He added, "We cannot waver under the necessity of uniting all socialist forces in both countries into a single organization."[10]

At the same time, Pilsudski was aware that his vision of unity among socialist organizations in Lithuania was going to be a hard sell in an era of national currents within socialism. His aim was to persuade Jewish and Lithuanian socialists that the common struggle against imperial Russia transcended the particular agendas of each party. "We are aware that doubts and even enmity have been building among our Jewish and Lithuanian comrades," he wrote, "[but] we nonetheless are convinced that with the development of political consciousness among working peoples . . . major misunderstandings and mistrust will disappear."[11] In another piece in this inaugural issue "On Patriotism," Pilsudski stressed that patriotism should not be confused with chauvinism. In Russia, chauvinism derived from official channels, "by the barbaric tsarist government, which seeks to prop up the tottering political system, throwing to its people—as one throws bones to attacking dogs—conquered countries to chew upon."[12] Russian chauvinism "contradicts the most basic desires for justice. It poisons the moral atmosphere of the conquerors and the conquered. Any decent person must oppose it. . . . There can be no division of opinion on this matter among the socialists. Eating away at them, socialists must conduct a life-or-death struggle, tearing away the mask to expose the human injustice."

Divisions between Lithuanians and Poles had to be overcome if the two peoples were successfully to mount resistance to Russian rule, Pilsudski argued: "Such sizable quarreling weakens us and enables the tsarist system to continue imposing oppressive rule over us. Down with this! Let's stamp out enmity between comrades of different origins, faith, or language. Against the raging storm of tribal hate, let harmony and brotherhood rule without regard to nationality or faith!"

Pilsudski continued to hammer away at the absolute need for programmatic unity. The precondition for raising social and economic standards in Lithuania was separation from Russia. "In the schools in Lithuania, not a single child hears the mother tongue," Pilsudski he wrote in October 1902. He reminded readers that Lithuania was a country in which the native peoples "have not a single library or newspaper of their own. Ethnic Lithuanians . . . are prohibited from publishing books in their own language. Another part of the native population—the Jews—are subject to limitations on their freedom of movement." The "burning issue on the tip of everybody's tongue" was to defend basic democratic rights.[13]

The struggle had to be waged not only against imperial Russian rule but also against conservative elements within Polish society. For Polish chauvinism also played a role in the moral decay. According to Pilsudski, the Polish ruling class continued to believe it had the historical right to leadership in the struggle for independence. Polish landed aristocrats "are of the opinion that working people should step aside and trust their 'older brothers' blindly." This upper crust of Polish society, including factory owners, was willing to throw its own kind under the bus for profit. The Polish poet Juliusz Słowacki had reminded readers in 1846 about the need to resist oppression from outside and exploitation from within. Pilsudski cited Słowacki's poem, which he characterized as calling for social revolution:

> When the world burns with suffering
> When the spirit of deeds rises
> He becomes a heavy, unmovable stone
> He does not allow any popular movement
> He wants to turn back into the old bed
> The new wave, the Lord's river
> Does not penetrate the aching hearts
> Does not hold the masses in the grave . . . [14]

Słowacki's poem, linking the idea of social revolution and independence, became a potent appeal. "Our lands, which gave birth to [Tadeusz] Kościuszko and [Adam] Mickiewicz," Pilsudski concluded, "have seen great patriots who fought not only against the conquerors but also against slavery of the common people among our own shadowy masters." In today's conditions, "we must use the most noble type of patriotism to fill our ranks under the red banner of socialism."[15]

Soon after the inaugural issue of *Walka* appeared, Pilsudski snuck back into tsarist Russia to participate in a conference of the party's central committee on November 6–7, 1902. He acknowledged that efforts thus far to mobilize the non-Polish nationalities in the borderlands had failed. The resolution of June 1902, calling on the Lithuanian Social Democratic Party (LSDP) and Jewish Labor Bund to merge with the PPS, had to be set aside for the time being. Nor was progress being made in relations with the Bund, to Pilsudski's chagrin. He could at least take comfort in reporting that the party's own Jewish Committee was putting out a paper in Yiddish and making progress in attracting Jews.[16]

Pilsudski remained in Russia during the last two months of 1902, and spent the winter months in Russia with his wife. To evade police detection, the couple left Vilna for Riga, where they stayed for the first three months of 1903.[17] In a letter from Riga, Pilsudski expressed grave concern about his lack of income, pleading with London to get him the meager stipend he relied on for basic expenses. The constant movement and travel, combined with the lack of a steady income, was beginning to wear on him. "As for me, I already long for rest," he wrote in December 1902. "I am devilishly exhausted and in weak health."[18]

Pilsudski nevertheless continued his forceful advocacy for an open society in the pages of a Kraków-based annual. "Russification" began with reference to two lines in Adam Mickiewicz's 1836 drama, *Les confédérés de Bar:* "The Muscovite is a bandit, a thief—a beast born cruel." Since the 1850s, demands for autonomy in the borderland areas inhabited by non-Russians grew more and more frequent. "When one takes into account that approximately half of the 125 million inhabitants of the Russian Empire are non-Russian, it is immediately evident how much the Empire's unity and inner strength is lost."[19]

Pilsudski was never able to stay away from Vilna for long. In June 1903 he visited the Lithuanian city to participate in a conference of the party's central committee.[20] The conference members noted that the party's connection with Lithuanian socialists was "inactive" at the time. The party's new paper, *Walka,* had few readers, and the party was not making inroads with ethnic Lithuanians. The conference also discussed relations with Jews and Belarusians. On the Jewish Labor Bund, Feliks Sachs expressed support for a separate Jewish party organization alongside the PPS. Pilsudski countered that such recognition was at odds with the party's position and maintained that the only way to achieve programmatic unity was for the Bund to merge with the PPS as an autonomous organization. But Adam Buyno, who along with Sachs represented the party's new, younger leadership, held that the old tactics of staunch opposition to the existence of other independent socialist parties in Lithuania was no longer viable. The old policy was undermining workers' solidarity. Pilsudski was given the task of responding to articles in the Lithuanian and Jewish press critical of its program.[21]

Returning to Galicia

Following the June 1903 conference, Pilsudski crossed the Austro-Hungarian border with his wife for Kraków. He dutifully reported on the meeting to his comrades in the foreign committee, expressing concern about two central committee members: Feliks Sachs and Adam Buyno. Sachs, he wrote, was closer in ideological conviction to Rosa Luxemburg's Social Democracy of the Kingdom of Poland and Lithuania, formed in 1899 from a union between the Social Democracy of the Kingdom of Poland and the Union of Workers in Lithuania. Seemingly opposed to the party platform, Sachs expressed solidarity with the right of Jews and Lithuanians to have separate parties, a view that some believed undermined the party program. With Adam Buyno, there was a clash of personalities, with Pilsudski claiming that "[Buyno] believes every word he utters as fact" and "distrusts all that others say." Buyno "doesn't understand or doesn't want to understand our organization, its principles, hierarchy and needs." Pilsudski stressed that he was not claiming that there was a conspiracy within the central committee or anything close to it, but the two did seem to want to change the party's direction.[22]

Upon posting his report to London in July 1903, Pilsudski left Krakow for Rytro, a mountainous village sixty miles south of Kraków, with his wife and stepdaughter. There he saw Ignacy Daszyński, with whom he had very good personal relations, so much so that he was the godfather to Daszyński's son.[23] In fact, since Pilsudski had settled in Kraków, Daszyński had been seeing quite a lot of him. Another person Pilsudski began to see frequently at this time was Michał Sokolnicki, whom he had first met in Lwów in 1901 as a fanatical admirer. "It was strange to actually meet Pilsudski in 1901, beaming with a halo and, already for me as well as for many, a bit of a legend," Sokolnicki commented. "Against the background of this legend, I remember him as a young, slim blonde with a small beard and keen, blue eyes. He had an extremely calm, restrained demeanor. In contrast to Jodko-Narkiewicz, he did not impose himself, speaking little with some hesitation. It was immediately apparent that he looked at people with mistrust and only reluctantly socialized."[24]

As much as Pilsudski appreciated the personal freedoms he enjoyed in Austria-Hungary, he was profoundly homesick. "You simply have no idea," he wrote his comrades in September 1903, "how lonely I feel—in thought, in my mind. I have thousands of projects and plans but no one to talk to about them (other than my enchanting wife)." To bring about real progress, he felt he had to operate out of Russia. He wondered aloud, at the same time, if part of the problem was his own nature. "I lack faith and trust in the feasibility of each project due in part to my mistrust of new people and to old vices and habits I developed from my early days in the PPS."[25]

Changing Position on the National Question
in the Borderlands

At this time Pilsudski reevaluated the party platform on relations with the borderland nationalities in Ukraine, Belarus, and Lithuania. Considering what was possible rather than what was desirable, he decided his campaign to unite all socialist parties under one banner had been ineffective. The Jewish Labor Bund, with centers in Lithuania and in the Kingdom of Poland, had grown in strength. The Ukrainians, Lithuanians, and Finns "were becoming visible," he noted, adding that "we must now be prepared to compromise, not control or conquer."[26] With the rise of socialist movements among borderland nationalities, "we must begin to conduct a foreign policy toward the Ukrainians, Russians, the peoples of the Caucuses, Lithuanians, Latvians, and even the Germans."[27]

After reassessing the situation on the ground, Pilsudski came out in favor of revising the party platform. The new direction was to consist of four principles. First, the PPS was to emphasize its all-Polish character, now referring to the German, Russian, and Austrian partitions "as a single whole." Second, the party needed a special focus on culture in order to compete with the National Democrats, its rivals who had demonstrated success in attracting a social base in this manner. Pilsudski thus recommended the establishment of Polish libraries, orchestras, and choirs in the three partitions. Third, he called for a more open party life. Lastly, the party was to henceforth demonstrate toleration toward other socialist organizations.[28]

During the second half of 1903, Pilsudski focused on a series of publications. Two of them were of particular importance because they contained autobiographical content. The first, a history of the underground press of the Polish Socialist Party, appeared in serialized form in *Naprzód* in Kraków. "They will pay me for my columns," Pilsudski noted with relief on August 15, 1903, "and this is income that I need to live on."[29] In its August 27 issue, *Naprzód* ran a notice about the forthcoming series, a serialized work it described as "colorfully written and highly informed."[30] After the first installment appeared in print on September 8, 1903, Pilsudski received his first payment of 50 Austrian kronen (the equivalent of $20 at the time). "I am greatly pleased!" he commented.[31] On the day of his thirty-sixth birthday—December 5, 1903—the fifty-sixth and final installment of the series appeared.

That same month *Naprzód* published the series in book form. Appearing under Pilsudski's real name, the study chronicled the history of the Polish Socialist Party in its first ten years, marking his debut as a serious writer. The most significant development on Polish lands, Pilsudski maintained, was the rise of the PPS and its newspaper, *Robotnik*. In painstaking detail, he described his harrowing work as the paper's editor between 1894 and 1900, when it was dangerous merely to possess a copy of the paper. Here, the author recorded his own firsthand account of the moment when, in February 1900, Russian secret police stormed his apartment in Łódź and carried away the printing press. "I stood by crushed, as if the coffin lid had closed on someone near and very dear to me," he recalled. "So many hopes, so much love, so much devotion were bound up with this scrap of iron, now condemned to silence and inactivity."[32]

The second publication of an autobiographical nature appeared in the Lwów-based monthly *Promień* (The Beam). In "How I Became a Socialist," Pilsudski described a childhood infused with the memory of national defeat. He recalled his mother's bedtime ritual of reading Poland's forbidden poets (Krasiński, Słowaki, and Mickiewicz). Home life, infused with patriotic zeal, was in stark contrast to what Pilsudski described as the stifling atmosphere of the Russian State Gymnasium in Vilna. The illegal study group he attended, which read patriotic and socialist literature, reinforced and deepened these sentiments. Here is how he characterized his childhood years in 1903:

> My cheeks burned that I must suffer in silence while my pride was trampled upon, listening to lies and scornful words about Poland, Poles, and their history. The feeling of oppression, the feeling of being a slave who can be crushed like a worm at any moment, weighed on my heart like a millstone. I always count the years spent in the Gymnasium among the most unpleasant of my life.[33]

Pilsudski then discussed the importance of his university experience, when he first came across Polish socialist literature. In his first year as a university student the arrest and execution of Polish socialist leaders solidified his socialist convictions.[34] After five years in Siberian exile, he returned to Vilna with the conviction that only a combination of socialist and national ideals could galvanize the masses. "I arrived at the conclusion," he wrote, "that my childish dreams and hopes should be combined with my youthful worldview. *The socialist in Poland has to demand inde-*

pendence for his country. For independence is the singular condition for the victory of socialism in Poland."[35]

"How I Became a Socialist" became a rallying cry for young Poles in Austrian Galicia. At the same time, the article invited mockery from the leader of the right-wing National Democrats.[36] In the pages of the Kraków-based *Przegląd Wszechpolski* (All-Polish Review), the leader of the National Democrats, Roman Dmowski, maintained that Pilsudski's article "does not in any way demonstrate the value of socialism. To the contrary, Pilsudski convinces us that his socialism, fashioned in Siberian seclusion, is outdated. He remains always the brave boy, the son of a mother-patriot, who dreams of the liberation of his homeland." Pilsudski, Dmowski concluded, was not a socialist. He merely used socialism as a tool to achieve patriotic ends.[37]

DURING THE YEARS Pilsudski lived in Kraków prior to World War I, his need for income gave him the incentive to publish considerably more writings. What was on his mind at the time is revealed in a piece published in October 1903 in which he discussed the legal suppression of Lithuanian culture. Particularly barbarous, he noted, was imperial Russia's ban on printing Lithuanian with Latin letters. Here, Pilsudski invoked the name of Prince Sviatopolk-Mirsky, the governor-general of Russia's northwestern provinces, who advocated a more liberal policy toward the nationalities. Even he, Pilsudski noted, conceded that efforts to block the illegal importation of Lithuanian books was hopeless but that such deeds nonetheless did not endanger the empire. He, therefore, according to Pilsudski, was not opposed to printing such literature in Vilna and Kowno. "Books, printed abroad and smuggled across the border in defiance of tsarist laws, find their way to all parts of Lithuania, entering nearly every home."[38] Those caught in the illegal book trade were given stiff sentences; many were sent to Siberia.

Set against government repression, Pilsudski continued, was a rise in pro-democracy movements in Russia. This could be observed throughout the Russian Empire: in Poland, in the Caucuses, in Russia proper, and in Ukraine. Beware, he concluded, of the government policy of inflaming anti-Jewish sentiment and anti-Jewish violence. Such a tactic was a government tool to divert attention from tsarist repression as a whole. That is exactly what was behind the Kishinev pogrom in the spring of 1903, he wrote: "We have been witness to this wretched, brutal method in April of this year."[39]

In the same issue of *Walka,* Pilsudski tried to allay the fears expressed by Lithuanian socialists. The PPS, he stated, had no intention of undermining Lithuanian aspirations for statehood. "This is not about fusing socialist organizations in Lithuania under the control of the PPS," he declared. "It is about forming a powerful union of all socialist parties in the territories of historic Lithuania. Victory cannot be achieved without a united front," he wrote.[40]

Pilsudski's key doctrinal statement emerged in the third article he penned for the same issue of *Walka.* Upon the withdrawal of Russian forces from Poland, Lithuania, and Ukraine, it would be crucial that the native peoples of these lands decide their fates without external coercion. In the next few lines we find what may be accurately called the Pilsudski doctrine on the fate of non-Polish nationalities in the eastern borderlands:

> When one portion of the socialist camp—the Russian and the Jewish parties—confine their demands to the transformation of Imperial Russia into a democratic, constitutional republic, without a solution for the nationalities problem, or even, to the contrary, explicitly favoring the present borders, then the other portion of the socialist camp—represented in large part by the Polish Socialist Party—pursues the total breakup of this house of captivity in which peoples and nations are suffocating. We strive for the total shattering of the chains that torment subjugated nations by a tsar who hampers their free development.[41]

The same doctrine applied to the substantial Jewish population in Lithuania: "We must work hard to improve these relations," Pilsudski concluded.[42]

The Russo-Japanese War

On February 8, 1904, Japan attacked a Russian fleet at Port Arthur off the Sea of Japan. Russia declared war two days later. For Pilsudski, the outbreak of the Russo-Japanese War signaled a new path. The importance he attached to it—and to its potential for benefiting the Polish cause—is revealed in a letter he wrote after the outbreak of hostilities. "There is a very sober atmosphere here," Pilsudski wrote from Russia, "with a sense that a special obligation has been imposed on us. We must in all haste mobilize a staff and a core of noncommissioned officers. We must create," he continued, "a warlike face. For this is the only way to capitalize on the atmosphere aroused by the war."

So many opportunities had presented themselves, Piłsudski noted, that a certain exhaustion had set in. "So be well," he concluded his letter to comrades in London. "I feel so rushed that it is hard to write coherently. I have not a moment to spare. I am meeting a host of new people, working hard like a dog, and am beat every evening. So I'll say amen."[43]

Piłsudski also perceived a change in the mood of the local population. "A revolutionary character is growing among the masses," he stated from Warsaw in February 1904. "Immediately after the outbreak of war, the situation changed. For a good amount of people, there is a sense of the uniqueness of the moment, requiring exceptional measures and actions on our part. This sense of the moment is already widespread. . . . The fact is that some kind of action from our side is necessary," he wrote, adding that "an indifferent, passive stand on our part would be a waste. After a certain amount of time, we will lose our influence and importance if we do not act."[44]

To Piłsudski, the outbreak of the Russo-Japanese War signaled the moment when the party had to do more than organize workers and distribute propaganda literature: it was time to take up arms. He informed party comrades in Kraków that the Lithuanian, Latvian, and Belarusian socialists had agreed to a joint declaration to this effect. "Comrades!" the declaration stated, "we are, above all, Russia's internal foes, representatives of the working peoples in Poland, Lithuania, Belarus, and Latvia. . . . We are children of lands conquered by the tsars and whose interests and needs are entirely neglected. Consequently, we are doomed to annihilation and ultimate ruin." The joint declaration, dated February 1904, ended by calling on the empire's non-Russian peoples "to work together in one implacable camp for the struggle against oppression and exploitation!"[45]

Piłsudski returned to Austria-Hungary to attend the funeral of his mentor from Siberian exile, Bronisław Szwarce, who passed away at age seventy on February 17, 1904. The PPS's foreign committee in London, meanwhile, reached out to Japanese officials. Jodko-Narkiewicz contacted the Japanese representative in Vienna, writing that in a war with Russia, the Poles should be regarded as Japan's closest allies. "In western Russia," he wrote, "one finds a strong, conquered Polish nation that, on more than one occasion, rose in armed revolt for the independence of its homeland without ever putting down its weapons." He added that "the Poles are born enemies of Russia, and the Japanese will meet only sympathizers among us. Polish national interests will in no way clash with Japanese policy."[46]

On March 16, 1904, Jodko-Narkiewicz met in London with Tadasu Hayashi, a Japanese representative. Following the meeting, he sent Hayashi a memorandum penned by Pilsudski that recommended the creation of a Polish Legion to assist the Japanese.[47] Hayashi reported to his superiors that he fully believed in Jodko-Narkiewicz's genuineness and the sincerity of his proposals for cooperation, but the idea of a Polish Legion operating within the Japanese military was "out of the question—the Japanese Govt. would never employ foreigners in their field army," he explained to Jodko-Narkiewicz in a letter.[48]

Pilsudski received notice about the contacts with Japanese officials. In a letter of March 19, 1904, he discussed internal party matters. He argued that "the main thing we need to think about are internal party affairs, for there will always be time to work out foreign policy. But unless there is internal party strength, we will achieve nothing abroad."[49] The comments demonstrate that Pilsudski at this time placed less emphasis on the Russo-Japanese War than did his comrades in the foreign committee. He remained more focused on internal party matters inside Russia. In a letter to Jodko-Narkiewicz in Lwów, he repeated his concerns about the younger, newer members of the party's central committee. "Relations with Jerzy [Adam Buyno]," he wrote, "are poor and unpleasant, and I don't know how things will continue, but as I sensed, he will go on quietly obstructing. *Nous verrons* [we will see]."[50]

The party's central committee inside Russia meanwhile became aware of contacts between the foreign committee and Japan. The central committee appealed to Pilsudski: "Can we, with the present condition of our military department, possess information important for Japan and harmful to Russia?"[51] Pilsudski replied that agencies within the PPS could observe Russian troop movements in real time and pass this intelligence on to the Japanese. Although the Japanese steadfastly opposed the idea of using a Polish Legion, they nonetheless became interested in the idea of sharing intelligence on the situation in Russia and Siberia. Translated into English, Pilsudski's proposal was forwarded to Japan's military attaché in London, Taro Utsunomiya.[52]

PILSUDSKI RETURNED TO KRAKÓW in April 1904. Soon after his arrival, he posted a detailed letter to London expressing his gratitude for receiving issues of the *Times*. The emphasis he put on the British daily demonstrated the importance Pilsudski placed on keeping abreast of international affairs.[53] Having just returned from Russia, he once again expressed reservations about the party's central committee. The party stewards, in his view—himself, Wojciechowski, Aleksander Malinowski, and Jodko-Narkiewicz—were all in exile. The leaders residing inside the country "are people who feel uncomfortable when presented with more serious assignments" while having an insufficient knowledge and acumen in foreign affairs. "The new, younger members of the central committee are still in need of mentors to guide them," Pilsudski maintained.[54]

Pilsudski described the qualities that he believed were necessary to truly lead. "In Leon [Bolesław Czarkowski] one observes a lack of courage and initiative. In Jerzy [Adam Buyno], there is a lack of education and the ability to exert significant influence on people." The others lacked charisma and inspired no confidence. "The rest," Pilsudski wrote, "are people who won't set the world on fire or, like Jan [Feliks Sachs], are deprived of energy and boldness of vision. I sometimes look upon the present situation with sadness. It has become plainly clear how few suitable people we have [inside Russia]. At all times," he continued, "there must be someone [inside tsarist Russia] who can raise the level of the party, one who will not allow it to be reduced to the level of socialist high-school students or merely revolutionary technicians."[55]

The pessimistic tone was also indicative of Pilsudski's failed hopes for a mass uprising in Russia's western provinces. Only a few minor protests had taken place thus far. "I returned to Kraków broken, almost ill. Where were these Poles from *Śpiewy Historyczne* [Historical Songs]," he wrote, referring to Julian Niemcewicz's nineteenth-century patriotic verses, or "from the poetry of Mickiewicz, Słowacki, and Krasiński? [Where were] these self-sacrificing knights, the dream of their mothers, the fiery spirits ready to take up arms at the first sound of the fight for freedom? This was the most difficult disappointment I have ever had."[56] Pilsudski's pessimistic mood changed abruptly on May 5, 1904, when he received an extraordinary cable from London. The Japanese general staff had invited him to Tokyo for a high-level meeting.[57]

CHAPTER 8

From a Tokyo Mission to the Union of Active Struggle

Our dream is to prepare a cadre of combatants to stand at the head of a future armed revolution leading to great things.

—JOZEF PILSUDSKI, ADDRESS TO THE FIRST CONFERENCE
OF THE COMBAT ORGANIZATION, KRAKÓW, JULY 1906

On May 13, 1904, Tytus Filipowicz informed Pilsudski that he was to meet the Japanese military attaché, Taro Utsunomiya, in Switzerland to work out the details of a visit to Japan.[1] Pilsudski left for Berne with his wife, Maria, holding meetings with the Japanese attaché on May 21 and 22. He was surprised to learn from Utsunomiya that other Poles were engaged in discussions with the Japanese, among them Roman Dmowski, who had been in Tokyo since May 15.[2]

Following the meeting in Berne, Pilsudski departed for Japan, stopping in several places. In London, he met on June 3 with the Japanese minister to Great Britain, Tadasu Hayashi. "Today I met with Count Hayashi," he wrote. "I confess that he made the best possible impression on me, so much so that I now have fewer worries and more hopes that our mission will succeed."[3] Pilsudski left London with letters of introduction for Japanese leaders in Tokyo. Hayashi, in turn, informed the Japanese foreign minister that he was sending Pilsudski along with Filipowicz—a trusted comrade and translator between Polish and English.[4]

Traveling on the SS *Campania* from Liverpool to New York, the two arrived on June 11, 1904, and made their way to their hotel on Lafayette Street in Manhattan's Soho neighborhood. "A wonderful city and strangely familiar," Filipowicz wrote of his first impressions of New York.[5] Pilsudski, suffering from seasickness, had little appetite for sightseeing. "I have been in New York for two days," Pilsudski wrote on June 13. "I caught a cold on the voyage. For a few days now I have had a wildly painful headache and toothache."[6]

On June 15, Pilsudski and Filipowicz left New York for San Francisco, where on June 22 they boarded a ship for Japan. The eleven days spent in the United States would remain Pilsudski's first and last visit to America. In a letter from San Francisco, Filipowicz described the six-day journey across the United States. The train from New York had gone north to Buffalo, and from Niagara Falls they journeyed across the country, including Manitou Springs in Colorado, the desert in Utah, and the Rocky Mountains. "We crisscrossed through snow-covered ranges of mountains," Filipowicz commented, "toward Sierra Nevada. Then we went from the tops of the snowy Sierras to Sacramento and toward San Francisco, where we saw palm trees and orange groves."[7] Inserted in Filipowicz's letter was a note from Pilsudski to his wife in Kraków. "Forward the enclosed letter to my wife," Pilsudski wrote, "and inform her about our movements so she knows where we are. Please do not forget!"[8]

Pilsudski composed a report on the voyage from San Francisco to Japan. Translated into English by Filipowicz, it was written for Japanese officials to introduce them to the program of the Polish Socialist Party. The report began with the statement that to a non-European country like Japan, Russia west of the Ural Mountains could easily appear homogeneous. "But in reality," he stated, "this homogeneity does not exist." Ethnic Russians, Pilsudski noted, made up less than half of the population. Not only were there different nationalities but there were vastly different cultures as well. "We have in the state's western region," he wrote, "Poland, Lithuania, Latvia, and Finland—countries that are, in the literal sense of the term, European—which have an entirely different social structure than Russia . . . as well as do the numerous peoples of Siberia and central Asia." He continued:

Allow me to add that a predominant part of the state was annexed to Russia by force in lands whose inhabitants—people who once lived entirely separate from Russia—feel themselves to be imprisoned. The difference in historical traditions as well as in the memory of past and present violence, therefore, deepens still further the heterogeneity of the tsarist state. This lack of uniformity in Imperial Russia is its central weakness, its Achilles' heel.[9]

The logic of a Polish–Japanese alliance, Pilsudski maintained, was clear. For starters, Poles had an "exalted boldness" in their pursuit of separation from Russia. *"The breakup of the Russian state into its main component parts,"* Pilsudski emphasized, *"and the granting of independence to the countries absorbed by force into the empire"* was widely desired. He added: "For the non-Russian nationalities, the victory of Japan has brought forth excitement and an inclination to fight actively against the enemy more than ever before." The outbreak of war "has consequently created a natural alliance between Japan and Poland."[10]

On July 11, 1904, Pilsudski and Filipowicz arrived at the Japanese port of Yokohama. Major Inagaki, from the General Staff of the Japanese Army, escorted them to Tokyo, where they checked into the Seiyoken Hotel, one of the oldest Western-style hotels.[11] The following day, Pilsudski and Filipowicz met with General Atsushi Murata and Toshitsune Kawakami, later to become Japan's first ambassador to the United States, who served as translator from English to Japanese. In this introductory exchange, Pilsudski handed Kawakami both his report and the letter of introduction from Hayashi.

Unbeknownst to Pilsudski at the time, his political rival, Roman Dmowski, had also submitted a proposal to the Japanese government. Filipowicz noted that he had a bad feeling about Dmowski and suspected he was going to undermine them.[12] Dmowski's report urged the Japanese to reject Pilsudski's proposals. Pilsudski's report represented "the oppositionist and revolutionary elements dissatisfied with the present rule in Russia" and should not be considered the last word on the subject. Representing the voice of the National League (National Democrats), Dmowski maintained that the vast majority of Poles opposed armed insurrection. Pilsudski's armed revolution, Dmowski continued, would be disastrous for the region, leading only to bloodshed and repression.[13]

Dmowski's memorandum had its desired effect. On July 23, 1904, Kawakami informed Pilsudski that Japan had decided against formal cooperation. "My government can't enter into a relation with you," Kawakami wrote on July 23, 1904, "in the fear that it will lead to some very serious and complicated international questions."[14] Kawakami is said to have been personally disappointed with his government's decision. Dmowski's counterproposal was undoubt-edly a major factor in the Japanese government's negative response to Pil-sudski. As historian Andrzej Fiszke noted, "Dmowski went to Japan in order to foil Pilsudski's plan to prepare an anti-Russian insurrection in Poland with the aid of the Japanese."[15]

Pilsudski and Filipowicz left Japan emptyhanded, arriving back in London in September 1904. But the mission to Japan was not entirely without results: the Japanese had agreed to provide the PPS with funds for arms and ammu-nition in exchange for intelligence on the movement of Russian troops.[16] As part of the agreement, Filipowicz translated intelligence reports into English for the Japanese. In London, meanwhile, Wojciechowski collected money from Taro Utsunomiya, which he used to purchase weapons for illegal trans-port to Russia.[17] During the course of the war with Russia, the Japanese pro-vided the PPS approximately £20,000 for arms purchase. Wojciechowski col-lected an additional $3,014 from Polish American organizations.[18]

The Combat Organization of the Polish Socialist Party

Meeting face to face with Japanese military officials led Pilsudski to revise his support for a mass uprising. He instead came to the conclusion that only a professional standing army could expel Russia from the Polish lands. Friends closest to him noted this new preoccupation in the weeks following Pilsudski's return from Japan. Leon Wasilewski, then residing in Kraków and working closely with Pilsudski, recalled the change in the party leader. "Ziuk [Jozef] started devoting long hours to the study of the military. I noticed more and more publications on military topics at his home. And at this time, Ziuk re-peatedly returned to military topics in conversation. . . . Sitting for hours over a map of the Russo-Japanese War theater, while reading Russian military periodicals, he soon began to impress us with an enormous wealth of knowl-edge about military topics."[19]

Pilsudski's new focus on the military was on full display at the conference of the party's central committee held in Kraków in October 1904. According to one of the participants, Pilsudski opened his address with details of his mission to Tokyo followed by a proposal for the creation of a Combat Organ-ization (Organizacja Bojowa). The party, he argued, must respond to orders of mobilization in the Polish provinces not with words but with "a tactic of deeds" (*taktyka czynu*).[20] The resolution passed. That all eight members of the central committee were there made this a historic decision all the more significant. Present also were Bolesław Jędrzejowski and Leon Wasilewski from the foreign committee as well the PPSD's leader, Ignacy Daszyński.[21]

There was no time to waste. Pilsudski designated Warsaw as the Combat Organization's command headquarters and called for local branches to be formed in every city and town with a party organization. For the task of the party's first armed action, Pilsudski turned to the head of the Warsaw branch, Józef Kwiatek, whom he summoned to Kraków for a meeting. Prior to the meeting, Pilsudski learned that mobilization had spread to the Kingdom of Poland. "I cannot remember how many sleepless nights I spent," Pilsudski later remarked, "pacing back and forth, smoking cigarette after cigarette, and drinking an inordinate amount of tea. I thought constantly about the form of our protest and what our position should be."[22] When Kwiatek arrived in Kraków in October 1904, Pilsudski presented his plan for an armed demonstration in Warsaw.

Kwiatek, excited about his new assignment, returned to Warsaw to prepare. He gave Walery Sławek six hundred rubles to purchase firearms and ammunition. On November 11, 1904, Sławek delivered thirty-eight revolvers. Weapons in hand, the party's Warsaw branch distributed a circular announcing the demonstration.[23] On the eve of the protest, the *Times* of London reported from Warsaw that "the Polish population actually rejoices at Russian defeat" and regarded the Russian mobilization order as an extreme provocation.[24]

On the crisp Sunday morning of November 13, 1904, a crowd gathered in Warsaw's Grzybowski Square to demonstrate against mobilization. According to eyewitness accounts, protesters began chanting, "We don't want to be soldiers of the tsar," followed by the singing of patriotic songs. When the crowd grew to more than three hundred, seventeen-year-old Stefan Okrzeja unfurled a red banner reading "P.P.S.: Down with the War and the Tsar. Long Live a Free Polish People!"[25] As police and Cossacks on horseback moved into the crowd to apprehend Okrzeja, the Combat Organization members opened fire and chaos ensued. Over four hundred people were arrested. Six were killed, and twenty-seven were wounded; of these, one dead and five wounded were policemen.[26]

One demonstrator, twenty-one-year-old Alexandra Szczerbińska—who later became Pilsudski's second wife—noted that the Grzybowski Square protest, the first armed demonstration on the Polish street since the 1863 uprising, had the impact of significantly slowing down Russian mobilization in the Polish provinces.[27] Another demonstrator, Walery Sławek, later reflected on the event: "I'll never forget the great joyfulness I saw on the faces of our fighters when a few police fled from the scene." That symbolic moment "constituted a great psychological turning point. The sight of policemen fleeing in panic made quite an impression."[28]

The Grzybowski Square demonstration was the Polish Socialist Party's first resort to force. The mastermind behind the event, Pilsudski, likely first got news of it in the November 15 issue of the Kraków daily, *Naprzód*. It was undoubtedly with a sense of exaltation that he read this line from the paper's Warsaw correspondent: "It is everyone's opinion here that there has not been such a demonstration since the year 1863." He likely also received copies of the foreign press, such as the *New York Times* article from November 17, 1904, with the words, "Never since the great revolt of 1863 had there occurred in Warsaw so determined a hand-to-hand struggle between the populace and the police and soldiers."[29] Vacationing with his family in Zakopane at the time, Pilsudski wrote to his comrades in London. "Make some noise in the English press regarding the incident in Warsaw," he implored. "If Europe makes more noise concerning [the Grzybowski Square] incident, it will make further mobilization that much more awkward for the [Russian] government."[30] For Pilsudski, it was clear that the demonstration had a definite impact on the national psyche, opening a new page in the history of the Polish Socialist Party and his country.

Outbreak of the 1905 Russian Revolution

On January 9, 1905, a Russian Orthodox priest, Father Gapon, led an estimated hundred thousand people in a peaceful march in St. Petersburg to present a petition to the tsar. It called for elections to a constitutional assembly, the immediate introduction of civil liberties, and an amnesty for political prisoners. Gapon also demanded a minimum wage, an eight-hour workday, and collective bargaining rights. But as the demonstrators approached the

Winter Palace, the royal guard opened fire, killing 130 people and wounding 299.[31] "Bloody Sunday," as it came to be known, sparked an empire-wide revolutionary upheaval. A vast spontaneous strike movement ensued. One day after the massacre, 160,000 workers stayed home in protest. By the end of January 1905, an estimated 410,000 workers had gone on strike, throwing Russia into complete disarray and ushering in a new era for the empire's labor movement.

In Warsaw, meanwhile, the head of the Polish Socialist Party's local branch issued an appeal titled "Our Political Declaration." Dated January 28, 1905, the declaration demanded individual civil rights, equality before the law regardless of religion or nationality, and the right of workers to strike and form trade unions. It called for "an independent national life," the use of Polish in schools, and a constituent assembly in Warsaw chosen by universal suffrage. In addition, the declaration demanded "the guarantee of free cultural development for the Jewish people and other national minorities."[32] The Warsaw organization's declaration coincided with a socialist-led general strike. By the end of January, 47,000 striking workers made Warsaw one of the empire's major revolutionary centers, with strikes in the Kingdom of Poland making up one-third of the 410,000 striking workers that January.[33]

It was in Zakopane that Pilsudski received news of the dramatic events in Russia. One of the visitors he received in February 1905 was twenty-five-year-old Michał Sokolnicki, who was surprised at Pilsudski's disinterest in the events in Russia. Pilsudski spoke instead about preparing a cadre of fighters for a future military and how to raise the necessary funds.[34] In Warsaw, meanwhile, the Young faction held a meeting of party leaders in imperial Russia in March 1905. In Pilsudski's absence, they declared the gathering to be the Seventh Party Convention, unexpectedly passing a fundamental change in the party platform. Henceforth, the resolution stated, the demand for independence was to be replaced by the demand for autonomy of the Kingdom of Poland in a democratic, constitutional Russia. The new central committee retained only two Old Guard members: Pilsudski and Alexander Malinowski. The convention also formed a Conspiratorial-Combat Department (Wydział Spiskowo-Bojowy) to oversee and direct combat units, placing Walery Sławek and Alexander Prystor at its head while naming Pilsudski as its director.[35]

Pilsudski attributed the change in the party platform to his absence. "I am convinced," he wrote on March 29, 1905, "that if I or even Leon [Wasilewski] had been at the convention, then much of what took place would have been prevented."[36] For Wasilewski, the Seventh Party Convention signaled the transfer of authority from the Old Guard to the party's Young faction. "At this moment," he remarked, "what was critical for us Old Guardists—me, Jodko-Narkiewicz, [Bolesław A.] Jędrzejowski, [Alexander] Sulkiewicz, and others—was the reaction of Ziuk [Pilsudski]. Were we to abide by the resolutions of the Seventh Party Convention or speak out against them and accept whatever consequences followed from that decision?"[37]

Recognizing the fissure that had just been created in the party, Pilsudski returned to Russia to reassert his authority. In the Warsaw suburb of Józefów, he gathered with the central committee for a two-day party conference on June 16 and 17, 1905. In his address, Pilsudski stated that he was in theory in favor of alliances with all revolutionary groups. "According to [Marian Bielecki]," Pilsudski said, referring to a representative of the Young faction who had earlier addressed the gathering, "the independence of Poland is impossible to attain. He proposed, as something in the realm of the possible, a federation with Russia. If [Bielecki] believes that a federation with Russia is more easily achieved, then I would call this optimistic. For a common struggle has to include common aims. Why is a common struggle for a federation possible but a joint struggle for independence impossible?" He continued: "I am in principle for [Bielecki's] resolution but I foresee difficulties in bringing them to fruition."[38]

Pilsudski's deliberations, combined with the weight of his personal influence, prevented a schism for the time being. The party council voted for a new central committee. Pilsudski remained on it, but the Young faction increased in number, adding new members like Max Horwitz. "After the Seventh Party Convention," Wasilewski remarked, "the situation for Old Guardists in the party was quite tenuous. We were ousted systematically from leadership as well as from journalistic and agitation work."[39] The latter point likely referred to changes in editorial oversight of *Robotnik*. After the arrest of Feliks Perl in August 1904, the printing press and staff had relocated to Warsaw, and the paper had come under the editorial control of the Young faction.

With the Young faction's takeover, Pilsudski retreated from party politics and focused his energy instead on the Combat Organization. Already having read extensively about the Napoleonic Wars, he took up the study of war more generally during this time, reading Carl von Clausewitz's *On War* (1832) while acquiring newly published studies on the Boer War (1899–1902) in South Africa. Upon learning of recent publications in English, he wrote Tytus Filipowicz in London to send him copies.[40] Shortly after, Pilsudski received two major English-language works on the Boer War for his personal library: Conan Doyle's *The Great Boer War* (1902) and the three volumes of *The Times History of the War in South Africa, 1899–1902* (1900–1904).

Outside of party affairs and the Combat Organization, big changes were taking place in Russia. Japan and Russia signed an armistice on September 5, 1905, bringing a formal end to the Russo-Japanese War. Social unrest followed, and labor unrest in Russia spiked when railroad workers in Moscow organized a general strike on October 4. Six days later, rail service in Moscow came to a complete halt, spreading to St. Petersburg. The railway strike spread to the Polish provinces—the third leading industrial center in imperial Russia—on October 11.[41]

Tsar Nicholas II had no choice other than to concede to the labor demands. On October 17, he issued the October Manifesto, introducing freedom of speech, freedom of the press, freedom of assembly, and freedom of religion. The historic declaration called for elections to a legislative parliament (Duma) to take place in April 1906. Overnight, clandestine organizations and their presses came out into the open.

The Warsaw branch of the PPS greeted the news of the October Manifesto with great enthusiasm. Its leaders appealed to Pilsudski to return from exile now that his illegal status was formally lifted. But for Pilsudski, such a move was out of the question. "Boy, we're living in extraordinary times!" he wrote after the October Manifesto was announced. "Interesting are the impressions of people and their feelings." It would be naive to believe the October Manifesto signaled the end of the clandestine struggle. "My prognosis about what the future holds," Pilsudski stated, "is that everything will end up in horrific chaos, leading to the weakening and exhaustion of Russia. The decay and disintegration of the Russian state will thus follow."[42]

Leon Wasilewski vividly remembered Pilsudski's reaction to the October Manifesto. "Ziuk [Pilsudski] had zero faith that the decrees of the October

Manifesto would remain in place," he wrote. "He looked upon them with great skepticism." Pilsudski was of the opinion that the Russian government, "dismayed by revolutionary turmoil, would react harshly and . . . roll back all the 'freedoms.'" To Michał Sokolnicki in November 1905, Pilsudski remarked that the unrest in Russia did not constitute a revolution: "'What is a revolution without a fight? And what is a fight with folded arms?'"[43] Clearly, Pilsudski's attitude toward Russia remained entirely unchanged.

Unmoved by the dramatic events in Russia, Pilsudski worked on forming a cadre of instructors for the Combat Organization. He opened the first training school in Kraków in November 1905. By the beginning of 1906 he had organized the opening of two more military training courses in Kraków. Instructors included Walery Sławek, Kazimierz Sosnkowski, and Alexander Prystor. Pilsudski gave lectures on organization and tactics. The three schools graduated approximately one hundred fighters by April 1906.[44] The newly trained instructors then crossed the border into Russia to form local chapters of the party's Combat Organization.

At the Eighth Party Convention, held February 1906 in Lwów, many Young faction representatives expressed unease with Pilsudski's control of the Combat Organization. Attended by 160 delegates, of whom 145 had voting rights, the convention lasted twelve days. Against the majority opinion of the central committee, the delegates voted to retain Pilsudski as head of the Combat Organization. The attempt to strip him of his powers led him to insist that the Combat Organization be independent. With a majority of delegates voting in favor, Pilsudski's motion passed. But his motion opposing the party platform changes on the national question failed.[45]

Leon Wasilewski was the only other Old Guardist present. "We took part in the Lwów congress very reservedly," he recalled. "Our leader was Ziuk [Pilsudski], who gave an extraordinary speech . . . in which he defended his position regarding the Combat Organization, describing it as 'a band of public cleaners, constantly demanding tsarist debris.'" Pilsudski "also defended the organizational independence of the Combat Organization. He spoke so convincingly that he commanded authority even over those on the party's left, including those who were seeing him for the first time."[46] One of the delegates from Łódź, Aleksy Rzewski, remembered a burst of applause. "It was not only the strength of the arguments from the leader of the Combat Organization," he recalled, "but also the extraordinary charm of persuasion that flowed from the whole figure of Mieczysław [Pilsudski] when he spoke about Poland and the armed struggle."[47]

IN APRIL 1906 the first Duma elections led to a resounding defeat for the Russian government. Of the 497-member Duma, the Labor Group of unofficial Socialist Revolutionaries gained 94 seats (18.9 percent) and the Social Democrats 18 seats (3.6 percent). The largest number of seats went to the liberal Constitutional Democrats, or Cadets, who gained 179 seats (36 percent), while the pro-government parties combined took a mere 32 seats (6.4 percent). In the Kingdom of Poland, where all socialist parties boycotted the elections, the right-wing populist National Democrats emerged victorious, gaining 34 of the 37 seats representing the Polish provinces.

Pilsudski's hunch that the tsarist regime would undermine the democratic process proved all too accurate. On May 6, 1906, five days before the first Duma in Russian history was scheduled to convene, Tsar Nicholas II promulgated a constitution. The document, known as the Fundamental Laws, retained for the tsar the title of "Supreme Autocrat" and gave him veto rights over all legislation passed in the Duma. The Duma, in turn, had no authority to override a veto, making it an impotent body. The constitution further gave the tsar the right to dissolve the Duma. Despite its severe shortcomings, the grant of a Duma and civil liberties signaled a new direction in Russian history. As Peter Kenez observed, "For the first time in Russian history, politicians were allowed to develop and to present to the electorate political platforms."[48]

Pilsudski's pessimism that the sweeping changes were little more than tsarist trickery to forestall revolution continued unabated. In his view, newly granted freedoms could be removed at any moment as long as the levers of power—the army and the police—rested solely with the tsar. The transformation of Russia into a constitutional monarchy thus in no way undermined Pilsudski's singular focus on cultivating an armed force. In the spring of 1906 the Combat Organization leadership selected a group of men and women to safeguard the clandestine arms and ammunition depots. In the course of 1906, these men and women created a chain of secret arsenals and magazines.

Twenty-three-year-old Alexandra Szczerbińska oversaw the Combat Organization's central arms depot in Warsaw, which supplied all weapons to local organizations. She recorded each transaction, distributing thousands of rifles, revolvers, and ammunition. In May 1906 Pilsudski came to inspect the depot. Szczerbińska later recalled, "I remember that when I was told to expect him I felt some curiosity to see this man whose name was fast becoming a legend in Poland."[49] She noted:

> I remember that my first thought of him was that here was a man whom Siberia had failed to break. It had not set its seal upon him either mentally or physically, as it had upon all the other returned exiles I had met. There was neither bitterness nor resignation in his face. Then I became conscious of the tremendous force of his personality, of that indefinable magnetism which enabled him, all through his life, to sway the minds of men, even against their will. I had somehow expected him to be a big man, powerfully built. I was surprised to find he was of medium height only with broad shoulders, a slender waist and a step as light as a girl's. He had a feline grace of movement which he retained even in old age.[50]

Pilsudski's control of the Combat Organization again came under scrutiny. At a party council in June 1906, the Young leadership passed a resolution for direct control of the Combat Organization.[51] Pilsudski countered by calling forth the First Conference of the Combat Organization, which opened in Kraków on July 5, 1906. "Having established a group of fighters," Pilsudski said in his opening remarks, "our dream is to prepare a cadre of combatants to stand at the head of a future armed revolution leading to great things."[52]

Opposed to small-scale street actions, Pilsudski argued that the party's armed forces were to be disciplined and its actions purposeful. The Combat Organization had a nobler purpose than indiscriminate, arbitrary acts of violence against government officials. Pilsudski's plan to expand the Combat Organization required financial backing. He therefore ordered a series of raids on government trains, with the funds acquired to be used for the maintenance of the fighting squads. In one raid on July 29, 1906, the Combat Organization came away with cash that, according to the exchange rate at the time, was the equivalent of $37,500. Casualties included the deaths of two Russian Army officials.[53]

While Pilsudski believed securing funds for the Combat Organization justified unintended casualties, he opposed political assassinations. This put him in conflict with the party's central committee. Pilsudski opposed the

Alexandra Szczerbińska, fellow member of the Combat Organization of the Polish Socialist Party and Pilsudski's future second wife, 1901.

attempted assassination of the Georgii Skalon, governor-general of Warsaw, in August 1906. He also opposed so-called Bloody Wednesday, when, on August 15, Combat Organization units carried out coordinated attacks in twenty locations on Russian police, gendarmes, state officials, and Russian soldiers. Innocent bystanders counted among the estimated eighty deaths.[54]

Pilsudski evidently was outraged that the central committee would order such an action. "I did not organize 'Bloody Wednesday' in 1906," Pilsudski clarified. "I was an opponent of terror against individuals and I never ever organized such assassinations."[55]

The image of the Combat Organization as bandits and thieves greatly disturbed Pilsudski. The events of Bloody Wednesday inspired him to publish a lengthy piece for the inaugural issue of the Kraków-based *Trybuna* (The Tribune), a periodical of the Old Guardists. Pilsudski maintained that the conditions for an armed uprising were not yet in place. The present task was the gradual, methodical preparation for a future uprising. Such preparation involved "a large-scale diffusion of our combat organization into small military units scattered throughout the Russian sector of Poland."[56]

In the international arena, Pilsudski observed a gradual shift in the European alliance system, changes that led to Russia's alienation from Germany and Austria-Hungary. To exploit these emerging divisions, Pilsudski began negotiations with the Austrian Army. He was not an entirely unknown figure. In 1905 his name had appeared in an Austrian security report: "In Kraków, Pilsudski has begun, in word and in deed, to spread the idea that for Polish independence to be more than just a dream, an army must be formed which, at the proper time, will take up armed struggle with Russia for the independence of Poland."[57] On September 29, 1906, Pilsudski met with Colonel Franz Kanik, chief of staff of the Austro-Hungarian 10th Corps in Galicia, as well as with Captain Edmund Hauser and Joseph Czernecki, tax commissioner in Lwów. Pilsudski presented his request for arms and permission to create a weapons storage depot in Galicia. In exchange, the Combat Organization of the PPS would share intelligence services on Russian military movements. In the event of war with imperial Russia, Pilsudski's fighters inside Russia would strike from behind enemy lines.[58]

In party affairs, meanwhile, the divide between Pilsudski and the central committee widened. Without consulting the central committee, he ordered several expropriation actions, and his combat units conducted raids on government trains on October 20 and 23. The party's central committee, irate at such independent actions, voiced concern. Pilsudski replied in deeds, ordering a postal train raid on November 8 at the Rogów station outside of Warsaw. While Pilsudski's fighting squad seized its largest booty to date—63,846 rubles ($31,284 at the time)—sixteen Russian soldiers were wounded.

One of the explosive devices used in the raid severed a Russian railway clerk's arm, and the *New York Times* referred to the attackers as "a band of terrorists."[59] Furious, the central committee ordered an immediate suspension of all Combat Organization actions. Pilsudski, ignoring the order, organized a conference of fighters in Zakopane. Defending his actions in Rogów, Pilsudski introduced a resolution opposing the central committee's platform of a federation with Russia.[60]

Breakup of the Party

The conflict between Pilsudski and the Young faction came to a head at the Ninth Party Congress of the PPS in Vienna in November 1906. The Young faction openly clashed with Pilsudski, representing the Combat Organization, and a few Old Guardists. "I was opposed to 'Bloody Wednesday'," Pilsudski said in his address to the 46-person convention. "The action was neither sensible nor necessary, nor did it raise our image in the eyes of the country."[61] The central committee replied that Pilsudski had employed tactics and passed resolutions "extremely divergent" from the party's, "aiming at the separation of the revolutionary movement in Poland from the general movement in the whole of the Russian Empire." The central committee put forth a resolution stating that the platform accepted at the recent Combat Organization gathering in Zakopane placed Pilsudski and his fighters "outside of the party's sphere."[62]

As the votes were tallied and the resolution passed by majority vote, Pilsudski and his supporters walked out in protest. The following day he issued a written rebuttal, declaring that "the political system that can respond to the economic and class interests of the country . . . can only be established in an independent democratic Polish republic."[63] Pilsudski and his supporters left Vienna on November 22, 1906, gathering the following day in Kraków to announce the creation of a new party—the PPS Revolutionary Faction, making the party schism official. The Revolutionary Faction organized quickly, putting out its first issue of *Robotnik* under Leon Wasilewski's editorship on November 30, 1906. The Young faction henceforth presided over a party now referred to as PPS Left.

To help oversee the new party's press, Pilsudski traveled to Warsaw. He stayed with Michał Sokolnicki, who recalled Pilsudski as distraught over the party schism. "He was, like always during his conspiratorial travels," Sokolnicki wrote, "calm and extremely careful. He examined every part of the apartment and behaved according to his surroundings. He thoroughly checked the area and conditions of the apartment building he was visiting. He did not speak much," Sokolnicki remembered, "and looked grim. With tea laid out in front of him, he smoked cigarettes incessantly. He was consumed by the fight against slow-witted, unbelieving people."[64] In December 1906, having just turned thirty-nine, Pilsudski returned to Kraków, now the center of the PPS Revolutionary Faction's central committee.

In the first three months of 1907, Pilsudski's Combat Organization performed thirty-three actions, seizing 6,500 rubles ($3,185) in one Warsaw raid. In addition to military affairs, Pilsudski was active in party politics, attending the nine-day First Congress of the PPS Revolutionary Faction. Taking place in March 1907 in Vienna, the party platform supported an independent Polish republic, arguing it was the only form that would give rise to true social democracy. For non-Polish inhabitants of the future state, the program guaranteed "the rights of national minorities in administration, schools, and the courts."[65]

Pilsudski, representing the party's Combat Organization, addressed the congress on tactics, funds, and supplies. He emphasized the centrality of the Combat Organization for the country's future. "We have been working in molehills, in the underground. It often seemed that in this type of work all the torments of us conspirators will be for nothing, and that we are constructing buildings on sand. But when the moment of battle arrives and the working classes begin to search for guidance," he said, "they will look to us! . . . Today, the revolutionary wave is waning, and everyone is gradually abandoning their lust for battle. But if we do not take advantage of the current period, if we do not capitalize on the tension caused by the general discouragement, then what will people say about us when a [revolutionary] wave returns?" He concluded: "We are fighting today for future leadership."[66]

Pilsudski discussed his aims in calling for armed action. The Combat Organization "must strive to block and obstruct the activities of the tsarist authorities by attacking state institutions. The more numerous the assaults become, the more difficult government administration will be, the more people will believe in the possibility of armed struggle with the government." The fighters, he continued, "shall be directed at institutions harmful to the revolution (police, gendarmerie) as well as at government stores of cash whose defense should become more and more burdensome and costly, and whose acquisition shall become one of the means by which to continue the fight against tsarism."[67] The Combat Organization was also to serve as self-defense units. Such units were to be used not only for ethnic Poles but for minorities as well, particularly against pogroms.

Pilsudski was well aware of the devastating wave of anti-Jewish violence that had swept through western Russia in 1905–1906, an estimated 657 pogroms leading to 3,103 Jews dead and 17,000 wounded.[68] He commented on the pogrom that had taken place September 1906 in the Kingdom of Poland. The outbreak of anti-Jewish violence in Siedlce began when the local Russian military chief ordered attacks on Jewish shops. Bloodshed followed, with the number of Jews murdered estimated between 23 and 100. Press reports maintained that the Russians assured local Poles not to worry because "our orders are only to kill Jews."[69] Pilsudski expressed shame that his Combat Organization failed to intervene. He attributed the outbreak to the Russian government's revenge for its officials killed in August. "The pogrom in Siedlce, which was an answer to Bloody Wednesday, met no response from the Combat Organization," Pilsudski commented in a 1910 publication. "It was a moral defeat, afterward followed by a material defeat. The Siedlce pogrom caused dismay in the whole party organization, because it was understood that with the help of the military, the government could organize such a pogrom at any point in the Kingdom [of Poland]. The Combat Organization had not sufficient means to counteract it."[70] Pilsudski believed he was obligated to protect all the inhabitants of lands he deemed Polish, regardless of religion and nationality.

Pilsudski increasingly focused his energy on military matters, even choosing not to run for a seat on the party's central committee. In the spring and summer of 1907, he ordered expropriation actions on Russian government trains in Łódź (April 22 and May 17), Warsaw (May 17), Lublin (May 26), and Kielce. At the time, the Combat Organization numbered 750 men and women in the Kingdom of Poland, divided into 150 five-person squadrons.[71]

Changes in Pilsudski's Private Life

In the fall of 1906, Pilsudski, Maria, and Wanda moved to a new, larger apartment at 16 Topolowa Street in Kraków. Maria began to regularly host key party figures as well as prominent writers, actors, and playwrights. One of the frequent visitors was Kazimiera Iłłakowiczówna, later to become one of Poland's most celebrated poets. "The [Pilsudski] home," Iłłakowiczówna recalled, "was always full of people. I met there, among others, [Walery] Sławek, Jodko-Narkiewicz, [Michał] Sokolnicki, [Alexander] Prystor, and [Tytus] Filipowicz."[72] Leon Wasilewski similarly recalled, "Madame Maria was undoubtedly an outstanding personality. Smart, well-informed, articulate, devoted to issues, she knew how to influence the people around her, especially when we take into account her pleasant appearance, social grace and cheerful mood."[73] Bogusław Miedziński, active in the PPS Revolutionary Faction, also frequently visited the Pilsudskis at this time. Maria, he remarked, "was extremely lively and talkative. She did not always uncritically echo the views of her husband."[74]

The fall of 1906 also marked a milestone in Pilsudski's family life. His older brother, Bronisław, finally returned home after nearly two decades in Siberian exile. When he arrived in Kraków, he moved into an apartment next door to his brother. It was undoubtedly an emotional reunion for the two brothers, both in their late thirties. During the nineteen years spent on Russia's Sakhalin Island in the North Pacific in forced exile, Bronisław had taken a keen interest in the language and culture of the island's indigenous Ainu people. Having become an ethnographer, Bronisław was preparing a study on Ainu language and folklore that would later appear in English in 1912. His study is still today considered a standard work on the subject.[75]

Another development in Pilsudski's personal life at this time was that his marriage was coming apart. In 1907 he spent more and more time away from home, often with a woman fifteen years his junior—Alexandra Szczerbińska. In Kielce in July 1907, the two coordinated the distribution of arms to fighting units in the Kingdom of Poland. Szczerbińska recalled a walk they took in a garden. "It was there that our acquaintance passed on to the plane of friendship," she wrote. "We used to go on long walks together." On one of those walks, "he told me that he loved me, and that he had loved me since those first days when we worked together at Zakopane."[76]

Leon Wasilewski remembered Pilsudski distancing himself from his wife at this time. "At first," Wasilewski noted, "Ziuk accompanied Maria to cafes. But gradually he began to gripe. When she wanted to stay late at 'Secession' café or at Jama Michalika coffee house, he started going home alone. It was against this background that one observed a certain cooling of Pilsudski's

Bronisław Pilsudski, after his return from
Siberian exile, Kraków, 1907. Forced in
1905 to leave behind his three-year-old
son and Japanese wife, then pregnant
with their second child, Bronisław today
has thirteen great grandchildren in Japan.
Because the male line ended in Poland, the
Pilsudski surname today is found only
in Japan.

relations with his wife, carefully hidden by him from even his closest friends.
But it was impossible for him to hide this."[77]

In November 1907, meanwhile, the Third Duma elections brought into
power a pro-tsarist legislature. The opposition political parties were forced
underground again, their printing presses were seized, and party leaders
were arrested.[78] To Pilsudski, the complete erosion of freedoms in Russia
was entirely unsurprising. "The revolution," he wrote at the time, "owes its
victory to moral forces, whereas its defeat and failure were due to the lack of
physical strength." Now that the revolution had failed, "our obligation is thus
to make use of today's revolutionary lull by preparing us for the future.
[This will ensure that] a future battle will not be characterized by the same
weakness that was recently shown."[79]

It was around this time, in December 1907, that Pilsudski began planning a
major expropriation action—a raid that he believed would yield a whopping

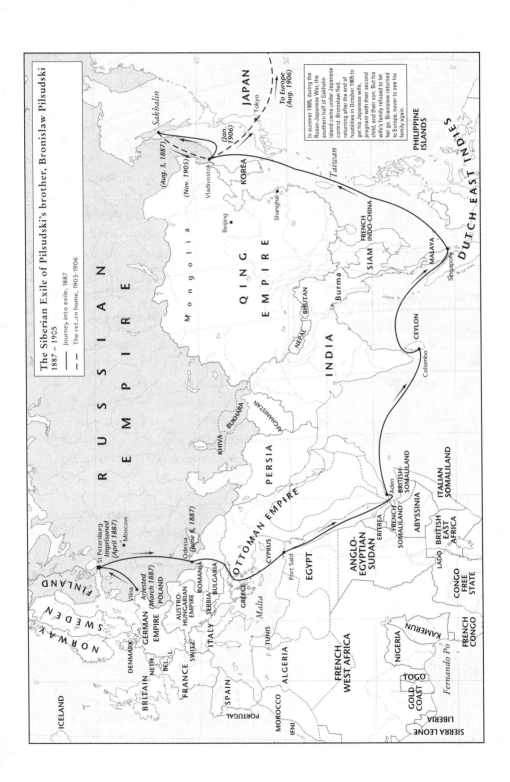

The Siberian Exile of Pilsudski's brother, Bronislaw Pilsudski
1887 – 1905

→ Journey into exile, 1887
--- The return home, 1905-1906

In summer 1905, during the Russo-Japanese War, the southern half of Sakhalin island came under Japanese control. Bronislaw fled, returning after the end of hostilities in October 1905 to get his Japanese wife, pregnant with their second child, and their son. But his wife's family refused to let her go. Branislaw returned to Europe, never to see his family again.

ICELAND

NORWAY
SWEDEN
FINLAND
DENMARK
BRITAIN
NETH.
BEL.
FRANCE
SWITZ.
GERMAN EMPIRE
AUSTRO-HUNGARIAN EMPIRE
POLAND
ROMANIA
SERBIA
BULGARIA
ITALY
SPAIN
PORTUGAL
MOROCCO
IFNI
ALGERIA
TUNIS
GREECE
Malta

St Petersburg
Imprisoned (April 1887)
Vilna
Arrested (March 1887)
Moscow
Odessa
(June 8, 1887)

RUSSIAN EMPIRE

Sakhalin
(Aug. 3, 1887)
(Nov. 1905)
(Jan. 1906)
Vladivostok

JAPAN
Tokyo
To Europe (Aug. 1906)

KOREA
Taiwan

Mongolia
Beijing
Shanghai

QING EMPIRE

OTTOMAN EMPIRE
PERSIA
KHIVA
BUKHARA
AFGHANISTAN

Port Said
CYPRUS
EGYPT
ANGLO-EGYPTIAN SUDAN

NEPAL
BHUTAN
INDIA
Burma
SIAM
FRENCH INDO-CHINA

CEYLON
Colombo

MALAYA
Singapore

PHILIPPINE ISLANDS

DUTCH EAST INDIES

Aden
ERITREA
FRENCH SOMALILAND
BRITISH SOMALILAND
ITALIAN SOMALILAND
ABYSSINIA
BRITISH EAST AFRICA
LADO
CONGO FREE STATE

FRENCH WEST AFRICA
SIERRA LEONE
LIBERIA
GOLD COAST
TOGO
NIGERIA
KAMERUN
FRENCH CONGO
Fernando Po

three hundred thousand rubles in a single action. To plan for the action, he spent the winter and spring of 1908 in Vilna. Not surprisingly, one of the Combat Organization members who joined him was Alexandra Szczerbińska, who arrived on February 14, 1908.[80]

Upon Pilsudski's return to Kraków, it became evident that the revolutionary decline in Russia had led to a loss of morale. "On the one hand, we sense everywhere a lack of confidence in the future of the Combat Organization," he wrote in May 1908. "On the other hand, when I think about the future, I start to calculate the number of people [we need] and it is hopeless. I feel now as if I am going from a wide road to a narrow path which then turns into a stump. And here, on this stump, the night has caught me by surprise."[81] The shift led Pilsudski to reconsider the future of the Combat Organization. Wishing for counsel with a trusted military advisor, he traveled to East Galicia to meet with Kazimierz Sosnkowski. Over tea at the American Café in Lwów, he expressed grave concern about the loss of faith in a brighter future. Pilsudski then declared that the history of the party's Combat Organization had come to an end.[82]

Sosnkowski responded with the suggestion that the time was ripe to form a new military organization, one that would represent Poland as a whole rather than a political party. In June 1908 several prominent figures, including Pilsudski, gathered in Sosnkowski's Lwów apartment. The result was the formation of the Union of Active Struggle (Związek Walki Czynnej) with Sosnkowski as commander. Historian Andrzej Chwalba has remarked that "there would never have been the Polish Legions without the creation in 1908 . . . of the clandestine Union of Active Struggle."[83] Soon after the gathering, Pilsudski crossed the border into imperial Russia en route to Vilna, where he stayed with family while coordinating the upcoming action.

AS HE APPROACHED THE AGE of forty at the end of 1907, Pilsudski had already declared his love not for his wife but for his mistress, Alexandra Szczerbińska. Maria had noticed the change. In a letter to her from Vilna, Pilsudski confessed to the affair. He expressed regret, asking Maria not to worry that "Miss Ola" (the pen name used to refer to Szczerbińska), was among the party comrades in Vilna. "I'm still tormented by the question of whether or not I did the right thing by speaking so openly to you," he wrote Maria in

March 1908. "I fear that I unnecessarily caused you many worries. If they are inevitable, it is better that they come later than sooner. If not, then they do not need to be added on to the distress I've already caused you." He ended the letter affectionately: "Write from time to time, my dear, so that I know something about how you're doing. Be healthy and content with happy thoughts."[84]

As the summer of 1908 set in, Pilsudski complained he was suffering from low morale. "My dear! I am still sunk in a state of apathy," he began in a letter to Maria in July or early August 1908, "and have surprised myself by even being able to pick up a pen and write." He appeared to feel that all his plans were on hold. "To the devil with them. Nothing, and I mean nothing, is progressing even one step."[85] The sense of despair was profoundly deepened that summer upon hearing tragic news from Kraków. On August 14, 1908, Pilsudski's nineteen-year-old stepdaughter, Wanda Juszkiewicz, died suddenly from inflammation of the gallbladder. Wanda's death plunged Maria into depression. Pilsudski had the difficult task of telling the bad news to Wanda's fiancé, his close comrade Walery Sławek, who was in Vilna as a Combat Organization member.

Yet a tiny light pierced the darkness. Maria, age forty-two, had been bedridden for days with symptoms—likely nausea and vomiting—that made her believe she was pregnant. She informed Pilsudski and asked him to come home. What she did not know is that he was days away from a huge expropriation action involving nineteen others. "Don't be mad at me for not coming home," Pilsudski wrote in September 1908. "God knows that I cannot. It would be a moral failure that I would not wish on anyone. I know and understand that it is a pregnancy, but I cannot come."[86]

Sources are vague about Maria's physical and psychological state during this time. Emotional and psychological fragility were inevitable in the wake of Wanda's death. But it was clearly more than that because Maria became ill and was hospitalized for unspecified reasons.[87] Wanda's death deepened the chasm that had already existed in the marriage. The combination of Wanda's death and Maria's illness led Pilsudski to avoid his grief-stricken Kraków home. At the end of 1908 Pilsudski asked for a divorce. "Maria replied," Alexandra later remarked, "that a woman such as she cannot be left behind."[88]

The request for a divorce in the same year as her daughter's death undoubtedly crushed Maria. She decided to send her thoughts on paper to her husband, in Vilna at the time. "I had decided not to write, thinking, 'to what end?'

Wanda Juszkiewicz, Pilsudski's
stepdaughter, age eighteen. Kraków,
ca. 1907.

After all, it takes ten days for letters to get to you and you aren't so eager to receive them anyway. I am not at all surprised as my letters aren't exactly pleasant. But you yourself understand that it cannot be any other way." Maria, despondent, alone, and defeated, continued:

> I am not a person devoid of feelings, anxieties, or even modest expecta-
> tions, especially because feelings that had once been aroused require at
> least some very minimal effort [to revive]. The sense of contentedness
> between us is no longer present. Promises on paper cannot satisfy even
> the most modest expectations on my part. For it's obvious that the feel-
> ings of someone else—for whom you say you do not have feelings—
> matter. Mine do not. That person . . . has undoubtedly had a more pleasant
> life than I whose past has consisted of unending breakdowns, anxiety,
> and traps of feelings. I cannot perceive this in any other way when I have
> to share you with someone else.
>   You have broken up with me for someone else without any grief or
> pangs of guilt on your part, or on hers.[89]

Maria pressed Pilsudski to return home and think things through before making a final decision. Her sense of despair leaps off the page: "In general, I cannot see any bright spots in my future. Things are getting worse with every passing year." Her depression and loss of hope were pronounced: "Previously, during major breakdowns, I was saved by the hope that maybe everything would finally work out. But even that hope has disappeared. What will happen next? I don't know."[90]

After Maria refused a divorce, Pilsudski and Alexandra decided to keep their relationship strictly private. "For almost the next ten years," Alexandra later remarked, "neither I nor Ziuk told our friends about us, figuring that Maria would eventually come around. But as the years passed by, and Pilsudski was getting old and wanted to have his own children, Maria still refused. Even after we had children, she would not give him a divorce, remaining married to him until the end of her life."[91] So an arrangement was made whereby Pilsudski continued to live with Maria in Kraków to keep up appearances. In 1909 he explained to Alexandra that at the present time there was no other option, assuring her that things would turn out for the better. "I feel that we are on the right path," he wrote Alexandra in early 1909, "that a lot of things have changed for the better to achieve a common understanding. The crisis, in my opinion, has passed and is advancing now to a quieter solution."[92]

CHAPTER 9

Building an Armed Force
for Independence

It is not despair, not immolation which guides me, but the desire
to conquer, to prepare victory.

—JOZEF PILSUDSKI (1908)

Since 1907 Pilsudski had been planning a large-scale raid on a government postal train, the largest expropriation action in the party's history. He was aware that the transport vehicle would be heavily guarded. With the possibility of fatalities on both sides, he composed a political last will and testament and sent it to Feliks Perl, one of his closest collaborators in the party, who agreed to use it as a basis for an obituary in the case of his demise. Written at age forty, Pilsudski's will serves as a window into how he perceived himself. "Of course, I don't want to dictate the estimate of my work and life—certainly not!" Pilsudski wrote to Perl. "I only beg you not to make of me 'a good officer' or 'a dreamer and sentimentalist'—that is, a man of self-sacrifice stretched upon the cross of humanity, or something of that sort. To a certain degree, I was that in the days of exalted and cloudy youth; now it is past, never to return."[1]

Pilsudski presented the attempt to undo the untenable situation of a partitioned homeland as his life's struggle. "It's not sentimentalism, not dreaming," he maintained, "it is simply being a man." For "without a fight, and even a fight with the gloves off, I am not even a babbler, but simply a beast submitting to stick and whip." The principal goal was to fight and prepare for victory. He continued, referring to the upcoming action:

My first idea, which I have never yet expounded, is the necessity in our circumstances of turning every party, and above all the socialists, into an organ of physical force. . . . I wanted to work out this idea in my actions during the last few years, and promised myself to achieve it or to die. I have already achieved a good deal in this direction, but too little to be able to rest on my laurels and occupy myself seriously with the immediate preparation for the fight, and now I am staking everything on one card. I have been called a noble socialist; I am a man about whom even his enemies do not publicly say foul things; a man, then, who has been of some little service in the general culture of the nation, and I wish to underline with my own person this bitter, this very bitter truth, that in a nation that does not know how to fight for itself, that withdraws every time someone strikes it in the face, men must even die in actions that are not lofty, beautiful, and great.[2]

Pilsudski's plan went into effect on September 26, 1908, when a group of nineteen fighters made their way to the railway station in Bezdany, fifteen miles north of Vilna. One of the four women participants was Alexandra Szczerbińska. This raid was be so significant that in 1933 historian Władysław Pobóg-Malinowski devoted an entire monograph to the event numbering 214 printed pages. When the government train pulled into the station in the dark of night, the fighters surrounded it. Armed guards responded with force and an exchange of gunfire ensued. Szczerbińska later recalled, "Pilsudski and Prystor burst into the mail wagon, dynamited the iron coffers and took possession of the banknotes. They stuffed them into mailbags and sacks, filling as many as they could before the sound of other trains approaching in the distance warned them that they had barely time to escape."[3] After forty-five minutes, the raid came to an end without any deaths or injuries on their side, but one local official was killed and five guards were wounded.

The fighters fled to a cottage in the forest that Szczerbińska had earlier rented as a safe house.[4] They all arrived in the early morning hours "after a long and perilous journey in the darkness through unfrequented tracks and by-roads of the forest."[5] After emptying the mailbags, they were pleasantly surprised when they counted 200,812 rubles—about $101,327 at the time— their highest yield to date.[6] On September 30, 1908, the *Times* of London reported that a gang of youths armed with revolvers and bombs "seized the small station of Bezdany, near Vilna, on Saturday night, killed a gendarme, bound and gagged the officials, and cut all the wires with a view to despoiling the mail train from Warsaw to St. Petersburg."[7] The Bezdany raid—the first one Pilsudski participated in directly—was but one of hundreds of raids that had been recently conducted: 678 in 1906, 469 in 1907, and 208 by the end of 1908.[8]

The morning after, the group separated into smaller units and went their separate ways. Pilsudski, Szczerbińska, and one other buried the mailbags of banknotes and silver in the forest near the cottage, making their way afterward to the local train station en route to Kiev. The station was full of police. "I could almost hear the beating of my heart when we walked into the station," Szczerbińska recalled, "but looking at Joseph Pilsudski, I saw that he was perfectly calm. There was not a shadow of emotion on his face as we passed through the barrier. All around us we heard people talking of Bezdany. The station was full of soldiers and police. . . . We fully expected to be stopped but fortunately no one took any notice of us, and we reached our destination without misadventure."[9]

After spending two months in Kiev, Szczerbińska returned to recover the buried loot, stopping on the way to visit family in her native city of Suwałki. With a helper, she transported the funds to Vilna. The money was then successfully smuggled across the Austro-Hungarian border to Kraków.[10] The Bezdany raid, which took nearly a year of preparation, was designed by Pilsudski to provide revenue to enable the new Union of Active Struggle (ZWC) to attract fighters from all walks of life, party members and nonmembers, socialists and nonsocialists alike.

After the Bezdany Raid

Pilsudski returned to Austrian Galicia in October 1908. He would not return to tsarist Russia until the outbreak of war in August 1914. One of the first party comrades in Kraków he met was Michał Sokolnicki. "[Pilsudski] was not in good health," Sokolnicki recalled. "He didn't look well, and I was struck by a deep gloom in his eyes. I also sensed in him new signs of hardness when he said, referring to the Combat Organization: 'As far as armed fighters are concerned—I have crossed them off.'"[11] Pilsudski himself made reference to the poor state of his health, writing to Alexandra

Szczerbińska that his doctor had recommended he leave the city for a period of two to three months for rest.[12]

Despite feeling under the weather, Pilsudski went about realizing his goal of forming a new military organization. In January 1909 he asked Jodko-Narkiewicz to come to Kraków for a gathering of top party leaders. "I want to touch on a few issues that are essential to me in order to determine where others stand," Pilsudski wrote. His proposal was to replace the Combat Organization with a new, nonpartisan union of fighters.[13] Present at the party gathering, held in Bolesław Jędrzejowski's apartment, was Jodko-Narkiewicz, Feliks Perl, Walery Sławek, Leon Wasilewski, Alexander Sulkiewicz, and Tytus Filipowicz. One of the recent developments weighing on everone's mind was the Austro-Hungarian annexation of Bosnia-Herzegovina in October 1908. All agreed that this brazen, provocative act would inflame tensions between Austria-Hungary and Russia—the traditional protector of Orthodox Serbs—for the foreseeable future. Although there was some resistance, Pilsudski received approval for his plan.[14]

In February, Pilsudski left with his wife, Maria, for the resort town of Abbazia, a Croatian coastal resort in Austria-Hungary alongside the Adriatic Sea dotted with villas. The Pilsudskis used the opportunity to stop in Vienna for social engagements. "At the moment," Pilsudski wrote from Vienna on February 21, 1909, "my health is much better than before. For two days now, I have been taking light walks which do me very well. It is only that I get tired very quickly and often have to take a rest." Five days later, Pilsudski sent a letter from Abbazia. The warm weather and fresh air were doing him good.[15]

The vacation on the Adriatic coast helped revive Pilsudski's health, and he felt upbeat upon his return to Kraków in the spring of 1909. One of the first things he did was to embark on a series of lectures with the theme "Our Revolutionary Tasks." The lectures reveal Pilsudski's new focus on the idea of building a national army. "It is understood that we must *fight* for the achievement of all our goals both political and social," he said in his first lecture. "And this is not only with words or with the dissemination of clandestine literature, but also with a gun in hand. We must stand up to the organized strength of the occupiers . . . with an armed force of the Polish masses. The revolution we are preparing is an armed, people's struggle against the army of a tsar who imposes his rule over us. Such a battle is our goal because only this kind of fight can result in victory." He continued: "But it is not enough to come to the conclusion that a military solution alone will bring about victory. . . . It is necessary to be aware of its character, to know what means our revolution will have at its disposal, to know the strengths and weaknesses of our enemy, as well as our own. Only then can we move forward with a plan for the revolution."[16]

In addition to building a national army, Pilsudski argued that a political representation had to be formed that could serve in the future as a provisional government. Such a body, composed of leaders of political parties advocating independence, would speak for society as a whole. But it would not gain real authority without an army and weapons. The task of the political body was "to form a revolutionary army and equip it with a sufficient amount of arms. Neither are easy to do, but war with the occupiers cannot be waged without them." Drawing on historical literature about modern warfare he had earlier so eagerly consumed, Pilsudski pointed to the example of the Second Boer War (1900–1902) between the British Empire and the Afrikaner (Dutch) colonists who had to acquire proper weaponry prior to the military engagement.[17]

In May 1909, meanwhile, Max Ronge, a career officer in the Austro-Hungarian Army in the directorate of military intelligence, reached out to Pilsudski. Ronge's objective was to gather military intelligence against Russia, and he directed Captain Józef Rybak to meet with Pilsudski. Walery Sławek accompanied Pilsudski when he went to Rybak's apartment in Kraków following his meeting with Ronge. At first they chatted about their backgrounds; when Rybak asked Pilsudski what he did for a living, Pilsudski replied that he was a journalist for the Kraków daily *Naprzód*.[18]

The two then got down to business, with Pilsudski agreeing to offer intelligence services on Russia in exchange for assistance in setting up a voluntary paramilitary force in Galicia that would fight alongside Austria-Hungary in the event of a military conflict with Russia. Rybak recalled that "when Pilsudski left my apartment, I thought through the idea of creating a Riflemen's Association. But not for long because I understood then that a legalized paramilitary organization could give us the same, if not greater, benefit as did the Union of Active Struggle. . . . I decided to legalize the Riflemen's Association for Russian citizens in Kraków. . . . I also convinced the local military commander to get weapons and instructors for the riflemen organization."[19] That proposal, after subsequent meetings with Pilsudski, extended to other areas of Galicia. "Beginning at this time," Rybak stated, "close ties were established between us."[20] The establishment of a close working relationship with a representative of the Austrian military was for Pilsudski a kind of quiet diplomatic victory. As Małgorzata Wiśniewska described the relationship, Pilsudski "jumped at the chance to realize his vision of creating a framework for . . . a national army, a plan only he had devised." Another historian noted, "Pilsudski entered the meeting [discussing] what was most important: building a Polish armed force that would be an important asset in a future campaign for an independent Poland."[21]

In the summer of 1909, Pilsudski traveled to Lwów to attend the first meeting of the ZWC's executive council. The council drafted a declaration of principles, and addresses were presented. Given that the ZWC had a mere 220 members, recruitment was high on the agenda.[22] In Vienna, meanwhile, party leaders met for the Second Party Congress of the PPS Revolutionary Faction. The new three-member central committee was chosen, consisting of Pilsudski, Jodko-Narkiewicz, and Filipowicz. The congress passed a resolution on the Bosnian crisis, recognizing that the conflict quite possibly could lead to war. The party, it concluded, had to prepare now for that likely outcome.[23]

THE PERIOD BEFORE WORLD WAR I was one of rising productivity for Pilsudski. Not only did he posses an innate compulsion to write, he had a financial incentive as well, for the bulk of his income derived from his writings. "These were lean times," Alexandra Pilsudska commented, "when [Pilsudski] lived only on the proceeds of his journalism and contributed articles to the Kraków newspapers, whose editors were willing enough to publish them since they attacked the Russian system and there was no love lost between Austria and Russia."[24] The frenzy of writing, combined with frequent public speaking appearances for which he had to prepare, was reflected in his home environment. In a letter from September 1909, Pilsudski noted the clutter on his desk. "The table is littered with maps and books and scraps of paper, some of it covered with writing; the rest blank. In fact it is in its usual perfect order. And if you must know it, you who are the very soul of order, I very much like this disorder of my table." The disorder was arranged in such a way that he could always find what he needed. For Pilsudski, neatness and an orderly desk worked in the opposite way. "Perhaps this disorder with which I am surrounded is an outward sign of the disorder within my own mind.

For instance, this passion of mine for working in fragments, without any method in what I do, concentrating on the things which interest me heart and soul."[25]

With the need for a steady income, Pilsudski was often juggling several writing projects simultaneously. "So you see how overwhelmed with work I am," he wrote to Alexandra in 1909, "work that is not yet finished and work which is only just begun. And then you must add to it all the work which I must undertake for the organization and lectures to the Riflemen after the holidays. You can imagine that my time is fully occupied."[26]

Pilsudski also delegated publication projects to trusted comrades, often those with advanced university degrees. In 1909, for example, he asked Michał Sokolnicki, a recent PhD from the University of Berne, to write a propaganda brochure on the necessity of building a Polish Army. Sokolnicki dutifully began work on the manuscript, frequently meeting Pilsudski at his new apartment on 31 Szlak Street in Kraków in the first half of 1910. Pilsudski stressed that military matters were to be discussed without regard to political parties, and that a Polish governing body had to be at the helm of such an armed force.[27]

Over cups of strong tea, Pilsudski began speaking openly about his future plans in a way he had never done before. "I got the impression at that time," Sokolnicki recalled, "that as he was devising plans increasingly of a military nature, Pilsudski's relations with the party were strained—that socialism was becoming a burden." Sokolnicki thus had the impression that Pilsudski was increasingly alone in his thoughts. "He was also for the most part gloomy, taciturn, and seemed tormented by many things around him. He cheered up with a lighter mood only when he was in a small circle of his close collaborators. Otherwise, during our conversations about the brochure at the end of 1909 . . . I came away with the impression of an immense sadness . . . not only over the loss of Poland's sovereignty but also over his country's collective soul. That is the background to my book, *Sprawa Armii Polskiej* (The Question of a Polish Army), which I wrote during the first months of 1910."[28] When Sokolnicki's book appeared in print later that year, he presented Pilsudski a copy, signing it, "To Pilsudski: the First Soldier of the new Poland."[29]

The mood swings Sokolnicki noted were likely related to bouts of fever and insomnia Pilsudski suffered at the time. "Today," Pilsudski wrote Alexandra on May 1, 1910, "I still have a fever. I didn't sleep all night. I feel beaten down and tired, reluctant to do anything, even to read military books. Pessimistic thoughts are running through my mind." He was "losing hope more and more."[30] He could only express hope in Alexandra's decision to apply for entry to the university. "I am pleased that you applied to study at the university. That was a good thing to do." Pilsudski became more positive when he began to feel better. "I don't get upset and irritated," he wrote later to Alexandra, "on account of recovery and the resultant return to poise and calm."[31]

The Riflemen's Association

The most important development in the history of the ZWC is the creation in 1910 of legal paramilitary organizations. By this time Pilsudski had become commander of the ZWC, with Sosnkowski named chief of staff. In its first two years the illegal but tolerated ZWC had a very modest following—64 members in November 1908, increasing to 219 by 1910.[32] A spike in membership began in the spring of 1910 with the formation of the Riflemen's Association (*Związek Strzelecki*) in Lwów, a legal paramilitary organization under the command of thirty-year-old Władysław Sikorski, a graduate of the school of engineering at Lwów Technical University. The Austro-Hungarian government formally recognized the Riflemen's Association on April 23, 1910, as well as its parallel organization in Kraków, Riflemen (*Strzelec*), on December 1, 1910.[33]

As legal organizations, the Riflemen and the Riflemen's Association trained in the open. "One of my most vivid memories of my husband," Alexandra recalled, "is of his holding the first parade of his Riflemen outside the House of Parliament in Lwów. He stood on the steps leading up to the building to take the salute as they marched past him, several hundreds of them." She described the officers' uniform—the simple blue tunic and trousers later adopted by the Polish Legions in World War I. "In later years when Poland was free," she continued, "I saw many parades of Polish troops, but I always remember that first march and the pride and joy in the eyes of Joseph Pilsudski as he watched it."[34]

With the establishment of the Riflemen organizations, Pilsudski focused more heavily on military matters. At a party council in Kraków in July 1910, he maintained that the new paramilitary organizations "today, above all, constitute a revolutionary army. Their wider task—preparation for battle." Analyzing the failure of the 1905 revolution, Pilsudski maintained that the problem was not the lack of popular support. "To ensure revolutionary victory," he said, "it is necessary that those working inside [the Russian sector] spread the idea of militancy [*bojowość*]."[35]

The rise of the Riflemen movement inspired Pilsudski to present a series of lectures on military history. He gave the first, "A History of the Combat Organization of the PPS," in July 1910 in Kraków and the second, on the 1863 Polish uprising, in November in Lwów. These were followed by lectures on military formations in imperial Russia's Polish provinces as well as on reforms in the Russian Army. In addition, in the fall of 1910 Pilsudski submitted an autobiographical essay on the 1887 prison rebellion in Irkutsk he participated in during his Siberian exile.[36]

Having just turned forty-three in December 1910, Pilsudski began the year 1911 by traveling with his wife to the Italian fishing village of Nervi south of Genoa. Letters from Nervi reveal a calm, relaxed disposition.[37] After their return to Kraków in the spring, Pilsudski visited Lwów, where he give a lecture to the Riflemen's Association on May 13. The unofficial reason for the side trip was to see Alexandra, who had been living in Lwów since she left Russia. Discussing historical changes in warfare, he noted that in ancient times, battles lasted for a period of hours. By the time of the Napoleonic Wars, however, battles lasted for an entire day, from morning until night. By the turn of the century, warefare had dramatically changed, as evidenced by the Boer and the Russo-Japanese wars. Present-day wars, he continued, lasted not days, but weeks at a time. "In the extended battles of today," Pilsudski said, "psychological symptoms have a huge significance." He concluded that "the scale of victory is determined in the heart, the will, the character and ability of man to endure. In a crisis, technical prowess gives way to character."[38]

IN THE MANY PUBLIC LECTURES Pilsudski gave during this period, his main theme was the rebellion of peoples subjected to foreign rule. On February 2, 1912, he spoke to university students in Kraków on the causes and consequences of the 1905 revolution. Sharply critical of the Young faction of the PPS that had taken over party leadership inside Russia, Pilsudski attributed the failure of the revolution to the lack of decisive action. What did the party do after the Japanese victory over Russia? "We trembled, afraid to mobilize in the Kingdom [of Poland], afraid to risk our lives. We did nothing to prepare for action." He concluded, "We did not pass the test. You, youth, saw the first light of daybreak with your own eyes. You believe in Dawn. Perhaps you will pass this exam for us. Perhaps your generation will not be afraid to act."[39]

Pilsudski argued that the 1905 revolution constituted a war over the type of rule in Rusia. The outcome rested on the interplay of moral and technical factors. Although the revolutionaries had the moral advantage, the government had the technical advantage—the army, police, and a countrywide administration. But in the long run, Pilsudski maintained, moral factors would lead to success. Following the Duma elections of 1906–1907, the revolution failed due to an inability to challenge government forces. After the 1905 revolution, Pilsudski continued, everything became crystal clear: there could be no victory without recourse to meaningful force, to an effective armed response. Without military backing, the revolutionary ideal would ring hollow.[40]

The lecture series with the most long-term impact was on the 1863 Polish uprising, which Pilsudski had been passionately interested in since age fifteen. "I have a plan," he wrote Alexandra in January 1912, "but I need to finish gathering materials, facts, figures, names, and dates, as well as citations, in order to give a somewhat academic lecture on 1863. It is taking a huge amount of time as I have a lot of this already in my head but in a terribly unorganized and unsystematic way."[41] While excited to engage in the research and writing, he was certainly not brimming with confidence about the upcoming public appearances, feeling he lacked academic credentials. "I have no practice in it, nor is it in my nature to use any regular method," he remarked on May 7, 1912, six days before the lecture series began. In a revealing aside, Pilsudski wrote that when he had so many things going on at once—lectures, publication projects, party work—he often had to relax for a few days to calm his nerves before he was able to resume writing.[42]

Between March 13 and May 17, 1912, Pilsudski gave ten lectures on the 1863 Polish uprising at the School of Social and Political Science in Kraków.[43] The talks amounted to a historical reckoning with the legacy of 1863 on the occasion of the upcoming fiftieth anniversary of the uprising. Far from providing a hagiographic, lachrymose conception of history filled with national martyrs and heros, Pilsudski intended the lectures to be a practical guide for the future, and a warning for the present. For Pilsudski, the purpose of studying history was to identify mistakes in the past so as not to repeat them. Consequently, the historical summary of 1863 was meant to be a detached

examination. Having seemingly read everything available on the topic, Pilsudski began his first lecture with a critical examination of the existing published and unpublished sources, including official records and memoir literature. "Anyone working on the history of 1863," he said to the audience, "is
struck by the acute lack of materials, and even more so with regard to the
military side of this history."[44]

The remaining lectures focused on the military history of the uprising, examining the causes of its demise. Pilsudski concluded that the uprising had
been called for prematurely: from a military standpoint, a national, armed
uprising should be ordered only under circumstances in which victory was
possible. A premature uprising did not serve the national interest. "An army
that is in the process of being organized is not fit for battle," Pilsudski remarked. "The outbreak of the [1863 uprising] was a surprise not only to the
Russian government but also to the Polish people. The entire nation cannot
pass from a state of subjugation to a state of open combat in one moment.
There has to be a period of psychological preparation, a period for building
faith and hope, and a period of time to create an organizational framework
[for war against the enemy]."[45]

In his tenth and final lecture, on May 17, 1912, Pilsudski discussed the
mental and intellectual toll that preparing the lectures had taken on him.
"I consoled myself," he said, "with the thought that you gentlemen would want
to understand my intentions, that you would want to understand how sin-
cerely I wish to build a bridge between the current generation and the generation of 1863. If I had before me the people of those days, I believe they would
tell me what I have often said to myself: 'We did not die in vain and from our
death may flow lessons for you.'"[46] Patrice Dabrowski points out that Pilsudski
identified two elements of the insurrectionary movement that facilitated the
uprising: the officers' training schools and the clandestine government that
provided armed units with a political representation.[47]

Pilsudski became aware that the Russians had complained to the Austrian
authorities about the activities of his paramilitary organizations and officer
training schools. On March 9, 1912, the Russian chargé d'affaires in Vienna
submitted a note to the Austrian minister of foreign affairs, Count Leopold
Berchtold, maintaining that Walery Sławek was teaching the Riflemen how
to make and use explosives for the purposes of sabotage and expropriation
actions inside Russia. Sławek and Pilsudski, the Russian official claimed, were

teaching officers in Kraków how to conduct anti-Russian terrorist attacks. The Austrian government was advised to dissolve the Union of Active Struggle and its Riflemen associations. The Austrians replied on July 31, 1912, that although the ZWC and the Riflemen associations were under surveillance, "Jozef Pilsudski . . . is not viewed unfavorably by the [Austrian] authorities."[48] To the chagrin of the Russian representatives in Vienna, the Riflemen associations continued to gain popular support. In June 1912 Pilsudski was named chief commander and Sosnkowski his chief of staff.[49]

Meanwhile, Pilsudski attended a party council in Kraków at which Witold Jodko-Narkiewicz reported on rising tensions between Russia and Austria-Hungary. The possibility of war between these two great powers over the Balkans looked increasingly likely.[50] The very notion of war between two countries that over a century ago had taken part in the partition of Poland led Pilsudski to draw up a plan for an armed uprising in the Kingdom of Poland in the event of such a conflict. The report, written in Zakopane for the Austro-Hungarian army, called on all Polish revolutionary organizations to unite under the command of the ZWC—that is, under Pilsudski's control. The uprising would be planned in close cooperation with Józef Rybak, the Kraków-based officer in the Austro-Hungarian Army's general staff.[51]

A keen observer of international affairs who always had one eye on the big picture, Pilsudski took concrete steps to form the nucleus of a national armed force by calling a meeting of all Polish pro-independence parties. Held in Zakopane on August 25–26, 1912, the conference consisted of leaders of the PPS Revolutionary Faction, the PPSD, the Polish Progressive Party (*Polska Stronnictwa Postępowego*), and the Polish Peasant Party (*Polskei Stronnictwo Ludowe*), among others. In total, thirty-three representatives attended, including Pilsudski, Jodko-Narkiewicz, Aleksander Sulkiewicz, Ksawery Prauss, Władysław Sikorski, and Ignacy Daszyński.[52] Pilsudski opened the conference with a proposal for the creation of a Polish Military Treasury to secure financial backing.

Pilsudski expressed grave concern about Poles' general attitudes toward the military idea, which he characterized as "reluctance, distrust, and even mockery." He empathized with those who did not want to repeat the failures of the 1863 uprising. But few, in his view, understood why the uprising had ended in defeat. "Not only has the military idea collapsed in Poland,"

Pilsudski said in a moment of profound pessimism, "but even the idea of the independence of Poland has disappeared from the horizons of the Polish spirit. The nation has fallen ill and has given up."[53]

At the same time, Pilsudski acknowledged the opposite trend in Galicia, with the activities of the ZWC and the Riflemen's associations. But the military organizations had low membership and the annual budget—which he estimated at 20,000 Austrian kroner [about $4,000 in 1912]—was pitifully small. "If we add to these deficits," Pilsudski commented, "the lack of supplies, the lack of implements, and the lack of the ability to conduct training exercises in the Polish provinces of Imperial Russia, where we also lack military schools, then we arrive at quite pessimistic conclusions."[54] One conference participant, Władysław Studnicki, recounted a passage of Pilsudski's that never made it into the transcript of the speech. "'Poles want independence," Studnicki quoted Pilsudski as saying, "but they hope it will cost only two cents of their spending money."[55]

Crisis in the Balkans

Soon after Pilsudski shared his pessimistic views about resignation and passivity in Polish society, war broke out in the Balkans. On October 18, 1912, Serbia, Bulgaria, Greece, and Montenegro jointly declared war on the Ottoman Empire, inaugurating the so-called First Balkan War. With Russia supporting the Balkan states and Austria-Hungary supporting the Ottoman Empire, the local conflict alarmed the capitals of Europe. On October 31, 1912, meanwhile, Pilsudski spoke in Vienna at a conference of German and Austrian social democrats. The Balkan war was on everyone's mind. "I address you at a time," Pilsudski said, "when a clap of thunder now reverberates throughout Europe. Your country, as well as ours, is threatened by this horrible war. In Poland today, which is spent by revolutionary struggle, it is difficult to endure the misery of war. We are not free of fear when we think about the dangers that await us. But nothing will deter us from fulfilling our duty. With your help, we will extend freedom to our lands."[56]

The Balkan war, which increased the likelihood of an Austria–Russia armed conflict, led Pilsudski to call into being a political counterpart to the paramilitary organizations. On November 10, 1912, leaders of seven pro-independence Polish parties formed a collective representative body, announcing the formation of the Provisional Commission of Confederated Independence Parties (Komisja Tymczasowa Skonfederowanych Stronnictw Niepodległościowych, KTSSN). On December 1, 1912, Piłsudski was named Military Commander (*Komendant Sił Wojskowy*). The new organization was established "with the aim of enabling the energetic joint action of Polish parties actively striving to regain independence, in the necessity of leading an armed struggle against the Russian state."[57]

As tensions rose in the Balkans, Piłsudski was frequently called upon for public comment. In November 1912, at the Society to Commemorate the Anniversary of the November Uprising—the Polish insurrection of 1830—he spoke on the topic of mass mobilization for armed revolt, past and present. Here, he declared that in his view the Riflemen associations constituted the nucleus a national army. A daily newspaper in Kraków reported that the speaker presented the subject with "an uncommon strength of conviction and directness of expression."[58]

With the arrival of the year 1913, Piłsudski stressed the importance of publicly marking the fiftieth anniversary of the 1863 January Uprising. On January 22 Piłsudski and Sosnkowski met with their Riflemen in uniform at the Lychakiv Cemetery in Lwów, where they laid a wreath on a hill in the cemetery, reserved for veterans, known as the 1863 January Rebels' Hill. Particularly significant for Piłsudski was the tombstone of Bronisław Szwarce, his old friend from Siberian exile whose funeral he had attended in 1904. From the cemetery, Piłsudski and Sosnkowski led a march of uniformed Riflemen through the city of Lwów. One of the men in uniform that day commented, "Taking part in those exercises under the command of Mieczyslaw [Jozef Pilsudski] to commemorate the 50th anniversary of the January Uprising on January 22, 1913, made a lasting impression on me."[59]

In the leadup to World War I, paramilitary associations in Galicia were expanding. In addition to the Riflemen and the Riflemen's Association under the command of the ZWC, this period saw the formation of the Polish Rifle Squads (*Polskie Drużyna Strzeleckie*), established in 1911 by former members of the National Democratic Party in the Kingdom of Poland who had broken ranks with their party by demanding the separation of Poland from Russia. After the failure of the Russian Revolution of 1905, this splinter group had

Pilsudski and Kazimierz Sosnkowski leading an officers' training school in
Zakopane, August 1913.

moved to Galicia. In February 1913, Pilsudski—as chief commander of the
Riflemen and military commander of the Provisional Commission—ordered
all three paramilitary organizations to meet for joint military exercises.[60]

During Pilsudski's stay in Lwów, he was interviewed in his apartment by
a Polish journalist who was also an activist in the National Democratic Party
in Vilna. The journalist described Pilsudski's living space as a modest,
student-like apartment with maps and studies on military matters spread all
about. "Middle-aged with an energetic expression on his face," the journalist
wrote, "he comes off as sincere, as reasoning . . . , and knows how to keep
up the appearance of being entirely matter-of-fact." When asked about his
study of military history, Pilsudski revealed an extraordinary level of self-
assuredness. "I have studied a few wars. I already know the Boer War and
the Russo-Japanese War in such detail that certainly there cannot be more
than a handful of people with similar knowledge."[61] Pilsudski noted that he
had never been a soldier, had never been in combat, and never received any

formal military training, but there were advantages to such a background. "I don't have prejudices. I see many things clearer," he said, evidently meaning that the lack of formal military training was an asset.

The journalist engaged Pilsudski in a discussion about the newly formed Provisional Commission of Confederated Independence Parties, noting that some were of the opinion that the Provisional Commission was a tool in the hands of the Austrians. Pilsudski replied that the new political body and paramilitary organizations were fully independent, and at the time were training hundreds of officers.[62] Walery Sławek, who was present at the interview, recalled something Pilsudski said that was cut from the published version for political reasons. Asked about the likelihood of a Europe-wide war, Pilsudski reportedly replied, "It seems to me that the Germans, with their technical advantage, will defeat Russia. The wealth and material resources of England and France, however, will prevail over German forces. This would be the best outcome for us, but it is difficult to predict the results of war."[63]

In May 1913 the Provisional Commission met in Kraków to coordinate strategy. Attended by, among others, Pilsudski, Daszyński, Sikorski, Jodko-Narkiewicz, and Sławek, the commission emphasized that its existence was as important in peacetime as it would be in a time of war. In their effort to prepare for eventual conflict, the commission called on all paramilitary organizations to unite under a single body.[64] As an intermediary stage, a Military Department was formed. "We see in the paramilitary Polish Rifle Squads a friendly and fraternal organization," the Central Council of the Riflemen's Association stated in June 1913. "The difference that exists between us can by no measure justify the separate existence of these organizations."[65] The Polish Rifle Squads nonetheless turned down the offer and retained their independence.

Pilsudski continued to expand the Riflemen's Association. In August 1913 he ran an officers' training school in Zakopane for more than two hundred young men. In addition, he played an important role in fundraising, including reaching out to Polish Americans for donations. The Polish Military Treasury, which included not only Pilsudski but also such figures as Walery Sławek and Leon Wasilewski, collected more funds from Polish Americans than from any other source.[66]

The summer of 1913 was also a time when Pilsudski spoke publicly about international affairs. After the conclusion of the First Balkan War on May 30,

1913, Pilsudski referred to the Balkans in an analysis of Polish resistance against imperial rule. He spoke in June 1913 about Galicia as the most politically active center of Polish society. After 1907, he noted, the politically active Polish elements in Russia either were behind bars or had emigrated. Pilsudski maintained that a single, unified paramilitary organization under one commander was sorely needed: "There is nothing more fatal in an army than collective leadership."[67]

Pilsudski's sense of urgency about the need to unify paramilitary organizations was prescient. On June 29, 1913, Bulgaria attacked Greece and Serbia over territorial disputes. The entry of Romanian, Turkish, and Montenegrin troops against Bulgaria inaugurated the Second Balkan War. Before the month-long conflict ended in Bulgaria's defeat on July 31, 1913, the Provisional Commission met in Kraków on July 21. The gathering included Pilsudski, Daszyński, Sikorski, Jodko-Narkiewicz, and Sławek, as well as leaders of the other five parties.[68] The result was a resolution stating that the Provisional Commission "is the first and only all-Polish governing body since the fall of the 1863 January Uprising." The heightened state of tension in Europe, it continued, "has awakened the irredentist aspirations of our nation. We would like to maintain uniform leadership over the whole of our military and civilian work aimed at rebuilding Poland."[69]

In the waning months of 1913 Pilsudski issued several orders as chief commander of the Riflemen's Association. "Begun five years ago in the Austrian partition [of Poland]," an order stated, "the military movement is today one of the most significant factors in Polish life. Among the latest turning points, when the fear of a European war on our land hangs over us, the military work we are doing is a bulwark against despair and provides hope for our countrymen."[70]

Pilsudski also issued an order to the Peasant Party in Galicia, one of the seven political parties in the Commission of Confederated Independence Parties (KSSN), which had removed "Provisional" from its title in November 1913. "The military banner should be held to the highest standard," Pilsudski wrote, "as a rallying point for the gallant, as a symbol of exertion, bravery and sacrifice, stimulated by an excitement for the finest efforts of a solder in battle."[71] He continued to call for the paramilitary organizations to merge into a single whole, going so far as to pass a resolution to this effect at a KSSN gathering in December 1913. In his deliberation, Pilsudski emphasized that even though members of the PPS headed the ZWC and the Riflemen's Association, both organizations were nonpartisan bodies.[72]

Anniversary of the 1863 Uprising

Pilsudski decided to mark the fiftieth anniversary of the 1863 uprising not only with commemorations but also with a major publication. Written over the course of three months, the study described the day of January 22, 1863, and appeared in print in December 1913 under Pilsudski's real name. The work was a testament to his belief in using the recent past as a guide for the present, as well as the importance of historical knowledge for mobilizing the masses. There is no doubt that the assistance of Michał Sokolnicki, who acted as Pilsudski's research assistant, allowed him to complete the manuscript in a timely fashion.[73]

Until 1913 the subject of the 1863 uprising had been taboo in certain Polish conservative circles. The rejection of the insurrectionary tradition had been widespread in Galicia, especially among the so-called Kraków conservatives who had benefited from Galician autonomy since the late 1860s. Changing attitudes in Galicia began with the rise of the paramilitary organizations in 1910, which led to a revival of interest in Poland's military past. "The rise of Polish paramilitary organizations at this time," Patrice Dabrowski noted, "is related to an early but significant impulse to celebrate the fiftieth anniversary of the January Insurrection. . . . While not as broadly public as commemorative parades, Pilsudski's [1912] lectures in a way inaugurated the 1913 anniversary year." Marking the fiftieth anniversary of the 1863 uprising thus represented a "sea change" in Galicia.[74] As the year 1913 ended, one of Pilsudski's first acts was to issue an order to the paramilitary organizations. On January 22, 1914, formal drills were to take place in public to commemorate the anniversary of the 1863 uprising.[75]

That the paramilitary movement was growing was evidenced by the formation of Riflemen's associations in France, Belgium, and Switzerland. In February 1914 Pilsudski went abroad to conduct inspections. His first stop was Switzerland, where he inspected the Riflemen Association in Geneva.[76] One member of the Swiss branch, Jerzy Śmigielski, recalled the excitement around Pilsudski's visit on February 13, 1914: "I assumed he must have been tall and broad-shouldered. But the gentleman who appeared was of average height, slightly bent over, with a black mustache and a pointed beard." Following a meeting with each member of Geneva's Riflemen Association, Pilsudski gave a public lecture on the 1863 uprising. Śmigielski described a large, packed venue and a lively atmosphere in which there were more people than seats available. "We were standing in the vestibule," he recalled, "and were proud that our Commander was received with such signs of respect." Śmigielski noted a moving scene at the end of the lecture when a veteran of the 1863 insurrection went up to Pilsudski "and gave him a long, hearty handshake to express his gratitude. I knew then," Śmigielski remarked, "that if this man called upon me for any reason, I would follow him always and everywhere."[77]

Pilsudski left Geneva that evening for France. In Paris he gave a speech at the Geographical Society on February 21, 1914, titled "The Polish Riflemen's Movement." Among those present was an agent of the Russian secret police. According to the agent's report, Pilsudski drew a large, enthusiastic crowd.[78] "The year 1863," Pilsudski began, "was a turning point in our history, a profound change in the mindset of the Polish people. Until that moment, the inhabitants of our partitioned country had passed on to the next generation a faith in the tradition of the armed movement as the means to regain our lost independence. But the uprising, drowned in a stream of blood, opened a new era marked by caution and reason." After the collapse of the uprising, "the idea of independence smoldered under ashes." But a revival of the independence movement was being led by the recently formed paramilitary organizations. Today, Pilsudski told the audience, the center of the Polish independence movement resided in Galicia.[79]

Another person present at Pilsudski's talk in Paris, the Russian exile Viktor Chernov, later claimed that the published version of the talk was incomplete. "With conviction," Chernov recalled, "Piłsudski predicted that an Austro-Russian war would break out in the near future over the Balkans. He did not have any doubt that Germany supports, and will stand behind, Austria-Hungary. He then expressed the belief that France will not have the luxury of remaining a passive witness to the conflict: the entry of Germany on the side of Austria will make it necessary for France—by virtue of the existing agreement—to intervene on the side of Russia. Finally, Piłsudski maintained that England will not be able to leave France to the mercy of fate. And if the combined forces of England and France are inadequate, sooner or later America will be drawn into the war on their side." This extraordinary insight, practically predicting the entire course of the coming war, was the outcome of a powerful native intellect, analytic reasoning skills, and the ability to ascertain the state of military readiness and military capabilities.[80]

On the eve of World War I, a former leader of the 1863 uprising passed away. On June 26, 1914, Pilsudski attended the funeral in Lwów of eight-two-year-old Józef K. Janowski, the former secretary of state of the National Government. Before family members of the heroic figure, Pilsudski gave an impassioned eulogy about the passing generation of fighters for freedom.[81]

TWO DAYS AFTER THE EULOGY in Lwów, the violent act of a nineteen-year-old Serbian nationalist changed the world forever. On June 28, 1914, Gavril Pincip assassinated the heir to the Austro-Hungarian throne, Archduke Franz Ferdinand, and his wife in Sarajevo. One of the most consequential assassinations in world history, this dramatic act of political violence threw Europe into disarray. Austria threatened war against Serbia, issuing an ultimatum it knew the small Balkan country could not accept. In the month that followed, Russia promised assistance to Serbia in the event of Austrian aggression. Germany, in turn, vowed to intervene on Austria-Hungary's behalf in the event of Russia's involvement. These three great powers knew that war between them would force France and Great Britain to intervene due to the alliance system then in place. Austria-Hungary, Russia, and Germany nonetheless continued on the path to war at an alarming pace. The assassination unleashed forces so strong that no leaders were able or willing to transcend the existing alliances to advocate for peace.

In Kraków, meanwhile, Pilsudski ordered the Riflemen associations to be battle ready. The Riflemen had grown to 7,239 fighters; the Polish Rifle Squads had an estimated four thousand members.[82] Since 1910 the Russian ambassador in Vienna had registered repeated complaints about the activities of Polish paramilitary organizations, with specific reference to Pilsudski. "At present," the Russian interior minister wrote in 1913, "the political center of the Polish question lies not in the Kingdom [of Poland] but in Galicia, where everything is boiling: there, riflemen divisions are being organized half-openly and openly under the leadership of Jozef Pilsudski, whom we foolhardily allowed to escape from prison."[83]

On the eve of World War I, Pilsudski had already carved out a place in his country's history. As chief commander of the Riflemen associations, as a member of the Polish Military Treasury, as military commander of the Commission of Confederated Independence Parties, and as a member of the central committee of the PPS Revolutionary Faction, Pilsudski's legend as a devoted son of the nation was already solidified. But with an uncertain future, and with several possible outcomes of a European-wide war, he remained profoundly apprehensive.

One of his collaborators at the time described Pilsudski as intensely engaged and often turned inward. Michał Sokolnicki recalled Pilsudski dividing his time between the Riflemen associations in the daytime, conferences in the evenings, and long conversations with close comrades in the late hours of the night. One had the sense, Sokolnicki remarked, that Pilsudski felt the weight of a nation on his shoulders. Sokolnicki recalled visiting the Pilsudskis in Kraków one spring night in 1914. A somber Pilsudski appeared "gloomy, entirely quiet, and preoccupied with heavy thoughts, with a worried look on his forehead, and with a kind of aversion for anyone who disturbed him with unnecessary chatter."[84]

Indeed, the first half of 1914 was a critical period in Pilsudski's life. He was now forty-six years old, and his views had gradually shifted in the preceding decade, beginning with his 1904 trip to Tokyo. Upon his return from Japan, comrades observed a new preoccupation. Conversations, one close friend noted, repeatedly returned to military topics.[85] The effect of his international travels—across the Atlantic, the North American continent, and the Pacific Ocean to Japan, and back again—was swift. In October 1904, one month after his return, he called for the creation of a Combat Organization. In November 1904 he ordered an armed action in Warsaw against the Russian gendarmerie. The international and Polish press reported on the event in Warsaw's Grzybowski Square, characterizing it as the first armed Polish action since 1863.[86]

The armed demonstration in Warsaw represented Pilsudski's emerging belief that routing Russian forces from Polish lands was to be achieved not by insurrection but as the result of war with a neighboring great power. The new emphasis on a military solution was plainly clear in Pilsudski's attitude toward the 1905 Russian Revolution. In February 1905, with the largest strike movement in Russian history then taking place, Pilsudski boarded a train from

Kraków to Zakopane for a party conference. Joining him was the young Michał Sokolnicki, who began speaking about the dramatic events in Russia. Pilsudski listened, said nothing, and then abruptly changed the topic. For the remainder of the train ride, Pilsudski spoke about one thing and one thing only: his new Combat Organization as the nucleus of a future national army.[87]

Between the 1905 Russian Revolution and the outbreak of war in 1914, Pilsudski put much of his energy into developing and training a Polish armed force for eventual combat with Russia. A stone's throw from the Russian border in Austrian Galicia, he cofounded the Union of Active Struggle in 1908, replacing it two years later with the Riflemen associations based in Kraków and Lwów. Pilsudski also established formal ties with the Austro-Hungarian Army. At the same time, he read voraciously to prepare publications and a series of high-profile lectures in the years 1910–1914, most notably the widely attended ten-lecture series in Kraków in 1912 on the coming fiftieth anniversary of the 1863 uprising.[88]

Not long after completing his lecture series in Kraków, the Second Balkan War broke out in June 1913. The bloody fratricidal conflict led Pilsudski, as well as many other observers, to the conviction that war between imperial Russia and Austria-Hungary was inevitable. His four-part article on the Balkan Wars published in the first half of 1914 provides a window into his thinking. Pilsudski argued that war between Russia and Austria-Hungary would serve as a lightning rod for the reawakening of the Polish cause.[89] The possibility of restoring sovereignty and dignity to Poland had never been more present.

CHAPTER 10

The Polish Legions and the Beginnings of World War I

Today, all are of the opinion that, at the very least, Pilsudski has
the makings of a historical figure. Sharing the fate of the Legions,
he is their personification, their symbol.

—RUDOLF STARZEWSKI, DIARY ENTRY OF DECEMBER 24, 1914

For more than a century, the goal of restoring statehood remained a singular dream of many Poles. The impulse to right the historic injustice of Poland's dismemberment became a common motif in nineteenth-century Polish art, literature, and even music.[1] Collective efforts to oust the occupiers through armed insurrections, from the Kościuszko Uprising of 1794 to the January Insurrection of 1863, had ended in resounding defeat. While the period of armed revolts gave way to an epoch of realism in Polish politics, focused on economic, social, and educational advancements on the Polish lands, the perennial Polish Question remained a thorn in the side of European statesmen. In 1862 British statesman Lord Acton commented that Poland's disappearance at the close of the eighteenth century "was an act of wanton violence, committed in open defiance not only of popular feeling but of public law. . . . This famous measure, the most revolutionary act of the old absolutism, awakened the theory of nationality in Europe, converted a dormant right into an aspiration, and a sentiment into a political claim."[2]

A half century after Lord Acton's public comment that the destruction of Poland was a moral stain on the conscience of Europe, Jozef Pilsudski had become the leading figure in the revival of the independence camp in Polish political life. A voracious reader of military history, Pilsudski concluded that the nineteenth-century model of armed insurrection was—in 1914—a recipe for disaster. The struggle for the separation of Polish lands had to be waged, he argued, in collaboration with Germany and Austria-Hungary at war with Russia. As a resident of Austrian Galicia for the previous twelve years, Pilsudski decided to form an alliance with Austria-Hungary that he hoped would eventually bring about the separation of Polish lands from Russia in the event of war between the partitioning powers. For Pilsudski, collaboration with Austria-Hungary was a purely tactical move, one he would be willing to abandon the moment he believed Polish interests were being compromised.

The opportunity for Pilsudski to realize his dreams began on July 28, 1914, when Austria-Hungary declared war on Serbia. In the previous six years he had solidified ties with constitutional Austria—where he was free to act without fear of repression—in the belief that these relations would enable him to defeat Russia. Bellicose Kaiser Wilhelm II of Germany, having given Austria-Hungary a famous "blank check" of support in case of Russian involvement, took the bold and provocative step of declaring war on Russia and France between August 1 and 3, followed by an invasion of Belgium. On August 4 Great Britain declared war on Germany, followed two days later by Austria-Hungary declaring war on Russia. Within the span of a week, the great powers of Europe were embroiled in a continental war.

With the outbreak of war, Pilsudski realized that all his prior military and diplomatic efforts had paid off. He would now have to play a delicate balancing act between serving the interests of Poland while operating under Austrian patronage. As a strategist who had thought through how to make such a conflict work out in Poland's favor, he had been preparing for this moment for quite some time.

According to a close comrade, Pilsudski had already devised a plan of action in case of war in Europe. In 1913 Stanisław Wojciechowski had met with Pilsudski in what would be the last time they saw each other before World War I. Recalling that exchange, Wojciechowski describes Pilsudski presenting a plan in the case of all-out war in Europe. At the moment war breaks out between Austria-Hungary and Russia, Pilsudski is reported to have said, a Polish armed force under his command would mount an invasion of the southern part of the Kingdom of Poland and announce the formation of a provisional national government.[3] It is not surprising, therefore, that within a week of the outbreak of war in August 1914, Pilsudski proceeded to act precisely in this manner.

On August 2 Pilsudski met with Austrian Army intelligence officer Captain Józef Rybak to coordinate the mobilization of a Polish armed force. Rybak supported the idea but with the stipulation that it would take place only after a formal declaration of war between Austria-Hungary and Russia.[4] Rybak also told Pilsudski that such a Polish force should enter the Kingdom of Poland through Miechów county and then proceed to the city of Kielce through Jędrzejów county. This was a surprise to Pilsudski, who had already dispatched a reconnaissance patrol to the industrialized Dąbrowa Basin in Piotrków province, which had a long history of labor unrest and support for the Polish Socialist Party.[5]

In Kraków, meanwhile, Pilsudski announced on August 3 the formation of the First Cadre Company (*Pierwsza Kompania Kadrowa*), a select group of the best soldiers chosen from the Riflemen and Rifle Squads. The First Cadre Company's 144 soldiers ranged in age from fourteen to thirty-nine. The majority were Catholic Poles, but among its ranks could also be found Jewish fighters, including twenty-three-year-old Bronisław Mansperl, as well as Evangelicals and Greek Catholics (Ukrainians). Pilsudski named Tadeusz Kasprzycki commander.[6]

In an emotional address, Pilsudski stated, "From this moment on, we are neither Riflemen nor Rifle Squads. All gathered here are one thing and one thing only: Polish soldiers." Beginning this day, the cadre company's symbol was to be the white-headed eagle. "Soldiers! You will have the extraordinary honor of being the first to march toward the Kingdom of Poland and cross the Russian border as the front line of a Polish Army, marching to fight for the liberation of our homeland."[7] Alexandra Pilsudska later commented, "It was one of the best moments in his life. At last, at the age of forty-six, he saw the realization of the dream of his boyhood, the creation of a Polish Army to fight against Russia." She wrote, "He was profoundly happy for he was serving the two ideals which had dominated his whole life. His love of Poland and his love of the army. He had so long been a voice crying in the wilderness, a solder in theory only, a mere writer on military strategy. Now the sword was in his own hand."[8]

Bronislaw Mansperl, a twenty-four-year-old Jewish officer in Pilsudski's First Brigade, who died on the battlefield in 1915.

On the same day, August 3, two leaflets appeared. The first, signed "National Government, Warsaw, 3 August 1914," announced the creation of a National Government in Warsaw and named Pilsudski commander of a Polish armed force. All Poles, the leaflet stated, had the duty to support the Polish armed force poised to enter Polish territories inside imperial Russia. They should likewise defer to Pilsudski's authority. A second leaflet, signed "Jozef Pilsudski, Chief Commander of the Polish Army," addressed the population of the Kingdom of Poland, the ten Polish provinces inside imperial

Russia. "The decisive hour has struck! Poland has ceased to be enslaved and now wishes to be the arbiter of her own fate, to build her own future. . . . Cadres of a Polish Army have entered the territory of the Kingdom of Poland, regarding themselves and the *Polish people* as the true and sole proprietors who fertilized and enriched this land with their hard work. The Polish Army has taken over in the name of the chief of state of the National Government."[9]

The National Government Pilsudski declared was, in fact, a fictional body. The announcement was intended as a ploy to inspire the newly liberated population to support and provide recruits for the Polish forces. Such a government would be formed in due time, but to give Pilsudski's armed forces a stamp of legitimacy, the National Government had to be prematurely announced. On August 4, Pilsudski dispatched a courier to Lwów with a letter for Alexandra Szczerbińska requesting that she and Leon Wasilewski travel to Warsaw to meet with Roman Dmowski to discuss the formation of a National Government.[10] On the same day, Pilsudski formed the Second Cadre Company and named Mieczysław Norwid-Neugebauer its commander.

IN THE EARLY MORNING HOURS of August 6, 1914, Pilsudski ordered the First Cadre Company, stationed in Kraków's Oleander Groves, to march northward into imperial Russia. "For many years, the land we are about to enter has been under captivity," the company commander, Tadeusz Kasprzycki, told his soldiers. "Let us liberate it and become the first regular branch of a Polish armed force to set foot there for decades."[11] At 9:45 a.m. the company crossed into Russia, stopping in Michałowice, the first town on the other side of the border.[12] The Austro-Hungarian incursion into the southwest corner of Russia's Polish provinces, the troops were told, had routed the Russians for the first time since 1815.

Pilsudski, meanwhile, remained in Kraków to attend a meeting of the Commission of Confederated Independence Parties (KSSN). He informed the members that the first troops were on their way to the Russian border and he had declared the formation of a National Government in Warsaw. When asked why the haste, Pilsudski replied, "A race against the Prussians to Warsaw."[13] The commission gave Pilsudski its stamp of approval.

Following the commission's meeting, Pilsudski left Kraków with his chief of staff, Sosnkowski, for the Austrian border town of Krzeszowice, a stone's

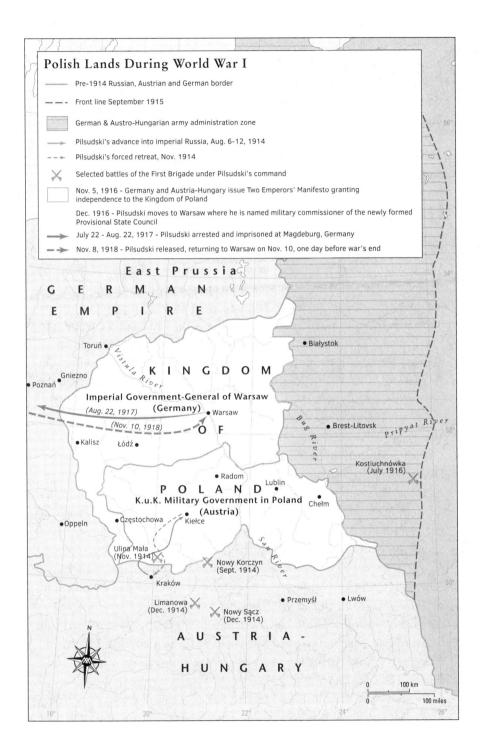

Polish Lands During World War I

——— Pre-1914 Russian, Austrian and German border

– – – – Front line September 1915

▨ German & Austro-Hungarian army administration zone

→ Pilsudski's advance into imperial Russia, Aug. 6-12, 1914

- - -▸ Pilsudski's forced retreat, Nov. 1914

✕ Selected battles of the First Brigade under Pilsudski's command

☐ Nov. 5, 1916 - Germany and Austria-Hungary issue Two Emperors' Manifesto granting independence to the Kingdom of Poland

Dec. 1916 - Pilsudski moves to Warsaw where he is named military commissioner of the newly formed Provisional State Council

➡ July 22 - Aug. 22, 1917 - Pilsudski arrested and imprisoned at Magdeburg, Germany

- -➡ Nov. 8, 1918 - Pilsudski released, returning to Warsaw on Nov. 10, one day before war's end

East Prussia

G E R M A N

E M P I R E

• Toruń
• Białystok

Gniezno
• Poznań

Vistula River

K I N G D O M

Imperial Government-General of Warsaw

(Aug. 22, 1917) (Germany) • Warsaw

(Nov. 10, 1918) O F

• Kalisz Łódź •

Bug River
• Brest-Litovsk
pripyat River

Kostiuchnówka
(July 1916) ✕

• Radom
Lublin •
P O L A N D
K.u.K. Military Government in Poland Chełm
(Austria)

• Oppeln • Częstochowa • Kielce

San River

Ulina Mała
(Nov. 1914) ✕
Nowy Korczyn
(Sept. 1914) ✕
• Kraków

Limanowa ✕
(Dec. 1914) Nowy Sącz ✕
(Dec. 1914)
• Przemyśł • Lwów

N

A U S T R I A -

H U N G A R Y

0   100 km
0   100 miles

throw from the Russian border. Waiting for them was Norwid-Neugebauer and his 535-strong Second Cadre Company. Pilsudski briefed the officers on the situation and verified that they possessed adequate arms and ammunition. Norwid-Neugebauer recalled that Pilsudski "reminded us of the importance of the moment, saying this was a turning point in the history of Polish captivity because it was the day in which a handful of Riflemen—in the name of the entire Polish nation—went to war for an independent existence."[14] From Krzeszowice, Pilsudski posted a letter to Rybak informing him about the imminent incursion into Russia. He also complained about the quality of weapons provided.[15]

It was not a coincidence that August 6, 1914, was the day Austria-Hungary declared war on Russia. With the objective of blocking the rail lines to Warsaw, but also of holding on to valuable oil wells in Eastern Galicia, the Austro-Hungarian Army advanced from Lwów into the Lublin province in southwestern Russia, some two hundred miles east of Pilsudski's position. The Germans, meanwhile, successfully staved off a Russian incursion into East Prussia. The initial success of the Austro-Hungarian and German armies allowed Pilsudski's forces to advance into imperial Russia unheeded. On August 7 the First Cadre Company passed through Miechów en route to the provincial capital, Kielce. Meanwhile the Second Cadre Company, under Pilsudski's command, crossed the border. The following day Pilsudski placed Władysław Sikorski in charge of all military formations in Galicia.[16]

The Russian withdrawal from the southern region of the Kingdom of Poland enabled Pilsudski to proceed on the fifty-mile journey to Kielce without incident. He stopped overnight in the city of Jędrzejów, twenty-four miles south of Kielce. In a circular, "The National Government to the People of Kielce Province," dated August 10, Pilsudski introduced himself as Chief Commander of the Polish Army. "The Russian Army," the circular stated, "has left our country. Together with the shameful violence of the enemy's army, the tsarist authorities—the most terrible promoters of disorder and anarchy—are in retreat and will not return to Poland." Authority now rested with the newly formed National Government, "the legitimate stewards of all that the Muscovite invaders had taken over."[17] The new government, the circular noted, would bring law and order, peace and security, while treating traitors and spies harshly.

On August 12, 1914, Pilsudski entered Kielce with a division of four hundred soldiers. The soldiers occupied the abandoned Governor's Palace, where the Russian authorities had been stationed. The Austrian and German military authorities would later take up residence elsewhere. To Pilsudski, the fact that he sat "in the Governor's Palace, formerly the seat of the principal authority, whereas the commanders of the German and Austrian forces had theirs somewhere else in the town . . . gave a fillip to a feeling of pride and optimism as to the future."[18]

The elation around the capture of Kielce was dampened by the reality on the ground. Entirely unexpected were the tepid, decidedly unenthusiastic reactions among the local Polish communities to the arrival of Polish troops. What's more, Pilsudski had to deal with the distinct displeasure of the Austrian authorities, who strongly frowned upon his independent military and political initiatives. On the day Pilsudski took Kielce, he received word that Austrian authorities had summoned him to Kraków for talks.[19] On August 13 he met in Kraków with Lieutenant-Colonel Jan Nowak of the Austrian Army general staff. Nowak told Pilsudski that the appearance of independent volunteer divisions inside enemy territory was unacceptable. Polish soldiers would have to formally enter the Austrian Army or be disarmed.[20] Pilsudski had no other alternative than to comply.

Meanwhile, the thrust of the Central Powers and Polish troops into the Kingdom of Poland led the Russian authorities to make a formal appeal to the Poles not only in Russia but in Austrian Galicia and Germany as well. On August 14, 1914, imperial Russia's commander in chief, Grand Duke Nikolai Mikhailovich, issued a manifesto. "Poles!" it began, tapping into collective Polish aspirations, "The hour has struck for the cherished dreams of your fathers and forefathers to be realized. A century and a half ago the living body of Poland was torn into parts, but her soul did not die. She lived in the hope that the hour of the resurrection of the Polish nation, of its fraternal reconciliation with Great Russia, would arrive."

The war had opened the possibility that Russia could reunite Polish territories from Austria and Germany and grant home rule to Poland under Russian tutelage. The manifesto dangled the promise of reunification: "Let the boundary lines which have cut the Polish nation asunder be obliterated. Let the Poles be reunited under the scepter of the Russian tsar." New freedoms were now being offered of home rule in an autonomous Poland with schools, religion, and administration under Polish control. "Under that scepter," the manifesto concluded, "Poland will be reborn, free in her faith, language and self-government."[21]

Although falling short of offering territorial independence, the manifesto represented a fundamental change in Russian policy. "We need not waste words on pointing out the momentous significance of this step," the *Times* of London commented on August 17, 1914.[22] While the Polish right-wing party, the National Democrats, endorsed the manifesto in the Duma, Pilsudski and the Galician Poles reacted with indifference, regarding it as merely another ploy to maintain Russia's ruthless hold on Poland.

Pilsudski meanwhile reorganized his company into the First Rifle Regiment on August 15, 1914, dividing it into five battalions. The commanders he chose included Edward Rydz-Śmigły, who later served as marshal of Poland after Pilsudski's death and commander of the Polish armed forces during the September 1939 campaign, as well as Michał Karaszewicz-Tokarzewski, who later served as commander in chief of the Polish Underground forces after the invasion of Poland in September 1939.

The Austrian rebuke of Pilsudski, combined with Russia's manifesto to the Poles, led Polish MPs in Austrian Galicia to take action. On August 16, 1914, Austrophile MPs in Vienna held talks with Austrian officials to propose the formation of a Polish armed division within the Austro-Hungarian Army. In Kraków, meanwhile, leaders of the Commission of Confederated Independence Parties met with the Polish Parliamentary Circle. The result was the creation of the Supreme National Committee (*Naczelny Komitet Narodowy*, NKN), which declared as its goal the liberation of Polish territories from Russia in alliance with Austria-Hungary, as well as the formation of Polish Legions under Austro-Hungarian auspices.[23] With the initial thrust of the Central Powers into Russia's western provinces, the NKN aspired to unite the Polish provinces of imperial Russia with Austrian Galicia and transform the Dual Monarchy of Austria-Hungary into a Triple Monarchy, with the Polish provinces constituting a third state.[24]

The Polish Parliamentary Circle issued a statement dated August 16, 1914. "To consolidate Polish national strength into armed Polish Legions," it read, "the Parliamentary Circle and *all Polish parties without exception* have decided to create a single, legal organization. Under Polish command and in close cooperation with the supreme command of the Austro-Hungarian Army, the Polish Legions will go into battle." The new NKN would serve as the political arm of the Polish Legions.[25] Juliusz Leo, mayor of Kraków and president of the Polish Parliamentary Circle, was named head of the NKN. The Polish Legions were to be divided into two regional branches: the Kraków-based Western Division, headed by Władysław L. Jaworski, a conservative and a Habsburg loyalist; and the Lwów-based Eastern Division, headed by a member of the National Democrats. The two branches, a resolution of the Polish Parliamentary Circle declared, "are to be used to fight against Russia in Polish lands in cooperation with the Austro-Hungarian Monarchy."[26] Władysław Sikorski was named head of the NKN's military department. After the NKN took a loyalty oath to the Habsburg monarchy, the Austrian military authorized it to furnish the Polish Legions with Polish uniforms and to employ Polish as the language of command. With the creation of the Supreme National Committee, the KSSN dissolved itself on August 17.[27]

Leo, Jaworski, and Sikorski jointly signed a circular addressed to the Polish Legions. "The time for action has come! A European war, for which our bards once prayed, and for which whole generations of Poles have waited, has broken out. The eastern theater of this war is being fought on Polish lands. The armies of the Austro-Hungarian Monarchy have set out against Russia, a violent occupier and tormentor of our people. Divisions of Polish riflemen are already engaged in battle in a heroic struggle against Moscow." The circular continued, "All Poles in Galicia are unified through the formation of the Supreme National Committee," whose purpose was to rally support behind the Polish Legions "who fight for the Fatherland, for the liberation of Poland."[28] That Pilsudski played no part in founding the Polish Legions and the NKN was by design. The Austrian authorities not only expressed extreme unease with his independent activities but also noted the lack of support for his cadre regiments on the Russian side of the border.

ONE OF THE OFFICERS in Pilsudski's regiment, Michał Sokolnicki, described the lukewarm reaction Polish troops received from the Polish inhabitants of Imperial Russia. He recalled that not a single person came out of their homes to greet them when his regiment arrived in Jędrzejów, a town halfway along the route from the Austrian-Russian border to Kielce, "When we passed an occasional house," Sokolnicki recalled, "they were shut and the residents inside hid from us, pretending the house was empty." The local population displayed "a deep apprehension" and did not take to the independence platform or the call for an uprising against Russia.[29]

The lack of local support for Pilsudski's regiment was starkly evident upon his return to Kielce on August 22, 1914. Sokolnicki recalled that Pilsudski's first order of business was to pay a visit to the local Catholic authorities, and Sokolnicki accompanied Pilsudski to the residence of the local Catholic bishop. The meeting was awkward and tense, as the two were received "dryly and formally." Pilsudski explained the reason for his visit, stating that as commander of the first Polish armed force to enter the Kingdom of Poland, he felt obligated to pay his respects to a high official of the church. "The bishop replied with an unfriendly expression and a hostile tone," Sokolnicki remembered, with the suggestion that unless Pilsudski's army consisted of pious churchgoing Catholics, the bishop had no intention whatsoever of giving his blessing.[30]

Following the dreadful meeting with the bishop, Pilsudski informed Nowak that he was formally accepting the order to merge with the Polish Legions. The First Rifle Regiment was no longer permitted to act independently and was henceforth a formal division within the Polish Legions. The Austro-Hungarian Army's supreme commander, Archduke Friedrich Karol Habsburg, renamed Pilsudski's unit the First Regiment of the Polish Legions.[31] Three days after the archduke's announcement, on August 30, 1914, the NKN issued a public statement that Pilsudski's concession represented a positive step toward the unity of Polish forces, the NKN's authority over all Polish military organization.[32]

Pilsudski, along with his soldiers, took the loyalty oath in Kielce on September 5, 1914, and the First Regiment of the Polish Legions was formally inducted into the Austro-Hungarian Army. "The ceremony that took place this morning at 9 a.m.," Pilsudski commented that afternoon, "was, for my armed forces, unpleasant."[33] Forced induction into the Austro-Hungarian Army and subordination to the NKN felt like the abandonment of independence. The palpable tension was part of a larger struggle for the independence of Polish armed formations. As Andrzej Chwalba has demonstrated, Pilsudski's Riflemen did not initially regard the Polish Legions positively. For when the NKN announced the creation of the Polish Legions on August 16, 1914, Pilsudski's Riflemen "were not happy at all with the new formation and regarded the term 'Legions' unfavorably, preferring to speak of themselves instead as 'riflemen.'"[34] Pilsudski did not hide his misgivings about joining the Legions, writing on September 5, 1914, that prior to joining, "our armed forces were regarded as autonomous Polish troops, allied with Austria but not a part of the Austrian Army."[35] In November 1914 he described this time of autonomy as "the first, romantic period of the war, when

I worked with my division with full independence, versus today, when the work of my division is taking place within a huge army, depriving me of all independence."[36]

Creating an Independent Military and Political Representation

Pilsudski's response was to create a counterpart to the Legions and the NKN in the newly liberated areas of the Kingdom of Poland that would be run by Poles native to the region. On the same day he took the oath, September 5, Pilsudski met with Michał Sokolnicki and Witold Jodko-Narkiewicz in Kielce and proposed that the two form a new organization to be called the Polish National Organization (*Polska Organizacja Narodowa,* PON). It would operate solely in the Kingdom of Poland, making it independent of Austria and the NKN. It was up to Sokolnicki and Jodko-Narkiewicz to organize the new body. "I will throw you into the water," Sokolnicki recalled Pilsudski saying; "now swim as you know how to."[37] That very day, a circular distributed in the name of PON announced that the new organization was to provide support for armed forces operating in the Kingdom of Poland, interact with the NKN as a co-equal counterpart, and serve as the nucleus of a Polish governing structure in the kingdom. Sokolnicki, who at the time served as commissioner of the Polish Army in Kielce, which was later dissolved under pressure from the NKN, was now named head of PON.[38]

Another role Pilsudski envisioned for PON was as a body that could deal politically with the Germans. In consultation with Pilsudski, Sokolnicki proposed sending a delegation to Berlin for talks with the German military.[39] Meanwhile, Pilsudski posted a letter to General Rajmund Baczyński, the Austrian-appointed commander of the Polish Legions in Western Galicia, complaining that he was unable to properly provide weapons and ammunition for legionnaires under his command. Despite their high morale, they were very poorly equipped. Unlike regiments in Galicia, the First Legion Regiment in Kielce had not yet received any funds.[40]

News from the front lent a sense of urgency to Pilsudski's appeal. On September 2, 1914, a Russian counteroffensive broke through Austrian lines. Russian troops entered Eastern Galicia and took Lwów. By September 13 the Austrians had retreated to the San River, abandoning Eastern Galicia to the

Russians. Pilsudski refused to stand idly by, leading a division of the First Legion Regiment out of Kielce on September 10 to help fortify the Galician front. He led his regiment forty-five miles southwest to Nowy Korczyn, where he took part in battles alongside the Austro-Hungarian Army. The NKN publicly praised Pilsudski for his efforts: "In the name of the Supreme National Committee, we warmly extend our gratitude to the command and soldiers of the First Legion Regiment, in recognition and genuine pride for the gallant courage they displayed in battle with our eternal enemy."[41]

In a further attempt to maintain a national character in Polish military units, Pilsudski dispatched First Lieutenant Tadeusz Żuliński to Russian-controlled Warsaw in October 1914 to organize a clandestine underground military organization. A member of the PPS Revolutionary Faction, Union of Active Struggle, and an officer in the Riflemen's Association before the war, Żuliński had become one of Pilsudski's most capable officers. On October 22, Żuliński announced the formation of the Polish Military Organization (*Polska Organizacja Wojskowa*, POW) in Warsaw. The announcement called for the creation of an independent Polish state carved out by a Polish armed force. The POW's soldiers were to be directed "against the most important enemy—Russia." By referring to Russia as one but not *the* only potential enemy, POW left open the possibility that it might eventually turn its forces against other partitioning powers. Its functions included intelligence gathering, propaganda, and underground military training schools.[42]

On the battlefront, meanwhile, the Austrians retreated further west, following a successful Russian advance. As the Russians recaptured the Kielce province, lost in the first weeks of the war, Pilsudski's First Legion Regiment was ordered to retreat along with the Austro-Hungarian forces. Not only Pilsudski but the entire staff of the Polish Military Organization evacuated the area. After marching sixty miles over several days, on November 8, 1914, they reached the town of Wolbrom at the southwestern tip of Kielce province, where Pilsudski ordered his men to halt.

As he watched Austrian troops sweep past them in full retreat, he realized they were heading in the direction of the German border, only thirty-seven miles away. He ordered three battalions and one cavalry brigade to reverse course and follow him in the opposite direction, to Kraków. Pilsudski later described why he made such a hasty, and possibly deadly, decision. "The First Corps," he commented, referring to the Austro-Hungarian First Army under

General Viktor Dankl, "could defend Prague and Vienna, Breslau and Berlin, but we free Polish Strzelcy [Riflemen] would not do that. We would try to die with honor, but we would die in our own land."[43]

His plan was to use a narrow corridor between the Russian advancing lines to slip into Austrian-controlled Kraków. On November 9, 1914, Pilsudski and his men marched nine miles through fields, ravines, and hills. That evening, after sending out surveillance patrols, Pilsudski stopped in the village of Ulina Mała for rest, between roads with advancing Russian troops. Enemy troops surrounded the village. Pilsudski's patrols informed him that the corridor leading south had been shut off by Russian troops. Pilsudski panicked, believing he had signed a death warrant for himself and his soldiers. "For the moment, I only heard a humming in my ear; I couldn't see; the blood pulsed violently in my temples. From some lumber-room of memory floated out 'Tu l'as voulu, Georges Dandin,'" he recalled, referencing a line in a Molière comedy, "You brought this upon yourself, Georges Dandin.'"[44]

Brooding for hours over the pros and cons of every possible way to get safely to Kraków, Pilsudski finally arrived at a decision: he would use patrols to determine the exact moment it was safe to march down a narrow path concealed by forest. Before delivering the order, he summoned two people for advice: his chief of staff, Sosnkowski; and a member of staff headquarters, Tadeusz Kasprzycki. Both argued the plan was too risky and advised against it. "Here was another blow," Pilsudski later commented. "The decision I had come to with such toil was shaken by their opinion. I relapsed into silence, and after walking up and down the room to think over my arguments, decided to stick to my first decision."[45]

At 3:30 a.m. on November 11, 1914, Pilsudski sent out surveillance patrols. When he received notice an hour later that the area was clear, he ordered his men to march south. Without a single soldier killed or injured, the maneuver proved successful. Pilsudski and his men arrived in Kraków that same day. With barely any sleep for days, Pilsudski went to his apartment on Szlak Street, rested and afterward composed a detailed report on the escape. "I confess," Pilsudski later reflected, "that it was only after Ulina [Mała] that I began to have confidence in myself and belief in my power. And perhaps just because of that I so often heard my solders say, 'Now we can follow our Commandant anywhere. If he could get us out of Ulina we need not worry!' It was like an examination that I passed both before myself and before my men."[46]

Pilsudski's bravery in escaping through enemy territory did not go unnoticed. On November 15 the Austro-Hungarian supreme commander, Archduke Friedrich Habsburg, promoted Pilsudski to the rank of brigadier general.[47] The treacherous march from Ulina Mała to Kraków, through the Vistula lowlands and swamps, led Pilsudski to contract a nasty cold. As in the past when contracting a virus, Pilsudski traveled to a warmer climate, this time in the Silesian town of Freistadt (today Fryštát, Czech Republic). In a letter, he commented on his unease with the idea of serving under foreign command. "We are spiritually and socially completely alien," he wrote, "and my regiment in the huge Habsburg Army feels as if it were a foreign body, some kind of cancer."[48]

Michał Sokolnicki, who visited Pilsudski in Freistadt, found him in a state of despair. "As always during difficult times," Sokolnicki commented, "Pilsudski was introverted and standoffish. It was as if a cloud hovered over him."[49] It

Pilsudski as commander of the First
Brigade, Kraków, December 1914.

was difficult to understand what was on Pilsudski's mind, "because Pilsudski did not always say everything in words: much of what he thought was indicated by long and meaningful periods of silence, of fits of anger in his eyes, murmurs of discontent and hand movements, and of unspeakable contempt or discouragement when he was not understood."[50]

Contributing to Pilsudski's despair was the unanticipated withdrawal from conquered territories of the Kingdom of Poland. With the Polish National Organization and its staff now in Western Galicia, the entire purpose of its existence had been undermined. PON now came under the authority of the NKN. It was also a time to rethink the structure of the Legions. On December 19, 1914, Pilsudski's First Legion Regiment was reorganized as the First Brigade of the Polish Legions, the name by which his division was henceforth known. The First Brigade was divided into three infantry regiments, six battalions, one cavalry, and two artillery divisions.[51]

RUSSIAN MILITARY VICTORIES in Eastern Galicia emboldened the pro-Russian camp in Polish politics. By December 1914, when Russian troops stood a mere thirty miles from Kraków, Roman Dmowski, with support from Polish conservatives who wished to further Polish aims through an alliance with Russia, had created a rival to the Supreme National Committee in Galicia. On November 25 they announced in Warsaw the formation of the Polish National Committee (Komitet Narodowy Polski, KNP), a narrow coalition of National Democrats and conservative Polish landowners, industrialists, clergy, and influential intelligentsia linked with the Party of Realpolitik (Stronnictwo Polityki Realnej). The new organization formally endorsed Grand Duke Nikolai's manifesto on Poland. In its first pronouncement, the KNP called for the liberation of Polish lands under control of the Central Powers and the unification of Poland under the scepter of the Russian monarch. Dmowski presided over the organization's executive council; the conservative landowning aristocrat Count Zygmunt Wielopolski was named president.[52]

Across the border in Austria-Hungary, where Polish leaders pinned their hopes on the victory of the Central Powers, Pilsudski continued to devise policies aimed at maximizing a desirable outcome for Poland. On November 24, 1914, he learned that PON had been formally dissolved because the Supreme

National Committee had extended its administration into the small sliver of the Kingdom of Poland still under Austrian rule.[53] Due to Russian military advances into Eastern Galicia, the NKN had already relocated to Vienna out of fear that Kraków might fall.

Pilsudski left the battlefield to attend meetings in Vienna with members of the Supreme National Committee and Polish politicians, arriving on December 18. Vienna's Polish daily newspaper announced the arrival of "Brigadier Pilsudski, the heroic commander of the Legion's First Brigade."[54] Among the entourage of legionnaires, journalists, and politicians who greeted Pilsudski at the train station was Rudolf Starzewski, editor in chief of the conservative Kraków daily *Czas*. Aligned with the conservative pro-Habsburg camp, Starzewski was not a Pilsudski supporter. But he was a seasoned, professional journalist who captured the moment. "At the train station," Starzewski noted in his diary on December 19, 1914, "Pilsudski was greeted by an honorary campaign of legionnaires, mainly unarmed wounded and sick." The crowd that amassed, he wrote, spontaneously broke out into patriotic songs.[55]

In Vienna, Pilsudski first met the chairman of the NKN, Władysław Jaworski. The two discussed the dramatic military setbacks. Jaworski expressed surprise at how little Pilsudski seemed discouraged by Russia's victories on the battlefield. According to Jaworski's account of the meeting, Pilsudski replied confidently that Russia would suffer "catastrophic" defeat in the near future. It was only a question of time.[56]

On December 21 the NKN held a dinner banquet in Vienna in Pilsudski's honor. Present were activists in the NKN, officers of the Polish Legions, and members of the Austrian parliament.[57] "What a site to behold," Jaworski commented, seeing leaders of the Polish socialist movement such as Daszyński, Pilsudski, and Sokolnicki alongside pro-Habsburg conservative Poles.[58] The banquet began with Jaworski's opening remarks. "The idea of freedom, of the independence of our Homeland," he said, "has been transformed in the form of the Legions. And here the creator of the Legions, Brigadier Pilsudski, is present among us, which gives us great joy. Mr. Brigadier—a legend is being created around you and your Legions that is radiating with fame." The Legions, Jaworski continued, "are defending the honor of the Polish nation. For this, you will be remembered in the annals of the history of Poland." What stood out to Sokolnicki in Jaworski's toast was the evocation of the legend idea around Pilsudski and his First Brigade.[59]

The weeks leading up to the dinner banquet in Vienna had been a dramatic time. After the escape from Ulina Mała to Kraków, Pilsudski had led two battles against Russian forces in Limanowa on December 5–6, and in Nowy Sącz on December 13. It is said that when he led his regiment into Nowy Sącz, he received enthusiastic support for the first time from local inhabitants, who lined the streets with flower and music.[60]

It is not surprising, then, that Pilsudski was moved by Jaworski's toast when he rose to say a few words. Raising a glass, he said the following: "Distinguished Gentlemen. I come from a country where the people are not accustomed to expressing their feelings [*uczuć*] openly. That is, from an unfree country. It is thus difficult to reply to such kind compliments and to accept these honors. One topic was brought up here, that more deeply related to Polish ambitions, which some believe that I represent. For many years what had pained me was that Polish society had no widespread momentum. I was crushed by the smallness of life and of the smallness of aspirations, the outcome of an unfree society." Yet for the first time, Pilsudski was seeing the beginnings of a change in Polish society. "As knights going out to war," he said, "we must have not only the strength of arms but the strength of the mind and heart behind them. This union of our people behind the Supreme National Committee can give us this. This state of mind can complete our victories in the field and justify the sacrifice of our blood."[61]

Later that evening Jaworski noted that Pilsudski's speech "made a big impression."[62] His view was reflected in press accounts. Rudolf Starzewski described the banquet as the most talked-about event in Vienna among Poles: "Until now, Pilsudski has been seen variously as a legendary hero by some, with indifference by other, and as a radical socialist, a revolutionary, by others. To the ill-informed, he was regarded merely as a bandit from the 1905 revolution, an outlaw. Today, all are of the opinion that, at the very least, Pilsudski has the makings of a historical figure. Sharing the fate of the Legions, he is their personification, their symbol."[63]

Starzewski expressed the opinion that Jaworski's toast was beautifully spoken but contained excessive praise, treating Pilsudski like a king or emperor. Yet it was true that the Legion's First Brigade and its commander had transformed a deep-seated pessimism into hope and pride. "The Legions defend not only Polish honor. They are the arms and mind of the committee," Starzewski wrote, referring to the Supreme National Committee.

Starzewski was of the opinion that Pilsudski had now become "not a so-cialist but a national hero" and thus the only figure who could represent Poland as a whole. "Pilsudski," Starzewski observed, "is the only cement in this historical process, the cement of blood, connecting the democratic ele-ments with the traditions of the Polish nobility [*szlachty*]."[64]

On December 22, 1914, regiments of the First Brigade left Nowy Sącz to defend positions on the railway lines south of Tarnów in the village of Łowczówek. Under the command of Pilsudski's chief of staff, Kazimierz Sos-nkowski, the Legions engaged in direct combat with Russian troops, holding them back in what was the bloodiest battle to date for Polish soldiers. The First Brigade is said to have taken six hundred Russian POWs. Although Pilsudski was away for the battle, tending to other areas of the Austrian-Russian front, the victory helped strengthen his growing legendary status.[65]

In the first days of 1915, Pilsudski expressed his gratitude to the fallen and wounded among the Legions. In an address to the First Brigade, he honored the bravery of his men in the battle of Łowczówek (December 22–25), singling out Sosnkowski and a few others for praise. He estimated that of the approxi-mately five thousand soldiers in the First Brigade, about one thousand had been killed or wounded since August 1914. Pilsudski reflected on the signifi-cance of 1914:

> In 1914, I was not concerned with settling the details of the military ques-tion in Poland, but simply with this—Was the Polish soldier to remain a mystical entity deprived of flesh and blood? In a great world war fought on Polish soil, when a solder with his bayonet and uniform would pen-etrate to every cottage and farm of our countryside, I wanted the Polish soldier to be something more than a pretty picture. . . . I wanted Poland, who had forgotten the sword so entirely since 1863, to see it flashing in the air in the hands of her own soldiers. Believe me, Mr. Chairman, if it were possible to ask her young soldiers sleeping in the graves, their sin-cere feeling about Poland—and the dead and dying do not lie—they would say with me, their leader, that we do not regret either blood or sacrifice if this dream of long years has been fulfilled. The Polish sol-dier created by Polish efforts has given his country a new value, which it did not before possess.[66]

Wacław Sieroszewski, who at age fifty-seven served in the First Cavalry Regiment in Pilsudski's First Brigade, wrote in 1915 what became the first biography of Pilsudski ever written. Published by the Military Department of the Supreme National Committee, it further burnished the emerging legend of Pilsudski from this time. "Soldiers' trust in Pilsudski's leadership, faith in his military abilities, in his foresight and care for the fate of his subordinates" was nearly absolute, Sieroszewski wrote. This extended to a belief "[in] the integrity of his character and in his genuine love for his country." Sieroszewski concluded: "For the broad masses of people, Pilsudski is regarded as a symbol of the unbending struggle for spiritual good, for the liberation of our homeland, for individual and national dignity, and for a better, more just . . . and brighter future."[67]

Dramatic Changes in the Fortunes of War

In 1915 the situation of the Central Powers changed dramatically for the better on the Eastern Front. Not only would Austria-Hungary take back the whole of Eastern Galicia, but a combined German-Austrian offensive forced the Russians out of the Kingdom of Poland and Lithuania, liberating those territories for the first time in a century. Pilsudski's prediction that Russia would suffer huge military defeats came true.

In January 1915 Pilsudski posted a letter to the high command of the Austrian armed forces, insisting that the Polish character of the Legions be maintained as a key component in attracting recruits. He also requested an increase in arms—especially machine guns, attributing the casualty rates to the lack of sophisticated weaponry with which to fight the Russians.[68] As the Legions attracted more members, Pilsudski continued to engage in the politics of maintaining full autonomy within the Central Powers. By the spring of 1915, propaganda for the Legions inside the Russian-controlled Kingdom of Poland increased. In Warsaw, the POW distributed an illegal circular in March informing the population that the Polish Legions were preparing to advance into the Polish provinces. The propaganda department of the POW introduced the Polish population behind enemy lines to the Legions and its leaders, characterizing the Legions as a "Polish Army" moving toward imperial Russia for the liberation of Polish lands. Here, the story of Pilsudski, introduced as chief commander of the Polish Army, was recounted through childhood, education, exile, and return. He now stepped fully onto the stage of history as head of the Polish armed forces, striving for the independence of Poland—a figure who had led the revolutionary movement "with the goal of fighting for the freedom of the Polish people. His whole life has been per-meated with the ideal of struggle with Russia as the biggest and most men-acing foe of Poland."[69]

By the spring of 1915 the Legions had expanded to more than eleven thou-sand members in Galicia and the areas of the Kingdom of Poland under Aus-trian rule. Among them were Jewish volunteers, who flocked to the organ-ization that promised, on paper, freedom and equality before the law without regard to religion in a future Poland. Indeed, efforts to recruit Jews into the Legions can be traced back to September 1914 when Michał Sokolnicki issued an appeal to Jews in the newly liberated areas to join the Polish Legions. The leaflet, "To Citizens of the Mosaic Faith," stated that the Polish Army in the Kingdom of Poland "extends to you our hand of brotherhood for a brighter future." The Poles were fighting the Russians, "who are also the most terrible enemy of citizens of the Mosaic faith. All the problems and antagonism in Polish-Jewish relations," the leaflet continued, "do not compare with the wretched Muscovite nightmare, by which the Jews—like the Poles—have been tormented. So come join us in a common struggle against an abomi-nable yoke. If you want to be free citizens with full equality in a free Poland—come with us. If you . . . do not want brutal Muscovite soldiers and Cossack units to torment inhabitants of our country, if you want to live in a thriving country under the rays of freedom—come with us!"[70]

In March 1915, Jewish members of the Polish Legions distributed a circular addressed to "the Jewish Youth" and signed, "Jewish Legionnaires, the Kingdom of Poland." Written by twenty-one-year-old Jacob Shatzky, a lieu-tenant in Piłsudski's First Brigade who would later become one of the most important historians of Polish Jewry, the circular called upon Polish Jewry to trust and support Piłsudski:

When the historical hour arrives for the Polish Nation, when the light of dawn brings freedom for all to the inhabitants of Polish lands without regard to religion or creed, we shall then understand that our civic ob-ligation is to exert all our strength to struggle with the Polish people for a better and more promising future. We must rise up against Russia and the Russian executioners—our greatest enemy and oppressor who has committed hundreds of massacres and pogroms upon a defenseless Jewish population—but not like slaves licking the feet of their master.

Having already spilled our blood on the battlefields, we have discovered that we possess human dignity, that we young Jews shall respond to oppression and persecution of our people with arms in hand. Today, we march under the banner of the Polish Legions in a common fight for the freedom of Poland—a Poland that for 800 years has taken us under its roof, a Poland that does not know violence and pogroms.

Yet the number of Jewish legionnaires compared with the Jewish population as a whole is very little. The Jewish youth in the Russian sector of Poland who evaded conscription [in the Russian Army] should join the ranks of the Polish Legions. Remember that Poland shall belong to those who fight for her. He who loves freedom and desires to be the citizen of a free country, who does not want to live in tsarist captivity, who does not want to rot and live a dull life under the Muscovite yoke, who wants to live and thrive in the light of freedom—come with us. Young Jews! The daily struggle for existence has not deadened the spirit of your desire for freedom, that in such a historically significance moment, we will differentiate justice from lawlessness. We hope that our voice will be heard and the rattle of arms in your hands will build respect even from your enemies.

Traces of Berek Joselewicz call upon you! To Arms! For the Freedom of Poland! For the freedom of all its citizens! To arms in the ranks of the Legions! Unite with us.[71]

The reference to the historical figure of Berek Joselewicz, a colonel in the Polish Army who commanded a Jewish platoon in the 1794 Kościuszko Uprising, was intended to inspire Polish patriotism among the Jews.

The combination of the Ulina Mała escape to Kraków in November 1914 and the lavish praise he received in December 1914 at the dinner banquet in Vienna appeared to give Pilsudski a greater belief in his own abilities and significance. On February 17, 1915, Jaworski commented that "[Pilsudski] has the army. How blind are those who cannot see this. How important it is to stay close to him and, if possible, influence him. His most significant conception," Jaworski continued, "is the following: the NKN—a national government; he—Pilsudski—*is* the Polish Army."[72] Rudolf Starzewski similarly commented at the time that many were acknowledging Pilsudski's "central place as initiator and creator" of the Legions.[73]

Part and parcel of Pilsudski's growing popularity was his continued insistence that the Polish forces retain their national character. In April and May 1915 Pilsudski communicated this central idea to Sikorski, head of the NKN's Military Department. Concerned that Sikorski was too conciliatory, Pilsudski increasingly insisted that the Legions had to be separate and fully autonomous from the NKN. The letter followed a correspondence from Sokolnicki to Pilsudski expressing concern about Sikorski and NKN.[74]

Pilsudski made his views known to several others as well. In a letter to three collaborators who were to be working for the POW in Warsaw after the anticipated Russian withdrawal, he instructed that the Kingdom of Poland should be independent of the NKN and its military department. "Demands for the Kingdom of Poland shall be the following: that the Kingdom be treated not as a country to be conquered in which the same benefits shall be extended as are in Galicia: Polish language in offices and schools, internal Polish autonomy." Such an arrangement could not be accepted, Pilsudski clarified.[75]

In a letter to Sikorski, Pilsudski stressed that when the Central Powers forced Russia out of Polish territories—which he believed would take place shortly—the NKN had to have in place separate demands for Polish sovereignty at the moment of the liberation of Warsaw.[76] That is why the POW was to become essential after the liberation of Polish lands from Russia. When in May 1915 he sent Ignacy Boerner as his emissary to Warsaw to work for the POW, Pilsudski instructed him to make preparations for the formation of a National Government, commenting on the future fortunes of the war: "Already, it is nearly entirely clear. Russia will be defeated, but the Central Powers will be defeated as well. In Russia, sooner or later, a revolution will break out, followed by a revolution in Italy, then in Austria and finally in Germany. At the moment Polish lands are liberated from the Russian yoke, the purpose of the Legions will come to an end, as the struggle to expel Russia will have been accomplished. We shall then build up our strength for the second phase in the history of the Legions, when we have to deal with Austria and Germany."[77]

That Pilsudski sent an emissary to Warsaw without the knowledge of the Austrian military was a source of friction. Rudolf Starzewski noted in February 1915 palpable tension between Sikorski and Pilsudski. "Those around Sikorski complain," he commented, "that Pilsudski is making his own 'politics,' that is, that he has his own representatives recruiting in the Kingdom of Poland; Pilsudski's followers point out that Sikorski has, until now, 'not been at the front.'" In June, Jaworski felt compelled to tell Piłsudski he was going down the wrong path, emphasizing "the necessity whenever possible of stressing unity between the Legions and the NKN."[78]

Russian Retreat from Polish Lands

In the spring of 1915, the German and Austro-Hungarian armies launched an offensive against Russia. On May 15, German forces crossed the San River into Eastern Galicia. After overwhelming the Russians, they took Przemyśl on June 3 and Lwów on June 22, crossing the Dniester River on June 27 into pre-1914 Russian territory. On July 13, German troops broke through the Russian lines of defense and advanced in the direction of Vilna, Warsaw, and Lublin.[79]

With the Russians out of Eastern Galicia and large parts of the western Kingdom of Poland, the NKN returned to Kraków from Vienna. What concerned Piłsudski was the NKN's decision to open an office in Piotrków, located in newly liberated lands of Imperial Russia. Piłsudski voiced his stern opposition: "You have impulsively built an NKN office in the Kingdom of Poland," he wrote the NKN's military department, "while I am working to organize the Kingdom separately, outside of the NKN." Piłsudski was trying to use the newly freed territories "as an argument against the unfair and foolish policy of the Austrians but also of the NKN."[80] Jaworski expressed concern over Piłsudski's position, commenting in his diary that Piłsudski's aim was command of the Kingdom and the removal from it of the NKN and its military department.[81]

In the first days of August 1915, Piłsudski met with Walery Sławek. At the time, German forces were poised to take Warsaw. Sławek recalled Piłsudski saying that "'the Central Powers cannot be allowed to recruit the local population into their armed forces. The Central Powers can receive local help. But in exchange they must formally legalize a Polish political authority to which it must give certain guarantees.'"[82] On August 6, 1915, the one-year anniversary of the entry of Polish troops into Imperial Russia from Kraków, Piłsudski gave a commemorative address to his soldiers. Speaking from the newly freed town of Lubertów, north of Lublin, he said:

A year ago, I began the war with a little handful of ill-equipped men. At that time the whole world had sprung to arms. I did not wish it to be possible that, when the new frontiers of states and nations were to be hacked out with swords on the living body of our country, Poles alone should stand aside. Nor, when the swords had been thrown into the scales of fate trembling above our heads, did I wish to permit the Polish sabre to be absent.

And now after a year of war, as at its beginning, we are Poland's only vanguard in arms, as also its moral vanguard, in that we know how to risk all when risk is necessary. Soldiers! Today, after a year of war and toil I am sad that I cannot congratulate you on tremendous triumphs, but I am proud that with greater assurance today than a year ago, I can call to you as in the past: "Forward, boys! Be it to death or life, to victory or defeat, go, awaken Poland to resurrection by deeds of war."[83]

ON AUGUST 5, 1915, German troops took Warsaw, liberating the historic Polish capital from Russian rule for the first time in a hundred years. With liberation, the Polish Military Organization came out into the open. Their first act was to occupy a former Russian government building.[84] In the course of August and September 1915, German units crossed the Bug River and took Brest-Litovsk, Grodno, and Vilna, only to be halted by the Russians after a three-hundred-mile thrust into prewar Russian territory. The German advance in Russia—its greatest victory during World War I—was a stunning turn of events.[85]

Without advance notice, Pilsudski arrived in Warsaw on August 15, stepping foot in a Warsaw free of Russian rule for the first time in his life. What he did not anticipate was the mixed reception he received. The divisive figure—whose suspicion of the Central Powers was known—caused conflict with the political leadership that favored accommodation with the Germans. Pilsudski, they feared, had come at an inopportune time and would only stir up trouble.

Politics aside, the announcement of Pilsudski's arrival created a stir in Warsaw. On August 16 an announcement appeared that there was to be a gathering in front of Hotel Francuski "in honor of the leader of our armed forces, the great warrior for Independence, Jozef Pilsudski."[86] Eighteen-year-old Tadeusz Katelbach came across the flyer. "I ran like crazy with a bunch of my peers to get to the hotel," he recalled. "It would be an exaggeration to say that all of Warsaw came, but there were thousands." When Katelbach arrived, he found a large crowd in front of the hotel chanting Pilsudski's name.[87] But someone else appeared on the balcony to announce that Pilsudski was ill and could not come out to greet them. According to Katelbach, many in the crowd swore at the Germans, accusing them of preventing Pilsudski from making an appearance.

The crowd's hunch seemed to be accurate. As it turned out, the show of support for Pilsudski had alarmed the Germans, who ordered Pilsudski to leave Warsaw, which he did the following day. Prior to his departure, he met with several Polish figures, issuing an order to increase the size of the Polish Military Organization, as well as to suspend recruitment from the Kingdom to the Legions. This policy concerned Sokolnicki, who wondered aloud about the wisdom of alienating both the military department of the NKN and the high command of the Austro-Hungarian Army.[88] Yet nothing swayed Pilsudski from asserting what he believed was in Poland's national interest. "Pilsudski is of the opinion," Jaworski commented on August 19, 1915, "that the people of his country back him, while the high command of the Central Powers stands in his way."[89] In a letter to Ignacy Daszyński from November 1915, Pilsudski wrote that "fighting alongside the Austro-Hungarian Empire as an institution testifies to the fact that Poland's military efforts are not independent."[90]

Meanwhile, Pilsudski's First Brigade was transferred to the front, where it sustained heavy casualties in battles with Russian forces. Among the officers who fell, Pilsudski singled out four by name, two of whom were Jewish. Bronisław Mansperl, now a company commander in the First Brigade, was killed on October 26 in the Battle of Kukle, just north of Białystok.[91] The symbolism of a Jewish commander in Pilsudski's Legions who gave his life for Poland was evident in Arthur Szyk's 1932 *Statute of Kalisz,* a series of forty-five paintings on the history of Jewish life in Poland. Szyk dedicated the volume to Pilsudski,[92] and included Mansperl in his gallery of paintings.

Pilsudski also mentioned by name two other Jewish legionnaires who fell in the Battle of Kukle, twenty-year-old Lieutenant Józef Blauer and forty-one-year-old Adolf Sternschuss. The Legion's weekly paper featured obituaries of all three Jewish soldiers who lost their lives for Poland.[93] In fact, Jewish officers and soldiers of the Polish Legions under Pilsudski's command were a significant component of this armed force: 10 percent in Austrian Galicia and

Dedication page of Artur Szyk's book *The Statute of Kalisz* (Paris, 1928) to Jozef Pilsudski with the intricately decorated initials, "JP." Between them, Szyk places the Polish coat of arms of a crowned white eagle. Below, a legionnaire holds a rifle, protecting a peasant sowing seeds and a young mother with her baby. On the upper part of the letter "P," a peasant in folk costume holds a sabre, attacking a two-headed dragon, the symbol of evil.

4 percent in the Kingdom of Poland.[94] Marian Fuks, former director of the Jewish Historical Institute in Warsaw, noted that "the role of Jews in the Legions has provided historical evidence of those participants' deep, patriotic sense of attachment to Poland; a sacrifice made of their own will for the Polish cause."[95]

THE DRAMATIC TRANSFORMATION in the fortunes of war for the Central Powers also affected the pro-Russian and pro-Entente Polish camp. The Russian withdrawal from Polish territories forced Roman Dmowski and the Polish National Committee to evacuate Warsaw and relocate to St. Petersburg in June 1915.[96] The Grand Duke's promise in August 1914 to reunite the Kingdom of Poland with Polish lands in Austria and Germany was no longer attainable given the new circumstances. Dmowski, having gained Russian political credentials, left the country in November 1915, settling in Paris to promote the Polish cause in Western diplomatic circles.[97]

Henceforth, there would be two major centers of Polish political life: in Central Europe, where the Polish camp was divided between the pro-Habsburg (NKN) and independence (Pilsudski) factions; and Western Europe, where the Polish National Committee under Roman Dmowski and Ignacy Paderewski led the pro-Entente wing, pinning Polish hopes on victory of the Western Allies and Russia.

CHAPTER 11

An Emerging National Leader

Pilsudski is leading a revolution behind the backs of the Germans.

—WŁADYSŁAW JAWORSKI, DIARY ENTRY, JULY 8, 1917

The changing fortunes of war confirmed for Pilsudski the wisdom of his basic assessment. Through his extensive readings and writings on military history, he had acquired an ability to meticulously weigh the strengths and weaknesses of warring parties. He concluded in May 1915 that the Central Powers would soundly defeat the Russians, repelling Russia from Polish lands. This development would usher in the second period in the history of the Polish Legions. Having fulfilled the task of liberating the Kingdom of Poland and Lithuania from Russian control, they would turn their attention to defending them through painstaking diplomatic and military maneuvers. Until then, it was necessary to preserve the national character of the Legions.

In an effort to maximize the probability of a desirable outcome of the war, Pilsudski uncompromisingly stuck to his principles. To prevent redrawing the map of the partitions, whereby the Russian sector of Poland was to be incorporated into the territories of the Central Powers, Pilsudski would dangle before them the most valuable trump card—the Polish soldier. That is why he concluded that after the liberation of Warsaw and Vilna, the Legions—formed as an auxiliary force within the Austro-Hungarian Army to fight against Russia—had outlived their purpose. Pilsudski told a gathering of supporters in September 1915: "I wanted to prove that we could put together an army that would be equal in quality to, or even better than, a professional army. I proved that. I wanted to show that the Polish soldier is superb. I demonstrated that. I wanted to prove that Poles are prepared to die for independence. I have proved that." Moving forward, however, the military and political tracks had to be redirected by wresting them from the control of the Central Powers: "A Polish Army can be formed only by a Polish Government."[1]

The Central Powers were concocting their own scheme. They divided the Kingdom of Poland into two occupation zones in an agreement signed on December 14, 1915. German General Hans Hartwig von Beseler was named governor-general in Warsaw for the northern zone while Austrian General Baron Erich Diller was named governor-general in Lublin for the southern zone.

For every act of the Central Powers, Pilsudski maneuvered in a way so as not to compromise what he perceived as his country's national interests. Nothing weakened his resolve, not even German concessions in Warsaw, where von Beseler granted Warsaw University and Warsaw's Technical High School permission to reopen as Polish institutions of learning and put into motion the beginnings of municipal self-government. Pilsudski's concern was not about the grant of concessions in the area of the Kingdom of Poland under German occupation, rights Poles had long enjoyed in Austrian Galicia. It would have come as no surprise to Pilsudski to know that, in private, von Beseler revealed upon assuming his post in Warsaw that one of his aims was to "contain or deflect political propaganda" in favor of Polish independence.[2]

As we have seen, on the eve of Germany's entry into Warsaw in August 1915, Pilsudski expressed the opinion that the Polish soldier should be used in the war against Russia only in exchange for certain demands. Among them was a legally recognized Polish political authority. With the division of the Kingdom of Poland into two zones, Pilsudski concluded that the best deal he could secure from the Central Powers was internal autonomy under the Austro-Hungarian monarchy, if the Germans could be persuaded.

Although a part of the Pilsudski cult claims he never compromised on full independence for his country, his realistic assessment at this time was that it was unlikely Poland would achieve postwar independence. In the fall of 1915 he concluded that the best he could hope for was the so-called Austro-Polish plan. "Let me begin by stressing from the outset," Pilsudski wrote on September 1, 1915, "that the political objective that I made for myself from the beginning of the war was, and is, the merging of Galicia and the Kingdom of Poland within the framework of the Austro-Hungarian Monarchy. I did not think then, nor do I today, that the war will bring a better outcome for Poland than the one described above." But the realization of that goal, Pilsudski cautioned, "depends to a great extent on this same Austria and its objectives. Unfortunately, Austrian aims for Poland are so vague, unclear, and irresolute, that it is very difficult to base anything on them."[3] We can regard these words, however, as his minimum program, one articulated back in February 1914. But for now it seemed he saw a path to full independence only later in the war.

And indeed, neither Germany nor Austria-Hungary gave any indication of a willingness to make clear commitments. In August 1915 Pilsudski had argued that in return for Polish men fighting alongside the Central Powers against Russia, Polish leaders had to first acquire autonomy for the Legions— that is, a legal agreement on the future status of Poland.[4] Before year's end, however, his aspiration for a fully autonomous Poland, carved out of a union of the Kingdom of Poland and Galicia, became more ambitious. Pilsudski decided that a political body composed of leaders native to the Kingdom of Poland had to be formed. On December 18, 1915, in Warsaw, political parties advocating independence created the Central National Committee (Centralny Komitet Narodowy, CKN). Pilsudski named longtime supporter Artur Śliwiński as head, with a staff composed of activists in the PPS Revolutionary Faction, the Polish Peasant Party, and the National Workers' Union. In its statement of aims, published in February 1916, the organization defined its principal goal as "the attainment of an independent Polish state protected by its own armed forces."[5] On May 16, 1915, Pilsudski laid out his vision for the CKN as a political center, one whose primary functions were to mobilize people through propaganda and raise funds.[6]

Several developments, both personal and professional, occupied Pilsudski in the first half of 1916. In February, in the wake of a severe illness, Pilsudski decided to convert back to Roman Catholicism. On the political front, he objected to the NKN's Military Department, which he regarded as part of an Austrian system of occupation. "Our policy is unchanged," he wrote in May 1916 to Walery Sławek. "That is to say: we will attack the Military Department and the work of the NKN in the Kingdom of Poland; we will protest against the Kingdom's division [into German and Austrian zones] and, above all, we will prohibit the NKN from becoming the vehicle for the internal consolidation of the Kingdom of Poland."[7]

The beginning of 1916 saw changes in the leadership of the Legions. Pilsudski was deeply suspicious of the individuals selected by the Austrian High Command. In February, the Command appointed General Stanisław Puchalski commander of the Legions, replacing Rajmund Baczyński. Both were career officers in the Austro-Hungarian Army whom Pilsudski regarded as excessively loyal and conciliatory. In March 1916 he put forth guidelines on how to wrest control of the Legions from Austrian command. "The central demands," Pilsudski wrote, "must be: the removal of Austrian officers [from the Legions]; I should be the Chief Commander of the Legions; and there should be a ban of the Military Department of the NKN from activities in the Kingdom of Poland."[8]

On March 25 the CKN in Warsaw turned Pilsudski's demands into an ultimatum in a letter to the NKN. "The creator of the Polish armed forces, Jozef Pilsudski," the letter stated, "enjoys the highest respect and is recognized by all stratum of our society. He is the most popular figure in the Kingdom of Poland and is today the property and pride of the entire nation." And yet, "despite his historical role, despite his distinguished and recognized virtues, Pilsudski was pushed aside at the beginning of the war and demoted to a secondary role. Until the chief command is placed in his hands, the Polish Legions will be unable to count on wide support in the Kingdom of Poland."[9]

The Supreme National Committee under Jaworski was well aware of the growing conflict. Yet the NKN, subordinated to the Austrians, could only persuade, not compel, the Austrians on the choice of Legions commander. In his diary Jaworski noted that a discussion about Pilsudski had led to a plan: If Austria openly committed to the independence of Poland, Pilsudski would likely agree to issue an order allowing recruitment in the Kingdom of Poland. He would then be named head of the Legions. "Solidifying ties between Pilsudski and the NKN is an important step to make," Jaworski commented in March 1916.[10]

At a banquet in Lublin in April 1916, Pilsudski said, "It is necessary to do that which heretofore the fatherland has not known: build faith in ourselves without the slightest sluggishness or hesitation." For "the most precious thing for every nation is its own sovereignty. Only things done with one's own hand carry great meaning, including the creation of the renewed military spirit of

Pilsudski, commander of the First Brigade, attending the opening of the art exhibition
"Art of the Legions," Kraków, 1916.

the Poles."[11] That same month Pilsudski was involved in the formation of the
Council of Colonels, an unofficial body made up of regiment commanders
in the Polish Legions. Primarily drawn from officers in the First Brigade, the
creation of the Council of Colonels represented a vote of no confidence by
Pilsudski in both Stanisław Puchalski, the Austrian-appointed chief commander of the Polish Legions, and in the Military Department of the NKN
under Sikorski.[12]

In May 1916, Pilsudski attended a dinner banquet at the Saski Hotel in
Kraków, where, in the presence of NKN Chairman Jaworski, he spoke of a
collective will to restore Poland's dignity. The people of Poland, Pilsudski
forcefully stressed, would not become once again the objects of history with
their national aspirations ruined and their people humiliated. "A mad ambition lives within us," Pilsudski said, "that by our own strength we can create
new Polish values" that would bring about desired outcomes of the war.[13]

Pilsudski in Kraków, 1916.

Following the banquet, Pilsudski left Kraków and headed to the Eastern Front to lead the First Brigade. The first contests took place 137 miles east of Lublin, along the Styr River north of Lutsk, in a series of battles that lasted into the summer of 1916. The fighting turned bloodier when Aleksei Brusilov, commander of Russia's 8th Army, launched the so-called Brusilov Offensive (June 4 to September 20) along the southwestern front. With the Habsburg forces taken by surprise and outnumbered by 132,000 Russian soldiers, the Austro-Hungarian Fourth and Seventh Armies retreated. By the end of June 1916 the Austro-Hungarian Army had sustained huge losses, estimated at 319,500 men, of whom 186,000 were taken as prisoners. In Galicia, Russian gains were modest, advancing thirteen to eighteen miles.[14]

In an effort to delay the Russian offensive, the Austrian High Command ordered all three brigades of the Polish Legions to engage Russian forces. Pilsudski led his First Brigade alongside other divisions of the Legions and the Austrian forces. The Battle of Kostiuchnówka (today Kostyukhnivka, Ukraine) began on July 4, 1916, when Pilsudski led the First Brigade in an attack on two Russian infantry and four Russian cavalry divisions. At the time, Pilsudski's First Brigade consisted of 5,500 men; the Second Brigade numbered 5,200 men, and the Third Brigade, 6,000. For the Battle at Kostiuchnówka, the Legions dispatched 5,350 infantry soldiers and eight hundred cavalry sabers, holding back Russian forces twice their size. For three days the Legions courageously held their positions in fierce fighting with Russian troops, which allowed Austrian forces to retreat in an orderly fashion and fortify new defensive lines.[15] After the third day of battle, the Legions received orders to retreat, and Pilsudski led his men thirty miles westward along the Stochód River (today: Stokhid, Ukraine), where the First Brigade's staff headquarters set up new positions and fortified their lines.

In an appeal to his soldiers issued on July 11, 1916, Pilsudski praised his men. "Despite the bloody and heavy sacrifices we made," he wrote, "we retreated only after we were almost entirely surrounded. We were the last to leave the front, holding back [as long as possible] enemy forces." Among the fallen soldiers Pilsudski paid tribute to in his address was twenty-six-year-old Major Tadeusz Furgalski, who fell on the first day of battle and "earned us so much fame. He trained many soldiers and boosted their morale with his humor and vigor. He was one of our best officers." In his formal report, Pilsudski put First Brigade losses at thirty-five officers and 604 soldiers killed or wounded.[16] Combined with losses in the Second and Third Brigades, killed and wounded amounted to approximately two thousand, making it the most significant battle in the Legions' history.

With high casualties among the Legions, and unsure whether the spilling of Polish blood was bringing about any gains for Poland, Pilsudski decided this would be his last Legions battle. With the Central Powers unwilling to commit to an agreement on Poland, he felt that the Legions had become a mere auxiliary force of the Central Powers. Pilsudski tendered his resignation from the Legions on July 29, 1916. He could no longer in good conscience submit to a situation in which he was fighting for Poland while simultaneously required to be loyal to Austria. By remaining in the Legions, Pilsudski concluded, he was being disloyal both to Austria and Poland.[17] Without the formation of a Polish government in the Kingdom of Poland and an autonomous Polish Army, he could no longer serve in good faith. "In this dilemma," he wrote to Ignacy Daszyński, "I had to settle my conscience and remain loyal only to Poland."[18] Jaworski was among those who felt relief upon hearing the news of Pilsudski's resignation, writing in his diary, "Pilsudski's request for dismissal is a turning point. . . . Gen. Puchalski said that if Pilsudski were to agitate, 'I'll deal with him.'"[19] In the end, the Austrian High Command accepted Pilsudski's request for dismissal on September 27, 1916, two months after he requested it.

Pilsudski reflected on the mixed legacy of the origins of the Legions and the NKN. In a letter to Jaworski, he expressed bitterness about the way in which the Legions had been founded: "The proclamation of August 16 [1914] was certainly splendid for Galicia and for all of Poland. Unfortunately, the mold into which the agreement poured Poland's effort could not have been worse for the success of our cause in the long run." Still worse was that when he was commanding troops in the newly freed areas of the Kingdom of Poland, "Galicia established the NKN and entered into an agreement with Austria behind my back, without any understanding with me."[20]

On August 6, 1916, Pilsudski issued an address to his soldiers to mark the two-year anniversary of the march from Kraków to the freed Polish areas of Russia. It struck a profound and emotional note in the immediate aftermath of his decision to resign from the Legions:

Two years have passed since August 6, 1914, a date memorable in our hearts, when our hands raised upon Polish soil the long-forgotten standard of Polish soldiers fighting in defense of their country. When I went into the field at your head, I was quite aware of the vast obstacles in our way. When I led you out from the walls of Kraków, which did not trust your strength, when I entered with you the towns and townships of the Kingdom [of Poland], I always saw before me a ghost, risen from the graves of our fathers and grandfathers, the ghost of the soldier without a country. . . . But today when we go into battle, we have a treasure to defend which is incontestably our own conquest. . . .

For this end, sacrifices must be made, both those that cost blood and those that do not. Two years have passed. The fate of our country still hangs in the balance. Permit me to wish you and myself that on our next anniversary my order may be read to free Polish soldiers on free Polish soil.[21]

Pilsudski meanwhile held a meeting of the Council of Colonels. The council drafted a petition to the NKN outlining its unified position and demanded that the Polish Legions be transformed into "a Polish Army that fights and dies for the independence of Poland." In addition, the commanders of the Legions "must be distinctly Polish and responsible solely to their own people and government."[22]

During the two-month period between submitting his request for dismissal and receiving a reply, Pilsudski returned to the headquarters of the First Brigade. A window into his fluctuating mood at the time is provided by Felicjan Sławoj Składkowski. "The commander was in good spirits today and joked around with everyone," he wrote in his diary on September 2, 1916. By the evening, Pilsudski's mood had shifted: "At night, however, he did not sleep. Instead, he paced back and forth in his room. So he has another hard thing to resolve and think about for all of us."[23]

Following the Austrian acceptance of Pilsudski's resignation, an exchange with NKN chairman Jaworski followed. "The name 'Pilsudski,'" Jaworski wrote him on October 5, 1916, "is inseparable from the Legions and from the idea of a Polish Army. Our homeland cannot be deprived of the strength which you have and which you provide." He implored him to create "something that will go down in history as inextricably tied to your name. . . . Everyone should feel obligated to help build a state over which shall rise the free White Eagle."[24] Despite sharing Pilsudski's aspirations for Poland, Jaworski cautioned against impulsive action. Pilsudski replied the following day:

I wanted the Polish soldier to be something more than a pretty picture. . . .
I wanted Poland, who had forgotten the sword so entirely since 1863, to
see it flashing in the air in the hands of her own soldiers. Believe me,
Distinguished Chairman, if it were possible to ask her young solders
sleeping in the graves, their sincere feeling about Poland—and the dead
and dying do not lie—they would say with me, their leader, that we do not
regret either blood or sacrifice if this dream of long years has been fulfilled. The Polish soldier created by Polish efforts has given his country
a new value, which it did not before possess.[25]

Pilsudski's emerging identification as a symbol of the nation—as irreplace-
able—was reflected in the next sentence: "I am proud, Mr. Chairman, that I
was the soul of these solders' work."

The CKN in Warsaw put out a statement on Pilsudski and the Legions, announcing that "the Legions' page of history has come to an end." Neither his
request for a National Government in Warsaw nor for an autonomous Polish
Army had been granted. The CKN pledged to continue: "We are proceeding
henceforth hand in hand with the Polish soldier. We have shown our combat
readiness and preparedness to fight against Russia."[26] On October 7, 1916, a
day after the CKN issued the statement, the Polish Legions' three brigades
were drawn back for rest. Under Austrian command, on October 20, the
Polish Legions were reorganized as the Polish Auxiliary Corps (Polski Kor-
pus Posiłkowy).

The Two Emperors' Manifesto

The resignation of Pilsudski no doubt led to dissension in the newly reorganized Polish Auxiliary Corps. Between the spring and fall of 1916, European
armies sustained staggeringly high losses. In the battles of Verdun and the
Somme on the Western Front, as well as in the Brusilov offensive on the
Eastern Front, the Central Powers and the Entente alliance sustained combined losses of over 2 million men in the east and 1.6 million in the west. The
loss of manpower by the Central Powers was crippling. At the Battle of Verdun
(February 21 to September 9, 1916), German losses numbered between 281,000
and 315,000. At the Somme (July 4 to November 18, 1916) they lost close to
500,000 (dead, wounded, missing, and captured). On the Eastern Front, between March and September 1916, the Austro-Hungarian Army lost upward

of 600,000 men, the majority taken as prisoners. The heavy losses reduced its forces by nearly one-half on the front with Russia.[27]

Desperate for new sources of manpower, the Central Powers turned their attention to the eastern borderlands for local recruits. In June 1916 Governor-General von Beseler pointed out that it would be difficult to recruit Polish soldiers without a decision on the independence of Poland. German chancellor von Bethmann-Hollweg and Austro-Hungarian foreign minister Stephan Burian were persuaded, and in August they presented a plan for an independent state, confined to the former Russian provinces of Poland, with an armed force under German command. The new Polish state, however, would not be allowed to conduct an independent foreign policy.[28]

In October 1916, von Beseler asked Józef Brudziński, rector of Warsaw University, to draw up a memorandum expressing Polish aspirations. Brudziński, a conservative Pole in the former Russian sector, completed it with the help of likeminded colleagues. Presented to Berlin on October 28, 1916, and subsequently to officials in Vienna, the memorandum stated that "though it is true that we are not the authorized representatives of Poland, we yet feel that we have the right to express in its name its unquenchable desire for the reestablishment of an independent Polish State. The circumstances brought about by the war demand an immediate proclamation by the Central Powers in which the fact is recognized that Poland is independent, with their full support."[29] That a Polish conservative could make such a bold statement to the leaders of the two occupying powers was a reflection of how far public opinion had changed since the outbreak of the war. Rumors circulated about an imminent announcement on Polish independence, and on November 3 Pilsudski sent guidelines to the CKN on how to respond if such a declaration was announced.[30]

On November 5, 1916, Kaiser Wilhelm II and Emperor Franz Joseph jointly issued the so-called Two Emperors' Manifesto announcing the establishment of an independent Kingdom of Poland. The new autonomous state would consist of Polish lands conquered from Russia and would be a constitutional monarchy. Its precise frontiers would be decided after the conclusion of hostilities in Europe. "While calling for the creation of a truncated state entirely subordinated to the Central Powers," Andrzej Nowak noted, "the decree nevertheless had a fundamentally positive significance for the problem of Polish independence. For it was the first decree in World War I of an international-legal matter devoted in its entirety to Poland, a decree issued by governments that actually ruled over Polish lands."[31] Adam Zamoyski has interpreted the manifesto differently, describing it as a sinister ploy. "Neither the Germans nor the Austrians," he wrote, "were in fact going to give up any of their own Polish territories, so it was a very strange Poland they were proposing. The future constitution was deliberately ill-defined, and it was fairly evident that the state would be no more than a puppet."[32] In his 1935 work, Leon Wasilewski viewed the manifesto as a rejection of the Austro-Polish proposal whereby the Kingdom of Poland and Austrian Galicia would be united into a single, autonomous Polish region. "The act of November 5 was decisive proof of the bankruptcy of the Austrian solution to the Polish question," he wrote.[33]

Despite the act's obvious shortcomings, Pilsudski used the opportunity to ruminate on its significance. The proclamation, he argued on the day the proclamation was announced, constituted nothing less than a watershed moment with far-reaching, precedent-setting consequences:

> For the first time in this world war, public utterances of fallen words long forgotten outside of Poland can be heard today in our cities from the mouths of representatives of the great armies and nations: "Polish Independence," "Polish Government," "Polish Army." Years ago, our fathers and grandfathers died on the battlefields for these words. We secretly walked forth with those words, sometimes sacrificing our liberty or even our lives, to create the building blocks of their essential substance. We tried to say these same words in the name of Poland on the memorable day of August 6, 1914.[34]

Those who shared Pilsudski's excitement included Wacław Jędrzejewicz, a twenty-three-year-old member of Pilsudski's First Brigade. Jędrzejewicz recalled that the Two Emperors' Manifesto "was one of the most important documents touching on Poland. It, indeed, placed the Polish question on an international scale for the first time . . . Those of us who lived in Warsaw at the time experienced this moment with great emotion, full of hope for the future."[35]

Although Pilsudski believed that the manifesto had set a landmark precedent in international affairs, he nevertheless knew in his gut that it was merely a cynical grab for Polish troops. Indeed, the German and Austrian governors-general in Warsaw and Lublin issued a second proclamation on November 9,

1916, calling on the inhabitants of the Kingdom of Poland to sign up for the new Polish Army.[36] At Pilsudski's urging, the CKN replied the following day: "A Polish Army can only be formed by a Polish State—the only legal dispenser of Polish blood."[37] And to make it clear that Poles—not the Central Powers— would choose their military leaders, the circular informed the Central Powers that "in Jozef Pilsudski, the steadfast creator of the Polish military movement, we have our commander in whose hands the Polish people shall place their sword with the utmost confidence." In a letter to the Warsaw University rector, Pilsudski had earlier made his position clear: "Soldiers . . . must have behind them a government that sets goals and appoints army chiefs and leaders."[38]

Sensing a challenge to his authority, Governor Beseler met with CKN leaders on November 10, 1916. In the course of the discussion, CKN head Artur Śliwiński put forth demands for a provisional Polish government and the formation of a Military Department headed by Pilsudski. "I know who Pilsudski is," Beseler replied. "He is the fiery patriot and great organizer. But your wanting to see him as head of the army is going too far. Such a position requires many years of experience and technical training. At the very least, however, having his cooperation in the creation of an army would be very desirable."[39]

Not long after, on December 13, Pilsudski met Beseler for the first time. They parted with mutual antipathy. Pilsudski said Beseler lectured him for an hour and a half and appeared annoyed whenever Pilsudski tried to interject or speak at all. Beseler, Pilsudski noted, "seems to be of the opinion that he understands the interests of Poland better than I do. He told me, 'you will have to relearn a few things in Warsaw,' to which I replied, 'I have been studying meticulously all aspects of the Polish question for 25 years. There is nothing left for me to learn.'"[40]

Pilsudski met with Beseler a second time to discuss his position on the formation of a Polish Army. But Beseler made it clear that all decisions relating to the Polish Army would be in German hands. After the second meeting, Pilsudski spoke about the exchange with Bogusław Miedziński, a legionnaire then active in the POW. "Beseler is an odd guy," Pilsudski told him, "some kind of unusual cross between a Prussian general and a German professor. This combination of a general's self-confidence, professional arrogance, and loquaciousness makes it impossible to reach an agreement with him." Beseler "toots his horn like a babbling goose, not understanding just how absurd it is to lecture me on what is in Poland's best interests."[41] Beseler, for his part, regarded Pilsudski as a military dilettante and demagogue.

Pilsudski's suspicions about German and Austrian motives were borne out as news filtered in about plans for the new Polish state. On December 13, 1916, the Central Powers selected Archduke Charles Stephen of Austria, brother of Austro-Hungarian commander in chief Archduke Frederick, as regent of Poland. A press account reported that "the Archduke Charles Stephen's only connection with Poland has been that one of his daughters, Archduchess Renée, is married to Prince Jerome Radziwill of Warsaw."[42] The press coverage was, in fact, misinformed for Archduke Stephen had genuine ties to Poland and Polish culture. Not only did he speak Polish but two—not one—of his sons-in-law were Polish: Archduke Stephen's second daughter, Archduchess Mechthildis, had married Prince Olgierd Czartoryski in 1913.[43]

Pilsudski meeting with Archduke Frederick, heir to the Austro-Hungarian throne and commander of the Austro-Hungarian Army, Jędrzejów, March 1915.

Pilsudski continued to apply pressure on Beseler about the formation of a Polish armed force. In a lengthy, detailed memorandum dated December 26, 1916, Pilsudski wrote the Warsaw governor-general that a Polish armed force linked to the new state had to not only be led by Poles but headed by an individual in whom the people had complete confidence.[44] Under Pilsudski's direction, the Central National Committee distributed a circular reinforcing this position. "Only a Polish government can . . . create a Polish Army," it stated. "Soldiers should take an oath of loyalty before Polish authorities. From the beginning of their existence, these soldiers should feel part of a free homeland." Pilsudski "is the only man to lead such an army. These are essential preconditions, the only ones that will guarantee that the history of the Legions—formed by Austro-Hungarian authorities—is not repeated."[45] In an interview with a Warsaw newspaper, Pilsudski reflected that the Poles "have not possessed a state for so long that they have cultivated a non-state culture."[46]

The Central Powers, meanwhile, made good on their promise to form Polish state institutions. On December 6, 1916, the German and Austrian governors-generals announced the creation of a Provisional State Council in Warsaw (*Tymczasowa Rada Stanu,* TRS). The new governing body was to be composed of twenty-five members selected by the occupying powers. The announcement effectively shifted the center of Polish political life under the Central Powers from Kraków to Warsaw. That is why on December 12, 1916, Pilsudski moved to Warsaw, where he took up residence on Służewska Street at the home of Michał Sokolnicki.[47]

The move to Warsaw had a significant impact on Pilsudski's personal life. For it signaled the de facto dissolution of his marriage to Maria Pilsudska. The two would remain separate for the rest of Maria's life. At the same time, the move to Warsaw allowed Pilsudski the freedom to advance his relationship with his longtime mistress, Alexandra Szczerbińska, who—after her release from prison at the end of 1916—had also settled in Warsaw. The forty-nine-year-old Pilsudski and thirty-four-year-old Alexandra, both childless, began trying to have a baby. Given that Maria refused to give Pilsudski a divorce, Jozef and Alexandra knew that such a child would be born out of wedlock. But given their ages, waiting longer was not an option.

In Warsaw, meanwhile, Pilsudski's nomination to the Provisional State Council became official on December 31.[48] The Council's opening ceremony took place on January 14, 1917, at the Royal Castle. In addition to German and Austrian commissioners, the Council consisted of six members from the CKN, nine from conservative groups, and ten nonparty representatives. Pilsudski was selected to head the TRS's Military Commission. Opening the ceremony, the body's chairman, landowner Wacław Niemojowski, proclaimed: "The formation of a national army under its own colors, ready to service the country, will be our task, beside the organization of the Polish State."[49]

At the beginning of March 1917, Pilsudski sat down with journalist Władysław Baranowski. "I am leading a war against Russia with the Germans only because it aids me in these efforts," Pilsudski said.[50] Pilsudski then handed the journalist a copy of a set of instructions he was about to present to the Provisional State Council. First, the instructions stated, Poland had to have an independent existence formed by a Polish armed force to regain and consolidate a state. Second, Poles had to form an army on Polish territory with the aid of the Central Powers, as long as the army's national character was preserved. The new Polish army was to be used *only* against Russia. Third, Poles would aid captive peoples in imperial Russia for the attainment of mutual, democratic aims. The fourth point Pilsudski emphasized was that Poland's true historic ties were not with the Central Powers but with the Western democracies: "Independent Poland cannot in the future find itself in opposition regarding its relations to the Western countries with whom she shall always have friendly ties."[51] Pilsudski could not have been clearer: Poles shared a common enemy with the Central Powers in Russia. The situation in the West was diametrically the opposite: Poles regarded France and Britain, against whom the Central Powers were waging war, as close friends and allies. The blood of Polish soldiers could be spilled only and exclusively on the Eastern Front. Pilsudski had thus drawn red lines around what he perceived to be his country's national interests, lines he absolutely refused to cross.

ON MARCH 16, 1917, thirteen days after Pilsudski's interview, the three-hundred-year rule of the Romanov dynasty in Russia came to an abrupt end. Tsar Nicholas II abdicated the throne, nominating his brother as successor, who politely declined the offer the following day, ceding power to the Duma. When Nicholas returned to St. Petersburg six days later, the newly formed Provisional Government placed him and his family under house arrest. For the first

time in Russian history, the acting heads of the government proclaimed a democracy. As Pilsudski had predicted, the collapse of tsarist rule led to a decisive change in Poland's favor. The new Provisional Government, severing itself
entirely from the tsarist regime, came out in favor of a free, independent Poland. By unanimous vote, the Provisional Government in St. Petersburg issued the following statement on March 30, 1917: "The Russian people, who
have thrown off the yoke of despotism, recognize the full right of the kindred
Polish people to determine equally their destiny according to their wishes."
The new, democratic Russia "considers the creation of an independent Polish
state in all territories where the Polish people constitute a majority of the population as a certain guarantee of durable peace in the remodeled Europe of the
future."[52] The Provisional Government's support for Poland was a watershed
moment for the Polish Question in World War I. For the fall of the tsar removed the central constraint on the Entente alliance with regard to Poland,
setting into motion an entirely new international climate favorable to Poland.

The abdication of the tsar in March 1917 also removed the one factor that
had united Poland with Germany. As head of the Provisional State Council's
Military Commission, Pilsudski had already placed the 11,200 fighters of the
Polish Military Organization in the council's service on January 16, 1917.[53]
This was both a goodwill gesture to the Provisional State Council as well as
a message to Beseler that Pilsudski's soldiers would take orders only from a
Polish authority. It is not surprising, therefore, that tensions between Pilsudski and Beseler steadily increased in the first half of 1917. Pilsudski, for
his part, did everything he could to ensure the autonomy of the future Polish
Army while Beseler worked to prevent it. At a meeting of the Military Commission on January 22, 1917, a German official stressed that Beseler was to be
head of the Polish Army, a view absolutely unacceptable to Pilsudski.[54]

Pilsudski voiced concern about the TRS's ability to assert Polish interests.
"The State Council," he wrote Leon Wasilewski on February 1, 1917, "is very
indecisive in all matters and fears taking any firm decisions." In a February 1917 session of the Provisional State Council, Pilsudski said he had a
bad feeling about German plans for a Polish Army: "Negotiations on the
whole matter of the Polish Army are taking place behind our backs—everything is in the dark." The Polish Army "must be national in character. It
must maintain close ties with the nation so as not to create a demarcation
line between it and the people."[55]

Pilsudski's suspicions of the Central Powers increased during this time. Much of the problem, he maintained in a letter to a Jagiellonian University professor on March 15, 1917, was the profound mistrust by the Central Powers of the Poles in general. This mistrust was evident in the conditions they had placed at every step in their Polish policy. "The Central Powers have never had respect for the autonomy of national cultures or the Polish nation's sense of honor and dignity," Pilsudski remarked. "In this way, one always has the impression that the Central Powers systematically destroy with one hand what the other one is trying to build." He added:

> That is one aspect of the matter, but we, the Poles, are dealing with the phenomenon of an upbringing in conditions of captivity, in a system of compromise with everyone and everything, without honor and dignity, with a feeling of fear of every major task that we take upon ourselves. That is why I do not remember a single moment or move in the past couple of years that would not be marked by this uniquely Polish trait of competing for who is worse, and of bidding to move us, not up but, on the contrary, downward.[56]

In short, life in the Kingdom of Poland after the Two Emperors' Manifesto was no different from life for the Poles in Austrian Galicia. To the TRS's department of internal affairs, Pilsudski said, "We have the freedom to create this army; we must have the desire to create this army; we have to build among us a mental state that, when the moment arrives for the creation of such an army, will allow us not to disappoint ourselves, but rather to form a sufficiently great force on which the Polish government shall ultimately rest."[57]

The ultimate proof of Pilsudski's misgivings about German aims came on March 25, 1917. The Provisional State Council, under pressure from Pilsudski, requested a meeting with the German and Austrian governors-generals in the Kingdom of Poland to discuss policy on the formation of the Polish Army. Beseler replied that there was no need for such a meeting. The Central Powers had no obligation to cooperate with the Provisional State Council on this matter.[58]

The rebuff led Pilsudski to lose all confidence in the Central Powers. At the first session of the Provisional State Council following Beseler's reply, Pilsudski announced that the Military Commission was suspending activities—for, in light of Beseler's position, the commission's purpose was entirely unclear.

Pilsudski therefore proposed that the commission begin preparing the formation of a national armed force in secret.[59]

On April 10, 1917, Austro-Hungarian emperor Charles I transferred the Polish Auxiliary Corps to German control, naming Beseler commander in chief of Polish forces. The Provisional State Council expressed distinct displeasure with the decision, characterizing it as proof that the Council would have no authority over the future Polish Army.[60] In a statement issued on April 16, 1917, the Central National Committee conveyed similar reservations. "The decision not to place the Polish Legions directly under the control of the Provisional State Council raises justified bitterness in our society and complicates the issue of forming a national army. Today . . . an army of our own—a national army—is for us indispensable." Nor could Pilsudski be cast aside, for "he is not only a symbol but a guarantee of our freedom." It was Pilsudski who was up to the task of "creating conditions in which a great, fighting National Army will emerge."[61]

Between May and June 1917, Pilsudski repeatedly proposed that the Provisional State Council dissolve itself in protest. At the Council session on July 2, Pilsudski announced his resignation. The entire staff of his Military Commission followed suit. In his address, he stated that the Provisional State Council no longer had the confidence of the public. Pilsudski was withdrawing not as a politician but as a military man who no longer harbored any belief that the Germans ever intended to allow the formation of an autonomous Polish Army.[62] To a group of senior Legionnaire officers immediately following his resignation, Pilsudski made the point clear: "All our interests and that of Germany are now at odds. Germany strives, above all, to defeat the Allies, whereas we desire that the Allies defeat Germany."[63]

Pilsudski's resignation set in motion what came to be known as the Oath Crisis. Fearing Pilsudski's next step, the German authorities ordered all Polish soldiers on July 9, 1917, to take an oath of loyalty to the armies of Germany and Austria-Hungary. At Pilsudski's urging, the commanders of the First and Third brigades of the Polish Legions refused. The majority of the Polish Military Organization's command headquarters, as well as most of its regional commanders, followed suit. The result was that an estimated 74 percent of legionnaires originating in the Kingdom of Poland refused to take the oath and were consequently placed in military custody. On July 14, German authorities arrested ninety members of the Polish Military Organization, including leaders Walery Sławek and Wacław Jędrzejewicz.[64] Some of the arrested legionnaires, while in transport to an internment camp, managed to smuggle out an illegal circular. "For our faithful loyalty to a principle," the leaflet stated, "we have been taken to an internment camp." It added that "before the band of Prussian lackeys and traitors stands one great Nation that, with arms in hand, fights for the independence of their Homeland." Germany was now regarded as an enemy.[65]

Władysław Jaworski, observing events from Kraków, had as far back as February 1917 expressed unease with Pilsudski's conspiratorial activities. The decision to withdraw from the TRS, in his opinion, went too far. "Since resigning from the Provisional State Council," Jaworski wrote in his diary on July 8, 1917, "Pilsudski is leading a revolution behind the backs of the Germans."[66] Another critic, Iza Moszczeńska, a leading feminist writer and wartime political activist, went public with her concerns, circulating an open letter to Pilsudski on July 11 cautioning against what she believed was radical subversion that could reverse all the gains that had been achieved. Back in January 1917, Moszczeńska had written Jaworski that "Pilsudski acts like a dictator. Such gestures are looked upon badly."[67]

Beseler made a last-ditch effort to bring an end to the Oath Crisis by calling Pilsudski into his office at the Belvedere Palace in Warsaw on July 20. Beseler proposed offering Pilsudski command of the Polish Army. Such an arrangement, Beseler reportedly said, would be to their mutual advantage. But the appeal simply came too late. "You are mistaken," Pilsudski is said to have replied, "You perhaps would gain one Pole, but I should lose a whole nation."[68] Seeing a possible opportunity to assert Polish control, Pilsudski drew up a list of conditions to be met for any such agreement in a letter to Beseler.[69] But before the letter ever reached the governor-general, Beseler decided it was too risky to have Pilsudski remain at large. On July 22, 1917, he gave the order to arrest Pilsudski and his chief of staff, Sosnkowski.

That evening, Pilsudski and Artur Śliwiński were having tea at Michał Sokolnicki's apartment. Sokolnicki recalled that "the mood was foul. There was no way to make light of the situation." Anxious about what was going to happen, "Pilsudski, as often was the case in such tense situations, was very preoccupied, closed in on himself more than usual, taciturn but infinitely kind."[70] Śliwiński recalled Pilsudski remarking that his arrest was imminent. German authorities entered Sokolnicki's home that same evening and took Pilsudski into custody. After being placed in a temporary facility, he was transferred to the military prison in Magdeburg, Germany, ninety-seven miles west of Berlin, on August 22, 1917. Pilsudski languished there for the remaining thirteen months of World War I.

Imprisonment

The arrest profoundly influenced Pilsudski's future. It dramatically strengthened his image as a national leader and symbol both at home and abroad. While his supporters were outraged, and the Provision State Council issued a formal protest, others who favored accommodation with the Central Powers were of the opinion that arresting Pilsudski was probably a good thing. "I regard the news of Pilsudski's arrest with a sense of relief," Jaworski wrote in his diary on July 24, 1917. "Yes, there will be outrage but I think things will calm down and be easier."[71]

A *New York Times* correspondent on July 29 reported large street demonstrations in Warsaw to protest the arrest. "General Pilsudski's following," the article stated, "is far greater than the German reports give any impression of," adding that "not merely single units of Polish legionaries refused to take the military oath, but whole regiments."[72] Following the distribution of illegal leaflets condemning the arrest, the *Boston Daily Globe* warned that "unless Gen. Pilsudski is released immediately, it is believed serious consequences will ensue," while the *Times* of London reported that all members of the Warsaw city council had stood in protest and chanted "Long Live Pilsudski!"[73] The London paper subsequently noted opposition even in Germany, citing the views of a prominent professor, Otto Hoetzsch, who argued that Pilsudski's arrest was proof of the bankruptcy of Germany's and Austria-Hungary's policy. The project for an independent Kingdom of Poland linked to the Central Powers, the professor wrote, "fails to observe that the Poles most decidedly do not want to receive this [Polish] kingdom from the Central Powers; they want to base it upon an international guarantee, with absolute freedom for their future relations and orientation of policy, and with all reserves concerning their wishes about Galicia and the Polish districts of Russia."[74]

The culmination of the Oath Crisis came on August 25, 1917, when the Provisional State Council dissolved itself in an act of protest. Scrambling to recover from the fiasco, Germany transferred supreme authority in the Kingdom of Poland to a three-man Regency Council on September 12.[75] The highly respected mayor of Warsaw, Prince Lubomirski, was named head of the new body at a ceremony held at the Royal Castle. The Regency Council had no popular sanction and was widely regarded as serving the interests of the Central Powers alone. Yet the Central Powers followed through with their pledge, entrusting the Polish-run Regency Council with the task of forming a government, albeit one that would not be permitted to conclude any international agreements while still under German-Austrian occupation.[76] In November 1917 the Central Powers approved the Regency Council's draft for a constitution as well as historian Jan Kucharzewski for prime minister. On December 7, 1917, Kucharzewski and his cabinet of ministers were sworn into office. Armies of the Central Powers still commanded the Polish forces, and the German and Austrian governments could revise or veto any legislation arising from the new Polish government. An illegal circular appearing at the time described the Regency Council as a sham, reminding readers of the thousands of Polish soldiers in internment camps. "We demand the freeing of their leader, Pilsudski! Only then will it be possible to form an independent Polish Army."[77]

More and more attention was paid to Pilsudski, sitting in a German military prison. An example of the imprisoned Pilsudski's powerful impact was revealed on July 30, 1917, in the private remarks of an Austrian government official: "Pilsudski's popularity as a martyr is growing. . . . After the war, he will return as a hero, a martyr and the most popular figure in Poland."[78] The *New York Times* reported on September 7, 1917, that "the Austro-German masters have dared to lay their hands on a man of whom the entire Polish nation is proud and who, in a sense, is the living symbol of Polish independence and freedom."[79] There is no doubt that the German arrest greatly raised Pilsudski's profile as a national leader. By sacrificing his own personal freedom for the cause of national dignity, he won the hearts of many of his opponents, thus making him into a truly national hero. To historians Daria and Tomasz Nałęcz, the significance of the German imprisonment was that it put to rest the accusation that Pilsudski had served as a German and Austrian agent during the war, while to historian Andrzej Chwalba, the arrest of Pilsudski "directly contributed to the strengthening of the cult of the commandant."[80]

AS THE CENTRAL POWERS moved forward in the establishment of Polish state institutions in the fall and winter of 1917, Pilsudski was far from forgotten.

In December 1917 four Warsaw-based political parties signed a petition stating that while the formation of a Polish government, cabinet, and constitution were positive developments, they were illegitimate in the eyes of the public as long as Pilsudski remained in prison.[81] In February 1918 a circular appeared in Warsaw claiming that the continued imprisonment of Pilsudski "builds in Polish society chronic vexation and unrest. The imprisonment of the Unshaken Leader has become a symbol that, like a nightmare, hovers over the life of the nation and poisons the atmosphere."[82]

In Magdeburg, meanwhile, Pilsudski was housed in a two-story wooden fortress. He described his living conditions as "very comfortable," with the entire second story to himself, including a bedroom, dining room, and a third room "that looked as if I was meant to receive people in it—which in my situation could only make me laugh." He was allowed to freely stroll in the garden outside, which always included an armed soldier on guard. "I was granted many comforts and unusual freedom," Pilsudski commented, "and thus had the freest prison life imaginable."[83] Although treated with respect due to his military rank, he was completely isolated. For twelve months, the only person he ever saw was the armed guard outside the fortress. The isolation became a form of psychological torment as German authorities refused all requests for visitors. Pilsudski passed his fiftieth birthday on December 5, 1917, alone with his thoughts. His isolation only came to an end in August 1918, when he was joined by Sosnkowski, with whom he spent the remaining months of the war.

In Warsaw, meanwhile, Alexandra Szczerbińska gave birth to Pilsudski's first child, Wanda, on February 7, 1918. Not only did German authorities deny Alexandra's repeated appeals for visitation rights, but for five weeks they withheld Alexandra's letters related to Wanda's birth. Pilsudski surely knew Alexandra was pregnant before his arrest. In a letter to Alexandra before he received the birth notice, he asked for the name Wanda in case the baby was a girl.[84] Upon receiving a birth notice, Pilsudski's elation leaped off the page at the news in a letter dated March 18, 1918; he was sorry only that he could not be there, hold her in his arms and gaze into her eyes. A month later he wrote to Alexandria, "Write and tell me more of the baby. I am grateful for even the most trivial details; as I cannot see her they make me imagine that we are all together."[85] A photo finally got through, for which he thanked Alexandra profusely in a letter.

In a terrible twist of fate, shortly after Wanda's birth, news arrived of a family tragedy. On May 17, 1918, Piłsudski's older brother, Bronisław, was found dead in the Seine River in Paris. Having drowned under mysterious circumstances, Bronisław evidently committed suicide.[86] The birth of Wanda and the death of Bronisław, combined with absolute isolation in a military prison, brought to the surface myriad tangled emotions for Piłsudski. One way to get his mind off the horrific news of his brother's suicide was to write. And write he did, composing a manuscript chronicling the military history of his First Brigade during World War I. Although the hundreds of hand-written pages remained in Magdeburg after Piłsudski's release, the German authorities returned the entire manuscript after the war. Piłsudski subsequently published his wartime study in 1925 under the title, *Moje Pierwsze Boje* (My First War Experience).

Woodrow Wilson on Poland

Across the Atlantic Ocean, the United States openly championed Polish independence for the first time during the war. President Woodrow Wilson's inclination was influenced by Colonel Edward House, his closest advisor. House first began to champion the Polish cause in November 1915 after meeting Ignacy Paderewski, the internationally renowned pianist and national activist who had moved to the United States in April 1915 as leader of the Polish relief effort. Paderewski was invited to meet with Wilson on November 6, 1916, at the president's country estate in Shadow Lawn, New Jersey, the day after the Central Powers had issued the Two Emperors' Manifesto announcing an independent Kingdom of Poland. Both Paderewski and Wilson were well informed about the manifesto. Not only had they likely received their own briefings, but the news was splashed over the front pages of the *New York Times* and *Washington Post*.

The meeting began with Wilson asking Paderewski his opinion about the proclamation. Paderewski expressed his view that it was merely a ploy by the Central Powers to enlist Polish soldiers. Wilson evidently replied that he agreed entirely with the assessment.[87] First Lady Edith Wilson, who was present at the meeting, later commented, "I shall never forget Mr. Paderewski's face as he stood pleading the cause of his country. It was so fine, so tragic, so earnest."[88] With Wilson's election to a second term that November,

Paderewski continued to use House to influence the president. "It was solely through Paderewski," House acknowledged, "that I became so deeply interested in the cause of Pound, and repeatedly passed upon [Paderewski's views to] the President which I had made my own."[89]

Wilson's advocacy for Poland was due not to a desire to garner the Polish American vote but to ideological conviction. On January 22, 1917, he made explicit reference to Poland in his address to the Senate. This first major foreign policy speech since Wilson was reelected is commonly known as his "Peace without Victory" address. He declared:

> No peace can last, or ought to last, which does not recognize and accept the principle that governments derive all their just powers from the consent of the governed, and that no right anywhere exists to hand peoples about from sovereignty to sovereignty as if they were property. I take it for granted, for instance, if I may venture upon a single example, that statesmen everywhere are agreed that there should be a united, independent, and autonomous Poland. [90]

Wilson's speech reverberated not only in the Polish world, but throughout the capitals of Europe, positioning America as a champion of the rights of all peoples to self-determination.

In Warsaw, the Provisional State Council issued a proclamation praising Wilson's address. Given that it was accepted unanimously, we know Pilsudski endorsed it. The statement read in part, "It is the first time in this war that the head of a powerful neutral State . . . has declared officially that, according to his conviction, the independence of the Polish State is the only just solution of the Polish question and an insurmountable condition of a lasting and just peace."[91]

Pilsudski commented on Wilson's landmark speech in a discussion on the Entente with a journalist in Warsaw. "As far as the Entente, and France in particular," Pilsudski said in the first days of March 1917, "I doubt that in the present moment, when France is so sensitive to Russian concerns due to the occupation of the entire Kingdom of Poland, that she could, or even wants to, follow Wilson's gesture." But eventually, Pilsudski added, France and Britain would have to back Wilson. "As a nation with democratic traditions and aspirations," Pilsudski said, "we expect from the great democratic countries the same encouragement and hope that Wilson's address has brought us."[92]

President Woodrow Wilson addressing the US Senate, proclaiming support for "a united, independent, and autonomous Poland" after the war. January 22, 1917.

The fall of the tsar in March played a role in the decision of the United States to enter the war. On April 2, 1917, Wilson asked Congress for a declaration of war against Germany. "The world must be made safe for democracy," Wilson said in his address. "Its peace must be planted upon the tasted foundation of political liberty."[93] Four days later Congress gave Wilson its approval, bringing the United States formally into World War I. (The United States declared against Austria-Hungary on December 7, 1917.) The American entry into the war greatly increased the weight and importance of US support for Polish independence. The United States was the only great power to have endorsed Polish independence prior to entering the war.

Poland in the International Arena

Between Pilsudski's imprisonment in July 1917 and the end of the war on November 11, 1918, huge changes took place in international affairs. The first was recognition by the Allied states of Western Europe and the United States

of a single Polish leadership body. In August 1917 the epicenter of Polish political life changed from Warsaw, where the Provisional State Council resigned, to Paris, where the pro-Entente Polish National Committee (Komitet
Narodowy Polski, KNP), established on August 15, in Lausanne, Switzerland,
opened its headquarters. Roman Dmowski was named president of the émigré
organization, which was staffed primarily by followers of his populist National Democratic Party. On August 22, 1917, the KNP invited Ignacy Paderewski to serve as the organization's delegate in Washington. Although
Paderewski accepted the invitation, he warned that "some members [of the
KNP] are highly unpopular." He pointed to Dmowski, whose pronounced
anti-Jewish prejudices made him a particularly unwise choice for president.
Paderewski tried to persuade the KNP that if it wanted to be regarded as
genuinely representative, it should include socialists, Jews, and members
of the Polish Peasant Party.[94]

Dmowski's anti-Jewish views, expressed openly since the 1890s, were unmistakable. Despite pressure on him to tamp down his rhetoric, he remained
vocally anti-Jewish. He wrote on July 18, 1917, "Our problem with Russia pales
in comparison with our problem with Germany. And our problem with Germany is, in fact, an easier one to solve than the problem of the Jews." Dmowski
likewise wrote on May 15, 1917, that "the Free-masons and Jews are the most
harmful element as far as the Polish question is concerned both in the Entente
and the neutral countries."[95]

In the end Dmowski refused to abide by Paderewski's suggestion to make
the KNP more representative of the Polish lands. At the same time, however,
Dmowski is rightly credited with furthering the Polish national cause. In October 1917 France approved his choice of General Józef Haller to command a
new Polish Army in France, a force that had grown to 57,300 by war's end.
By the fall of 1917 the Western Allies recognized the KNP in Paris as the official representative body of Poland and the Polish Army in France as a co-
belligerent of the Entente. The KNP received formal recognition as representatives of Poland by France (September 20), Great Britain (October 15), Italy
(October 30), and the United States (November 10).[96] Earlier Dmowski had
expressed his wholehearted faith in the United States and Britain to support
an independent Poland with access to the sea. "As it is today, so during the
peace negotiations," Dmowski wrote in May 1917, "the most important part
will be played by the Anglo-Saxons, i.e., Great Britain and the U.S.A. This

general statement holds good also for the Polish question. In its solution the above States will play a decisive role."[97]

The fall of 1917 was a time of more cataclysmic changes in Russia. On November 7–9, Vladimir Lenin and the Bolsheviks seized power in St. Petersburg. The fall of the Provisional Government had huge consequences for the course of the war. The new Bolshevik government vowed to withdraw from the war and conclude a separate peace with Germany, throwing the entire international order into disarray. Regarding the fate of non-Russian peoples, the new, anti-imperialist Russian government issued a "Declaration of the Rights of the Peoples of Russia" on November 15, 1917. It included a sweeping statement in support of "the right of the peoples of Russia to free self-determination, even to the point of separation and the formation of an independent state."

It was in the field of foreign policy that the Russian Revolution so starkly altered the course of the war. On December 22, 1917, Bolshevik Russia's chief negotiator, Leon Trotsky, entered into talks with Germany at Brest-Litovsk, leading to the suspension of hostilities. For all practical purposes, Russia had left the war. Prior to the commencement of peace talks, the Polish prime minister in Warsaw, Jan Kucharzewski, formally requested Polish representation at Brest-Litovsk, but Germany denied the request, leaving the Poles entirely out of the peace talks.[98] In the end, two peace treaties were signed. In the first, concluded on February 9, 1918, between the Central Powers and Ukraine, Germany and Austria-Hungary formally recognized a Ukrainian state. As news leaked about the details of the agreement, Poles expressed outrage: Germany and Austria-Hungary had ceded the Chełm district—part of the Kingdom of Poland—to the Ukrainian People's Republic, limiting a future Poland to a narrow ethnic frontier.[99] With additional rumors that Austria-Hungary had secretly offered Eastern Galicia to Ukrainians as a separate crownland, Warsaw was wracked with a wave of strikes. On February 17, 1918, the Kucharzewski government resigned in protest, followed by the Regency Council, bitterly condemning what they referred to as a "new partition."[100]

The second peace agreement at Brest-Litovsk, signed on March 3, 1918, formally ended Russia's involvement in World War I. The Treaty of Brest-Litovsk was a far-reaching agreement that one historian has called "a peace of decolonization."[101] By ceding Finland, Ukraine, Belarus, the Baltic States, and Poland, Russia released the non-Russian populations of imperial Russia's western rim—an estimated population of fifty million.

In Washington, meanwhile, the third major development during Pilsudski's imprisonment took place. On January 8, 1918, Wilson boldly advocated for the Polish cause in an address to a joint session of Congress, outlining his blueprint for a postwar peace: "An independent Polish state should be erected, which should include the territories inhabited by indisputably Polish populations, which should be assured a free and secure access to the sea, and whose political and economic independence and territorial integrity should be guaranteed by international covenant." That the new Poland would be "guaranteed by international covenant" was the basis for Wilson's final point No. 14. Here, Wilson argued that the new Poland could gain permanent and lasting form only through an international framework of security: "A general association of nations must be formed under specific covenants for the purpose of affording mutual guarantees of political independence and territorial integrity to great and small states alike."[102]

Wilson's advocacy for Poland was a milestone. His insistence that the independence of Poland be incorporated as an Allied war aim placed pressure on the Entente countries to follow suit. In January 1917, when France and Britain had been fighting alongside Russia against the Central Powers and the United States was still neutral, the French and British did not dare compromise their alliance with Russia by pressing them on Polish independence. But such diplomatic restraints on the Western democracies had gradually dissolved in the aftermath of the dramatic events of 1917, which saw the fall of the tsar, US entry into the war, and the Bolshevik Revolution. Russia's withdrawal from the war, combined with Dmowski's diplomacy in Paris, led France, Britain, and Italy to accept the American position on Poland.

The new orientation found concrete form on June 3, 1918, when France, Britain, and Italy issued a joint declaration endorsing the restoration of Poland with access to the sea.[103] The stage had been perfectly set for the return of Pilsudski at the conclusion of hostilities in Europe. That moment came at 11 a.m. on November 11, 1918, when Germany and Austria-Hungary put their signatures on the armistice agreement imposed by the Allies. The guns of Europe—after four years, three months, and eleven days of ruthless and bloody war—fell silent.

CHAPTER 12

The Father of Independent Poland

Kościuszko has been avenged. One of the most inspiring and
dramatic struggles ever made by a race to regain freedom and to
restore its once glorious fortunes is drawing to a happy end in the
basin of the Vistula.

—*NEW YORK TRIBUNE*, NOVEMBER 16, 1918

On the crisp, chilly morning of November 8, 1918, two German officers visited Pilsudski and Sosnkowski in prison in Magdeburg. The war was coming to an end and they were free, the German officers informed them. Overjoyed, the two gathered what belongings they could carry and prepared to leave. Pilsudski had no civilian clothing and left the gates of Magdeburg in the uniform of the Polish Legions.[1] Escorted to a military vehicle, they sped off in the direction of Berlin. They were brought to the Hotel Continental and told to wait for further instructions. The two slept that night as free men for the first time in over a year. Awakened the following morning by commotion in the street, they observed crowds outside the hotel. The waiter gave them the dramatic news that Kaiser Wilhelm II had abdicated the throne and a republic had been proclaimed. Due to the ensuing chaos, the daytime train to Warsaw had been canceled. They would have to wait for the overnight train.

A representative of the German Foreign Ministry appeared in the hotel to invite the two ex-prisoners to lunch. Regarding Pilsudski as the likely leader of a future independent Poland, the German official treated him with ministerial honors. In Warsaw, meanwhile, "the whole city was bursting with excitement," Alexandra Pilsudska recalled.[2] Rumors of Pilsudski's arrival had spread the day before. As a result, crowds had gathered at the central train station in Warsaw beginning on the evening of November 8 to catch a glimpse of the legendary leader. By the evening of November 9, the crowds disappeared, not knowing if the rumors were true.

Back in Berlin, the Germans placed Pilsudski and Sosnkowski on the overnight train to Warsaw on November 9. After their departure, German authorities cabled Prince Lubomirski of the Regency Council in Warsaw, confirming that Pilsudski was to arrive in Warsaw the following morning on November 10 at 7 a.m.[3] When Lubomirski arrived in his chauffeured government vehicle at the central train station in Warsaw, he was greeted by Adam Koc, commander of the Polish Military Organization (POW) and a few of his underlings standing on the platform. The two Polish leaders—one appointed by German authorities and the other clandestine—had never met before. Koc approached Lubomirski, introducing himself as a veteran of the First Brigade and chief commander of the Polish Military Organization. "Regent Lubomirski," Koc recalled, "was visibly very moved by the moment, repeating the words, 'Please God, let him arrive. Please God.'"[4]

As the train pulled into the station, Pilsudski was overwhelmed by the moment. Not only was he about to set foot on free Polish soil for the first time in his life, he was also going to see his nine-month-old daughter, Wanda, for the first time. Stepping out of the train, Pilsudski was greeted by Lubomirski and Koc. "He looked pale," Koc observed, "and, of course, exhausted. But his strength was intact."[5] Koc welcomed Pilsudski to Warsaw in the name of the Polish Military Organization and its commander. Prince Lubomirski put out his hand, warmly welcoming Pilsudski back to his country. He directed Pilsudski and Koc to his automobile, inviting them to his home for tea and breakfast.[6] In the course of their drive to Lubomirski's residence, Pilsudski was spotted. Crowds gathered on the streets as news of Pilsudski's arrival spread through the city. The car slowly waded through adoring crowds before arriving at its destination.

After breakfast, Lubomirski invited Pilsudski into his study for a private conversation, and then Koc took Pilsudski to the apartment he had secured for him at 2 Moniuszko Street.[7] A crowd gathered in front of the apartment, chanting "Long Live Our Commander, the Leader of the Nation!" Exhausted, Pilsudski emerged on the balcony and managed to say a few words: "My beloved fellow countrymen. Rest assured that I will devote all my strength and being to the service of our country. I thank you from the bottom of my heart for such a genuine and warm welcome."[8] The following day, inhabitants of Poland woke up all over the country to the headline that Pilsudski was back home after sixteen months of captivity.

Pilsudski's first order of the day was to leave inconspicuously for the suburbs of Warsaw, where Alexandra and Wanda lived. Just as he was about to leave, Pilsudski got a visit from Wacław Jędrzejewicz, whom Koc had sent with a care package of basic supplies. "He did not look well at all," Jędrzejewicz recalled. "His complexion was ashen, and he was very tired."[9]

Pilsudski set off for Alexandra's immediately after his visitor left. When word got out, crowds gathered in front of her home. "They lined the streets outside the house where I was living," Alexandra recalled, "and stood waiting patiently in the rain for hours. When at last his carriage drew up at the gate, they almost mobbed him." Wanting to avoid a spectacle, Alexandra waited upstairs while a friend opened the front door. When Pilsudski reached the second floor, he embraced Alexandra while setting eyes on their firstborn child for the first time. Alexandra tenderly captured the moment: "I had been afraid that Wanda would be shy and give him an unfriendly reception, but apparently in the first few seconds of their acquaintance she made up her mind to love her father. She regarded him gravely, head a little on one side, and then held out her arms to him with a radiant smile."[10]

ON THE DAY OF PILSUDSKI'S ARRIVAL—November 10—Prince Lubomirski announced he was severing all ties to the German authorities. "The German occupation," he stated in an open letter, "has ceased to exist. Commander Pilsudski is now in Warsaw. We are calling upon representatives of all parties to come to Warsaw to form a national government."[11] After meeting with Pilsudski, Lubomirski saw crowds marching on the streets of Warsaw, raising the red banner. Demanding the abdication of the Regency Council, marchers chanted Pilsudski's name. As the slogans got louder and louder, Lubomirski realized the crowd was moving in the direction of his residence on Wiejska Street. "To my astonishment," Lubomirski recalled, "I found armed guards waiting for me at my home, stationed there for my personal protection. I regarded these street processions in Warsaw as a threat to public order that could cause serious disturbances and even lead to a revolution."[12]

On the streets of Warsaw, Lubomirski heard only talk of Pilsudski's return. As historian Piotr Wróbel described it, "News of Pilsudski's arrival spread like wildfire throughout the city. Nearly everyone pinned great hopes on the man they regarded as a savior."[13] Some conservatives, on the other hand, reacted to Pilsudski's arrival with uncertainly and fear. On November 10, 1918, the former chairman of the Supreme National Committee, Władysław L. Jaworski, jotted down in his diary: "I got word that Pilsudski arrived in Warsaw, that he met with the Regency Council, that the Regency Council will disband and Pilsudski will take over as dictator."[14]

Lubomirski briefly explored the idea of using force to quell the street disturbances. He summoned his military advisor, Henryk Minkiewicz, to discuss establishing order. Minkiewicz strongly advised against forcibly dispersing the crowds, explaining that he simply had too few soldiers at his disposal.[15] It was then that Lubomirski realized he had no other option than to share power with Pilsudski.

Pilsudski spent the entire evening of November 10 with Alexandra and Wanda, arriving back at his sleeping quarters in the morning hours. He was able to get only a modicum of sleep that night. Alexandra described the significance of the day: "It was indeed an hour of great joy to him. [Pilsudski] was back in Warsaw again, in that free Poland for which he had worked since his boyhood, and he knew that at last he held the confidence of his own people. Yet I think that in all that day of triumph no moment was so sweet to him as when he felt Wanda's arms thrown round his neck."[16]

News of the war's end was greeted with jubilation in Poland. With the imminent German withdrawal, law and order had to be maintained. In this moment of uncertainly, all eyes in Poland turned to a single man—Jozef Pilsudski. On the night of November 10, before receiving any official title, Pilsudski made an agreement with the German Military Council for an orderly withdrawal of the estimated 80,000 German troops in the Kingdom of Poland. In an address to German soldiers the following morning, Pilsudski stated he had no ill will toward them; they had served their country honorably and he would ensure their safe passage as long as they complied with the order to hand over their weapons prior to entering Germany.[17]

As the dramatic news of the armistice reached Poland in the afternoon of November 11, 1918, the Regency Council summoned Pilsudski for high-level talks. The gravity of the moment was apparent to everyone. At approximately

5 p.m., the three-member body announced it had handed over control of the armed forces to Pilsudski, bestowing upon him the title of commander in chief. It had also entrusted Pilsudski with the task of forming a national unity government. Upon the successful formation of such a government, the Regency Council would voluntarily disband. Lastly, the council formally declared the independence of Poland. "Given the increasing strength of Pilsudski's authority," Prince Lubomirski later noted, "all parties from the extreme right to the extreme left demanded that we hand over rule to Pilsudski. I was sure that this decision would have a very positive effect on morale."[18]

On the day Poland declared independence and the armed forces came under Pilsudski's control, the press got caught up in the exuberance of the moment. "The Commandant has returned! Since yesterday morning, the joyful news has spread throughout Warsaw," stated Warsaw's progressive daily.[19] Another paper, in an article titled "Leader of the Nation," wrote, "Today is unquestionably Commander Pilsudski's moment. Behind him stands a wall of trust by the people. True, there have not yet been elections. But he has already been elected because he is the nation's first representative. Such a title is fitting for the Commander to become the supreme authority of the republic. He has no need to take power [as power has already been placed in his hands]."[20]

Although formally independent, rival centers of authority still existed at home and abroad. In France, the Polish National Committee was recognized by the Allies as Poland's official representative. In Warsaw, the former capital of German-occupied Poland, the Regency Council governed. In the former Austrian-controlled areas, Polish governing bodies emerged in Kraków and Lublin while a fifth declared itself in German-controlled Poznań. The Polish Liquidation Committee, set up in Kraków on October 28, 1918, declared itself as the provisional government of Western Galicia in the wake of the Austro-Hungarian Empire's disintegration. With centers in Kraków and Lwów, its acting head was Wincenty Witos.

On November 6, 1918, meanwhile, a Provisional Polish People's Republic (Tymczasowy Rząd Ludowy Republiki Polskiej) had been proclaimed in Lublin, with Ignacy Daszyński as prime minster and Edward Rydz-Śmigły as military commander. The Lublin government was the initiative of Organizational Council A (Konwent Organizacji A), a representation of leftist political parties that had the backing of the POW, the powerful Pilsudskiite

Embattled Poland, 1918 - 1921

– – – Border of the Polish-Lithuanian Commonwealth, 1772

------ Front line Poland-Russia, May 1920

– – – Front line Poland-Russia, August 1920

—— Final border of the Second Polish Republic

The Territories administered by reborn Poland on Nov 11, 1918

Lands under Polish control by May 1920

⊙ Seat of Symon Petliura's Ukrainian Republic (April – June 7, 1920)

① Conflict with Ukraine over Lvov/East Galicia 1918-1919

② Conflict with Lithuania over Vilnius area 1919-1920

③ Conflict with Germany over Poznań/ Greater Poland, 1919-1920

④ Conflict with Germany over Upper Silesia 1919-1920

⑤ Conflict with Czechoslovakia over Cieszyn Silesia, 1919-1920 military organization. On November 7, when Rydz-Śmigły referred to himself as "Pilsudski's deputy commander," the self-proclaimed government issued the Lublin Manifesto. The body called for a republican form of government and robust social legislation.[21] On the day of Polish independence, Poznań became the fifth location of a Polish governing body to form. Capitalizing on the collapse of German authority, on November 11, 1918, Polish nationalists led by Wojciech Korfanty, then a deputy in the German Reichstag, organized a Supreme Peoples' Council (Naczelna Rada Ludowa), called for elections to a parliament, and proclaimed itself the new provisional government of the Poznań region.

Pilsudski's ability to unite these five disparate governmental bodies under Warsaw's control made him the most significant figure in the foundation of the state. He appeared as a potent symbol of national unity. On November 11, Daszyński informed Pilsudski that the Lublin government was now at his disposal. That evening, as Poland was proclaimed independent, Pilsudski and Daszyński spoke by telephone. Daszyński recalled being gripped with emotion during the conversation: "Upon hearing Pilsudski's voice on the telephone, . . . my heart overflowed with joy at the Commandant's release from prison and the hope that now all of Poland could be unified." Daszyński boarded a train to Warsaw and paid Pilsudski a visit. He saw the toll imprisonment had taken: "Pilsudski had a yellow, rather unhealthy complexion resulting from his 16 months in prison."[22]

On the following morning, Daszyński attended a conference Pilsudski organized to discuss the creation of a national government with representatives of the main political parties. According to press accounts, several meetings took place from 2 p.m. until late into the night.[23] The first was held at Warsaw's Kronenberg Palace. Pilsudski reportedly told party leaders that he first and foremost intended to create a unity government, a coalition representing the population as a whole, including the minorities.[24] That is why, during the second round of talks, Pilsudski invited leaders of Jewish political parties. Most attended, including the heads of the Folkist Party, the Zionist Party, the Labor Zionist Party, and the Orthodox Agudas party. The Jewish Labor Bund abstained, instead sending its requests in a letter.[25]

The Zionist leader, Yizhak Gruenbaum, spoke on behalf of Polish Jewry as a whole. "All of Poland," he reportedly said to Pilsudski, "sees in you, Commandant Pilsudski, the person who has been chosen to create a Government."

At the conclusion of the talks, Pilsudski promised to consider the concerns presented to him.[26] The very fact that Pilsudski invited Jewish leaders for talks reinforced the perception of him as a benevolent figure. Commenting on the meeting, historian Szymon Rudnicki remarked, "It is for this reason that from the beginning of statehood all Jewish political parties supported Pilsudski, who favored granting national minorities full civil rights and constructing Poland as a federal state."[27] Following the day of talks, Pilsudski issued a communiqué informing the population about discussions in the capital, in particular on the Regency Council's request that he form a national government.[28]

On military matters, Pilsudski issued his first Order of the Day as commander in chief on November 12. "I have assumed command of the armed forces," the order stated, "at a moment when the heart of every Pole beats strongly and lively, when the light or freedom shines on the children of our land. I am, together with you, experiencing the emotion of this historic hour. I pledge my life, blood, and sacrifice for the good of the fatherland and the welfare of its citizens." That he pledged to defend the rights of all "citizens" rather than "Poles" reflected Pilsudski's commitment to equality for all inhabitants regardless of nationality and religion. As military commander, he called on his soldiers "to make an effort to remove differences and friction, cliques and provincialism, in the army in order to quickly create an atmosphere of comradeship that facilities cooperation."[29]

On November 12, 1918, the Warsaw City Council unanimously passed a resolution naming Pilsudski a national hero.[30] His popularity was partly linked to a pro-America spirit encompassing Warsaw. The conservative daily *Kurier Warszawski* (Warsaw Courier), for example, ran an editorial on November 14, 1918, proposing that the city erect a monument to Woodrow Wilson and reported on the enthusiastic response to an American flag hung on a building in Warsaw. A leaflet by a group of high school students declared, "The eyes of the entire nation are turned to Pilsudski as the only person able to unify the country under a democratic banner. . . . [By supporting Pilsudski] we are spreading the principles of democracy by creating a Homeland of Freedom and Equality."[31]

The legitimacy of the Regency Council meanwhile came under increasing scrutiny. On November 13, 1918, a Warsaw liberal daily called on it to disband. "The Regency Council is today merely a shadow," *Nowa Gazeta* (New Gazette) stated, "which gives way to a well-deserved oblivion."[32] In contrast, the press anointed Pilsudski as the true, authentic leader. "In the midst of the chaos that has prevailed in Poland during the last few weeks, the name 'Pilsudski' inspires hope and faith. There is a sense that only he, with the popularity and trust he enjoys among a broad part of the masses, will save Poland from a deeper internal upheaval."[33]

The awesome responsibility bestowed upon Pilsudski, combined with his national popularity, led to a growing consensus that the Regency Council had to go. On November 14, 1918, the council dissolved itself, declaring that Jozef Pilsudski was henceforth both commander in chief and head of state. Regency Council member Archbishop Kakowski commented that "Pilsudski was the only person at that moment who could spearhead the reconstitution of Poland."[34]

To some, the abrupt transfer of power to a single man was unsettling. When news of the Regency Council's dissolution broke, the eminent novelist Maria Dąbrowska jotted down her reaction in her diary. "Today the Regency Council placed its authority in the hands of Pilsudski," she wrote on November 14, 1918, "who is now a de facto dictator. . . . To date, Pilsudski's steps and appeals have been exceptionally wise, full of moderation while rising to the occasion to address all issues of the day. God, let him turn out to be not only a fetish of the nation but indeed a helmsman."[35]

Anticipating concerns that he intended to abuse his power, Pilsudski announced his choice for prime minister on the day he was named head of state. In a statement printed in the papers that very evening, he announced the nomination of Ignacy Daszyński, his longtime collaborator and head of the Polish Social Democratic Party, to form a national government. "Convinced that only a freely elected Legislative Sejm [Parliament] has the authority to pass laws," the announcement stated, "I have ordered that elections be set in the shortest possible time."[36] Presenting himself as nonpartisan, Pilsudski noted that he had received broad input from various political parties that would help to shape the future government.

IT WAS AN EXTRAORDINARY MOMENT for Pilsudski. At age fifty, after a life of conspiracy, deprivation, incarceration, and exile, he was presiding over the reconstitution of Poland under his leadership. Many, then and today, linked this watershed moment to Pilsudski's return to the country on November 10. Not only was his presence a factor in the declaration of independence on November 11, 1918, but within three days the acting authorities of reborn Poland voluntarily handed over power to Pilsudski, entrusting him with the responsibility of government and security. "From the moment of November 14, 1918," historian Grzegorz Nowik writes, "the Regency Council placed in the hands of Jozef Pilsudski the responsibility of creating a national government and . . . formally granted him unlimited, dictatorial power until a Legislative Sejm was to be elected."[37] And indeed, until a freely elected Legislative Sejm held its first session ninety-eight days later on February 20, 1919, Pilsudski wielded absolute power.

In November 1918, the term "dictator" began to be attached to Pilsudski's name. He himself marveled at being given so much power so quickly. In a 1923 speech he said (referring to himself in the third person):

> In the course of a few days, without this man making any efforts, without any violence on his part, without any bribery, without any concession, . . . without any so-called "legal" occurrences, something most unusual became a fact. This man became Dictator. When I was preparing today's speech, I thought over this term "dictator." I don't wish to use any far-fetched term or coin any special title for myself. I only wish, as a historian, to define the phenomenon which cannot be otherwise described.[38]

With the Regency Council dissolved, Pilsudski proceeded to do everything possible to make good on his promise to form a national unity government. Although Pilsudski denied affiliation with any political party, even though he had been one of the founders and leaders of the Polish Socialist Party, his choice of the socialist Ignacy Daszyński as prime minister raised concerns. The day after the Regency Council dissolved, Prince Lubomirski asked about this, to which Pilsudski reportedly replied, "I owed this to my friend."[39] There was a certain logic to the choice of Daszyński, a longtime collaborator whom Pilsudski had known for almost two decades and who had served for many years in the Austrian parliament. Daszyński was unacceptable, however, to many conservatives, especially to the National Democratic Party. Władysław Konopczyński, a prominent historian and National Democratic Party member, noted in his diary on November 15, 1918, "In the course of the day, it has come to light that Pilsudski nominated Daszyński prime minister. This is very bad news."[40] Another conservative, Władysław L. Jaworski, commented, "Pilsudski couldn't choose anyone else because he was under pressure to choose a socialist and a non-Jew," adding, "Pilsudski and Daszyński will simply jump at whatever the street tells them to do."[41]

The discomfort extended to the powerful center-right leader Wincenty Witos of the Polish Peasant Party (Polskie Stronnictwo Ludowe—"Piast"; PSL-Piast), who made his opposition to Daszyński clear. On the morning of November 17, a large demonstration in Warsaw organized by the National Democrats demanded "a real national government" rather than a socialist one.[42] Unable to garner any support from the National Democrats for a coalition government, Daszyński stepped down on November 17. Pilsudski accepted his decision, praising Daszyński for his devotion and service to the country. Daszyński dissolved the Lublin government, instructing its twelve ministers to back Pilsudski.[43]

Pilsudski turned to forty-eight-year-old Jędrzej Moraczewski. A moderate Galician socialist active in the PPSD since the 1890s and a mechanical engineer by training, Moraczewski had represented his party in the Austrian parliament in Vienna from 1907 to 1918, joining the First Brigade of the Polish Legions during World War I. A candidate acceptable to the rightist National Democrats and to the center-right, Moraczewski worked with Pilsudski to create a cabinet of ministers under his premiership drawn from the leaders of the main political parties. Negotiations on the formation of a coalition government included a meeting between Pilsudski and Witos, who told him that "forming a government that included representatives from all three areas of pre-partition Poland was an absolute necessity, not only because Polish society demands this but also because it was in the interests of the state as well."[44]

The first government in reborn Poland formally came into being on November 18, 1918. As it was announced at 2 a.m. at a makeshift press conference, one daily, *Kurier Polski* (Polish Courier), was able to splash the headline on the morning edition's front page on November 18. In a joint statement, Pilsudski and Moraczewski announced the names of twenty-one new ministers. Nine were selected from the dissolved Lublin government. Pilsudski was named minister of war. The cabinet consisted of six socialists, five Peasant Party members, two members from parties of radical intellectuals, and two

Independent Poland's first government, convened on November 18, 1918. Members
include (*sitting from left*) Interior Minister Stanisław Thugutt, Prime Minister
Jędrzej Moraczewski, Minister of War and Head of State Jozef Pilsudski,
Justice Minister Leon Supiński, and Foreign Minister Leon Wasilewski.

nonparty members. In addition, two seats were reserved for members of the
National Democratic Party from Poznań in West Prussia.[45]

Key posts were given to longtime Pilsudski collaborators, such as Leon
Wasilewski (minister of foreign affairs) and Ksawery Prauss (minister of education).[46] Despite the inclusion of center-right and rightist party representatives, figures like Wincenty Witos complained that Moraczewski filled the
majority of cabinet posts with socialists.[47] Kraków conservatives like
Władysław Jaworski, former chairman of the Supreme National Committee,
did not look kindly upon the new government: "Oh God, what a sad oper-
etta! Moraczewski is a dull fanatic—a shallow, rather harsh, undereducated
historian."[48]

The sense of unease with the new government's socialist orientation was
for some directly linked to the head of state. On November 19 a leaflet appeared in Warsaw characterizing the new government as a group of radicals

who were raising the red banner over the country. The homeland, it warned, was in danger: "Pilsudski, an enemy of the tsarist system, has learned to govern by its example, just like Lenin. Pilsudski wants to establish here a Russian hell. Who, then, is Pilsudski? Poles! Shall we allow Poland to submit to the authority of adventurers and perjurers?"[49]

The formation of a provisional national government was nonetheless a landmark achievement for Pilsudski. Foreign Minister Wasilewski visited him at the end of the day on November 18 and found him mentally alert but physically in tatters, so tired he was unable to get out of bed. "Pilsudski suffers from exhaustion," Wasilewski noted in his diary, "for he has gotten a mere 1½ hours of sleep in the last few days."[50]

In the next few days, Moraczewski, who was relatively unknown on a national scale, issued a proclamation to announce the aims and goals of his government. He stressed that the new government was a provisional one whose purpose was to administer the state until elections to a legislative Sejm (Parliament). All power would then be handed over to the country's elected government. The Sejm, he continued, would be based on universal, direct suffrage for all citizens aged twenty-one and over, without regard to sex, nationality, or religion. Reborn Poland, Moraczewski maintained, was the inheritor of a rich, historical tradition of tolerance in a multiethnic and multireligious state. "In the field of equal civil rights," Moraczewski proclaimed, "Poland shall inherit the most glorious tradition of the old Polish-Lithuanian Commonwealth—religious toleration." He added, "With all means at our disposal, we shall eradicate any legal restriction on the rights of any part of society that remain from the old regimes of the partitioning powers."[51]

Following Moraczewski's proclamation, Pilsudski outlined his own powers in an effort at transparency. These included the following: "Art. 1: As Provisional Head of State, I assume the responsibility of the highest authority of the Republic of Poland. I shall remain so until the convocation of the Legislative Sejm; Art 2: The government of the Republic of Poland is appointed by me and is responsible to me until the elected Sejm meets with its prime minister."[52] The tone of Pilsudski's notice was unnerving to some, with the leading socialist daily in Kraków, *Naprzód* (Forward), headlining its front-page story on November 23, 1918, "The Dictatorship of Pilsudski." But those fears began to dissipate when Pilsudski made preparations for national elections.

The Pilsudski government introduced its first regulation on November 23, 1918, mandating an eight-hour workday.[53] It followed with a historic election law, introduced on November 28, that set elections to the Sejm for January 26, 1919.[54] Among other things, the landmark election law, by Pilsudski's insistence, granted women the right to vote, making Poland one of only four countries in the world in 1918 to do so, alongside Canada (May 24), Germany (November 30), and Austria (December 18). The United States (1920), Great Britain (1928), and France (1944) followed later. Despite concerns in Pilsudski's own progressive circles that the majority of women voted for conservative Catholic parties and the populist National Democrats, Pilsudski unhesitatingly granted women's suffrage. He argued that thousands of women, like his wife, Maria, and his future wife, Alexandra, had filled the ranks of the independence movement and had fought alongside men in the Polish Legions. Alexandra Pilsudska later wrote, "The women who served with the Legions, the P.O.W. and other organizations during the war, he [Pilsudski] said, had carried out work as important as that of the men. As they had shared equal dangers in liberating the country they were entitled to have an equal voice in its ruling."[55]

Next on Pilsudski's agenda was foreign policy. His first diplomatic overture came on November 16, when he appealed to the Allied states for recognition and military aid. To the governments of the United States, Great Britain, France, Italy, Japan, and Germany, Pilsudski formally announced his country's independence. "As commander in chief of the Polish Army," he wrote to all six countries, "allow me to notify the governments and peoples . . . of the existence of an Independent Polish State consisting of all the lands of a united Poland." He continued: "The revival of Poland's independence and sovereignty has become an accomplished fact thanks to changes arising from the great victories of the Allied armies."[56]

Pilsudski singled out the American president in a telegram to Woodrow Wilson: "Poland, which regards you as her first champion, views your support as proof of sympathy for the Polish cause." To the marshal of France and commander in chief of Allied Forces, General Ferdinand Foch, Pilsudski asked that General Józef Haller's Polish Army be released from its obligations and transferred to Poland.[57] At the time Haller's forces numbered 57,300 men. Pilsudski's appeals for strong ties with the Western democracies and for democratic norms were well received. The *New York Tribune*, for example, commented:

[Poland's] independence and restoration as a nation have been guaranteed to her. She is entitled not only to Galicia but to Posen and to most of West Prussia. She will undoubtedly receive them back at the peace conference. Meanwhile, she is staking out her claim. Kościuszko has been avenged.[58]

Settling the Frontiers

Pilsudski's emphasis on building a robust national army, in part through bringing home General Haller's Polish Army in France, was linked to the problem of the frontiers. At the time, Warsaw controlled only the Kingdom of Poland and West Galicia, a small portion of the country's historic lands. Over the next two years Pilsudski expanded the borders in every direction, leading to armed conflicts with Ukrainians, Germans, Russians, Lithuanians, and Czechs. Two of these armed conflicts began at the moment of Poland's restoration in November 1918. In perhaps his first act as commander in chief, Pilsudski sent army officers to Poznań (Posen) in West Prussia. As a result, German authorities in Poznań surrendered power on November 16, 1918.[59] Within two weeks Pilsudski's troops seized most of Poznań province, largely without bloodshed. In the course of the next few months, Polish troops took control of the region from Germany.

The end of World War I and the restoration of Poland took place during the height of a global pandemic—the Spanish flu. In October–November 1918, the Spanish flu reached its peak in Poland. By October an estimated twenty thousand people in Kraków alone were infected. In Lwów, according to the local press, the spike in Spanish flu cases had made it difficult to bury all the dead.[60] In Eastern Europe, the epidemic coincided with the outbreak of a new war between Ukrainians and Poles in East Galicia. On November 1, 1918, while Pilsudski was still in prison in Magdeburg, the last Habsburg viceroy in Lwów had handed over the city's control to Ukrainians. The Ukrainian National Council seized the opportunity and proclaimed independence. The West Ukrainian National Republic (ZUNR) came into being, with its capital in Lwów. Ukrainian forces in the city, numbering between 1,350 and 1,500 fighters, raised the national flag at the town hall and captured most of Lwów, including its Jewish quarter. The Ukrainians seized government buildings, the main railway station, telephone and telegraph services, as well as the post office. The Ukrainian National Council proclaimed East Galicia as Ukrainian territory as Ukrainian forces took Przemyśl, which was then 45.6 percent Polish, 38.3 percent Jewish, and 15.6 percent Ukrainian.[61]

At the time, Lwów's 197,400 inhabitants were 51.5 percent Roman Catholic (Polish), 29.4 percent Jewish, and 17.5 percent Greek Catholics (Ukrainian).[62] It is not surprising, then, that the city's majority Polish population responded by mounting an armed uprising. Five days later, Lwów's Polish insurgents grew to 1,428 fighters with weapons and ammunition, including twenty-eight machine guns.[63] By the time World War I ended on November 11, a Polish-Ukrainian War was in full swing. When Pilsudski became commander in chief on November 11, 1918, one of his first orders was to send military assistance to the Polish insurgency in Lwów. He had the full backing of his political opponents in the Polish National Committee in Paris, who, on November 13, told the American ambassador in France that East Galicia should be defended as Polish territory.[64]

On November 16, 1918, Pilsudski ordered General Bolesław Roja, the Polish Army chief in West Galicia, to advance on Lwów with four infantry regiments. Roja's troops reached Lwów on November 19, and Ukrainian units now faced a combined force of 6,022 Polish soldiers.[65] Fighting engulfed the city for the next three days. In the early hours of November 22, 1918, the Ukrainian Army fled and Polish forces hoisted the national flag atop city hall. Roja declared Lwów liberated and vowed to keep law and order. He dispatched patrols led by officers "to use guns with all ruthlessness" against any individual, civilian or military, who engaged in looting or violence of any kind. Victory came at a high cost for the Poles, with 210 soldiers killed and 762 wounded.[66]

For many inhabitants of Lwów, Roja's call for law rang entirely hollow. The estimated 340 civilian casualties included a considerable number of Ukrainian victims. A Ukrainian study published in 1934 referred to the conquest of Lwów as "Poland's colonial war" in Ukraine. "On the morning of 22 November [1918], amid the general rejoicing of the Polish inhabitants," Vasyl Kuchabsky wrote, "Polish troops occupied the areas of the city vacated by the Ukrainian troops. Immediately, as in Przemyśl, Ukrainians were interned and all Ukrainian national institutions were looted. . . . The loss of Lviv represented the beginning of the war between the newly established Polish state and Western Ukraine. Only now did the population of Western Ukraine realize the true significance of what had happened in Lviv, and it was only the war with all of Poland that forced them to invest energy in the creation of a state and military organization."[67] In New York, meanwhile, the Ukrainian Federation of the United States issued a strongly worded protest: "The Polish attempt forcibly to incorporate Ukrainian districts into Poland is an infringement of principles laid down by President Wilson in regard to the self-determination of peoples."[68]

Outbreak of Anti-Jewish Violence

Ukrainian losses were largely seen as the byproduct of a Polish-Ukrainian military conflict in which civilians were in the crossfire but not a target. This was not the case with the 57,000-strong Jewish community. The controversy that reverberated far beyond the borders of Poland was a two-day orgy of anti-Jewish violence that followed in the immediate wake of Poland's takeover of Lwów. According to contemporaneous accounts, Lwów's Jewish community declared neutrality during the conflict. But it was claimed that shots were fired from within the city's Jewish district at Polish soldiers during the siege. So when the Polish Army took the Jewish district, rumors that the Jews had sided with the Ukrainians led to the outbreak of a full-scale pogrom on November 22, 1918. Polish troops ransacked the city's Jewish quarter, pillaging shops and stores. Homes and synagogues were set on fire while soldiers attacked Jews. The violence was abruptly halted two days later with the imposition of martial law. When the dust settled and the destruction to people and property could be assessed, the local Jewish Rescue Committee counted 73 Jews dead and 437 wounded.[69] The Jewish Rescue Committee also reported that two synagogues had been burned to the ground, more than five hundred Jewish businesses were destroyed, two thousand Jews were made homeless, and seventy Jewish children lost both parents.[70]

The pogrom in Lwów was only one of many outbreaks of anti-Jewish violence in November 1918 that came in the wake of Poland's rebirth. The first occurred on the day Poland declared independence, November 11. In Kielce, a town in the Kingdom of Poland that had been under Austro-Hungarian rule since 1915, and which was indisputably Polish, representatives of Jewish political parties and their supporters gathered in a theater to discuss their future. At the conclusion of the meeting, with an estimated three hundred people present, a crowd gathered outside. Some militants entered the theater and drove the Jews out into the street. A mob, armed with clubs and bayonets, attacked the Jews, leading to four dead and many wounded.[71] Jewish socialists could be found among the party leaders present. Accusations of pro-Bolshevik sympathies triggered the violent outbreak. As historian William Hagen wrote, Kielce "was the crucible in which Warsaw-centered Polish opinion on the postwar pogrom wave was forged, with anti-Bolshevism as most potent ingredient rather than the paranoia over Jewish loyalty and revengefulness towards supposed economic exploitation that pervaded discourse over Galician pogroms."[72]

In contrast to Lwów, where perpetrators accused Jews of disloyalty during the military conflict with the Ukrainians, the pogromists in Kielce targeted what they claimed were "Judeo-Bolshevists." The right-wing Warsaw daily, *Kurier Warszawski,* described the Kielce pogrom as an expression of patriotic zeal in the face of "Judeo-Bolsheviks" (*żydzi-bolszewicy*). Maintaining that "Bolshevik agents and Jews" in Kielce could be heard chanting "Down with the White Eagle. Down with Poland! Long Live Trotsky," the paper stated that local Poles understandably rose to defend their country's honor on the very day Poland declared statehood. "The result of the behavior of these types of Jews at a time when patriotic Polish enthusiasm was at its height," the paper continued, "was unrest among Kielce inhabitants. If in Kielce there were excesses in which Jews fell victim, then Jewish agitators of Bolshevism were to blame."[73]

The pogroms in Kielce and Lwów were not isolated incidences. In the remaining nineteen days between Polish independence on November 11 and the end of November 1918, more than one hundred locations in Polish-held areas recorded outbreaks of anti-Jewish violence, nearly all of them in West Galicia. The number of Jews killed in November 1918 in West Galicia—excluding the Lwów and Kielce pogroms—was not less than fifty-nine and likely more.[74] The death of Jewish civilians in Polish-held territories in the first nineteen days of independence led one Polish Jew from Galicia to comment, not inaccurately, that "the birth of Poland was accompanied by rivers of Jewish blood."[75]

The spread of anti-Jewish violence tarnished Poland's image at the very moment of the country's rebirth. A German correspondent in Lwów filed a story that got picked up in several American newspapers. Giving figures that later proved to be wildly exaggerated, the *Berliner Tageblatt* reported that eleven hundred Jews had been killed in Lwów. This figure was repeated in American newspapers from New York to San Francisco. The Berlin dispatch included the following: "Immediately upon entering the city, the Poles proceeded to sack and burn the Ghetto district. The streets were filled with the charred bodies of murdered Jews, many of whom, in the frenzy of despair, had leaped from the burning buildings, which were surrounded by Polish troops. The Polish authorities were indifferent and declined to take measures to halt the slaughter."[76]

Pilsudski addressed the crisis by receiving two Jewish delegations on November 25 and 29, 1918. The first meeting, reported in detail in the press, included a representative of the Kielce Jewish community, Noah Braun, as well Warsaw's Yitzhak Gruenbaum and Rafał Szereszowski.[77] After presenting a memorandum on the Kielce pogroms, Braun asked Pilsudski to dispatch an investigative team to Kielce to apprehend the perpetrators and to inquire about the role of the local military and municipal leadership during the pogrom. "As Polish Jews," Braun stated in the memorandum presented to Pilsudski, "we welcome the establishment of a Free, United and Independent Poland, affirming our willingness to build a Polish State for which we are prepared to sacrifice our blood." At the same time, Polish Jews "expect that the Government treat the Kielce pogrom with all seriousness and gravity so as not to perpetuate the notion that everything is permitted in relation to Jews and that crimes committed against them go unpunished."[78]

According to press reports, Pilsudski is said to have replied that the whole problem of anti-Jewish rioting would be addressed in a comprehensive manner upon the convocation of the country's elected parliament in February 1919. He emphasized that he was aware of the serious nature of anti-Jewish violence and attributed it to the breakdown of law and order in the aftermath of the war's end. The government in Warsaw, he said, did not yet possess the means to halt every incident. Two days later, a Warsaw daily described the exchange:

The attorney Y. Gruenbaum remarked to Pilsudski, 'the pogromists in Kielce, just like those in West Galicia, are opposed to your government, and to you, Commandant Pilsudski,' to which Pilsudski replied, 'Yes, [they are] against me. I am aware of this.' Commandant Pilsudski reported, furthermore, that news was reaching him from all over the country of inflamed relations with the Jews. The government, he underscored, does not yet possess adequate strength to respond; the army is only in the process of being formed. The Commandant further stated that, particularly as the son of an oppressed people, he would not allow any person or group to be persecuted. In the end, Pilsudski replied that an investigation of the military, as well as of the civilian authorities, had already begun.[79]

In his second meeting with Jewish leaders on November 29, 1918, Pilsudski received a delegation from Kraków. Headed by the Zionist leader Ozjasz Abraham Thon, the delegation also included Yitzhak Gruenbaum and Max Lesser. As in the previous meeting, the delegation presented Pilsudski a memorandum detailing the scale of anti-Jewish violence in West Galicia and in Lwów. As described in the Yiddish and Polish press, Pilsudski listened carefully and pledged his support for investigating the role of the military and municipal authorities during the pogrom. The memorandum asked the Polish government to compensate Jewish victims, to care for widows and orphans, and to aid the homeless. Finally, Pilsudski was asked to issue a statement condemning the anti-Jewish actions. Pilsudski replied that he had already issued an order to the army to intervene on behalf of the Jews, and he had confirmation that commanding officers had communicated the order to subordinates.[80]

Tension rose when Thon asked Pilsudski to make this order public because no one knew about it. Pilsudski's reply raised eyebrows among the Jewish delegation. "I am not an autocrat," Pilsudski is reported to have said, "and I cannot issue proclamations of a political character other than at the request of the government. The Jewish question is a very entangled one (zawikłany). Jews have equal rights and will have the opportunity to participate and put forth demands in the future Legislative Sejm in a proper forum. Solving these problems cannot take place before the convocation of the Legislative Sejm."[81] Gruenbaum in particular regarded Pilsudski's response as entirely inadequate. "Stopping Anti-Jewish Pogroms," Gruenbaum replied, "is not something that can wait for the convocation of the Parliament!"[82] A contemporaneous report on the pogroms by the Jewish Socialist Labor Confederation in

London, a Labor Zionist organization, did not take kindly to Pilsudski's refusal to issue a public statement, commenting, "So in the name of democracy the pogroms are not to be prohibited before the constituent assembly meets!"[83]

Reflecting on this meeting nine years later, Thon remarked that "we went as a delegation and presented to Pilsudski the horror of the Lwów events. Did this move him? My impression, then and now, is that it certainly did. But in words he was rather stern—not in such a harsh way as to disregard the catastrophe of the shedding of blood. But he addressed the tragedy in a soldierly fashion."[84] Thon, who in January 1919 was elected to the first legislative parliament of Poland, further ruminated on his impressions of Poland's head of state:

> This first audience immediately made me aware of Pilsudski's relation to the Jewish question in Poland: that he had not taken a moment of his free time to think it through. There was no doubt that the Jews had no reason whatsoever to believe any harm would come to them from this man. Pilsudski is simply not a wrongdoer. But at the same time there is no likelihood or justified hope that the Jews can count on him for anything positive on their behalf.[85]

Thon was intrigued by Pilsudski's personality and sharp intellect, and noted that he could "listen splendidly and respond perfectly. No word, no gesture escapes his attention."[86] Writing in December 1927, Thon commented that if at the time of writing Pilsudski believed a positive solution to the Jewish problem in Poland was an issue of primary importance in the very formation of the Polish state, he had not at all been of this opinion when the two first met on November 29, 1918.

Assessing his exchanges with Jewish leaders, it appears Pilsudski was entirely taken by surprise by the spread of anti-Jewish violence. On January 23, 1919, he met with British Zionist Israel Cohen, who commented at the time: "General Pilsudski candidly admitted to me that the Poles were no philo-Semites, and the only hope he held out was that the present anti-Jewish hostility could not last."[87] However Pilsudski understood the problem of anti-Jewish violence abruptly rising and rapidly spreading in Poland, what is certain is that its impact in international circles was resolute and immediate. In Washington, D.C., the Polish National Committee's US representative,

Paderewski, was reading press account after press account about the pogroms in American papers. On November 20, 1918, he recommended that the US State Department dispatch a fact-finding mission to Poland consisting of Jewish American and Polish American leaders with the objective of assessing the scale of violence and making its findings public.[88]

The situation meanwhile deteriorated further, leading Jews from America and Britain to appeal for Allied intervention. "We have none but the friendliest feelings for the new Poland . . . ," the *Jewish Chronicle* of London stated on November 29, 1918, "but the revived State will find but a poor pathway to international sympathy in the continuous ill-treatment of its Jewish inhabitants." It continued, "The necessity for intervention is pressing, and we trust that the Allied Powers may find it possible to exercise some joint and instant pressure. But far better would it be if the enlightened leaders of Poland would themselves put an end to incidents which are as painful to Jews as they are unhappily discreditable to the Polish good name." The British Jewish daily pointed to Pilsudski as the man of the hour, communicating its pleasure with the telegram recently received from Polish representatives in Paris "that the Polish military leader, Pilsudski, is taking steps to prevent further disorder. Pilsudski would appear to have the means at his disposal, and with the help of the friendly Liberal parties will, we hope, soon re-establish respect for life and order."[89]

Despite Pilsudski's stated efforts to curb the violence from the top, anti-Jewish disturbances continued. In response, an estimated eight thousand people staged a protest in New York City's Madison Square Garden on December 11, 1918, calling for "justice for Jewish victims in Poland."[90] The organizers read aloud a declaration demanding guarantees for Polish Jews at the forthcoming peace conference in Paris. The *Times* of London characterized the problem of anti-Jewish violence in reborn Poland as only one of several problems facing the new state: reconstruction, unemployment, the Jews, and the Bolshevik danger. "Of these," the newspaper remarked, "the Jewish problem has already attracted foreign attention, because of pogroms at Lemberg and elsewhere." The *Jewish Chronicle* of London likewise stated, "Lemberg is but a symbol of the whole Jewish question overhanging the future of Poland."[91]

The pogrom wave did not affect Pilsudski's increasingly positive image in the international press. After initial expressions of concern over his absolute authority, the foreign press began to soften its view. "General Pilsudski, while he is the military head of the Government," stated the *New York Times* on December 17, 1918, "signs all Government decrees and is considered the civilian head also." The Warsaw-based correspondent stated that the Polish leader was "a slightly built, nervous man, bent with ill health, but keeps long hours at his post. His eyes are blue and his eyebrows are heavy." The paper expressed the opinion that Pilsudski's motivation was not dictatorship. Rather, it was to provide an orderly and stable transition to parliamentary, democratic rule.

The present state of affairs, Pilsudski told the correspondent in the same interview published December 17, 1918, was temporary: "Our present task is to keep peace and order while waiting for the elections." He attributed Poland's sovereignty to the Allies. He had not only gratitude that the Allied victory made possible Poland's independence, but he shared with them the democratic idea as well. "Let me first say," Pilsudski told the *New York Times*, "how happy I am that there is a united Poland. Our independence is due entirely to the Allies, otherwise it would always have been a fiction." He added, "I am a strong admirer of America. It was my good fortune to visit there in 1904, although it was only for a few days during a jump across the continent."[92]

The view of the foreign press was that Pilsudski calmed the waters on matters relating to Jews and other minorities by maintaining a tone of civility and tolerance. But no one denied that the first nineteen days of Polish independence were a rude awakening. With fighting in East Galicia and West Prussia, combined with the outbreak of anti-Jewish violence around the country that proved impossible to fully quell, Pilsudski understood immediately the profound challenges that lay ahead.

CHAPTER 13

Statesman and Diplomat

A century and a half of struggle, often entailing blood and
sacrifice, has found its triumph this day. A century and a half of
dreams of a Free Poland has ended in realization.

—JOSEF PILSUDSKI, ADDRESS TO THE INAUGURAL SESSION
OF POLAND'S FIRST ELECTED PARLIAMENT, WARSAW,
FEBRUARY 10, 1919

On November 29, 1918, Pilsudski moved out of his modest apartment
on 50 Mokotowska Street into Warsaw's nineteenth-century Belvedere Palace.
The neoclassical structure had been the residence of former German governor-
general Hans von Beseler and, before him, of imperial Russian officials. There
was symbolic significance in the fact that Pilsudski became the first Polish
head of state to set foot in the regal Belvedere.

Having formed independent Poland's first government on November 18,
1918, and set a date for elections to a legislative Sejm for January 26, 1919, Pilsudski turned his attention to foreign affairs. Prior to the war's end, as we
have seen, the Allied Powers had recognized the Polish National Committee
(KNP) in Paris as Poland's official representatives. This state of affairs remained
intact after the war's end, with the Paris Poles openly opposing the socialist-led
government in Warsaw. Pilsudski quickly realized that the establishment of
diplomatic relations with France, Great Britain, the United States, and Italy
depended on a negotiated settlement with the KNP.

Pilsudski approached the issue on two fronts. Aware of being a virtual
unknown outside of Central Europe, he used the international press to introduce himself to the Western European and American publics. In the

winter of 1918–1919, American, British, French, and Italian readers became acquainted with the enigmatic ruler of independent Poland. Pilsudski stressed his desire for close ties with the Entente, his unambiguous support for constitutional, parliamentary government, for rule of law, and for minority rights. When pressed about his socialist past, Pilsudski told the Associated Press, "I am neither a Socialist nor a Bolshevik but a Democrat."[1]

Pilsudski's second approach was to make his views known to foreign diplomats, who initially saw the Polish leader through the eyes of his political rivals in Paris. These diplomats were troubled by Pilsudski's wartime collaboration with the Central Powers as well as his socialist past. The very fact that Pilsudski was granted his authority by the Regency Council, a body created by the wartime Central Powers, tainted him to varying degrees in Western eyes. "Pilsudski's service in the forces of the Dual Monarchy and his brief collaboration with the Germans in the Council of State," Harold H. Fisher observed in 1928, "had not been forgotten by the Allies. More damaging at this particular moment to Pilsudski's standing in the west were his socialist opinions and his long revolutionary career."[2] The fear of Bolshevism, Fisher emphasized, was at its height, with the Bolsheviks replacing the Germans as the West's new enemy. One of Pilsudski's tasks, therefore, was to convince the Allies of his absolute commitment to protect Poland's eastern frontiers from the spread of communism.

Pilsudski was largely unknown in American diplomatic circles. He did not speak English and had no personal ties with the United States, having only passed through the States once in June 1904 on his way to Japan. In his 1932 study, British author Robert Machray noted the difficulties Pilsudski faced in his efforts to establish ties with the Allied Powers:

> The Allies knew little of Pilsudski, and did not like very much what they knew; they remembered how his Legions had fought for Austria, and how he had collaborated with the Germans in the Council of States; they did not give proper value to his reason for resigning from the body and his consequent imprisonment at Magdeburg; they had no clear idea of the work he was doing in Poland in organizing the country and in stemming the Bolshevik tide. . . . For several months the French Foreign Office supported Dmowski as against Pilsudski. For a while it had seemed as if there were two Polish Governments, one in Warsaw and the other in Paris.[3]

Roman Dmowski (*seated, center*) with fellow members of the Polish National Committee
(KNP) in Paris. Members included Count Maurycy Zamoyski (*seated, left*), Erazm Piltz
(*seated, right*), and, among others, Marian Seyda (*standing, second from right*). For the
first three months after World War I, France, Britain, and the United States recognized
the KNP as the official representatives of Poland.

As Pilsudski took steps to create a parliamentary democracy, voiced his
staunch opposition to Bolshevism, and sought close ties with the Western Allies, his image abroad gradually changed. Western diplomats took increasing
note of Pilsudski's public declarations, such as the one on December 15, 1918,
in which he said that Poland's role in Europe was "to guarantee the frontiers
against Bolshevism." He added, "I think the Bolshevik danger is imminent
in Poland unless we are able to put up a fence against the Russian influence."
It was a matter of urgency, Pilsudski declared, that the Allies aid Poland in
the fortification of that barrier: "It is necessary," he said, "that our Government be recognized by the Allies. At present there are certain difficulties. The
Polish Committee in Paris represents parties not in accord with the others
here, but this internal matter is being arranged."[4]

Pilsudski was alluding to talks that had begun in December 1918. They were set in motion by the KNP on November 16, when it resolved to send a representative to Warsaw to meet with Pilsudski. The Paris committee chose Stanisław Grabski to head the mission. A participant in the founding congress of the Polish Socialist Party (PPS) in 1892, Grabski was active in the PPS until 1901, when he began to flirt with the nationalist camp. In 1907 he switched allegiances and joined Roman Dmowski's National Democratic Party. Due to his long acquaintance with Pilsudski, Grabski was regarded as the best candidate, and at the November 16 meeting in Paris, he called for face-to-face talks with Pilsudski, whom he believed held the key to the political situation. Others, like the conservative journalist and publicist Erazm Piltz, agreed that establishing ties with Pilsudski was in the committee's best interests, while Józef Haller, commander of the Polish Army in France, recommended that one of his officers should accompany Grabski to Poland.[5]

The KNP position hardened two days later when Poland's first government under Prime Minister Moraczewski was announced. Holding an emergency session, the Paris committee—made up of conservative landowners and nationalists belonging to the National Democratic Party—expressed great concern. One member was "of the opinion that the committee must demand the overthrow of the leftist government while keeping Pilsudski in power. Sending a mission of our representatives at once to meet with Pilsudski is an urgent necessity." Count Maurycy Zamoyski, the KNP vice chairman, went further, arguing that the committee should conduct a smear campaign to "disqualify the socialist government."[6]

The First Round of Talks

Accompanied by Tadeusz Malinowski, an officer in Haller's army, Grabski arrived in Warsaw on December 5, 1918. In his first meeting with Pilsudski, held that same day, Grabski presented him with a mandate from Paris. It called for the appointment of a national unity government representing all the political currents in Poland but with a large share reserved for the National Democratic Party.[7]

The two identified areas of commonality. First, both agreed on the need for a single representation at the upcoming Paris Peace Conference. Second, they agreed that Haller's army should be transferred to Poland, with Grabski stressing that this could happen only after a national unity government was formed. Grabski came away from the first day of talks under the impression that he had the upper hand. "I have Pilsudski wrapped around my finger," Grabski commented to a friend that evening.[8] In their second meeting, held on December 7, 1918, Grabski told Pilsudski that the Moraczewski government threatened national unity at a moment when such unity was absolutely necessary.[9] Pilsudski replied that he had installed a socialist government not for ideological reasons but to offset the influence of the Bolshevik tide. Present at the meeting was Polish foreign minister Leon Wasilewski, who noted in his diary that the talks were tense and difficult.[10]

Pilsudski realized he could not make a deal at the present time. When he proposed expanding the Polish National Committee in Paris to include representatives of the Warsaw government, Grabski responded in the negative. Grabski added that the Polish National Committee would remain independent even after the formation of a national unity government. This independent body operating outside of Warsaw's auspices would negotiate on Poland's behalf at the Paris Peace Conference.[11] That Dmowski would conduct foreign policy independently, without consulting with Warsaw, was to Pilsudski an outrageous demand.

The talks concluded on December 10, 1918, without an agreement. The Grabski Mission had failed. Back in Paris, Count Zamoyski reassured the French that a coalition government would eventually be formed in Warsaw despite the setback.[12] Grabski, historian Kay Lundgreen-Nielsen observed, "had come to Poland to get the Moraczewski Government removed and a national coalition government appointed, with National Democrats in the most important posts. His task had not been successful in December, but his strength during the negotiations had been that he could point to the fact that Allied help could only be arranged via the KNP in Paris."[13]

The breakdown of talks in Warsaw elicited a strong response in Paris. At a session of the KNP held on December 11, 1918, one committee member proposed a coup d'état: "A growing opposition of the whole of Polish society against the partisan Moraczewski government and even against Pilsudski . . . is so pernicious that we can no longer delay actively intervening to bring about a change in the government."[14] The same speaker claimed that Bolsheviks were now sending huge sums of money to Poland to spread propaganda.

Grabski tried to go around Pilsudski by appealing to the public. Holding a press conference at Warsaw's Hotel Bristol on December 20, he proposed replacing the Moraczewski cabinet with a national unity government, providing the press with a list of twenty-four ministers, including Pilsudski as head of state and minister of war. "Today," Grabski said, "we are a nation allied with the Victorious Powers. Only a *national government* can enjoy the full authority and responsibility for the fate of the nation, no differently than in the years 1830 and 1863. At present, the existence of a head of state and a cabinet without a parliament does not serve the interest of Poland."[15]

The failure of talks in Warsaw similarly concerned the Allies, who favored a pro-Entente, stable government in Poland. The American liaison officer to the French General Staff, Major Julian L. Coolidge, remarked on December 11, 1918, that "there is a de facto Government of General Pilsudski recently released from a German prison, but that Government lacks stability. Moreover, the Bolshevik danger is very acute. The government of Lenin is spending large sums of money in Bolshevik propaganda in Poland."[16]

Coolidge emphasized that Poland needed a robust army to defend itself and Europe from Bolshevism. But sending Haller's army to Poland was beset with political difficulties because the Allied governments recognized the Polish National Committee in Paris "as the basis for the constitution of the future Polish State." If the Paris and Warsaw Poles failed to conclude an agreement, Coolidge concluded, "the Peace Congress will deem Poland incapable of Self Government and will be little disposed to aid the Polish Cause, but it is easier to approve of unity in theory than to carry it out in practice. . . . It is to be hoped that a solution will be quickly found as, otherwise, Poland is sure to become a seat of Bolshevist revolution."[17]

Pilsudski similarly emphasized the importance of a strong military. In his letter to President Woodrow Wilson dated December 9, 1918, he requested Polish American volunteers be sent not to France to join Haller's army but directly to Warsaw to serve in reborn Poland's armed forces. For since the summer of 1917, some sixteen thousand Polish Americans already had crossed the Atlantic to join Haller's Polish Army in France.[18]

Pilsudski Sends a Mission to Paris

After the failure of the Grabski Mission, Pilsudski sent a delegation to Paris to negotiate on his behalf on December 17, 1918. By entering into direct talks with the Allies, Pilsudski hoped to bring enough pressure to bear on the KNP to force its hand. He chose Kazimierz Dłuski, a physician who had completed medical school in Paris, to lead a four-person delegation to Paris. The others included Michał Sokolnicki, Bolesław Wieniawa-Długoszowski, and Antoni Sujkowski. Alongside talks with the KNP, Pilsudski instructed Dłuski to establish direct contacts with Western diplomats.[19]

Prior to their departure, Pilsudski asked the delegation to hand-deliver two letters. The first was to Marshal Foch, commander in chief of the French and Allied armies. Pilsudski expressed his sincere gratitude for Foch's role in ridding Poland of its three occupiers. "I owe the freedom of my country to your armies," he wrote the marshal. "For this I am eternally grateful." The second letter, addressed to Roman Dmowski, offered an olive branch. Pilsudski argued that old divisions had to be set aside for the good of the country: "For the purposes of reaching an agreement with the Polish National Committee in Paris," Pilsudski wrote, "I have dispatched to Paris a delegation. . . . I humbly request that you be willing to do everything to facilitate such negotiations. Please regard it as genuine when I say that I wish, above all, to avoid having two bodies representing Poland with the Allies: only one common representation will result in our demands being heard." He concluded, "Based on our long acquaintance, I hope that now in such a critical moment, at least some individuals—if not all of Poland—can rise above the interests of parties, cliques, and groups."[20]

What the Pilsudski delegation did not expect was the cold reception it received from the French, who had formally recognized the KNP as Poland's government on November 13, 1918.[21] On behalf of his government, France's ambassador to the United States, Jean Jules Jusserand, cabled US secretary of state Robert Lansing on November 26, urging the US government to extend formal recognition to the Polish National Committee in Paris as Poland's de facto government. Such a move, the ambassador stressed, was not only warranted but urgently needed due to the rapid spread of Bolshevism in the east.[22]

Aware that the precondition by the Western allies for recognition was an agreement with the Polish representatives in Paris, Pilsudski pinned his hopes on the Dłuski Mission conducting parallel talks with the Allies. "I can speak with [George] Clemenceau without the KNP present," Pilsudski said on December 26, 1918, referring to France's prime minister.[23] Pilsudski decided to accompany members of the Dłuski Mission to Kraków, where they stopped on their way to Paris. Among those traveling with him was Sokolnicki, who described "welcoming celebrations and large crowds" at the Kraków train station to greet Pilsudski on his first visit as head of state.[24] With great fanfare, the Kraków Labor Council issued a statement to welcome the country's head of state: "Kraków workers! The head of the Republic of Poland and commander in chief of its armed forces, Jozef Pilsudski, has arrived in Kraków. Working peoples welcome him warmly and express their feelings of respect and gratitude for his work, for his struggle, for his years behind bars, and his relentless will for victory. Long Live Freedom, Independence, and the Unity of Poland!"[25]

A special edition of *Naprzód* (Forward), Kraków's socialist daily, greeted Pilsudski warmly. "To You, Chief of the Republic," the paper stated, "we have one demand: that you pave the way for a republic [with] frontiers reaching as far as the Polish people live, and to a Freedom that accomplishes human rights." The paper joyously concluded:

> Kraków greets you, Pilsudski, with bells of hearts beating louder than bronze bells; Kraków greets you with a hymn of freedom, more prominent than a thundering orchestra; Kraków greets you at the thresholds with which the legendary procession of the first Polish soldiers began; Kraków greets you with the memorable words with which you blessed a handful of heroes facing a terrible battle on August 6, 1914: "Long Live Free Poland!"[26]

In contrast, the conservative Kraków daily, *Czas* (The Times), reported on Pilsudski's arrival with extreme skepticism. It charged that his goal was to impose socialism on the country. "Today," the paper stated on December 20, 1918, "we are unsatisfied with Pilsudski's policies regarding the most important issues facing the country." It warned the following day readers not to take Pilsudski's words at face value: "Head of State Pilsudski, who by his actions supports the socialist government, in words takes every opportunity to express his support for a 'national' cabinet."[27]

The Dłuski Mission meanwhile departed for Paris, and Pilsudski returned to Warsaw. There, on December 26, he sat down with journalist Władysław Baranowski. "Commandant Pilsudski received me very kindly, one could say almost warmly," Baranowski commented.[28] Baranowski proceeded to ask Pilsudski about foreign policy. The first objective, Pilsudski replied, was the establishment of diplomatic relations with the victorious Allies. "Above all, and more than at any time including that of the war," Pilsudski said, "we depend on the Allies. As victors, they are now in charge. The borders of Poland will depend on them. We must . . . at least take into account their authority, particularly the prestige of France." The problem to address, Pilsudski emphasized, was the necessity of preventing a situation in which there were two, separate Polish delegations at the Paris Peace Conference. "We cannot afford to be a spectacle," he said. "I won't allow it."[29]

Baranowski then turned to an awkward subject. Had the commandant considered preserving his dictatorial power instead of going ahead with parliamentary elections? The question itself made Pilsudski's blood boil. "I do not desire, nor am I able, to impose a dictatorial state by any measure," he shot back in a raised voice. "Not only does this contradict my beliefs and my sense of freedom, but it would also create an illegal situation that is unsustainable and that could harm Poland in the opinion of the world." Poland, Pilsudski said, had to proceed in the very opposite direction, one in which it underwent a process of "legalization" through the formation of a parliamentary government and recognition by the Allies. "Despite everything," Pilsudski added, "people here and abroad will become more amenable to our country when they realize that Bolshevism will be halted at our doorstep."[30]

When Woodrow Wilson arrived in England on December 26, 1918, he was greeted by a message of gratitude in a joint statement by the Polish Information Committee in London and the Council of the Polish Community in Great Britain. "We cannot forget—no Pole will ever forget—that on January 22, 1917, at a moment when all was obscure in the European outlook, and the cause of Poland was clouded with doubts and difficulties, your clear and unwavering declaration in your message to the Senate of the necessity of a 'united, independent, and autonomous Poland.' It brought hope to every Polish heart, and provoked manifestations of the greatest enthusiasm before the American Consulate in Warsaw, even amid the terrors of the German occupation." The message urged Wilson to support the Pilsudski government in Warsaw:

> It is a subject of great joy to us that Poland now possesses a Government formed of the most stable and progressive elements of the country, and headed by a heroic soldier, General Pilsudski. It is our confident hope that under your wise guidance, this Government may soon be acknowledged by the Associated Powers, and that the work of the reconstruction of our country's social and national life may then be taken up without any further delay.[31]

Other supporters of Pilsudski included William J. Rose, a Canadian who had spent the war years in a Polish district of Silesia near Cieszyn (Teschen). Concerned that the Polish National Committee was maliciously misrepresenting Pilsudski's views, Rose published an article in a London periodical in support of the Warsaw government and its leader. Having arrived in Paris in November 1918, Rose observed the hostility of the Polish National Committee toward the Pilsudski government. It was scandalous, he wrote in the pages of the London-based *Polish Review* in December 1918, that "the Polish mission dispatched from Warsaw two weeks ago to present the whole case to the Entente in Paris has been stranded, for some reason or other, in Switzerland . . . Somebody seems somewhere to be afraid of something."[32] From the moment a government emerged in postwar Poland, Rose continued, the Polish National Committee had been, behind his back, erroneously telling Western diplomats that Pilsudski was making Poland Bolshevik. These misleading messages, Rose maintained, had spilled over into the Western press, which was describing the Warsaw government as radical socialist and even Bolshevik. That Rose's observation had merit is evidenced by a piece from the *Times* of London, dated December 31, 1918, that characterized Prime Minister Moraczewski as one who "warms to the sight of the Red Flag, diluted or not to some shade of pinkness."[33]

Rose's advocacy for Pilsudski included a December 1918 feature piece in a British weekly review of foreign policy, a publication that had favored Wilsonian principles of national self-determination for various Slavic peoples. Rose cautioned readers against stereotyping Poland's leader as a socialist. "Imbued with the traditions of the old Polish fighters for liberty of the Legionaries who had followed Napoleon, and of the Polish Democrats who had started the insurrections of 1830 and 1863," Rose wrote in the pages of *New Europe*, "he is a spiritual descendant of the Europe of Garibaldi and Mazzini."[34] During the war, Rose emphasized, Pilsudski used the Central Powers for patriotic ends only, going to prison rather than swearing an oath of allegiance to Germany. "Pilsudski is the most determined anti-German leader in Poland," Rose stated. "Pilsudski's brilliant qualities as a soldier should not be allowed to overshadow his statesmanship. His personality, which has a Napoleonic touch about it, has produced by now a Bonapartist legend. What remains to be seen is whether even that is sufficient to control starving masses, land-hungry peasants and incurable reactionaries."[35]

Despite growing public support in Great Britain and the United States, Pilsudski understood well that the establishment of diplomatic ties with the Allies depended on concluding an agreement with the Paris Poles. After the Dłuski delegation left Kraków for Paris on December 24, 1918, they were delayed in Berne, Switzerland, waiting for their French visas. The unexpected delay turned out to be a blessing in disguise.

While in Berne the Dłuski delegation crossed paths with a number of Allied representatives. First it stumbled upon Richard Kimens and Rowland Kenny, the heads of the British Mission to Poland. Second, it met Sir Horace Rumbold, a career diplomat then serving as Great Britain's ambassador in Berne who later that year became Britain's ambassador to Poland. Dłuski described the exchange with British diplomats as going "quite smoothly," showing sympathy with the plight of the Pilsudski mission.[36]

The Dłuski delegation also met with American diplomats in Berne, including Archibald C. Coolidge, head of an American delegation known as the Coolidge Mission, who had been assigned the position by US secretary of state Robert Lansing. The encounter with Coolidge gave Dłuski an opportunity to correct many misconceptions the Americans harbored, such as the assertion that Bolshevism was rampant in Poland. "So we tried to steer the Americans away from this erroneous view," Dłuski remarked, "demonstrating that Moraczewski's ministry, despite its faults, is . . . the best security cover against the threat of Bolshevism that was in close proximity to our border."[37]

These face-to-face encounters with British and American diplomats on January 1–2, 1919, quickly paid off. As the Dłuski Mission stood on the platform in Berne waiting to board the train to Paris on January 3, a courier appeared, handing Dłuski a telegram. "The purpose of the British mission to

Warsaw," the telegram read, "is to establish *de facto* relations with the Polish Government. His Majesty's Government will do everything in its power to restore Poland." The telegram concluded that it had asked August Zaleski, then representing Pilsudski's government in the Polish consulate in Berne, to transmit the cable to Warsaw.[38]

Boarding the train to Paris, the delegation had high hopes. But skepticism also ran high, in awkward anticipation of entering into negotiations with longtime political rivals who did not share their core principles of a free society for all citizens, and whom they believed sowed hatred among peoples through ethnocentrism and anti-Semitism. In Berne, Sokolnicki had jotted down the day's important developments on January 1, 1919. Knowing that Pilsudski hoped to add his own delegates to the Polish National Committee and subordinate it to Warsaw, Sokolnicki pondered what it would mean to sit in the same organization with the likes of Roman Dmowski. "By joining the [Polish National] Committee," Sokolnicki wrote on January 1, 1919, "we will bring upon ourselves the hatred of Jews and the distrust of the left in European countries."[39]

In Warsaw, meanwhile, Pilsudski's popularity among the rank and file was as solid as ever. On December 29, 1918, twenty-five-year-old Wacław Jędrzejewicz attended a speech Pilsudski gave at a meeting of the Polish Military Organization. "My friends," Pilsudski said, after speaking at length about Polish soldiers during the war, "let me conclude with a slogan that my grandparents and parents were willing to die for, and for which so much Polish blood has been spilled: Long Live Poland!"[40] Jędrzejewicz remembered the emotions Pilsudski's speech evoked in him: "One can only imagine the impression those words made on us, young officers being inducted into the Polish Army."[41] Pilsudski addressed many of his speeches at this time to his soldiers. To mark New Year's Day on January 1, 1919, Pilsudski addressed his soldiers with the following words: "Let every soldier, from the highest-ranked commander to the newest recruit, remember that his consciousness at work and his efforts depend on whether we secure the rights to which all nations are entitled—independence and full freedom to run our own affairs in a sovereign homeland."[42] Prime Minister Moraczewski commented on Pilsudski's influence among his soldiers, observing in 1919 that "as a leader, Pilsudski is able to win over the hearts of the solders he commands, to awaken blind faith in his abilities and in the success of every battle he had fought."[43]

A flyer circulated by volunteer soldiers reflected the aura of legend and invincibility surrounding Pilsudski. "Thousands of young Polish men serve today in the armed forces to fight Bolshevism," the circular stated. "Nearly all see that the commander in chief of the Polish Army and head of state, Pilsudski, [is] a wholly trustworthy man [who] thinks only about his country and the welfare of its people. His whole life has been devoted to his country. Having spent time in prisons and in dungeons, he never lost faith in his ideals and today works for the Polish people. In these difficult times, we should show the Chief of State gratitude and offers of help."[44]

In Paris, meanwhile, the Dłuski Mission was aware of the reserve with which it was regarded in France. Indeed, not a single member of the Polish National Committee was among the several dozen people who greeted the mission when it arrived in Paris on January 4, 1919. One of the first things the Dłuski Mission did was to invite William Rose to their place of residence at the Hôtel Lutetia.[45] Rose's advocacy for the Pilsudski government, along with his ties to Anglo-American diplomatic circles, had made him a person of note. As expected, Rose came through for them, arranging a meeting between Sokolnicki and the assistant director of intelligence for Britain's Foreign Office, James Headlam-Morley. The latter agreed to Rose's request on condition that the meeting be considered unofficial. "I thanked him," Rose recalled, "pointing out that it would be a pity if the people best qualified to explain the situation in Poland should be kept in the background and not allowed to meet with the very circles who most needed the information they could give. He agreed, and results came quickly."[46]

The objective of Pilsudski's delegation was elucidated in the press. The *Times* of London reported on January 5: "Its errand is to establish diplomatic relations with the French Government. . . . The mission stated that the special objective of their presence is to obtain recognition of the Polish State, of which General Pilsudski is chief, and to obtain military assistance as well as food supplies, of which Poland is urgently in need."[47] The first encounter between the Dłuski Mission and Entente officials made a positive impression. The following day, Headlam-Morley informed Rose that two members of the British delegation to the Paris Peace Conference, Sir Esmé Howard and Sir Valentine Chirol, had requested a meeting with Sokolnicki. "We arrived and were received by Headlam-Morley in person," Rose recalled. "Speaking in French, Sokolnicki presented the whole situation in Poland in plain terms.

He was nearly an hour in doing so, after which questions were asked. The atmosphere was most cordial, and one felt that, 'official' or not, the ice was
now broken."[48] After the day's gatherings with British diplomats, Sokolnicki
commented, "During the meeting, I clearly noticed the tendency of certain
English circles to free us from the unilateral sphere of French influence, contrasting our delegation with the [Polish] National Committee. It was suggested, for example, that our delegation have an audience with King George
in London."[49]

The Dłuski delegation finally held talks with the Polish National Committee starting on January 6 and ending on January 11. To the Warsaw delegation, Roman Dmowski came off in a rough and uncompromising manner.
He demanded a guarantee that he alone be in charge of negotiations with the
Allies, to which Sokolnicki replied that the KNP would have to recognize the
Pilsudski government.[50] Although Dmowski responded that he would consider it, he told his colleagues in private something different. "The Polish delegation to the Paris congress," Dmowski said at a KNP session on January 6,
1919, "cannot rely on a government that can fall or challenge our congressional
mandates." The minutes of the meeting record some as not only agreeing with
Dmowski but opposing any agreement with the government in Warsaw as
long as Pilsudski was in charge.[51] What is clear is that Dmowski did not hide
his antipathy toward Pilsudski in the meeting with the Warsaw delegation.
Sokolnicki wrote in his diary the day of the meeting, "Dmowski began with
an attack, saying that Pilsudski was a weak and hesitant man; that he had
surrendered to the views of the people around him, and that the time had
come to end Pilsudski's dictatorship."[52]

American officials in France were informed of Dmowski's position. The
US secretary of state's special representative in Paris, General T. Bliss, met
with Dmowski on January 7. Dmowski was explicit about where he stood,
telling Bliss that he could not accept the Warsaw government's proposal.
Dmowski, Bliss wrote, was willing to recognize Pilsudski as head of state on
condition that all the terms of the Polish National Committee were met, including replacing the current cabinet and exclusive control over representation at the Paris Peace Conference. Bliss's pronouncedly negative impression
leaps off the pages: "Dmowski seems to be a good deal of a reactionary," he
remarked, noting Dmowski's surprising statement that it would be "a great
danger" if Germany became a liberal democracy. "When I asked him in what

way this would be a danger to Europe," Bliss recalled, "he merely stared at me in quiet amazement."[53] When a journalist asked Pilsudski his views on Dmowski and the National Democratic Party on January 13, 1919, he did not mince words, calling them "reactionary, anti-Semitic and unacceptable to the people at large."[54]

Several foreign diplomats who met Pilsudski for the first time in January 1919 recorded their impressions. R. C. Foster, a representative of the American mission to Poland, drew up a report on January 14, 1919, the day he first met Poland's head of state. "My whole impression of Pilsudski, he observed, "was that he was working for Poland and he spoke with a certain force and conviction that I had not expected to find as a result of the impression given me by the other people."[55] Other American officials who met Pilsudski included William R. Grove and Vernon Kellogg of the American Relief Administration's mission in Poland. Following their face-to-face meeting with Pilsudski on the day of their arrival in Poland on January 4, 1919, Grove jotted down his impressions the same day. "We found him to be a very agreeable man," Grove remarked, "with a sense of humor. The discussion was informal. At this and subsequent meetings, he was very plainly dressed; no frills, no bunk."[56]

Just how much was at stake in fostering ties with the victorious Allies and receiving much-needed aid was soon revealed. On January 5, 1919, the Red Army entered Vilna, repelling the makeshift Polish forces that had been briefly occupying the city. The ease with which the Red Army took Vilna highlighted Poland's military weakness. "The Polish troops," the *Boston Daily Globe* reported on January 10, 1919, "had no cannon and only a few cartridges per rifle." The inability of the fledgling Polish Army to halt the Bolshevik advance on Vilna was a stark reminder of Poland's need for a modern, robust army to server as a bulwark against the spread of communism. For Poland to receive urgently needed military and food aid, however, required a political settlement between the Paris and Warsaw Poles. "General Pilsudski and other leaders," the *New York Times* reported on January 10, 1919, "are being told very plainly that the Allies will help only when Poland is internally united."

The conservative French daily, *L'Écho de Paris,* agreed. "Until a union is accomplished we cannot recognize a Cabinet which, in our eyes, does not represent the entire country," the paper stated. "What we demand of the Polish Government is that it should not aim at keeping up the appearance of neutrality but should assume an attitude distinctly favorable to the Entente."[57]

Herbert Hoover, head of the American Relief Administration (*seated, center*), with Pilsudski to his left and the Polish prime minister, Ignacy Paderewski, on his right. Behind Hoover sits Interior Minister Stanisław Wojciechowski. Warsaw, August 15, 1919.

Pilsudski found such declarations baffling given his repeated statements in support of the Allies.

The mounting pressure abroad to replace the Moraczewski cabinet could also be felt at home. An army intelligence memorandum from January 8, 1919, reported that the mood of the population was in favor of a coalition government to be formed as soon as possible.[58] Western correspondents filed multiple dispatches from Warsaw based on interviews with Pilsudski. One British correspondent reported on the urgent need for the announcement of a coalition cabinet. "It would seem, therefore," the correspondent wrote on January 11, 1919, "that the first duty of all Polish politicians, of whatever party, should be to come together and form a Coalition Government, with which the Allies could talk directly." In the paper's opinion, waiting for elections was not an option: "The present situation is intolerable from two points of view—first, that of Poland, which, with the Bolsheviks pressing on its frontiers and besieging its cities, is unable to obtain help from the Entente; and, second, that of the Allies, who cannot further their natural interest by making Poland into a strong barrier against Russian anarchy, all because of a few men clinging to office for three weeks longer in Warsaw."

General Pilsudski, the correspondent stated further, "said that once the Polish State was firmly established he would serve it like a dog. In this phrase he gave a clue to his character." The paper encouraged Pilsudski to set aside his differences with the Polish National Committee in Paris and form a new government: "These three weeks are very important for Poland by reason of the advance of the Bolshevists," he wrote. "It is of paramount important during this period that relations with the Allies should be intensely close, which, unfortunately, they are not at present, with all the country, none the less, crying desperately to have them and the need as urgent as need ever was."[59]

The Bolshevik takeover of Vilna greatly concerned Paderewski. "Poland cannot defend itself," Paderewski wrote Colonel Edward House, Wilson's chief advisor on January 12, 1919. "We have no food, no uniforms, no arms, no munitions." What's more, the political situation was dire, Paderewski emphasized: "The present Government is weak and dangerous, it is almost exclusively radical-socialist. I have been asked to form a new cabinet, but what could I do with the moral support of the country alone, without the material assistance of the Allies and the United States?"[60]

Wilson's press secretary, R. S. Baker, expressed growing confidence in Pilsudski. He maintained that the Polish leader was competently running the country, building an army, and putting forth a democratic program of reforms. Pilsudski's foreign policy agenda, moreover, was in full accord with President Wilson's, Baker emphasized.[61] A French foreign ministry memorandum expressed support for a compromise rather than advocating for the KNP. "We can recognize General Pilsudski as Head of State provided he governs with a coalition cabinet where Dmowski, Paderewski, and their colleagues play a role."[62] In contrast to the French, American and British governments were beginning to view the KNP as a political party rather than a representative body. William J. Rose observed this dynamic when he arrived in Paris after the war's end. "I knew that 'Poland' for the Allies, particularly for the French, meant the [Polish] National Committee in Paris," he wrote, "composed chiefly of National Democrats, and with the eminent Roman Dmowski as their head."[63]

At their first meeting with the Dłuski Mission on January 6, the KNP discussed Pilsudski's December 21 letter to Dmowski as well as Pilsudski's statement of aims. Dmowski interpreted Pilsudski's letter as a demand for subordination to Warsaw. That evening, he commented privately about Pilsudski's letter: "He writes to me like a king by whose grace I can be granted a ministerial post."[64]

Pilsudski Talks with Paderewski

As the negotiations in Paris between the Dłuski Mission and the Polish National Committee dragged on without results, Ignacy Paderewski saved the day. The internationally renowned pianist-politician had lived in the United States during the war, had close ties with American diplomats, and knew Woodrow Wilson personally. A fluent speaker of English and French, Paderewski was acceptable to the Allies, the Polish National Committee, and Pilsudski alike. When he propitiously arrived in Warsaw on January 1, 1919, adoring crowds lined the streets to greet him. The following day Paderewski appeared in a horse-drawn buggy headed for Warsaw's elegant Bristol Hotel. One eyewitness recalled that the surrounding streets "were filled with tens of thousands of people. The windows of tenements were swarming with hundreds of viewers, with one balcony collapsing under the weight of those gathered. There was no end to cheers and shouts."[65]

Paderewski had arrived in a country wracked with political, social, and economic problems brought on by the war's devastation. Only a few days earlier Pilsudski had dispatched to Paris his aide-de-camp, Stanisław Hempel, to impress upon the Allies the urgent need for aid. Holding a press conference in the French capital, Hempel said that food aid was desperately needed, and that the Polish Army was dangerously short of artillery, clothing, and boots, crippling its lines of defense against an advancing Red Army.

Hempel's message, presented as diplomats arrived from all over the world to attend the upcoming Paris Peace Conference, made an impact. A *New York Times* correspondent filed this report on December 29, 1918:

> Unless Poland receives food supplies and clothing from the Allies immediately, there is grave danger that the population, which is facing starvation, will join the Bolshevik movement and thereby menace the

stability of the new Government, according to Lieutenant Stanislaw Hempel, aide-de-camp to General Joseph Pilsudski, military head of the Polish Government. Lieutenant Hempel, who arrived in Paris a few days ago from Poland on a diplomatic mission, has issued an urgent plea through the newspapers that the United States rush food to his country. In this plea he declared there were only two or three weeks' supplies left and that, while the people thus far had steadfastly refused to accept Bolshevism, they might be expected to revolt unless provided with the necessaries of life.[66]

Hempel's press conference came on the heels of the news that the Bolsheviks had captured Minsk on December 12, 1918, and were now advancing in the direction of Vilna. Hempel's words reverberated even more strongly in Allied circles when, on January 1, 1919, the Bolsheviks declared Minsk the capital of a Belarusian Soviet Socialist Republic. The Red Army was approaching, the *Times* of London warned, "the part which most directly concerns Western Europe; that is, the part bordering on ex-Russian and ex-Austrian Poland."[67]

Pilsudski's aide-de-camp emphasized that assistance to Poland served the interests of the Allies. Driving home Hempel's warning were new reports of pro-communist demonstrations. A correspondent in Warsaw filed a firsthand account on December 29, 1918, of a demonstration of thirty-five hundred people in the Polish capital "with red banners, on which were emblazoned, 'Long Live the Social Revolution!,' 'Long Live the Dictatorship of the Proletariat!' and the like. I watched them pass and they . . . shouted, 'Down with the Government!,' 'Down with Pilsudski!'" Speaking to concerned onlookers, the reporter heard people saying that Allied help was needed "and that not an hour should be lost in sending General Haller's disciplined Polish Army from France here."[68] In fact, Poland's secret intelligence service at the time confirmed an uptick in Bolshevik agitation linked to the activities of the Polish Communist Party (KPP), formed on December 16, 1918, in Warsaw, leading to the arrest in Warsaw of close to a thousand people who were described as communist sympathizers.[69]

Such reports of communist agitation in Poland sent a clear message to the Allies about how much was at stake in the Paderewski-Pilsudski talks. Their negotiations began on January 4, 1919, when Paderewski presented terms mirroring those of Stanisław Grabski, terms that Pilsudski rejected. Paderewski reacted by abruptly leaving Warsaw for Kraków on the same day. Later that evening, a group of conservatives attempted to overthrow Pilsudski. Led by military commander Colonel Marian Żegota-Januszajtis and conservative politician Prince Eustachy Sapieha, the action began with the arrest of Prime Minister Moraczewski, Foreign Minister Leon Wasilewski, and Interior Minister Stanisław Thugutt, as well as the commander of the Warsaw garrison. Armed with revolvers and hand grenades, the conspirators then entered the Belvedere Palace looking for Pilsudski.[70]

The insurrectionists were no match for the palace guard, the head of state's personal protection squad and the guard duty platoon of the 7th Lancers, which wrestled the palace intruders to the ground and disarmed them. The commander of the regiment reportedly told Pilsudski, "A coup d'état is taking place, Commandant, but it is a farce, not a coup." The commander then called for reinforcements, telling Pilsudski that a threat to his security was still a concern. With characteristic calm and self-assuredness, Pilsudski reportedly waved his hand in dismissal, replying, "Don't be afraid. They will do nothing here."[71] He nevertheless took action, calling on the head of the General Staff, General Stanisław Szeptycki, to reinforce the capital. The ill-conceived plot collapsed in a matter of hours. Moraczewski, Wasilewski, and Thugutt were freed by the next morning.

The failed coup had the immediate effect of increasing confidence in Pilsudski. "On the whole," the *Times* of London reported in a dispatch dated January 6, 1919, a day after the coup, "the doings of yesterday have not been without advantage, as they have shown that . . . the Army, young as it is, does not consider itself a political instrument, but a military organization subject to discipline, encouraging the stability of the country." The Warsaw correspondent continued: "General Pilsudski's hands have been strengthened by what has happened, and if, when M. Paderewski returns tomorrow, he comes to an agreement with him for the reconstruction of the Cabinet, then Poland will at last have come in sight of the corner he has got to turn." Polish novelist Maria Dąbrowska echoed this sentiment, writing in her diary on the day after the coup that "this has undoubtedly strengthened the position of the acting government."[72]

The failed coup also made the need for a political settlement crystal clear. And on January 5, Pilsudski dispatched General Szeptycki to Kraków to ask Paderewski to return to the capital to restart talks. At their meeting in Warsaw on January 7, 1919, Pilsudski asked Paderewski to form a new government and serve as prime minister. A window into Paderewski's view of Pilsudski at the time comes from American officials William Grove and Vernon Kellogg, who sat down with Paderewski on the same day he agreed to form a government. Grove reported, "Paderewski considers that Pilsudski is a good man, but that he represents a party only, and not the whole of Poland." Grove was nonetheless optimistic, commenting that Paderewski and Pilsudski appeared equally committed to forming a coalition government acceptable to the Allies.[73] For the next seven days, the two hammered out the details. Meanwhile, a circular appeared in the streets of Warsaw urging people to support the negotiations. "At every turn," the circular stated, "loudly give your support for a National Government and for Jozef Pilsudski as Commander of the Polish Army. Long Live the Government, the Army and Commandant Pilsudski!"[74]

As negotiations continued in Warsaw, it became clear that Pilsudski's preference to wait until the January 26 parliamentary elections was no longer a viable path forward. On January 7, Pilsudski told Vernon Kellogg about his intention to meet with socialist leaders to explain why an accord with Paderewski was necessary. "[Pilsudski] is devoting all of today," Kellogg reported, "to conferences with the Socialists endeavoring to get them to accept the new situation and really support it. He is pointing out to them that this is the only hope of Allied aid and American recognition and assistance—and that all the needs of Poland i.e., supplies for its army, a loan, supplies of food and raw materials, etc. will be quickly met once a stable representative government is formed in Poland and recognized by the Allies and America."[75] British officials had likewise told Pilsudski, Kellogg remarked, that no military aid would be forthcoming as long as the present socialist cabinet remained in power. In Kellogg's view, this was a positive development, demonstrating that Pilsudski was now fully aligned with the American position and was working on steering his supporters in the same direction.

With pressure mounting on Pilsudski to strike a deal, he began to feel the squeeze. "No one understands the position I am in or the situation in general," he told a journalist on January 13, 1919. "This is not about the Left or the Right. Enough of this kind of talk! I act for all. This is about the army that is only in the process of being formed. Everything I do must be for the armed forces. That is what I am razor focused on," Pilsudski said. "It is therefore also about the Haller Army and about Gen. Żeligowski, matters which Marshal Foch has to settle." Paderewski was the best candidate to lead a unity government, Pilsudski emphasized, because "he has a common language with the Allies. Anyway, I really count on Paderewski. We agree on almost all the main issues. He is even a fiercer advocate of 'federalism' than I and he will moderate Dmowski's views. Paderewski, you say, bows in all directions; and I say, let him bow. Bring me whatever he needs." Pilsudski concluded by saying, "I will have everything in the palm of my hands when I have an army."[76]

To the surprise of both delegations in Paris, which were working feverishly on draft agreements, the impasse was broken in Warsaw. On January 14, Paderewski informed Dmowski that an agreement had been reached with Pilsudski for a coalition government. Dmowski received the telegram during a meeting with the Dłuski Mission. According to Sokolnicki, Dmowski was shocked at the news.[77] The agreement stipulated that Paderewski would form a government as prime minister while Pilsudski would remain head of state and commander in chief. The KNP in Paris would now add ten delegates of Pilsudski's choosing, including Dłuski, Sokolnicki, Herman Diamond, Stanisław Thugutt, and Wasilewski. Henceforth, the KNP would no longer to be merely a mouthpiece of the National Democratic Party. In addition, a three-member body composed of Dmowski, Paderewski, and Wasilewski would represent Poland at the Paris Peace Conference.[78]

As disappointed as Dmowski was, he put country above party. On January 15, 1919, he cabled Paderewski that the Polish National Committee had accepted the agreement. The historic accord became official on January 21, 1919, when the KNP extended formal recognition to the Warsaw government. In the Polish National Committee's next session, held on January 30, 1919, three new members were welcomed: Kazimierz Dłuski, Michał Sokolnicki, and Antoni Sujkowski.[79] These developments represented an enormous victory not only for Pilsudski but for Poland as a whole, for it was only in the wake of the accord that the Allies began extending urgently needed aid. "I made an entry in my diary on January 15 in Paris," the British diplomat Sir Esmé Howard recalled, "that Poland was saved. This was perfectly true. In spite of their great dissimilarities of outlook, character, education, manner, in fact of almost everything that goes to make a friendship, Paderewski's obvious sincerity had somehow charmed Pilsudski into as much of the spirit of union as was necessary for the time being."[80] The agreement was a victory for

Pilsudski and his persuasive powers. For it fulfilled his primary aim of in-corporating political parties from the left into the KNP and placing it under Warsaw's control.

Meanwhile, steps were taken in Warsaw to implement the Pilsudski-Paderewski agreement. On January 16, 1919, Prime Minister Moraczewski tendered his resignation, expressing the hope that the new Paderewski cab-inet would be able to remove the hardships that had led to the cabinet's dis-missal.[81] Pilsudski, in turn, named Paderewski prime minister and presented the names of ten cabinet members. Paderewski was to serve as both premier and foreign minister while Pilsudski remained provisional head of state and commander in chief. Three Moraczewski cabinet members were retained—the minister of justice (Leon Supiński), minister of labor and social welfare (Jerzy Iwanowski), and the minister of provisions (Antoni Mińkiewicz). Pilsudski appointed longtime collaborator Stanisław Wojciechowski to the post of in-terior minister. Nonparty specialists oriented to the center-right, including four from Galicia, two from Poznań province, and the rest from the former Kingdom of Poland, filled the remaining positions.[82] "There is immense joy among all responsible sections of the people at the news, which is spreading through the city rapidly," a Warsaw correspondent for the *Times* of London reported on January 16, 1919. It was an extraordinary development in the early history of reborn Poland, marking the moment when the de facto existence of two Polish governments had been eliminated.

To his delegation in Paris, Pilsudski explained that the agreement was reached for three reasons: (1) to obtain military, financial, and food aid from the Allied Powers; (2) to diminish domestic unrest prior to the Sejm elections; and (3) to fortify the frontiers.[83] Pilsudski stressed that the vacuum caused by the hasty German withdrawal from Lithuania and Belarus, an action he had expected would take place three months later, was a critical factor. The Bolshevik advance in the immediate aftermath of the German withdrawal "caused the question of the assistance of the Entente to become more urgent. I believe this assistance will be granted only after constituting Paderewski's government."[84] For it was through Poland, Pilsudski emphasized, that the Bolsheviks were to reach Central and Western Europe, a process that began with the recent conquest of Vilna at the beginning of January 1919. But there was an additional reason for the agreement. While the need for Allied recognition played a central role, Pilsudski added, "the moral gain of the change is that Paderewski, in taking power from my hand, recognized me as the Head of State."[85] The formation of a Paderewski government, therefore, had effectively sealed the deal with the Allied Powers.

It is thus not surprising that the Paderewski-Pilsudski agreement led to a diplomatic breakthrough. Colonel House, upon learning of the agreement, advised President Wilson to extend formal recognition to Poland. "Now that Paderewski has formed a Government in Poland which is apparently being supported by Pilsudski and the other more prominent leaders," House wrote on January 21, 1919, "I suggest that you, on behalf of the United States, immediately recognize this Government as a de facto Government. I believe that we should take the lead in this matter."[86] The expert on Eastern Europe in the British delegation in Paris, James Headlam-Morley, similarly expressed support for his country's recognition of Warsaw. On January 22, 1919, he reported on a meeting he had had in Paris with a vehement supporter of Pilsudski. "It was quite essential," Headlam-Morley paraphrased the gentleman, "that Pilsudski should be supported. He was the only person who could keep things together. If he fell there would be revolutionary outbreak at once. He spoke repeatedly, with great admiration, of Pilsudski as a national hero."[87] Headlam-Morley likewise wrote to Lewis Namier, then serving in the Political Intelligence Department of the British Foreign Office. Responding to Namier's concerns that the Paderewski government was linked too closely to Dmowski, Headlam-Morley replied that Paderewski was a good alternative, liked by the Allied Powers, and had no known anti-Semitic leanings. "Though of course," Headlam-Morley commented, "I agree with you that the support ought to be based not merely on the principle that we are supporting Paderewski, but that Pilsudski should be put much more in the foreground than he has been."[88]

The formation of the Paderewski cabinet led the Allied governments to reassess their policy toward Poland. They were also aware of growing popular support for the fledgling new state. At a rally on January 26, 1919, in Washington, D.C., an estimated eight thousand people, including government officials and community leaders, called on the United States to recognize the new government in Warsaw.[89] The march in Washington coincided with extraordinary events taking place that same day in Poland.

Sejm Elections and Reinstatement as Head of State

A fundamental step toward the formation of a democratic state took place on January 26, 1919, when elections to the legislative Sejm were held. Military conflicts were still ongoing in East Galicia and in Poznania, and with the Bolsheviks in the northeast provinces, elections could only be held in the Kingdom of Poland and West Galicia. To the 296 deputies elected were added 44 unelected seats for Poles who had formerly served as members of the German parliament from Poznań or West Prussia or of the Austrian parliament from East Galicia.[90]

Prior to the elections Pilsudski had expressed concern about a divided parliament. "Responsibility for state affairs will fall on those who, receiving the majority of votes, will take power into their own hands," he wrote on the eve of Election Day. "The worst outcome, I suppose on the other hand, is that the Sejm will have no clear majority."[91] Before election results were made public, an Italian journalist asked Pilsudski if he would give up power as he had promised, to which Pilsudski replied, "I am a servant of the people and I will hand over my authority to the assembly, however it is constituted." He added, "I regard this Sejm as the free expression of the people and I will devote all my soldierly work to the Homeland."[92]

On Election Day, a periodical published by Jan Jędrzejewicz ran an editorial, "Piłsudczycy" (Pilsudskiites). The mere biography of Pilsudski, it stated, served as a model of patriotism and sacrifice. "Who is a Pilsudskiite?" the article asked: "A person who cannot lead a private life. A person who lives a life of service in his work and beliefs." Pilsudski, as their leader, had demonstrated an ability to realize his aims before and during the Great War. "Responsibility for the fate of the nation must be placed in the hands of those who are worthy of this responsibility. For generations, people grew up under the sign of service to the national cause. The day of their spiritual birth is August 6, 1914," the article stated, referring to the day Pilsudski led troops into imperial Russia to mark Polish entry into World War I, "the flagship day that will forever shine in our souls."[93]

The 340 deputies in reborn Poland's first elected assembly were divided along partisan lines, with 34.2 percent of the seats going to the rightists, 30.8 percent to centrists, and 30.5 percent to leftists. By region, the National Democrats received 45 percent of the votes in the former Kingdom of Poland as against 22 percent for the Polish Socialist Party, while dominating in the areas taken from Germany. National minorities received 3.5 percent of the seats, with eleven going to representatives of Jewish political parties and two to the German People's Party.[94]

The impact of the elections on Poland's standing abroad was immediate. On January 30 the United States became the first Entente country to establish formal diplomatic relations with Poland. "The formal recognition by the United States of the new Polish Government," the *New York Times* stated on January 31, 1919, ". . . shows the confidence of our Administration, and incidentally of the allied Governments, in the new regime." The paper expressed a new optimism. "The Poles are really united politically in support of the present Provisional Government of Paderewski and Pilsudski," the *New York Times* stated on January 30, 1919, "and that the Constitutional Assembly, to which delegates have just been elected, will begin the orderly work on February 9 of building their new State." The other Entente powers followed suit in recognizing the new state, including France (February 23), Great Britain (February 25), and Italy (February 27).

THE HISTORIC CONVOCATION of Poland's first elected legislature took place on February 10, 1919. Alexandra Szczerbińska vividly recalled the celebratory mood in Warsaw. "Flags were flying, bands playing," she wrote. "Crowds paraded the streets, laughing, singing patriotic songs, carried away on one great tide of enthusiasm, in the realization that at last Poland's reproach among nations had been taken away. We were once again a free people with a parliament of our own."[95]

Alexandra, who with Pilsudski had a one-year-old daughter, waited patiently for the event to commence. She described the dramatic moment of anticipation:

The public gallery was crowded hours before the ceremony; hundreds of people had fought for admission. Cabinet Ministers and members filled the benches in the center, facing a platform draped with the national flag. Just before the hour struck, a hush fell over the whole assembly, and I remember wondering whether the people around me were feeling even as I was the unseen presence of all those who had lived

Pilsudski and Prime Minister Ignacy Paderewski, on their way to the opening session of
Poland's first parliament, Warsaw, February 10, 1919.

and fought and shed their blood to give us this victory. . . . Then I
heard a burst of cheering from the crowds outside and a moment later
Joseph Pilsudski took his place on the platform to open the Diet. He wore
the simple blue uniform of the Legions and behind him were four
aides-de-camp.[96]

Among the deputies present was the influential Peasant Party ("Piast")
leader, Wincenty Witos. "A crowd of thousands had already begun to sur-
round the parliament building in the early morning," he recalled. "In front
of the building, on top of which fluttered the country's flag, stood an honorary company of soldiers. At the strike of 9 a.m., parliamentary deputies
began to enter, followed by their guests. Every single seat in the parliament
hall had been filled," Witos added, continuing, "The arrival of the Head of
State, who was to perform the historic act of opening the first Sejm in Independent Poland, was eagerly awaited."[97] American diplomat William
R. Grove was among the foreign dignitaries present. Sitting in the balcony,
Grove jotted down these words in his diary: "Congress formally called to

attention when Pilsudski, Chief of State, entered; all stood while he read his speech; was in Polish but said to have been excellent."[98]

Before the newly elected Sejm, guests, the press, and foreign dignitaries from the United States, France, Britain, and Italy, among others, Pilsudski opened his historic address:

> A century and a half of struggle, often entailing blood and sacrifice, has found its triumph this day. A century and a half of dreams of a Free Poland have ended in realization. The nation is celebrating today a great and happy occasion, following a long, bitter period of suffering. At this moment, when all Polish hearts are beating fast, I am pleased to have been given the honor of opening the Polish Sejm, which will be the sole master and ruler of our country.[99]

He then turned to foreign affairs:

> In our foreign relations there is one ray of hope, the tightening of the bonds of friendship, which unite us with the Entente Powers. There has long been the closest sympathy between Poland and the democratic peoples of Europe and America, who do not seek glory in the conquest and oppression of other nations but base their policy on the principles of right and justice. This sympathy has increased since the victorious armies of the Allied Powers, which broke the last vestige of the power of our oppressors, have freed Poland from her servitude.[100]

The speech galvanized the crowd. Following Pilsudski's reference to the United States, spontaneous applause rippled through the assembly accompanied by chants of "Long Live Wilson!"[101]

Pilsudski concluded on a somber note, warning that the country's borders were far from secure. Military conflicts to the north, east, south, and west were in the process of being resolved. "Hateful currents of our neighboring states are threatening our frontiers," he said. The country's soldiers had to take up arms to defend Poland's borders in order to ensure the country's free development. "We will not give up one inch of Polish soil and we shall not permit our borders, to which we have a right, to be diminished in any way, shape, or form," Pilsudski said, followed by rapturous applause.[102]

Several present recorded their reaction to Pilsudski's speech. Witos recalled that "Pilsudski was frequently interrupted with increasingly thunderous applause, especially when he spoke about the army and the alliance with the Allies, France in particular." Grove jotted in his diary the same day that Pilsudski referred to aid from the entente, when "crowds cheered enthusiastically and feelingly."[103] The international press similarly noted the assembly's enthusiastic response to the call for close ties with the Allies. "General Pilsudski," the *New York Times* reported on February 12, 1919, "referred to the close bonds between his country and the Allies. His words were cheered."

Deputies chose a speaker on February 14, the position narrowly going to the National Democrat from Poznań, Wojciech Trąmpczyński, who received 155 votes to Wincenty Witos's 149.[104] "I am delighted at the speed with which this country's political system is being developed and organized," Pilsudski told a French daily on February 19. "Despite the difficulties involved, the elections were held without incidents and the opening of the Legislative Sejm took place smoothly. This miracle," Pilsudski continued, "can only be explained by the elevated disposition of the masses, evoked by the sense of a profound national victory over our eternal enemies. If the unemployed laborer, barefoot and on an empty stomach, happily exercised his right to vote, that was because one thought was prevailing over all others: 'Poland Has Risen from the Dead!' This slogan is now stronger than hunger and cold, filling the hearts of all Poles."[105] At a dinner Pilsudski hosted at the Belvedere Palace for foreign dignitaries on February 18, he toasted the guests with the words, "The people of Poland are your most faithful allies. You have earned our gratitude and affection."[106]

One of the most important and symbolic acts in Pilsudski's political career came at the Sejm's third session on February 20, 1919. Formally resigning as provisional head of state, he handed his power over to the speaker, saying: "My role has come to an end. I am pleased that, obedient to my soldierly oath and to my convictions, I can place at the disposal of the Sejm all power that I have heretofore exercised. I hereby declare that I am submitting my position as Head of State into the hands of the Speaker."[107] Pilsudski then exited the chamber while the assembly deliberated on two items. First, it approved regulations governing the powers between the two branches of government, placing firm limits on the authority of the head of state.

The regulations, which became known as the Little Constitution, consisted of fewer than 250 words:

RESOLUTION OF THE LEGISLATIVE SEJM, FEBRUARY 20, 1919

I.   The Sejm accepts Jozef Pilsudski's declaration entrusting the office of the Chief of State to the Sejm and expresses its gratitude for His hard work in the service of the homeland.

II.   Until the legal adoption of a Constitution, which in essence will determine the regulations governing the organization of supreme authority in the Polish State, the Sejm entrusts to Jozef Pilsudski the further office of the Head of State based on the principles:

> 1.   The sovereign and legislative authority in the Polish State is the Legislative Sejm; the speaker of the Sejm, countersigned by the prime minister and the relevant cabinet members, issues laws.
> 2.   The Head of State is the state's representative and the executor of the Sejm's resolutions in civilian and military matters.
> 3.   The Head of State appoints the government on the basis of an agreement with the Sejm.
> 4.   The Head of State is responsible, together with the government, to the Sejm for the exercise of his office.
> 5.   Every act of the Head of State requires the signature of the relevant ministers.

Signed, Speaker W. Trąmpczyński and Prime Minister I. J. Paderewski[108]

The second act of the assembly was a unanimous vote to reinstate Pilsudski as head of state. Upon returning to the chamber, he was greeted by shouts from leftist deputies of "Long Live Pilsudski!" and received bouquets of flowers. "Commandant Jozef Pilsudski!" Speaker Trąmpczyński said. "The Legislative Sejm today has unanimously decided to return to you the title of Head of State. Pursuant to this resolution, the supreme authority of the state, which you have placed in my hands, entrusts You again to exercise this authority for the benefit of the people and of the country."[109]

Pilsudski turned to the assembly. Thanking the deputies, he said he felt he had too arbitrary a temperament, due to his "Lithuanian stubbornness," to carry out the duties of a position that required the conciliatory attributes of a statesman. "But as a soldier," he said, "I obediently accept your resolution, the resolution of an assembly representing the country as a whole. It is my hope that the trust you have placed in me will ease the burden that has been placed on my shoulders."[110]

The very act of voluntarily giving up power served as a weighty confirmation of Pilsudski's reputation for trustworthiness, a commitment to democratic government, and a sign of loyalty to the Allies. Foreign journalists praised the legal transfer of power. The Associated Press stated that by the events of February 20, 1919, "Europe's newest parliament . . . was marked by the formal turning over by General Joseph Pilsudski of his authority as dictator and the returning of it to him, subject to the approval of the Diet." It continued that "the presence of peasants in national costume, with here and there priests and rabbis, testified that the assembly was not ruled by a clique of landed nobility."[111]

WESTERN DIPLOMATS WHO MET Pilsudski at this time came away with a positive impression. "We Americans had to learn about Pilsudski," Grove remarked. "He was a national character in Poland but in the armistice period was scarcely known outside of Central Europe. That accounted for our lack of knowledge of the real character of the man. But as the weeks and months passed and we heard so much about him and saw what he was accomplishing, our respect for his administrative and military talents increased rapidly."[112]

Following the session of the Sejm on February 20, 1919, Pilsudski could look back on the three months and nine days that had passed since the end of the Great War and be dazzled by the accomplishments achieved. His role in the establishment of the state, the government, and the armed forces had made permanent his place in history. As reborn Poland's first head of state and commander in chief, history had anointed him modern Poland's founding father. Piotr Wandycz observed, "The nomination of Paderewski's cabinet, reconciliation between the National Committee in Paris and the regime in Warsaw, elections to the Sejm which confirmed Pilsudski's position as chief of state, and the Allied recognition of Poland . . . amounted to crystallization of the Polish state. An independent Western-oriented republic established itself; no Bolshevik revolution had taken place."[113]

Yet the coalition government's interior minister, Stanisław Wojciechowski, rightly observed that the seed of the future conflict between Pilsudski and the Sejm was firmly planted in the contents of the Little Constitution. The excitement around the consolidation of the Paderewski cabinet and the reinstatement of Pilsudski as head of state, as well as recognition by the Allies, had obscured this reality. According to the Little Constitution, Wojciechowski remarked, "The Head of State was now deprived of the right to appoint the government at his own discretion . . . and he became responsible before the Sejm, along with ministers, for the implementation of laws because they were henceforth promulgated by the Speaker rather than by the Head of State."[114] For the time being, however, extreme hardship, border wars, and the need for Allied assistance gave way to a spirit of compromise.

CHAPTER 14

The State Builder

I do not want to see Poland control large stretches of territory
inhabited by unfriendly people. But to give freedom to a neighboring people would be the pride of my life as a statesman
and soldier.

—JOZEF PILSUDSKI, FEBRUARY 12, 1920

The year 1919 became a crucial one for Pilsudski, for Poland, and for
Europe as a whole. It was in this year that Pilsudski's efforts to establish parliamentary government, to strike an agreement with the Polish National
Committee in Paris, and to gain recognition from the Allies all came to fruition. Key achievements in January and February coincided with the start of
the Paris Peace Conference, which had begun on January 19, 1919. With the
naming of Paderewski as prime minister, elections to the Sejm, and the assembly's decision to reinstate Pilsudski as head of state, Pilsudski's leadership
became legitimized at home and abroad. Although the new system of government, modeled on that of the French Third Republic, made ministers
responsible to the Sejm and severely limited the powers of the head of state,
Pilsudski's considerable influence remained intact as commander in chief of
the Polish armed forces.

Having stabilized the political system and gained recognition from the
Great Powers, Pilsudski now turned his gaze to the settlement of the frontiers. While he knew that the western border with Germany would be largely
imposed at the Paris Peace Conference mostly in Poland's favor, the country's
eastern borders would depend upon the prowess of Poland's armed forces.

Pilsudski thus put forward a two-pronged strategy for settling Poland's frontier. The first was diplomatic pressure on the Western Allies. The second was a much more complex and multilayered policy in the east—a combination of expanding Poland's eastern frontiers and pushing back the Russian military presence far to the east to create a belt of independent borderland states tied to Poland either in a loose federation or as independent states. This controversial federalist idea gained some traction at the time but ended up in total failure by 1921. Poland's eastern frontiers were to be formed during this period through armed conflict.

The most important concrete result of establishing formal diplomatic ties with the Western Allies and the United States was large-scale aid relief. This could already be seen with the first shipment of American aid reaching Danzig on February 17, 1919. By the end of February, fourteen thousand tons of American food had reached Poland.[1] In Paris, meanwhile, the Supreme Council—composed of representatives of the principal powers (the United States, Great Britain, France, Italy, and Japan)—received a Polish delegation on January 29, 1919, when it listened to a presentation of Poland's case by Roman Dmowski. The Supreme Council then appointed an Inter-Allied Mission to Poland composed of American, British, French, and Italian representatives assigned to assess conditions and the needs of the country.[2]

The Inter-Allied Mission arrived in Warsaw on February 12, 1919. One of the British members, fifty-five-year-old Sir Esmé Howard, later reflected on how little Western diplomats knew about Poland at the time. "Most Englishmen of my age at least," Howard remarked, "were brought up in such complete ignorance about everything concerned with Poland that before attempting to deal with the Polish question at the Paris Conference it was practically necessary to go through a course of instruction on the subject.... Poland indeed," he continued, "was like a closed and forgotten book put away on the topmost shelf."[3]

Pilsudski received the Inter-Allied Mission at the Belvedere Palace on February 14, 1919. "His is a strange and fascinating personality," Howard noted in his diary that same day, "very simply dressed in a grey military tunic and black trousers. He has a spare figure and a small, thin, worn face, very deep set eyes and black eyebrows which meet; a moustache which quite covers his mouth, and a well chiseled nose and chin. He has occasionally a wonderful smile." Pilsudski, Howard continued, "is fanatically Polish and patriotic."[4]

Howard was seated next to Pilsudski at a dinner held in honor of the Inter-Allied Mission on February 18. He recalled the following exchange with the Polish head of state:

> He asked me what part of England I came from and whether I had any sentiment about it. I told him about my devotion to Cumberland and that I never felt really at home anywhere but there. 'Oh,' he said, 'then you will understand what I feel for my native district near Vilna in Lithuania. I am never really happy except there. So strong was this feeling with me that when I was a fugitive proscribed by the Russian police I never could let a year go by without seeing my own homeland, though of course the risk of capture was infinitely greater because they were always on the lookout for me.'
>
> Then I began to understand why this man would never consent to separate Vilna from Poland. . . . After that conversation I felt Pilsudski was a real human being whom I could understand, and I had a genuine fellow feeling for him.[5]

The second British member of the Inter-Allied Mission, General Carton de Wiart, came away from these meetings with the impression that Pilsudski was a standout among statesmen. "Since those days," Wiart later reflected, "it has been my destiny to meet many of the great men of the world, but Pilsudski ranks highly among them—in fact, for political sense, almost at the top." Pilsudski's appearance, he continued, "was striking to a degree and his air that of the conspirator. He had deep-set eyes of searching penetration, heavy brows and a drooping moustache which was peculiarly characteristic."[6] The American official, Arthur Goodhart, was similarly intrigued upon meeting the enigmatic leader in Warsaw. "To the people, he symbolizes Poland's century-long desire for freedom," Goodhart commented on July 14, 1919. "He has the reputation of never telling a lie, a characteristic which apparently is quite exceptional here, for three different people mentioned the fact to me during the course of this evening's reception."[7]

At the time of the first meetings with the Inter-Allied Mission, Pilsudski was directing ongoing military operations with Ukrainians in East Galicia. In the Lithuanian-Belarusian territories, encounters with the Red Army had already begun. An Italian journalist sat down with Pilsudski on February 1, 1919, to discuss the various conflicts. Pilsudski told him:

War, which has ended in Europe, is now beginning to envelope our country's borders. The Ukrainians threaten Lwów, the Bolsheviks have seized Vilna and are at the gates of Brześć and Grodno, saying as they advance that their aim is Warsaw and all of Poland. The Czechs invaded the Polish region of Cieszyn as well as Polish counties of Spiz and Orawa. The Germans are fighting against us in Poznań. We are surrounded on all sides by foes and isolated from the world.[8]

The situation in Poznań, Pilsudski continued, "is particularly difficult and painful." Parts remained under German control and awaited a decision at the Paris Peace Conference. Fighting could break out at any moment, he warned, if the peacemakers did not announce a final German-Polish frontier soon. In an interview that caught the attention of the Allies, he made his views on Danzig (Gdańsk) quite clear: "Danzig is the gate to the Vistula, our historic and geographic port on the Baltic Sea, absolutely necessary for our trade as well as our national life. That is why we demand that Danzig be unequivocally recognized as a Polish possession."[9]

Pilsudski also elaborated on the question of East Galicia. "I cannot predict what will be the future border between us and the Ukrainians," he said. "But there is strong support here for incorporating the whole of East Galicia, which would give us a common frontier with Romania. That border would provide Poland a link to the Black Sea, something desirable from the economic point of view." In Pilsudski's view, the conflict with the Ukrainians was destined to resolve itself: "I believe in the Ukrainian national movement and there are many points upon which we can agree."[10] To the French minister in Warsaw, he gave a second reason for the significance of East Galicia: to give Poland a frontier with Romania so that, in case the German border was cut off in a military conflict, Poland would have a link to the Allies.[11] His general feeling about the situation in Poland as a whole was expressed in a second interview on February 7, 1919. "At the moment," he said bluntly, "Poland is, in fact, without frontiers. Everything we shall gain on our Western border depends on the Entente and how much it is willing to squeeze out of Germany. Our Eastern frontier is something different altogether: here there are doors that open and close, and it depends who opens them and how forcefully."[12]

The opening shots of the Polish-Bolshevik conflict took place in mid-February 1919. The immediate trigger was a German withdrawal in the first week of February 1919 from a seventy-two-mile stretch of territory east of Poland's boundary via a rail line that ran from Volkovisk in Belarus to Białystok and Łapy. As German troops pulled out of the area, Polish and Bolshevik troops filled the vacuum from opposite directions. The first clash took place on February 14, 1919, in the Belarusian village of Bereza Kartuska.[13] Fortifying a Lithuanian-Belarusian front under General Szeptycki, the Polish forces took Kowel, Brześć (Brest-Litovsk), and parts of Volhynia on February 9. They then advanced ninety-six miles north, taking Białystok on February 19.[14]

Polish military successes continued in the spring of 1919, beginning with the capture of Pinsk on March 5 and Grodno on April 15, in a thrust that moved north in the direction of Lida and Vilna. Upon Pilsudski's return to Warsaw on April 29, 1919, General Haller waited at the Warsaw central train station, where the two men shook hands in a high-profile exchange. Upon visiting Grodno on June 1, 1919, Pilsudski said, "As a son of this land, I know perfectly well all the hell of misery that you had to endure here. It was my dream upon entering this soil to give you what you lacked most—liberty and the freedom to decide your own destiny."[15] Back in Warsaw, meanwhile, Pilsudski held an audience with military officials on March 6, 1919, to brief them on operations. Bogusław Miedziński, who had come from the command headquarters of the Kielce district, recalled Pilsudski expressing concerns that the army was dreadfully short of supplies: "I have no ammunition, no artillery and the treasury is empty."[16] Pilsudski stressed the urgent need to transport Haller's Polish Army in France, an army that "would also bring weapons, ammunition, and cannons to Poland, tested and ready for use." The import of military aid, Pilsudski continued, rested solely with France and General Foch's support. Obtaining French military assistance was thus the most pressing priority. The following day Pilsudski sent a cable to France's prime minister, George Clemenceau, expressing gratitude for having extended formal recognition to Poland.[17]

Pilsudski aired his views to the French public in an interview on March 19, 1919, that appeared on the front page of the popular Paris newspaper *Le Petit Parisien*. The interview began with the question of whether Pilsudski belonged to any political party. He replied unambiguously that he had no party affiliation. Was it not true, the paper asked, that Pilsudski fought against Russia during World War I and thus contributed toward weakening the Entente? He replied, "I harbored a deep feeling of hatred toward Russia, which had tormented my country in a manner so horrific that it is difficult for the French to understand." Pilsudski's profound distrust of Russian state officials came to the surface when asked about a possible peace agreement with Russia. "But we cannot believe anything Russia promises," he said. "For Russia promises when it is forced to do so and then goes back on its word from the moment its strength is renewed."[18]

Pilsudski's deep-seated mistrust of Russia guided his thinking about Poland's eastern borders. Make no mistake about it, Pilsudski told the French reading public, the Soviets intended not peace but war and annexation. "I am convinced," he told *Le Petit Parisien,* "that Russian Soviets will attempt to attack Poland." The civil war in Russia, Pilsudski predicted, would last for a long time. "Without regard to who will govern, Russia is fiercely imperialistic. One could even say it is the fundamental feature of its political character. We experienced imperialism under the tsars; today, we see Red-communist imperialism. Poland constitutes the barrier against Slavic imperialism, whether it be the tsarist or Bolshevik form." In Pilsudski's view, removing Ukraine from Russian control—whether White or Bolshevik—was the key to the security of Poland and Europe as a whole: "Their attack on Poland depends in the first place on the Ukrainian question: material considerations and, above all, hunger influences Soviet policy. They have to obtain supplies in agriculturally rich Ukraine. That is why if Ukraine falls to them, then they will move on Poland."[19]

Pilsudski expanded on his views in April 1919. "You know my views on Lithuania and Belarus," he wrote to Leon Wasilewski, who had arrived in Paris on March 6 to join the Polish delegation at the Paris Peace Conference, "which are based on the principle that I desire to be neither an imperialist nor a federalist." But he then added that meetings with Entente officials and comments about the brotherhood of peoples and nations based on American ideas were making him more conducive to the federalist principle. The main goal, Pilsudski explained, was to free Poland's borders from Bolsheviks.[20]

As Pilsudski discussed his views on foreign affairs publicly and privately, his military campaign in the Lithuanian-Belarusian borderlands continued unabated. Szeptycki took Lida on April 17, Nowogródek on April 18, and Baranowicze on April 19. Commanding the operation himself, Pilsudski ordered a surprise attack on Vilna using the 1st Cavalry Brigade of Lieutenant-Colonel

Władysław Belina-Prażmowski, with 840 men, nine machine guns, and two field guns, as well as the 2nd Legionary Infantry Division under General Rydz-Śmigły, with 2,270 men and two batteries of field guns.[21] The units entered Vilna on April 19, and heavy fighting repelled the Red Army, which fled the city by the following day. Pilsudski's personal command of the Vilna operation, despite Szeptycki's advice to stay a safe distance from the front, put him at considerable risk and was another example of his iron will and faith in his own instincts.

Three days before the planned military strike on Vilna, Pilsudski sent a Lithuanian Pole and Vilna native, Michał Romer, to Kaunas to conduct secret negotiations with the Lithuanian government on April 16 and 17, 1919. But when the negotiations failed due to the Lithuanian government's insistence on two separate states, Pilsudski ordered the military takeover of Vilna. He had told Romer on April 6 that "if [negotiations] should prove a failure due to the Lithuanians, there shall be no other way left but to assume the imperialist consequences of the Polish military effort, implementing the partition of Lithuania and annexation of Vilna to Poland."[22]

The failure of the Kaunas negotiations led Pilsudski to take decisive action. On April 21, 1919, he entered Vilna, the city of his childhood, triumphant and proud to rid his ancestral homeland of Russian forces. In his "Proclamation to the Inhabitants of the Former Grand Duchy of Lithuania," Pilsudski announced his intention to allow the local population to determine its own fate and to further his larger aim of a single Polish-Lithuanian federalist state. "I shall give you the opportunity to resolve internal national and religious matters as you see fit," he said, "without any coercion or pressure from Poland. That is why, despite the fact that guns continue to thunder and blood is still being shed, I am introducing not a military but a civilian government to which I will appoint local people, sons of this land."[23] When news of Pilsudski's proclamation reached Paris, Allied officials regarded it positively, as did Hugh Gibson, the first American minister to Poland, who had just taken up residence in Warsaw. The foreign press also reported on the proclamation favorably. "General Pilsudski has issued a proclamation to the Lithuanians," the *Times* of London stated in its edition of May 2, 1919, "declaring that he is not there to annex the country; that the form of Government will be a civil one; and that the plebiscite is devised to show the will of the population to belong either to Poland or to Lithuania."

Yet Polish and Lithuanian nationalists buried Pilsudski's dream of a single federal state, a modern-day reconstitution of the eighteenth-century Polish-Lithuanian Commonwealth that would have allowed Vilna to be part of Lithuania. In Warsaw, Pilsudski's political opponents—the right-wing National Democratic Party—were outraged that Vilna was to be regarded as anything other than an integral part of Poland. In Kaunas, on the other hand, the Lithuanian government viewed the proclamation as a thinly disguised Polish plan for annexation.

For Pilsudski, the capture of Vilna had deep emotional resonance. "For me the Vilna question had always been of the first importance," he said, reflecting back on the capture of Vilna in a lecture delivered in August 1923. "It occupied me more than any other. My heart was in it most of all."[24] The decision to take Vilna by force was a strategic one, based both on an intelligence report indicating that the Lithuanian Army was planning to march on Vilna and on a determination that the Vilna operation had to be carried out before the Paris Peace Conference had made any decision on the city's final status.

By the time of the Vilna operation, the combined forces of the Polish Army fighting in Lithuania-Belarus and East Galicia numbered 127,117 men.[25] Vladimir Lenin, outraged at the Polish surprise action, ordered a counterattack to retake Vilna. Between April 26 and 30, 1919, Polish troops repelled the Russian counteroffensive so successfully that by the beginning of May, the Red Army had been moved forty-five miles east of Vilna. Having reached the line of the German wartime trenches, Pilsudski ordered the offensive halted and turned his attention to defeating Ukrainian forces in East Galicia.

It was fortuitous that on April 21, 1919—the day Polish troops captured Vilna—Pilsudski received a telegram from General Józef Haller informing him that his long-awaited Polish Army in France, numbering approximately fifty thousand, had arrived in Poland. Pilsudski cabled Haller, "On my behalf please express to the officers and soldiers my joy at their arrival in their homeland and confidence that, like every righteous Polish soldier, they will defend victoriously our threatened borders."[26]

Pilsudski could revel in his successes for only a few moments before addressing conflicts in other parts of the country. In March 1919 the Ukrainians had begun an offensive in East Galicia to take back Lwów. On the other side of the country, the Germans resumed attacks on Polish armed defenses in the Poznań region. Pilsudski—who had promised the Allied Powers that the

Polish soldiers pose after the capture of Vilna, July 6, 1919. Behind them hang portraits of
General Thaddeus Kościuszko, commander of the Polish insurrectionary forces in 1794,
and their commander, General Pilsudski.

Haller army would be used to defend Poland against Bolshevik Russia—broke
his promise and dispatched Haller's forces to the Ukrainian front. On May 21,
1919, Prime Minister Clemenceau of France, at the request of the Council of
Four, cabled Pilsudski to remind him that Haller's forces were not to be used
against the Ukrainians.[27] Moving far enough to create a border with Romania, Polish forces secured East Galicia after Pilsudski took command of a
new offensive, arriving in the area on June 22, 1919. Upon reaching the Zbrucz
River on July 17, the war in East Galicia came to an end. The Allied Supreme
Council asked Pilsudski to withdraw to an Allied-approved line of demarcation. Pilsudski refused, threatening to resign if forced to do so.[28]

The conquest of East Galicia came at a time when various Polish armed
units stationed abroad, including General Haller's Polish Army, were arriving
in Poland. General Lucjan Żeligowski's 4th Polish Rifle Division returned
from Odessa in June 1919; in May 1919, the commander of the Polish armed
units in Poznań formally turned over control of his forces to Pilsudski.[29] The

fact that ten rifle divisions of the Haller and Żeligowski armies fought in the last stage of the battle in East Galicia demonstrated the significance of their incorporation into Poland's armed forces. The complete unification of the armed forces came in July 1920 with the return to Poland of the 5th Polish Rifle Division under the command of General Kazimierz Rumsza, formed in 1918 as a Siberian regiment in Józef Haller's forces tasked to fight the Bolsheviks. Formally incorporated into the Polish Armed Forces in November 1919 by order of Piłsudski, the 5th Polish Rifle Division was defeated by the Bolsheviks in January 1920. Forced to flee eastward to evade capture, the approximately one thousand officers and soldiers continued eastward in a harrowing trek back to Poland via Japan and China.[30]

Pogroms in the Borderlands

There is no more delicate topic in the life of a new country than the accusation that its armed forces are guilty of wrongdoing. So it is not surprising that Piłsudski's initial reactions to the outbreak of anti-Jewish violence were mixed, guarded, sometimes defensive, and at other times condemnatory. But it is significant that the head of state and commander in chief chose not to issue any public statement on the subject.

In the wake of Poland's successes on the battlefield, the outbreak of pogroms rattled the Jewish community and received major international attention. Two of the pogroms—in Pinsk and Vilna—took place in the immediate aftermath of the Soviet withdrawal amid accusations of Jewish collusion with the enemy. One of the worst outbreaks took place in Pinsk, a town of 38,686 in 1913, of whom 28,063, or 72.2 percent, were Jewish. On April 5, 1919, the regional commander of the Polish armed forces headquartered in Pinsk, Major Aleksander Łuczyński, led a squad of fifteen soldiers to the Jewish community building, where about a hundred Jews had assembled to discuss arrangements for the distribution of Passover provisions provided by the American Food Commission. All were taken out of the building, marched to the marketplace, and arrested on suspicion of pro-Bolshevik ties. Thirty minutes later, thirty-five "Bolsheviks" from among the arrested—among them women and children—were lined up and executed by firing squad.[31]

Major Łuczyński declared two days later that the town's Jews as a whole had displayed communist sympathies and "blatant ingratitude" toward the

Polish authorities.[32] At first, press accounts, such as those of the *New York Times* and *Washington Post* from April 9, named the victims simply as "Bolsheviks." Once reports surfaced on what actually took place, in the major papers at home and abroad, a tale about Bolshevik traitors turned into a story about massacres of innocent Jewish civilians at the hands of the Polish Army. A British journalist who traveled to Pinsk two weeks before the executions paid a visit to the military commander, Major Łuczyński, who remarked that a spy was present in every Jewish home. "This belief that all Jews are Bolsheviks was held by every Polish officer [in Pinsk]," the journalist noted.[33]

The shocking news of the execution of Jewish civilians was followed by more anti-Jewish violence along the Polish-Bolshevik front. The most egregious was in Vilna when, on the day Polish troops entered the city on April 19, 1919, between fifty-four and sixty-five Jewish civilians were murdered.[34] Press accounts proliferated, sowing enmity in the West for the new Poland. A US state department report from June 1919, based on a visit of American officials to Vilna, found that Jews in Vilna were very apprehensive, desired compensation for property damage during the pogrom, and were concerned about their physical safety, yet they had maintained a positive attitude to Pilsudski in the aftermath of the pogrom.[35] British journalist H. N. Brailsford came away from a face-to-face meeting with Pilsudski at the time with a similar view: "Pilsudski, a humane and liberal man, is not strong enough to prevent the oppression and even slaughter of the Jews."[36]

Reports on Pilsudski's reactions to anti-Jewish violence were mixed and often contradictory, ranging from critical remarks on Jewish attitudes to calls for cracking down on the perpetrators. In March 1919 Pilsudski received a Jewish delegation in Warsaw and characterized Polish Jews as "hostile" to Poland. "Asked what the proofs of this were, he replied that there were none, but that this was the general feeling."[37] In an article in the *Jewish Chronicle* in London appearing on March 7, 1919, Pilsudski explained his comment with the aside that Polish Jews had drawn the attention of the world to the pogroms. In its next issue appearing on March 14, 1919, the *Jewish Chronicle* stated that Pilsudski's comments "are far from reassuring. We state here . . . that there is not a scintilla of ill-feeling on the part of Jews towards the new Poland. On the contrary, they wish the resurrected State well with all their hearts." When the British Zionist Israel Cohen asked Poland's head of state to publicly condemn anti-Jewish violence, Pilsudski replied that such a declaration was unnecessary. "It is understood," Pilsudski is reported to have said, "that the Government doesn't approve of the pogroms or of violence of any kind against anybody."[38]

Pilsudski now vowed to do everything in his power to stem the tide of anti-Jewish violence. On May 9, 1919, he received Noah Prylucki, a Jewish member of the Polish parliament, and promised to take into consideration Jewish concerns and read carefully the petitions provided.[39] Pilsudski clarified his position to Hugh Gibson, the American ambassador to Poland. "Have had long frank talk with Chief of State regarding Jewish situation in general," Gibson reported on May 31, 1919. "General Pilsudski was evidently alarmed and indignant. He said that [to persecute] the Jews brought shame upon the name of Poland and could not but harm the country." Pilsudski then said: "The Government as well as all good Poles are strongly opposed to any persecution for we know that we cannot settle down to peaceful development while there is discord among clement of our own population. For the good of the country the Government is determined to put down any anti-Jewish activities with an iron hand."[40] The US State Department found Gibson's cable important enough that it issued an official announcement on June 3, 1919. Pilsudski, the statement read, "is not only opposed to persecution of Jews but has given strict instructions to maintain order and to protect the Jews."[41]

Despite Pilsudski's assurances, anti-Jewish violence continued in the wake of the Polish military campaign. The persistence of anti-Jewish violence prompted US president Wilson to agree in May 1919 to set up an American commission to investigate the matter. Headed by the Jewish American Henry Morgenthau Sr., it included Brigadier General Edgar Jadwin, who was Polish American, and Mr. Homer H. Johnson. The Morgenthau Commission arrived in Poland on July 13, 1919. After a two-month fact-finding mission, the commission left Poland on September 13, completing its final report in October.[42]

Pilsudski initially had greeted the Morgenthau Commission with displeasure, making it clear that he regarded the mission as intrusive and potentially harmful. Nearing the end of the mission, however, Pilsudski expressed more understanding for its purpose. "He said," Morgenthau recalled, "that the Poles and Jews must live together, that their relations could never be perfect, but that the Government would really do its best to avoid friction. . . . He had no objection to private investigations, and, so far as our mission was concerned, he admitted it had already had a good effect. He hoped our report would satisfy the world enough to end such inquiries, for he did feel that interference from foreign nations was bad for the prestige of the government at home."[43]

The Treaty of Versailles

In Paris, meanwhile, the peacemakers issued the Treaty of Versailles. Passed on June 28, 1919, the settlement of Germany's borders signaled a diplomatic victory for Poland. Back in March, the Paris Peace Conference had established a Commission on Polish Affairs to tackle the German-Polish frontier. It recommended that Danzig, part of West Prussia, most of Poznań, and Upper Silesia where Poles made up a compact majority, be assigned to Poland. Opposed to these terms was British prime minister Lloyd George, who was unwilling to press the Germans too hard. The result was that the Treaty of Versailles assigned Poznań and most of West Prussia to Poland, allowing it access—albeit narrow—to the Baltic Sea. Due to different positions among the great powers, Britain in particular, the treaty met Pilsudski's demand for Danzig only halfway. Danzig was to be severed from Germany but proclaimed a Free City under the auspices of the League of Nations, within the Polish customs area. Plebiscites would determine the final status of the disputed territories in Upper Silesia and the southern strip of East Prussia. At the Spa Conference in Belgium, held in July 1920 under the auspices of the Supreme Council of the League of Nations, Polish foreign minister Władysław Grabski and Czechoslovak foreign minister Edvard Beneš agreed to a division of the disputed Cieszyn / Teschen region into Polish and Czechoslovak zones.[44] But when the Conference of Ambassadors worked out the final details, it left 139,000 Poles under Czechoslovak rule. Far from bringing a rapprochement to troubled Polish-Czechoslovak relations, the Spa Conference deepened the mutual enmity.

The Treaty of Versailles also issued a resolution on the status of Jews and other minorities. Due to the unabated spread of anti-Jewish violence in borderland regions newly under Polish control, especially in Pinsk and Vilna, the Council of Four (the United States, Britain, France, and Italy) persuaded Poland to sign an agreement to protect its Jewish and other minority populations. The Polish Minorities Treaty was adopted, with Poland's reluctance, during the Treaty of Versailles. The necessity of the Minorities Treaty was bolstered on August 8, 1919, following the Polish capture of Minsk. The Polish takeover of Minsk witnessed the outbreak of anti-Jewish violence in which thirty-one Jews were killed in a pogrom.[45] The pogrom in Minsk was followed by the release of the Morgenthau Commission report in October 1919, which estimated that 280 Jews had been killed in pogroms in Polish-controlled territories between November 1918 and August 1919.[46]

The Polish-Bolshevik Conflict Intensifies

For Pilsudski and Poland, the summer of 1919 was cause for great optimism. In the United States, many Polish Americans rallied behind Pilsudski, as evidenced in a three-day convention held in Boston by the left-leaning Polish National Defense Committee. The organization gathered to "celebrate Pilsudski's leadership," raise funds, and encourage American support for Poland's leader.[47] The Treaty of Versailles, which laid down Poland's western frontiers, was followed in July 1919 by Poland's defeat of the Ukrainians in East Galicia. This allowed Pilsudski to turn his attention to repelling Bolshevik forces from the Belarusian-Lithuanian borderlands. He explained his position in a 1924 study:

> As early as 1918, with no aid from outside, I had come to a clear conclusion about the objectives of our war against the Soviets. Amongst other things, I had decided to make every possible effort to remove as far as possible from the places where the new national life was burgeoning and taking shape, any attempt that might be made or any snare that might be set with a view to imposing once more a foreign life upon us, a life not organized by ourselves. In 1919, I accomplished this task.[48]

The grand scheme was to create a belt of independent states from the Baltic Sea to the Black Sea, which would include a sovereign Ukraine. One of the hallmarks of Pilsudski's foreign policy at this time was his refusal to get entangled in the Russian Civil War between the Red Army and the White Army, made up of anticommunist forces ranging from social democrats to extreme right-wing monarchists. This ambitious program put him at odds with the Allies, who were openly siding with the Whites in the Russian Civil War.

Despite pressure from the Western Allies to assist the White Army, Pilsudski insisted on remaining natural.

The summer of 1919 saw significant new developments in the bloody Russian Civil War. General Anton Denikin, commander of the White Army's southern front, took Kiev in August 1919 and Orel, 205 miles from Moscow, on October 14. As the Whites gained ground, a British military advisor to Denikin arrived in Warsaw to ask Pilsudski to join the anti-Bolshevik offensive. Pilsudski flatly refused, stating that Denikin would fail to take Moscow and soon retreat back to the Black Sea. One of those present at the exchange was General Carton de Wiart, a British member of the Inter-Allied Mission then stationed in Warsaw, who vividly recalled the scene in his memoirs. "In view of Denikin's rapid advance this seemed a fantastic statement to make," General Wiart wrote, "but Pilsudski's judgment rarely failed, and I had such confidence in him that I reported this at once to the War Office." Pilsudski, Wiart continued, "had never put me wrong. Within a very few weeks Pilsudski had proved a good prophet, for Denikin was back in the Black Sea."[49] The turn of events was astonishingly quick, with the Bolsheviks recapturing Kiev in December 1919. "At the height of the White successes in 1919," historian Adam Ulam aptly observed, "the Polish armies kept their positions in the undeclared war with Soviet Russia, offering not one bit of help to Kolczak or Denikin."[50] Pilsudski's pledge of noninterference in the Russian Civil War led to Denikin's stinging accusation that Pilsudski "saved Bolshevism from collapse."[51] The charge seemed to ricochet off Pilsudski easily. "Poland," Pilsudski said, "can have nothing to do with the restoration of old Russia. Anything rather than that—even Bolshevism." Regretfully, he added, "there is no third Russia. Where is it, where? For we, too, long for it and seek it."[52]

Pilsudski nonetheless continued with his goal of clearing Bolshevik troops from the borderland regions. On August 8, 1919, Polish troops captured Minsk. On his visit to the captured city on September 19, Pilsudski issued a manifesto declaring, "I am a son of these same lands as are you and so I am able to understand the poverty and discontent experienced here." Poland, he said, was bringing democratic ideas and institutions. "Poland marches everywhere with the slogan of freedom. Poland marches not with the desire to oppress under the brutal boot of her soldiers nor with the desire to impose on anybody adherence to its laws."[53] In October 1919, Pilsudski traveled to Vilna to speak at the newly opened Stefan Batory University, an institution with profound historical resonance as the alma mater of the nation's nineteenth-century bards Juliusz Słowacki and Adam Mickiewicz. "The fate of these walls mirrors the fate of this borderland region," Pilsudski said, adding that it was a sheer miracle that it was once again a Polish university.[54]

With Moscow threatened by the White Army, the Bolsheviks offered generous peace terms, ceding territory on their western frontiers with Estonia, Finland, Latvia, and Lithuania in August–September 1919. They initiated peace talks with Poland on October 11, 1919, in Mikaszewicze (today Mikashevichy, Belarus). The talks exposed irreconcilable differences between the two parties. Expressed through his representatives, Pilsudski's position consisted of the following: (1) Polish troops would not advance beyond the line they were currently holding; (2) the Soviet government would establish a neutral zone six miles wide by an act of withdrawal from their current lines with Poland; (3) the Soviets would cede Dunaburg to Latvia; (4) the Soviets would cease communist agitation within the Polish Army; and (5) the Bolsheviks would cease attacks on the Ukrainian armed forces under the command of Symon Petliura.[55] The Soviets responded with a counterproposal for each point, not one of which Pilsudski accepted. The talks ended on December 15, 1919, with no agreement. It is likely that Soviet negotiators intended to delay any agreement that would put a halt to their own military movements westward. Unbeknownst to Soviet negotiators, Polish representatives were in possession of secret intercepts of Soviet military intelligence proving Soviet plans to advance the Red Army further west before any agreement was reached.[56]

At the same time, Pilsudski overestimated Soviet weaknesses, demonstrated by his unwillingness to compromise on any of his positions. As he said in an interview with the *Times* of London published on October 16, 1919: "I have no fear for Poland in a war against the Bolsheviks. Both in morale and in training the Polish Army is superior . . . [and] I cannot image any situation in which they would get the better of us." When the *Times* of London asked Pilsudski in its edition of February 14, 1920, if he feared the Red Army, Pilsudski replied, "No, they're such bad soldiers. The Polish soldier is a far better man. We've always beaten them. Why should I be afraid of them?"

Pilsudski meanwhile had to respond to a political crisis at home. The Supreme Council in Paris ruled on November 21, 1919, that Poland's rule over East Galicia was recognized for a period of twenty-five years, after which a plebiscite would determine its ultimate fate. This decree, unacceptable to most Polish leaders, led Paderewski to tender his resignation on November 27. Pilsudski asked him to form a new cabinet, but Paderewski's efforts failed.[57] So Pilsudski asked the Sejm deputy, Leopold Skulski, to form a cabinet, which Skulski succeeded in doing on December 13. Poland's new foreign minister, Stanisław Patek, gained strong French support, convincing the Supreme Council on December 22 to rescind the decree on East Galicia, thus recognizing it as a permanent part of Poland.[58]

Just as Pilsudski's new foreign minister scored a diplomatic victory on East Galicia, the Supreme Council in Paris proposed a provisional eastern border of Poland based on the suggestions of British foreign secretary Lord Curzon. The recommendation identified Brest-Litovsk and the Bug River as Poland's eastern border with Russia, stretching from the Carpathians west of the Rawa Ruska to East Prussia. The British proposal was a blow to Pilsudski, who had insisted on the absolute necessity of a buffer zone with Russia. Holding back Polish forces, Pilsudski believed, would merely lead to a Russian incursion and prevent the rise of an independent Ukraine. With regard to the Lithuanian-Polish demarcation line, French general Ferdinand Foch proposed a Lithuanian-Polish frontier on July 26, 1919. Referred to as the Foch Line, the proposal granted Poland the Białystok region while ceding the northern part of Suwałki province to Lithuania.[59]

The breakdown of the Polish-Bolshevik talks escalated the conflict in the eastern borderlands. With diminishing Allied support for Polish territorial claims in the east, Pilsudski concluded that his only hope for pushing Russia back closer to its ethnic frontiers was to forge an alliance with the Ukrainian military leaders in a quest to form a belt of independent states to push Russia back to frontiers corresponding to the old Polish-Lithuanian Commonwealth. But the grand scheme did not succeed. This was first evident in August 1919 when Pilsudski failed to impose his federalist plans on Lithuania. After the Lithuanians expressed no interest in a federal union with Poland, Pilsudski staged a poorly planned coup in Kaunas, seat of the Lithuanian government, on August 28, 1919. Intended to install a Lithuanian government sympathetic to Pilsudski, idea was to install a Polish Lithuanian, Stanisław Narutowicz, as its leader. But Pilsudski's order did not reach all the persons involved. When the plan went into effect, only scattered acts of sabotage took place in Kaunas. In the course of the failed coup, Lithuanian authorities arrested 150 ethnic

Poles who had allegedly taken part in the event.[60] It is not surprising that the failed coup entirely undermined confidence in any subsequent Polish expressions of goodwill toward Lithuania.

Pilsudski emerged from the failed peace talks with the Bolshevik regime and the failed coup more isolated. With regard to his scheme for an independent Ukraine, the war-weary members of the Sejm, such as the PPS leaders, favored peace negotiations, while the National Democrats were hostile to Pilsudski's eastern borderland schemes. What's more, Pilsudski was unable to secure British support. But he forged ahead, holding talks in Warsaw on December 9, 1919, with Petliura, who was then head of the Directory of the Ukrainian National Republic and commander of its armed forces. At the same time, Pilsudski was clear with the Allies, telling them, in part through interviews with the foreign press, that Poland was on the front lines against a Bolshevik invasion of Europe and needed more support for its policies.[61]

In the process of forming a military alliance with Petliura, Pilsudski— believing he now had more leverage—reached out again to Soviet leaders. In March 1920 he proposed a settlement with the Bolsheviks in exchange for a free hand in the borderlands, including the creation of an independent Ukraine and Belarus. The Soviets replied in the negative. For Pilsudski, the second breakdown in talks with the Bolsheviks proved that Russian armies could be removed from Ukraine only by force. Pushing Pilsudski to a military solution was also the discovery of a secret Russian report on Soviet strategy toward Poland. Presented to Trotsky by the Red Army's chief of operations on January 27, 1920, the report called for an energetic and decisive strike against Poland in May 1920 to seize western Belarus and Ukraine.[62]

The secret report reinforced Pilsudski's hunch about Russian intentions for Poland. It is not surprising, then, that he proceeded to finalize a political agreement with Petliura on April 21, 1920, that recognized the independence of Ukraine and was followed by a military agreement signed on April 24. The central compromise for Petliura was conceding East Galicia and western Volhynia in exchange for securing Polish military assistance to free Ukraine. Needless to say, West Ukrainian leaders hotly resented the decision to give up East Galicia.[63]

Military action immediately followed the signing of the Polish-Ukrainian accord, known as the Treaty of Warsaw. On April 25, 1920, Pilsudski ordered a military offensive in Ukraine, his troops marching eastward in conjunction with Petliura's forces. Pilsudski was full of zeal. "The spirit of the army is magnificent," he wrote Poland's prime minister Skulski on April 26, 1920.[64]

Anticipating substantial criticism in Entente circles, Pilsudski issued a proclamation to the people of Ukraine the day after his troops crossed the front line. It was an extraordinary appeal of an invading force, almost Napoleonic in zeal. Its central idea was that the Polish Army's intention was to spread liberty, without imperialistic aims, into an area of Europe under threat of Russian dominance. The proclamation stated that "the Polish armed forces will remain in Ukraine only as long as it will be necessary to transfer the administration to a legitimate Ukrainian government. When the national government of the Ukrainian Republic has established its authority, when the troops of the Ukrainian people have taken hold of its frontiers to protect their country against new intrusions, when the free nation itself is in a position to decide its destiny, then the Polish soldiers will withdraw." Until that time, the Polish armed forces would guarantee protection and rights without regard to nationality or religion.[65]

One of the Polish soldiers on active duty was Kazimierz Sokołowski, a nineteen-year-old Warsaw University student volunteer. On April 28, 1920, he jotted down his reaction to the movement of Polish troops in the direction of Kiev. "The Polish Army, personally led by Commandant Pilsudski," he wrote, "has broken through Bolshevik lines, seizing Żytomir yesterday morning, taking many prisoners, and is now advancing toward Kiev." Sokołowski attached great importance to Pilsudski's message to the Ukrainians, writing, "the significance of Pilsudski's appeal to the Ukrainians is—morally speaking—enormous: through his mouth flows the slogan of Polish democracy—'free with the free, equal with the equal'—the ancient act of the Union of Hadiach," he wrote, referring to the seventeenth-century act providing for Ukraine to be a third constituent member of the Polish-Lithuanian Commonwealth. "Poland wants a free Ukraine," Sokołowski concluded, "because it well knows that without it, Russia will be right at our doorstep."[66]

The *Irish Times* reported on May 1, 1920, that "messages received in London from Warsaw announced that the Poles have published declarations recognizing Ukrainian independence." The American military attaché in Warsaw, Lieutenant Colonel Elbert Farman, expressed the opinion that Pilsudski was making every effort to counter the imperialist charge being leveled at him by Western diplomats.[67]

In a parallel manifesto, Petliura communicated to his fellow Ukrainians that Pilsudski's army had come not as conquerors but as allies. They would withdraw once the war with Russia had come to an end.[68] Some questioned Pilsudski's sincerity in promising a future withdrawal. Yet his past statements, public and private, were consistent on this point. When a foreign correspondent had asked Pilsudski in February 1920 what his policy was toward Lithuania, Ukraine, and Belarus, he replied that his aim was not conquest—history had taught him that conquest never ended well in the long run—but the spread of liberty. "I do not want to see Poland control large stretches of territory inhabited by unfriendly people," he said. But "to give freedom to a neighboring people would be the pride of my life as a statesman and soldier."[69] That sense of a Polish mission to extend Western democracy to the east was reflected in another remark Pilsudski made in 1920: "I think that the mission of Ukraine is the historical heritage of Poland of spreading the culture of the West."[70]

Some foreign press accounts in New York and London reported the movement of Polish troops positively, citing Pilsudski's proclamation as evidence that the purpose of the drive was not imperial aspiration but to free Ukraine. Additional statements came from the Polish Foreign Ministry. "The Polish Government affirms the right of the Ukraine to an independent national existence," the Foreign Ministry declared, affirming its government's recognition of Petliura as head of the Ukrainian Republic.[71]

As Polish troops moved swiftly eastward, the Bolshevik army withdrew. A telegram to Petliura, dated May 6, 1920, revealed Pilsudski's belief that promoting Ukrainian independence was part of Poland's mission. "At a time when the Polish Army fights a common enemy side by side with the brave Ukrainian troops in the name of the old Polish slogan, 'For Our Freedom and Yours,' this successful joint struggle between the Ukrainian Republic and Poland will bring forth lasting prosperity to both nations."[72]

The Kiev Campaign

On May 7, 1920, units of Pilsudski's cavalry entered Kiev, followed by Polish and Ukrainian infantry. Here, at the peak of his Ukrainian campaign, Pilsudski issued an order to his top commanders, revealing that what he said in private was consistent with his public statements. "It is in the Polish interest," he wrote, "to withdraw our troops from the occupied Ukrainian territories as soon as possible in order to establish friendly neighborly relations with the new Ukrainian state.... The Polish occupation of Ukraine must be calculated in months and not in years."[73] With the aim of separating Ukraine from Russia, Pilsudski now fought for an independent Ukraine on the Dnieper River, linked to Poland by a political and military alliance. In a letter to his prime minister, he commented on the mood of the local population. Having traveled the whole front, he reported that Jews seemed unenthusiastic to see Polish troops, fearing violence.[74] After Kiev fell, it was reported that Ukrainian forces had taken Odessa. These developments, a correspondent for the *Times* of London observed on May 13, 1920, were received positively in Ukraine due to disdain for the Bolsheviks. Excitement gripped the people of Poland as news arrived about the fall of Kiev to Polish forces. "Kiev has finally been taken! Long live Poland, Long Live Commander Pilsudski and the victory of our army," Sokołowski jotted down in his diary on May 9, 1920.[75]

Pilsudski publicly denigrated the Red Army as weak and poorly organized, estimating in a May 16 interview with the British *Daily Mail* that thirty thousand Russian POWs were being held. He noted that the campaign he was leading had opened up new possibilities for the Ukrainians. We can discern Pilsudski's mindset at this particular time through an address he delivered on May 17 in Vinnytsia, seat of government of the Ukrainian Republic, 437 miles east of Warsaw, where he met with Petliura. Both Poland and Ukraine, he proclaimed, had endured long periods of captivity marked by persecution. Poland could not remain sovereign as long as the peoples of the borderlands between it and Russia remained unfree. "Poland, having achieved the great treasure—freedom—has decided to reject all that threatens it as far as possible from its borders." He thus championed "a free parliament in a free Ukraine."[76] After Pilsudski returned to Warsaw the following day, the Sejm gathered and hailed Pilsudski as a hero. Sejm speaker Trąmpczyński stated, "Our army bears freedom to long-downtrodden peoples, and peace to people of goodwill. In thee . . . we see the symbol of our beloved army, an army mightier than in the days of our greater glory."[77]

Critics of Pilsudski at home meanwhile continued to voice concerns, cautioning that the Kiev campaign constituted reckless overreach. The National Democratic Party chairman of the Foreign Affairs Committee, Stanisław Grabski, wrote that the war against Soviet Russia "should be about the estab-

Pilsudski and his Ukrainian counterpart, Symon Petliura, during the
Kiev military offensive. Vinnytia, Ukraine, May 17, 1920.

lishment of the Polish-Russian border, and we should not be concerned about
Ukraine." He warned that "to have Kiev in permanent possession, it would
be necessary to go far beyond the Dnieper, and such a march would threaten
[Poland] with a defeat like Napoleon's in 1812."[78] To an American diplomat in
Warsaw, on the other hand, Pilsudski seemed like the one hope for diminishing Bolshevik Russia's hold on European soil. "The longer I remain here,"
wrote an American official in Warsaw on May 29, 1920, "the more firmly I
believe that Pilsudski is the only agency through which, at present, we can
hope to down Bolshevism."[79] The Allies did not share the same enthusiasm
for Pilsudski's Kiev venture. British prime minister Lloyd George was openly
critical, warning that Pilsudski's military ventures threatened the peace
in Europe.

The Soviet commander of the northwestern front, Mikhail Tukhachevsky,
began a counterattack on May 14, earlier than expected. Faced with a full
counteroffensive, Pilsudski entrusted the vice minister of war, General

Sosnkowski, with a response. As the Red Army offensive picked up speed, Pilsudski more closely supervised the Polish effort to hold its position. He visited the headquarters of General Szeptycki's 4th Army in Molodeczne on June 3 and then Sosnkowski's Army Reserve headquarters in Vilna the following day, helping to successfully repel two of Tukhachevsky's divisions.[80]

While Pilsudski helped secure the northern front, the Russians launched an offensive from the opposite side of the theater of war from the south. General Semion Budenny's 1st Cavalry Army attacked Polish forces on June 5 at Samhorodok, eighty-one miles southwest of Kiev, breaking through Polish lines and sweeping into the Polish rear. Budenny's forces, instead of moving eastward to encircle the 3rd Polish Army in Kiev, advanced west in the direction of Żytomir. On June 8 Pilsudski ordered Polish forces to evacuate from Kiev, then under the control of General Rydz-Śmigły's 3rd Polish Army, and retreat to Żytomir with the aim of halting Budenny's forces. General Rydz-Śmigły, however, did not receive the order in time and, instead, evacuated from Kiev on June 10 and 11 but not in the direction of Żytomir. Pilsudski's plan to encircle and destroy Budenny's 1st Calvary Army had failed. On June 13, 1920, the last Polish soldiers withdrew, leaving Kiev to the Soviets.[81]

In Warsaw, meanwhile, the retreat from Kiev caused a cabinet crisis. With the right-wing parliamentarians blasting Pilsudski for unnecessarily putting the country at risk, Prime Minister Skulski and his entire cabinet tendered their resignation. The crisis was resolved on June 23 when Władysław Grabski, a National Democrat, was named prime minister, giving the post of foreign minister to Eustachy Sapieha.[82] In its issue of June 15, 1920, meanwhile, a British reporter for the *Daily Mail* asked Pilsudski if some circles in Poland had imperialist aims in Ukraine. "That is contrary to our nature and anyone who states that does not know Poland," he replied. Polish and Ukrainian forces, meanwhile, were in rapid retreat as Budenny's cavalry forces from the southern front and Tukhachevsky's forces from the northern front made rapid gains, repelling all Polish forces from Ukraine by early July 1920.

At dawn on July 4, 1920, Tukhachevsky began a second offensive with twenty infantry divisions and three cavalry divisions. One day earlier, on July 3, he had issued a proclamation to all Russian soldiers on the Western Front. The Red Army, he wrote, will defeat the "criminal government" of Pilsudski: "In the West the fate of World Revolution is being decided. . . . On our bayonets we will bring happiness and peace to the toiling masses of mankind. The hour of attack has struck! To the West! On to Vilna, Minsk,

Warsaw—Forward!"[83] Szeptycki's thirteen infantry divisions were unable to halt the advance, forcing them to retreat to the Berezino River, seventy-six miles southeast of Minsk, on July 8. In the course of the next two weeks, Tukhachevsky's forces rolled into Minsk (July 11), Vilna (July 14), Grodno (July 19) and Pinsk.

In Warsaw, meanwhile, a Council of National Defense (*Rada Obrony Państwa*, ROP) was formed. Headed by Pilsudski, it consisted of nineteen cabinet and military officials given supreme power to defend the country. In a proclamation in its name, Pilsudski wrote the following: "To the Citizen of the Republic! The Homeland is in Need." The proclamation called for volunteers to enlist to help defend the country. "The Polish soldier, bloodied on the front, must know in his heart that the entire nation stands behind him, ready to aid at any moment."[84]

With the Polish retreat continuing unabated, Pilsudski came under vociferous press attacks. Disheartened, he offered to resign at a meeting of the ROP on July 19. "I am under the fire of accusation of all kinds," Pilsudski is reported to have said. "I myself am disgusted with a country that treats its highest representative in this way."[85] But the council refused to accept his resignation. A member of the US Legation in Warsaw reported on July 20, 1920, "It angers me the way the Poles have turned on Pilsudski now that things are going badly and forgetting all that he has done for them."[86] As the Red Army moved closer to Polish territory, Pilsudski formed a Government of National Unity on July 24, 1920, naming Wincenty Witos as prime minister, Ignacy Daszyński deputy prime minister, and Sosnkowski to the post of minister of war.[87]

The gravity of the situation was reflected in the arrival of the Inter-Allied Mission to Warsaw in July 1920. The mission included General Maxime Weygand of France, then head of the Entente's War Council, and Britain's Viscount D'Abernon, the British ambassador in Berlin. Among the French staff serving under Weygand was twenty-nine-year-old Charles de Gaulle, an infantry instructor to the Polish Army. Pilsudski welcomed the Allied officials at Belvedere Palace. "Pilsudski impressed me," Weygand recalled, "with his sharpness of mind, and in the field of strategy, with his intuition and understanding of the role of maneuver and action."[88]

D'Abernon similarly noted his first impressions of Pilsudski. "The dominant personality here," he wrote in his diary on June 28, 1920, "is unquestionably Marshal Pilsudski, Head of State and Commander-in-Chief of the Army. . . . An ardent patriot, and a man of immense courage and force of character." Pilsudski was "in appearance, so striking as to be almost theatrical. None of the usual amenities of civilized intercourse but all the apparatus of somber genius. . . . The Polish ministers who, theoretically, are supposed to advise him, possess in truth little real influence or authority."[89] In its first report, dated June 28, 1920, the Anglo-French Mission requested the immediate dispatch of munitions and the deployment of hundreds of French and British officers.[90] In the end, only France came through, dispatching military aid, and by the second week of August, an estimated six hundred French officers arrived in Warsaw to join the French Mission.[91]

The situation grew more dire when the Red Army took Białystok on July 28, 1920, and Brest-Litovsk on August 1. Soviet talk of peace and respect for the sovereign right of its neighbors now gave way to open calls for spreading revolution. In Białystok, a Provisional Polish Revolutionary Committee formed to take power in Warsaw after Pilsudski's anticipated collapse. Headed by Polish communist leaders Julian Marchlewski and Feliks Dzierżyński, their manifesto declared that peace in Poland was possible only under communist rule.[92] Following the overthrow of "the bourgeois landowner government of Pilsudski," a Polish Soviet Republic was to be formed. Among foreign delegations in Warsaw, nonessential personnel were ordered to leave on August 1.[93] In London, meanwhile, attempts by Lloyd George and Lord Curzon to broker a ceasefire agreement on August 4 failed.

It was at this critical juncture, with Poland in the throes of an existential crisis, that Pilsudski prepared a grand plan for the defense of Warsaw. With the weight of his country—and of Europe—on his shoulders, he left Warsaw to ponder a military plan on his own. Three days later, on August 5, Pilsudski returned to Warsaw and met with his three top military advisors: Minister of War Sosnkowski, chief of the general staff General Tadeusz Rozwadowski, and General Weygand. Pilsudski was most partial to the proposal by Rozwadowski, and asked him to prepare a battle order. Although he approved of the battle plan as a whole, Pilsudski insisted on multiple amendments and the two sat for hours making revisions. One day later, on August 6, 1920, a revised draft was prepared and Rozwadowski issued a comprehensive plan for a counteroffensive against the Red Army.[94] Weygand cabled Marshal Foch in Paris the same day, informing him that he had given Pilsudski his full approval.[95]

The plan Pilsudski adopted called for a decisive Polish counterattack to come from the southern front at the Wieprz River, a tributary of the Vistula

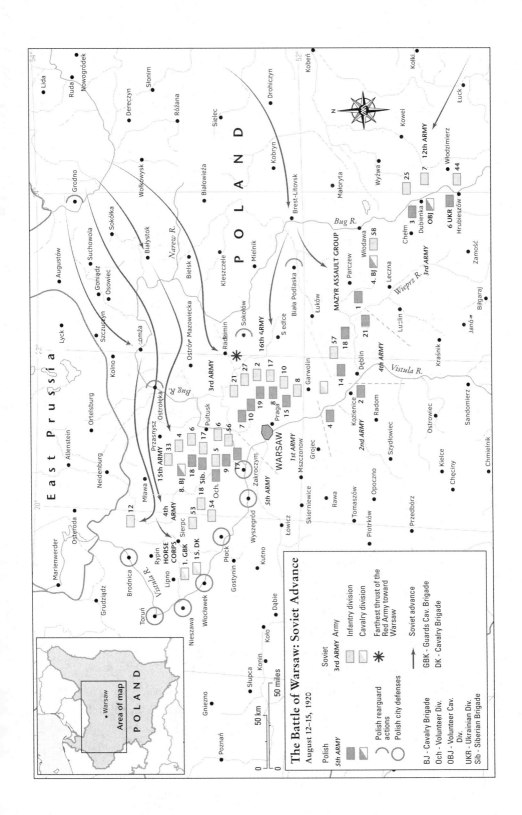

The Battle of Warsaw: Soviet Advance
August 12–15, 1920

Polish

5th ARMY
Polish rearguard actions
Polish city defenses

Soviet

3rd ARMY Army
Infantry division
Cavalry division
Farthest thrust of the Red Army toward Warsaw
Soviet advance

BJ - Cavalry Brigade
Och - Volunteer Div.
OBJ - Volunteer Cav. Div.
UKR - Ukrainian Div.
Sib - Siberian Brigade
GBK - Guards Cav. Brigade
DK - Cavalry Brigade

POLAND

East Prussia

Area of map
POLAND
Warsaw

about fifty miles south of Warsaw. This military strike would severely weaken Tukhachevsky's western front. Tukhachevsky's northern forces, meanwhile, were to be paralyzed by General Sikorski's Fifth Army. At the same time, General Franciszek Latinik's First Army was to protect the capital outside of Warsaw. Pilsudski himself was to command the so-called striking group to violently attack and disorient Russian troops. The Polish offensive was to be launched on August 16, 1920. On August 12 Pilsudski met with Prime Minister Witos, Deputy Prime Minister Daszyński, and his interior minister. Witos recalled that Pilsudski "was very preoccupied, very serious, and I thought depressed. He came off as uncertain, hesitant, and quite anxious. In his conversation with us, he was extremely cautious with a very pessimistic outlook on current affairs. He announced that he was betting on the last card with no certainty of winning."[96] That evening the commander left the capital to prepare for battle.

On the way to his headquarters in Puławy, seventy miles southeast of Warsaw near the Wieprz River, Pilsudski visited Alexandra, two-year-old Wanda, and his second daughter, five-month-old Jadwiga. "He bade good-bye to his children as though he was going to his death," Alexandra recalled, "and was impatient with me because I would not admit that this offensive might end in disaster for Poland."[97] Once in Puławy, he inspected units of his strike group, part of the 4th Polish Army, on August 15, in the presence of Weygand, who described the dramatic moment: "He electrified his strike group. He poured from his own soul into the souls of the fighting men the confidence and will to overcome all obstacles."[98]

On August 14, 1920, the Red Army came within six miles of Warsaw. Panic set in as local residents watched foreign diplomats evacuate, unaware this was part of Pilsudski's risky strategy to lure Soviet forces and mount a surprise counterpunch from the rear. "If Polish freedom dies," the Council for National Defense stated in a desperate appeal to foreign governments for aid, "tomorrow yours will be threatened. A Bolshevik victory on the Vistula threatens all Western Europe."[99] Public critique of Pilsudski, whose Kiev debacle was now blamed for the possibility of a Bolshevik takeover of Warsaw, was palpable and biting. Confidence in Pilsudski waned, with Roman Dmowski proposing a motion in the Council for National Defense to separate the powers of the army's supreme command and the chief of staff, both in Pilsudski's hands. The motion failed to garner enough votes.[100]

"Miracle on the Vistula"

At dawn on August 16, 1920, with Russian troops at the gates of Warsaw, Pilsudski launched a massive counteroffensive. His strike group (*Grupa Uderzeniowa*), consisting of the most elite units of the southern front and reinforced by the 4th and 3rd Polish Armies, rapidly advanced from the south and spread over large areas in the direction of Mińsk Mazowiecki, Brest-Litovsk, and Siedlce. After repelling Soviet troops near Kock, eighty-one miles south of Warsaw, Pilsudski directed his forces to the rear of Tukhachevsky's troops, penetrating what he believed was the weak center of the Soviet line. Pilsudski meanwhile directed the 1st Polish Army to hold Warsaw itself, the 2nd Polish Army to hold Warsaw's southern sector, while General Sikorski's 5th Army, stationed thirty miles north of the city, halted the advance of the Soviet 15th Army. Pilsudski's infantry meanwhile took Garwolin, now finding itself on the left flank of the 16th Soviet Army trying to cross the Vistula River. With Polish forces having reached the rear of the Soviet 16th Army, Tukhachevsky's forces went into a tailspin the following day when, on August 17, 1920, Polish forces took Siedlce, fifty-six miles east of Warsaw, followed by Biała Podlaski, moving Polish forces to the deep rear guard of the 10th Soviet Army.

With Polish divisions attacking on all sides, the Soviet offensive was reversed. Within two days Polish forces had staved off a Soviet takeover of Warsaw. On August 18, the Soviet 16th Army—which had stood at the gates of Warsaw two days earlier—was in retreat. Pilsudski returned to Warsaw the same day to command the counteroffensive. The Bolshevik government, Pilsudski wrote in an appeal, "has sent to Warsaw hordes of savages in the false hope of conquering us," but they were now in full retreat.[101] By the time Pilsudski arrived in Warsaw on August 18, he was hailed as a hero whose military plan was brilliant.[102] One day later the Soviet Armies had been driven back more than twenty-five miles from the capital. "Warsaw is saved," the *New York Times* declared on August 20, 1920. Other foreign papers, such as the *Boston Daily Globe,* marveled at the scale of victory, observing that Pilsudski's march was unstoppable. At the same time, the profound relief at the reversal of the Red Army advance gave way to fears of a renewed Kiev-style Polish thrust into the east. To reassure the Allies, Prime Minister Witos issued a statement that the Polish government was still committed to peace talks,

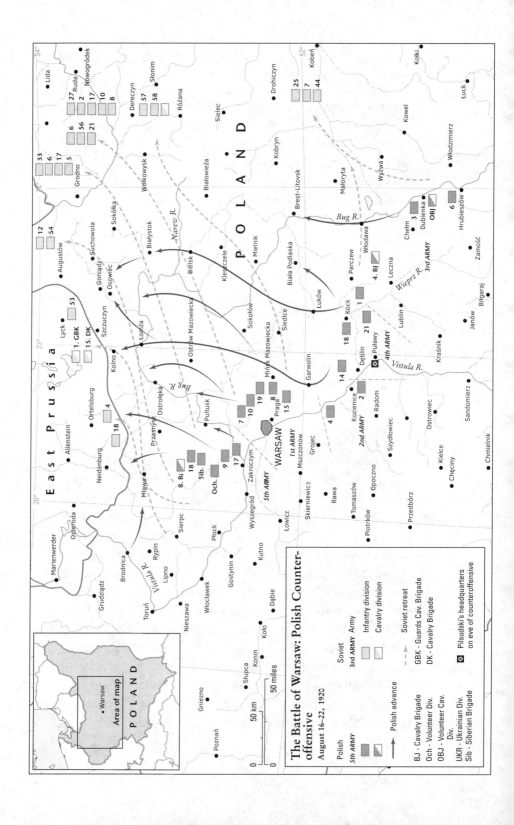

The Battle of Warsaw: Polish Counteroffensive

August 16–22, 1920

Polish   Soviet

5th ARMY   3rd ARMY Army

         Infantry division

         Cavalry division

         Soviet retreat

—→ Polish advance

BJ - Cavalry Brigade   GBK - Guards Cav. Brigade
Och - Volunteer Div.   DK - Cavalry Brigade
OBJ - Volunteer Cav.
     Div.
UKR - Ukrainian Div.   ⊠ Piłsudski's headquarters
Sib - Siberian Brigade   on eve of counteroffensive

Area of map

POLAND

Warsaw

0   50 km
0   50 miles

affirming, "We do not desire to annex foreign lands."[103] And indeed, Poland agreed to renew formal peace talks, which opened in Minsk on August 21.

On August 25, 1920, the Battle of Warsaw came to an end. Pilsudski reached the East Prussian frontier, expelling the last Soviet division from the country.[104] Not only Poland but the Western world breathed a collective sigh of relief. Casualties on the Polish side included forty-five hundred killed, twenty-two thousand wounded, and ten thousand missing in action. The Soviet forces lost twenty-five thousand men in battle and fifty thousand were taken as prisoners.[105] Despite the armistice, the conflict continued. When Tukhachevsky opened a new front on the Niemen River in September 1920, Pilsudski resumed the Polish offensive. After a five-day battle, Polish forces took Grodno on September 26. In another battle in Western Belarus, meanwhile, Polish troops recaptured Pinsk. In a chaotic series of moves to demarcate borders prior to a formal peace agreement, battles between Polish and Soviet forces continued.

In Vilna, which the Soviet government had cleverly handed over to independent Lithuania on August 26 after defeat in the Battle of Warsaw, the situation had become singularly complicated. Pilsudski could not allow the Soviets to decide the fate of Vilna. "Not only from the point of view of personal sentiment and ties of feeling, which undoubtedly played an important role in explain his actions," Andrzej Garlicki writes, "but also for political reasons. If he wished to remain as leader he could not afford to allow the public to see failure at Kiev repeated in the loss of Wilno, a juxtaposition made by the political press of his opponents."[106] At the same time, however, Pilsudski could not be seen dismembering a neighboring state by occupying its self-declared capital. In a rather fantastical "revolt" by a friend and officer of Pilsudski's, the Lithuanian-born Lucjan Żeligowski and his troops entered Vilna on October 9 and easily took the city from the Lithuanian forces. In a proclamation Żeligowski announced not incorporation into Poland but the creation of an independent Middle Lithuania.

On October 12, 1920, Żeligowski issued a decree as self-proclaimed supreme commander of Middle Lithuania's armed forces. He established a Temporary Governance Committee to administer the infant state's affairs. On December 1, 1921, it issued a law for the upcoming elections that were to take place on January 8, 1922. After Middle Lithuania's first elected parliament met on February 8, 1922, it decided shortly afterward to merge with Poland by a vote of 96 votes for and 6 abstaining. On March 2 a delegation from Vilna arrived in Warsaw, and on April 6, 1922, the parliament voted in favor of a formal incorporation of Middle Lithuania into Poland.[107] From the Lithuanian point of view, the whole affair amounted to a takeover of about one-fifth of the land they considered Lithuanian. Yet, as historian Theodore Weeks has pointed out, Lithuanian leaders dismissed entirely the reality of Polish cultural domination in Vilna and the city's historical links to Poland.[108]

The incorporation of Vilna into Poland was hugely controversial, with the French, English, and Italian ambassadors in Warsaw calling a meeting with Polish officials to express their view that annexing Vilna was highly problematic. But Pilsudski refused to back down, visiting Vilna on April 18, 1922, where he announced the dissolution of the Middle Lithuania Republic and its union with Poland. He gave a moving, lengthy speech on the meaning of Vilna for himself and for the country. The heritage of Vilna, he said, was inextricably bound with Poland. He regarded Lithuania proper, with its capital in Kowno, very kindly and hoped for peaceful relations.[109]

Soviet-Polish peace talks meanwhile moved from Minsk to Riga. On October 12, 1920, Polish and Soviet representatives signed a preliminary agreement. On October 18, when the armistice went into effect, Pilsudski issued an order for his troops to stand down.[110] A final agreement was not reached until the spring of the following year. The Treaty of Riga, signed on March 18, 1921, formally ended the Polish-Soviet War. As part of the agreement, Soviet Russia recognized Polish sovereignty over the Vilna region and East Galicia, as well as over the lands between them—western Belarus and western Volhynia. In exchange, Poland recognized Soviet control over the eastern Belarusian and Ukrainian borderlands. The Treaty of Riga marked the collapse of two grand aspirations: Pilsudski's federalist program and Lenin's wish for a communist revolution in Central and Western Europe. As historian Jerzy Borzęcki has noted, both sides received their vital demands. The Poles got their Polish ethnic territory in the east while the Soviets held on to most of Ukraine and Belarus.[111] By halting these colliding ambitions, the Riga agreement brought relative stabilization to the region.

The Internment of Jewish Soldiers in Jabłonna

In Jewish collective memory in Poland, the Polish-Soviet War of 1920 cannot be disentangled from an event involving Jewish soldiers in the Polish Army. On August 16, 1920—the day Pilsudski launched a counteroffensive—

Jozef Pilsudski receiving bread and salt from the Jewish community in Dęblin, after its
capture during the 1920 Polish-Soviet War. This famous photograph has become the
iconic symbol of Pilsudski's favorable image among Jews. Dęblin, August 1920.

Minister of War Sosnkowski issued a notorious order to intern Jewish soldiers,
officers, and volunteers at a camp in the town of Jabłonna, fourteen miles
north of Warsaw. The order called for the removal of Jews from army offices
and military formations due to "the continuous increase in cases testifying
to the harmful activities of the Jewish element."[112]

The order from Poland's minister of war was a stinging rebuke, amounting
to what the late Jerzy Tomaszewski characterized as "a scandal with great
meaning."[113] The Jewish Parliamentary Club expressed outrage in a letter to
Sosnkowski dated August 16, 1920: "We cannot comprehend why Jews in the
army are treated in this way while, at the same time, they are accused of a lack
of patriotism and of an unwillingness to sacrifice their blood for the defense
of the state." The order to intern Jewish soldiers "demonstrates that the military
authorities are not in favor of the participation of Jews in the army but rather

strive, in all ways, contrary to the principle of equality of rights, to remove Jews from military formations and to impose on them conditions worse than for Christian soldiers." The order "makes the predicament of the Jews extremely difficult at the present moment. It intensifies and fuels an anti-Jewish atmosphere and may lead to unpredictable consequences."[114] On August 19 the Jewish Parliamentary Club sent another letter to General Sosnkowski, arguing that "such orders instill a conviction that Jews are enemies of the state."[115] Despite protests from Deputy Prime Minister Daszyński, the Council decided to keep the order in place for the Jabłonna camp.

Although there is no evidence that Pilsudski gave the order, there is also no record of him objecting to it. We can discern his views on the matter from an interview he gave to *Kurier Poranny* (Morning Courier) on August 26, 1920. When asked about Jewish soldiers in the Polish Army, Pilsudski gave a characteristically nuanced view, essentially saying that the behavior of Jewish soldiers varied. "Jews did not behave poorly everywhere. In the Łomża and Mazovia provinces, they bravely held back the Bolshevik advance. In Mazovia, many were killed. On the other hand," he continued, "not far away in Łuków, in Siedlce, in Kałuszno, in Białystok and, further away, in Włodowa—and sometimes even on a mass scale—treason could be found on the Jewish side."[116]

The first press account appeared on September 1, 1920, when a Polish newspaper printed a firsthand account from a reporter who had visited the camp on August 29. In "The Riddle of Jabłonna," the reporter estimated about three thousand Jews were held at the camp. Among the Jewish soldiers "were a great many volunteers, intellectuals and academics plucked from various branches of the army. No one knows what is going on." These internees were not accused of any crime but appeared to have the status of prisoners. The reported stated. The writer supported his claim with the story that when he returned to Warsaw, he visited four Jewish soldiers from the Jabłonna camp who needed medical treatment unrelated to the internment. "They are being treated as prisoners," he reported.[117] When the Jewish inmates were released from Jablonna twenty-four days after their internment on September 9, it was reported that the camp held 17,680 Jewish soldiers.[118]

On the floor of the Polish parliament Yitzhak Gruenbaum demanded an explanation from the minister of War, Sosnkowski. "Jabłonna was ordered," the parliamentary minutes record Sosnkowski as replying, "at a time when the enemy was at the gates of our capital, when Praga was aflame." The internment of Jewish soldiers, General Sosnkowski continued, came about due to reports of Jewish soldiers deserting and joining the Red Army on the eastern front. Gruenbaum interjected to demand that the general provide the single name of a Jewish soldier who had committed treason. Sosnkowski was unable to respond.[119]

Pilsudski's role in the Jabłonna affair has never been established. But it is highly unlikely that an order by his minister of war to intern Polish soldiers of Jewish background during the Battle for Warsaw was issued without his approval. Although Pilsudski's role cannot be definitively determined, the

Jewish soldiers on the day they were freed from the internment camp in Jabłonna, where Jewish soldiers of the Polish Army accused of Bolshevik sympathies during the Polish-Soviet War were sent. Jabłonna, September 8, 1920.

Jabłonna camp impacted Polish-Jewish relations throughout the entire interwar period.

The Significance of the Battle of Warsaw

For many, Pilsudski's real significance lay in the role he played in halting a Bolshevik conquest of Europe in 1920. The British statesman Lord D'Abernon most dramatically expressed this idea when he referred to the 1920 Polish-Soviet War as one of the eighteen decisive battles of world civilization. "The history of contemporary civilisation knows no event of greater importance than the Battle of Warsaw, 1920," Lord D'Abernon remarked in a 1930 interview marking the tenth anniversary of the battle. He continued:

> never had Poland's service been greater, never had the danger been more immediate. The events in 1920 also deserve attention for another reason: victory was attained above all thanks for the strategic genius of one man and thanks to the carrying through of a maneuver so dangerous as to necessitate not only genius, but heroism. . . . It should be the task of political writers to explain to European opinion that Poland saved Europe in 1920, and that it is necessary to keep Poland powerful and in harmonious relations with Western European civilization.[120]

In his evaluation of the Polish victory in 1920, historian Norman Davies noted: "Had Pilsudski and Weygand failed to arrest the triumphant advance of the Soviet Army at the Battle of Warsaw, not only would Christianity have experienced a dangerous reverse, but the very existence of Western civilization would have been imperiled."[121] And in the field of military history, the plan that Pilsudski and Rozwadowski devised for the Battle of Warsaw is counted among the twenty-five wars in world history revealing "tactical genius in battle."[122] At the time, Pilsudski's political opponents as well as French military circles put forth the thesis that the battle plan was devised not by Pilsudski and General Rozwadowski, but entirely by General Weygand. Yet Weygand himself never made that claim, publicly attributing the victory to Polish military strategy and execution. In an interview appearing on August 21, 1920, a French journalist asked Weygand to comment on the title he had been given in the French press as "the savior of Warsaw." Weygand replied in the following manner: "I beg you to fix French opinion on that important point. This is a purely Polish victory. The preliminary operations were carried out in accordance with Polish plans and by Polish generals." Weygand reinforced this view in his memoirs, emphasizing that Poland's victory in the 1920 Battle of Warsaw could be attributed "to the military genius of Rozwadowski and his consistent cooperation with the commander-in-chief [Pilsudski]."[123]

CHAPTER 15

From the First Years of Peace to the 1926 Coup

Poland is aware of its peaceful and civilizing mission which has
fallen to it in Eastern Europe and which corresponds to the
mission of France in the West.

—JOZEF PILSUDSKI, PARIS, FEBRUARY 1921

The year 1921 saw the dawn of the Second Polish Republic, an extraordinary time marked by international treaties, the settlement of frontier conflicts with Bolshevik Russia, and the establishment of independent Poland's constitution. It also marked the beginnings of the normalization of Poland's place in Europe. This process was symbolized by Pilsudski's first official visit to a foreign country in peacetime, a high-profile trip to France. Pilsudski would arrive in Paris not only as head of state but also as first marshal, a title bestowed upon him on March 19, 1920.[1] At the time of his visit to France, Pilsudski's standing in Entente circles was mixed to poor, with much unease relating to his military ventures in the eastern borderlands.

Now, at the beginning of 1921, the most serious concern of the Entente powers regarding Pilsudski was his capture of Vilna from the Lithuanians the previous October. The decision to wrest Vilna from Lithuania continued to trouble them. Lithuanian resentment over the capture of Vilna was such that until 1938, Pilsudski's death, Lithuania insisted that a formal state of war existed between the two countries. But the direction toward peace with Russia was positive. The agreement in Riga between Poland and the Soviets on October 12, 1920, marked the end of hostilities in a conflict that had been going on for almost two years.

On the last day of 1920, Pilsudski issued a New Year's address to his soldiers. "For the first time in independent Poland, we observe the New Year not in war but in peacetime," he remarked. Yet he cautioned against false complacency: "Poland is surrounded by foes" who "lie in wait for any display of weakness on our part," looking for the opportunity to undo Poland's independence. His central message to the soldiers was: "The more reliable, the more efficient and capable a soldier will be, the more the freedom of the homeland will be protected. Thus, the easier will be peaceful work on the scarring of wounds inflicted by a prolonged war."[2]

His New Year's address also included an announcement about new regulations for the armed forces in peacetime. Now that military conflicts had ended, Pilsudski introduced a decree on January 7, 1921, for the reorganization of the country's military. The leading military institutions were now divided into two branches. The first was the War Council (Pełna Rada Wojenna), an advisory body chaired by the president. The second was the Inner War Council (Ścisła Rada Wojenna), a body led by a general who in times of war was to serve as commander in chief. The latter was responsible for defense of the state, and its decisions were binding on the minister of war, making it an independent, nonpartisan body.[3] Pilsudski's aim in introducing the new regulation was to keep the army out of political fluctuations of government. The army decree was thus a conscious anticipation of the country's first constitution, which he knew would subordinate the War Council to the minister of war.

Pilsudski then turned his attention to foreign affairs. First on his agenda was the alliance with France, a friendship that had yielded huge benefits thus far. As we have seen, France—the dominant military power in continental Europe—was the only country that had provided experienced officers and military aid to Poland during the 1920 Polish-Soviet War. Pilsudski was therefore genuinely delighted to receive an invitation for a state visit from France's prime minister. On February 1, 1921, Pilsudski left Warsaw for Paris, journeying to France with Foreign Minister Sapieha and Minister of War Sosnkowski.[4] On February 3, Pilsudski and his ministers arrived in Paris, where they were greeted at the railway station by Prime Minister Aristide

Briand, Minister of War Louis Barthou, and a group of French generals, including General Maxime Weygand.[5]

During Pilsudski's three-day stay in France, which took place in a very favorable and friendly atmosphere, he had a packed schedule of luncheons and dinners with the French president and other officials. He gave a series of addresses in French that laid out Poland's vision and the importance of strong French-Polish ties. Pilsudski commented that it was France's president Alexandre Millerand, with whom he had the best rapport and who understood in detail the Polish position.[6] At a luncheon on February 3, Pilsudski spoke about his understanding of Poland's role in Eastern Europe: "Poland is aware of its peaceful and civilizing mission which has fallen to it in Eastern Europe and which corresponds to the mission of France in the West. Poland will fulfill its mission persistently and in an ever closer relationship with France, remaining faithful to the great principles that led the Allies to victory."[7]

Pilsudski (*center, left*) with French president Alexandre Millerand (*center, right*), Paris,
February 1919.

The significance of his statement should not be overlooked. According to this view, Poland was spreading the democratic ideal in Eastern Europe, the principles for which the Allies fought the war. Pilsudski believed independent Poland was an outpost of Western democracy in Eastern Europe. He wanted France to know it had a loyal ally in Warsaw in every sense of the word. At a reception held at City Hall, Pilsudski told the mayor of Paris that the trip to the French capital would be a memory dear to his heart.[8]

At the farewell luncheon in Pilsudski's honor, held on February 5, the basis for a political-military agreement between the two countries was discussed. Sapieha and Sosnkowski remained in France after Pilsudski's departure to hammer out the details. On February 19 the French-Polish Agreement was signed. For France, the agreement had a strong anti-German component. For the Poles, the agreement had a strong anti-Soviet motif. On February 21 Sosnkowski signed a secret military convention with General Foch. Both agreements were among the most important features of Poland's foreign policy in the interwar period.[9]

During the Paris visit, Pilsudski also took the opportunity to honor those who aided his country. On February 5 he presented General Foch with the Polish Order Virtuti Militari for his service to Poland. Upon his departure from Paris, he stopped in Verdun, where Marshal Pétain gave him a tour of the famous battleground. Pilsudski took the opportunity at Verdun to present Pétain with the Virtuti Militari.[10] Pilsudski's first foreign visit was a resounding success. Upon his return home, he solidified ties with Romania, signing a political and military convention on March 3, 1921.

It was at this time that Poland reached a milestone. On March 17, 1921, Pilsudski attended a session of the Sejm in which it approved the country's first constitution. The ceremony around the event had great symbolism, with Pilsudski, the Sejm speaker, and Sejm deputies proceeding to a cathedral to lay a wreath at the statue of Stanisław Małachowski, former marshal of the Sejm when that body passed the constitution of May 3, 1791.[11] For Pilsudski, it was a bittersweet moment. On the one hand, he had been waiting for this moment his whole life. On the other hand, the document, modeled on the constitution of France's Third Republic, heavily limited the authority of the president. A nine-person commission selected in 1919 by the Legislative Sejm drafted the constitution. Its chairman, Professor Edward Dubanowicz of Lwów University, was a constitutional lawyer closely linked to the National

Democrats, who made sure the constitution would call for a weak president and an all-powerful Sejm.[12] Pilsudski and his supporters never accepted this arrangement—not because it limited executive authority, something Pilsudski fully supported, but because it made the office impotent.

Pilsudski and his supporters knew that the National Democrats under Dmowski had used the constitution as a check on Pilsudski's power rather than devising a constitutional system that was good for the country. "The President of the Republic," the constitution states, "exercises the executive power through ministers responsible to the Sejm and through officials subordinated to the Ministers."[13] The president's authority was thus subordinated to the 444-person Sejm, elected for a five-year term by proportionate representation. The constitution gave the president, elected for a seven-year period, the additional title of commander in chief but imposed severe limits on that role as well. First, the president could declare war and conclude peace only after obtaining the Sejm's consent (Section III, Art. 50). Second, the president "may not exercise chief command of the armed forces in times of war" (Section III, Art. 46). The Peasant Party leader, Wincenty Witos, emphasized the importance of these articles in constraining Pilsudski's military ventures.[14] Thus, the president was formally head of state but his powers were so limited that his authority was restricted to formal duties. The National Democrats had scathingly criticized Pilsudski for the Kiev debacle and the near collapse of Poland, and insulted him by attributing the Polish victory over the Red Army to the French alone. In fact, the term by which the Polish-Soviet War came to be known, "Miracle on the Vistula," was, ironically, coined at the time by a National Democrat supporter in order to attribute victory to divine providence rather than to Pilsudski. But as long as he remained commander in chief, Pilsudski successfully kept his January 1921 army decree intact by preventing the introduction of the constitutional articles limiting his control over the armed forces.

Just days after the passing of the constitution, the fate of Upper Silesia was decided. On March 20, 1921, the long-awaited plebiscite took place. The result, made public on April 23, was that 707,605 residents voted in favor of incorporation into Germany while 479,359 voted for Poland.[15] This did not please the Poles, who believed that many of the German votes were cast illegally, and they used the occasion of Kościuszko Day on May 3 to launch an uprising. Chaos ensued when a German volunteer Free Corps and German self-defense units arrived on the scene to quell the revolt, halting the uprising on May 21. Allied troops reasserted control of the plebiscite region after a ceasefire went into effect. But casualties occurred even among Allied forces, and Pilsudski personally expressed his condolences to the king of Italy for killed and wounded Italian soldiers.[16] In the end, the League of Nations divided Upper Silesia, with Poland receiving 46 percent of the population and the bulk of Upper Silesia's industry.

At the end of April 1921, Pilsudski gave two memorable public addresses. First he spoke in Kraków when the Jagiellonian University's faculty of law bestowed upon him an honorary doctorate. There, at Poland's oldest and most illustrious university, Pilsudski began by marveling at the course of his life. He had grown up in imperial Russia where lawlessness prevailed and afterward, as a soldier, where law was really brute force and military discipline. He was proud to be presiding over a state that operated under the rule of law. "My first decision [as head of state]," he said, "was establishing the law and strengthening a sense [for it] through the whole society."[17] He understood that spreading the value of respect for the rule of law was a long, gradual process.

The second public address Pilsudski gave was on the occasion of the one hundredth anniversary of Napoleon's death on April 29, 1921. In a talk published in the daily press, Pilsudski characterized the French general as "the greatest soldier that ever lived," one who applied his genius in the service not only of freedom in general but to Polish liberty in particular. "Soldiers! Under the command of Napoleon, our grandfathers and great-grandfathers, who worshiped him as supreme commander, once fought and bowed their banners to him."[18]

Pilsudski had retained from his younger days a special interest in military history, and an unbounded admiration for Napoleon. A copy of Jacques-Louis David's painting *Napoleon Crossing the Alps* hung in his office at the Belvedere Palace, and he sometimes took copies of Napoleon's letters with him to read over and over again while traveling. On May 5, 1921, when the anniversary ceremonies began, the National Museum in Warsaw opened an exhibition on Napoleon with artifacts on loan from Paris; it is not surprising that Pilsudski attended the opening.[19] He saw in Napoleon a combination of a military genius who used the armed forces for the purposes of liberating and bringing freedom to neighboring peoples, as did Napoleon for Poland.

At this time a huge change took place in Pilsudski's personal life. On August 17, 1921, Maria Pilsudska passed away in Kraków. Maria had never granted Pilsudski a divorce. She was buried at the Rossa Cemetery in Vilna alongside her daughter, Wanda Juszkiewicz. Pilsudski did not attend the funeral, sending in his place his brother Jan.

Maria's death entirely changed Pilsudski's personal life. Alexandra had purchased a house in Sulejówek, outside of Warsaw, in a secluded area in a pine forest. She spent the summer of 1921 with the girls there, and Pilsudski visited when possible. On October 25, 1921, Alexandra and Pilsudski were married at the Łazienki Palace chapel in Warsaw. Alexandra and the girls— now ages three and one—could finally move into the Belvedere Palace, where they occupied its west wing. The normalization of Pilsudski's private life, whereby Alexandra could serve openly as first lady and the family could live together, was a milestone after years of concealment and awkwardness.

Meanwhile, Pilsudski toured the western part of the country, stopping in Toruń in Pomerania to give a speech in which he spoke rather elegantly about history and geography. German troops did not leave Toruń until January 1920, when they vacated the city as part of a Treaty of Versailles mandate. All nations, Pilsudski said, had historical monuments marking their history. "Poland has many of these temples of history, but to me, there is no grander temple than the boundaries that once severed our country." He continued, discussing the meaning of frontier towns like Toruń. "The message that came to us from these frontier posts not so long ago," Pilsudski concluded, "was 'Forget.' Today the message is 'Remember.'"[20]

Not long after the visit to Toruń an important change took place in the cabinet of ministers. On June 11, 1921, Pilsudski appointed Konstanty Skirmunt, the Polish ambassador in Rome, to the post of foreign minister. A career diplomat with center-right political leanings, Skirmunt came to the job with the goal of improving Poland's image abroad. He laid out principles in August 1921 in a diplomatic circular intended to counter the views in Western diplomatic circles that Poland was imperialistic and aggressive, and that Pilsudski in particular was unpredictable. The circular emphasized respect for international treaties, cooperation with smaller neighbors, and normalization of relations with Germany and Soviet Russia. To develop as a new state, Poland needed peace above all, Skirmunt wrote. This meant support for existing state borders and strong ties with the Western democracies.

A second document, adopted by the Council of Ministers in January 1922, related to foreign policy from the viewpoint of state security. In a position that became a staple principle of foreign policy during the interwar period, the document stated that Poland's principal foreign policy goal was peace and preserving the status quo. Poland would use its armed forces only if attacked or to aid an ally, like France or a Baltic republic, against German or Soviet aggression. Poland's security was intricately linked to a strong alliance with France.[21]

Soon after Skirmunt put out his circular, a cabinet crisis ensued. In early September 1921, Prime Minister Witos, who had been serving since July 1920, tendered his resignation. Pilsudski, who opposed Witos's decision, had no choice but to name a new government. On September 19, 1921, he named Antoni Ponikowski, a professor at the Polytechnic Institute in Warsaw, to head a new cabinet. Ponikowski retained Skirmunt as foreign minister and Sosnkowski as minister of war. Pilsudski approved the cabinet the following day.[22]

Six days later, on September 25, Pilsudski went to Lwów to attend a banquet in his honor. While he was leaving City Hall on his way to the theater, a Ukrainian nationalist tried to assassinate him, firing three bullets at close range. The gunman narrowly missed and Pilsudski was not injured. But Kazimierz Grabowski, Lwów's district governor, who was accompanying him, was shot in the leg. According to one press account, Pilsudski "directed his chauffeur to drive to a hospital, and, after being assured that Grabowski's wound was not serious, insisted on going to the theater as he had intended. He was enthusiastically cheered by the audience when he entered."[23] The assassination attempt in Lwów was a stark reminder that many Ukrainians considered Polish control of East Galicia illegal.

The Warsaw government experienced another cabinet crisis, this one connected to the Treaty of Rapallo, signed on April 16, 1922, between Germany and Soviet Russia. The treaty highlighted the threat posed by the strengthening of ties between Poland's neighbors, who had been weakened only temporarily in the war. The treaty itself came out of the 1922 Genoa Economic and Financial Conference of major European powers that had begun on April 10. In protest of the Treaty of Rapallo, Polish foreign minister Skirmunt abruptly left the Genoa conference. Pilsudski criticized the Polish delegation, and Prime Minister Ponikowski tendered his resignation on April 16, 1922.

What followed was a two-month political crisis. A parliamentary struggle ensued, during which Pilsudski challenged the Sejm over the limits on executive power. In June 1922 the Sejm voted to extend his right to choose a new prime minister on his own initiative.[24] By June still no new cabinet was formed, and the crisis continued when another candidate for prime minister failed to form a cabinet. Finally, on June 24, 1922, Pilsudski named Artur Śliwiński prime minister. The new cabinet replaced Skirmunt with Gabriel Narutowicz as foreign minister. But that government was short-lived, falling on July 7 when parliament's vote to approve the cabinet came up six votes short.[25]

Pilsudski relinquished his right to initiate the formation of a new government. Thus, the parliament's Main Commission recommended Wojciech Korfanty as premier. This merely prolonged the cabinet crisis. After a narrow vote by the Sejm in support of Korfanty, Pilsudski utterly refused to support this leader of the right-wing Polish Christian Democratic Party. He explained his position in a letter to the Sejm speaker on July 14, 1922, indicating he would resign if Korfanty headed a new cabinet.[26] Pilsudski went back to the Sejm to request in writing a clarification of Article 3 of the Little Constitution, which gave the head of state the right to form a government "on the basis of an understanding with the Sejm." The Sejm replied in writing, confirming that the head of state had the right to appoint a prime minister but if he does not make a nomination or if the Sejm votes against his nomination then the Sejm, by a majority of votes, designates a new prime minister.[27]

After Pilsudski threatened to resign, which created a stir in the parliament, the National Democrats organized anti-Pilsudski meetings in various halls in Warsaw. On July 26, 1922, the National Democrats put forth a resolution to remove Pilsudski as head of state. The vote failed to pass, with 205 opposed versus 187 in favor and four abstentions.[28] On this issue, Witos's Peasant Party (Piast) stood on Pilsudski's side. The National Democrats, on the other hand, bitterly claimed it was the vote of the Jewish and German members of parliament that tipped the scale against the motion.[29]

The long crisis came to an end when the Sejm, revising the interpretation of the Little Constitution, asked Pilsudski to name a premier on July 29. He chose Julian Nowak, rector of Jagiellonian University, who was not affiliated with any party. Supported by the left and center parties, the Sejm approved Nowak with a vote of 240 to 164.[30] The impasse was broken with a semblance of stability, as Nowak's government, consisting mostly of ministers from the previous cabinet, remained in place until December. Given the new prime minister's nonpartisan portfolio, this had been a battle of personalities unrelated to parliamentary principles and programs. As head of state, Pilsudski insisted on veto power over the choice of the head of the cabinet of ministers (prime minister).

The cabinet crisis and struggle with the Sejm embittered Pilsudski. It was thus significant that a new base of support for Pilsudski emerged in the summer of 1922 with the convening in Kraków of the first convention of the Union of Polish Legionnaires. Taking place August 5–7, 1922, and attended by some twenty-five hundred people, it constituted a powerful affirmation of support for Pilsudski unrelated to any political party.[31] Pilsudski's speech to the gathering electrified the crowd. Entirely in his element, he referred to the pivotal moment of the Legion's entry into World War I. "The decision of August 6 [1914], which I chose," he said, "gave Poland soldiers, created what Poland had never had before—strength and perhaps a new type of man. I, my comrades, can be proud, because on August 6, I began a fabulous and unknown career on Polish lands . . . I passed my life exam."[32]

Marshal Pilsudski on a foreign visit with King Ferdinand I of Romania, Bucharest, September 1922.

Meanwhile, Pilsudski accepted an invitation from King Ferdinand of Romania for a state visit. Accompanied by several officials and his foreign minister, Gabriel Narutowicz, they set out on September 12, 1922, for a three-day visit. The rapport with Romania's Queen Maria and King Ferdinand was well established and ties between the countries, based on the earlier agreement signed in March 1921, were strengthened. His interview with a Romanian paper and address to King Ferdinand and Queen Maria demonstrated his genuine appreciation for friendly ties, emphasizing the significance of their common border, acquired with the incorporation of East Galicia. Before leaving Romania, Pilsudski spoke with one of the Polish officials present, Władysław Baranowski, revealing how much the conflict with parliament had rattled him: "Neither the war with the Bolsheviks, nor our various other complications," Pilsudski said to Mr. Baranowski, "compares to the impact on me of the struggle with the Sejm in a stinking atmosphere full of venom and meanness." It was for this reason, Pilsudski continued, that the visit to Romania had been so relaxing, especially being away from Warsaw where "I am like a caged animal that anyone can take a jab at."[33]

Parliamentary and Presidential Elections

The interview in Romania demonstrated not only how contentious Polish politics had become but also that unstable government was eroding confidence in the country's parliamentary system. With the cabinet crisis behind them, and successful passage of the new election law in July under Prime Minister Nowak, hopes were high that the parliamentary elections in November 1922 would stabilize government and restore a semblance of calm. But as it turned out, the events of November–December 1922 would shatter Pilsudski's hopes for such an outcome. It was nevertheless an important moment in the history of the Second Republic, as the first parliamentary elections after the passing of a constitution. This new body, representing the collective will of the voters, was to be tasked with naming Poland's first president.

We should recall that on the eve of parliamentary elections, the center parties—with 60 percent of the Sejm seats—enjoyed an absolute majority over the Right and Left, which had about 18 percent each. The elections of November 1922, however, revealed significant changes in the political makeup of the Sejm. The center lost 24 percent of its seats, mainly to the national minority parties, who gained 21.6 percent of the seats. The leftist parties increased their share by 5.5 percent but the right-wing parties gained many more, with a 12 percent increase. The main outcome of the elections, therefore, was to strengthen the Right, the Left, and the national minorities at the expense of the Center. In the end, the National Democrats and their associates emerged as the strongest single bloc, gaining 30.1 percent of the votes, with the leftist parties gaining 25.2 percent, the centrist parties, 21 percent, and the National Minorities parties, including the Minorities Bloc, receiving 21.6 percent of the seats, almost one-fifth of the Sejm.[34]

The proportion of national minority representation in the Sejm was not surprising. The substantial increase from the 1919 elections was due to territorial expansion in the east during the wars of 1918–1920, where national minorities constituted a majority of the local population. The first complete census, issued in November 1921, revealed that national minorities made up 30.8 percent of the population, including Ukrainians (14.3 percent), Jews (7.8 percent), Germans (3.9 percent), and Belarusians (3.9 percent).[35]

At the opening session of Poland's new parliament on November 28, 1922, Pilsudski addressed the assembly. Unlike his first address to the Sejm in February 1919, when Poland was at war, the current session was taking place in peacetime. With a note of optimism, Pilsudski referred to the significance of the moment: "We are presiding over the first Sejm based on a constitutional republic. This constitutes a turning point in the life of the state which— exiting the period of transition—has now entered the path to normal development." But a democratic political culture remained weak, and Pilsudski warned that few in government had demonstrated a willingness to compromise. "I call on you, gentlemen, to set an example for everyone to see that in our country there is a possibility of loyal cooperation of people, parties, and state institutions."[36]

When it came time to elect Poland's first president, Pilsudski surprised the country by announcing on December 4, 1922, that he was withdrawing his candidacy. He explained in a gathering of the Council of Ministers that the president had to be someone with a different temperament, a compromiser "with a heavy step but a light hand." The president, as prescribed in the constitution, had "too many ceremonial duties, not enough real authority."[37] Prior to Pilsudski's decision to bow out of the race, his presumed candidacy had split the rightist coalition in the new parliament, when Witos's PSL-Piast delegates broke ranks with the National Democrats and came out in favor of a Pilsudski presidency. This meant that Pilsudski had the support not only of the traditional leftist parties—the Polish Socialist Party, the Polish Peasant Party-Liberation, and the Polish Workers Party—but also both the Piast Peasant Party and the powerful Minorities Bloc. Pilsudski's victory would have been a foregone conclusion.

Pilsudski's position on the office of the president as laid out in the construction was clearly communicated at the time to his future foreign minister, August Zaleski. "Pilsudski refused to stand as a candidate," Zaleski recalled in his unpublished memoirs, "because he considered that the new constitution did not give the president any possibility of a political authority. In fact," Zaleski continued, "the position of the President of Poland was modeled on that of the King of England. He could act only on advice of responsible ministers. Pilsudski considered that such an attitude on the part of the legislature was appropriate in case of a heredity monarchy but was superfluous in the case of an elected head of state." Further summarizing Pilsudski's position, Zaleski concluded: "And if you had to elect a nonentity as a mere figurehead, it was just as well or even better to have a monarchy which gives to the Head of State the prestige the crown still carries with some people. In this respect, the marshal was decidedly inclined more to the American than the French model of republican constitution."[38]

Tragedy Strikes

On December 9, 1922, presidential elections took place in Poland. Of the five candidates, including socialists and right-wing National Democrats, fifty-seven-year-old Gabriel Narutowicz, Pilsudski's choice, came out ahead, 289 to 227.[39] That evening, Alexandra Pilsudska visited the president-elect. "On arrival at the simple little house where he lived with his niece I found him in poor health and suffering from a deep depression which he tried in vain to shake off," she recalled. "He confided to me that he had a strange premonition which warned him not to accept the Presidency."[40]

A swearing-in ceremony on December 11 was conducted and Narutowicz prepared to move into the Belvedere Palace. "I shall not take over the Marshal's study," he is quoted as saying. "I shall keep that exactly as he leaves it so that

I can be constantly reminded of his example."[41] Pilsudski later made note of this gesture as a reflection of how respectful Narutowicz was as a person.[42]

Witos's Piast members, having supported Narutowicz, were harassed outside the parliament house by mobs shouting "Traitors!" Chants outside the parliament building of "Down with the Jewish president!" and "Down with the Jews!" could also be heard.[43] That the right-wing parties in Poland would scream loudly in protest was not surprising. Prior to the election, the National Democrats put forth what they referred to as the Doctrine of the Polish Majority, arguing that the choice of a president should reflect the will of ethnic Poles and ethnic Poles only. But because the support of the national minority parties helped tip the balance in favor of Narutowicz, a storm of incendiary criticism followed, with the National Democrats and their allies bombastically arguing that Narutowicz was put in office by a Jewish conspiracy to take over Poland. "Narutowicz, president of the Jews," read the headlines in right-wing papers.[44]

In the first days after the election, National Democrats claimed the presidency was illegitimate because Narutowicz was elected not by the Polish people but by minorities, particularly Jews. The relentless campaign was meant to cast a shadow of illegitimacy over Narutowicz. This, in turn, created a toxic atmosphere. On the day after the election, the Christian Alliance of National Unity declared that it could not support "a government created by a president imposed by foreign nationalities: Jews, Germans and Ukrainians."[45] A National Democratic member of the Sejm likewise warned the Jews that they had gone too far, writing, "How could the Jews dare to impose their president on us?"[46]

To Pilsudski, the incendiary campaign against Narutowicz by the National Democrats and their associates was an outrage. On December 11, 1922, he told the new Sejm speaker, Maciej Rataj, "I cannot give up power at a time when a band of gangsters is disturbing the peace, insulting the President and the Government does nothing. Give me power, and I will quiet the streets. If not, I will do it alone—I cannot give way to these conditions."[47] Meanwhile, Pilsudski moved out of Belvedere Palace to a private apartment on December 13, attending a palace ceremony the following day to welcome the president-elect into his new residence. It was a symbolic moment of the legal transfer of power.

But Pilsudski was unable to suppress the vicious campaign against Narutowicz. On December 16, 1922, five days after being sworn in, Narutowicz

Pilsudski and President-Elect Gabriel Narutowicz, December 14, 1922,
two days before Narutowicz was assassinated.

attended an exhibition at Warsaw's National Gallery of Art. The British
ambassador to Poland, Sir William Max-Miller, congratulated him on his
victory. "You should offer me your condolences instead," Narutowicz gloomily
replied.[48] Shortly after this exchange, a fifty-three-year-old painter named
Eligiusz Niewiadomski, a National Democratic Party sympathizer, slipped
in with a concealed weapon and shot Narutowicz to death at close range. A
fellow Pole had murdered independent Poland's first president after only five
days in office.

At his trial, which took place on December 30, 1922, the murderer's guilt
was never in question. Not only did Niewiadomski proudly admit that he had
assassinated Narutowicz and that his deed was premeditated and carefully
planned, but he expressed no remorse whatsoever. The lead prosecutor, Kazimierz Rudnicki, asked when he first planned to kill the president. Niewa-
domski replied that he decided on the morning of December 6, the day he
learned Pilsudski had withdrawn his candidacy for president. In a bombshell
statement, Niewiadomski testified that he had originally planned to murder
Pilsudski and was, in fact, going to kill him on December 6 at the opening of
an art exhibition in Warsaw the marshal was scheduled to attend on December 6. When asked why, Niewiadomski replied that Pilsudski was the

creator of "Judeo-Poland."[49] Pilsudski's decision to pull out of the presidential election—one he was overwhelmingly favored to win—threw Niewiadomski into a state of despair and he decided to call off the planned assassination of Pilsudski.

After answering questions from the prosecutor, Niewiadomski was given permission to address the court. In a rambling speech, read out loud from a prepared statement, the accused repeatedly linked Pilsudski with an alleged Jewish conspiracy to rule Poland. Niewiadomski argued that Narutowicz's support from Jewish voters had rendered the election result null and void. The assassination of Narutowicz thus constituted "one of the episodes in the fight for the nation, the fight for the Polishness of Poland. As such, my action is its own defense, and speaks for itself," the accused said. He added:

> I believe that as a human being, as a professor, as a husband, and as a father, Narutowicz was a good, noble, admirable person. . . . For me he existed not as a human being but as the symbol of a certain political situation . . . a symbol of shame. My shots removed this badge of shame from the forehead of Poland. Through my deeds spoke not partisan fury, but the conscience and the offended dignity of the nation.[50]

After hearing the murder's statement, the court rendered its verdict on the same day: Niewiadomski was found guilty and sentenced to death by firing squad. An interview Pilsudski gave the following day, December 31, 1922, offers insight into his thinking at the time. It was a dramatic moment as Niewiadomski admitted Pilsudski had been his original target. Pilsudski expressed outrage at the act itself, and guilt that Narutowicz had stood in his place. He was bitter over the incendiary campaign against the Narutowicz presidency, which rendered the National Democrats culpable in his eyes. "I must take note of how childish the base of political thought is here," he said. For in most countries presidential elections engage the citizenry peacefully out of genuine interest in electing qualified candidates, and these citizens then accept the democratically chosen president-elect, he said, adding, "In Poland, it is the opposite. Here, people look to our politicians for lies and base their policies on these lies."[51]

Equally shocking to Pilsudski was the abrupt change in the attitude of the National Democrats and the right-wing press to the trial. In the days between the assassination and the trial, right-wing party leaders had characterized

Niewiadomski as a madman, but the publication of the complete transcript of the assassin's remarks at the trial in the press of the National Democrats resulted in a reassessment based on the assassin's expressed position. What followed was a shift in the murderer's image from a lone, deranged gunman to a national hero. For in the weeks that followed the trial, the newspapers of the National Democratic Party openly praised the assassin's views.[52] In the pages of a National Democratic Party weekly, for example, a well-known writer put forth the thesis, on January 6, 1923, that the assassin "cannot but provoke admiration for [his] strength and capacity for sacrifice." Niewiadomski's remarks at the trial constituted "a monument to a man of great character . . . a noble soul!" The writer praised the assassin for clarifying that the Jews alone were the problem, not other national minorities. "This is about that one national minority, the demon of humanity, this singular anti-Christian minority, the disease known as Jewry, the demon with which Europe and the entire world are now leading a struggle to the death."[53]

At 6:30 a.m. on January 31, 1923, Niewiadomski was taken to the execution site outside the gates of the Warsaw Citadel. Theatrical down to his last breath, Niewiadomski carried a single rose in his hand and was granted a request not to wear a blindfold. As the six-man firing squad raised their rifles, the murderer is said to have called out, "Shoot me in the head and heart. I am dying for Poland which Pilsudski has destroyed."[54] In its coverage of the execution, Warsaw's National Democratic daily concluded that "with his sacrifice he gave witness to the idea of the nation."[55] At the funeral, held on February 6 in Warsaw, the crowd was estimated to number ten thousand mourners. The result was a pile of flowers and wreaths so high that it was visible from far away.[56]

In the month that followed Niewiadomski's execution, police records from Poznań reveal that some began to view the assassin not as a disgrace but as a national martyr. Public displays of support for Niewiadomski became frequent enough that on February 16, 1923, the Polish parliament passed a resolution banning open praise of the murderer.[57] Poznań police files from February 1923 contain investigative reports into violations of the new regulation. On February 21, for example, the district court in Poznań began proceedings against the owner of a bookstore who had displayed Niewiadomski's image in the store window. Another police report found that on February 13, a mass was held for Niewiadomski in a church in Poznań's city center.[58] Still other police records reported that in Poznań during February 1923, people put altars in their windows and that images of Niewiadomski were widespread in the city streets.[59]

The assassination of Poland's first president, and the mixed reaction of the public to the crime, was a huge blow to the country in general and to Pilsudski in particular. "This crime did more than any other stroke of fate to make the Marshal an embittered man," William F. Reddaway remarked in his 1939 biography, adding, "the gravest consequence of the assassination, however, was probably its effect upon Pilsudski's mind."[60] Wacław Jędrzejewicz, who had served in Pilsudski's government and knew him personally, went further: "This national tragedy was also a deep personal tragedy for Pilsudski, who never got over it. The death of Narutowicz changed his character. Profound indignation and disgust with the situation in Polish political parties—as expressed by this death—was to be a characteristic trait of the Marshal in the later years of his life."[61] American historian Richard M. Watt similarly maintained, "As Pilsudski viewed it, the Right had supported the murder of his friend, and they would have applauded his own assassination. The Marshal's close associates now detected a subtle but definite alteration in his view of Poland's people and their future. Pilsudski had begun to speculate— what manner of people were these?"[62]

Meanwhile, Rataj nominated Władysław Sikorski to head a so-called Cabinet of Pacification. The Sikorski cabinet enjoyed support from center-left and center-right parties. To Pilsudski went the position of chief of the general staff. On December 20, 1922, the Sejm sat in session to elect a president. Stanisław Wojciechowski, one of Pilsudski's oldest collaborators who by then was a member of the PSL-Piast party, was elected with 298 votes. The chasm between Pilsudski and the National Democrats was irreparable; Witos's Piast party remained unaligned with the rightest parties, allowing for a center-left cabinet.

The beginning of 1923 emerged in the shadow of Narutowicz's assassination and the vicious right-wing campaign that had preceded it. On January 19, 1923, Prime Minister Sikorski called for the normalization of Polish political life. With the support of left and center parties, he attempted to bring calm to the frayed nerves of Poland's political life. The moment of calm quickly gave way to new challenges. The center-left orientation of the PSL-Piast abruptly changed when, on March 17, Witos and the rightest parties agreed to a pact in Warsaw. Although seventeen Piast deputies abandoned their support in protest, the right-center coalition bloc still constituted a parliamentary majority. On May 26, 1923, Sikorski resigned and Witos formed a new center-right government, with some posts going to the National Democrats and other rightist parties.[63] Pilsudski was outraged that rightest deputies who six months earlier had been part of the smear campaign against Narutowicz were now holding cabinet posts. Unable to bear political life in Warsaw any longer, he left his official residence to move with his family to their home in Sulejówek. This marked the beginning of his full retreat from government and the army.

Retreat from Politics

For Pilsudski, the transition from public to private life could only have taken place at a time of peace and stabilization in international affairs. Significant in this regard was the resolution of the Conference of Ambassadors, acting in the name of the Allied Powers. Signed in Paris on March 15, 1923, the agreement formally recognized the Polish-Lithuanian frontier and the Treaty of Riga, which demarcated the Polish-Soviet border.[64] International recognition of Poland's eastern border ended Poland's four-year struggle over the frontiers. This critical moment, when the Allies finally recognized Poland's borders, played a role in Pilsudski's decision to withdraw from public service (especially in the military) now that the country was secure.

From July 1923 to May 1926, Pilsudski lived in Sulejówek with his family. These years "were some of the happiest times we ever spent together," his wife commented. By all accounts, Pilsudski was quite attached to this home, partly for the way it came into his possession, when after World War I the army had secretly collected funds and purchased it as a gift to the family. In front of the red-roofed, white manor house set back in a garden, tables on both sides of the porch bore the inscription "The Soldier of Reborn Poland Offers This House to His Commander." The house "seemed to have absorbed something of the warmth and friendliness that had gone into its building [and] became our home. After all the tempestuous troubles we had known, it was a haven, the first place where we could live the simple family life we had always dreamed of," Alexandra commented.[65]

On June 9, 1923, Pilsudski resigned his position as chief of the general staff. "The honor of serving is like a soldier's banner with which the soldier parts

Pilsudski with his wife, Alexandra, and their daughters, Wanda and Jadwiga,
Sulejówek, 1924.

with his life," he said in his announcement on June 13.[66] A journalist asked
what he was planning to do, to which Pilsudski replied, "Well, I will rest
fully."[67] He took further action to withdraw from government service. On
July 2, he handed President Wojciechowski two resignation letters, the first
as head of the Inner War Council and the second for his post in the Full War
Council. The only official position Pilsudski retained was that of the chancellor of the Order of Virtuti Militari, which was not a political position. Retaining this sole function was not merely honorary. It gave Pilsudski a pretext for widening his contacts in the military, something he knew he might
need in the near future.

July 3, 1923, was the first day since the end of World War I that Pilsudski
was a free citizen, unencumbered by official duties. At Warsaw's Bristol Hotel

he gave a speech. This extraordinary address, delivered in the company of his adoring associates, revealed publicly for the first time Pilsudski's bitter resentment about the Narutowicz assassination. Directing his sharp feelings toward the National Democrats, he said, "This gang, this band, which questioned my honor, was out for blood. Our President was murdered in what amounted to a street brawl, by these same people who had once showed similar base hatred toward [me, the first Head of State] . . . they committed a crime. Murder is punished by law."[68]

Not long after the Hotel Bristol address Pilsudski prepared a memorial essay on Narutowicz's legacy. A moving tribute to Poland's first president, Pilsudski began by mentioning that Narutowicz's family had come from the same region of Lithuania as he did and shared the same social background of landed gentry.[69] Pilsudski recalled his meeting with Narutowicz after he became president-elect. The first thing Narutowicz did was to show Pilsudski a gun he said he was henceforth to carry with him everywhere he went. Pilsudski recalled Narutowicz's despair in the wake of the hysterical reaction to his election by the right-wing deputies and their presses, quoting Narutowicz as saying, "This is not Europe. Those people felt better under those who trampled their necks and beat their mouths." Pilsudski then describes how Narutowicz "showed me a pile of anonymous letters full of invectives, dirt, and threats." Narutowicz was a man of high culture and education, elegantly mannered, and remained to the end "an unusually loyal minister in my government." According to Pilsudski, Narutowicz's central concern in foreign affairs was improving Poland's standing in Western Europe. After being elected, Narutowicz became alarmed at the campaign against him. Pilsudski noted, "There was bitterness in his profound disappointment." He concluded with this tribute: "You died from bullets . . . from countrymen to whom you brought your gospel of love and work."[70]

In the country as a whole, meanwhile, tensions rose over runaway inflation and the social unrest that followed in its wake. As the Polish mark fell in value, Prime Minister Witos started cracking down on strikers, sending the military to put down a railway strike in October 1923.[71] A general strike, organized by the socialists, crippled the country in November 1923. The value of the Polish mark continued to decline, and by December 1923 had become worthless, exchanging at 4.3 million to $1 down from 52,000 marks to $1 in

May.[72] Grabski's monetary reforms had simply collapsed. Witos's own party split over a land reform bill, with some fearing Witos was too willing to make concessions. The Witos government lost its parliamentary majority as strikes and dramatic hyperinflation weakened his popularity. On December 14, 1923, Witos tendered its resignation. On December 19 Władysław Grabski was named the new prime minister. A former treasury secretary, he headed a government that was nonpartisan. This government ruled until November 1925, making it the longest-serving cabinet in this period. Given the dramatic fluctuation in the country's currency, the Grabski government attempted to reform the country's financial system; in April 1924 it created a new central bank, Bank Polski.

For Pilsudski 1924 was a year of both political retreat and extraordinary productivity. First and foremost was his writing. He published the two key works at this time—his history of the 1863 uprising and his study of the 1920 Polish-Soviet War. The historian Andrzej Garlicki points out that the year 1924 was also the time when work was done on perpetuating Pilsudski's legacy. This began with the decision of the Legionnaire's Association to celebrate Pilsudski's name day, May 19, nationally, which would be repeated in subsequent years. "I am relaxing these days for the first time in years," Pilsudski said in 1924 to a visitor in Sulejówek. "I am taking a break from the state, from politics. I breathe clean air." He continued, "I admire nature on this small patch of garden given to me, I enjoy my farm. And although I have to work for myself and my children, I don't feel tired and it seems extremely easy to me."[73]

On January 20, 1924, Pilsudski gave a series of lectures on the topic of 1863. As we have seen, he had already spoken publicly on this subject in 1912; those lectures were later published in 1929. The lectures, given in 1924 and covering the main aspects and significance of the uprising, were published in the same year in a fifty-two-page booklet. Pilsudski somewhat personalizes the story in his discussion of the rise of the Central National Committee in 1862. One of its members, Bronisław Szwarce, whom Pilsudski met in Siberian exile, became an important mentor and personal inspiration.

Pilsudski also emphasized the enormous symbolism the National Government of 1863 occupied in Polish collective memory. As in his earlier studies, Pilsudski emphasized that the insurrectionary spirit extended beyond the Polish community to the Jews. This was a source of pride for Pilsudski, who

emphasized the significance of Jewish participation in the 1863 Polish uprising. "Let me choose from these memories [of the uprising] perhaps the
most original, seemingly incredible, and testifying to . . . the strong power of
the National Government. I am referring to the large-scale participation of
Jews in the uprising." He concludes his lecture with the question, "And when
I raise the question, 'Greatness, by what name shall I call you?,' I get the reply:
'The greatness of our nation lies in the epoch of 1863.'"[74]

Pilsudski's best-known work, however, was his history of the 1920 Polish-
Soviet War. It would remain his longest publication, appearing in 1924 as a
225-page study. The impetus for the work was General Tukhachevsky's lectures of February 1923. Tukhachevsky argued that the essential cause of the
Red Army's failure was not Pilsudski's counteroffensive plan but instead the
inadequate training of commanding officers for their duties and the lack of
technical materials—circumstances the inexperienced officers were unable to
overcome. Tukhachevsky issued a warning to Europe with the statement
that if the Red Army had taken Warsaw, the revolutionary movement "would
not have stopped at the frontiers of Poland. It would have reached across the
whole of Western Europe."[75]

Pilsudski begins his study with the statement that he felt compelled to
respond to Tukhachevsky's lectures. He then methodically discusses war
strategy and battle plans, including the extraordinarily precarious situation
he found himself in, and the painful need to derive a plan to save Warsaw from
capture. He discussed the strategic calculation he considered as well. There
is no shortage of self-praise. "I attempted . . . to win victory for the troops
under my command and for the country which I was defending," he wrote.
He continued:

> I will content myself with the statement that throughout this two-years'
> war I gained victory after victory. On each occasion in which I took the
> direction of events into my hands, I gained victories which were mo-
> mentous in the history of the war. They were always strategically victo-
> ries and did not derive merely from the utilization of a tactical superi-
> ority. I compelled the enemy to change his strategic dispositions and to
> seek some means of reorganizing his war machine, since as a result of
> my victory, his former preparations had been rendered null and void in
> the actual smoke of battle.[76]

The main takeaway for Pilsudski was his belief in the central significance of the 1920 Polish victory for Europe and the world: "I will say only that it all but affected the destinies of the entire civilized world."[77]

In lecturing and publishing on the 1920 Polish-Soviet War, Pilsudski was continuing a pattern of writing on military history. This was, though, his first military history about a battle he himself took part in. The year 1924 also saw him pen more lectures and also prefaces, as one contemporary recalled.[78] One preface he wrote was for a work by Colonel Tadeusz Kutrzeba on the importance of the commander in chief as a position independent of the minister of war and chief of the general staff. During times of war, Pilsudski wrote, the chief commander would join the government, and he included an extraordinary analysis of chief commanders ranging from Napoleon to those in World War I. For Pilsudski, the experience of war shapes a people. "War," he wrote, "is always an extraordinary harness of human strength, energy and nerves, and it is not surprising that the various feelings and work of the soul are manifested more strongly and vividly in these eras [of war]."[79]

Among the speeches Pilsudski gave in 1924, one stands out for what it reveals about his self-image. In "Democracy and the Army," Pilsudski acknowledged the tension between the open, democratic society that guarantees civil rights versus the principle of honor and obedience in the army. "Honor," he wrote, "is the God of the army which brings with it obedience. Its power is so striking that it can bring about death." He concluded the essay by saying that he spent his whole life with fighters for freedom while at the same time leading a military formation. "We balance love for power and might with love of freedom. To date, I have not settled the matter," he wrote, adding that "honor is a mighty force." He also commented on his own understanding of why he had been given so much authority by so many officials: "God has instilled in me the elements of power and authority of command that can bring forth obedience. He gave me in embryo form, in feeling, a love for power and might."[80]

Pilsudski was very keen to mark historic anniversaries. One with profound personal significance was the tenth anniversary of the founding of the Polish Legions. To mark the occasion, Pilsudski published a thirty-one-page anniversary essay on August 10, 1924. He reminded readers that on the eve of 1914, the Polish population as a whole had no interest in war. For it was not the generation, he stated, that admired Adam Mickiewicz's call for national rebirth. That is why the rise of the Polish Legions, providing an alternative model, was so important in spreading national pride. The Legions gave Poles new vision and new possibilities.[81] From Chicago, the consul general of Poland sent Pilsudski a letter with a check for $15, funds raised by the Anniversary Celebration Committee to mark the Legions' anniversary.[82] The committee put out a leaflet for the occasion, honoring Pilsudski's order in August 1914 to cross the border from Austria into the Russian-held Kingdom of Poland. "Measuring the strength of his intentions, Pilsudski once again took up armed struggle that had brought down our grandfathers and fathers in 1794, 1831, 1863. . . . Let's honor Jozef Pilsudski. Let's Honor the Polish Soldier! Long Live Poland!"[83]

The year 1924 was a time of relative calm and stability. Prime Minister Grabski's government ruled uninterruptedly, making this the only year in the period of liberal parliamentary democracy from 1919 to 1926 that passed without a change in government. But instability and uncertainly returned in 1925 and the first half of 1926 when new developments in international affairs, combined with hyperinflation, gravely underscored Poland's vulnerabilities once again. The deteriorating situation was signaled by the rise of a stronger and more assertive Germany. In the summer of 1925 a German-Polish tariff war—in which Germany raised the tariff on Polish coal imports—led to a decline in the value of the Polish złoty, hurting the economy badly due to its dependence on the German market. In international affairs, meanwhile, Poland was blindsided by the Treaty of Locarno, an agreement perceived to have seriously undermined Polish security. It included a German treaty with France and Belgium guaranteeing their respective frontiers unconditionally, but Germany refused to recognize its frontiers with Poland and Czechoslovakia. German foreign minister Gustav Stresemann was clear about his country's three great foreign policy goals: "the readjustment of our eastern frontiers; the recovery of Danzig, the Polish corridor; and a correction of the frontier in Upper Silesia."[84]

That the agreement allowed Germany's eastern border to remain unresolved alarmed the Czechoslovaks and Poles, Pilsudski in particular. France tried to reassure Poland by signing on October 18, 1925, a Franco-Polish Treaty guaranteeing military aid in the event of a conflict with Germany. But the Franco-Polish agreement could not seriously alter the reality of Locarno.[85] Poland's Foreign Minister Alexander Skrzyński, upon returning from Locarno, told the French ambassador in Warsaw that Locarno was "a dagger thrust in the back of the alliance between our two countries."[86] It left Poles and Czechoslovaks with a sense that the Western Allies now believed the Polish-German and German-Czechoslovak borders were up for negotiation. For Pilsudski, Locarno represented Poland's misguided foreign policy in the period since his retirement in 1923. "Every decent Pole," Pilsudski is said to have remarked, "spits when he hears the word [Locarno]."[87] This was further evidenced with the Treaty of Berlin between Soviet Russia and Germany, signed on April 24, 1926, in which the two countries pledged neutrality in the event that one of them attacked a third party. Alarmed by the German-Soviet agreement, Pilsudski grasped immediately the danger it presented. "Our army," he said, "is very badly armed and poorly clad. We have lost time because of the [political] crisis, and the Germans since Locarno have made their second approach to the Russians since Rapallo. . . . Already the pincers are beginning to squeeze."[88]

Prior to the German-Soviet agreement, Poland had been hit with more political instability. In November 1925 the Polish economy experienced a currency exchange crisis brought on in part by the German-Polish tariff war. The złoty, already in decline, slipped further in value. Prime Minister Grabski asked the Bank Polski to intervene but it refused. On November 14, 1925, Grabski tendered his resignation. The crisis brought Pilsudski out of isolation. On the day of Grabski's resignation, Pilsudski left for Warsaw, where he met with President Wojciechowski to deliver a note demanding that neither Sikorski nor Szeptycki be named minister of war in the new cabinet.[89] The note was leaked to the press and splashed over the front page of the daily papers the following day. The news that Pilsudski felt compelled to tell the country's president whom he should and should not appoint as minister of war was taken as an indication that he had decided to reinsert himself back into government affairs. A high-ranking Soviet diplomat wrote that no name had surfaced for minister of war but that Pilsudski's followers fully expected his name to be at the top of that list.[90]

After returning to Sulejówek, Pilsudski woke on November 15, 1925, to the news that a crowd of soldiers and generals were gathering outside his home to demand proper oversight of the armed forces. The Soviet diplomat in Warsaw, Pyotr Voykov, estimated a crowd of twenty generals and approximately one thousand officers. There was no mistaking, the Soviet officer remarked, the importance of Pilsudski's influence.[91] General Dreszer-Orlicz appealed to Pilsudski to restore order and return to his command position. The general reminded Pilsudski that upon returning from Magdeburg on November 10, 1918, "you restored to us Poland's long forgotten glory; you crowned our banners with victory. Today, we are once again in the midst of doubts and troubles. We ask you not to leave us in this crisis, for you will desert not only us, your loyal soldiers, but Poland."[92]

It became clear that any choice for minister of war that did not meet with Pilsudski's explicit approval would lack legitimacy. On November 20, 1925, the country's foreign minister, Alexander Skrzyński, was asked to form a new government. Skrzyński retained his current post of foreign minister while also serving as prime minister. His unity cabinet represented the main political parties, giving posts to members of the National Democrats, Christian Democrats, PSL-Piast, National Labor, and the Polish Socialist Party. But it turned out to be a particularly ineffective cabinet, composed of parties with vastly contrasting fiscal and economic policies in a time of financial crisis.

On November 30, 1925, Prime Minister Skrzyński named a longtime Pilsudskiite to the post of minister of war, General Lucjan Żeligowski. It was a choice that the prime minister knew was acceptable to Pilsudski and his supporters. And it was not only the demonstration that influenced the decision. Pressure on the government to place Pilsudski (or Pilsudskiite candidates) in control of the armed forces came from places like the leftist PSL-Liberation (Peasant Party). The PSL-Liberation Party in fact came out publicly, arguing that the country needed a strong military commander: "That commander," the PSL-Liberation stated, "is Jozef Pilsudski, the man who built Poland and defended the country against her enemies."[93]

In setting up a cabinet, meanwhile, the National Democrats insisted on assigning one of their own to the post of finance minister. The prime minister conceded, appointing Jerzy Zdziechowski, who assumed the position at the very moment of another currency crisis. Between November 20 and mid-December 1925, the value of the Polish złoty fell from 6.5 to 10.5 per $1. The złoty then began a downward spiral in March and April 1926, when it fell further to 17.5 per $1. As panic set in and deposits were withdrawn, many banks went bust. One result was a frightening rise in the unemployment rate, increasing to one-third of industrial workers by April 1926.[94] Finance

Minister Zdziechowski's actions exacerbated the social unrest. He reduced pensions by 35 percent and laid off twenty-five thousand railroad employees. He then cut compensation payments to the sick and the disabled, all the time raising taxes to replenish shrinking government revenues. The policy of draconian deflation became wildly unpopular.

When, at the beginning of 1926, Max Muller of the British Legation in Poland returned to Warsaw, he sensed tension in the air. "Since my return to Warsaw a fortnight ago," he wrote on January 20, 1926, "the air has been full of rumors concerning Marshal Pilsudski's political activities." Muller was of the opinion that whatever choice Pilsudski made, "he would never be a party to any revolutionary act against the interest of the state."[95] It was an extraordinary vote of confidence. At the time of Muller's comments, prices were rising at an alarming rate on basic goods such as gas, electricity, salt, and alcohol precisely at a time when the national currency was losing value. When the finance minister announced on April 20, 1926, that the salaries of state employees were to be lowered until the start of 1927, the socialist members of the cabinet resigned in protest. The cabinet crisis led Prime Minister Skrzyński to resign on May 5, 1926.[96]

Coup d'État

After days of scrambling to reconstitute the government, President Wojciechowski made the fateful decision of asking Wincenty Witos to form a new government. On May 10, 1926, Witos announced a center-right cabinet with deputies from the National Democrats, the Christian Democrats, the Christian National Party, the National Workers' Party, and the PSL-Piast.[97] Pilsudski regarded the new center-right cabinet under Witos as an extreme provocation, due in particular to the choice of General Juliusz Malczewski, a sworn opponent of the marshal, for the post of minister of war.

There followed a sharp, public critique of the new Witos cabinet. In a bombshell interview appearing in the morning edition of a Warsaw daily on May 11, 1926, the day Witos was to be sworn in, Pilsudski publicly attacked the new government in biting language. "I knew in advance that with such a Government there would be internal corruption and the misuse of governmental authority in every direction for party and private advantage," Pilsudski said. He further claimed that under the previous Witos cabinet, he had been surrounded by paid spies in Sulejówek. He concluded that he doubted anyone in the army would be willing to die for this government.[98] Witos took the extraordinary step of ordering the confiscation of the paper but was unable to prevent some copies from circulating clandestinely.

On the following morning, May 12, 1926, Pilsudski set out from Sulejówek at 9:30 a.m. for the army camp at Rembertów, where troops loyal to him were stationed. By 2:30 p.m. Pilsudski and his men reached the bridgehead in Praga to central Warsaw. They crossed the bridge, meeting no resistance. Pilsudski later explained that he believed a show of force would achieve his goal and that he never thought there would be violence of any kind. Critics of Pilsudski are not so sure.[99] When he approached government officials on the other side of the bridge, including Poland's president, Pilsudski demanded the formation of a new government. But President Wojciechowski stood his ground and unexpectedly refused. For Pilsudski, earlier in May, had given his word to the president that he was not planning a coup. The president had even assured Skrzyński that Pilsudski had given him his word.[100] Pilsudski now had to decide whether to submit or to use force. He chose the latter.

For the next two days, troops loyal to Pilsudski fought pitched battles with troops loyal to the government. During the battles, Pilsudski's approximately two thousand fighters and three artillery battalions faced a totally unprepared government force of some seven hundred soldiers.[101] The major turning point was the declaration of the PPS on May 14 in support of Pilsudski, calling for a general strike. The Railway Workers' Union joined, bringing transportation to a screeching halt and preventing pro-government forces from reaching Warsaw.[102] When Pilsudski's forces took the Belvedere Palace on May 14, 1926, Prime Minister Witos and President Wojciechowski resigned at 7 p.m. On principle, Wojciechowski refused to continue serving. Blood had been spilled on the streets of Warsaw in a three-day civil war. Casualties were high, with the deaths of 215 fighters (25 officers and 173 soldiers) and 164 civilians, while more than nine hundred were wounded.[103]

Pilsudski's wife, Alexandra, had stayed in Sulejówek with the children during the coup. She later called those two days and two nights "the most anxious days of my life." On the evening of May 14 or 15, she left Sulejówek to visit Pilsudski. What she saw gravely concerned her: "I was appalled at the changes in him. In three days he had aged ten years. The flesh seemed to have fallen from him; his face was parchment white and the skin had taken on a

Pilsudski entering Warsaw with his military entourage on the day of his coup,
May 12, 1926.

strange transparency, almost as though it was lighted from within. His eyes were hollow with fatigue. Only on one other occasion did I ever see him look so ill, and that was within a few hours of his death."

In Alexandra's view, the coup changed Pilsudski forever. "Those three days of civil war left a mark on him for the rest of his life. He was never so calm as before, never so completely master of himself. Thereafter, he carried always a burden."[104] The American specialist on the 1926 coup, the late Joseph Rothschild, observed, "That he, the restorer of the Polish state, the father of its army, the protagonist of a strong presidency, should lead a revolt against the state authorities, sunder the unity of the army, and overthrow a constitutional presidency—for Wojciechowski refused to legitimate the coup by remaining in office—were facts that would haunt Pilsudski for the remaining nine years of his life."[105]

The coup shook the country to its core. In the most undemocratic of ways, Pilsudski removed the government by force. The question now was whether Pilsudski would assume the role of dictator. But he chose a different route, forming a ruling government and restoring a de facto balance of power in the parliament. For the time being, Pilsudski asked Sejm speaker Maciej Rataj to serve as acting president.[106] Rataj appointed Kazimierz Bartel, a self-educated locksmith who became a mathematics professor at Lwów Polytechnic, to form a government. Pilsudski was named minister of war with a cabinet of four nonparty specialists and five senior civil servants. Bartel's cabinet had no political orientation and lasted only from May to September 30, 1926. Poland was now under Pilsudski's thumb.

CHAPTER 16

The Path to Authoritarian Rule

Our aim is the total and final liquidation of the dictatorship of
Jozef Pilsudski.

—CENTROLEW (CENTER-LEFT COALITION), SEPTEMBER 11, 1930

Pilsudski's coup d'état of May 1926 hit the country hard. Not only did Poland's resurgent leader remove the legally constituted government by force, but the population witnessed two Polish armed forces battling one another for three days in the nation's capital. Casualties were high, causing fear and uncertainty throughout the country. Just as when he was handed absolute power in November 1918, Pilsudski chose in May 1926 not to impose a dictatorship. Instead, he sought to reform the country's parliamentary system to allow for a strong executive branch, a more compliant Sejm, and a stable cabinet that could serve for extended periods of time, would be loyal to him, and could actually get things done.

In the immediate aftermath of the coup, Pilsudski put in place a respectable cabinet, announcing a date of May 31, 1926, for presidential elections. The socialists demanded the dissolution of the Sejm and new parliamentary elections. Pilsudski rejected this idea, precisely to prevent the resurgence of the Left.[1] This, ironically, found favor with the rightist deputies. The cabinet under Prime Minister Kazimierz Bartel functioned smoothly at first. There could have been no other post for Pilsudski than minister of war, an office he would occupy until his death in 1935.

The reaction of foreign diplomats and the international press provides a window into how the coup was seen abroad. On May 21, 1926, an official in the British Foreign Office based in Warsaw commented on a conversation he had just had with a prominent Polish socialist. According to the unnamed figure, the vast majority of the citizenry supported Pilsudski's actions. "He said," the diplomat reported, "that however regrettable the methods employed for upsetting the existing administration might have been, it was generally considered in Poland that the time had come to put an end to the constant changes of government. . . . At least 80% of the country welcomed Pilsudski's main effort to bring some sort of order into administrative conditions at home, particularly with regard to finances."[2]

Meanwhile, Pilsudski issued his first Order of the Day to soldiers as minister of war. Appearing on May 22, 1926, it got the attention of the foreign press and was translated in full in the *New York Times* on June 30. "Soldiers!" he wrote, "I am once again at the helm as Your Commander. You know me. Without regard for my own welfare, I have always stood among you in your worst hardships. You know me and if not all of you favor me, each of you must respect me as the one who led you to many victories."[3] In an interview with a French newspaper appearing on May 25, Pilsudski was asked to discuss his foreign policy agenda. "Our country, exhausted by war, touched by internal upheaval, necessarily needs peace," Pilsudski said. "We do not desire any more territory, for we want to live in—and strengthen—peace. If someone were to attack us, we know how to defend ourselves. That is part of my nature," he said, "and that is also the nature of the Polish people."[4]

Pilsudski also commented in the same interview on the challenges of ruling diverse lands with different legal and administrative traditions. "We live in legislative chaos," he said. "Our state inherited the laws and regulations of three countries. New laws and regulations were then imposed on these." He then discussed desirable models of governments for Poland. "This must be simplified by giving power to the President. We are not speaking here of imitating the United States per se, where the states are given wide autonomy [and the president wide power]. There, a main feature is that the central authorities have wide powers and that the president is a significant figure."[5]

The French reporter expressed concern about the degree of power Pilsudski now enjoyed in the aftermath of the coup. Pilsudski reassured the French with the following reply: "No! I am not in favor of dictatorship in Poland," he said. "I imagine the head of state differently: he must have the right to take decisions quickly in matters relating to the national interest. Parliamentary harassment will only delay the most indispensable solutions." He then alluded to the day he was named head of state on November 14, 1918. "When I returned from Magdeburg nearing the war's end," he remarked, "I had in my hands absolute power. I could have abused it, but I realized that Poland should be cautious. It is young and poor. We must avoid risky experiments."[6] In an Order of the Day dated May 22, 1926, Pilsudski remarked that the most important thing was "morality in public life" after the "demoralization" of society during the partitions and war.[7] Asked about the coup one week later, he replied, "I will not enter into a discussion about the May events. I decided in accord with my conscience, and I don't see any need to have to explain it."[8] Henceforth, the Pilsudski ruling camp was to be called Sanacja, literally "healing," reflecting Pilsudski's program of ridding the political system of the negative features that existed before the coup.

Across the Atlantic, *Time* magazine published several articles on the events in Poland. In its first piece after the coup, the American weekly portrayed Pilsudski rather positively, noting that Prime Minister Witos had chosen for his minister of war "Pilsudski's avowed enemy, the Marquis of Malczewski." Another reason for the marshal's coup, the magazine maintained, was Pilsudski's concerns "that this Nationalist Cabinet would begin the old game of oppressing the Jews and racial minorities, whereas Pilsudski and the Socialists desired to weld the country into a compact unit." On June 7, 1926, Pilsudski appeared on the cover of *Time*, which featured an article characterizing Poland's leader as "a living yet piquantly legendary hero."[9]

The Sejm held presidential elections on May 31, 1926. The leftist parties nominated Pilsudski, and the rightist parties, led by the National Democrats, nominated Adolf Bniński. Pilsudski's negative views of the office had not changed since the adoption of the constitution in 1921. This time around, however, he allowed his name to be cast. He told a journalist that the president should be someone who could intermingle easily and make a good name for Poland abroad. He himself would prefer to be in a guidance and advisory role for the president.

When the votes were cast for president on May 31, 1926, Pilsudski, the clear favorite, got the support of the Left, a portion of the center parties, and the national minorities.[10] The final vote—cast jointly by the Sejm and Senate—was 292 for Pilsudski (60.2 percent) versus 193 for Bniński (39.8 percent). In a move that caught many by surprise, Pilsudski respectfully declined the position, saying he would not serve as president until amendments were made to the constitution restoring an appropriate balance of power between the branches of government. Nonetheless, the significance of his decisive victory could not be overstated. Both houses of the country's parliament gave Pilsudski a resounding stamp of approval. With its vote, he reasoned, the parliament had in effect legalized the coup. That is all he wanted. The presidency should go to someone else.

In the wake of Pilsudski's decision, disappointing to many who voted for him, a second round of elections took place. Pilsudski nominated longtime acquaintance and former socialist comrade Ignacy Mościcki, then a professor of chemistry with no party affiliation. Mościcki ran against the same conservative candidate as did Pilsudski, as well as a third candidate from the PPS. The national assembly cast its votes on June 1, 1926, resulting in a win for Mościcki. It was a clear victory for Pilsudski's camp with support from the same parties that had favored Pilsudski, including the Jewish and German minority deputies.[11] In a piece meant to introduce Mościcki to the general public, Pilsudski praised the new president. In the pages of the pro-government *Kurier Poranny* (Morning Courier) the day after the elections, he recounted his long friendship with the new president, going back to his early days in London. He praised the professor's intellect and measured judgments. "The president is independent-minded," Pilsudski wrote. "His is a mind that can never be shoved into the framework of doctrines."[12]

In the immediate post-coup era, many open letters criticizing Pilsudski circulated. Dated May 29, 1926, "An Open Letter to Jozef Pilsudski" asked, "You, former Brigades commander, are Your hands clean? Well, not so in some cases, but very filthy in others. They are dirty with the traces of fraternal blood that were just spilled on the streets of Warsaw." This blood will leave a permanent stain on Pilsudski's legacy, it continued; "none of it will wash away." Another open letter, by a former adjutant in the Belvedere Palace, "A Former Pilsudskiite to Marshal Pilsudski," criticized Pilsudski for taking the law into his own hands.[13]

There were also many publications, for and against the new regime at this time. One such brochure printed in the immediate aftermath of the 1926 coup attacked Pilsudski and his circle of supporters. Members of the communist party likewise vilified Pilsudski after the coup, referring to him as a "fascist dictator."[14] In contrast, his avid supporters put out numerous writings praising their leader. One of the best-known promoters of the new regime was Antoni Anusz. As a member of the Sejm in 1927, he published a propaganda brochure, *First Marshal of Poland, Jozef Pilsudski: Builder and Resurrector of the Polish State,* reminding readers of Pilsudski's central role in the restoration of independence. The brochure maintained that Pilsudski seized power in 1926 to restore much-needed order and stability to the country, wresting control from "wrongdoers" who "subordinated party interests to the interests of the country as a whole."[15]

The process of forming a new government and the selection of a new president was a critical step providing a sense of stability in the aftermath of the coup. Pilsudski did not introduce a new political or economic program nor did he speak of a new political system. He spoke of the new government's intention to "cleanse" the system of corruption. It was at this time that Pilsudski took up the issue of constitutional reform. "The constitution was drafted," Pilsudski told his trusted advisor, Kazimierz Świtalski in May 1926, "with dislike for me." But he stressed that he was not a foe of parliamentary government. "I do not want to be Mussolini nor do I want to go around with a whip. . . . ," he said. "I don't think there would be enough time to rewrite the entire constitution. There would be a flood of words in such a debate in the Sejm and this would extend the proposed bill immeasurably." Rather than craft a new document, Pilsudski worked with the cabinet on a bill to amend the existing constitution. Constitutional reform "requires thought," Pilsudski told Baranowski in June 1926. "It is not about the written Constitution, but good morals."[16]

The bill to amend the constitution came before the Sejm on August 2, 1926, passing overwhelmingly by a vote of 246 in favor and 95 opposed.[17] It ironically got the backing of the rightist parties, who feared that new parliamentary elections (something the Left was demanding) would go badly for them. The amendment reconfigured the balance of power between the executive and legislative branches of government, strengthening the office of the president in significant ways. The president could dissolve the Sejm and rule by decree with the force of law until a new Sejm convened, at which time the decrees had to get the Sejm's approval.[18] The government could not spend money exceeding the scale of the previous year's budget if the Sejm failed to pass a new budget. Prior to the vote, the foreign press had speculated that Pilsudski would create a strong presidency and a very weak parliament, "especially in the face of a dictator who is likely to come back with a demand for an even greater reduction in the functions of the National Assembly." More foreign papers began referring to Pilsudski as a dictator. "The dictatorial forces have demonstrated that Marshal Pilsudski's policies must be obeyed," the *New York Times* stated on June 24, 1926.

The constitutional bill also allowed President Mościcki to create an Inspector General of the Armed Forces. Soon after, he nominated Pilsudski for the job, who now served in two capacities as minister of war and inspector general of the armed forces. When Pilsudski was asked about the constitutional amendments on August 26, 1926, he replied, "Perhaps the American example is the direction we are going towards with our constitution."[19]

Political Realignment

Although Pilsudski gained power in 1926 through support of the Left, he subsequently decided he could only stabilize the state with the support of conservatives. So he reached out to a certain group of landowning aristocrats from the eastern borderlands. One of his goals was to draw them away from the National Democrats. On October 2, 1926, Pilsudski became prime minister after a budget crisis led Kazimierz Bartel to resign. Pilsudski chose former prime minister Jędrzej Moraczewski of the PPS for the post of public works minister. He then nominated two center-left members of his camp, Kazimierz Młodzianowski as interior minister and Antoni Sujkowski as minister of religion and public education.[20] The foreign ministry went to the very capable August Zaleski, a career diplomat and graduate of the London School of Economics who had formerly held posts in Switzerland, Greece, and Italy. He had also represented Pilsudski's government in the Polish consulate in Berne in 1918–1919, and had been an envoy to the League of Nations.

The appointment of two conservatives had the effect of weakening the influence of the National Democrats by shifting some conservative support to Pilsudski. The presence of Moraczewski in a conservative cabinet raised eyebrows in socialist circles. Uncomfortable with a party member serving in a conservative cabinet, the PPS issued a statement that Moraczewki represented only himself, not the party. In fact, the PPS suspended Moraczewski from the party a few weeks later and subsequently expelled him altogether.

The allocation of key cabinet posts to conservatives signaled a new phase for Piłsudski. The wish to cultivate ties with the conservatives culminated in his visit, on October 25, 1926, to the Radziwiłł Castle in Nieśwież, east of Warsaw near the Polish-Soviet border. At the luncheon held in Piłsudski's honor, Jerzy Potocki described the atmosphere. He Piłsudski appeared genuinely happy to be present, and "the entire time," Potocki wrote, "the Marshal was in good humor." Piłsudski toasted the Radziwiłł family, "in hopes they remain as eternal as the old walls of Nieśwież."[21] The visit led to an alliance with the conservative group that included such individuals as Artur Potocki, Eustachy Sapieha, Albrecht Radziwiłł, and Janusz Radziwiłł, its leader. The Polish Socialist Party (PPS) reacted with mounting criticism of the new government. In a move that marked the Left's increasing disenchantment with Piłsudski, the PPS leadership on November 10, 1926 put out a statement opposing the "monarchist and reactionary elements" in the new cabinet.[22]

In a reprieve from the sharply divisive political climate, Piłsudski marked the eighth anniversary of independence on November 11, 1926, with a homespun radio address about children. "Sitting next to me are two girls, beautiful girls, and they are asking me to play games with them," he said. "And the autumn sunshine will warm up, the wind will be gentle in the face and then we will find rebirth from the soul together with a happy smile from living with a great and reborn soul."[23]

Piłsudski subsequently made time to address his soldiers and the Legionnaires. To mark the anniversary of August 6, 1914, when Piłsudski's army crossed the border from Austria to Russia, he spoke not only about the events of August 1914 but also about the moment he returned from Magdeburg on November 10, 1918. "At that time, I began to work on building the Polish State, serving as its chief. It is hard to describe the wild chaos I stumbled upon after my release from Magdeburg: crazy chaos of the courts, of the political groupings; altogether a brainteaser nearly impossible to solve," he said. "These discrepancies were so great, so enormous, that I consider it a kind of miracle that I was able to lead you out of this chaos into a different path."[24]

Another address on a subject dear to Piłsudski's heart took place on June 27, 1927, surrounding the return of Juliusz Słowacki's remains to Poland seventy-eight years after the exiled poet died in Paris. On Piłsudski's initiative, Słowacki's remains were brought from Paris to the crypt at Kraków's Wawel

Castle alongside Polish royalty. In was an extraordinarily symbolic moment when the remains of one of Poland's three nineteenth-century bards whose verses Pilsudski cherished was being laid to rest in a sovereign Poland. In one of his most famous speeches, Pilsudski declared Słowacki "an equal of the kings." In words layered with meaning, he remarked that "there are people and their works so strong and powerful that the impenetrable gates of death do not exist, that they live on and are present among us." Słowacki, Pilsudski concluded, "bears witness to the Polish soul."[25] Foreign journalists noted the symbolism of the event, filing articles that appeared in *Le Temps* of Paris, the *New York Times,* and the *Scotsman*, among others.

The year 1927 also witnessed the second celebration of Independence Day (November 11) as a national holiday. The ritual now involved a military parade ending at Pilsudski's official residence, speeches, and patriotic music. The commemorations were meant to inculcate the citizenry with patriotic zeal and to inscribe this historic day in collective memory. The fact that Pilsudski was at the center of the ceremony was a reflection of his increasing supremacy in national life.[26]

National Minorities after the Coup

Due to the fact that Pilsudski's government actively sought to improve relations with the national minorities, their attitude toward the regime change was generally positive. For it brought to power a leader and cabinet starkly more favorable toward minorities than the center-right government it had replaced. As with probably the majority of ethnic Poles, Pilsudski's personal popularity was high coupled with the widespread desire for an end to a fractious, unstable system of government and economic instability. The country's ethnic Germans, numbering approximately 740,000, welcomed the coup, chiefly because it led to the diminished influence of the National Democrats. German citizens of Poland were generally of the opinion that the coup would lead to more tolerant minority policies and an improvement in their situation.[27]

The same could be said of the Jewish minority, numbering 3.1 million, or 9.8 percent of the population, by 1931. At a plenary session of the Chief Zionist Council held on May 16, 1926, delegates voted overwhelmingly in support of Pilsudski.[28] Decisive support for Pilsudski could also be seen in declarations of the Jewish parliamentary members. The first session of the Jewish Parliamentary Club after the coup gave full backing to Pilsudski.[29] Yitzhak Gruenbaum, a Jewish member of parliament and a leader of the National Minorities Bloc, wrote on June 19, 1926, "From our point of view, the current government is, it seems to me, the best kind in comparison to all we've had thus far."[30] In his celebrated history of the Jewish problem in the Polish parliament between the two world wars, Szymon Rudnicki found that the vast majority of Jews welcomed the coup. "Some fully recognized that despite its anti-constitutional character, the coup stood to rescue Poland," Rudnicki commented. "For Jews, Pilsudski's coup meant the end of the extreme nationalist authorities of the hated nationalist camp for whom the struggle with the Jews was a staple part of their program."[31]

A prominent Jewish member of the Polish parliament, Apolinary Hartglas, spoke to one of Pilsudski's close advisors after the coup. Asked about the new government's policy toward the Jews, the advisor reportedly replied in the following: "Pilsudski is of the opinion that the equality of the Jews should exist not only on paper but in practice."[32] Hartglas himself was relieved that Pilsudski returned to power. The sheer chaos enveloping the country, Hartglas reasoned, required Pilsudski's return to power to restore order and stability. The vast majority of Polish Jews, Hartglas remarked in February 1928, shared the view that the collapse of the Pilsudski government would result in the establishment of a markedly anti-Jewish regime strongly influenced by the right-wing National Democrats.[33]

The collective relief felt by Polish Jewry following Pilsudski's return to power was likewise noted by Jewish organizations abroad. The American Jewish Congress, for example, went on record stating that Pilsudski's government, in contrast to previous administrations, had put a decisive end to a hostile atmosphere toward the Jews. "With the advent of Marshal Pilsudski," the American Jewish Congress stated in February 1927, "the attitude of the government has become more friendly."[34]

The feeling among the Jewish population that a more secure and favorable climate prevailed under the Pilsudski government was almost universally expressed. On May 24, nine days after the coup, the newly appointed interior minister, Kazimierz Młodzianowski, declared: "The Government intends to follow a sincere and open policy in what concerns the affairs and interests of the National Minorities."[35] In June, Leon Wasilewski—known for his tolerant views toward national minorities—was appointed head of the new Committee of Experts on the Eastern Provinces and the National Minorities. Government policy on national minorities was addressed in detail at an August 18, 1926, cabinet meeting, which issued a resolution renouncing national assimilation as a state policy toward minorities. "The political aim in relation to national minorities," the resolution stated, "is state assimilation (*asymilacja państwowa*) of the people. Such a goal can be achieved only by creating favorable living conditions for the people and thus linking them to the state." It continued, "State and national assimilation by means of coercion is impossible to achieve; the influence of Polish culture can only work in an atmosphere of harmonious relations [with the national minorities]."[36]

By rejecting the call for national assimilation in favor of "state assimilation," whereby loyalty to the state rather than polonization was demanded, the government signaled its aim to improve relations with the national minorities. Prime Minister Bartel, who explicitly promised equality for the Jews, reinforced the new emphasis on improving ties with the Jewish community and other national minorities.[37] Following the resolution on national minorities, the government took a series of steps to ameliorate the position of the Jews. Gustaw Dobrucki, the new minister of religious denominations and education, came out unambiguously in opposition to the *numerus clausus* on January 20, 1927, reissuing a 1925 circular forbidding its application in institutions of higher education. He reaffirmed this position in an address to Jewish members of the Sejm, saying, "the government of Marshal Pilsudski is absolutely against the *numerus clausus*."[38] Felicjan Sławoj Składkowski, who replaced Młodzianowski as interior minister on October 2, 1926, issued a decree on February 1, 1927, that henceforth the right to use Yiddish in public places was guaranteed.[39] Perhaps the most consequential decree was introduced in November 1927, when Pilsudski instructed Interior Minister Składkowski to resolve once and for all the issue of Jews who, due to the fact that they were born in lands that were at the time located in Soviet Russia, had been denied Polish citizenship. "Give them Polish passports," Pilsudski instructed Składkowski. "Poland cannot have within its borders second-class citizens who despise her."[40] With the stroke of a pen, Składkowski granted citizenship to approximately thirty-three thousand Jews who had immigrated to Poland from the east during the Russian Revolution and civil war.[41]

The grant of citizenship to Jewish refugees was one of a series of decrees issued in the first period of rule after the coup. Pilsudski's government also addressed several long-standing Jewish grievances. One of the factors that inspired confidence among the Jews was Pilsudski's choice of Kazimierz Bartel for prime minister. The Jewish community generally regarded Bartel as a friendly figure who had a good reputation in Jewish circles. "As a person, he has very liberal convictions and is devoid of anti-Semitism," Hartglas stated.[42] To the Jews, and also other minorities, Bartel was thus a reflection of Pilsudski's support for a more open and tolerant climate.

The German minority also saw Pilsudski's coming to power in a favorable light. Pilsudski conceded that the German masses had little or no feeling of loyalty to Poland. But he also believed that they had "demonstrated in the course of their history an ease of assimilation and possess an innate streak of loyalty toward the state. The utilization of this minority for the state, with the prospect of political assimilation, is possible and probable. The government should be just but powerful toward the Germans."[43] Pilsudski's position demonstrated an optimism that was a reflection of the peaceful international climate, spirited hopes, and economic prosperity of the second half of the 1920s.

As Pilsudski tried to improve relations with the national minorities, tensions were growing with Lithuania. The persistent conflict with its neighbor affected Poland's ties to its Lithuanian minority, a community of some eighty-three thousand by 1931. At the end of 1926 Pilsudski gave an interview in which his resentment against the Lithuanian government was palpable. For Lithuania was the only neighboring state that saw itself in a state of war with Poland. Pilsudski emphasized that Lithuanian relations with Poland were an exception in Europe because Lithuania did not recognize the frontiers between it and Poland despite the international accord signed in March 1923 by the Western Allied powers. Lithuania was, Pilsudski remarked, "our restless neighbor who so easily utters the word 'war' and with such difficulty mumbles the word 'peace.'"[44] In a meeting with the interior minister and Kazimierz Świtalski, among others, he vented his frustrations over Lithuania's inflexible position. "Pilsudski's aim," Świtalski wrote in his diary on December 18, 1926, "is to place diplomatic pressure on Lithuania; to force her to stop proclaiming that they are 'in a state of war' with Poland."[45]

Growing Conflict with Parliament

On the domestic front, meanwhile, Pilsudski's conflict with parliament dominated political life in the years 1928–1930. The first period of extreme acrimony—down to the summer of 1929—coincided with a time of economic growth and rising incomes, giving a boost to Pilsudski's ruling government. Industrial production rose by 20.8 percent in 1927, by 12.7 percent in 1928, and by 2.3 percent in 1929.[46] The onset of the Great Depression in the fall of 1929, however, gradually worsened the political crisis and led to even sharper critiques from the opposition.

In anticipation of the parliamentary elections to take place in March 1928, Pilsudski devised the idea of forming a nonpartisan, pro-government bloc consisting of various parties and individual deputies. This diverse body of deputies, he reasoned, would make it possible to gain a parliamentary majority and circumvent the extreme fragmentation and instability of the parliamentary system that had led to rapid changeovers of government. If successful, his new plan would also diminish the influence of the right-wing National Party and thus create a stable government. He entrusted the project to his longtime confidant, Walery Sławek, who created the Nonparty Bloc for the Support of the Government (*Bezpartyjny Blok Współpracy z Rządem*, BBWR). The BBWR was a heterogeneous group that had no unified program and was held together by two guiding principles: service to Poland and loyalty to Pilsudski. In the run-up to elections, a variety of groups campaigned, including high church officials who supported Pilsudski's bloc. Janusz Radziwiłł told Pilsudski that the majority of conservatives would likely back him as well. Meanwhile, the BBWR vigorously campaigned on the local level with the message that a vote for it was a vote for Pilsudski.[47]

The first parliamentary elections since the coup took place on March 4, 1928, with an extraordinary voter turnout of 78.3 percent. As a single bloc, the BBRW received the largest number of votes, gaining 27.6 percent of the seats against 8.6 percent for the Right, 10 percent for center parties, and 26.3 percent combined for leftist parties. The combined national minority parties got 21.3 percent of the seats.[48] The 1928 election clearly strengthened Pilsudski's position and significantly weakened his rivals. The combined center-right share of seats dropped from 57.9 percent in the 1922 parliamentary elections to just under 20 percent in 1928. The Left increased its support

Polish-Yiddish campaign poster urging Jews to vote for the Pilsudski bloc in the 1928 parliamentary elections. Stanisławów, November 1928.

from 22.1 percent in 1922 to 26.3 percent in 1928, with the combined national minorities share increasing from 20 percent to 21.6 percent.[49] The outcome was more favorable for Pilsudski in the Senate, where his pro-government bloc got 41.5 percent of the total vote.

Despite initial optimism that the BBWR and the noncommunist Left—who together totaled over half the Sejm delegates—could work together, things got off to a bad start. Pilsudski put forth Kazimierz Bartel as his candidate for speaker of the Sejm. Pilsudski appeared to expect the Sejm to merely accept his candidate without discussion as a goodwill gesture. This was unacceptable to many, and the PPS put forward its own candidate, Ignacy Daszyński, on March 23. "The choice of Daszyński will be regarded by the Commandant as a *casus belli* [extreme provocation]," Świtalski jotted down in his diary the following day.[50]

On March 27, 1928, the Sejm held elections for speaker, casting 260 votes for Daszyński and 141 for Bartel. The pro-government press expressed fury,

Political cartoon, "How the Right Sees the Government of Marshal Piłsudski," 1928, portraying Pilsudski as an Orthodox Jew enjoying challah and gefilte fish while reading a Yiddish newspaper by the light of a menorah.

calling the election of Daszyński a provocation. At the end of March, the newly elected Sejm opened its first session. Pilsudski addressed the assembly dressed in his blue marshal uniform with a saber on long raps.[51] When he began, three deputies of the Polish Communist Party interrupted the proceedings with shouts of "Down with the fascist government of Pilsudski!"[52] After the deputies refused to remain quiet and Speaker Dasznski had them removed from the chamber, Pilsudski resumed his speech. He noted that unlike at his first address to the Sejm in February 1919, when the state borders were still being decided on the battlefield, Poland's borders in 1928 were stable and internationally recognized. The linchpin of security, he concluded, was the special alliance with France and Romania.

Pilsudski turned his attention once more to constitutional reform. Though highly critical of Poland's parliamentary system, he was steadfast in defending democratic government in general. In meetings with government officials, he disavowed any support for one-party, totalitarian systems, citing the examples of Italy and Soviet Russia as types of government he wholly rejected. Pilsudski appeared to see the United States and Great Britain as the best models of stable government.[53] But many parliamentary systems suffered from inadequacies and inefficiencies, he believed.

Pilsudski's initiative for constitutional reform was delayed by a health scare that frightened the government and alarmed the country. On April 17, 1928, Pilsudski suffered an apoplectic attack, losing partial use of his right arm for a few days. The public was falsely informed that he had been hospitalized for a few days due to a pain in one of his hands. On May 2, 1928, news broke that on doctor's orders, sixty-year-old Pilsudski would take a break from government work while he recovered. Persistent feelings of frailness and weakness led Pilsudski to tender his resignation as prime minister on June 25, 1928. The acting deputy prime minister, Kazimierz Bartel, replaced him. The Bartel cabinet retained August Zaleski as foreign minister and Sławoj-Składkowski as interior minister, and added Kazimierz Świtalski as minister of education.[54] The Bartel cabinet served for ten months, bolstered by a period of economic growth.

Shortly before resigning, Pilsudski had expressed again his strong desire for constitutional reform, requesting that the BBWR leaders prepare a resolution for a vote in the fall.[55] Less than a week after stepping down as premier, Pilsudski was interviewed by a Warsaw daily about his resignation. Pilsudski sharply castigated the Sejm, causing a stir in parliamentary circles and driving deeper the wedge between him and the opposition. He complained bitterly that because the president had such limited authority, the burden of government fell entirely to the prime minister and that in reality the premier could do little without the agreement of the Sejm. Such agreements were painfully difficult to achieve, and therefore little got done. "The duties of the prime minister, as our constitution stipulates, fills me with inner disgust," Pilsudski said. Compounding this impotency, he continued, Sejm deputies had the right to scream and shout, to hurl insults and print slanderous stories. So he resigned because he could no longer endure this state of affairs. At the same time, the president was a mere figurehead under the constitution who "had not even the right to appoint his personal staff." What most exacerbated the tensions between Pilsudski and the Sejm was his pronouncement that what he really desired was to physically beat the deputies who exhibited traits he abhorred: "If I had not overcome my impulses, I would do nothing else than beat and kick the MPs without pause, because they have a method of work that precludes all efficiency and productivity."[56] He was being driven to madness, he said.

The fallout from the interview was immediate and swift. The PPS passed a protest resolution. The government, in a turn toward authoritarianism, warned the party not to publish the resolution. The PPS defiantly went ahead, printing its statement of protest in its newspaper *Robotnik* (The Worker). The government responded by confiscating the issue. In compliance with the government censor, the issue eventually came out on July 3, 1928, but with a blank space appearing at the top of the front page where the resolution was supposed to appear. With no explanation, the censors allowed the article title to remain, demonstrating to the reader precisely what content had been removed.[57] By censoring the press, the government had violated the constitutionally protected right to freedom of the press.

For the remainder of 1928 Pilsudski kept up a schedule of speeches and appearances. He reiterated his full confidence in Kazimierz Bartel. Education minister Świtalski noted in his diary on July 17, 1928, that Pilsudski "is of the opinion that Bartel is someone fully loyal. That is why the commandant is appealing to us not to spoil Bartel in his work." At the same meeting Pilsudski switched topics, weighing in on the subject of youth and education, speaking about the need to improve primary and secondary schools as well institutions of higher learning. He recommended an educational reform bill.[58]

On August 12, 1928, Pilsudski spoke in Vilna at a convention of Legionnaires. He alluded—as he often did in speeches—to the time he returned to Warsaw in November 1918. As he forged a new state in the nation's capital, he recalled, he longed all the time for the city he grew up in. Contemplating his own mortality, Pilsudski used the opportunity to announce that upon his demise he wanted his heart to lie in Rossa Cemetery in Vilna alongside his mother.[59] Soon after his stay in Vilna, Pilsudski embarked on a six-week vacation to Romania for rest and recuperation. Returning home on October 3, 1928, he seemed fit and healthy, and went back to work full-time the following day.

An important marker in the history of interwar Poland was the tenth anniversary of independence on November 11, 1928. The celebrations were on a higher scale than in the previous year. Military demonstrations marked the day, with Pilsudski and President Mościcki reviewing the estimated thirty-two thousand troops in Warsaw before approximately fifty thousand onlookers.[60] An American official in Warsaw described the peoples' reaction to Pilsudski: "One long remembered the endless line of men, women and children of all classes parading past Marshal Pilsudski as he stood in front of the reviewing stand receiving the spontaneous cheers of civilians, soldiers, and war-crippled veterans, an infinitely deserved tribute of love and devotion."[61]

The Polish-American scholar M. Biskupski points out that "Pilsudski was always featured in speeches and pronouncements, and his double role as the vanquisher of the Bolsheviks in 1920 and a hero of 1918 were common motifs."[62] Sejm speaker Ignacy Daszyński urged citizens to remember that the day Pilsudski returned to Poland on November 10, 1918, marked the birth of the republic. The Warsaw City Council announced that Saski Square in Warsaw was to be renamed Jozef Pilsudski Square.[63] Representing France at the celebrations was the second in command of the French Army's General Staff, Louis Maurin, who presented Pilsudski with a profoundly meaningful gift—a gilded saber that Napoleon had presented to his most courageous soldiers.[64]

While the Jews of Poland appeared in large numbers during the celebrations, the country's other minorities reacted quite differently to the Independence Day festivities. The German, Belarusian, and Ukrainian parliamentary clubs kept a distance, never officially recognizing the day or participating in any events. When the Polish parliament sat for a special session on November 11 to mark the anniversary, the German, Ukrainian, and Belarussian deputies were absent.[65] The Jewish Parliamentary Club, on the other hand, publicly urged the Jewish community to partake in the celebrations. And indeed, the Jewish community outwardly expressed its patriotism. An estimated ten thousand Jewish schoolchildren and university students marched to the grave of the Unknown Soldier in Warsaw to lay a wreath before marching to the Belvedere Palace. According to press reports, Pilsudski and Mościcki greeted them, warmly.[66]

Political Conflict Escalates

The year 1929 saw a distinct escalation of Pilsudski's conflict with the Sejm opposition. Frustration with Pilsudski had led the center-left parties to form a new organization to counterbalance the BBWR. In the autumn of 1928, three left and three center parties formed Centrolew, the Center-Left Coalition, consisting of deputies from the PPS, PSL-Liberation, PSL-Piast, the Peasant Party, the Christian Democrats, and the National Workers' Party. The conflict between Centrolew and Pilsudski deteriorated gradually, especially with the so-called Czechowicz Affair, when in February 1929, the Sejm voted to establish a special committee headed by socialist Herman Lieberman to investigate Treasury Secretary Gabriel Czechowicz, who was accused of spending considerably more than the previous year's budget allocated. The affair led Czechowicz to tender his resignation on March 8, 1929. But this was not enough for the opposition. On March 20, the Sejm passed a measure to bring Czechowicz before a state tribunal to investigate the matter.

The Sejm's actions outraged Pilsudski. In the pages of a pro-government daily on April 5, 1929, he reminded readers that this was the first time in the history of reborn Poland that a cabinet member was brought before the state tribunal. In a bitter and hostile tone, Pilsudski characterized some of the Sejm members in damning terms, charging them with purely partisan motives and conducting themselves like "apes." He repeated that as prime minister in 1928, he, not the accused, was responsible for the budget. Czerchowicz was merely carrying out instructions. If anyone was guilty of wrongdoing, therefore, it was himself. Czerchowicz's accusers, Pilsudski continued, were people "who cover themselves with their own excrement."[67] Needless to say, many were shocked by Pilsudski's choice of words and the razor-sharp tenor of his attacks.

Pilsudski told a close confidant that he regarded the state tribunal as an anachronistic remnant of the period of Sejm domination before the coup.[68] Meanwhile, as the opposition tried to block every government initiative, deadlock set in and Prime Minister Bartel resigned on April 14, 1929. The government that followed with Kazimierz Świtalski as prime minister became the first of Pilsudski's "colonels cabinets" headed by one of his close ex-legionary followers. In the new government, six of the fourteen cabinet members were high-ranking military officers. This group of close collaborators would henceforth remain more or less the same, consisting of such figures as Walery Sławek, Alexander Przystor, Józef Beck, Bolesław Wieniawa-Długoszowski, Kazimierz Świtalski, Bogusław Miedziński, and Janusz Jędrzejewicz.[69]

The state tribunal began its trial against Czechowicz on June 26, 1929. On the first day Pilsudski submitted a declaration in which he took full responsibility for the actions of the former treasury minister. "I cannot but say that in the trial of Czechowicz, I see the desire to falsify the historical record, make myself ashamed, and insult me." On the other hand, he had become accustomed to this kind of chicanery. "I confess," he wrote, "that I am proud of my work and find great merit in limiting the Sejm's excessive power." He continued with sharp words: "This is a trial of ritual murder committed on a man who is answering for an act he did not commit. I cannot restrain myself from saying that this system is vile and despicable."[70] In the end the trial was short-lived. Only four days after proceedings began, the state tribunal determined it was unable to deliberate further without a separate inquiry by the Sejm to assess motivation. In the end, the Sejm never undertook such an investigation and the Czechowicz affair ended. But the bitter taste it left persisted.

Sejm speaker Daszyński visited Pilsudski at the Belvedere Palace on June 24, 1929, in an attempt to achieve cooperation between the government and the Sejm. Despite his efforts, the pro-government and anti-government groupings dug in their heels and refused to budge.[71] Pilsudski, observing gridlock and an opposition determined to undermine the government, wrote a scathing piece on the emerging political crisis. In the pages of a pro-government paper, his disgust with the opposition was palpable, as he criticized its refusal to cooperate with the governing cabinet. With contemptuous references to Daszyński and the Sejm opposition, the tone of the article deeply offended many deputies.[72]

Pilsudski's sharp, public attack on the Sejm led to a new phase in the conflict. His indelicate words provoked the opposition to question the legitimacy of his authority and to demand both his and the president's removal from power. "The time is absolutely ripe," the Peasant Party's Parliamentary Club resolved on October 1, 1929, "for the immediate resignation of the whole of the present Cabinet and the liquidation of the entire Sanacja regime."[73] When the Peasant Party's newspaper printed the resolution, the government—characterizing it as incitement to violence—confiscated the issue.[74] The PPS expressed similar grave disappointment with their former founder and leader, Pilsudski. "The Pilsudski of 1905, of 1914, of 1918 or of 1920, belongs to history," the PPS newspaper stated on October 1, 1929. "The Pilsudski of 1926–1929 is the leader of the disappearing world of Old Poland, the Poland of the aristocratic societies," wrote Mieczysław Niedziałkowski, editor in chief of the party's newspaper and co-founder of Centrolew.[75]

The growing conflict between Pilsudski and the Sejm found dramatic expression on October 31, 1929. An ordinary session of the Sejm was to take place, but the speaker, Daszyński, was informed that Prime Minister Kazimierz Świtalski was under the weather and had sent Pilsudski to speak on his behalf. Pilsudski, who we recall served as minister of war, arrived expecting to address the Sejm. As news spread of Pilsudski's imminent arrival, army officers gathered in the main hall of the Sejm, an area open to the public. Alarmed by the unexpected development, Daszyński decided the presence of armed officers in support of Pilsudski—estimated at one hundred—was highly inappropriate and postponed the Sejm meeting.[76] Baffled by the decision, Pilsudski marched into the Sejm speaker's office rather irate and asked Daszyński what was going on. "I will not open the Legislative Chamber," Daszyński replied, "in the presence of bayonets, rifles and swords."[77] After some protest by Pilsudski, who said he could easily have instructed them to leave if asked, he left the building after expressing his distinct displeasure. The opposition did not take well to what they interpreted as an act of intimidation through a show of force.

It is telling that in the midst of the growing crisis in government, Pilsudski found time to compose a piece commemorating a historical event, the twenty-fifth anniversary of the Grzybowski Square demonstration in November 1904, when the Combat Organization of the PPS engaged in armed struggle with the Russian police for the first time. This event, Pilsudski wrote, "influenced the fate of Poland in a way much more significant than one had supposed at the time."[78]

The postponement of the Sejm led to more mayhem. The main socialist party was outraged, passing a resolution declaring that the postponement of the Sejm was a move to prevent the parliament's control over government policy. Demonstrations protesting the government's dealings with the Sejm spread to many cities. In Lwów, protesters reportedly chanted "Down with Pilsudski," while armed motorcades tried to disburse the crowds. There were also anti-government protests in Kraków and Łódź as well as in many other towns where protesters clashed with police.[79] When the Sejm reopened on December 5, 1929, PPS delegates initiated a vote of no confidence against the Świtalski cabinet, garnering 243 votes for and 119 against the motion. Forced to resign, Świtalski was replaced by Bartel. At a gathering of parliamentary clubs on December 17, the pro-government parliamentary bloc (BBWR) presented a plan for a new constitution, but Centrolew refused to be a part of any initiative on constitutional changes. On December 29, 1929, Bartel formed a new cabinet, retaining most of the ministers from the previous government.[80]

The confrontation between the government and the Sejm deteriorated even further. On February 2, 1930, the central committee of the PPS passed a resolution appearing on the front page of its paper. In words that could be interpreted as plans for a coup, the resolution called for "the liquidation of the hidden dictatorship in favor of democracy as the foundation of the Polish Republic."[81] The resolution accused Pilsudski of deliberately sharpening his rhetoric in a manner that could once again, as it did in 1926, lead to violence.

Barely a moment passed before another cabinet crisis arose. On March 15, 1930, Centrolew forced Bartel to resign. To the disappointment of the opposition, which did not want to see the return of a colonels cabinet, the post of prime minister went to Walery Sławek, Pilsudski's longtime collaborator and loyalist, who formed a new government on March 29, 1930. The Sejm, meanwhile, had been scheduled to convene on May 23 at the request of the Centrolew opposition, which had complained that parliament was being silenced. But on the opening day of the Sejm, President Mościcki declared a thirty-day postponement, ratcheting up the tension between the government and the parliamentary opposition. On May 28, 1930, the central committee of the PPS distributed an ominous circular to its regional branches, stating in part, "We are entering a new period of the political struggle which cannot be resolved by the Sejm."[82]

The obstruction of parliament continued unabated. When a special session of the Sejm met on June 20, President Mościcki postponed it for another thirty days. The willful suppression of the parliamentary right to convene brought the conflict to a breaking point. Centrolew convened a meeting of all its Sejm and Senate deputies, who issued a declaration of aims. The Polish president was sharply criticized for undermining the parliament. Centrolew demanded the resignation of "the government of the dictator, Jozef Pilsudski," and the restoration of parliamentary rule.[83]

With seemingly no other options, Centrolew embarked on a campaign of mass demonstrations. On June 29, 1930, it convened a massive convention in Kraków, attended by some fifteen hundred delegates, along with approximately thirty thousand supporters.[84] Representatives of Centrolew's six parties drafted a resolution that explicitly called for the overthrow of the government and the end of what they referred to as Pilsudski's dictatorship. "For the last four years," the resolution began, "Poland has been living under the power of the actual dictatorship of Jozef Pilsudski. The will of the dictator is carried out by changing governments. The president of the republic is likewise subordinated to Pilsudski's will." The resolution stated that leaders who came to power by extralegal means in 1922 could no longer legally remain in power, and that due to the dictatorial government, the huge opposition blocs in the Sejm had been deprived of a voice in domestic and foreign policy.[85]

The point that drew blood, so to speak, was the following: "We declare," the resolution stated, "that without the abolition of dictatorship, it is impossible to get the economic depression under control or to solve the great domestic problems which Poland must solve on behalf of her future." The organization bloc resolved:

> That the struggle for the abolition of Jozef Pilsudski's dictatorship has been undertaken jointly by all of us and will be continued jointly until victory; that only a government possessing the confidence of the Sejm and of the nation will meet with our determined support and the assistance of all our forces; that any attempt at a coup d'état will be met with most determined resistance; that in relation to the government in power by the coup the nation will be free from any duties, and the obligations of the illegal government towards foreign countries will not be recognized by the Republic. . . . We further declare that the President of the Republic, Ignacy Mościcki, unmindful of his oath, has openly taken his stand with the dictatorship [of Pilsudski] against the will of the country and . . . should resign.[86]

The resolution, read aloud, galvanized the participants. But to the government, it appeared as an open plot to overthrow it. Later that same day, June 29, a mass meeting was held at Kleparski Market. Party activists condemned the government for its obstruction of parliament. A leader of the PPS urged the crowd, "all to the front, all to the war of liberty against dictatorship!"[87] Wincenty Witos described a demonstration marching in the direction of the Adam Mickiewicz monument in Kraków's Main Market Square. Chants of "Pilsudski to the gallows!" and "Down with the puppet, President Mościcki," could be heard.[88] In response, the government ordered the confiscation of the resolution while successfully prohibiting its publication in the press. But copies had been provided to the foreign media beforehand. In its edition of June 30, 1930, the *New York Times* cited the resolution at length in a peace title, "20,000 Vote Protest on Pilsudski's Rule. Six Parties at Meeting in Cracow Call on President Moscicki to Resign."

The resolution was the opposition's furthest step yet in its bid to take power. Witos indicated that a number of Centrolew leaders believed that Mościcki would resign. Witos countered that nothing short of force would topple Pilsudski.[89] And indeed, far from intimidated, the government acted swiftly. On June 30, 1930, Prime Minister Sławek and Interior Minister Sławoj Składkowski visited Pilsudski at his country home, where Pilsudski instructed them to begin legal proceedings against the Centrolew leadership.[90] Upon their return to Warsaw, Sławek and Składkowski began preparing an indictment against thirty-three Centrolew leaders who had organized the Kraków convention. The former Sejm speaker, Maciej Rataj (himself a PSL-Piast member), announced that he was pleased the case was being brought before the court. Since the Sejm seemed to be permanently closed, he remarked, a trial "will become the platform from which we shall explain to the nation and to the world why we called this Cracow congress—as a protest against the suppression of our constitutional rights and the laws of the country."[91] But on July 11 the public prosecutor announced there was insufficient evidence to move forward.

The left-wing branch of Centrolew appeared as determined as ever to expose and challenge the suppression of parliamentary proceedings. The PPS newspaper *Robotnik* remarked that the peasants and workers had an unbroken will, a "desire to overthrow the hated dictatorship."[92] On August 22, 1930, Pilsudski informed the cabinet that he intended to dissolve the Sejm and arrest members of Centrolew. The following day, Prime Minister Sławek tendered his resignation and Pilsudski replaced him as premier on August 25.[93] Pilsudski gave an interview two days later in which he publicly insulted members of the Sejm, condemning the behavior of the parliamentary opposition, and expressed a strong desire for a new constitution. He complained bitterly that regarding work with the Sejm, "all attempts to date have resulted in complete fiasco. The MP in Poland today is a vile phenomenon because he allows himself to be humiliated by his behavior . . . all the work in the Sejm stinks and infects the air everywhere." He went on in a manner others perceived as a threat when he remarked, "In every office the deputy should be removed outside the door; if they do something to him, then so be it."[94]

Pilsudski had been expressing profound disappointment with Poland's parliamentary system for several years. As far back as June 1926, when asked about the Sejm, he had said, "First, one has to force the politicians to stop talking or smash them, break them, destroy them, whether those on the right or left."[95] And now his contempt for parliament was so pronounced that it incited some of his followers to violence. On August 29, 1930, unnamed army officers in broad daylight harshly attacked and severely beat Jan Dębski, the head of the Peasant Party and a leader in the Centrolew opposition.[96]

The Brześć Affair

The opposition was dealt a double blow. On the same day that Dębski was physically assaulted, President Mościcki dissolved the Sejm. He called for new elections to be held November 16 (Sejm) and November 23 (Senate). Pilsudski was determinant to root out the leaders of Centrolew on charges of conspiracy to overthrow the government. Now that the Sejm was dissolved, parliamentary immunity no longer applied. And it did not help their case that the opposition made explicit reference to a planned takeover of government. On September 1, Sławoj Składkowski presented a list of deputies to Pilsudski, who proceeded to mark the names of those he wanted arrested.[97]

The announcement of the forthcoming November elections led Centrolew to form a new voting bloc. On September 9, 1930, they announced the creation of the League for the Defense of Law and People's Freedom. "Our aim," the League stated on September 11, 1930, "is the total and final liquidation of the dictatorship of Jozef Pilsudski."[98] On the night of September 9 and the early morning hours of September 10, 1930, Pilsudski ordered the arrest of fourteen opposition members of the Sejm, including eleven from Centrolew. They included Wincenty Witos, a three-time prime minister, as well as the leaders from all six parties that made up Centrolew, including Herman Lieberman and Adam Ciołkosz of the PPS.[99] Karol Papiel, a leader of the National Workers' Party in Centrolew, was dragged out of his house the night of September 9. "One of the gendarmes," an eyewitness stated, "grabbed him by the head and the other by his legs. He was then knocked down on a stool, a wet cloth was thrown onto the crosses, and about 30 blows were meted out with an iron tool. Popiel fainted." After the beating, the captain overseeing the arrest reportedly said, "Enjoy how little was done. Next time Marshal Pilsudski will order a bullet to your head."[100]

In an interview appearing on September 13, 1930, Pilsudski dismissed criticism and downplayed the political nature of the arrests. He explained that he arrested members of parliament because they were abusing their rights to immunity, which they used as a cover to break the law.[101]

Pilsudski's unprecedented move to arrest members of the Sejm coincided with a serious crisis in East Galicia. The Organization of Ukrainian Nationalists (OUN), formed in early 1929, began a violent campaign against Polish officials. In a series of Ukrainian actions in the summer and fall of 1930, Polish officials were attacked and Ukrainian sabotage left Polish houses, barns, mills, and other buildings in ruins.[102] The conflict created more sympathy for the government and made it easier to accuse Centrolew of disloyalty, of siding with forces hostile to Poland.

On September 16, 1930, the Polish government launched a program to suppress Ukrainian nationalists. Polish soldiers entered Ukrainian villages to apprehend known activists, but many civilians fell victim to police misconduct. The mass arrests included thirty Ukrainian current and former members of the Sejm plus nearly one hundred Ukrainian politicians. The pacification program, which ended in November 1930, significantly deepened the conflict between Ukrainians and Poles.

Meanwhile, the country prepared for elections to take place in November 1930. These were not normal elections because arrests continued throughout the electoral period. By mid-October it is estimated that several thousand had been placed in custody, including eighty-four Sejm and Senate deputies, mostly in the military prison in Brześć.[103] These political prisoners were allowed no contact with the outside world. The wife of PPS activist Adam Ciołkosz, for example, recalled that although she sent care packages and letters, she never once received a reply nor was she ever given permission to visit until her husband's release.[104] On September 25, 1930, Wojciech Korfanty—a former deputy prime minister back in 1923—was arrested and transferred to the Brześć fortress. The arrests, by order of Interior Minister Sławoj-Składkowski, were made without a court order, violating due legal process.[105]

It was in this climate of intimidation and government arrests of the opposition that elections to the Sejm took place. Helped by government interference to favor the BBWR and by a severely weakened opposition, the results
were a resounding victory for the government camp.[106] With 74.8 percent
voter turnout, the elections resulted in Pilsudski's long-sought-after parliamentary majority: the BBWR received 55.6 percent of the votes, securing 247
of 444 deputies. In contrast, Roman Dmowski's National Party got 14 percent,
the center parties (Christian Democrats, PSL-Piast, and the National Workers
Party) received 9 percent, the left parties (PPS, PSL-Liberation, and Peasant
Party), 12.9 percent, and the minorities, 7.4 percent. The government bloc received an even greater majority in the Senate (67.6 percent) and thus gained
control of both branches of parliament. On December 9, 1930, the Pilsudski
loyalist Kazimierz Świtalski was nominated as Sejm speaker while W. Racz-
kiewicz became Senate speaker; both were from the BBWR. Pilsudski himself had briefly accepted the post of prime minister but resigned on December 4, with Walery Sławek replacing him. Pilsudski nonetheless continued
to serve as minister of war.

With the elections complete and the new government in place, Pilsudski
needed an extended period of rest, recommended by his doctor after bouts
of illness and general exhaustion. He went on a three-month vacation to
the Portuguese island of Madeira. With some peace of mind that the situation in Poland had stabilized, he departed on December 15, 1930, having
just turned sixty-three. He was accompanied by two physicians.[107] Speculation that Pilsudski had an affair while in Portugal with one of the doc-
tors, thirty-four-year-old Eugenia Lewicka, got the attention of his wife,
Alexandria, shortly after his return to Poland on March 29, 1931. No longer
allowed to see Pilsudski once they were back in Poland, Lewicka—who
is said to have knocked on Pilsudski's door in Warsaw only to be told by
Alexandra to leave—was later found unconscious at her place of work on
June 27, 1931. Eugenia Lewicka died two days later, having ingested a poisonous chemical.[108]

During his time on Madeira, Pilsudski could derive comfort from the fact
that the pro-government bloc was firmly in power with a majority in both
the Sejm and the Senate. The precedent set between the coup of May 1926
and the arrest of his political opponents was nonetheless ominous.

Pilsudski's Foreign Policy

It was understood that Pilsudski, regardless of the position he held in the government, determined the priorities and tasks of the country's foreign policy, even if Foreign Minister Zaleski had a certain degree of flexibility. Between 1926 and 1930, Polish foreign policy operated in the shadow of Locarno (October 1925), as well as the German-Soviet Treaty (April 1926). Since 1926 Pilsudski had responded to the two accords by trying to fill the security gap. One means was to allay fears that Pilsudski still had military designs on his neighbors. Immediately after the coup, Pilsudski clearly expressed his desire for peaceful relations with all his neighbors, stressing he no longer had any territorial claims whatsoever. The Polish foreign minister, August Zaleski, likewise sought to minimize fears in the West that Pilsudski would resume military operations. As Piotr Wandycz has argued, the central concern for Poland during the second half of the 1920s was the probability of a premature Allied evacuation of the Rhineland.[109]

After Locarno, when Germany recognized its frontiers with France and Belgium but left open the question of its frontiers with Poland and Czechoslovakia, German foreign minister Stresemann argued that Allied troops no longer needed to occupy the Rhineland, or any German territory. The problem Pilsudski and Zaleski faced was how to adjust Poland's foreign policy to the Franco-German dialogue without compromising the security advantage of the French-Polish alliance.[110] Poland's primary aim was to achieve a nonaggression pact with Germany, with Foreign Minister Zaleski proposing a triple French-German-Polish security pact. He used as leverage Poland's willingness to accept a premature Allied evacuation from the Rhineland. The Germans simply refused the offer outright, saying Poland had no say in the matter. What was becoming clear was that France began to regard its alliance with Poland as an obstacle to improving ties with Germany. Aware of this emerging trend, Zaleski made a point of being conciliatory to the Germans.

In the summer of 1927, Paris made overtures to Washington in a bid to strengthen the security framework. The result was the Kellogg-Briand Pact, signed on August 27, 1927, by US secretary of state Frank Kellogg and France's foreign minister, Aristide Briand.[111] The agreement—Poland and Germany were two of the initial thirty-three signatories—condemned war as an instrument of national policy and committed pact countries to peaceful, diplomatic resolutions of disputes. Pilsudski, due to the fact that no means of enforcement was provided, dismissed the Kellogg-Briand Pact as having little real value. In contrast, France's ambassador to Poland, Jules Laroche, told Foreign Minister Zaleski that the pact was an important development. Due to France's efforts, he said, the Kellogg-Briand Pact had given Poland the equivalent of a nonaggression agreement with Germany, which had now explicitly rejected war as a means of settling its conflict over the German-Polish frontiers.[112]

The French diplomat's interpretation did not impress Zaleski, who placed pressure on Paris to refrain from making new concessions to Berlin on the Rhineland issue. Zaleski then appealed to public opinion, creating a stir in Germany and France when he publicly expressed his opposition to an early withdrawal of Allied forces from the Rhineland. The German refusal to recognize the frontiers with Poland and Czechoslovakia, Zaleski maintained, threatened peace in the region. "We see in the occupation [of the Rhineland]," Zaleski told a German newspaper, "a guarantee of general security."[113] Editorials in the German press responded that Poland had no business inserting itself into this matter. The German ambassador to France, Leopold von Hoesch, said in response to Zaleski's statement that his government would not discuss this matter with Warsaw, nor would it recognize the German-Polish borders. Privately, French foreign minister Briand assured von Hoesch on June 28, 1928, that he did not intend to include Poland in the negotiations.[114]

Pilsudski was cognizant that the continued absence of diplomatic ties with Lithuania was undermining the message he put forward to the West that Poland had stable borders and peace with its neighbors. He decided to reopen the issue. While the Council of the League of Nations was meeting in Geneva, Pilsudski went to meet with the Lithuanian prime minister to try to overcome the impasse in the presence of a host of world leaders. At a session on December 9, 1929, Pilsudski attended a meeting at which Lithuanian prime minster Augustinas Voldemaras was present, in addition to Briand of France, Stresemann of Germany, and leaders of Britain and Italy. The Council witnessed a rare moment in which the leaders of Poland and Lithuania held direct talks about war and peace.

German foreign minister Stresemann remembered his exchanges with Pilsudski. "Pilsudski gave the impression of having an honest soldiery nature," Stresemann remarked. "Toward the Germans, he was to some degree amicable and had good reason to want to communicate with us."[115] But Pilsudski was less than amicable with the Lithuanian leader. In the presence of Pilsudski and major Western European premiers, Lithuanian prime minister Augustinas Voldemaras delivered opening remarks. Pilsudski then turned to Voldemaras and, according to one account, "struck the table with his open hand so hard that the water pitcher rattled, and he screamed at the Lithuanian, 'I have not made the long trip from Warsaw to Geneva, Mr. Voldemaras, just to hear your long speech.'" Briand evidently tried to calm him down, but Pilsudski continued, "I just want to know whether you are for war or peace." Voldemaras, intimidated and under pressure to respond in a manner not too discordant with the wishes of the Council, reportedly answered "peace," at which Pilsudski declared the matter settled.[116]

Hoping this exchange signaled a possible breakthrough in Lithuanian-Polish relations, diplomats seized the moment by drafting a formula for a resolution. The Council reconvened that evening to hear the Dutch representative present a draft declaration stating that a state of war between Lithuanian and Poland no longer existed. The two leaders agreed they would attend future talks on opening consular and diplomatic offices in their respective countries. The Council likewise registered Pilsudski's statement recognizing the independence and territorial integrity of Lithuania. The Council set a date of March 30, 1928, in Königsberg for direct Lithuanian-Polish talks. The resolution was adopted and hailed in Warsaw and Paris, where it was characterized as a victory for Briand. The Polish-Lithuanian dispute, it was believed, would be resolved shortly, relieving a source of great tension in Europe.[117]

Upon his return to Lithuania, however, Voldemaras quickly succumbed to domestic criticism and withdrew his support for the resolution. As the March 1928 conference was approaching, Voldemaras insisted on Polish concessions to reopen recently closed Lithuanian-language schools and to readmit ethnic Lithuanians of Polish citizenship who had been expelled. He also raised the issue of the 1923 Conference of Ambassadors resolution on Vilna. The French press criticized the Lithuanian prime minister for obstructionism, maintaining he constituted "a permanent menace to the peace of Europe."[118] Briand referred to Voldemaras as an "unsteady and dangerous personality," while Zaleski complained of his "disagreeable tone."[119] Strese-mann likewise registered a rather negative opinion of the Lithuanian prime minister.

It was not surprising, then, that the Königsberg conference produced no results. A second round was scheduled for June 1928, but nothing came of those either. Just before the second round of talks were to be held in June, Voldemaras gave an interview in which he revealed his position. He told the *Times* of London on June 14, 1928, that he had no intention of coming to a settlement as long as Vilna remained in Polish hands. "Our position is clear," Voldemaras said, "for Vilna is not in our hands but in theirs. Judging from Mr. Zaleski's statement that the Vilna question does not exist for the Poles, it is difficult to expect good results from further negotiations."[120] Needless to say, the second round of talks ended without an agreement. The two coun-tries did not exchange ambassadors, and the common border between them remained closed, a state of affairs that remained unchanged until after Pil-sudski's death. For the rest of his life Pilsudski remained bitterly disappointed at his inability to establish diplomatic ties with the country of his ancestors. It also symbolized the failure of his federalist schemes that Lithuania flat out rejected.

Pilsudski was equally eager for a nonaggression pact with Soviet Russia. The opportunity to apply the Kellogg-Briand Pact to relations between the Soviet Union and its western neighbors came on December 29, 1928, when the Soviet representative Maxim Litvinov proposed to Poland that the two countries sign an agreement bringing in the Baltic States and eastern Euro-pean countries. But German foreign minister Stresemann refused to take part, saying that it smacked of an eastern Locarno.[121] Pilsudski dispatched a representative to the gathering and the so-called Litvinov Protocol was signed in Moscow on February 9, 1929, by Soviet Russia, Poland, Estonia, Latvia, and Romania. The signatory countries were now committed to "the renunciation of war as an instrument of national policy."[122]

While a positive development, the Litvinov Protocol seemed to pale in comparison to the events of June 1930, when Allied forces prematurely or-dered evacuation from the Rhineland without a German guarantee to respect the territorial integrity of Poland and Czechoslovakia. Prior to the evacua-tion, Pilsudski spoke with two British officials about relations with Ger-many. Due to the weak terms of the Treaty of Versailles, Pilsudski did not believe Germany posed an immediate threat. Instead, he was preoccupied with the border with Bolshevik Russia. In contrast to the German Army, numbering 100,000 men in 1932, the Polish armed forces had 265,980 active troops, and the French Army had 402,255 active troops. In a meeting with the British ambassador to Poland on December 20, 1929, Pilsudski spoke primarily about his fears of Bolshevik Russia. But he remarked that in the long term, the threat from Germany would be even greater. The Polish general staff knew Pilsudski's position. In April 1930 the British military attaché in Warsaw, Colonel Martin, reported to London that the Polish general staff was of the opinion that "in the present situation Germany does not constitute a direct threat to Poland" but that "long range, Germany remains the greatest danger for the integrity and security of Poland."[123]

CHAPTER 17

Poland in a Changing World

Poland believes that there is at almost any moment the danger of
the invasion of Polish territory by German irregular troops. If this
should occur, the whole Polish army would be immediately
mobilized and march into Germany to settle the thing once and
for all, and they would not be influenced by any action of the
League of Nations or anyone else.

—JOZEF PILSUDSKI, LETTER TO PRESIDENT HERBERT HOOVER,
OCTOBER 22, 1931

The Brześć Affair involving the arrest of the ruling government's political opponents undoubtedly cast a shadow over the remaining years of
the Pilsudski regime. The affair made it easier for the opposition to hurl at
Pilsudski stinging accusations ranging from "dictator" to "fascist." Few inhabitants of Poland were neutral on the subject of their leader. Instead, the
citizenry became deeply polarized between Pilsudski's loyal, often fanatic
followers and his haters. Those wishing he would return to private life regarded him as a threat to democratic government, a supporter of national
and religious minority rights, and an egoist with a lust for power who willfully disregarded legal procedures and rules. Pilsudski, his opponents argued, believed only he was able to safeguard the country's national interests.
He was "Poland's scourge and villain," as historian Eva Plach characterized
his opposition's views.[1]

Pilsudski's opponents also were of the opinion that Brześć was not the result of a real existential threat to the government but instead the inevitable
outcome of Pilsudski's authoritarian style of rule. These opponents, both so-

cialists and nationalists, were very vocal. One left-wing pamphleteer in 1930 published a biting attack, "The Dictator Jozef Pilsudski and 'Pilsudskiites.'" From the moment Pilsudski took power in 1918, Marian Porczak wrote, he "positioned himself unambiguously" against democratic government. The author's unfavorable opinion of Pilsudski's politics was linked to an unflattering portrait of a personality characterized as one of supreme arrogance and conceit.[2] The first "Pilsudskiite," Porczak argued, was Pilsudski himself. He wrote: "Pilsudski regards himself as being providential, as . . . standing above all rights and above the nation." He "is full of self-admiration, often referring to his distinguished military merits, to his greatness, and to his fame." Pilsudski, the pamphleteer concluded, "has ruined the political system of the Republic without replacing it with anything new or better."[3]

Pilsudski's standing abroad after the Brześć Affair likewise deteriorated. Nowhere was this more evident than in the figure of H. N. Brailsford, the left-wing British journalist who had come away from his first interview with Pilsudski in 1919 with the view that Poland's head of state was "a humane and liberal man."[4] Eleven years later, in October 1930, the same journalist charged that Pilsudski was steering Poland in the direction of fascism.[5] The *Manchester Guardian* referred to the arrests of opposition leaders as "Pilsudski's campaign of terrorism." In its edition of September 11, 1930, two days after the arrest wave began, the Warsaw correspondent for the same newspaper reported, "To-day's events in Poland should be enough to destroy any illusions that Poland is a democracy or that Marshal Pilsudski has any ultimate resources other than of violence." The sole reason for the arrests, the paper argued, was fear of defeat in the upcoming parliamentary elections scheduled for November 1930. Notably absent was any mention of Centrolew's resolution demanding the dissolution of the Pilsudski government by force.

Several other Western papers that reported on the arrests drew similar conclusions. The *New York Times*, for example, reported on November 4, 1930, that Pilsudski's rule constituted a dictatorship but a moderate one, pointing out that of the sixty-four former politicians arrested, all but one was allowed to run for office in the upcoming parliamentary elections, even if from a prison cell. Henceforth, in the aftermath of the Brześć Affair, the phrase "the Polish dictator" was now almost universally affixed to Pilsudski's name in the foreign press. Even the Pilsudski loyalist Roman Debicki, a career diplomat who served in the Foreign Ministry under Pilsudski and who after 1945 taught international relations in the United States at Georgetown

University, conceded on this point. In his classic study of Polish foreign policy between the world wars, published in 1962, Debicki maintained that the Brześć Affair, during which opposition members reportedly were treated harshly, had a detrimental impact on Poland's image abroad. The arrests "gave some color of truth to unfriendly charges that the Pilsudski regime was a strong-man dictatorship, and these charges were not without effect on foreign opinion."[6]

Despite the unease with the crackdown on his opponents, Pilsudski never lost the ability to charm the foreign press. This was evident in the aftermath of his electoral victory in November 1930. In "Daughter, 11, Boss of Polish Dictator," the *Washington Post* portrayed Poland's ruler as a devoted father dedicated wholly to his daughters. When he was younger, the reporter stated, Pilsudski had delighted in playtime with them and kept well informed of their activities in school. A unique story illustrated the close relationship he had with his children:

> When the new school year began this fall the marshal was in session with several cabinet ministers on an important matter concerning the forthcoming elections for Parliament.
>
> Suddenly, the two girls burst into the room. It appeared that instead of going straight home after their first school day they decided that they must tell their dad right away of their first impression of new teachers and new classmates. The marshal excused himself before the cabinet ministers, interrupted the conference and had a chat with his girls for half an hour.[7]

The image of a beloved father continued to be presented in the foreign press. Upon Pilsudski's return from a vacation in Portugal, one paper described the scene: Pilsudski "came back today . . . but the official reception was sidetracked while two little girls flew into their father's arms. The official salute was booming and Premier Sławek, accompanied by government officials, stood aside while Wanda and Jadwiga hugged Pilsudski and kissed the marshal."[8]

THE NOVEMBER 1930 elections changed entirely the political scene in Poland. With a parliamentary majority, Pilsudski's bloc could now comfortably

Pilsudski with his two daughters, Wanda and Jadwiga, Sulejówek, 1926.

rule and the political situation began stabilizing. With the stabilization of government after some five years, Pilsudski finally felt comfortable leaving domestic matters to his trusted cabinet. He could now focus almost entirely on his two greatest interests: foreign policy and the army. In this last period of Pilsudski's rule, between 1931 and his death in May 1935, the dramatic conflict between the government and the parliament quieted down considerably. But international events were about to fundamentally change the position of Poland.

It was a time of steep economic decline, as the global economic depression continued to impact the country. In Europe as a whole, industrial output fell 27 percent between 1929 and 1932. The impact on Poland's economy was greater, with its industrial output falling by 37 percent during the same time. The decline in the price of agricultural goods during the Great Depression fell by one-half, with a devastating effect on Poland, an agricultural country.[9]

The situation outside Poland's borders changed dramatically with the dramatic electoral victory for the Nazi Party. In elections to the Reichstag in September 1930, the Nazi Party surged from 810,000 votes in 1928 (2.6 percent) to 6.4 million votes (18.3 percent), making it the second largest political party in Weimar Germany. In the July 1932 elections, the Nazi Party more than doubled its representation, gaining 13.1 million votes (37.4 percent), making it the single largest party in the Reichstag. President Paul von Hindenburg was forced to name Adolf Hitler chancellor of Germany on January 30, 1933. In these fast-changing circumstances in international and domestic affairs, it is not surprising that Pilsudski became laser focused on foreign affairs.

With the abrupt and unanticipated rise of the Nazi Party and the consequent shifting balance of power in Europe, Pilsudski began to reconsider his role. The first evidence of this change in role comes from President Mościcki, who recounted the exchange he had with Pilsudski upon his return to Poland from his extended vacation. On the day he returned to Poland from Madeira, Portugal—March 31, 1931—Pilsudski discussed this matter. He told President Mościcki that his health was such that he could no longer carry the burden of so many responsibilities and would now limit himself to overseeing the army and foreign policy.[10] Pilsudski communicated his decision to his closest collaborators—Świtalski, Sławek, Prystor, Beck, and Mościcki—in a meeting on April 29, 1931. In his diary entry from the day of the meeting, Świtalski's noted that Pilsudski had been disturbed by press accounts describing him as a threat to democracy in the light of the Brześć Affair. Compelled to explain his actions, Pilsudski described himself as someone who always chose "right over might," and he emphasized that the 1926 coup had been legalized by a vote of the legislature.[11]

Despite the stabilization of the domestic political scene, changes in government personnel still occurred. On May 27, 1931, Colonel Sławek resigned and the president appointed Alexander Prystor to form a government. Only two new ministers of the outgoing cabinet were replaced, one of which raised charges of nepotism. Pilsudski's younger brother, Jan Pilsudski, who had earlier served as a judge in Vilna, assumed the post of finance minister.[12] His appointment "seems to guarantee that the marshal's wishes in that sphere will be closely followed," the New York Times reported on May 28, 1931. More concerning was the fact that the new finance minister had no economic background "but has presumably been selected for the post in order to facilitate the participation of Marshal Pilsudski in the shaping of financial policy," the *Times* of London speculated on May 28, 1931. The PPS newspaper *Robotnik* likewise criticized the appointment in its edition of May 28. *Robotnik* printed resolutions of a party conference that characterized the regime as "the dictatorship of Pilsudski," saying that is why Centrolew had been so important as a necessary formation constituting "self-defense in the face of dictatorship."[13]

Robotnik was referring to a growing perception that cabinet shuffles no longer had an impact on political life. Instead, the pro-Pilsudski orientation of the cabinets remained intact regardless of who occupied government positions. This phenomenon gave Pilsudski the assurance that he could step away from domestic matters with a leadership he trusted.

The stabilization of Poland's political life was rudely interrupted by an assassination that rattled the country. On August 29, 1931, Tadeusz Hołówko, vice chairman of the Sejm and a leader of the BBWR, was assassinated while on a visit to East Galicia.[14] The suspect was a member of a secret Ukrainian organization, which brought back to the surface Poland's vexing Ukrainian problem. Pilsudski was terribly distraught about the killing, which removed from the political scene a staunch supporter in the Sejm and longtime ally. Hołówko had been a former member of the PPS and an activist in the Polish Military Organization and had been badly injured in the 1920 Polish-Soviet War.[15] It was thus a deeply personal loss for Pilsudski. "In the person of the deceased," Pilsudski wrote in a letter of condolence to Hołówko's family, "Poland has lost one of its best sons—a passionate patriot, a fighter for independence and a tireless worker in the field of hard, daily peace work. May your anguish be diminished by knowing that the country as a whole mourns this great and heavy loss."[16]

Declining Health

Pilsudski's declining health continued to take a toll. In a meeting with advisors on October 9, 1931, Sławoj Składkowski noted in his diary that "the commandant does not look well. His cheeks are flush and he complains of feeling week."[17] With the persistence of weakness and fatigue, Pilsudski traveled to a warmer climate to rest, departing on October 11, 1931. Accompanied by a physician, he arrived at Carmen Sylva, a health resort on the Black Sea coast in Romania, where a villa had been reserved for him. But heavy rain, cold, and wind led Pilsudski to become quite ill, and he contracted pneumonia and a high fever.[18] One of those accompanying Pilsudski, Colonel Roman Michałowski, noted the intensity of the marshal's illness in his diary.[19] On October 29 the marshal returned to Warsaw. He made his first public appearance after his return on November 29, 1931, for festivities marking the 101st anniversary of the Polish uprising of November 1830.[20]

The serious bout of illness Pilsudski suffered in Romania had frightened him. It led him to conclude the end of his life was near and to contemplate what legacy he would leave behind. One week after his return—on November 4, 1931—he summoned a longtime comrade and former prime minister Artur Śliwiński. He asked Śliwiński to write an official biography. Pilsudski proposed a series of conversations in which he would agree to answer any and all questions about his life. Although Śliwiński agreed, and sat down with him on four separate occasions in November 1931 to interview him, he never completed the biography. Instead, after Pilsudski's death, Śliwiński published the full transcript of the interviews, complete with his own comments on Pilsudski's facial expressions, mood, and tone of voice.

In the first interview, Pilsudski commented on his earliest childhood memories. "From as early as I can remember," he said on November 9, 1931, "I thought about serving Poland. I dreamed of greatness." Śliwiński responded that such dreams were common in young boys. The difference, Pilsudski rejoined, was that "I never parted from these thoughts. This conviction of my childhood was preserved."[21]

After discussing a host of issues relating to his family background, upbringing, and political beliefs, Śliwiński asked Pilsudski to comment on the most pressing issue of the day—the Brześć trials of his political opponents that had begun two weeks earlier, on October 26, 1931, in Warsaw. Those standing trial, accused of conspiracy to overthrow the government, included such major political figures as Wincenty Witos and Wojciech Korfanty. "I have nothing to hide about myself," he said to Śliwiński, adding, "I am not ashamed of anything as I am prepared to speak on all matters that a biographer finds relevant." Arresting the conspirators was, Pilsudski said, something he dreaded but considered necessary. "Poland was in danger. I had to resort to very harsh measures, even such as Brześć," Pilsudski said in a broken voice, with pauses between each sentence.[22] In the text of the interview, Śliwiński commented that discussing the topic of Brześć exhausted Piłsudski.

Although Piłsudski withdrew from domestic matters, he could be assured that the parliamentary majority prevented the country's rightest parties from passing antidemocratic measures. And in this context, Piłsudski's government stood firmly opposed to anti-Jewish bills put forward by the right-wing opposition. This was clearly shown on March 4, 1932, when right-wing, populist deputies brought before the Sejm a bill proposing to limit the number of Jews admitted to Polish universities. The measure was defeated by a large margin. A member of the Sejm's Educational Committee, Józef Stypiński, clarified that the proposed bill violated Articles 96 and 111 of the constitution.[23]

The Conduct of Foreign Policy

As the Great Depression ravaged the economies of Europe in the early 1930s, hitting both Germany and Poland particularly hard, the political landscape in Germany experienced dramatic shifts to the extreme right. Following Germany's groundbreaking 1930 elections that made the Nazi Party the second largest party in parliament, Piłsudski felt the need to respond. In December 1930 he appointed the dynamic Colonel Józef Beck to the position of undersecretary of state at the Ministry of Foreign Affairs.[24] Beck, with a more forceful and less conciliatory disposition than Foreign Minister Zaleski, now became more central in shaping the country's foreign policy.

Meanwhile, Piłsudski took more aggressive steps to implement his so-called policy of equilibrium in foreign affairs. This principle called for concluding peace agreements with Germany and Soviet Russia. His approach was first to focus on achieving a settlement with Soviet Russia. Such an agreement, he believed, would strengthen Poland's hand in dealing with Germany. At the time Piłsudski was keenly aware of an emerging sympathy in Western diplomatic circles for German revisionist claims on Polish territory. In a cable to the US secretary of state, Henry L. Stimson, the American ambassador to Poland remarked that Poland's foreign minister had expressed concern over growing sympathy for German claims on the Corridor (the strip of western Poland allowing access to the Baltic Sea), a trend that was having a disquieting effect on public opinion in Poland.[25] Piłsudski's concern about sympathies in the West for German revisionist sentiments was confirmed by the views of France's prime minister, Pierre Laval. When the US secretary of state met with Laval in London on July 24, 1931, the American secretary was struck by the French premier's leanings toward Germany on the question of the Corridor. "We discussed the Franco-German situation first of all," Stimson commented. "He . . . told me of his talks with [German Chancellor] Brüning. The underlying problem which could solve everything else was the question of the Polish Corridor. If that could be solved France would have no other real trouble with Germany."[26]

The French prime minister's views raised serious concerns in Poland. When news reached Warsaw that Prime Minister Laval was scheduled to visit Washington at the end of October 1931, Pilsudski ordered his ambassador to the United States, Tytus Filipowicz, to cut short his vacation and return immediately to Washington. Arrangements were to be made for a meeting between the Polish ambassador and President Herbert Hoover ahead of Laval's arrival.[27] The American president granted Filipowicz an audience on October 21, 1931. Present at the meeting was the US undersecretary of state, who filed an official memorandum on the meeting the following day that provides a valuable window into Pilsudski's thinking at the time. "Marshal Pilsudski instructed the ambassador," the report states, "that Poland would not consider any settlement of the Polish corridor other than the maintenance of the *status quo*. Poland would absolutely refuse to enter into any discussion whatsoever of that subject with any neutral nation." The summary of Pilsudski's instructions continued:

> Poland believes that there is at almost any moment the danger of the invasion of Polish territory by German irregular troops. If this should occur, the whole Polish army would be immediately mobilized and march into Germany to settle the thing once and for all, and they would not be influenced by any action of the League of Nations or anyone else.
>
> On the other hand, the intentions of Poland are purely pacifist. Poland would like nothing better than to live on the most cordial terms with Germany, co-operate with Germany economically and politically, but has reached the point where the violent and anti-Polish propaganda in Germany must be stopped if the peace is to be kept.[28]

Pilsudski's communiqué revealed the outlines of his foreign policy. Poland was to unwaveringly defend its territorial integrity, with or without the

West. The US chargé d'affaires in Poland, John C. Wiley, filed a report on December 2, 1931. Pilsudski, Wiley wrote, "may have thought that by alarming the American government with the danger of war, it would, out of anxiety for the security of things in Germany, take effective steps to put an end to Corridor discussions in the United States." Wiley wondered aloud if Pilsudski understood that government cannot muffle a free press. "That political personages and the press in the United States should be free in their utterances from the influenced of government pressure is doubtless not fully understood by Marshal Pilsudski." Wiley warned that "should a situation arise in the future, such as foreseen in the message of Marshal Pilsudski, the threat of an immediate Polish attack on Germany is probably not an empty one; at least not if the Marshal still presides over Polish affairs."[29]

The record of Pilsudski's message to President Hoover indicated a growing concern about the rising popularity of German revisionism. From the military point of view, however, Pilsudski understood the German threat as a distant one due to Germany's status as a demilitarized country. At the same time, he was perfectly aware that the highest German officials in the Weimar government favored a revision of the borders.

In August 1930 a conservative member of the German cabinet, Gottfried Treviranus, loudly lamented the lost territories in the chambers of the Reichstag. Treviranus was quoted in the *Manchester Guardian* on August 12, 1930, as having said, "The future of our Polish neighbor . . . can only be assured if Germany and Poland are not kept in perpetual unrest by unjust frontiers." The view that a border adjustment on the Polish-German frontier would go a long way to stabilizing this troubled region of Europe was finding more and more adherents in the West. In Washington, D.C., for example, William E. Borah, chairman of the US Senate Foreign Relations Committee, expressed support in October 1931 for both returning the Polish Corridor to Germany and restoring to Hungary its prewar boundaries.[30] Outraged by such a provocative statement, Hoover instructed the White House to issue a clarification. "A press statement that the President has proposed any revision of the Polish Corridor is absolutely without foundation. The President has made no suggestion of any such character."[31] It was thus clear that Pilsudski, concerned about the growing sympathy toward Germany in Western diplomatic circles, felt the need to let the American administration know that Poland was unwilling to bend to any degree on the question of borders.

President Hoover's comments clarifying the U.S. position did not calm Pilsudski's nerves. Evidence of this can be seen in Pilsudski's emotional outburst in October 1931 with a young aide. "'Are you aware of the gravity of the internal and external dangers facing Poland?' Pilsudski exclaimed, losing his cool. 'What will happen when I am gone? Who will be able to look reality in the eye? If all the Poles understand what I'm saying, they will get to work in defense of the nation's interests. If not, . . . Poland will disappear in ten years.' The marshal then threw the cards on the table, covering his face with outstretched arms, and seemed to weep."[32]

Sympathy for revisionist principles could be detected not only across the Atlantic but also across the English Channel. This became painfully apparent during the official visit of Poland's foreign minister, August Zaleski, to Great Britain in December 1931. On December 10 and 11, Zaleski met with the British foreign secretary, Sir John Simon, to discuss the system of alliances and security for Poland and other new states. Zaleski emphasized that a British military and naval guarantee of the German-Polish frontier was essential. To Zaleski's surprise, Simon wavered, instead raising the question of whether Poland had any room for compromise on this question.[33] The troubling exchange, communicated back to Pilsudski, contributed to Pilsudski's emerging realization that Poland could not rely on Great Britain's active support even for preserving the status quo.

It was the loss of faith in the commitment of the Western democracies to defend Poland's frontiers that led Pilsudski to originate the policy of equilibrium, calling for the normalization of relations with Germany and Soviet Russia. Pilsudski chose Józef Beck to carry out this policy, especially after 1932. It was a strategy Pilsudski had first formulated after the 1926 coup. The late Piotr Wandycz described the policy as consisting of two parts: "one, strict neutrality between Germany and Russia, so that each of them would be absolutely certain that Poland would not go against it with the help of the other; and two, alliance with France and Romania as a guarantee of peace."[34]

Pilsudski implemented the first phase of his foreign policy by entering into negotiations with Soviet Russia for a nonaggression pact. To get a firsthand update on Germany, he summoned to Warsaw his special envoy in Berlin, Alfred Wysocki, on June 7, 1932. Germany was embroiled in domestic political problems, Wysocki reported, and was in no position to initiate any aggression against Poland. Wysocki's report reinforced Pilsudski's view that the Soviet Union was a greater short-term military threat than demilitarized

Germany. He nonetheless paid close attention to German politics and, in fact, was alarmed by the German cabinet formed by Franz von Papen on May 31, 1932. Especially concerning to Pilsudski was von Papen's choice of General Kurt von Schleicher as his new minister of defense. Von Schleicher's open hostility to Poland was well known.[35]

Tensions flared when a dispute arose over Poland's rights to use Danzig as a naval port. Pilsudski ordered the Polish destroyer *Wicher* (Gale)—on which he had arrived from Portugal the previous year—to sail into the Danzig harbor on June 14, 1932. The Polish navy was ostensibly acting as host to a visiting British Royal Navy flotilla. After official visits between officers of the two vessels, the Polish destroyer returned to Gdynia the afternoon of June 15 amid vigorous protests from the Free City of Danzig's senate.[36] "This was a typical Pilsudski coup," Wandycz commented, "a notice served on the powers that Warsaw would not tolerate the slightest derogation of its rights and interests, and was not afraid to act forcefully."[37] The *Wicher* affair displayed Pilsudski's tactic of carrying out military maneuvers on the German frontiers as a form of deterrence.

A breakthrough in negotiations came on July 25, 1932, when the Polish ambassador in Moscow, Stanisław Patek, signed a long-sought nonaggression pact with the Soviet Union. The Russians recognized Poland's eastern frontiers, and the two countries pledged friendly ties for a period of three years. The agreement pledged that the contracting parties "undertake to refrain from taking any aggressive action against or invading the territory of the other Party, either alone or in conjunction with other Powers."[38] It was an unqualified success for Polish diplomacy, one that secured its eastern borders, allowed for more economic cooperation, and strengthened Poland's position in relation to Germany.

Meanwhile, a convention of Legionnaires took place in Gdynia. Pilsudski, who had earlier made every effort to speak in person at such gatherings, instead sent a written address to be read aloud. It was a moving tribute to his followers. The address began by saying that he grew up in an era when the fighters of 1863 were shunned for bringing calamity on their country. But they had given their lives out of patriotic zeal, something he did not want lost in collective memory: "With regard to me, I have on multiple occasions said in those times that I was afraid when sons spit on the tombs of their fathers for the latter's foolishness, for shedding their blood for Poland. To remove this bitterness from Polish life, I gave much of myself, I gave my hardest efforts,

Pilsudski receiving US general Douglas MacArthur. Warsaw, September 1932.

and lost much of my health in the process—and I do not think that my work was in vain."[39]

In the fall of 1932 General Douglas MacArthur, chief of staff of the United States Army, did a tour of major European countries. On September 10, 1932, he visited Warsaw, where he met with Pilsudski at Belvedere Palace. "In Poland," MacArthur later recalled, "I saw a hundred thousand superb cavalry measured by the standards of fifty years before, and Marshal Jozef Pilsudski, its premier, at his wits end trying to figure out a way to avoid certain disaster, caught up geographically as he was between Germany and Russia."[40]

Hitler's Rise to Power

On July 31, 1932, the first German elections to the Reichstag in two years revealed a massive surge in support for the Nazi Party. The Nazis more than doubled their representation in the Reichstag from 6.4 million to 13.1 million votes, making them the largest party, with 230 seats. In this most successful election cycle in the history of the Nazi Party, it got 37.4 percent of the popular vote.[41] In the remaining five months of 1932, Pilsudski strengthened the Foreign Ministry. His longtime foreign minister, August Zaleski, had served for six years. On November 2, 1932, Pilsudski named Józef Beck his new foreign minister. The replacement of Zaleski reflected Pilsudski's decision to adapt Poland's foreign policy to a new, increasingly hostile international arena.

On that fateful day of January 30, 1933, German president Paul von Hindenburg reluctantly named Hitler chancellor of Germany. In an interview with the London-based *Sunday Express* on February 12, 1933, Hitler was asked about his views on the Versailles Treaty. He replied that it constituted a tragic mistreatment of the Germans. "Another hideous injustice to Germany," he added, "is, of course, the Polish Corridor. The present position is hateful to all Germans . . . the Polish Corridor must be restored to us."[42] This public declaration less than two weeks after his assumption to power hit a raw nerve in Poland. In the Sejm, the influential Bogusław Miedziński, who also served as editor of the semi-official government daily *Gazeta Polska* (Polish Gazette), echoed the government position when he said, "If Hitler wants the Polish Corridor, let him try to take it." He followed his aside in parliament with an editorial directing the following message to Adolf Hitler, as quoted in the *New York Times* on November 3, 1933: "Our reply to all German claims is our guns." Hitler's statement in the *Sunday Express* also appeared to have emboldened Germans in the Free City of Danzig. On February 15, 1933, the Danzig Senate revoked a 1923 agreement allowing a detachment of harbor police under Polish control to help guard the stockpile. Danzig notified Polish authorities in March 1933 that it would replace the detachment with one of their own.

Pilsudski reacted immediately and decisively. On March 6, 1933, he ordered a Polish naval transport vessel to enter Danzig's harbor, off Westerplatte, and 120 Polish troops disembarked to reinforce the garrison.[43] Strong protests in Germany were echoed in Geneva, where League of Nations officials called foul play on Poland's part, turning it instantly into an international incident. Others cautioned that it was an absurd exaggeration to suggest, as did some German papers, that Pilsudski was attempting to annex Danzig with 120 men.

Hitler backed down, choosing not to respond militarily, and thus Pilsudski's show of military force was a success. The Polish vessel and its 120 troops withdrew on March 16, 1932, after the Danzig Senate agreed to restore the Polish harbor police force.[44] As a sign of goodwill, two of the Free City of Danzig's representatives traveled to Warsaw for a meeting with Pilsudski, who reportedly remarked, "I am very glad that you sought the only sensible way for our mutual relations." If the Danzig Senate had voted differently, Pilsudski is reported to have said, it would have ended badly, "much worse that you could imagine."[45]

Although Pilsudski's action achieved its aim, it did violate the terms of the 1923 agreement regulating the status of Danzig. The Western powers thus formally condemned the maneuver. Pilsudski's bold move was above all an act of deterrence, intended to send a message that he was willing to act preemptively against Germany if a threat to Poland was anticipated.

That the conflict with Germany was part of a larger problem of Western attitudes toward the successor states of Eastern Europe after 1918 was confirmed by the so-called Four Powers Pact. Though never actually ratified, the pact was signed on March 18, 1933, in Rome. Among the foreign diplomats present were British prime minister Ramsey MacDonald and Foreign Secretary Sir John Simon, to whom Mussolini formally presented a draft of the Four Powers Pact.[46] Intended for Italy, France, Great Britain, and Germany, it allowed for treaty revisions when such changes were deemed to avoid military conflicts. Poland was alarmed to discover that Mussolini's draft included a clause recognizing equal rights in armaments for Germany. The draft of the Four Powers Pact made public was immediately seen as a concession to territorial revisionism. The Poles were shocked to discover that the Four Powers Pact even included a provision for connecting East Prussia to the German mainland by means of annexing the Polish Corridor. "The four Powers," the draft stated, "reaffirm . . . the principle of a revision of the peace treaties given the existence of conditions which might lead to a conflict between the states."[47] Although it is true that France and Britain were later able to remove this provision, in private Mussolini assured German foreign minister Baron von Neurath that he would support the German demand for the elimination of the Polish Corridor. "Mussolini had authorized the Ambassador to state that he fully recognized and would support the claims of Germany to have East Prussia connected again with the Reich through elimination of the dividing corridor," the German foreign minister reported in a memorandum dated March 14, 1933. When word got out, Mussolini qualified his statement, saying that "the moment had not yet arrived for pursuing an active policy of revision, since Germany [is] at present not even a match for the Polish Army."[48]

The Four Powers Pact served to strengthen Pilsudski's suspicions about the reliability of his French ally. In Poland, news of Mussolini's draft came as a bombshell. The Polish press, from socialists to nationalists, condemned the draft of the Four Powers Pact, accusing its framers of endangering the stability and sovereignty of Europe's new states. *Gazeta Polska,* the Warsaw daily linked to the ruling government, issued a powerful rebuke: "If the plan means the peaceful revision of the Versailles Treaty, its framers make a grave error in supposing that Poland will ever agree to any revision of boundaries in whatever way it may be proposed to her."[49] Observing firsthand the strong reactions, the German ambassador in Warsaw filed a report to the German foreign minister. "That France is becoming less and less inclined to go to war for the Corridor," he wrote on April 27, 1933, "is a fact which is causing as much indignation here as anxiety."[50]

A "Preventive War" against Nazi Germany?

In 1962 British historian Alan Palmer described Pilsudski as "one of the first statesmen to perceive the danger to Europe of a Nazi Germany."[51] A popular historian who had written extensively on Eastern Europe, Palmer was referring to Pilsudski's alleged proposal to the French for a preventive war against Nazi Germany immediately after Hitler's rise to power. Yet more than a half century after Palmer's statement, there is still no consensus about whether or not such a plan was ever proposed. What is not in dispute, however, was Pilsudski's ability to see Hitler's threat clearly and earlier than other statesmen. Sir Robert Vansittart, who served as permanent undersecretary in the British Foreign Office in 1933, remarked that most heads of state saw the real intentions of European dictators too late. But Pilsudski was an exception. "Pilsudski was almost alone," Vansittart wrote in his autobiography, "in seeing them precisely from the start. Unfortunately for the West the Marshal had no name there except a tarnished one." The British diplomat continued: "Here was Hitler freshly planted, with no time to strike roots. . . . Pilsudski was man enough to see that this unbalanced half-man might set the world alight, and he put out feelers to find whether anyone would join in removing the growth cheaply."[52]

In March 1933 Pilsudski reached out to French officials through unofficial channels to assess their willingness to deter German aggression. What took place next is shrouded in mystery, with scholars and diplomats divided into two camps—one claiming that there was a secret proposal made to France, and the other claiming that such a proposal never took place.[53] According to the available documents, we know that in March and April 1933 the German government received reports that Pilsudski was planning a preventive war. If, as has been claimed by Pilsudski loyalists, one of Pilsudski's secret envoys presented such a plan to members of the French military or government, no document in the French military or diplomatic archives has been uncovered attesting to such an exchange (although there are references to a French reply to such a proposal). According to Foreign Minister Beck, Pilsudski carefully examined the pros and cons of a preventive war at two points in the spring and fall of 1933. Beck does not, however, make reference to any proposal being presented to the French.[54]

For Pilsudski, the Westerplatte episode was meant to test the German reaction to Polish military threats. Having flexed Poland's military muscles, Pilsudski decided at the beginning of April 1933 to apply diplomatic pressure on Germany to publicly renounce territorial revisionism. On April 4, 1933, Pilsudski instructed his envoy in Berlin, Alfred Wysocki, to arrange a top-secret meeting between Hitler and Jan Szembek, the Polish undersecretary for foreign affairs.[55] Szembek was to demand that Hitler publicly recognize Poland's rights in Danzig. Pilsudski was willing to resort to the most extreme measures if such a request was denied.

When Wysocki replied that Hitler refused to meet with a lower-level diplomat, Pilsudski proposed the meeting take place with Wysocki. On April 18, 1933, Wysocki received new and updated instructions: "Please tell the Chancellor that, in the opinion of some, he is held responsible, whether as Chancellor of the Reich, or as head of his party, for attempts to intervene in the internal affairs of Danzig, contrary to other rights and legal interests of Poland." Wysocki should then ask Hitler "publicly to denounce such action, thus putting an end to Polish suspicions." Wysocki was to make clear that failure to comply might result in military action, telling Hitler that "continuation of the situation as it now exists would, in our opinion, unnecessarily create difficulties that would force us to draw dire conclusions." Wysocki was to ask

Hitler to publish a communiqué in the German and Polish press, "stating therein that the Chancellor is against any action directed against Polish rights and legal interests in the Free City of Danzig." "The Marshal," the instruction stated, "considers this conversation extremely important in view of the necessity of establishing our policy on Danzig, which to a great extent would depend on the result of this exchange."[56] Wysocki was granted an audience with Hitler for May 2, 1933.

Meanwhile, in case diplomatic initiatives failed, Pilsudski worked out a contingency plan for a military option. On April 18, 1933, he presented a plan for military action in the case of war with Germany. The secret plan, written by hand, was presented to Pilsudski's adjutant, Captain Lepecki. The plan stipulated that in the case of war with Germany, a Government of National Unity and Defense was to be formed. The original proposal, including a signed, handwritten note by President Mościcki giving his approval, was never publicly revealed. Lepecki recalled asking if Pilsudski believed Germany planned a military strike in Danzig, to which Pilsudski is said to have replied, "Even if we attacked Germany, it would be a defensive act."[57] Although some have questioned whether this document really existed, a recent study has confirmed its authenticity.[58] One piece of evidence is the record of an earlier meeting of cabinet members at which time—according to the notes of the meeting written the same day—Pilsudski outlined the same plan for a war government in case of German aggression.[59]

Pilsudski's plan for a war cabinet completed on April 18, 1933, demonstrates that he seriously contemplated, and drew up plan for, a preventive war against Germany. Although no evidence has been uncovered of a Polish proposal to France for joint military action, it is clear that Pilsudski wanted the Germans and West European officials to believe that a Polish strike was imminent. We know this from diplomatic exchanges at the time. For example, Sir Horace Rumbold, then the permanent undersecretary in the British Foreign Office, remarked from Berlin on April 7, 1933, "It is known that in France responsible people are talking of a preventative war. . . . There is no doubt that Poland is now being held back by France, but would invade Germany in the case of a preventative war. It is to be doubted whether any French Government would undertake the responsibility for leading the country into war again. In any case, the German Government is determined to avoid conflict."[60]

It is clear from contemporaneous German diplomatic records from this time that the rumor of a Polish preventive war plan reached the German Foreign Office. The rumors themselves appeared to be having the precise effect Pilsudski intended. At a conference of ministers held at the Reich Chancellery in Berlin on April 7, 1933, the German foreign minister, Baron von Neurath, made explicit reference to Pilsudski's supposed proposal to France for a preventive war against Germany. "It is known," von Neurath remarked on April 7, 1933, "that Poland is playing with the idea of a preventive war on account of our territorial demands." Yet what von Neurath had to say about German-Polish relations at this same meeting merely confirmed Pilsudski's calculation of German aims. "Reaching an understanding with Poland," von Neurath commented, "is neither possible nor desirable . . . for the reason that in this way the interest of the world in a revision of the German-Polish border will not die down."[61]

The latter document demonstrates that the German government, in the first week of April 1933, was convinced France had received from Poland a proposal for joint military action against Germany. In Warsaw, where German officials had the most up-to-date information about Polish government affairs, Germany's ambassador to Poland, forty-eight-year-old Hans von Moltke, expressed skepticism about the rumors. There was, in his view, "no reason for believing there were Polish offensive plans" even if he acknowledged that the possibility of a Polish invasion of East Prussia was still being investigated.[62] That rumors of a Polish plan for a "preventive war" were being widely discussed by German officials is beyond dispute. In a cable from Warsaw dated April 23, 1933, von Moltke specifically referred to such rumors, writing that "in the discussion of a preventive war it is often pointed out—in my opinion, correctly—that there is no clear war aim that justifies the stakes involved. No doubt there are people here who dream of a conquest of East Prussia and Upper Silesia, but even if Poland should succeed . . . she could hardly fail to realize that this booty cannot remain a permanent possession." Von Moltke opined further that Pilsudski's main objective was to warn supporters of revisionism. On the other hand, von Moltke acknowledged that he was entirely unable to figure out Pilsudski's game plan. The marshal's objectives were impossible to discern. Pilsudski, he reported, was generally considered an opponent of a conflict with Germany. "But no one knows what he thinks or what he wants, and his plans are veiled in impenetrable obscurity."[63]

Other evidence of the presence and influence of rumors about a Polish-initiated preventive war plan is the recollection of Heinrich Brüning, who served as German chancellor from 1930 to May 1932. When asked in 1947 if he recalled rumors about a preventive war in 1933, he replied: "The fact that as soon as Hitler came to power, Marshal Pilsudski proposed to France joint preventive military action, indicated how well-grounded our fears were."[64] Reflecting further, he stated that "according to information received from our diplomatic and military agencies, Pilsudski took steps to find out if France would be ready to exert, together with Poland, military pressure on Germany. I was asked insistently . . . to inform Hitler, as energetically as possible, of the magnitude of the danger involved."[65]

Another valuable piece of evidence is a letter by Anatol Muhlstein, minister counselor at the Polish Embassy in Paris, dated April 17, 1933. He reported that rumors of a plan for a Polish preventive war were circulating "among very important political circles" in Paris.[66] The Belgian ambassador in Paris, Gaiffier d'Hestroy, similarly noted that rumors of Pilsudski's plan for a preventive war were being discussed in French government circles.[67] Still, no official French records exist of any such proposal ever having been presented. Historian Paweł Duber has argued reasonably, based on the available evidence, that Pilsudski used the threat of a preventive war to compel Hitler to make concessions but likely never put forward the plan directly to the French.[68]

What the evidence demonstrates is that Pilsudski made several inquiries into French willingness to respond militarily to German aggression against Poland. And he got a crystal-clear answer: France would not use military force to aid Poland under any circumstances. Pilsudski gleaned this information from various sources, beginning with the emissary he sent to Paris in January 1933, Jerzy Potocki, his former aide-de-camp. Potocki spent two months in Paris on the secret mission, meeting personally with French prime minister Joseph Paul-Boncour. The Potocki mission, kept secret even from the Polish ambassador to France, had been a way to gauge French interest in curbing the growth of radicalism in Germany.[69] The second emissary Pilsudski sent to Paris was Colonel Bolesław Wieniawa-Długoszowski, dispatched in March 1933 to ascertain the possibility of support for joint mobilization against Germany. But Wieniawa-Długoszowski failed to secure a meeting with any top military officials. Both missions to Paris nonetheless brought back to

Pilsudski news of France's unwillingness to act militarily to stop German rearmament.

The British also became aware of France's reluctant attitude at this time. On March 13, 1933, for example, British prime minister Ramsey MacDonald and British foreign secretary Sir John Simon asked Frence's prime minister if he was willing to use a military threat to halt German rearmament. A record of the meeting, drawn up that same day, states: "Mr. Paul-Boncour has the impression that whatever was done it would be impossible now to stop German rearming."[70] The French ambassador to Poland, Jules Laroche, shared the view of Prime Minister Paul-Boncourt. In a meeting in Warsaw with his German counterpart on February 22, 1933, Laroche "has foreseen that only new friction and lasting enmity between Poland and Germany would result from the system of Corridor." Laroche further told the German ambassador, von Moltke, that "it was in the interest of Poland to reach a rapprochement with Germany, and he understood that that was not possible without eliminating the Corridor." When asked whether he had communicated these opinions to Polish officials, Ambassador Laroche reportedly replied that he had made a point not to express such views in Polish company.[71]

The French ambassador's views represented a current in Western diplomacy of which Pilsudski was fully aware. We can discern Pilsudski's thinking from the record of a conversation he had with Lieutenant-Colonel Kazimierz Glabisz, first officer of the marshal's staff. According to Glabisz's report, dated April 18, 1933, Pilsudski said, "Germany dreams of cooperation with Russia—like in Bismarck's era. Such cooperation would be our undoing. We cannot let it happen." Although an alliance between Nazi Germany and Soviet Russia was unlikely, Pilsudski reportedly said that "the strangest alliances have been made in this world." Pondering how to prevent this from happening, he said: "It will be a difficult game on account of the paralysis of will among the Western Powers and their shortsightedness, and the failure of my own federalist plans."[72] In other words, Pilsudski seemed to be saying, the failure to erect an independent Ukraine, which would have provided a buffer between Poland and Russia, had rendered Poland unable to defend itself against a joint German-Russian invasion.

Pilsudski meanwhile left the capital for Vilna on April 20, 1933, for celebrations marking the fourteenth anniversary of the reoccupation of the city. For the event, which took place on April 21, officials gathered an esti-mated thirty-five thousand troops for a parade before Pilsudski in full battle order. Foreign observers closely monitored yet another outward dis-play of military strength by Pilsudski. Some saw it as a maneuver to make a public show of strength, a kind of dress rehearsal for full mobilization. "A surprise order had been issued through the country," the *New York Times* reported on April 26, 1933, "and all men, tanks and other war equipment were rushed to Vilna. This demonstration is said to have satisfied Marshal Pilsudski and the Ministers regarding the war preparedness of the Polish Army." The military parade included not only tanks but armored vehicles and several squadrons of airplanes.

The massive military parade in Vilna was closely observed in Berlin, where "no doubt its significance was fully debated, particularly as rumors of the im-minence of a 'preventative war' directed against Germany were widely cur-rent. It was represented that Pilsudski sounded France regarding her joint participation in such a war, but finding her not feeling strong enough to en-gage in it, he had determined that Poland should undertake it alone."[73] The mood in Berlin was reflected in a statement by the German vice-chancellor, Franz von Papen, who told the *Times* of London on April 27, 1933, that the rumor of a preventive war against Germany "was not only a crime against Germany and her European mission but a crime against the existence of Western civilization. The German Government would take all necessary mea-sures to enlighten world opinion about the source and the motives of such sinister plans against world peace and would take the most rigorous measures to preclude any possibility which would give occasion to foreign Powers to realize such dark schemes."[74]

Using the threat of military force as leverage, Pilsudski paved the way for a favorable outcome in negotiations. On May 2, 1933, the long-awaited meeting took place between Pilsudski's special envoy in Berlin, Wysocki, and Hitler. "I take this opportunity to draw the Chancellor's attention," Wysocki said to Hitler, "to Poland's vigilance with regard to all questions connected with her access to the sea and the rights she acquired in Danzig under the Treaty of Versailles." In the name of the Pilsudski government, Wysocki asked Hitler to issue a declaration "that neither he nor the Government of the Reich has any desire to encroach upon Poland's rights and interests in the Free City of Danzig."[75]

Wysocki was more than pleased with Hitler's response. Turning to Foreign Minister von Neurath, Hitler instructed him to draft such a letter. The following day, the German government press agency released a statement stating that "the Chancellor stressed the firm intention of the German Government to keep its attitude and actions strictly within the limits of the existing treaties."[76] Although the statement directly contradicted Hitler's remarks to the *Sunday Express* from February 1933, it nevertheless introduced a reprieve from the rising tension and rumors of a preventive war. Perhaps the most judicious and sober assessment came from the Berlin correspondent of the *Times* of London, who wrote on May 5, 1933, that it was too optimistic to maintain that this communiqué represented the beginning of a new era in Polish-German relations: "The most that seems to have been accomplished is a return to correct relationships and a dispersal of the dangerous feeling that an early war was likely or inevitable." In contrast, the Berlin correspondent for the *New York Times* on May 5 struck an optimistic note, stating that the agreement represented "a decisive improvement in German-Polish relations."

Two weeks after the communiqué was issued, Hitler's speech to the Reichstag similarly struck a conciliatory note. Calming growing tensions around his coming to power, Hitler stated that his government wished to resolve any conflicts with its neighbors peacefully without military solutions, and that it respected "the understandable demands of Poland."[77] The pro-government *Gazeta Polska* stated on May 5, 1933, that the meeting in Berlin "has had a calming effect on Polish-German relations."

In Warsaw, meanwhile, Pilsudski met with General Max Schindler, the German military attaché in Poland. Meeting Poland's sixty-five-year-old ruler for the first time, Schindler described Pilsudski as appearing older than he was by at least ten years, commenting that "[his] gait is shuffling and tired, his posture bent over." He continued that "his bushy eyebrows as well as the sparse white mustache which is brushed far back under the lower lip lend his appearance at first a somewhat somber character which may be intentional." The marshal's sober disposition changed once the conversation got going, and "his whole personality acquires a certain charm." Schindler noted that "a certain undertone of kindness is unmistakable."[78] The German military attaché concluded his portrait: "It is indisputable that a certain suggestive power emanates from Pilsudski, which explains the fact that his entourage clings to him with such fanaticism. His great successes have certainly contributed to increasing within himself the consciousness of the value of his personality. It is impossible to escape the impression of being confronted with a particularly striking personality."[79]

In Berlin, meanwhile, conciliatory rhetoric of Germany's new regime continued during the summer of 1933. Pilsudski, aware that the new direction in German foreign policy was likely the direct result of his military action and threats, instructed Wysocki to organize a second meeting with Hitler. The meeting coincided with changes of personnel in the Polish ambassadorial staff. Pilsudski reassigned Wysocki to Rome while naming thirty-nine-year-old Józef Lipski the new ambassador to Germany on July 2, 1933. In a farewell meeting with the German chancellor on July 13, 1933, Wysocki reported that Hitler spoke in a "peaceful and friendly tone" and said that "his Party and the Government, . . . so long as he was at their head, could not have any aggressive designs against any State, nor therefore against Poland." What's more, Wysocki continued, "the Chancellor also told me he had given orders in Danzig that quarrels with Poland were to be avoided, and he was prepared to believe that the atmosphere created there would give the best results."[80]

In June 1933 Pilsudski left Warsaw for a seven-week stay in Pikieliszki, an eighteenth-century manor farmstead north of Vilna. He asked Wysocki to visit him prior to his departure for Rome, and on July 21 Wysocki arrived with Beck. "I noticed immediately that he was not in good spirits," Wysocki recalled. "His uniform was unbuttoned, without a halter, and on his ear, as usual, traces of aftershave soap. He put out his hand to us in silence."[81] From Wysocki's account, we learn that Pilsudski expounded in detail on key elements in Polish foreign policy that he wanted the new ambassador to Italy to express abroad. First, he told the two diplomats, the foundation of Polish foreign policy was the principle that the country's security depended on the maintenance of existing treaties, especially where borders were involved. In Eastern Europe, Poland desired stable relations with Soviet Russia and unambiguous support for the territorial integrity of the Baltic states. For the first time in the history of the Second Republic, Pilsudski could breathe a sigh of relief—at least temporarily—due to Poland's two treaties with Soviet Union and Nazi Germany. At the same time, he reiterated that it was the alliance with France that formed the basis of his national policy.[82]

Unable to attend the twelfth annual convention of Legionnaires in Warsaw on August 6, 1933, Pilsudski instead sent a statement in writing, which would be his last address to this annual meeting. "When I am sitting on the shore of a beautiful lake near Vilna," he wrote from Pikieliszki, "and listening to the soft murmur of a gently plummeting wave, I recalled the history of my turbulent and adventurous past."[83] He then excerpted Juliusz Słowacki's epic poem, "Beniowski," from the part published posthumously in 1849 that portrayed the young hero during the time of the fight against the Russians during the Confederation of Bar (1768–1772):

> For when I scratch through Poland's ashy relic,
> Then on the harp-strings touch with my pure hand,
> Ghosts rise up from the grave, so sweet and grand!
> Transparent, bright! So lively, fresh-bestowed,
> That I can't cry for them with heart on sleeve.[84]

Pilsudski appeared inspired, sitting in rural solitude and calm, peaceful surroundings. "Moments, when the heart broke with pain and fatigue, when foreheads were dewy not only with sweat but often with blood—I had to call forth endurance." He continued that "in the blue water of the lake I can see my eyes . . . the eyes of a child, full of delight and full of curiosity. And I shall always think that living as I lived—there was value in it—was worth the pain and suffering."[85]

In Germany, meanwhile, Pilsudski's foreign policy strategy seemed to be working as intended. Hitler's speech to the Reichstag of May 17, 1933, publicly committed Germany to recognize existing treaties. No previous German chancellor had made similar pronouncements. The former secretary of state in the Reich chancellery, Otto Meissner, later remarked that Hitler had been informed in March 1933 that Pilsudski had proposed a preventive war to the French. Fearing France may accept, he decided to emphasize peaceful relations with Poland in his speech as a result.[86] Brüning speculated that Hitler's conciliatory speech to the Reichstag, vowing to respect all existing international treaties, was the outcome of this news. In Brüning's opinion, Hitler's conciliatory message had gone too far because, as he wrote, by mid-May 1933, "our information from Paris indicated that France hesitated to accept Pilsudski's proposal."[87] The marked improvement in Polish-German relations thus led Pilsudski to put on hold a military option. But Pilsudski's suspicions were revived on October 14, 1933, when Hitler pulled Germany out of the League of Nations and withdrew from the Conference on Disarmament.

The announcement took all of Europe by surprise. The Western press reacted with great concern. In its cover-page article appearing on October 15, 1933, the *New York Times* warned that "any increase in [Hitler's] military strength is a danger to the security of France and her allies. It is perfectly true to say that the political situation in Europe today is the worst the Old World has seen since the end of the World War."

Pilsudski regarded Germany's announcement as extremely worrisome. Pilsudski acted quickly and decisively, calling forth a meeting with Foreign Minister Beck and his undersecretary of foreign affairs, Szembek. Up-to-date information on the state of German armaments was urgently needed, Pilsudski said. This involved, he continued, reaching out to French intelligence agencies possessing the most current figures. Pilsudski asked that Beck and Szembek request that a reply be provided within no more than six days. He therefore instructed his foreign minister and undersecretary to make contact with French government and military officials. The French should be told as sternly as possible, Pilsudski said, that these talks absolutely had to be kept secret. Pilsudski had no wish to be an alarm bell for journalists.[88]

To maintain secrecy, Pilsudski decided to pursue talks outside of official diplomatic channels. He chose Captain Ludwig Morstin, a former officer in the First Brigade, and, in 1919–1920, a liaison officer with the Polish High Command to the French General Staff. During his time in Paris, Morstin had been on very good terms with General Maxime Weygand, a tie Pilsudski wanted to capitalize on. So he sent Morstin on a mission to Paris with instructions to ask Weygand to present two questions to the French government in the name of Poland, a request to which Weygand agreed: Would France order the mobilization of her armed forces if Germany attacked Poland; and in case of such German aggression toward Poland, would France move her armed forces to the German border?

Morstin left for Paris on October 21, 1933. Weygand and his wife greeted him warmly, and insisted he stay as a guest in their home. Weygand was able to pull the necessary strings. A few days later, he presented Pilsudski's questions to the French foreign minister, Joseph Paul-Boncour, who then met with French president Albert Lebrun to discuss the matter. A few days later, Paul-Boncour gave Weygand the French government's answer to Pilsudski's questions: no to both. France could only promise military aid to Poland in the form of staff, armaments, and ammunition. Sometime at the end of October or early November, Morstin traveled back to Warsaw and informed Pilsudski in person about the French reply.[89]

Pilsudski had no other option than to conclude that the French-Polish alliance contained, in practice, no military guarantee of Poland's borders. He pondered the idea of a preventive war for a second time in the fall of 1933 "before taking the decision to negotiate with Germany in view of France's position."[90] On November 5 Pilsudski held a meeting in Warsaw with Ambassador Lipski, whom he had summoned from Berlin, and Foreign Minister Beck. After listening to Lipski's detailed review of the situation in Germany by Lipski, Pilsudski turned to Beck and remarked that it was time to move forward on a negotiated agreement with Germany. In the planned meeting between the Polish ambassador and the German chancellor, Lipski was to present a set of concerns from Pilsudski. He was first to say that Poland based its security, in part, on the adherence of European states to existing treaties guaranteed by the League of Nations. But Germany's withdrawal from the League had removed that element of security. Thus, the German chancellor had to reassure Poland. "Pilsudski," Lipski recalled, "laid special stress on the sentence about 'the necessity of [Hitler] taking steps to reinforce security. . . . *This you must tell him.*'" Pilsudski further instructed Lipski that security had to be guaranteed not only for the present but for the future as well. "Pilsudski was at the time in a very serious mood," Lipski wrote, "and it was obvious that he had a weighty decision on his mind."[91] That evening Lipski left for Berlin, after having leaked news of his conference with Pilsudski. The daily press, such as the *Manchester Guardian* on November 10, 1933, revealed the forthcoming conference with Hitler.

On November 15, 1933, Lipski and Hitler had their high-profile meeting. In the presence of German foreign minister von Neurath, Lipski conveyed to Hitler Pilsudski's regards and wishes for the development of peaceful ties through direct negotiations. He then communicated, explicitly in Pilsudski's name, the request that Germany take concrete steps to assure Poland's security. "What can it offer to Poland to reassure her," Lipski asked. Hitler replied, Lipski wrote, "that he had no intention whatsoever of effecting any change by resort to war. The Chancellor was anxious for good relations with Poland, and a favorable atmosphere, so that the common life of the two nations would take a normal course." What's more, Hitler is reported to have said, "Poland is an outpost against Asia. The destruction of Poland would be a misfortune for the States which would consequently become neighbors of Asia."[92] According to Lipski, Hitler never uttered the words "frontier" or "corridor" during the meeting.

On November 16, 1933, the German, Polish, and international press published an official German communiqué. Chancellor Hitler and the Polish ambassador in Berlin, the document stated, "renounce all application of force in their mutual relations, with a view to strengthening European peace."[93] The communiqué no doubt calmed nerves in Europe and abroad. Pilsudski's reaction was echoed in the pages of the semi-official government daily, *Gazeta Polska,* which characterized the agreement as an advance of fundamental importance in the country's foreign affairs. "The Locarno Agreement brought a mutual commitment on nonaggression between Germany and France," *Gazeta Polska* stated on November 16, 1933. "Yesterday's declaration brings the same thing between Germany and Poland. In this sense, it can be said without hesitation that one of Locarno's main gaps was closed yesterday."

The London correspondent of the *Manchester Guardian,* in its edition of November 17, 1933, tapped into the heart of the matter when he stated that the crux of the issue "turns on the question of the Polish Corridor. That was the chief concern of the German Revisionist propaganda . . . for the last ten years," the paper stated, adding significantly, "but it does not seem to be so important to the Third Reich." And, in fact, Pilsudski and his foreign affairs minister emphasized Hitler's Austrian origins, contrasting them with the Prussian statesmen who preceded him. The Austrian background, they believed, made Hitler more willing to compromise on the Polish Corridor. During his meeting with Pilsudski on November 5, 1933, for example, Lipski noted the great weight Pilsudski attached to the Prussian influence on prior German leaders. The German government moved swiftly to the signing of a formal nonaggression pact. On November 24, 1933, Foreign Minister Neurath informed von Moltke in Warsaw that Hitler had approved the draft of a

German-Polish declaration. Hitler requested that von Moltke present it in person to Marshal Pilsudski in the name of the Reich chancellor.[94]

Pilsudski welcomed von Moltke at Belvedere Palace on November 27, 1933. In the presence of Polish foreign minister Beck, von Moltke proceeded to read out loud the draft in German. Pilsudski, von Moltke noted, "expressed his desire to put German-Polish relations on a friendly basis, but emphasized with a bluntness that I had hardly heard before from Polish politicians that the thousand-year-old anti-German feelings of the Polish people would place great difficulties in the way of the implementation of this policy."[95] Von Moltke wrote that "the Marshal . . . gives the impression of being intellectually fresh, but physically old beyond his years and almost frail."[96]

Later that same day Pilsudski left Warsaw for an extended stay in Vilna. With the German draft in hand, he took his time reviewing the text, making several changes. Prior to presenting his revised draft to the Germans, Pilsudski received two German representatives of the Danzig Senate—Hermann Rauschning and Arthur Greiser—on December 11, 1933, in a goodwill gesture that helped further relax German-Polish tensions. After another month he cabled Ambassador Lipski the revised Polish version of the Declaration. On January 9, 1934, Lipski handed Pilsudski's revised draft to the German foreign minister, and all the changes were accepted.[97] Pilsudski returned to Warsaw on January 15, 1934.

ON JANUARY 26, 1934, a ceremony in Berlin was held at the signing of the Polish-German Declaration, which the press referred to as a nonaggression pact. Signed by German foreign minister Baron von Neurath and Polish ambassador to Germany Józef Lipski, the declaration, lasting for a ten-year period, committed both governments "to settle directly all questions of whatever nature which concern their mutual relations peacefully" in which "in no circumstances . . . will they proceed to the application of force. . . . The two Governments base their action on the fact that the maintained and guarantee of a lasting peace between their countries is an essential prerequisite for the general peace in Europe."[98] After ratification of the treaty by the two countries' parliaments, and the approval of the German and Polish presidents, the agreement went into effect on February 24, 1934, at a ceremony attended by von Moltke and Beck in Warsaw.

The landmark agreement was seen by Pilsudski as an important achievement. It was the culmination of a gradual shift in the period 1932–1934 away from reliance on France toward a policy of equilibrium between Poland's two powerful neighbors. Right below the surface of his joy at achieving diplomatic success, though, Pilsudski was brutally pessimistic about the long-term prospects of peace. Alexandra Pilsudska recalled the first exchange she had with her husband after the signing of the German-Polish Declaration. "It was a diplomatic victory," she wrote, "but it did not deceive my husband. 'It will give us longer to prepare our defenses . . . ,' he said to me afterwards. 'But it is only a question of putting off the evil day. While Germany looks toward the Corridor and Russia has her eyes on the west there can be no lasting security for us.'"[99]

Pilsudski revealed his fears about the prospects for security at an extraordinary meeting at Belvedere Palace with current and former prime ministers. He spoke in the company of President Mościcki, Foreign Minister Beck, Prime Minister Alexander Prystor, Minister of Education Jan Jędrzejewicz, Sejm speaker Kazimierz Świtalski, as well as all former prime ministers. Reflecting on the state of Polish foreign policy in the previous two years, Pilsudski is reported to have said the following: "The commandant does not believe that this arrangement of peaceful relations between Poland and its two neighbors was to last," Świtalski wrote in his diary entry for March 7, 1934. "The Commandant estimates that good relations between Poland and Germany will last for another four years," Świtalski noted.[100]

The immediate reaction to the Polish-German accord was exuberance and relief. Stockholm announced that Pilsudski's name had been put forward for a Nobel Peace Prize "as the man who has done most for the maintenance of world peace."[101] Some called it a diplomatic miracle, considering the two countries were on the brink of war nine months prior. "This remarkable Treaty," the London-based *Observer* stated on January 28, 1934, "represents nothing less than a fundamental change in the conditions of European diplomacy. . . . Both Herr Hitler and Marshal Pilsudski are to be congratulated, but Herr Hitler more." The *New York Times,* reporting on January 27, went further, calling the accord "an international political move of the highest importance, marking Poland's efforts to secure peace and relieve the political tension of Europe."

On the day the pact was signed, Foreign Minister Beck distributed a communiqué to Polish embassies abroad describing the agreement as "an act of great political importance."[102] The Warsaw correspondence for the *Times* of London, in its edition of January 19, 1934, was full of praise for Poland's leader, describing "the German-Polish non-aggression pact further evidence of the political skill and vision of marshal Pilsudski." The paper's correspondent in Berlin remarked in the same edition of the paper that past German chancellors in the Weimar Republic could have concluded the same agreement with Poland. "They would, however, have been attacked as traitors if they had attempted any such thing," the corresponded remarked.

Hitler reinforced the spirit of the treaty in his address to the Reichstag on January 30, 1934, marking the first anniversary of Hitler's coming to power. The government of Germany, Hitler said, "has made efforts since its first year to arrive at new and better relations with the state of Poland." Germany, he continued, "is happy to find in the Chief of the actual Polish State, Marshal Pilsudski, the same larger-minded conception, and so to be able to fix this conception in a treaty which will not only be of service equally to the German people and the Polish people, but will also constitute a great contribution to the maintenance of the general peace."[103] Pilsudski understood perfectly that Hitler's words constituted nothing more than hollow rhetoric but that the agreement at least bought Poland some time.

In Western Europe, meanwhile, some Western diplomats saw the treaty as a public breach in the French alliance system. The secrecy with which the Polish-German negotiations were conducted had aroused suspicion and mistrust. The French ambassador to Germany, André François-Poncet, was livid. For two days before the German-Polish Declaration was announced, he had met with his Polish counterpart in Berlin, Ambassador Lipski, who did not breathe a word about the upcoming signing ceremony. "From then on," François-Poncet remarked, "there could be no trust. We could no longer treat him as an ally."[104]

There was speculation, for example, that Poland had agreed to end its opposition to German revisionist aims in Austria and Czechoslovakia. To allay these fears, Pilsudski met with the French ambassador to Poland, Jules Laroche, on January 29, 1934, to assure him the rumors were baseless. "Don't look in the Declaration for anything other than what is in it," Laroche, in a report drawn up that day, quoted Pilsudski as saying.[105]

Paris's influential newspaper of record, *Le Temps*, devoted much of its leading articles to the topic, with an exuberant, positive editorial. Its evaluation of the German-Polish Non-Aggression Pact (the term the paper used) was significant. "It would be undoubtedly risky to conclude that the Germany of Hitler has renounced its Pan German gaze on the East," *Le Temps* stated. "But no matter what the real thoughts of Berlin are, the prospect of a ten-year pause in the German-Polish conflict is a very important development for the situation in Europe. We have no doubt that this will serve the cause for peace."[106] The paper added that the accord with Germany in no way invalidated the existing treaties Poland had with France, Romania, and Soviet Russia. In its edition of January 29, 1934, the *Times* of London took a more cautious view, arguing that France was in part to blame for Poland's drift from the Western alliance system. "It is hoped here that France will learn a lesson from the pact. Poland . . . has now detached herself from the constellation of Western Europe, and will go her way alone and peaceful."

It was the Soviet Union that expressed the gravest concern about the new diplomatic arrangement. In its first communiqué on the subject, issued on January 30, 1934, Soviet authorities castigated the agreement as a victory for Germany alone. "If Germany has recognized the frontiers with Poland," the official Soviet news agency stated, "that would mean either full capitulation in its foreign policy by the Hitler government or else some great political maneuver."[107] Described by the French military attaché to Poland, Charles d'Arbonneau, as a policy of "sacré égoisme" (sacred egoism) and by Stalin as "a policy of zigzags," the French and Soviets clearly misunderstood Pilsudski's policy of equilibrium. As historian Marek Kornat has argued, the British and French policy of appeasing Germany in the period 1925–1933 gave Pilsudski no alternative but to seek friendly ties with his two giant neighbors.[108] Hitler, seeking to avoid a military confrontation while his country was still demilitarized, took the rumors of a preventive war seriously. For he realized that a rapprochement with Poland was for the time being necessary while he rearmed. Pilsudski was well aware of the fragility of maintaining friendly ties with Nazi Germany and Soviet Russia. As he told his undersecretary for foreign affairs in April 1934, the diplomatic game of navigating relations with Nazi Germany and Soviet Russia was comparable to "sitting on two stools that cannot last long. We must know which one we shall fall off first and when."[109]

In the aforementioned meeting of current and former prime ministers held at Belvedere on March 7, 1934, Pilsudski reflected on the German-Polish pact. The trigger that led him to pursue an agreement with Berlin, Pilsudski said, was Germany's withdrawal from the League of Nations in October 1933. "The commandant explained," Kazimierz Świtalski noted, "that he took advantage of the moment Germany withdrew from the League of Nations and put forward the issue in the following manner: since Germany was no longer restrained by the League of Nations, it has to give Poland some security guarantees. Without Germany's acquiescence, the commandant intended to put together a defensive military system explicitly directed against Germany. Unexpectedly, however, Hitler agreed to the terms at once. On this turn of events," Świtalski summarized Pilsudski as saying, "Hitler came out bravely against the Prussians; he began to enunciate recognition of Poland as a state."[110]

In the next part of his talk, Pilsudski discussed his views of German-Polish relations moving forward. "The commandant does not much appreciate the signed accord," Świtalski remarked in his diary on March 7, 1934, "but rather stresses more that the attitude of Hitler is changing the psychology of the German people towards Poland. The consequence is that even if Prussians return to power, which would be the worst for Poland, this psychological change among the Germans will be an obstacle for them to revert back to the old anti-Polish politics."[111] The March 7 meeting with the highest dignitaries of the Second Polish Republic revealed Pilsudski's thinking about foreign relations in the immediate aftermath of the German-Polish Declaration. The record of the March 7 gathering, historian Piotr Wandycz maintained, "is without doubt the most important document providing a window into Pilsudski's reasoning and conception behind the German-Polish Declaration."[112]

CHAPTER 18

Pilsudski's Last Year

It was said that when Marshal Pilsudski died, not a single burglary took place in Warsaw; the criminal world too felt the solemnity of the moment.

—IRENA PROTASSEWICZ

In the last year of his life, Pilsudski focused on maximizing Poland's security in the face of a dramatically changing international landscape. Although he placed great importance on his achievements in signing non-aggression pacts with his two large neighbors, Pilsudski continued to regard the alliance with France as the key to security. An important development in this regard was a change in the French government in Poland's favor. On January 27, 1934, Joseph Paul-Bancour's tenure as France's foreign minister came to an end. On February 9, the newly named prime minister, Gaston Doumergue, appointed seventy-one-year-old Louis Barthou to the post of foreign minister. Unlike his predecessor, Barthou opposed the Four Powers Pact, putting him in distinct favor with the Polish government.

The change in attitude was reflected in Foreign Minister Barthou's decision to make an official state visit to Warsaw on April 22, 1934. The trip was highly symbolic as the first official visit of a French foreign minister to re-born Poland. That ties between the new French foreign minister and Pilsudski would be close was anticipated. The two had known each other since 1921, when Barthou took part in the signing of the Polish-French accord. Now, thirteen years later, Barthou sat with Pilsudski in Warsaw in an effort to restore ties in the wake of the German-Polish Declaration.

The two-hour meeting at the Belvedere Palace took place on April 23 in the presence of Poland's foreign minister, Beck, its undersecretary for foreign affairs, Jan Szembek, and the French ambassador to Poland, Jules Laroche. The talks began with Barthou assuring Pilsudski that as France's new foreign minister, he would take a hard stand on Germany. On German revisionism, Barthou told Pilsudski that he stood firmly and unwaveringly opposed. Pilsudski nodded approvingly, then presented what he referred to as the three pillars of Polish foreign policy: improving relations with its two giant neighbors; maintaining Poland's alliances with France and Romania; and strengthening the country's relations with the League of Nations.[1]

Laroche's contemporaneous report of the meeting described a natural rapport between Barthou and Pilsudski, along with a cordial atmosphere. "Marshal Pilsudski," Laroche wrote, "gave Mr. Barthou an exceptionally friendly welcome. I noticed that his face lit up when he saw it." He continued, "Mr. Beck told us that the Marshal had never shown so much friendship toward a foreign personality."[2] In the discussion about foreign policy, Laroche described an exchange in which "Marshal Pilsudski forcefully affirmed his government's commitment to its alliance with France." On the other hand, Pilsudski emphasized that his policy was dominated by the reality of his two powerful neighboring countries, Germany and the Soviet Union. According to Laroche, Pilsudski commented that the nonaggression pacts concluded with them "leave my hands absolutely free."[3]

Barthou then reassured Pilsudski that the new French cabinet stood firmly opposed to German rearmament. He was surely surprised at Pilsudski's reply—essentially that it was in the French national character to concede. "In my view," Pilsudski remarked to Minister Barthou, "you will yield." According to Szembek's account, Minister Barthou was quite taken aback by the remark, stating, "That is very harsh, Marshal. Let me assure you that the decisions of the present French government are extremely firm and absolutely final." Pilsudski then alluded to the problem of rapidly changing governments in France, leading to shifts in policy, and reminded Barthou of an exchange they had had during his 1921 visit to France. When he and Barthou strolled together in Verdun alongside Marshal Pétain, Barthou tripped over a pebble and almost fell. Barthou, Pilsudski reminded him, had then remarked, "No worries. I'm used to falling. I've been a minister thirteen times." Pilsudski

French foreign minister Louis Barthou (*center*) meeting with Pilsudski (*center, left*), along with French ambassador Jules Laroche (*left*), Poland's foreign minister Jozef Beck (*second from right*), and Poland's undersecretary of foreign affairs, Jan Szembek (*right*). Warsaw, April 22, 1934.

then added, "Maybe you yourself will not wish to yield but then either you would withdraw from the Cabinet or you would be outvoted."[4] The Warsaw meeting between France's foreign minister and Pilsudski lasted for two hours and "was permeated with a warm and cordial atmosphere, with Marshal Pilsudski frequently reminiscing in a pleasant manner about his time with Barthou in Paris back in 1921."[5]

Pilsudski's assurances that the German-Polish nonaggression pact in no way undermined the French-Polish alliance affirmed Barthou's position. "The French-Polish alliance," Barthou said at a press conference, "is intact and indissoluble."[6] The Warsaw correspondent of the *New York Times,* in its edition of April 25, 1934, commented, "Mr. Barthou's two-day stay here proved beyond doubt that the alliance is still strong and healthy." Meanwhile, the Polish government declared that "the long conversation which the French Minister for Foreign Affairs had with Marshal Pilsudski at the Belvedere yesterday [demonstrates] that the basis of the alliance between Poland and France remains absolutely immutable and that this alliance constitutes an element eminently constructive in European politics."[7] The pro-government daily, *Gazeta Polska,* devoted detailed and resoundingly positive coverage of the event.[8]

The Paris daily *Le Temps* characterized the Warsaw meeting as a positive step in European security. Barthou's exchange with Pilsudski demonstrated, the paper stated, that the Polish-French alliance was "unshakable." The paper continued that France had always been in favor of a détente in German-Polish relations and that the German-Polish nonaggression pact in no way diminished the importance of the French-Polish alliance. The paper quoted Foreign Minister Beck's words that the French-Polish alliance was an essential, long-lasting element of Poland's foreign policy whose goal was peace. "In the midst of these complex and troubling European problems," Barthou said in his Warsaw address, "the friendship between France and Poland constitutes a factor for peace, stability, order and security." *Le Temps* credited Pilsudski with dramatically improving Poland's position in Europe, stating that since France and Poland signed the alliance in 1921, "Poland has become a stronger power and no longer feels it is caught between a Russia that is hostile and a Germany that knows no other method than that of threats and intimidation."[9]

Without mentioning Locarno (1925) or the Four Powers Pact (1933), Barthou promised that France would no longer enter into international agreements affecting Poland's security without consulting Poland first.[10] Pilsudski understood French priorities in foreign policy well. In particular, Pilsudski knew that reaching an agreement with Germany would give Poland more leverage in negotiations with France. Poland's pro-government daily, reporting on the Barthou-Pilsudski exchange, called the French-Polish alliance "permanent and unwavering."[11]

Reporting on the Russian perspective, *Le Temps* interviewed Soviet officials who said they were watching closely in hopes that Pilsudski would emerge with a clear, unambiguous French orientation. For, as one Soviet official said, "by its geographic position, Poland can serve as either a buffer between Germany and Soviet Russia or as the front line in a German attack."[12] Pilsudski's view of the Franco-Polish alliance was also shaped by a rather pessimistic perception of French power. When asked in June 1934 about relations with France, Pilsudski is said to have replied, "I fear for the fate of France in a war against Germany. France will not win this war."[13]

The optimism coming out of the Barthou-Pilsudski meeting was further bolstered by more good news on the diplomatic front. On the day of Barthou's meeting with Pilsudski, Moscow announced that negotiations had begun with Polish officials on extending the Soviet-Polish nonaggression pact for another ten years.

The rumors about a new Polish-Soviet agreement became reality on May 5, 1934, when the two countries signed a few protocols in Moscow. The strengthening and reaffirmation of the 1932 Soviet-Polish Non-Aggression Pact was intended, the agreement stated, as "fresh proof of the unchangeable character and solidarity of the pacific and friendly relations happily established between them." The two countries thus declared a ten-year extension of the 1932 accord until December 31, 1945. In the second protocol, Poland and Soviet Russia affirmed that neither country is at present, nor will be in the future, party to any agreement that might conflict with peace between the two countries. The two countries furthermore renounced all designs on the territory of the other.[14] "The Soviet-Polish reaffirmation concerning territorial design," the *New York Herald Tribune* remarked on May 6, 1934, "is considered of special interest because of alleged German National Socialist plans for territorial adjustment, under which the so-called Corridor or other Polish territory would be returned to Germany, and Poland would receive in compensation part or all of the Soviet Ukraine."

Another newspaper maintained that the second protocol "settles the question of whether Germany and Poland have had some secret agreement which might menace the Soviet Union." The Moscow correspondent of the *New York Times* further reported on May 6, 1934, that the signing of the protocol "is taken here as a demonstration that there is no secret German-Polish agreement. By the terms of the peace treaty between Poland and the Soviet Union . . . both nations renounced further territorial claims against each other."

The strengthening of Poland's accord with Soviet Russia, coming on the heels of Barthou's trip to Warsaw, marked in large part the culmination of Pilsudski's aims in foreign affairs. He had achieved international calm and security, temporarily suspending any chance of compromising his country's security. Second, Pilsudski raised Poland's status in the eyes of the Western democracies, sending the strong message that wavering on guarantees of frontiers would lead Poland to do whatever necessary to ensure its own security.

A Diplomatic Breakthrough

Despite Pilsudski's extraordinary achievement establishing his policy of equilibrium, the pact with Nazi Germany undoubtedly led to a series of awkward photo exchanges. The most notable was the visit of Nazi propaganda minister Joseph Goebbels to Warsaw.

Arriving on June 13, 1934, Goebbels had been invited by a Polish organization to speak at Warsaw University. Concerned about its image abroad, the Polish government emphasized that it regarded the visit as private, not official.[15] The private nature of the visit did not prevent such figures as Poland's new prime minister, Leon Kozłowski, from attending. Pilsudski chose not to attend. By his absence, Pilsudski made known his evident unease with Goebbels's presence. The lecture Goebbels gave, "The Ideology of National Socialism and Its Achievements in the Third Reich," was not received well. The estimated thousand people in attendance reportedly reacted "politely but with very unenthusiastic applause."[16]

The very fact that Pilsudski did not agree to meet Goebbels until a day after his arrival was indicative of the marshal's discomfort. But he decided to do so in the end, hosting Goebbels at Belvedere Palace with a thirty-minute time limit on the afternoon of June 14, 1934. By all accounts, it was a cordial exchange but politics was evidently not discussed.[17] The photograph of Pilsudski with Goebbels at Belvedere revealed an unsmiling Pilsudski, standing physically distant from Goebbels. "The strange manner of his arrival," the *Jewish Chronicle* of London reported on June 22, 1934, "the numerous anti-Nazi demonstrations that greeted him, the lecture itself and the fact that Marshal Pilsudski kept him waiting for twenty-four hours before agreeing to receive him, made this first visit of the Nazi minister to the Polish capital a very disappointing affair."

Meanwhile, the presence of Nazi Germany's propaganda minister met with an enthusiastic response from Poland's tiny fascist-style political party. Founded on April 1934, the National-Radical Camp (*Obóz Narodowo-Radykalny*, ONR) issued its Declaration of Principles openly hostile to democratic government and seething with hatred toward the Jews. "The Jew cannot be a citizen of the Polish State," the ONR founding program stated. "As long as Jews live on Polish lands, their property will be regarded as belonging to the Polish State." It further stipulated that "the de-Judaization [*odżydzenie*] of Polish cities and towns is an essential precondition for the healthy development of the Nation." The latter program was intended, the program emphasized, to facilitate mass Jewish emigration.[18]

It is not surprising, then, that the ONR's broadcasting of its antigovernment and anti-Semitic views spiked when Goebbels arrived in Warsaw. So alarmed was the Polish government at the propaganda appearing in the ONR's newspaper, *Sztafeta* (Relay Race), on the day of Goebbels's speech in Warsaw on June 13, 1934, that its agents entered the offices of the newspaper, removed the printing press, and ordered the paper banned, arguing that the paper was a threat to public safety. As the press reported, the Polish interior minister, Bolesław Pieracki, ordered the action against the ONR.[19] The following day, on Thursday, June 14, the ONR's organizing committee chairman, Jan Mosdorf, phoned the offices of the Interior Ministry and asked to speak with Minister Pieracki. Informed that the interior minister was out of the office until Monday, Mosdorf reportedly replied, "That will be too late."[20]

The following day, Pieracki had lunch with colleagues at the Social Club in Warsaw. As he exited the building onto the street, two men shot him at close range, killing him instantly. The interior minister was on his way to announce on national radio the decision to outlaw the ONR. Outraged at the assassination, the government, probably at the direction of Pilsudski, announced its intention to declare the ONR illegal, and hundreds of its members were arrested.[21] Jewish periodicals around the world praised the government. In its edition of June 22, 1934, the *Jewish Chronicle* in London stated that, although the murderer had not yet been captured, "the Government is taking drastic action against the leaders of [the National Radical Camp]. Many of them have been arrested including the chief leader, Jan Mosdorf. After thorough house searches, all seventeen clubs of the National Racial Party in Warsaw have been closed down." The paper continued, "Mr. Kozlowski, the Premier, speaking at the funeral, said that the Government is determined to take drastic measures to put a stop to criminal violence." Other papers praised Prime Minister Kozłowski's vow to ruthlessly suppress the National Radical Party. In his speech at the railway station in Warsaw at which the coffin of the late Interior Minister Pieracki was being transported to the funeral,

Kozłowski was said to "declare war" on extremist groups that advocated violence. "The moral responsibility for this crime," he said, "rests with every political group fostering terrorist methods."[22]

Within an hour of the assassination, meanwhile, Prime Minister Kozłowski met with Pilsudski. Present was Pilsudski's adjutant, Capt. Lepecki, who described the dramatic exchange between Poland's' two top leaders. Kozłowski was said to have pointedly proposed creating an "isolation camp" for extreme, violent radicals bent on threatening public safety. Pilsudski gave his consent on the condition that such an internment camp would be temporary, lasting for not more than one year.[23] The site of the internment camp, they decided, would be Bereza Kartuska in eastern Poland near the Soviet border, isolated but with direct access by rail from Warsaw. The result of the meeting was that Prime Minister Kozłowski, with the signatures of the president and cabinet of ministers—including Pilsudski's—issued a ministerial decree on June 17 authorizing the creation an internment camp for individuals who were deemed a menace to public order and security. On July 2, 1934, meanwhile, Sejm speaker Kazimierz Świtalski, in a meeting with Prime Minister Kozłowski and Foreign Minister Beck, among others, noted that Bereza Kartuska was discussed in detail.[24]

Shortly afterward, during the evening and early morning hours of July 6–7, 1934, the top leadership of the ONR as well as the Young Section of the right-wing National Party, were arrested. They became the first inmates at the Bereza Kartuska camp. On July 10, 1934, the Polish government declared the ONR dissolved and illegal. The organization, the announcement stated, constituted a threat to public safety.[25] By July 12, 1934, the government's semi-official newspaper reported that the Bereza Kartuska camp was holding 210 inmates. The reason that over two hundred inmates were now interned there was the discovery, in the beginning of July, that the organization responsible for the assassination of Interior Minister Pieracki was not the ONR but the Organization of Ukrainian Nationalists (OUN).[26] The discovery of the Ukrainian connection was followed by more than a hundred arrests of Ukrainians involved in the organization, all brought to Bereza Kartuska.[27] To be sure, the OUN, a terrorist organization openly espousing violence against Polish officials, had been targeted earlier when, on June 14, OUN leader Stepan Bandera and twenty other party members had been arrested in Lwów. By the end of June 1934 an estimated eight hundred OUN members were in Polish prisons. The man who pulled the trigger, twenty-one-year-old Hryhorii Matseiko, shooting the interior minister in the back of the head, fled Warsaw for Lublin and then Lwów, staying with members of the OUN. Armed and with money supplied by the OUN, Matseiko crossed into Czechoslovakia on August 5, 1934, living out the rest of his life in exile under the name Petr Knysz, dying of natural causes in 1966.[28]

WHILE COMBATTING INTERNAL ENEMIES, Pilsudski set about creating a secret intelligence cell to monitor the internal affairs of Nazi Germany and Soviet Russia. The idea began to take shape in May 1934, when Pilsudski summoned the vice minister of war, General Kazimierz Fabrycy, and asked him to head an intelligence network of primary importance: to dispatch agents to monitor the internal affairs of Poland's two giant neighbors.[29] After preparing a detailed plan, Pilsudski presented it to Fabrycy in June 1934. The secret intelligence cell was to be headed by Fabrycy and would consist of undersecretary Szembek, the Polish ambassador to Soviet Russia, Juliusz Łukasiewicz, and the Polish ambassador to Germany, Józef Lipski. Lieutenant-Colonel Kazimierz Glabisz would be added to Fabrycy's staff. Pilsudski reminded Fabrycy that the most important indication of a country's likelihood for aggression against its neighbor could be known by an assessment of its internal situation. "No government, or for that matter, dictator, commenced a war while internal chaos pervaded its country," Pilsudski said. "That government or dictator must, above all, possess strong authority in its hands and feel confident in this regard. Thus, the development of the internal situation in Russia and Germany in the political and economic arena has to be, at the very least, intimately studied by your cell."[30]

Emphasizing the need for scrupulous work on the internal affairs of Germany and Soviet Russia, the secret intelligence cell became known as the Laboratory.[31] Fabrycy summarized what Pilsudski told him: "For Poland, lying between two such powerful and hostile neighbors as Russia and Germany, it is immeasurably important to know in advance with which one a conflict will likely occur first, and which of them is most dangerous." By November 1934, the Laboratory was fully operational, its first monthly report on Pilsudski's desk.[32]

In foreign affairs, meanwhile, two important events took place in the fall of 1934. The first was an outcome of Poland's new independent foreign policy after Pilsudski achieved his policy of equilibrium. At a meeting of the League of Nations in Geneva on September 13, 1934, Foreign Minister Beck announced that Poland was officially pulling out of the Minorities Treaty signed in 1919 in Paris. Prior to his speech, Beck spoke to Pilsudski by phone and is said to have obtained the marshal's unhesitating approval. The withdrawal, Foreign Minister Beck remarked, was put forward "as a symbol of our basic attitude in international relations."[33] Connected to Poland's new assertion of independence, both Beck and Pilsudski claimed no specific intention to compromise the legal status of minorities in Poland. And indeed, Beck publicly reassured the Jews that no ill intention on his or his government's part was behind the decision. In Geneva, Beck put forward his position in an interview with the *Jewish Telegraph Agency* on September 16. Poland, he said, would never permit infringements on the rights of any citizens regardless of their religion, ethnicity or native tongue. After all, he remarked, Poland's constitution guaranteed minority rights.

Not a single Jewish leader bought Beck's line. Neville Laski of the Board of Deputies of British Jews, as well as Nahum Goldmann of the Committee of Jewish Delegations, met with Beck to express their displeasure.[34] This was followed with public denunciations by American, French, and Italian government officials. The League of Nations likewise expressed "shock" at the news.[35] One day after Beck's announcement, one newspaper stated that the Polish foreign minister's statement "is widely interpreted as a declaration of the intention to arrive at a closer relationship with Germany, and as the first important result of the German-Polish Pact between marshal Pilsudski and Herr Hitler."[36]

Polish Jews, however, appeared less concerned. The president of the Jewish Parliamentary Club, Rabbi Dr. Ozjasz Thon, reminded readers that under Pilsudski's rule, no Jews had appealed to the League of Nations. "I do not wish to make a Jewish case out of this affair," Thon wrote in the pages of Kraków's Jewish daily. "So far the declaration has not hurt us, since we derive no benefit from the minority treaty and this affair is therefore an inessential aggravation for us."[37]

More dramatic were the shocking events of the following month. On October 9, 1934, Foreign Minister Barthou of France received King Alexander I of Yugoslavia in Marseille, France, on an official state visit. Barthou greeted the king as he disembarked from the ocean vessel, accompaning him to a motorcade from which the two began to ride toward their regal hotel. Unbeknownst to them, a Bulgarian nationalist was among the crowd lining the streets. When the car approached, he ran to the automobile and shot Alexander I dead. During the scuffle that followed the gunshots, Barthou was killed by a stray bullet fired by French police at the assassin. The news shocked the world.[38] Characterized as one of France's greatest living statesmen, seventy-two-year-old Barthou had first served in the government forty years earlier. Barthou's diplomatic mission to create an Eastern Pact to curb German power—a pact consisting of all the East European–collapsed with his death.[39] Pilsudski was devastated by the news of Barthou's death.

As the months passed from the fall of 1934 to the winter of 1934–1935, Pilsudski's health deteriorated significantly—especially at the beginning of 1935. Those closest to him testified that he remained cognitively lucid. Also at this time Pilsudski experienced a profound sense of loss at the death of his older sister, Zofia, who passed away in Warsaw on February 3, 1935.

On February 6, Zofia's body was transported to Vilna, where Pilsudski took part in the funeral along with family and government officials. "We were terrified by the poor appearance and frailty of the Commandant," observed one of the officials attending the funeral. "His face was literally truncated with suffering and pain."[40]

ALTHOUGH PILSUDSKI HAD REMAINED increasingly aloof from domestic affairs after he became ill, constitutional reform had been part of his broader plan for Poland since the early 1920s. Issued on April 23, 1935, and signed into law by the president and the cabinet of ministers, it was the last government document on which Pilsudski affixed his signature before his death. The new constitution was approved by a narrow interpretation of lawful parliamentary procedures that had allowed a vote in the legislature to take place without members of the opposition in attendance. With Pilsudski's health in rapid decline, the government leadership (Sanacja) succeeded in passing the new constitution before the marshal's death.

So drastic was the recalibration of the balance of power in favor of a strong executive that some foreign observers argued that the new constitution signaled the end of parliamentary democracy in Poland. According to the new constitution, the office of the president was defined as "the one and indivisible authority of the State" (Art 2, par. 4). In place of checks and balances, the new law declared that the Parliament, the Senate, the armed forces, and the courts were "organs of the State subordinate to the President" (Art. 3, par. 1). The president appointed the prime minister and nominated candidates for the ministerial posts (Art. 12). The president was also permitted to dissolve the legislature if he saw fit.

If the president chose not to run for reelection at the end of his seven-year term, or to resign, he was authorized to name one of two candidates running to succeed him (Art. 13). Allowing the president to choose his successor guaranteed that the present government would stay in power. The 1935 constitution further stripped power from the legislature by stipulating that the president himself would appoint one-third of the members of the senate (Art. 47).

At the same time, the new law kept intact the guarantees of civil liberties and religious freedom and preserved the rights of opposition parties and their presses. "The State," the constitution stated, "assures its citizens the possibility of developing their personal capabilities, as also liberty of conscience, speech and assembly" (Art. 5, par. 2). These civil rights "cannot be restricted by origin, religion, sex, or nationality" (Art. 7, par. 2). With regard to religious freedom, the 1935 constitution was explicit: "Freedom of conscience and of religion shall be guaranteed to all citizens. No citizen shall by reason of his faith or his religious convictions be limited in his access to rights" (Art. 111, par. 1). What's more, the Polish state, the constitution stipulated, would not encourage or support policies that pitted the majority against any minority: "The State aims at uniting all its citizens in harmonious cooperation for the common good" (Art. 9). The constitution also guaranteed free, secret, equal, direct, and proportional suffrage, but more generally it was designed to do away with the "Sejmocracy", or rule of the parliament, that had been a hallmark of the 1921 law.

Pilsudski, who did not seem to have been consulted prior to the announcement of the establishment of the constitution, was uneasy with the process by which the document was approved. When, back in January 1934, he observed the procedural trickery used to pass through constitutional proposals, he told Sławek and Świtalski that it was not the contents of the bill he opposed, but "it was not healthy that a Constitutional Law should be adopted by a trick or joke."[41] As historian Antony Polonsky has maintained, Pilsudski expressed the opinion then that only detailed discussion of the constitution in parliament would make the final outcome legitimate. Indeed, it was not until January 16, 1935, in the Senate and March 23, 1935, in the Sejm that the new constitution was approved, more than a year after Pilsudski cautioned against a speedy passing of a constitutional bill. "The new constitution," Polonsky observed, "was intended to give lasting form to the principles of government for which Pilsudski had fought for so long, and which he believed he had implemented since the coup."[42]

ON THE DAY THE CONSTITUTION WAS PASSED, April 23, 1935, a doctor who had been brought to Warsaw from Vienna visited Pilsudski to assess his state of health. No one expected good news. Pilsudski's wife recalled, "During the month of March [1935] the slightest exertion became too much for him."[43] The diagnosis was nonetheless devastating. Pilsudski, the doctor concluded, had advanced, incurable cancer of the liver. Despite this terrible news, Pilsudski had no choice but to carry on his duties in military and foreign affairs. For on March 16, 1935, Hitler had introduced universal conscription. The demilitarization clause of the Treaty of Versailles was henceforth null and void, the decree announced, as Germany was to expand its armed forces to twelve army corps and thirty-six divisions, totaling 480,000 men. Pilsudski's first response was to order Colonel Glabisz to draw up a report on the matter.[44]

The last major foreign dignitaries Pilsudski hosted at the Belvedere Palace in Warsaw were British foreign minister Anthony Eden and British prime minister Sir John Simon. The meeting took place on April 2, 1935, in the presence of Mr. Eden's Polish counterpart, Foreign Minster Beck. Pilsudski traveled to the Belvedere by automobile and was greeted by his adjutant, Aleksander Hrynkiewicz. "The commandant got out of the car sluggishly, with difficulty," Hrynkiewicz wrote in his diary that day. He accompanied Pilsudski to the building entrance, noting that "he walked slowly, sliding the soles of his shoes across the floor." Pilsudski's face looked "very pale. His complexion was sallow, like someone ill." In the few days that had passed since the last time Hrynkiewicz had seen him, "he clearly lost weight, which was immediately obvious, as the free space of the collar in the circumference had increased."[45]

Pilsudski carried on what was described as a very cordial meeting with Britain's top officials. Pilsudski told Eden that prior to 1918 he had regarded the British Intelligence Service as the best in the world. But that changed during the Russian Civil War, Pilsudski continued, when British intelligence inaccurately evaluated the White Army's potential and ignored Pilsudski's own assessment that the Whites would be defeated, thus wasting a huge number of resources in support of the losing side. Pilsudski also took the opportunity to reveal his dislike of Lloyd George, who had served as British prime minister and who had openly stood against Pilsudski's policies. "I always answer letters," Pilsudski told Mr. Eden, "but it happened that I received a long political letter from Lloyd George to which I did not reply. I abstained from answering it because the reply would have had to be offensive, and I did not want to do so in respect of a [prime minister]."[46]

Eden devoted some attention to this meeting in his memoirs. Recalling that day, Eden remarked, "The Marshal was universally revered, and deservedly so, for his brilliant military service in the liberation of Poland after the Russian Revolution. His opinions, or what were thought to be his opinions, for he now rarely emerged in public, were accepted with the utmost loyalty and respect." Eden then described the meeting: "My interview took place in circumstances very different from those I had expected. I went into the room with Beck, who was almost too anxious to please Pilsudski and make the meeting a success. The Marshal's mind was failing but his authority was undiminished. Nobody had warned me how ill he was, for I suppose that nobody knew who might have told me; it was a closely kept secret."[47]

In a report cabled to London the following day, Eden commented in greater detail. "The conversation was not carried on easily," Eden wrote on April 3, 1935, "because a great part of the Marshal's remarks, all of which were spoken in French, were unintelligible whether to myself or to two ministers who were present." He continued, writing, "I had the impression of a man now very feeble physically who . . . lived completely in the past." Foreign Minister Eden concluded that "so far as he seems to have visualized his own country's position in the present conditions it is as a country which clings to its pacts with each of its great neighbors and refuses resolutely to move from its position or to face any events which might compel it to revise the attitude which it has taken up."[48] When the meeting ended, after roughly forty-five minutes, the two statesmen shook hands and said their goodbyes.

When the British diplomats exited the room, Pilsudski immediately walked to the bedroom to lie down. "I looked at him anxiously," Colonel Lepecki remarked in his diary. "He gave the impression of a very exhausted and feeble man. I stood by the bed helpless, not knowing what to do. I nevertheless struck up a conversation, saying, 'It was very nice to have had such a visit,' to which Pilsudski replied, 'Yes. True. One always has to have the backing of the English.'"[49]

Reporting on the exchange, a foreign correspondent in Warsaw remarked that "the British underestimated the tenacity and shrewdness of Marshal Pilsudski, who fully realizes that Poland holds the key position in the European situation and who will not surrender it without adequate reassurances regarding Poland's fears of invasion and, perhaps, not without proper 'compensation.'"[50]

As the spring of 1935 came into full bloom, Pilsudski was ill enough that travel was out of the question. Plans to observe Easter at his country home in Sulejówek had to be canceled. He read a great deal, pondering in particular the significance for Poland's security and international relations of Hitler's public declaration on rearmament. "He used to sit at his desk," Alexandra Pilsudska recalled about March and April 1935, "anxiously studying the map."[51] Compounding his fear was the belief that he had no real successor with equal abilities to safeguard the country's security. Pilsudski had revealed his apprehension for what would happen to his country after his death. Kazimierz Świtalski recorded him saying on March 7, 1934, that "it will be very difficult to maintain" the country's policy of equilibrium "because the country's commander must have the gift of inventiveness in delaying or changing things when necessary."[52]

A Country in Mourning, a World in Disarray

With the general population shielded from news about the marshal's health, the announcement on May 12, 1935, of Pilsudski's death came as a shock. Although he had obtained near-absolute power, it was known that Pilsudski never sought personal material gain from his office. To many, it was not surprising to learn a year before his death that Pilsudski refused to accept a pay increase passed by the Polish parliament, and that for years he handed over his entire salary earned as minister of war to orphanages and charities.[53] This was a familiar story to the public at large. As Antony Polonsky noted, "The regime had become increasingly alienated from public opinion but Pilsudski himself had been widely respected as honest, far-seeing, and noble."[54]

As news of the marshal's passing spread, the country as a whole went into collective mourning. His death was splashed across the pages of the foreign press all around the world as well. For it was widely known that Pilsudski had been the mastermind behind Poland's foreign policy. His abrupt and sudden disappearance left countries from the Soviet Union to Great Britain concerned about the implications. Despite common reference to him as a "dictator," praise reverberated around the world. In a radio address on the evening of his death, the French foreign minister, Pierre Laval, expressed deep regret at the loss of "that illustrious soldier, who is the personification of the courage, honor, and patriotism of the Polish nation."[55] The day after his death, the *Times* of London stated that Pilsudski's death "removes one of the most romantic and remarkable figures from the high places of Europe. He was the product of a period of oppression, war, and revolution, and emerged from it as the builder of a modern State." The editorial then described Pilsudski's place in the national life of his country: "Pilsudski . . . had a shrewd sense of what was practicable, and an absorbing determination to serve his country. A great soldier and capable master of statecraft, he preferred to keep himself in the background and to act through others; but his countrymen came to look to him at all the critical moments of their checkered modern career."[56] A second editorial in the *Times* of London remarked that Pilsudski "combined the gifts of foresight and rapid decision" with an intellect that "enabled him to acquire a knowledge of the theory of war, and, besides that, he was a born leader." Pilsudski, the editorial continued, "received a place in his lifetime among the great commanders of Polish birth and was the author of the restored army's tradition."[57]

Some veterans of the Polish Legions wrote to their local newspapers. In a letter that appeared in the *Hartford Courant* on May 15, 1935, one man wrote: "I knew Pilsudski. I fought under him as a member of the Polish Legions. No armchair general was he. No, sir, not Pilsudski. Freezing in the dread Russian winter, sweltering in the arid summer, this man, probably the last of his race of generals, squatted with his men in the front line trenches."

In Warsaw, President Mościcki delivered a moving speech the evening of Pilsudski's death. "With a lifetime of effort he built up the power of a nation. With the genius of his mind, and the supreme exertion of his will, he created a State. . . . From the depths of past ages," he continued, "this man, the greatest in the whole vast sweep of our history, drew the strength of his spirit, and with superhuman exertion of mind, sought out and found the roads for the future."[58]

On May 15, 1935, Pilsudski's body was transported three miles in a solemn procession from the Belvedere Palace to St. John's Cathedral, with an estimated half million onlookers standing on the streets to pay their respects.[59] The body was then placed in a gun-carriage on an open train car for viewing en route to Kraków for the official funeral. The journey took over fourteen hours, stopping in each hamlet to allow its inhabitants to pay homage to their leader. In Kraków, a procession took the coffin to Wawel Castle, where generals of the Polish Army lowered it into the church crypt alongside the tombs of Queen Jadwiga, King Stanisław Poniatowski and King Jan Sobieski, and General Tadeusz Kościuszko, as well as the great bards of the nation. One hundred and one guns were fired as a salute, and a minute's silence was observed all over the country.[60] On May 22, 1935, Lithuania granted Poland's request to have the body of Pilsudski's mother, Maria Pilsudska, exhumed and relocated to a cemetery in Vilna, where it would be reburied with Pilsudski's heart.[61] At the procession were bearers with silver trays carrying earth from the grave of Pilsudski's mother, at whose feet his heart was to be placed in June.

Across the Atlantic, meanwhile, the US Congress heard an address honoring the life of Pilsudski. On May 24, 1935, a Mr. Sadowski of the Polish Club of Washington presented a lengthy speech, "Joseph Pilsudski: The Father of the Polish Republic," which was entered into the official record book. "Marshal Pilsudski is to Poland," Mr. Sadowski began his address, "what George Washington is to our country. He is truly the Father of Poland." He added:

> [Pilsudski] was a statesman possessing tremendous powers but never abused them. He was not a despot, he was not a conqueror, he was not a ruthless warrior fighting for the sake of conquest; he was like General Washington—a man who loved his country and his people and fought bravely for freedom and liberty. Although it is difficult to say that the birth of any nation should be regarded as the work of one individual,

Pilsudski's funeral procession, Warsaw, May 17, 1935.

yet so powerful was the personality of Marshal Joseph Pilsudski that not only the creation of the Polish Republic but its domestic and foreign policies bear the stamp of his individuality.[62]

Sadowski then paused to read aloud the eulogy that Reverend John J. Rolbiercki of Catholic University in Washington had recently delivered. "In a sense," the eulogy read, "the life of Pilsudski may be taken as a symbol of

Poland's struggle for liberty." He added that "his real monument is the new Poland. If Poland is united, if it has definite national aims and a strong national spirit, these are but concrete and actual expressions of the mind and soul of Pilsudski."[63]

Pilsudski also received genuine praise from the country's large Jewish community. While Catholic Poles were bitterly divided over the marshal and his legacy, the largest Jewish community in Europe, which was also the world's second largest, was nearly universally united in their positive view of Pilsudski. "Polish Jewry," the *Jewish Chronicle* in London stated on May 24, 1935, "has passed this week in the depth of mourning for Marshal Pilsudski." As Antony Polonsky maintained, Pilsudski's death was "greatly mourned by the bulk of Poland's Jewish population."[64] Many Polish Jews testified that the authoritative figure had deterred anti-Jewish violence. When Pilsudski, the protector and "grandfather" of the Jews, passed away, the threat of anti-Jewish violence was once again real. One Jew from Grodno in Eastern Poland recalled that several Polish youths approached him days after Pilsudski's death. "In Grodno," Ilya Karpenko recalled, "some local Poles did not hesitate to say to us, 'your "grandfather" has died. Now we'll show you.'"[65]

One can also find, among the hundreds of memorial books of the Jewish communities of Poland published after World War II, frequent references to Pilsudski as a positive figure. In the memorial book of Kielce Jewry, for example, one testimony states that "as long as Pilsudski was alive, the Polish anti-Semites did not dare to attack us openly."[66] In the memorial book of the Jews in Dąbrowa Tarnowa, one finds a similar sentiment. "When Pilsudski died in 1935," one testimonial states, "the Polish Jews lost a good friend who had denounced anti-Semitism."[67] In his oral testimony given to the Shoah Foundation Archive at the University of Southern California, Sam Kudewitz, born in 1910, recalled that life in his native Poland on the eve of World War II had become unsettling for the Jews because of a rise in anti-Jewish violence, a hostile university environment, and a government that openly called on the country's Jews to find a home elsewhere. To Mr. Kudewitz, however, the Poland of Pilsudski was remembered as a different country altogether. "But when Pilsudski was still alive," he commented, "it was very good for the Jews at that time in Poland." When, around 1930, Sam got married, he was asked if he and his wife considered emigrating to the United States where they had family. "When Pilsudski was alive," Sam replied, "we didn't need America. We had it very good in Poland. I had a nice shop and we had a nice home."[68]

Another Polish Jew giving oral testimony to the Shoah Foundation was asked directly what she thought about Pilsudski. In 1926, Stella Faiek was age twelve. After high school, she worked at Janusz Korczak's orphanage and recalled Pilsudski and his family visiting. "Pilsudski was a very nice person," Stella said. "Very good to the Jews. I saw him a few times. Everybody liked him. He was a different person than the other Poles."[69] Another Polish Jewish Holocaust survivor interviewed by the Shoah Foundation held similar views, saying he always thought of Pilsudski as a protector of the Jews.[70]

THE VIEW OF PILSUDSKI since his death has gone through many twists and turns. In the remaining years of the Second Polish Republic (1935–1939), as fascism and authoritarian rule spread to many European countries, Pilsudski's successors were unable to restrain Nazi Germany and Soviet Russia. As Poland's two powerful neighbors became ever more threatening in the last years before World War II, Pilsudski's image grew increasingly positive.

In the first two decades of communist rule in Poland (1948–1968), the regime launched an assault on Pilsudski's legacy, practically erasing him from memory. In the 1970s and 1980s, his chief biographer in Poland, Andrzej Garlicki, was harshly critical. At the same time, however, Garlicki acknowledged the central role Pilsudski played in the life of the country. At the end of his meticulous biography, published as a single volume in 1988, Garlicki concluded: "It was a long path from his early childhood in Zułów through Siberian exile, the socialist movement, the Legions, Magdeburg, Belvedere, Sulejów, and back to Belvedere—to the royal tombs at Wawel Castle. He was an extraordinary personality who has left his mark on several decades of Polish history. He was a legend even during his lifetime who became the symbol of Poland's rebirth."[71]

The political legacy Pilsudski left behind did not serve Poland well after he was gone. For he had devised a system that the historian M. B. Biskupski insightfully characterized as "an almost indefinable amalgam of democratic practice and authoritarian rule."[72] Insomuch as the government operated smoothly in 1930–1935, it did so only because Pilsudski was at the helm. His death led to widespread chaos and instability, with no competent successors to replace him. One of the consequences of this crisis of government was the breakdown of law and order in the form of anti-Jewish violence in what was otherwise a time of peace for Poland without any immediate threat to the country's frontiers.

Unlike in the era of Pilsudski's rule in peachtime, when it was known that anti-Jewish excesses would not be tolerated, his death was followed by a wave of pogroms that his successors were either unable or unwilling to halt. The first took place on June 7, 1935, in Grodno, less than a month after the marshal's passing. In the course of one day, forty Jews were wounded, two of whom later died.[73] The anti-Jewish rioting spread to other towns with an estimated eighty Jews injured by June 12.[74] We recall that Pilsudski's death was directly related to the outbreak of anti-Jewish violence was reflected in the testimony of one victim in Grodno. As two Polish youths approached him, one reportedly said, "Your 'grandfather' is dead, now we will show you."[75]

Anti-Jewish violence continued through 1936 and 1937, with an estimated one hundred incidents that left seventeen killed and two thousand seriously injured.[76] In addition, Pilsudski's heirs moved the country increasingly toward a politics resembling that of Pilsudski's enemies, the right-wing National Democrats. This included the imposition of repressive measures on minorities. These measures were meant to limit their rights, to pressure Jews to emigrate, and to allow so-called ghetto benches in Polish universities.

In foreign relations between Pilsudski's death and the outbreak of World War II, Foreign Minister Józef Beck led the country astray, unable to skillfully navigate the increasingly precarious international arena without Pilsudski's guidance. Nor was Beck able to discern Hitler's ultimate intentions and act in a way to protect the country from total ruin. In the first nine months after Pilsudski's death, Beck adhered to the policy of equilibrium between Poland's two giant neighbors. Afterward, Beck steered the country toward a pro-German orientation. In his first trip abroad following Pilsudski's death, on July 3, 1935, the symbolism was plain for all to see when Beck chose to travel to Berlin. Earlier, in a foreign policy speech given three weeks after Pilsudski's death, Beck offered a new vision. Whereas Pilsudski had said he believed the accord with Germany would not last for more than four years, Beck expressed the view that the German-Polish Non-Aggression Pact of January 1934 was the basis for a lasting, and possibly a permanent, peace with Germany.[77]

The change from Pilsudski's policy of balance toward a pro-German orientation gradually crystallized. On March 7, 1936, when the German armed
forces entered the demilitarized Rhineland for the first time since 1918, Beck
made no public comment. Having determined that France would confine
its reaction to public condemnation without military action, Beck played
the duplicitous game of informing the French that Poland would help in
any manner requested while simultaneously informing the Germans that
he would not oppose their actions. Unlike Pilsudski, who stood firmly against
German remilitarization of the Rhineland, Beck appeared to believe that it
posed no real danger for Poland.[78] That he would continue to give the Third
Reich a green light in foreign matters as long as Poland's borders remained
secure is evident in Beck's attitude to Czechoslovakia. In an aside in June
1935 to his undersecretary, Beck said he would not oppose a German advance
on Czechoslovakia.[79] On a state visit to Rome in March 1938 just days before the German annexation of Austria, Italy's foreign minister, Galeazzo
Ciano, asked Beck his opinion on Hitler's threats to take Vienna by force.
"With regard to the Anschluss," Ciano wrote in his diary on March 7, 1938,
"[Beck] feigned a disinterest which appears out of proportion to the importance the problem could take for Poland."[80]

It is not surprising, therefore, that historians of interwar Europe have evaluated Colonel Beck in a decidedly negative light. "Beck was as much disliked
and distrusted in London as in Paris," the late historian Zara Steiner commented. The American historian Gerhard L. Weinberg similarly observed,
"In his exaggerated self-esteem, [Beck] appears to have been unaware of his
own unpopularity in English as well as French government circles."[81] When
American reporter and writer, Louis Fischer, traveled to Warsaw in 1936, he
secured an interview with Foreign Minister Beck. "He received me in the
ministry," Fischer recalled, "and before he had talked five minutes I thought
of an eel. It was impossible to pin him down, and when I believed he was
pinned down to one point he had evaded my question and delivered a dis-
quisition on an abstraction. I knew I would never know what he had said
when he got through."[82]

One former minister in Pilsudski's cabinet in the early 1930s who was increasingly alarmed at the direction Beck was taking the country in the late
1930s was Wacław Jędrzejewicz. In his memoirs, Jędrzejewicz recalled that
in January 1939, after Germany had annexed Austria and dismembered

Czechoslovakia the previous year, Beck organized a banquet in Warsaw to mark the fifth anniversary of the German-Polish Non-Aggression Pact. With Germany's foreign minister Joachim von Ribbentrop in attendance, Jędrzejewicz was struck by the optics of this bizarre event. Colonel Beck, he commented, appeared to be under the illusion that Germany would remain committed to the nonaggression pact.[83] By turning a blind eye to German aggression elsewhere, Beck was placing Poland in an increasingly exposed position.

Several other diplomats recorded their concerns. "We have certainly sought to do our best with Colonel Beck," British foreign secretary Anthony Eden noted in July 1937, "but with little success I fear. He is an unsatisfactory individual to work with and shifty even to the extent of injuring his own country."[84] After Beck's abovementioned visit to Rome, Italy's foreign minister, Ciano, jotted down impressions in his diary: "Beck doesn't seem to be particularly strong or remarkably intelligent. Above all he is not clear in his presentation: his reasoning does not clearly express his ideas nor is it geometric. He is rather unsystematic, and strays and digresses further into least essential and imprecise facts."[85]

Not long before he passed away, Pilsudski greatly feared what would happen to Poland following his death. In October 1931 he broke down under the weight of a sinking feeling of despair. "What will happen when I am gone? Who will be able to look reality in the eye?" he said, covering his face with his hands, distraught.[86] Pilsudski's premonition proved accurate all too soon.

Epilogue

The life of Jozef Pilsudski, spanning the last third of the nineteenth century and first third of the twentieth, stands out among those of other statesmen of that era. His legacy—which was already discussed during his lifetime—has increased in importance at various times since his death. "Always modest and aloof, seldom seen in public," one foreign observer remarked in 1931, "Pilsudski is already a legend."[1] His untimely death at age sixty-seven in 1935 threw the country into disarray at the moment of Nazi Germany's rise to power and the strengthening of Stalinist rule in Soviet Russia. Foreign observers noted that Pilsudski's absence was felt everywhere. On a visit to Warsaw in February 1939, for example, Italian foreign minister Galeazzo Ciano observed how much Pilsudski's absence pervaded the political scene: "The only voice that counts in Poland is that of a dead man, Pilsudski, and there are far too many who vie for the title of being the true depositories of his wisdom."[2]

An American travel writer, Robert McBride, similarly felt the marshal's absence during a 1937 trip to Poland. "Three illustrious names in Polish history dot the centuries from the late sixteenth to the early twentieth," he wrote. The first two were the sixteenth-century king Stephen Batory and the eighteenth-century general Tadeusz Kościuszko. "And the last is Joseph Pilsudski, revolutionist from boyhood, who not only became the chief creator of the modern state but drove back the invading Russians from the gates of Warsaw in 1920 and established for his country frontiers more extensive than those granted by the framers of the Treaty of Versailles."[3]

The cruel visitation of fate that befell the country after Pilsudski's death made the story of Poland one of the most tragic in modern history. Ravaged by Nazi and Soviet occupiers in World War II, Poland came under communist captivity for the next two generations. The country was forced by no decision of its own to fall behind the Iron Curtain and into obscurity. Despite his historic role in the creation of an independent state, the subject of Pilsudski in communist Poland became taboo until 1989. Yet the communist regime could not wholly suppress the memory of independent Poland's founding father. Pilsudski thus periodically surfaced in communist Poland as a potent symbol of resistance and democratic ideals.

Pilsudski's place in Polish collective memory deepened during the Cold War. In 1978, the anticommunist writer and essayist Kazimierz Brandys commented that Pilsudski was regarded as "a supreme authority. There was greatness in him."[4] The potency of Pilsudski's memory was immediately evident to an American visitor to Poland in 1988. As a foreign exchange student in Kraków, Danusha Goska came across graffiti of Pilsudski's image stenciled on city streets. "When I saw it, as I walked to my morning classes, my heart was glad. In the afternoon, as I walked home, a different sight greeted my eyes. The handsome, chiseled silhouette of the Marshal would be painted over with white paint. Similar white paint covered the word 'Solidarity.'"[5]

Goska's discovery of Pilsudski's popularity was shared by many during the 1980s. When communist authorities first allowed the public to mark the anniversary of independence on November 11, 1981, the awkward efforts to dismiss Pilsudski's place in that history were unsuccessful. On the radio, songs of the First Brigade—Pilsudski's wartime armed force—were played for the first time since 1939. "He is almost a mystical symbol of nationhood to millions of Poles," wrote the Warsaw bureau chief of the *New York Times* on November 11, 1981. "Now, veneration of Marshal Pilsudski is a national passion. Workers at a Gdansk ship repair yard announced today that they were renaming their yard the Jozef Pilsudski Shipyard. His photograph, instantly recognizable for its drooping walrus mustache, hangs over many a hearth. Marchers today wore it as a postcard-size badge."[6]

On the eve of the fall of communism in 1989, another foreign correspondent in Warsaw noted, "Joseph Pilsudski . . . has become a cult figure for his strong defense of Polish independence."[7] In the immediate aftermath of the fall of communism, Pilsudski surged in popularity. On the day of postcommunist Poland's first presidential elections in November 1990, the *New York Times* journalist Stephen Engelberg marveled at the prevalence of Pilsudski imagery. "The mustached figure of Marshal Pilsudski," he observed, "has hovered over the presidential campaign in various subtle guises. Some of the posters with pictures of Lech Walesa, the Solidarity chairman, who also has a mustache, were photographed from an angle that evoked old pictures of the marshal."[8] Engelberg spoke to a young factory worker waiting in line at the voting booth in Sulejówek who expressed his admiration for Pilsudski's record of opposition to anti-Semitism. "'We had a lot of Jews in Pilsudski's time, and things were better then,'" he commented. The reporter followed the latter statement with the following commentary: "The consensus of historians is that Marshal Pilsudski resisted the rising tide of Polish anti-Semitism in the early years of the Depression, and envisaged a Poland in which Jews and members of other minorities would live side by side with their fellow Poles."[9] Former Solidarity leader Adam Michnik referred to Pilsudski, along with Kościuszko and Nobel Prize recipient Czesław Miłosz, as among "the best of our people."[10]

On the occasion of the centennial of Polish independence in November 2018, a liberal Catholic weekly emphasized Pilsudski's mixed legacy, with views of him ranging from heroic to despotic. "The founding father of Polish independence, a brilliant military man, an experienced politician, an outstanding strategist and visionary," noted Kraków's *Tygodnik Powszechny,* "but also a dangerous terrorist, a dark dictator and madman . . . an enemy of democracy who hated opposition."[11] In Warsaw, meanwhile, the then-president of the European Council, Donald Tusk, spoke of the outstanding leaders who helped bring about Poland's independence in November 1918. "But also," he remarked, "we always really think of that one symbolic figure, who was actually, not just symbolically, the father of Polish independence: Józef Piłsudski. . . . After all," he continued, "it was Jozef Piłsudski who said that a nation which does not respect its past does not deserve a good future. So let us emphasize this once again as clearly as possible: the hero and father of our independence is Jozef Piłsudski."[12]

Today, outside of Poland, Pilsudski is largely unknown. Yet for many who are descendants from Polish lands, Pilsudski remains a potent symbol, not only as the country's founding father but also as a visionary of a tolerant and ethnically diverse commonwealth. Iwona Korga, a historian who immigrated to the United States in the early 1990s and today serves as president of the Jozef Pilsudski Institute of America, reflected on the meaning of Pilsudski. "As a historian, I strongly believe that Pilsudski gave his life for Poland," she remarked. "He devoted himself to planning, organizing, fighting, and ruling. Above all, he was never attached to luxury but rather ruled by modesty, by devotion to family, and devotion to his soldiers. It is important to add," she concluded, "that Pilsudski built a free and democratic state, with rapid advancement in industry, education, and culture."[13]

Pilsudski envisioned the new Poland, carved out of the dissolution of the Russian, German, and Austro-Hungarian empires, as a space inhabited by a multinational, multilingual, and multireligious population. For Pilsudski, then, Poland was to serve as an outpost of liberal democracy in Eastern Europe, spreading its principles eastward to the neighboring peoples between Poland and Russia. During the first period of his rule in 1918–1921, Pilsudski tried to realize his vision by pushing Russia back to its ethnic frontiers by championing the independence of Ukraine, and even Belarus, states that would serve as a buffer between Russia and the West. He conceived of a sovereign Ukraine not merely as a security wall to prevent Russian aggression but as an outpost of Western liberal democracy. "There can be no independent Poland," Pilsudski is quoted as saying in 1919, "without an independent Ukraine."[14] He was not successful, having been thwarted by the Red Army, and he regarded the failure to create a Ukrainian state as a grave misfortune for Europe. Subsequently, after concluding that the Polish alliance with France was a purely political one without border guarantees, Pilsudski signed nonaggression pacts with both Nazi Germany and Soviet Russia in the years 1932–1934. He was under no illusion that the ten-year pacts were a guarantee of security, stating in private that the agreement with Nazi Germany in particular would last no more than four to five years. Poland, cursed by its geographic position, had to prepare for what he believed was inevitable war.

The most controversial aspect of Pilsudski's legacy was the 1926 coup and the turn to authoritarian rule. I have argued that this transformation was not the outcome of any shift in Pilsudski's ideological beliefs in democratic institutions, minority rights, the rule of law, and strong ties with the Western democracies. Rather, it was the result of economic and political chaos that befell Poland in 1918–1926, a period that saw sharp fluctuations in the value of currencies and thirteen short-lived governments. Pilsudski thus did not lose faith in the democratic ideal or in democratic government. He lost faith in the Poland that was emerging before his eyes—in Polish society's ability to exercise its new freedom responsibly, to respect the constitutionally guaranteed right to equality before the law for all citizens, and to accept the outcomes of free elections even if the results were disappointing. The man who presided over the establishment of a genuine liberal democracy while serving as head of state in the years 1918–1922 did not become himself a foe of the very institutions he worked to build.

The watershed moment that changed Pilsudski forever was the assassination of President Gabriel Narutowicz on December 16, 1922, just days after his election. The brutal murder had followed five days of a relentless, vicious smear campaign by Pilsudski's right-wing opponents, who repeatedly referred to the president-elect as "Mr. Narutowicz, President of the Jews," based on the claim that Narutowicz could never have won without the Jewish and minority vote.[15] The politicians of the Right, despite having taken part in the drafting of the constitution adopted in March 1921, were clearly unwilling to live by the most fundamental tenet of a democratic state laid out in that very constitution: the equal right of all citizens to have their votes counted and that the results of a free and fair election be respected without recourse to violence and intimidation. For Pilsudski, it was not only the assassination but the shocking praise the murderer received after his trial and execution. Reporting on the trial in the pages of a National Democratic Party weekly, the well-known columnist Adolf Nowaczyński remarked on January 6, 1923, that the assassin "cannot but provoke admiration for his strength and capacity for sacrifice." The assassin's trial testimony, he concluded, constituted "a monument to a man of great character."[16] The open praise of the assassin in the right-wing press further embittered Pilsudski, leading him to routinely characterize his political opponents henceforth as "scumbags, scoundrels, and thieves."[17] In his seminal three-volume history of modern Poland, Władysław Pobóg-Malinowski commented on the impact of the Narutowicz assassination: "The Right's murder of Narutowicz, and the complete impunity of the chief instigators, led Pilsudski to the conviction that nothing can be achieved in Poland through kindness and persuasion, that force and extortion are the only way and that one has to be tough and ruthless."[18]

Pilsudski's death in May 1935 left Poland virtually leaderless. His successors were unable to skillfully balance diplomacy and security, the foreign minister investing too much trust in his German neighbors to keep their word, leaving the country entirely unprepared for what was to come in September 1939. The late historian and political scientist Joseph Rothschild encapsulated Pilsudski's ultimate significance when he asserted that however one regarded Pilsudski's style of rule, which became authoritarian after

1926, "it must be acknowledged that Piłsudski merits primary credit for the fact that today the notion of a Europe without a Polish state is no longer conceivable."[19]

In his biography published in 1939, the career Polish diplomat Anatol Muhlstein reflected on Pilsudski's character. "In thought," Muhlstein wrote, "Pilsudski was always ahead of his time. He lived in the future. His mind was, so to speak, a machine for creating something new." As a person, as a human being, the trait that made him so popular, the Polish diplomat concluded, "was his selflessness and his simplicity. In an age in which money was king, Pilsudski felt contempt for opulence and luxury. He led a simple life without pomp or ostentation, the beauty of which was perceptible in the eyes of the populace."[20] For Poland and Europe, Pilsudski indeed had a singular vision for a democratic, pluralistic state in which all citizens had the equal right to have their votes counted without regard to sex, religion, or nationality. But when faced with political crisis, his vision failed him. In the last nine years of rule, Pilsudski relied on force as a means of restoring a democratic future, thus leaving a mixed legacy.

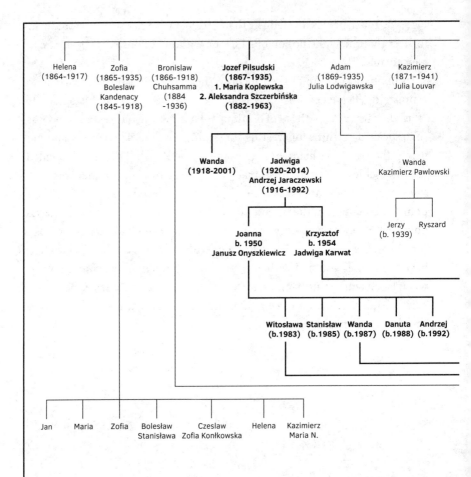

Helena
(1864-1917)

Zofia
(1865-1935)
Boleslaw
Kandenacy
(1845-1918)

Bronislaw
(1866-1918)
Chuhsamma
(1884
-1936)

Jozef Pilsudski
(1867-1935)
1. Maria Koplewska
2. Aleksandra Szczerbińska
(1882-1963)

Adam
(1869-1935)
Julia Lodwigawska

Kazimierz
(1871-1941)
Julia Louvar

Wanda
(1918-2001)

Jadwiga
(1920-2014)
Andrzej Jaraczewski
(1916-1992)

Wanda
Kazimierz Pawlowski

Joanna
b. 1950
Janusz Onyszkiewicz

Krzysztof
b. 1954
Jadwiga Karwat

Jerzy   Ryszard
(b. 1939)

Witosława
(b.1983)

Stanisław
(b.1985)

Wanda
(b.1987)

Danuta
(b.1988)

Andrzej
(b.1992)

Jan   Maria   Zofia   Bolesław
Stanisława

Czeslaw
Zofia Konłkowska

Helena   Kazimierz
Maria N.

Pilsudski's Family Tree

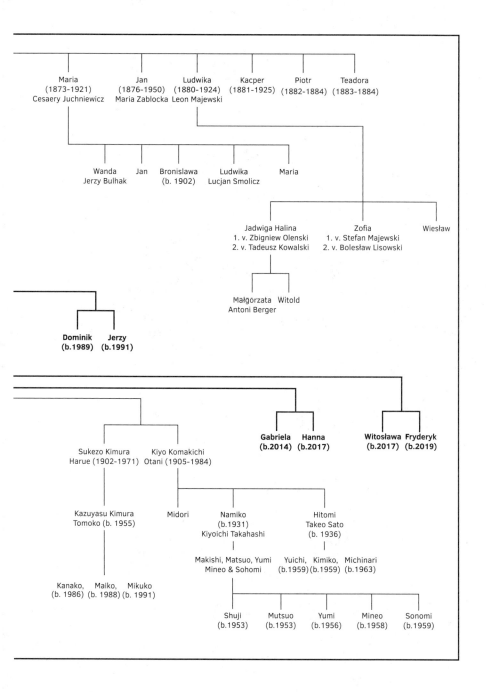

Maria
(1873-1921)
Cesaery Juchniewicz

Jan
(1876-1950)
Maria Zablocka

Ludwika
(1880-1924)
Leon Majewski

Kacper
(1881-1925)

Piotr
(1882-1884)

Teadora
(1883-1884)

Wanda
Jerzy Bulhak

Jan

Bronislawa
(b. 1902)

Ludwika
Lucjan Smolicz

Maria

Jadwiga Halina
1. v. Zbigniew Olenski
2. v. Tadeusz Kowalski

Zofia
1. v. Stefan Majewski
2. v. Bolesław Lisowski

Wiesław

Małgorzata Witold
Antoni Berger

Dominik
(b.1989)

Jerzy
(b.1991)

Gabriela
(b.2014)

Hanna
(b.2017)

Witosława
(b.2017)

Fryderyk
(b.2019)

Sukezo Kimura
Harue (1902-1971)

Kiyo Komakichi
Otani (1905-1984)

Kazuyasu Kimura
Tomoko (b. 1955)

Midori

Namiko
(b.1931)
Kiyoichi Takahashi

Hitomi
Takeo Sato
(b. 1936)

Makishi, Matsuo, Yumi
Mineo & Sohomi

Yuichi,
(b.1959)

Kimiko,
(b.1959)

Michinari
(b.1963)

Kanako,
(b. 1986)

Maiko,
(b. 1988)

Mikuko
(b. 1991)

Shuji
(b.1953)

Mutsuo
(b.1953)

Yumi
(b.1956)

Mineo
(b.1958)

Sonomi
(b.1959)

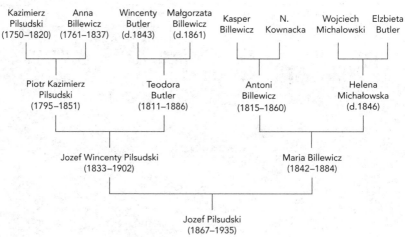

Kazimierz Pilsudski (1750–1820) — Anna Billewicz (1761–1837) — Wincenty Butler (d.1843) — Małgorzata Billewicz (d.1861) — Kasper Billewicz — N. Kownacka — Wojciech Michalowski — Elzbieta Butler

Piotr Kazimierz Pilsudski (1795–1851) — Teodora Butler (1811–1886) — Antoni Billewicz (1815–1860) — Helena Michałowska (d.1846)

Jozef Wincenty Pilsudski (1833–1902) — Maria Billewicz (1842–1884)

Jozef Pilsudski (1867–1935)

Notes

The following abbreviations are used for frequently cited works and archives:

AAN   Archiwum Akt Nowych, Warsaw

CBW   Central Military Library (Centralna Biblioteka Wojskowa), Warsaw

DU   Leaflets / Circulars (Druki Ulotne)

Kalendarium   Wacław Jędrzejewicz and Janusz Cisek, *Kalendarium życia Józefa Piłsudskiego,* 3rd ed. (Kraków: Instytut Książki, 2006). 4 vols.

PAN   Archives of the Polish Academy of Sciences, Warsaw

PIA   Archives of the Pilsudski Institute of America, Brooklyn

PIL   Archives of the Pilsudski Institute in London

PZ   Jozef Pilsudski, *Pisma zbiorowe,* vols. 1–10 (Collected Writings)

PZU   Piłsudski, *Pisma zbiorowe uzupełnienia,* vols. 1–2 (Collected Writings, Supplement)

Introduction

Epigraphs: Adam Michnik, "Shadows of Forgotten Ancestors (1973)," in *Letters from Prison and Other Essays,* trans. Maya Latynski (Berkeley: University of California Press, 1985), 213; Andrzej Garlicki, *Józef Piłsudski, 1867–1935* (Warsaw: Czytelnik, 1988), 164–165.

1. Eva Hoffman, *Exit into History: A Journey through the New Eastern Europe* (New York: Penguin, 1993), 33.

2. Declaration of the Polish parliament, Warsaw, May 12, 1995, quotation from *Polish Review* 61, nos. 1–2 (2011): 8.

3. Konrad T. Naylor, *100 postaci, który miały największy wpływ na dzieje Polski: Ranking* (Warsaw: Plus, 1996), 5.

4. Marcin Święcicki, former mayor of Warsaw, email message to the author, July 29, 2020.

5. "Poland's Disputed Past," *Economist,* November 21, 1998, 7; Święcicki, email to the author, July 29, 2020.

6. See *Polityka* 3 (May 2015), special issue, and the weekend edition of *Gazeta Wyborcza*. May 14–15, 2015, which included a free copy of a picture album: *Józef Piłsudski: Unikatowe zdjęcia*, 2 vols. (Warsaw: Dom Wydawniczy PWN, 2015).

7. Michael T. Kaufman, New York Times correspondent in Warsaw, quotation from Kaufman, *Mad Dreams, Saving Graces: Poland—A Nation in Conspiracy* (New York: Random House, 1989), 56.

8. Lawrence Weschler, *The Passion of Poland: From Solidarity through the State of War* (New York: Pantheon, 1984), 65, 122.

9. Jan Kubik, *The Power of Symbols against the Symbols of Power: The Rise of Solidarity and the Fall of State Socialism in Poland* (University Park: Pennsylvania State University Press, 1994), 219.

10. Bartłomiej [Adam Michnik], "Cienie zapomnianych przodków," *Kultura* 5 (1975); Engl. trans.: "Shadows of Forgotten Ancestors (1973)," in Adam Michnik, *Letters from Prison and Other Essays*, trans. Maya Latynski (Berkeley: University of California Press, 1985), 210, 212.

11. Sisley Huddleston, "Pilsudski and the New Poland," *Fortnightly Review,* February 1920, 263; Charles Phillips, *The New Poland* (London: George Allen and Unwin, 1923), 111; Dmitry Merezhkovsky, *Joseph Pilsudski,* trans. Harriet E. Kennedy (London: Sampson Low, 1921), 7–8; E. Alexander Powell, *Embattled Borders: Eastern Europe from the Balkans to the Baltic* (London: Century Co., 1928), 280–281.

12. Vincent D'Abernon, *The Eighteenth Decisive Battle of the World: Warsaw, 1920* (London: Hodder and Stoughton, 1931); Lord D'Abernon, interview in *Gazeta Polska* (Warsaw), August 17, 1930, quotation from Robert Machray, *Poland, 1914–1931* (London: George Allen and Unwin, 1932), 165.

13. Machray, *Poland,* 15.

14. "Marshal Pilsudski," *Times* (London), May 13, 1935, 17; "Pilsudski Showed a Relentless Will," *New York Times,* May 13, 1935, 6; "The Legacy of Pilsudski," *Times* (London), May 18, 1935, 15; Grace Humphrey, *Pilsudski: Builder of Poland* (New York: Scott and More, 1936), 297–298.

15. Roy Devereaux, *Poland Reborn* (London: Chapman and Hall, 1922), 66.

16. Olivier d'Etchegoyen, *The Comedy of Poland,* trans. Nora Bickey (London: George Allen and Unwin, 1927), 118–119 (orig. pub. French 1925).

17. Jan Lipecki [Irena Panenkowa], *Legenda Piłsudskiego,* 2nd ed. (Poznań: Wielopolska Księgarnia Nakładowa Karola Rzepeckiego, 1923), 81.

18. Marjan Porczak, *Dyktator Józef Piłsudski i "piłsudczycy"* (Kraków: self-pub., 1930), 14.

19. Brian Porter-Szucs, *Poland in the Modern World* (Chichester, UK: Wiley-Blackwell, 2014), 101.

20. Quotation from Janusz Cisek, "Pilsudski's Federalism," in *Wilsonian East Central Europe: Current Perspectives,* ed. John S. Micgiel (New York: PIA, 1995), 45.

21. See, among others, *Żydzi w Polsce odrodzonej*, ed. I. Schiper, A. Tartakower, and A. Hafftka (Warsaw: Nakładem Wydawnictwo, 1933), 2:341; L. Dobroszycki and B. Kirshenblatt-Gimblett, *Image before My Eyes* (New York: Schocken, 1977), 141–144; Joseph Marcus, *Social and Political History of the Jews in Poland, 1919–1939* (Berlin: Mouton, 1983), 214, 286, 293, 313; Ezra Mendelsohn, *The Jews of East Central Europe between the Two World Wars* (Bloomington: Indiana University Press, 1983), 69; I. Gutman and S. Krakowski, *Unequal Victims* (New York: Holocaust Library, 1986), 5; I. Gutman et al., *The Jews of Poland between Two World Wars* (Hanover, NH: University Press of New England, 1989), 11, 31, 45; Jerzy Tomaszewski, "Niepodległa Rzeczpospolita," in *Najnowsze dzieje Żydów w Polsce w zarysie*, ed. Józef Adelson (Warsaw: Wydawnictwo Naukowe, PWN, 1993), 224; "Pilsudski, Jozef," *Encyclopaedia Judaica* 16 (2007), 163–164; Natalia Aleksiun, "Regards from My Shtetl: Polish Jews Write to Pilsudski, 1933–1935," *Polish Review* 61, nos. 1–2 (2011): 57–71; *Polin: 1000 Year History of Polish Jews*, ed. B. Kirschenblatt-Gimblet and A. Polonsky (Warsaw: Museum of the History of Polish Jews, 2014), 241; *Jews, Poles, Legions, 1914–1920*, ed. Artur Tanikowski (Warsaw: Museum of the History of Polish Jews, 2014), 170–171; L. Dulik and K. Zieliński, *The Lost World: Polish Jews* (Lublin: Wydawnictwo Boni Libri Leszek Dulik, 2015), 198, 213; Marcek Gałęzowski, *Na wzór Berka Joselewicza: Żołnierz I oficerowie pochodzenia żydowskiego w Legionach Polskich* (Warsaw: IPMN, 2010).

22. Interview in the documentary film *Image before My Eyes* (1980).

23. Rafael F. Scharf, *Poland, What Have I to Do with Thee?* (London: Vallentine Mitchell, 1998), 69.

24. Irena Bronner, *Cykady nad Wisłą i Jordanem* (Kraków: Wydawnictwo Literackie, 1991), 48.

25. Alexander Blumstein, *A Little House on Mount Carmel* (London: Vallentine Mitchell, 2002), 7.

26. Diary entry of May 13, 1935, Lwów, in Wiktor Chajes, *Semper Fidelis: Pamiętnik Polaka wyznania mojżeszowego z lat 1926–1939* (Kraków: Księgarnia Akademicka, 1997), 177.

27. See Joshua D. Zimmerman, "Feliks Perl on the Jewish Question," *Polin: Studies in Polish Jewry* 27 (2015): 321–334; Zimmerman, "Jozef Pilsudski and the 'Jewish Question,' 1892–1905," *East European Jewish Affairs* 28, no. 1 (1998): 87–107.

28. Neal Ascherson, *The Struggles for Poland* (New York: Random House, 1987), 80.

29. Mendelsohn, *Jews of East Central Europe*, 69.

30. "85th Anniversary of Marshall Józef Piłsudski's Passing," May 12, 2020, POLIN Museum of the History of Polish Jews, https://polin.pl/en/anniversary-pilsudskis-passing.

31. Jan Karski, *Emisariusz własnymi słowami*, ed. Maciej Wierzyński (Warsaw: PWN, 2012), 12.

32. Andrzej Garlicki, *Przewrót majowy* (Warsaw: Spółdzielnia Wydawnicza "Czytelnik," 1979), 387–388.

33. On this point, see Antony Polonsky, *Politics in Independent Poland, 1921–1939: The Crisis of Constitutional Government* (Oxford: Oxford University Press, 1972), 510.

34. Maria Korzeniewicz, email message to the author, July 26, 2020.

35. For more on the Brześć trials, see Marian Leczyk, *Sprawa brzeska: Dokumenty i materiały* (Warsaw: Książka i Wiedza, 1987). For a firsthand account by one of those arrested, see Herman Lieberman, *Pamiętniki* (Warsaw: Wydawn. Sejmowe, 1996).

36. See Szymon Rudnicki, *Obóz Narodowo-Radykalny* (Warsaw: Czytelnik, 1985).

37. For a historiographical discussion of the pact, see Anna Cienciala, "The Foreign Policy of Józef Pilsudski and Józef Beck, 1926–1939: Misconceptions and Interpretations," *Polish Review*, 61, nos. 1–2 (2011): 115–117.

38. On the 1935 constitution, see Polonsky, *Politics in Independent Poland*, 386–390.

39. Wacław Sieroszewski, *Józef Piłsudski* (Kraków: Drukarnia Narodowa, 1915), 85–86.

40. Janusz Jędrzejewicz, *Józef Piłsudski* (Warsaw: Nakładem Księgarni "Ogniwo," 1919), 7.

41. A. Bruce Boswell, *Poland and the Poles* (New York: Dodd, Mead, 1919), 296–297.

42. Huddleston, "Pilsudski and the New Poland," 263–264.

43. Devereaux, *Poland Reborn*, 64–65.

44. Roman Dyboski, *Poland* (New York: Charles Scribner's Sons, 1933), 208.

45. Ibid., 180.

46. Humphrey, *Pilsudski*, 297–298.

47. Robert Machray, *The Poland of Pilsudski* (London: George Allen and Unwin, 1936), 70.

48. W. F. Reddaway, *Marshal Pilsudski* (London: George Routledge, 1939), 171.

49. Władysław Pobóg-Malinowski, *Józef Piłsudski, 1867–1901: W podziemiach konspiracji* (Warsaw: Gebethner i Wolff, 1935); Pobóg-Malinowski, *Józef Piłsudski, 1901–1908: W ogniu rewolucji* (Warsaw: Gebethner i Wolff, 1935).

50. Józef Piłsudski, *Pisma zbiorowe*, 10 vols. (Warsaw: Instytut Jozefa Piłsudskiego, 1937–1938) (PZ).

51. W. F. Reddaway, ed., *The Cambridge History of Poland: From August II to Pilsudski, 1697–1935* (Cambridge: Cambridge University Press, 1941), 2:601.

52. Ibid., 613.

53. Ibid., 615.

54. O. Halecki, *A History of Poland* (New York: Roy, 1943), 299.

55. G. Missalowa and J. Schoenbrenner, *Historia Polski* (Warsaw, 1953), 226.

56. Ibid., 258.

57. Jędrzej Giertych, *Józef Piłsudski, 1914–1919*, 3 vols. (London: Wydawnictwa Towarzystwa im. Romana Dmowskiego, 1979–1990).

58. For the only publication of documents on the Brześć trials, see Leczyk, *Sprawa brzeska.*

59. Garlicki, *Józef Piłsudski,* 136.

60. Ibid., 178.

61. Michnik, "Shadows of Forgotten Ancestors," 201–222.

62. Ibid., 213–214.

63. Ibid., 217.

64. Wacław Jędrzejewicz, *Pilsudski: A Life for Poland* (New York: Hippocrene Books, 1982). In 1995 Garlicki's biography appeared in an abridged English translation without notes. See Garlicki, *Józef Piłsudski, 1867–1935,* ed. and trans. John Coutouvidis (London: Scolar Press, 1995).

65. Jędrzejewicz, *Pilsudski,* 370.

66. Ibid., 374.

67. See, for example, Daria Nałęcz and Tomasz Nałęcz, *Józef Piłsudski: Legendy i fakty* (Warsaw: Młodzieżowa Agencja Wydawnicza, 1986); Andrzej Chojnowski, *Piłsudczycy u władzy: Dzieje Bezpartyjnego Bloku Współpracy z Rządem* (Wrocław: Zakład Narodowy imienia Ossolińskich, 1986).

68. See, for example, Janusz Faryś, *Piłsudski i piłsudczycy: Z dziejów koncepcji polityczno-ustrojowej, 1918–1939* (Szczecin: Uniwersytet Szczciński, 1991); Bohdan Urbankowski, *Józef Piłsudski: Marzyciel i strateg* (Warsaw: Alfa, 1997). Popular biographies include J. Odziemkowski, *Józef Piłsudski: Wódz i polityk* (Warsaw: Ministerstwo Obrony Narodowej Wojkowe Biuo Badań Historiycznych, 2007); Joanna Wieliczka-Szarek, *Józef Piłsudski, 1867–1935: Ulustrowana biografia* (Kraków: Wydawnictwo Ryszard Kuszczyński, 2007); Sławomir Koper, *Józef Piłsudski: Życie prywatne Marszałka* (Warsaw: Bellona, 2010); and Joanna Wieliczka-Szarek, *Józef Piłsudski, 1867–1935: Wszystko dla niepodległej* (Kraków: Wydawnictwo AA, 2015). Popular photo albums and coffee table books on Pilsudski proliferated. See Andrzej Garlicki, *Józef Piłsuski: Życie i legenda* (Warsaw: Kancelaria Sejmu, 1993); M. Całęzowski and A. Przewoźnik, *Gdy wódz odchodził w Wieczność. Uroczystość* (Warsaw: Rada Ochrony Pamięci Walk i Męczeństwa Instytut Józefa Piłsudskiego Poświęcony Badaniu Najnowszej Historii Polski, 2006); and J. Englert and Grzegorz Nowik, *Marszałek Józefa Piłsudski: Komendant—Naczelnik— Państwa—Pierwszy Marshałek Polski* (Warsaw: Muzeum Józefa Piłsudskiego w Sulejówku, 2014).

69. Włodzimierz Suleja, *Józef Piłsudski* (Wrocław: Zakład Narodowy im. Ossolińskch, 1995).

70. Ibid., 6.

71. See, for example, the work by Jędrzej Giertych's son: Maciej Giertych, *Dmowski czy Piłsudski?* (Wrocław: self-pub., 1995); or Antoni Położyński, *Marszałek Józef Piłsudski odbrązowiony* (Warsaw: self-pub., 1998).

72. I am grateful to Agnieszka Marczyk and Adam Michnik for their comments on this paragraph.

73. *New York Times,* December 17, 1918, 13.

74. Minutes of the first session of the Legislative Sejm, February 10, 1919, in *Sprawozdanie stenograficzne z 1. posiedzenia Sejmu Ustawodawczego z dnia 10 lutego 1919*, 3.

75. Pilsudski, speech to the Legislative Sejm, February 10, 1919, reprinted in *PZ*, 5:56–57.

76. Jules Sauerwein, "Une déclaration du maréchal Pilsudski," *Le Matin* (Paris), May 26, 1926, 1.

77. Ibid.

78. Diary entry, second half of May 1926, in Kazimierz Świtalski, *Diariusz 1919– 1935* (Warsaw: Czytelnik, 1992), 144.

79. "P.P.S. wobec wywiadu marsz. Piłsudskiego. Uchwały" ("Our Reaction to Marshal Pilsudski's Interview"), originally appeared in *Robotnik* (Warsaw), July 3, 1928, 1.

80. Piłsudski, "Gasnącemu światu," *Głos Prawdy,* September 22, 1929, in *PZ* 9:185–192; *Gazeta Chłopska,* October 10, 1929, cited in Antony Polonsky, *Politics in Independent Poland, 1921–1939* (Oxford: Oxford University Press, 1972), 294n4.

81. John Wiley, Warsaw, to the secretary of state, Washington, December 2, 1931, in *Papers Relating to the Foreign Relations of the United States, 1931*, vol. I (Washington, D.C.: US Government Printing Office, 1946), 604.

82. M. Laroche, French ambassador in Warsaw, to the French foreign ministry, Paris, April 24, 1934, in *Documents Diplomatiques Français, 1932–1939,* first ser., vol. 6 (Paris: Imprimerie Nationale, 1972), 333–334.

83. "Goebbels' 'Warm' Welcome: a Fiasco," *Jewish Chronicle* (London), June 22, 1934, 35.

84. "Koledzy i Koleżanki!," Warsaw, November 12, 1918, CBW, DU-1334.

1. Childhood and Adolescence

Epigraph: "Dziennik Bronisława Piłsudskiego z lat 1882–1885," diary of Bronisław Pilsudski, entry of February 8, 1883, in Pilsudski Institute of America Archives (PIA), RG 1, folder 13.

1. PIA, RG I, folder 73—Pilsudski family tree; Archives of the Pilsudski Institute, London, RG 1, folder 1, fol. 5; Tadeusz Kubalski, *Zułów: Wczoraj i dzisiaj* (Warsaw: Nakładem Zarządu Głównego Związku Rezerwistów, 1938), 28; Władysław Pobóg-Malinowski, *Józef Piłsudski,1867–1901: W podziemiach konspiracji* (Warsaw: Nakład Gebethner i Wolff, 1935), 14–15; Andrzej Garlicki, *Józef Piłsudski* (Warsaw: Czytelnik, 1990), 7.

2. Letter of Bronisław Pilsudski to Wacław Sieroszewski, quotation from Wacław Sieroszewski, *Józef Piłsudski* (Chicago: Nakład Centralnego Komitetu Obr. Nar., 1915), 7.

3. Alexandra Piłsudska, *Pilsudski: A Biography by His Wife* (New York: Dodd, Mead, 1941), 152. Alexandra Pilsudski's second wife never met Pilsudski's father. The description derives from conversations with her husband.

4. Ludwik Krzywicki, *Wspomnienia* (Warsaw: Czytelnik, 1959), 3:261.

5. Elga Kern, *Marja Piłsudska: Matka marszałka* (Warsaw: Nakłade Głównego Księgarni Wojskowej, 1935), 20; Kubalski, *Zułów,* 37; Garlicki, *Józef Piłsudski,* 7; Władysław Pobóg-Malinowski, *Józef Piłsudski, 1867–1914* (1964; repr., Łomianki: Wydawnictwo LTW, 2015), 13.

6. Kern, *Marja Piłsudska,* 20; Pobóg-Malinowski, *Józef Piłsudski, 1867–1914,* 15.

7. Kern, *Marja Piłsudska,* 20.

8. Pobóg-Malinowski, *Józef Piłsudski, 1867–1914,* 15.

9. Kern, *Marja Piłsudska,* 26; Pobóg-Malinowski, *Józef Piłsudski, 1867–1914,* 19; Garlicki, *Józef Piłsudski,* 7.

10. Kubalski, *Zułów,* 37; Janusz Cisek, "Dziecko płci męskiej stanu szlacheckiego," *Rzeczpospoita,* February 4, 2009.

11. Adam Zamoyski, *The Polish Way* (New York: Franklin Watts, 1987), 284–285; Piotr Wandycz, *The Lands of Partitioned Poland* (Seattle: University of Washington Press, 1974), 179.

12. Stefan Kieniewicz, *Powstanie Styczniowe* (Warsaw: Państwowe Wydawnictwo Naukowe, 1983), 666.

13. Ibid., 737; Andrzej Chwalba, *Historia Polski, 1795–1918* (Kraków: Wydawnictwo Literackie, 2000), 341; Jerzy J. Lerski, *Historical Dictionary of Poland, 966–1945* (Westport, CT: Greenwood Press, 1996), 224.

14. Archives of the Pilsudski Institute, London, RG 1, folder 2, fol. 5. Helena, who never married and had no children, was born with an intellectual disability. See Krzywicki, *Wspomnienia,* 3:265.

15. Jacque de Carency, *Joseph Pilsudski: Soldat de la Pologne restaurée—Étude biographique* (Paris: La Renaissance du Livre, 1929), 20; Kubalski, *Zułów,* 55.

16. Alexandra Pilsudska, *Pilsudski: A Biography by His Wife* (New York: Dodd, Mead, 1941), 152.

17. Quotation from Krzywicki, *Wspomnienia,* 3:265.

18. Krzywicki, *Wspomnienia,* 3:262.

19. Grace Humphrey, *Pilsudski: Builder of Poland* (New York: Scott and More, 1936), 20.

20. Conversation with Felicjan Sławoj Sławkowski, quoted in Felicjan Sławoj Sławkowski, *Strzępy meldunków* (Warsaw, 1936), 300.

21. Pobóg-Malinowski, *Józef Piłsudski, 1867–1914,* 18; Garlicki, *Józef Piłsudski,* 8; Pilsudska, *Pilsudski,* 152; Humphrey, *Pilsudski,* 25.

22. "Childhood and Education," in *Joseph Pilsudski: The Memories of a Polish Revolutionary and Soldier,* trans. and ed. D. R. Gillie (London: Faber and Faber, 1931), 11.

23. Letter of Bronisław Pilsudski to Wacław Sieroszewski, cited in Sieroszewski, *Józef Piłsudski,* 6.

24. Cisek, "Dziecko płci męskiej stanu szlacheckiego"; Kubalski, *Zułów,* 26, 28, 41; Henryk Cepnik, *Józef Piłsudski: Twórca niepodległego państwa polskiego,* 3rd ed. (Warsaw: Instytut Propagandy Państwowo-Twórczej, 1935), 24; D. R. Gillie, introduction to chap.1, in *Joseph Pilsudski: The Memories,* 10; letter of Bronisław Pilsudski, quoted in Sieroszewski, *Józef Piłsudski,* 6–7.

25. *Joseph Pilsudski: The Memories,* 11.

26. W. F. Reddaway, *Marshal Pilsudski* (London: George Routledge and Sons, 1939), 8.

27. Letter of Bronisław Pilsudski, quotation from Sieroszewski, *Józef Pilsudski,* 6.

28. Humphrey, *Pilsudski,* 20.

29. Letter of Bronisław Pilsudski to Sieroszewski, quotation from Sieroszewski, *Józef Piłsudski,* 8.

30. Pilsudski, "Jak stałem się socjalistą," *Promień,* nos. 8–9 (1903), English translation in *Joseph Pilsudski: The Memories,* 11.

31. Letter of Bronisław Pilsudski, quoted in Sieroszewski, *Józef Piłsudski,* 8–9.

32. Pilsudska, *Pilsudski,* 153–154.

33. Pobóg-Malinowski, *Józef Piłsudski, 1867–1901,* 27.

34. Pilsudska, *Pilsudski,* 153.

35. Roman Koropeckyj, *Adam Mickiewicz: The Life of a Romantic* (Ithaca, NY: Cornell University Press, 2008), 200.

36. *Poems of Adam Mickiewicz,* ed. George R. Noyes (New York: Polish Institute of Arts and Sciences, 1944), 414–415.

37. Zygmunt Krasiński, "Psalms for the Future," reprinted in translation in Monica M. Gardner, *The Anonymous Poet of Poland: Zygmunt Krasinski* (Cambridge: Cambridge University Press, 1919), 276. Maria Pilsudski's biographer, as well as Jozef and Bronisław, confirmed that Krasiński was Maria's favorite poet. See Kern, *Marja Piłsudska,* 138; letter of Bronisław Pilsudski to Wacław Sieroszewski, quotation from Sieroszewski, *Józef Piłsudski,* 9; *Joseph Pilsudski: The Memories,* 11.

38. Zygmunt Krasiński, *Irydion* (1837), in Gardner, *Anonymous Poet of Poland,* 167.

39. Manfred Kridl, *A Survey of Polish Literature and Culture* (The Hague: Mouton, 1967), 301.

40. *Joseph Pilsudski: The Memories,* 11.

41. Jozef Pilsudski, *Walka rewolucyjna w zaborze rosyjskim: Fakty i wrażenia o ostatnich lat dziecięciu* (Kraków: Nakł. wydawn. "Naprzodu," 1903), 1:4, in *PZ,* 2:58.

42. Humphrey, *Pilsudski,* 24.

43. Maria Dernałowicz, *Juliusz Słowacki* (Warsaw: Interpress, 1987), 129. For the complete poem, see Juliusz Słowacki, "Odpowiedź na *Psalmy przyszłości*," in Słowacki, *Wiersze i Poematy* (Warsaw: Państwowy Instytut Wydawniczy, 1983), 1:469–480. For a partial English translation, see Słowacki, "To the Author of the Three Psalms," in *A Polish Anthology,* ed. T. M. Filip (London: Duckworth, 1944), 355–357.

44. Julian Krzyżanowski, *A History of Polish Literature* (Warsaw: PWN, 1978), 269.

45. *Joseph Pilsudski: The Memories,* 11.

46. Garlicki, *Józef Piłsudski,* 9; Pobóg-Malinowski, *Józef Piłsudski, 1867–1914,* 21; *Kalendarium,* 1:7.

47. Census of the City of Vilna, 1875 and 1897, in Theodore R. Weeks, *Vilnius between Nations, 1795–2000* (DeKalb: Northern Illinois University Press, 2016), 61; Joshua D. Zimmerman, *Poles, Jews and the Politics of Nationality* (Madison: University of Wisconsin Press, 2004), 16; Antony Polonsky, *The Jews in Poland and Russia,* vol. 2 (2010), 205.

48. The gymnasium was a European high school that prepared students for entry into the university.

49. *Joseph Pilsudski: The Memories,* 12. On Pilsudski's schooling, see Humphrey, *Pilsudski,* 28.

50. Śliwiński, "Marszałek Piłsudski o sobie," *Niepodległość* 43 (1937): 369.

51. Report of the Vilna Gymnasium on Jozef Pilsudski, quotation from Garlicki, *Józef Piłsudski,* 11.

52. Władysław Nowicki, "Wspomnienie," *Kurier Czerwony,* June 1, 1935, in *Kalendarium,* 1:8; quotation from Karol Niezabytowski, "Od szkolnej ławy—z Piłsudskim," *Wiadomości* no. 3 (January 15, 1950): 2.

53. Diary of Bronisław Pilsudski, entry of February 10, 1883, PIA, RG 1, folder 13.

54. Humphrey, *Pilsudski,* 29.

55. Quotation from Sieroszewski, *Józef Piłsudski,* 16.

56. F. K., "13-letnie chłopię—Ziuk Piłsudski: Poetą i redaktorem 'Gołębia Zułowskiego,'" *Kuryer Literacko-Naukowy* (Kraków), August 19, 1935, 1; Pobóg-Malinowski, *Józef Piłsudski, 1867–1914,* 40; Kubalski, *Zułów,* 67; *Kalendarium,* 1:9.

57. F. K., "13-letnie chłopię," 2.

58. Adam Borkiewicz, "Źródła do biografii Józefa Piłsudskiego z lat 1867–1892," *Niepodległość* 19 (January–June 1939): 392; Pobóg-Malinowski, *Józef Piłsudski, 1867–1914,* 18; *Kalendarium,* 1:9. For example, Pilsudski copied down the fable "Lis i Osioł" (The fox and the donkey), from *Poezye Józefa Grajnerta: Bajki i przypowiastki* (Warsaw: Główny skład w Księgarni M. Glucksberga, 1874), 49–50.

59. Émile De Saint-Hilaire, *Historya Napoleona,* trans. Leon Rogalski (Warsaw: Nakładem Augusta Emmanuela Glucksberga, 1844), from Saint-Hilaire, *Napoléon du Conseil d'État* (Paris: V. Magen, 1843). On Pilsudski's early admiration for

Napoleon at this time, see Sieroszewski, *Józef Piłsudski,* 18; Borkiewicz, "Źródła do biografii Józefa Piłsudskiego," 392; Garlicki, *Józef Piłsudski,* 12; Pobóg-Malinowski, *Józef Piłsudski, 1867–1914,* 33, 40.

60. *Joseph Pilsudski: The Memories,* 12.

61. Artur Śliwiński, interview with Marshall Pilsudski, 1931, in "Marszałek Piłsudski o sobie," *Niepodległość* 45 (1938): 26–27.

62. Wacław Studnicki-Gizbert, "W 50-tą rocznicę 'Spójni,' 1-go kółka uczniow-skiego w Wilnie po powstaniu 63 r.," *Kurier Wileński,* May 12, 1932, quotation from Bohdan Urbankowski, *Józef Piłsudski: Marzyciel i strateg* (Poznań: Zysk i S-ka, 2014), 27; Garlicki, *Józef Piłsudski,* 12; Pobóg-Malinowski, *Józef Piłsudski, 1867–1914,* 42; Pobóg-Malinowski, *Józef Piłsudski, 1867–1901,* 45–46, 49; Sieroszewski, *Józef Piłsudski,* 21; *Kalendarium,* 1:20.

63. Pobóg-Malinowski, *Józef Piłsudski, 1867–1901,* 47.

64. Pilsudski, "Jak stałem się socjalistą" (1903), *PZ,* 2:45.

65. Letter of Bronisław Pilsudski to Wacław Sieroszewski, quotation from Sieros-zewski, *Józef Piłsudski,* 19–20.

66. Pilsudska, *Pilsudski,* 157.

67. Bolesław Limanowski, *Historja ruchu narodowego od 1861 do 1864 r.,* 2 vols. (Lwów: Księgarnia Polska, 1882); Walery Przyborowski, *Wspomnienia ułana z 1863 roku* (Poznań: Calier, 1878). For a discussion of these works, see Urbankowski, *Józef Piłsudski,* 29; and Kazimiera Cottoam, *Boleslaw Limanowski* (Boulder, CO: East European Quarterly, 1978), 76–78.

68. Diary of Bronisław Pilsudski, entry of December 4, 1883, PIA, RG 1, folder 13.

69. Adam Bromke, *Poland's Politics: Idealism vs. Realism* (Cambridge, MA: Harvard University Press, 1967), 25.

70. Jozef Pilsudski, *Rok 1863* (Warsaw: "Ignis," 1924), quotation from Bromke, *Poland's Politics,* 25. All of Pilsudski's writings and speeches on 1863 appear in Jozef Pilsudski, *Rok 1863,* ed. Stefan Kieniewicz (Warsaw: Książka i Wiedza, 1989).

71. Mieczysław B. Lepecki, *Józef Piłsudski na Syberji* (Warsaw: Główna Księgarnia Wojskowa, 1936), 201; *Kalendarium,* 1:28.

72. *Joseph Pilsudski: The Memories,* 13.

73. Quotation from Lepecki, *Józef Piłsudski na Syberji,* 11.

74. Śliwiński, "Marszałek Piłsudski o sobie," *Niepodległość* 43 (1937), 367.

75. *Joseph Pilsudski: The Memories,* 13.

76. Diary of Bronisław Pilsudski, entry of June 9, 1883, PIA, RG 1, folder 13.

77. Ibid., entry of February 8, 1883.

78. Ibid., entry of March 31, 1883.

79. Ibid., entry of March 12, 1883.

80. Ibid., entry of August 31, 1883.

81. Ibid., entry of October 23, 1883.

82. Śliwiński, "Marszałek Piłsudski o sobie," *Niepodległość* 47 (1938): 349.

83. Quotation from Śliwiński, "Marszałek Piłsudski o sobie," *Niepodległość* 43 (1937), 371.

84. Ibid., 372–373.

85. Śliwiński, "Marszałek Piłsudski o sobie," *Niepodległość* 45 (1938), 29–30.

86. University application (July 23, 1885), in Lepecki, *Józef Piłsudski na Syberji*, 199, and in *PZ*, 1:9.

87. Śliwiński, "Marszałek Piłsudski o sobie," *Niepodległość* 47 (1938), 204.

88. *Kalendarium*, 1:26.

89. Pilsudski, Kharkov, to aunt Stefania Lipmanówna, Vilna, March 18, 1886, in *PZU*, 1:12n1; Włodzimierz Suleja, *Józef Piłsudski* (Wrocław: Zakład Narodowy im. Ossolińskch, 1995), 13.

90. Pilsudski, "Jak stałem się socjalistą" (1903), *PZ*, 2:50.

91. Lucjan Blit, *The Origins of Polish Socialism: The History and Ideas of the First Polish Socialist Party, 1878–1886* (Cambridge: Cambridge University Press, 1971), 141; R. F. Leslie, ed., *The History of Poland since 1863* (Cambridge: Cambridge University Press, 1980), 52.

92. In his memoirs, Pilsudski reflects on this time and the discovery of Dickstein's work; in *Joseph Pilsudski: The Memories*, 15–16. Dickstein's work appeared as Jan Młot [Szymon Dickstein], *Kto z czego żyje* (Warsaw: n.p., 1881). Also see Janusz Jędrzejewicz, *Józef Piłsudski* (Warsaw: Nakładem Księgarni "Ogniwo," 1919), 7; Pobóg-Malinowski, *Józef Piłsudski, 1867–1914*, 53.

93. Pilsudski, Kharkov, to aunt Stefania Lipman, Vilna, March 18, 1886, in *PZU*, 1:12.

94. *Kalendarium*, 1:28.

95. Śliwiński, "Marszałek Piłsudski o sobie," *Niepodległość* 47 (1938), 203–204.

96. Pilsudski, Vilna, to the university rector, Kharkov, August 2, 1885, in *PZ*, 1:10.

97. Quotation from Lepecki, *Józef Piłsudski na Syberji*, 209.

98. Pilsudski, Vilna, to the university rector, Kharkov, December 12, 1886, in Lepecki, *Józef Piłsudski na Syberji*, 207.

99. Śliwiński, "Marszałek Piłsudski o sobie," *Niepodległość* 43 (1937), 368.

100. *Joseph Pilsudski: The Memories*, 15.

101. The brochures in translation included Wilhelm Liebknecht, *W obronie prawdy* (Geneva: Nakł. i staraniem stowarzyszenia "Lud polski," 1882); Karl Marx, *Kapitał: Krytyka ekonomii politycznej*, vol. 1 (Leipzig: E. Kasprowicz, 1884).

102. Garlicki, *Józef Piłsudski*, 15.

103. Pobóg-Malinowski, *Józef Piłsudski, 1867–1914*, 55.

104. Garlicki, *Józef Piłsudski*, 16; Pobóg-Malinowski, *Józef Piłsudski, 1867–1914*, 57.

105. Jędrzejewicz, *Pilsudski*, 9; Pobóg-Malinowski, *Józef Piłsudski, 1867–1914*, 56–57.

106. Pobóg-Malinowski, *Józef Piłsudski, 1867–1914*, 57.

107. *Kalendarium*, 1:30; Jędrzejewicz, *Pilsudski*, 9.

108. Suleja, *Józef Piłsudski*, 14; Garlicki, *Józef Piłsudski*, 16; *Kalendarium*, 1:30–31; Pobóg-Malinowski, *Józef Piłsudski, 1867–1914*, 59–60; Jędrzejewicz, *Pilsudski*, 9–10.

2. Exile and Romance

Epigraph: Pilsudski, Tunka, March 4, 1891, to Leonarda Lewandowska, Orla, reprinted in *Piłsudski, Pisma zbiorowe uzupełnienia,* eds. Andrzej Garlicki and Ryszard Świętek (Warsaw: Krajowa Agencja Wydawnicza, 1992), I:66.

1. Pilsudski, Krasnoyarsk, to Stefania Masłowska, Vilna, July 18–19, 1887, in *PZU,* 1:13.

2. Ibid., 13.

3. Ibid., 14.

4. Pilsudski, letter to Stefania Masłowska, Vilna, October 22 to November 30, 1887, in *PZU,* 1:14.

5. Ibid., 15.

6. Pilsudski, "Mutiny in Irkutsk Gaol 1887," in *Joseph Pilsudski: The Memories of a Polish Revolutionary and Soldier,* trans. and ed. D. R. Gillie (London: Faber and Faber, 1931), 22–23.

7. Ibid., 26.

8. *Kalendarium,* 1:34; Mieczysław B. Lepecki, *Józef Piłsudski na Syberji* (Warsaw: Główna Księgarnia Wojskowa, 1936), 75.

9. Pilsudski, Kirensk, to the ministry of the interior, St. Petersburg, October 5, 1888, in *PZU,* 1:16–17.

10. "Landy Stanisław (1855–1915)," *Polski Słownik Biograficzny* 16 (1971): 478; Lucjan Blit, *The Origins of Polish Socialism: The History and Ideas of the First Polish Socialist Party, 1878–1886* (Cambridge: Cambridge University Press, 1971), 35; Maciej Demel, *Aleksander Landy: Życia i dzieło* (Warsaw: Państwowe Wydawnictwo Naukowe, 1982), 21.

11. Felicja Landy, "Stanisław Landy na Syberji," *Kronika Ruchu Rewolucyjnego w Polsce,* no. 2 (1936): 104; Demel, *Aleksander Landy,* 21–23.

12. Andrzej Garlicki, *Józef Piłsudski* (Warsaw: Czytelnik, 1990), 21; Janusz Jędrzejewicz, *Józef Piłsudski* (Warsaw: Nakładem Księgarni "Ogniwo," 1919), 13–14.

13. Landy, "Stanisław Landy na Syberji," 106.

14. "Landy Michał (1844–1961)," *Polski Słownik Biograficzny* 16 (1971): 477.

15. For a translation and discussion of Cyprian Norwid's poem "Polish Jews" (1861), see Harold B. Segel, *Strangers in Our Midst: Images of the Jew in Polish Literature* (Ithaca, NY: Cornell University Press, 1996), 87–88. For a color reprint of Lesser's painting, see Ezra Mendelsohn, *Painting a People: Maurycy Gottlieb and Jewish Art* (Hanover, NH: University Press of New England, 2002), plate 14. On Michał Landy, see Israel Bartal and Magdalena Opalski, *Poles and Jews: A Failed Brotherhood* (Hanover, NH: University Press of New England, 1992), 43–57.

16. Mendelsohn, *Painting a People,* 211.

17. Pilsudski, Tunka, to Leonarda Lewandowska, April 8–9, 1891, in *PZU,* 1:70.

18. Pilsudski, Kirensk, to Stanisław Landy, Irkutsk, December 31, 1889, in *PZU,* 1:16.

19. Pilsudski, Tunka, November 29, 1890, to Leonarda Lewandowska, Orla (?), in *PZU,* 1:50; Garlicki, *Józef Piłsudski,* 23.

20. Pilsudski, Kirensk, March 19, 1890, to Stanisław Landy, Irkutsk, in *PZU,* 1:18.

21. Ibid.

22. Pilsudski, Kirensk, March 25, 1890, to Leonarda Lewandowska, Irkutsk, in *PZU,* 1:19. I am grateful to Julian Bussgang for helping me render this passage in English.

23. Ibid., 20.

24. Pilsudski, Kirensk, April 8, 1890, to Leonarda Lewandowska, Irkutsk, in *PZU,* 1:22.

25. Ibid., 23–24.

26. Pilsudski, Kirensk, April 22, 1890, to Leonarda Lewandowska, Irkutsk, in *PZU,* 1:25.

27. Pilsudski, Kirensk, May 4, 1890, to Leonarda Lewandowska, Irkutsk, in *PZU,* 1:26.

28. Pilsudski, Kirensk, May 19, 1890, to Leonarda Lewandowska, Irkutsk, in *PZU,* 1:27.

29. Ibid.

30. Garlicki, *Józef Piłsudski,* 24.

31. Pilsudski, Irkutsk, July 29, 1890, to Celina Bukont, Vilna, in *PZU,* 1:31.

32. Pilsudski, Irkutsk, July 21, 1890, to Wincenty Pilsudski, Vilna, in *PZU,* 1:29.

33. Pilsudski, Irkutsk, July 29, 1890, to Celina Bukont, Vilna, in *PZU,* 1:31.

34. Pilsudski, Irkutsk, July 21, 1890, to Wincenty Pilsudski, Vilna, in *PZU,* 1:30.

35. Pilsudski, Irkutsk, July 31, 1890, to Leonarda Lewandowska, in Pilsudski, Vilna, in *PZU,* 1:32.

36. Pilsudski, Irkutsk, August 3, 1890, to Leonarda Lewandowska, Vilna, in *PZU,* 1:33.

37. Lidia Łojko, *Ot 'Zemli i Voli' k VKP, 1877–1928: Vospominanija* (Moscow: Gosudarst. izdat., 1929), 96.

38. Stefan Juszczyński, "Z pobytu w Tunce," *Niepodległość* 4 (1931): 180; "Juszczyński Stefan," *Polski Słownik Biograficzny* 9 (1964–1965): 350.

39. "Mancewicz Michał," *Polski Słownik Biograficzny* 19 (1974–1965): 468.

40. Pilsudski, Tunka, August 13, 1890, to Leonarda Lewandowska c/o Celina Bukont, Vilna, in *PZU,* 1:34.

41. Juszczyński, "Z pobytu w Tunce," 181.

42. Pilsudski, Tunka, October 15, 1890, to Leonarda Lewandowska, Orla, in *PZU,* 1:40; *Kalendarium,* 1:42.

43. Pilsudski, Tunka, August 13, 1890, to Leonarda Lewandowska c/o Celina Bukont, Vilna, in *PZU,* 1:34–35.

44. Alexandra Piłsudska, *Pilsudski: A Biography by His Wife* (New York: Dodd, Mead, 1941), 163.

45. M. K. Dziewanowski, *Joseph Pilsudski: A European Federalist, 1918–1922* (Stanford, CA: Hoover Institution Press, 1969), 30.

46. Pilsudski, Tunka, August 20, 1890, to Leonarda Lewandowska c/o Celina Bukont, Vilna, in *PZU*, 1:36–37.

47. Ibid., 1:36.

48. Ibid., 37.

49. Ibid., 38.

50. *PZU*, 1:30n2.

51. Pilsudski, Tunka, October 15, 1890, to Leonarda Lewandowska, Orla, in *PZU*, 1:39.

52. Ibid., 40. I am grateful to Julian Bussgang for helping me render this passage in English.

53. Pilsudski, Tunka, October 22, 1890, to Leonarda Lewandowska, Orla, in *PZU*, 1:42.

54. Pilsudski, Tunka, October 29, 1890, to Leonarda Lewandowska, Orla, in *PZU*, 1:43.

55. Pilsudski, Tunka, November 5, 1890, to Leonarda Lewandowska, Orla, in *PZU*, 1:46–47.

56. Ibid., 46.

57. Pilsudski, Tunka, November 26, 1890, to Leonarda Lewandowska, Orla (?), in *PZU*, 1:50.

58. Ibid., 51.

59. Ibid.

60. Ibid., 52–53.

61. Pilsudski, Tunka, December 30, 1890, to Leonarda Lewandowska, Orla (?), in *PZU*, 1:56.

62. Pilsudski, Tunka, January 13, 1891, to Leonarda Lewandowska, Orla (?), in *PZU*, 1:57–58.

63. Pilsudski, Tunka, January 20, 1891, to Leonarda Lewandowska, Mikołajew, in *PZU*, 1:59–60.

64. Ibid., 61.

65. Pilsudski, Tunka, February 16, 1891, to Leonarda Lewandowska, Orla, in *PZU*, 1:62.

66. Pilsudski, Tunka, March 4, 1891, to Leonarda Lewandowska, Orla, in *PZU*, 1:65.

67. Pilsudski, Tunka, March 11, 1891, to Leonarda Lewandowska, Orla, in *PZU*, 66.

68. Ibid., 1:66–67.

69. Ibid., 67.

70. Pilsudski, Tunka, March 24, 1891, to Leonarda Lewandowska, Orla, in *PZU*, 1:68.

71. Pilsudski, Tunka, April 8, 1891, to Leonarda Lewandowska, Orla, in *PZU,* 1:70.

72. Pilsudski, Tunka, April 8, 1891, to Leonarda Lewandowska, Orla, in *PZU,* 1:70.

73. Pilsudski, Tunka, January 20, 1891, to Leonarda Lewandowska, Mikołajew, in *PZU,* 1:60.

74. Pilsudski, Tunka, May 20, 1891, to Leonarda Lewandowska, Orla, in *PZU,* 1:74–75.

75. Ibid., 75.

76. Pilsudski, Tunka, June 24, 1891, to Leonarda Lewandowska, Orla, in *PZU,* 1:75.

77. Pilsudski, Tunka, September 16, 1891, to Leonarda Lewandowska, Orla, in *PZU,* 1:76.

78. Ibid.

79. Pilsudski, Tunka, December 11, 1891, to Leonarda Lewandowska, Odessa, in *PZU,* 1:77–78.

80. Władysław Pobóg-Malinowski, *Józef Piłsudski, 1867–1914* (1964; repr., Łomianki: Wydawnictwo LTW, 2015), 82.

81. Garlicki, *Józef Piłsudski,* 21, 31.

82. Łojko, *Ot "Zemli i Voli,"* 92–93.

83. Juszczyński, "Z pobytu w Tunce," 181.

84. "Michał Mancewicz (1860–1930)," *Polski Słownik Biograficzny* 19 (1974).

85. *Joseph Pilsudski: The Memories,* 16.

86. Landy, "Stanisław Landy na Syberji," 107.

87. Garlicki, *Józef Piłsudski,* 24; Bohdan Urbankowski, *Józef Piłsudski: Marzyciel i strateg* (Poznań: Zysk i S-ka, 2014), 68.

88. Jozef Pilsudski, "Rok 1863," in Pilsudski, *Pisma zbiorowe* (Warszawa: Instytut Józefa Piłsudskiego, 1937), 6:158, 162.

89. Pilsudski, "How I Became a Socialist" (1903), in *Joseph Pilsudski: The Memories,* 16.

90. Pilsudski, 1931 interview, in Artur Śliwiński, "Marszałek Piłsudski o sobie," *Niepodległość* 43 (1937): 368.

3. Socialist Leader and Conspirator

Epigraph: Wiktor [Pilsudski], Taurogi, September 7, 1895, to the ZZSP, London, in *PZU,* 1:129–130.

1. Zygmunt Nagrodzki, Vilna, to Stefania Lipman, Woroneż, July 3, 1892, in *PZU,* 1:401–402.

2. *Kalendarium,*1:47; Henryk Cepnik, *Józef Piłsudski: Twórca niepodległego państwa polskiego,* 3rd ed. (Warsaw: Instytut Propagandy Państwowo-Twórczej, 1935), 53.

3. PIA, RG 1, folder 73—Pilsudski family tree.

4. Wacław Jędrzejewicz, *Pilsudski: A Life for Poland* (New York: Hippocrene Books, 1982), 16.

5. Bohdan Urbankowski, *Józef Piłsudski: Marzyciel i strateg* (Poznań: Zysk i S-ka, 2014), 74.

6. Włodzimierz Suleja, *Józef Piłsudski* (Wrocław: Zakład Narodowy im. Ossolińskich, 1995), 22.

7. Andrzej Garlicki, *Józef Piłsudski, 1867–1935* (Warsaw: Czytelnik, 1990), 42.

8. Urbankowski, *Józef Piłsudski,* 74; *Kalendarium,* 1:47–48; Jędrzejewicz, *Piłsudski,* 16.

9. Wacław Sieroszewski, *Józef Piłsudski* (Piotrków: Departament Wojskowy Naczelnego Komitetu Narodowego, 1915), 19.

10. Pilsudski, "Jak stałem się socjalistą" (1903), in *PZ,* 2:53. Also see Suleja, *Józef Piłsudski,* 22.

11. *Kalendarium,* 1:47–49; Garlicki, *Józef Piłsudski,* 37.

12. [Stanisław Mendelson], "Szkic programu Polskiej Partyi Socjalistycznej," in *Polskie programy socjalistyczne, 1878–1918,* ed. Feliks Tych (Warsaw: Książka i Wiedza, 1975), 253–254; in translation, "Outline of the Polish Socialist Party (1892)," in *For Your Freedom and Ours,* ed. Krystyna Olszer (New York: F. Unger, 1981), 150–151.

13. Stanisław Wojciechowski, *Moje wspomnienia* (Lwów: Książnica-Atlas, 1938), 1:90.

14. [Mendelson], "Szkic programu Polskiej Partyi Socjalistycznej," 259.

15. [Jozef Pilsudski], "Wilno, 1 lutego," *Przedświt* (London), no. 3, March 1893, in *PZ,* 1:18–21.

16. [Jozef Pilsudski], Vilna, February 15, 1893, to the editors of *Przedświt,* in *PZ,* 1:79.

17. [Jozef Pilsudski], "Wilno, 17 lutego," *Przedświt* (London), no. 3, March 1893, in *PZ,* 1:22–23.

18. Rom [Jozef Pilsudski], "Wilno, 4 marca," *Przedświt* (London), no. 4, April 1893, in *PZ,* 1:25.

19. Joshua D. Zimmerman, *Poles, Jews and the Politics of Nationality: The Bund and the Polish Socialist Party in Late Tsarist Russia, 1892–1914* (Madison: University of Wisconsin Press, 2004), 40–41.

20. Z. Kopelson, "Evreiskoe rabochee dvizhenie kontsa 80-kh i nachala 90-kh godov," in *Revoliutsionnoe dvizhenie sredi evreev,* ed. Shimen Dimanshtein (Moscow: Izd-vo politkatorzhan, 1930), 72–73; Pilsudski, London, to W. Gumplowicz, Zurich, January 16, 1902, in *PZU,* 2:92–93.

21. Rom [Jozef Pilsudski], "Wilno, 4 marca 1893," *Przedświt* (London), no. 4, April 1893, in *PZ,* 1:25–26.

22. Leon Wasilewski, "Kierownictwo P.P.S. zaboru rosyjskiego (1893–1918)," *Niepodległość* 11 (1935): 352; Feliks Perl, "Szkice dziejów P.P.S.," n *Księga pamiątkowa*

P.P.S. w trzydziestą rocznicę (Warsaw: Nakładem Spółki Nakładowo-Wydawniczej "Robotnik," 1923), 5; Jędrzejewicz, *Pilsudski*, 17.

23. [Jozef Pilsudski], "Do towarzyszy socjalistów Żydów w polskich zabranych prowincjach," *Przedświt* (London), no. 5, May 1893, in *PZ*, 1:30.

24. Wojciechowski, *Moje wspomnienia*, 1:63.

25. Ibid.

26. Ibid., 66–67.

27. Leon Wasilewski, *Józef Piłsudski jakim go znałem* (Warsaw: Towarzystwo Wydawnicze Rój, 1935), 60–61.

28. [Pilsudski], "Wilno, 8 lipca 1893," *Przedświt* (London), no. 7, July 1893, in *PZ*, 1:40; Rom [Pilsudski], "Wilno, 25 lipca 1893," *Przedświt* (London), no. 7, July 1893, in *PZ*, 1:42.

29. [Jozef Pilsudski], "Stosunek do rewolucjonistów rosyjskich," *Przedświt* (London), no. 8, August 1893, in *PZ*, 1:43.

30. Ibid., 44–45.

31. Andrzej Nowak, *Polska i Trzy Rosje: Studium polityki wschodniej Józefa Piłsudskiego do kwietnia 1920 roku*, 3rd ed. (Kraków: Arcana, 2015), 26.

32. *Kalendarium*, 1:53–54; Jędrzejewicz, *Pilsudski*, 17; Władysław Pobóg-Malinowski, *Józef Piłsudski, 1867–1914* (1964; repr., Łomianki: Wydawnictwo LTW, 2015), 103; Pobóg-Malinowski, *Najnowsza historia polityczna Polski, 1864–1945* (Paris: Gryf, 1953), 1:51; Wasilewski, "Kierownictwo P.P.S.," 353.

33. [Pilsudski], "Wilno, w końcu grudnia," *Przedświt* (London), no. 12, December 1893, 21; authorship confirmed in *PZ*, 1:51.

34. Ziuk [Jozef Pilsudski], Vilna, December 1893, to Stanisław Wojciechowski, London, in *PZU*, 1:83–84.

35. [Jozef Pilsudski], "Sprawozdanie z II zjazdu Polskiej Partii Socjalistycznej," in *PZU*, 1:88.

36. Wasilewski, "Kierownictwo P.P.S.," 353; Garlicki, *Józef Piłsudski*, 46–47; Pobóg-Malinowski, *Józef Piłsudski, 1867–1914*, 103.

37. [Jozef Pilsudski], "Sprawozdanie z II zjazdu Polskiej Partii Socjalistycznej," in *PZU*, 1:87.

38. Napoleon Czarnocki, "Przyczynki do historii P.P.S.," in *Księga pamiątkowa PPS w trzydziestą rocznicę* (Warsaw: Nakładem Spółki Nakładowo-Wydawniczej "Robotnik," 1923), 59.

39. Zimmerman, *Poles, Jews and the Politics of Nationality*, 76; On Pilsudski's role in providing Yiddish literature to the Vilna Group, see Frants Kursky, "Di 'tsukunft' in untererdishn rusland," in *Gezamelte shriftn* (New York: Farlag der veker, 1952), 253.

40. Ziuk [Pilsudski], Vilna, to the ZZSP, London, April 29, 1894, in *PZ*, 1:89.

41. Rom [Pilsudski], Vilna, to the ZZSP, London, May 1894, in *PZU*, 1:93. On *Der arbeter* (1893–1896) in Galicia, see Jacob Bross, "The Beginnings of the Jewish Labor Movement in Galicia," *Yivo Annual of Jewish Social Science* 5 (1950): 66–82;

Walentyna Najdus, *Polska Partia Socjalo-Demokratyczna Galicji i Śląska, 1890–1919* (Warsaw: Państwowe Wydawnictwo Naukowe, 1983), 168; Joshau Shanes, *Diaspora Nationalism and Jewish Identity in Habsburg Galicia* (New York: Cambridge University Press, 2012), 103–104.

42. *25 yor: Zamlbukh* (Warsaw: Di Velt, 1922), 112; Malinowski, *Materiały*,1:91, 101. See Pilsudski, Vilna, to ZZSP, London, July 1894, in *PZU*, 1:97, where he referred to the arrival of the typesetting machine with Hebrew typeface.

43. Czasowy [Pilsudski], "Wilno we wrześniu," *Przedświt* (London), no. 9, September 1894, in *PZ*, 1:61.

44. Ibid., 62.

45. Ibid., 63.

46. Ibid.

47. Ibid., 65–66, 68.

48. Rom [Pilsudski], Vilna, to the ZZSP, London, May 1894, in *PZU*, 1:92–93.

49. Rom [Pilsudski], "Wilno, 18 maja," *Przedświt* (London), no. 5, May 1894, in *PZ*, 1:56–58.

50. [Pilsudski], "Walka z rządem," *Robotnik*, September 24, 1895, in *PZ*, 1:116, 119.

51. Police reports are summarized in *Kalendarium*, 1:57–58.

52. Z. Kormanowa, *Materiały do bibliografii druków socjalistycznych na ziemiach polskich w latach, 1866–1918*, 2nd ed., rev. (Warsaw: Książka i Wiedza, 1949), 67; *Kalendarium*, 1:58.

53. Z [Pilsudski], Vilna, to the ZZSP, London, July 15, 1894, in *PZU*, 1:96.

54. [Pilsudski], "Od Redakcyi," *Robotnik*, July 12, 1894, 1.

55. *Kalendarium*, 1:58–59; Jędrzejewicz, *Pilsudski*, 19.

56. Quotation from Sieroszewski, *Józef Piłsudski*, 21–22.

57. Perl, "Szkice dziejów P.P.S.," 6.

58. On Pilsudski's reports, see Kazimierz Pietkiewicz, "O czasach pepeesowych i przedpepeesowych słów kilka," in *Księga pamiątkowa PPS w trzydziestą rocznicę* (Warsaw: Nakładem Spółki Nakładowo-Wydawniczej "Robotnik," 1923), 35.

59. Wasilewski, "Kierownictwo P.P.S.," 353; Garlicki, *Józef Piłsudski*, 47–49; *PZU*, 1:100n11.

60. Pietkiewicz, "O czasach pepeesowych," 37.

61. Wiktor [Pilsudski], March or April, 1895, Vilna, to the ZZSP, London, in *PZU*, 1:107.

62. [Pilsudski], "U nas i gdzieindziej," *Robotnik*, October 27, 1894, 3.

63. Polish Socialist Party [Pilsudski], "Odezwa na śmierć cara Aleksandra III," Warsaw, November 9, 1894, in *PZ*, 1:73.

64. Z [Pilsudski], London, December 1894, to Aleksander Sulkiewicz, in *PZU*, 1:101.

65. Ignacy Mościcki, "Autobiografia," *Niepodległość* 12 (1979): 108–109.

66. *PZU*, 1:115n4; *Kalendarium*, 1:68.

67. Czarnocki, "Przyczynki do historii P.P.S.," 59.

68. Ziuk [Pilsudski], March or April 1895, Vilna, to the ZZSP, London, in *PZU*, 1:106.

69. [Jozef Pilsudski], "Rosja," *Robotnik* single issue (jednodniówka), April 1895, in *PZ*, 1:79–80.

70. Ibid., 91.

71. Central Workers' Committee of the Polish Socialist Party [Pilsudski], Warsaw, May Day Circular, May 1895, in *PZ*, 1:76–77.

72. Wiktor [Pilsudski], Vilna, April 1895, to the ZZSP, London, in *PZU*, 1:112.

73. Wiktor [Pilsudski], Vilna, June 1895, to the ZZSP, London, in *PZU*, 1:115.

74. Wojciechowski, *Moje wspomnienia*, 1:95.

75. *Robotnik*, June 7, 1895, in *PZ*, 1:91–92.

76. [Jozef Pilsudski], "Na posterunku," *Robotnik*, June 1895, in *PZ*, 1:92–93.

77. Ibid., 95.

78. "Uchwały III-go zjazdu Polskiej Partyi Socjalistycznej," *Robotnik*, August 1895, 6. The third conference resolution is reprinted in *PZU*, 1:120–123; and in Malinowski, *Materiały*, 1:144–150. On the importance of this resolution, see Nowak, *Polska i Trzy Rosje*, 27.

79. According to the 1897 census of the Russian Empire, ethnic Russians constituted 44.3 percent of the population. See H. Seton-Watson, *The Decline of Imperial Russia, 1855–1914* (New York: Praeger, 1967), 31.

80. [Pilsudski], "Rusyfikacja," *Robotnik*, July 3, 1895, 1, in *PZ*, 1 97–98, 100.

81. [Pilsudski], "Nasze Hasło," *Robotnik*, August 15, 1895, in *PZ*, 1:102.

82. [Pilsudski], "Czym jest Polska Partia Socjalistyczna," *Robotnik*, August 15, 1895, in *PZ*, 1:107.

83. [Pilsudski], "W rocznicę," *Robotnik*, February 9, 1896, in *PZ*, 1:121.

84. Wiktor [Pilsudski], Taurogi, September 7, 1895, to the ZZSP, London, in *PZU*, 1:129.

85. Jewish members of the Polish Socialist Party, Warsaw, to the Central Workers' Committee, December 1895, in Malinowski, *Materiały*, 1:161–162.

86. Wiktor [Pilsudski], Taurogi, September 7, 1895, to the ZZSP, London, in *PZU*, 1:129–130.

4. Into the International Arena

Epigraph: Henry Hyndman, London, to the ZZSP, London, January 31, 1896, AAN, sygn. 305 / II / 15, folder 28.

1. "Jędrzejowski Bolesław Antoni," *Polski Słownik Biograficzny* 11 (1964–1965): 239; *Kalendarium*, 1:74; Wacław Jędrzejewicz, *Pilsudski: A Life for Poland* (New York: Hippocrene Books, 1982), 20–21.

2. Wiktor [Pilsudski], London, to Witold Jodko-Narkiewicz, Berne, March 23, 1896, in *PZU*, 1:140.

3. *Robotnik*, July 3, 1896, 16, in *PZ*, 1:146.

4. Antonio Labriola, Rome, April 1, 1896, in *Pamiątka majowa: Wydawn. Polskiej partyi socyalistycznej z pod trzech zaborów* (London: Związku Zagranicznego Socjalistów Polskich, 1896), 55.

5. *Robotnik,* July 3, 1896, 16, in *PZ,* 1:147.

6. Jan Kancewicz, *Polska Partia Socjalistyczna w latach, 1892–1896* (Warsaw: Państwowe Wydawnictwo Naukowe, 1984), 427.

7. [Jozef Pilsudski], "Nasze Pismo," in *Pamiątka majowa* (1896), in *PZ,* 1:133.

8. Ibid., 137, 139.

9. *Przedświt* (London), no. 5, May 1896, in *PZ,* 1:145–146. For a discussion of this Yiddish circular—the PPS's first—see Pinchas Shwartz, "Di ershte yidishe oysgabes fun der PPS (1895–1898)," *Historishe shriftn* (Vilna, 1939), 3:530.

10. "Święto majowe w kraju," *Robotnik,* July 3, 1896, 5.

11. Wiktor [Jozef Pilsudski], London, to the Central Workers' Committee c/o Aleksander Sulkiewicz, June 9, 1896, in *PZU,* 1:222.

12. Bolesław Miklaszewski, New York, to the ZZSP, London, April 5, 1896, in *PZU,* 1:177n1.

13. *Pamiętniki Bolesława Miklaszewskiego* (Warsaw, 1928), 72, unpublished manuscript in PAN archives, sygn. 61.

14. Pilsudski, London, to Bolesław Miklaszewski, New York, April 24, 1896, in *PZU,* 1:176.

15. See "Z emigracji z Ameryki," *Przedświt,* no. 5, May 1896, 18. On the Jewish Socialist Post in America, see Władysław Pobóg-Malinowski, *Józef Piłsudski: W podziemiach konspiracji, 1867–1901: W podziemiach konspiracji* (Warsaw: Gebethner i Wolff, 1935), 297–298.

16. Wiktor [Jozef Pilsudski], London, to the Central Workers' Committee c/o Aleksander Sulkiewicz, May 7, 1896, in *PZU,* 1:181.

17. Wiktor [Jozef Pilsudski], London, to the Central Workers' Committee c/o Aleksander Sulkiewicz, August 4, 1896, in *PZU,* 1:254. The Yiddish brochure appeared as Ben N. [Benjamin Feigenbaum], *Dos gan-eydn hatakhton: A vunderlikhe emese mayse, vi men is dergangen dem veg tsum gan-eydn oyf der velt, un vi menshen foren ahin* (Warsaw, 1875). The brochure's publication date, 1896, and place of publication, New York, were changed to "Warsaw, 1875" to elude the censors.

18. Al. Dębski [Jozef Pilsudski], London, to Jewish Post from America to Poland, New York, June 10, 1896, in *PZU,* 1:227–228.

19. Wiktor [Jozef Pilsudski], London, to Bolesław Miklaszewski, New York, June 24, 1896, in *PZU,* 1:231–232. Emphasis in the original. The work "kraj" (country) was used to refer specifically to the Russian partition of Poland. See Leon Wasilewski, *Józef Piłsudski jakim go znałem,* ed. A. Friszke (1935; Warsaw: Muzeum Historii Polski, 2013), 121.

20. Quotation from Michał Romer, *Litwa: Studium o odrodzeniu narodu litewskiego* (Lwów: Polskie Towarzystwo Nakładowe, 1908), 278.

21. Wiktor [Jozef Pilsudski], London, to the Central Workers' Committee c/o Aleksander Sulkiewicz, June 25, 1896, in *PZU,* 1:233.

22. Wiktor [Jozef Pilsudski], London, to Witold Jodko-Narkiewicz, Berne, May 27, 1896, in *PZU,* 1:201.

23. Wiktor [Jozef Pilsudski], London, to the Central Workers' Committee c/o Aleksander Sulkiewicz, July 6, 1896, in *PZU,* 1:243; Wiktor [Jozef Pilsudski], London, to the Central Workers' Committee c/o Aleksander Sulkiewicz, July 15, 1896, in *PZU,* 1:247.

24. Henry Hyndman, London, to the ZZSP, London, January 31, 1896, in AAN archives, sygn. 305/II/15, folder 28.

25. "Wnioski," reprinted in B. A. Jędrzejowski, London, to Antonio Labriola, Rome, April 28, 1896, in Antonio Labriola, *Korespondencja* (Warsaw: Książka i Wiedza, 1966), 494.

26. Wiktor [Jozef Pilsudski], London, to the Central Workers' Committee c/o Aleksander Sulkiewicz, May 7, 1896, in *PZU,* 1:182.

27. B. A. Jędrzejowski, London, to Antonio Labriola, Rome, April 28, 1896, in Labriola, *Korespondencja,* 492–493. The 1866 congress resolved in favor of "the necessity of reducing the power of Russia in Europe . . . by the reconstitution of Poland on a Socialist and Democratic basis." See *Full Report of the Proceedings of the International Workers' Congress: London, July and August 1896* (London: Labor Leader, 1896), 4.

28. B. A. Jędrzejowski, "Socialism in Russian Poland," *Justice* (London), special May Day issue, May 1, 1896, 10–11.

29. [Rosa Luxemburg], "Neue Strömungen in der polnischen sozialistischen Bewegung in Deutchland und Österreich," *Die Neue Zeit,* April 19 and May 6, 1896; [Rosa Luxemburg], "Neue Der Sozialpatriotismjus in Polen," *Die Neue Zeit,* July 1, 1896, 459–470. The latter were reprinted in *Rosa Luxemburg: Gesammelte Werke* (Berlin: Dietz Verlag, 1972), vol. 1, bk. 1, pp. 14–51.

30. Karl Kautsky, "Finis Poloniae?," *Die Neue Zeit,* July 1, 1896, 484–491. For a summary of these two pieces, see J. P. Nettl, *Rosa Luxemburg* (London: Oxford University Press, 1969), 62–63.

31. Paul Frölich, *Rosa Luxemburg: Her Life and Work* (New York: Monthly Review Press, 1969), 36.

32. Antonio Labriola, Rome, May 3, 1896, to B. A. Jędrzejowski, London, in Labriola, *Korespondencja,* 496; B. A. Jędrzejowski, London, to Antonio Labriola, Rome, May 5, 1896, in Labriola, *Korespondencja,* 500.

33. Wiktor [Jozef Pilsudski], London, to the Central Workers' Committee, May 13, 1896, in *PZU,* 1:188.

34. Wiktor [Jozef Pilsudski], London, to the Central Workers' Committee, May 20, 1896, in *PZU,* 1:198.

35. Pilsudski, May 20, 1896, quotation from *Kalendarium,* 1:81.

36. Wiktor [Jozef Pilsudski], London, to the Central Workers' Committee c/o Aleksander Sulkiewicz, June 9, 1896, in *PZU,* 1:221–222. The reference here is to a verse from the song of the Polish Legions stationed in Italy in 1797, commanded by Gen. Jan Dąbrowski. In 1927 the song was adopted as the country's national anthem.

37. Wiktor [Jozef Pilsudski], London, to the Central Workers' Committee c/o Aleksander Sulkiewicz, June 25, 1896, 233.

38. Rosa Luxemburg, "La questone polacca al congresso internazionale di Londra," *Critica Sociale,* July 16, 1896; the article appeared simultaneously in Polish as "Kwestia polska na Międzynarodowym Kongresie w Londynie," *Sprawa Robotnicza,* July 1896. For an English translation, see Rosa Luxemburg, "The Polish Question at the International Congress in London," in *The National Question: Selected Writings of Rosa Luxemburg,* ed. Horace B. Davis (New York: Monthly Review Press, 1976), 49–59.

39. Luxemburg, "The Polish Question," 51–52.

40. Ibid., 57–58.

41. Wiktor [Jozef Pilsudski], London, to the Central Workers' Committee, July 15, 1896, in *PZU,* 1:247.

42. Georges Haupt, *La deuxième intérnationale, 1889–1914* (Paris: Mouton, 1964), 150.

43. "The International Workers' Congress," *Times* (London), July 30, 1896, 11. For more on this incident, see *Full Report,* 19.

44. *Full Report,* 32.

45. Wiktor [Jozef Pilsudski], London, to the Central Workers' Committee, August 4, 1896, in *PZU,* 1:253.

46. *Full Report,* 85.

47. Ignacy Mościcki, "Autobiografia," *Niepodległość* 12 (1979): 109.

48. Wiktor [Jozef Pilsudski], Kraków, to the ZZSP, London, August 24, 1896, in *PZU,* 1:263; Wiktor [Jozef Pilsudski], Lwów, to the ZZSP, London, August 29, 1896, in *PZU,* 1:264.

49. Wiktor [Jozef Pilsudski], Lwów, to the ZZSP, London, August 29, 1896, in *PZU,* 1:265; for the publication referred to, see Bronisław Szwarce, ed., *Wydawnictwo materiałów do historii powstania, 1863–1864* (Lwów: Nakładem "Kuriera Lwowskiego," 1894).

50. Wiktor [Jozef Pilsudski], Lwów, to the ZZSP, London, August 29, 1896, in *PZU,* 1:265; Joshua Shanes, *Diaspora Nationalism and Jewish Identity in Habsburg Galicia* (New York: Cambridge University Press, 2012), 103–104.

51. Wiktor [Jozef Pilsudski], Lwów, to the ZZSP, London, September 15, 1896, in *PZU,* 1:267.

52. Ibid., 268.

53. Ibid. Note that in contrast to autocratic Russia, Austria-Hungary was a constitutional monarchy where political parties and their publications operated openly and legally.

54. Ziuk [Jozef Pilsudski], the Russia partition, to the ZZSP, London, September 16, 1896, in *PZU*, 1:269.

55. Jewish members of the PPS, Warsaw, to the Central Workers' Committee of the PPS, September 1896, in A. Malinowski, ed. *Materiały do history PPS* (Warsaw: Wydawnictwo dzieł społeczno—politycznych, 1907), 1:217–221.

56. Wiktor [Pilsudski], Vilna, to the ZZSP, London, October 6, 1896, in *PZU*, 1:272.

57. Wiktor [Pilsudski], Vilna, to the ZZSP, London, December 12, 1896, in *PZU*, 1:280.

58. Wiktor [Pilsudski], Vilna, to the ZZSP, London, October 24, 1896, in *PZU*, 1:275; on borrowing on credit, see Wiktor [Pilsudski], Vilna, to the ZZSP, London, October 6, 1896, in *PZU*, 1:272.

59. [Pilsudski], "Z kongresu," *Robotnik,* October 4, 1896, in *PZ*, 1:147–148, 150.

60. "Kler przeciw ludowi," *Robotnik,* November 11, 1896, 2–4; "Podróż z cara," *Robotnik,* October 4, 1896, in *PZ*, 1:151.

61. Wiktor [Pilsudski], Vilna, to the ZZSP, London, December 12, 1896, in *PZU*, 1:281–282.

62. Pilsudski, Vilna, to the ZZSP, London, November 1896, quotation from Stanisław Wojciechowski], *Polska Partya Socyalistyczna w ostatnich pięciu latach* (London: Polish Socialist Party, 1900), 42–43.

63. [Pilsudski], "Niewola," *Robotnik,* December 6, 1896, in *PZ*, 1:156.

5. Party Leadership and Arrest

Epigraph: [Jozef Pilsudski?], "W kwestyi żydowskiej," *Robotnik,* February 13, 1898, 3.

1. Andrzej Garlicki, *Józef Piłsudski, 1867–1935* (Warsaw: Czytelnik, 1990), 61.

2. Leon Wasilewski, *Józef Piłsudski jakim go znałem,* ed. A. Friszke (1935; Warsaw: Muzeum Historii Polski, 2013), 111.

3. Ibid., 112.

4. [Pilsudski], "W rocznicę," *Robotnik,* January 24, 1897, 1.

5. Ibid.

6. From Zygmunt Krasiński, "Przedświt" (Dawn, 1843), in Monica M. Gardner, *The Anonymous Poet of Poland: Zygmunt Krasinski* (Cambridge: Cambridge University Press, 1919), 234.

7. [Pilsudski], "W rocznicę," *Robotnik,* January 24, 1897, 1.

8. Pilsudski, Vilna, to the ZZSP, London, February 12, 1897, in *PZU*, 1:292.

9. Jan Kancewicz, *Polska Partia Socjalistyczna w latach, 1892–1896* (Warsaw: Państwowe Wydawnictwo Naukowe, 1984), 405.

10. For a list of the ten-person Polish delegation, see *Kalendarium*, 1:87.

11. Aleksander Dębski, London, to Pilsudski, Vilna, no date, quotation from *Kalendarium*, 1:97.

12. [Pilsudski], Vilna, to the ZZSP, London, February 12, 1897, in *PZU*, 1:292.

13. Walentyna Najdus, *Ignacy Daszyński, 1866–1939* (Warsaw: Czytelnik, 1988), 120.

14. Joshua Shanes, *Diaspora Nationalism and Jewish Identity in Habsburg Galicia* (New York: Cambridge University Press, 2012), 104.

15. [Pilsudski], "Po wyborach," *Robotnik,* April 15, 1897, 1.

16. Ignacy Daszyński, *Pamiętniki* (Kraków: Nakładem Z.R.S.S. "Proletarjat," 1925), 1:105.

17. Wiktor [Pilsudski], Vilna, to the ZZSP, London, May 30, 1897, in *PZU*, 1:300.

18. [Pilsudski], "Prawo a urzędnicy," *Robotnik,* June 29, 1897, 4.

19. [Pilsudski], Vilna, to the ZZSP, London, July 24, 1897, in *PZU*, 1:304.

20. Andrejs Plakans, *The Latvians: A Short History* (Stanford, CA: Hoover Institution Press, 1995), 102–103; Andrejs Plakans, *A Concise History of the Baltic States* (Cambridge: Cambridge University Press, 2011), 264.

21. Eriks Jekabsons, "Początek stosunków Łotwy i Polski: Pierwsze kontakty, wiosna-jesień 1919 roku," *Res Historica* (Lublin), no. 42 (2016): 246.

22. [Pilsudski], Vilna, to the ZZSP, London, July 24, 1897, in *PZU*, 1:303.

23. R. F. Leslie, ed., *The History of Poland since 1863* (Cambridge: Cambridge University Press, 1980), 46–47, 55; Piotr Wandycz, *The Lands of Partitioned Poland, 1795–1918* (Seattle: University of Washington Press, 1974), 289.

24. "Czar's Visit to Warsaw," *New York Times,* September 13, 1897, 5.

25. A. Woźniak, "Gruziński wielkorządca w Warszawie: Rządy księcia Aleksandra Imeretyńskiego w Królestwie Polskim (1897–1900)," *Pro Georgia,* no. 11 (2004): 75–78.

26. [Pilsudski], "Towarzysze! Robotnicy!," Central Workers' Committee of the Polish Socialist Party, Warsaw, August 30, 1897, in *PZ*, 1:177.

27. Ibid., 178–179. For a discussion of this circular, see Wacław Jędrzejewicz, *Pilsudski: A Life for Poland* (New York: Hippocrene Books, 1982), 24.

28. [Pilsudski], Vilna, to the ZZSP, London, October 2, 1897, in *PZU*, 1:305.

29. Ibid., 305–306.

30. [Pilsudski], Vilna, to the ZZSP, London, October 18, 1897, in *PZU*, 1:309.

31. John Mill, "Arkadi un der ershter tsuzamenfor," in *Arkadi: zamlbukh tsum ondenk fun grinder fun 'bund' arkadi kremer, 1865–1935* (New York: Unzer tsayt, 1942), 164.

32. Leonas Sabaliunas, "Social Democracy in Tsarist Lithuania, 1893–1904," *Slavic Review* 31, no. 2 (June 1972): 340; Sabaliunas, *Lithuanian Social Democracy in Perspective, 1893–1914* (Durham, NC: Duke University Press, 1990), 38.

33. [Pilsudski], "Czwarty zjazd naszej partii," *Robotnik,* February 13, 1898, 1.

34. Ibid., 2.

35. [Pilsudski], "Od redakcji," *Robotnik,* December 12, 1897, 1.

36. For the list of participants, see *PZU*, 2:14n1.

37. [Jozef Pilsudski?], "W kwestyi żydowskiej," *Robotnik,* no. 26, February 13, 1898, 3.

38. Ibid., 4.

39. Wiktor [Pilsudski], Vilna, to the editor of *Przedświt* (Leon Wasilewski), London, February 15, 1898, in *PZU*, 2:26.

40. Ibid., 27. I am grateful to Filip Mazurczak for helping to render this passage in English.

41. Karl Kautsky, *Niepodległość Polski* (London: Wydawnictwo Polskiej Partyi Socyalitycznej, W drukarni ZZSP, 1896), which subsequently appeared in Yiddish as Karl Kautsky, *Di unobhendgigkeyt fun poyln*, trans. Leon Gottlieb (London: PPS, printed by the ZZSP, 1901).

42. Wiktor [Pilsudski], Vilna, to Bolesław Antoni Jędrzejowski, May 10, 1898, in *PZU*, 2:41.

43. Wiktor [Pilsudski], Vilna, to the ZZSP, London, March 3, 1898, in *PZU*, 2:32.

44. Wiktor [Pilsudski], Vilna, to the ZZSP, June 4, 1898, in *PZU*, 2:43.

45. Woźniak, "Gruziński wielkorządca w Warszawie: Rządy księcia Aleksandra Imereyńskiego w Królestwie Polskim (1897–1900)," *Pro Georgia*, no. 11 (2004): 86; *Kalendarium*, 1:113.

46. Wiktor [Pilsudski], Kraków, to Bolesław A. Jędrzejowski, London, June 22, 1898, in *PZU*, 2:45. On the secret memorandum, see Woźniak, "Gruziński wielkorządca w Warszawie," 86; and *Kalendarium*, 1:113.

47. *Tajne dokumenty rządu rosyjskiego w sprawach polskich: Memoriał ks. Imeretyńskeigo. Protokóły Komitetu Ministrów. Nota Kancelaryi Komitetu Ministrów* (London: n.p., 1898). For a reprint of Pilsudski's introduction, see "Wstęp do Memoriału Księcia Imeretyńskiego," in *PZ*, 1:203–218.

48. [Pilsudski], "Książę Imeretyńsky o sprawie robotniczej," *Robotnik*, July 10, 1898, 1, in *PZ*, 1:222.

49. Woźniak, "Gruziński wielkorządca w Warszawie," 87; Garlicki, *Józef Piłsudski*, 66; Jędrzejewicz, *Pilsudski*, 25.

50. "Secret Official Report on the Condition of Poland," *Times* (London), August 13, 1898, 11.

51. "Le Tsar, La Pologne et Le Prince Imeretinsky," *Le Temps* (Paris), August 17, 1898, 1.

52. Wiktor [Pilsudski], London, to Kazimierz Kelles-Krauz, Paris, July 7, 1898, in *PZU*, 2:45; Wiktor [Pilsudski], London, to Feliks Perl, Lwów, July 7, 1898, in *PZU*, 2:46. The 31-page brochure, Res [Perl], *Adam Mickiewicz* (London: PPS, 1898), appeared later that year.

53. [Pilsudski], "Z pola walki," *Robotnik*, July 10, 1898, 3, in *PZ*, 1:222.

54. Patrice M. Dabrowski, *Commemorations and the Shaping of Modern Poland* (Bloomington: Indiana University Press, 2004), 150–153.

55. [Pilsudski], "Jubileusz Mickiewicza," *Robotnik*, July 10, 1898, 11–12. Authorship is confirmed in *Kalendarium*, 1:115. For the monument committee's subsequent album on the monument, see *Pomnik Mickiewicza w Warszawie, 1897–1898*, ed. Zygmunt Wasilewski (Warsaw: Nakładem Komitetu Budowy Pomnika, 1899).

56. Wasilewski, *Józef Piłsudski*, 120.

57. Wiktor [Pilsudski], London, to Maksymilian Horwitz, Ostend (Belgium), July 26, 1898, in *PZU*, 2:54.

58. Joanna Olczak-Ronikier, *In the Garden of Memory: A Family Memoir* (London: Phoenix, 2005), 57.

59. Wiktor [Pilsudski], Lwów, to the ZZSP, London, August 19, 1898, in *PZU*, 2:59.

60. Wiktor [Pilsudski], Vilna, to the ZZSP, London, September 11, 1898, in *PZU*, 2:61.

61. Wiktor [Pilsudski], Vilna, to Bolesław Antoni Jędrzejowki and Aleksander Malinowski, London, September 22, 1898, in *PZU*, 2:64.

62. Wiktor [Pilsudski] to the ZZSP, London, October 23, 1898, reprinted in *Niepodległość* (London) 11 (1978): 14.

63. Wiktor [Pilsudski] to B. A. Jędrzejowski, London, August 31, 1899, reprinted in *Niepodległość* (New York) 17 (1984): 10.

64. [Pilsudski], "Pomnik kata," *Robotnik*, October 11, 1898, 1, in *PZ*, 1:227. On the Muraviev monument, see Theodore R. Weeks, "Monuments and Memory: Immortalizing Count M. N. Muraviev in Vilna, 1898," *Nationality Papers* 27, no. 4 (1999): 551–564.

65. [Pilsudski], "Pomnik kata," *Robotnik*, October 11, 1898, 1. in *PZ*, 1:227. Muraviev was released from his duties in 1865.

66. Ibid., 1:228–229.

67. [Pilsudski], proclamation dated November 1898, [Vilna], in *PZ*, 1:234.

68. Dabrowski, *Commemorations*, 151.

69. [Pilsudski], "Bankructwo Ugody," *Robotnik*, October 11, 1898, in *PZ*, 1:229.

70. [Pilsudski], "Odezwa do robotników w sprawie pomnika Mickiewicza w Warszawie," Warsaw, December 16, 1898, in *PZ*, 1:240–241. Also see Pilsudski's two other commentaries: "Od redakcji," *Robotnik*, December 19, 1898, and "Pomnik Murawjewa," *Przedświt*, no. 12, December 1898, both in *PZ*, 1:235–239.

71. Wiktor [Pilsudski], Vilna, to the Conspiratorial Commission of the ZZSP, London, February 2, 1898, in *PZU*, 2:21.

72. Wiktor [Pilsudski] to B. A. Jędrzejowski, London, January 11, 1899, reprinted in *Niepodległość* (New York) 16 (1983): 7.

73. Wiktor [Pilsudski] to B. A. Jędrzejowski, London, January 11, 1899, reprinted in *Niepodległość* (New York) 16 (1983): 7.

74. Stanisław Wojciechowski, *Moje wspomnienia* 1 (Lwów: Książnica-Atlas, 1938), 130–132.

75. Wiktor [Pilsudski], Vilna, to the ZZSP, London, August 1898, quotation from Wojciechowski, *Moje wspomnienia*, 1:126.

76. Jan Pilsudski, recollections preserved in the Pilsudski Institute, London, quotation from *Kalendarium*, 1:127–128.

77. *Kalendarium*, 1:132–133; Garlicki, *Józef Piłsudski*, 63; Włodzimierz Suleja, *Józef Piłsudski* (Wrocław: Zakład Narodowy im. Ossolińskich, 1995), 42.

78. [Pilsudski], "Po manifestacjach," *Robotnik,* June 4, 1899, in *PZ,* 1:257.

79. [Pilsudski], "Pięciolecia 'Robotnik,'" *Robotnik,* July 23, 1899, in *PZ,* 1:264.

80. Wiktor [Pilsudski] to B. A. Jędrzejowski, London, May 15, 1899, reprinted in *Niepodległość* (New York) 17 (1984): 15–16.

81. Wiktor [Pilsudski] to B. A. Jędrzejowski, London, May 27, 1899, reprinted in *Niepodległość* (New York) 17 (1984): 17; Wiktor [Pilsudski] to B. A. Jędrzejowski, London, August 31, 1899, reprinted in *Niepodległość* (New York) 17 (1984): 9–10.

82. [Pilsudski], "Z powodu strejków tegorocznych," *Robotnik,* October 1, 1899, in *PZ,* 1:274–275.

83. Wiktor [Pilsudski], Łódź, to the ZZSP, London, October 8, 1899, reprinted in *Niepodległość* (New York) 17 (1984): 12–13.

84. Wiktor [Pilsudski], Łódź, to Leon Wasilewski, London, November 19, 1899, reprinted in *Niepodległość* (New York) 18 (1985): 11.

85. Ibid., 11–12.

86. Ibid., 14. Emphasis in the original.

87. Wasilewski, *Józef Piłsudski* [1935 edition], 36–46.

88. L. Płochocki [Leon Wasilewski], *We wspólnym jarzmie: O narodowościach przez carat uciskanych* (London: PPS, 1901), 11.

89. [Pilsudski], "Nowy okres," *Robotnik,* December 3, 1899, 1, in *PZ,* 1:276, 279.

90. [Pilsudski], "W rocznicę," *Kurierek Robotnika,* January 24, 1900, 1–2, 4.

91. Wiktor [Pilsudski], Łódź, to the ZZSP, London, January 15, 1900, reprinted in *Niepodległość* 19 (1986): 9.

92. Wiktor [Pilsudski], Łódź, to the ZZSP, London, February 7, 1900, reprinted in *Niepodległość* (New York) 19 (1986): 18.

93. Wiktor [Pilsudski], Łódź, to the ZZSP, London, January 7, 1900, reprinted in *Niepodległość* (New York) 19 (1986): 5.

94. Wiktor [Pilsudski], Łódź, to the ZZSP, London, February 8, 1900, reprinted in *Niepodległość* (New York) 19 (1986): 22.

95. Ziuk [Pilsudski], Tenth Pavilion of the Warsaw Citadel, April 1900, report for party comrades, in *PZU,* 2:81–85.

96. Wasilewski, *Józef Piłsudski* (1935 edition), 47.

6. An Extraordinary Escape and a New Home in Austrian Galicia

Epigraph: Robotnik, August 5, 1902, 2–3.

1. W. Pobóg-Malinowski, *Józef Piłsudski, 1867–1914* (1964; repr., Łomianki: Wydawnictwo LTW, 2015), 175–176n20.

2. *Kalendarium,* 1:148.

3. Wasilewski, "Kierownictwo P.P.S. zaboru rosyjskiego (1893–1918)," *Niepodległość* 11 (1935): 355; "Sachs, Feliks," *Polski Słownik Biograficzny* 34 (1992–1993); "Rożnowski, Kazimierz," *Polski Słownik Biograficzny* 32 (1989–1991), 471; Stanisław Wojciechowski, *Moje wspomnienia,* vol. 1 (Lwów: Książnica-Atlas, 1938), 138.

Rożnowski was sentenced to six years of exile in Siberia, Malinowski to eight years.

4. Wojciechowski, *Moje wspomnienia*, 138; Andrzej Garlicki, *Józef Piłsudski, 1867–1935* (Warsaw: Czytelnik, 1990), 70.

5. Wojciechowski, *Moje wspomnienia*, 139.

6. *Robotnik* (London), April 26, 1900, 1.

7. From a 1903 article reprinted in *Joseph Pilsudski: The Memories of a Polish Revolutionary and Soldier,* trans. and ed. D. R. Gillie (London: Faber and Faber, 1931), 127.

8. *Joseph Pilsudski: The Memories,* 127, 134.

9. Pilsudski, Warsaw Citadel prison, April 1900, in *PZU,* 2:81–83.

10. [Pilsudski], June 1, 1900, Warsaw Citadel prison, to Wanda Juszkiewicz, in Adam Borkiewicz, "Źródła do biografii Józefa Piłsudskiego z lat 1867–1892," *Niepodległość* 19 (January–June 1939): 392; and in *PZU,* 2:85.

11. M. Paszkowska, "Zorganizowanie przewiezienia J. Piłsudskiego z Cytadeli w Warszawie do Petersburga," in *Uwolnienie Piłsudskiego: Wspomnienia organizatorów ucieczki* (Warsaw: Towarzystwo Wydawnicze "Ignis," 1924), 17–18.

12. Alexandra Pilsudska, *Pilsudski: A Biography by His Wife* (New York: Dodd, Mead, 1941), 176–177.

13. Paszkowska, "Zorganizowanie przewiezienia J. Piłsudskiego," 17; Maria Paszkowska, "Dziwny człowiek: Intendent X pawilonu," in *Księga pamiątkowa PPS w trzydziestą rocznicę* (Warsaw: Nakładem Spółki Nakładowo-Wydawniczej "Robotnik," 1923), 102.

14. Paszkowska, "Ucieczka: Mój udział w wykradzeniu Józefa Piłsudskiego," in *Księga pamiątkowa P.P.S.* (Warsaw: Nakł. Spółki nakładowo-wydawniczej "Robotnik," 1923), 105.

15. Paszkowska, "Zorganizowanie przewiezienia J. Piłsudskiego," 22.

16. Mazurkiewicz, "Wyprowadzenie ze szpitala," in *Uwolnienie Piłsudskiego,* 40–41.

17. Ibid., 46.

18. Ibid., 47. My gratitude to Julian Bussgang for helping render these passages in English.

19. Ksawery Prauss, "Przyjazd do Kijowa," in *Uwolnienie Piłsudskiego,* 49–51.

20. "Ucieczka tow. Piłsudskiego," *Robotnik* (Kiev), June 26, 1901, 10.

21. J. Miklaszewski, "Przeprowadzenie przez granicę," in *Uwolnienie Piłsudskiego,* 57. For a photograph of the monument that today marks the spot where the Pilsudskis first set foot on Austrian soil, see Joanna Wieliczka-Szarkowa, *Józef Piłsudski, 1867–1935: Wszystko dla niepodległej* (Kraków: Wydawnictwo AA s.c., 2015), 72.

22. *Statystyka miasta Krakowa* (Kraków: Nakładem Gmindy Miasta Krakowa, 1907), pt. 2, vol. 9, p. 18; Nathaniel D. Wood, *Becoming Metropolitan: Urban Self-*

hood and the Making of Modern Cracow (Dekalb: Northern Illinois University Press, 2010), 36–37; and Andrzej Żbikowski, *Żydzi krakowscy i ich gminy w latach 1869–1919* (Warsaw: Wydawnictwo DiG, 1994), 42.

23. *Statystyka miasta Krakowa*, pt. 2, vol. 9, p. 3.

24. *Encyclopedia of Ukraine* 3 (1993): 223; and Christoph Mick, *Lemberg, Lwów, Lviv, 1914–1947: Violence and Ethnicity in a Contested City* (West Lafayette, Indiana: Purdue University Press, 2016), 5.

25. *Kalendarium*, 1:156.

26. Adam Uziembło, *Niepodległość socjalisty* (Warsaw: Ośrodek Karta, 2008), 34.

27. Uziembło, *Niepodległość socjalisty*, 10.

28. Adam Uziembło, "Pierwszy portret Ziuka," *Kultura* (Paris), no. 3, 1956, 100.

29. Ziuk [Pilsudski], June 20, 1901, Lwów, to Bolesław A. Jędrzejowski, London, in *Niepodległość* (New York) 11 (1978): 24.

30. Helena Tołłoczko, Brzuchowice, letter of November 7, 1933, reprinted in Zygmunt Zygmuntowicz, *Józef Piłsudski we Lwowie* (Lwów: Nakładem Towarzystwa Miłośników Przeszłości Lwowa, 1934), 5–6.

31. Stanisław Siedlecki, letter of October 1933, in Zygmuntowicz, *Józef Piłsudski*, 7. On Siedlecki's background, see "Siedlecki Stanisław," *Polski Słownik Biograficzny* 36 (1995–1996). Note that news of Pilsudski's escape appeared in the Kraków-based PPSD newspaper *Naprzód* (Forward), as well as in a Lwów paper, *Kurier Lwowski*.

32. Siedlecki, in Zygmuntowicz, *Józef Piłsudski*, 7–9.

33. Ziuk [Pilsudski], July 15, 1901, Lwów, to Bolesław A. Jędrzejowski, London, in *Niepodległość* (New York) 11 (1978): 25–26.

34. Ziuk [Pilsudski], July 25, 1901, Kraków, to Bolesław A. Jędrzejowski, London, in *Niepodległość* (New York) 11 (1978): 28.

35. Lesław Dall, "Józef Piłsudski w Zakopanem," *Wierchy* (Kraków), no. 65 (1999): 63.

36. Ziuk [Pilsudski], August 14, 1901, Zakopane, to Bolesław A. Jędrzejowski, London, in *Niepodległość* (New York) 11 (1978): 32.

37. Ziuk [Pilsudski], September 3, 1901, Zakopane, to Bolesław A. Jędrzejowski, London, in *Niepodległość* (New York) 11 (1978): 33–34.

38. Ziuk [Pilsudski], September 5, 1901, Zakopany, to Bolesław A. Jędrzejowski, London, in *Niepodległość* (New York) 11 (1978): 34. See *Robotnik* (Kiev), August 9, 1901.

39. Leon Wasilewski, *Józef Piłsudski jakim go znałem* (Warsaw: Towarzystwo Wydawnicze "Rój," 1935), 54.

40. Ziuk [Pilsudski], December 19, 1901, Southbourne-on-Sea (England), to Bolesław A. Jędrzejowski, London, in *Niepodległość* (New York) 19 (1986): 23–24; Ziuk [Pilsudski], December 25, 1901, Southbourne-on-Sea (England), to Bolesław A. Jędrzejowski, London, in *Niepodległość* (New York) 19 (1986): 26.

41. Wojciechowski, *Moje wspomnienia*, 1:152–153.

42. *PZU* 2:107n1; Wojciechowski, *Moje wspomnienia*, 1:153.

43. Wasilewski, *Józef Piłsudski*, 65.

44. On the Bund's fourth congress and its declaration on Jewish nationality, see Jonathan Frankel, *Prophecy and Politics: Socialism, Nationalism, and the Russian Jews, 1862–1917* (New York: Cambridge University Press, 1981), 220; and Joshua D. Zimmerman, *Poles, Jews and the Politics of Nationality: The Bund and the Polish Socialist Party in Late Tsarist Russia, 1892–1914* (Madison: University of Wisconsin Press, 2004), 119–123.

45. Józ[ef] Pilsudski, London, to Władysław Gumplowicz, Zurich, January 16, 1902, in *PZU*, 2:95; Ziuk [Pilsudski], London, to Witold Jodko-Narkiewicz, Lwów, February 12, 1902, in *PZU*, 2:105.

46. Zetterbaum, a member of the PPSD, believed Jews should identify as Poles of the Hebrew faith.

47. Ziuk [Pilsudski], London, to Kazimierz Kelles-Krauz, Vienna, February 17, 1902, in *Niepodległość* (New York) 13 (1980): 9–10.

48. Jozef Pilsudski, London, to Władysław Gumplowicz, Zurich, February 17, 1902, in *PZU*, 2:108–109.

49. Ziuk [Pilsudski], London, to Central Committee of the Polish Socialist Party, Tsarist Russia, January 27, 1902, in *PZU*, 2:100–101.

50. Ziuk [Pilsudski], February 17, 1902, London, to Stanisław Wojciechowski, Southbourne-on-Sea, in *PZU*, 2:106.

51. Ziuk [Pilsudski], February 20, 1902, London, to Central Workers' Committee, in *PZU*, 2:115.

52. Ziuk [Pilsudski], March 25, 1902, London, to Stanisław Wojciechowski, Southbourne-on-Sea, in *PZU*, 2:121; Ziuk [Pilsudski], April 1, 1902, London, to Stanisław Wojciechowski, Southbourne-on-Sea, in *PZU*, 2:122.

53. Ziuk [Pilsudski], April 5, 1902, London, to W. Jodko-Narkiewicz, Lwów, in *PZU*, 2:123; Ziuk [Pilsudski], April 8, 1902, London, to Stanisław Wojciechowski, Southbourne-on-Sea, in *PZU*, 2:138.

54. Quotation from Antonia Domańska, recollection in *Kalendarium*, 1:171.

55. Ziuk [Pilsudski], April 21, 1902, Lwów, to Bolesław A. Jędrzejowski, London, in *Niepodległość* 13 (1980): 14.

56. W. F. Reddaway, *Marshal Pilsudski* (London: George Routledge and Sons, 1939), 41.

57. Walery Sławek, "Wspomnienia (1895–1910)," *Niepodległość* 17 (1985): 133; see 132 for Sławek's comment on Wanda's role in introducing them.

58. Ziuk [Pilsudski], May 13, 1902, Vilna (?), to the foreign committee of the PPS, London, reprinted in *Niepodległość* (New York) 13 (1980): 18.

59. Ziuk [Pilsudski], May 31, 1902, Vilna (?), to B. A. Jędrzejowski, London, in *Niepodległość* (New York) 14 (1981): 3–4.

60. Sławek, "Wspomnienia (1895–1910)," 133; Wasilewski, "Kierownictwo P.P.S. zaboru rosyjskiego," 355–356. Resolutions of the Sixth Party Congress were first published as "VI zjazd PPS," *Przedświt,* no. 8, August 1902, 281–285; and as "Szósty zjazd PPS," *Robotnik,* August 5, 1902, 1–3. They are reprinted in *PZU,* 2:139–144.

61. Resolutions of the PPS's Sixth Party Congress (June 1902), in *PZU,* 2:142.

62. Ibid., 142–143.

63. Ibid., 143. For the original, see "Szósty zjazd PPS," *Robotnik,* August 5, 1902, 1. This section of the resolutions, titled "The Socialist Movement among the Jews," was reprinted in *Robotnik* as the congress's first resolution and appeared on the issue's cover page.

64. *Robotnik,* August 5, 1902, 2–3.

65. Quotation from Walery Sławek, "Wspomnienia (1895–1910)," *Niepodległość* 17 (1985): 134–135.

66. See [Pilsudski], July 9, 1902, Brzuchowice, to B. A. Jędrzejowski, London, in *Niepodległość* 14 (1981): 5.

67. Feliks Sachs, Vilna, to the foreign committee of the PPS, London, August 7, 1902, AAN, sygn. 305 / VII / 34, folder 1, fols. 52, 61.

68. Ziuk [Pilsudski], July 28, 1902, Brzuchowice, to foreign committee, London, reprinted in *Niepodległość* (New York) 14 (1981): 7.

69. Ziuk [Pilsudski], May 30, 1902, Vilna (?), to B. A. Jędrzejowski, London, reprinted in *Niepodległość* (New York) 13 (1980): 18. Also see Pilsudska, *Pilsudski,* 180–181; Grace Humphrey, *Pilsudski: Builder of Poland* (New York: Scott and More, 1936), 87.

70. Ziuk [Pilsudski], July 28, 1902, Brzuchowice, to foreign committee, London, reprinted in *Niepodległość* (New York) 14 (1981): 8.

7. Creating a Party Platform

Epigraph: Walka (Kraków), October 1902.

1. *PZ,* 2:8.

2. Ibid.

3. Ibid., 9.

4. Leon Wasilewski, introduction, in *PZ,* 2:2.

5. [Pilsudski], "Wilno, we wrześniu 1902 r.," *Walka,* October 1902, in *PZ,* 2:18.

6. Ibid., 19.

7. Ibid, 20–21.

8. Ibid., 21.

9. Ibid.

10. Ibid., 22.

11. Ibid.

12. [Pilsudski], "O patriotyzmie," *Walka*, October 1902, in *PZ*, 2:24; quotation taken in part from the translation in *For Your Freedom and Ours*, ed. Krystyna M. Olszer (New York: Frederick Unger Publishing Co., 1981), 158.

13. [Pilsudski], "O patriotyzmie," *Walka*, October 1902, in *PZ*, 2:25.

14. Ibid., 27. Verse from *Dzieje Juliusza Słowackiego*, vol. 4 (Lwów: Nakładem Księgarni polskiej, 1894), 335. I am grateful to Roman Koropeckyj for helping me render these verses in English.

15. Ibid., 27.

16. Report of the congress of the Central Workers' Committee of the Polish Socialist Party, November 15, 1902, in *PZU*, 2:149.

17. *Kalendarium*, 1:172; Grace Humphrey, *Pilsudski: Builder of Poland* (New York: Scott and More, 1936), 87.

18. Mieczysław [Pilsudski], December 16, 1902, Riga, to the foreign committee, London, in *Niepodległość* (New York) 15 (1982): 9; Ziuk [Pilsudski], March 27, 1903, Riga, to Bolesław A. Jędrzejowski, London, in *Niepodległość* (New York) 15 (1982): 12.

19. [Pilsudski], "Rusyfikacja," *Kalendarz Robotniczy* (1903), in *PZ*, 2:28–31. According to the 1897 census of the Russian Empire, ethnic Russians made up 44.5 percent of the country's 125.6 million inhabitants. See Hugh Seton-Watson, *The Decline of Imperial Russia, 1855–1914* (New York: Praeger, 1967), 31.

20. *Niepodległość* (New York) 12 (1979): 11; *Kalendarium*, 1:178. For the conference protocols, see Conference of the Central Committee of the PPS, June 4–6, 1903, Vilna, in *PZU*, 2:155.

21. *PZU*, 2:158, 162–163.

22. [Pilsudski], July 26, 1903, Kraków, to the foreign committee of the PPS, London, in *Niepodległość* (New York) 12 (1979): 14–15.

23. Ziuk [Pilsudski], August 6, 1903, Rytro, to the foreign committee of the PPS, London, in *Niepodległość* (New York) 12 (1979): 20, 23; and Ignacy Daszyński, *Pamiętniki* (Kraków: Nakładem Z.R.S.S. "Proletarjat," 1925), 1:214–215.

24. Michał Sokolnicki, *Czternaście lat* (Warsaw: Instytut Badania Najnowszej Historii Polski, 1936), 74.

25. Ziuk [Pilsudski], September 14, 1903, Rytro, to party comrades, London, in *Niepodległość* (New York) 19 (1986): 56.

26. Ibid., 54.

27. Ibid., 55. On this passage, see Andrzej Nowak's analysis in his *Polska i Trzy Rosje: Studium polityki wschodniej Józefa Pilsudskiego do kwietnia 1920 roku*, 3rd ed. (Kraków: Arcana, 2015), 35.

28. Ziuk [Pilsudski], September 14, 1903, Rytro, to party comrades, London, in *Niepodległość* (New York) 19 (1986): 51–53.

29. Ziuk [Pilsudski], August 15, 1903, to Bolesław A. Jędrzejowski, London, in *Niepodległość* (New York) 12 (1979): 28.

30. *Naprzód* (Kraków), August 27, 1903, 1.

31. Ziuk [Pilsudski], September 10, 1903, Rytro, to party comrades, London, in *Niepodległość* (New York) 19 (1986): 41. For the first installment, see D.C.N. [Pilsudski], "Walka rewolucyjna pod zaborem rosyjskim," *Naprzód* (Kraków), September 8, 1903, 1.

32. Jozef Pilsudski, *Walka rewolucyjna w zaborze rosyjskim* (Kraków: Nakładem Wydawnictwa "Naprzodu," 1903), 136–137; English translation from "Bibula—Secret Printing Pressess," in *Joseph Pilsudski: The Memories of a Polish Revolutionary and Soldier,* trans. and ed. D. R. Gillie (London: Faber and Faber, 1931), 90.

33. J. Pilsudski, "Jak stałem się socjalistą," *Promień* (Lwów), September–October 1903, 343–344. Quotation from the English version in Pilsudski, "How I Became a Socialist" (1903), in *Joseph Pilsudski: The Memories,* 13.

34. Pilsudski, "How I Became a Socialist" (1903), 15–16.

35. *Promień* (Lwów), September–October 1903, 348. Emphasis in the original. This passage in the original Polish is missing from the abridged English translation.

36. Stanisław Siedlecki, "Założenie 'Promienia,'" *Niepodległość* 4 (1930): 80.

37. Sk. [Roman Dmowski], "Historia szlachetnego socjalisty: Przyczynek do psychologii politycznej społeczeństwa," *Przegląd Wszechpolski* (Kraków), October 1903, 49–50.

38. [Pilsudski], "Wilno, październik 1903," *Walka,* November 1903, in *PZ,* 2:214–216, quotation on 216.

39. Ibid., 218. On this pogrom, see Steven Zipperstein, *Pogrom: Kishinev and the Tilt of History* (New York: Liveright, 2018).

40. [Pilsudski], "Nasze stanowisko na Litwie," *Walka,* November 1903, in *PZ,* 2:223.

41. Ibid., 220.

42. [J. Pilsudski], "Kwestia żydowska na Litwie," *Walka,* November 1903, in *PZ,* 2:226.

43. Ziuk [Pilsudski], February 1904 (after the outbreak of the Russo-Japanese War), Tsarist Russia, to party comrades, London, in *Niepodległość* (New York) 15 (1982): 19–21. For comment on this letter, see *PZU,* 2:183–186.

44. Ziuk [Pilsudski], February 1904, Warsaw (?), to party comrades, Kraków, in *Niepodległość* (New York) 15 (1982): 22, 24.

45. "Odezwy naszej partii," *Przedświt* (Kraków), no. 3, March 1904, 133–135. The circular was also printed in *Naprzód* (Kraków), March 15, 1903, 1, signed by the PPS, the Lithuanian Social Democrats, the Belarusian Revolutionary Party, and the Latvian Social-Democratic Party.

46. Witold Jodko-Narkiewicz, Lwów, to His Excellency, Nobuoki Makino, Vienna, February 8, 1904, in *Zeszyty Historyczne* 27 (1974): 5.

47. Witold Jodko-Narkiewicz, Lwów, to His Excellency, Nobuoki Makino, Vienna, March 19, 1904, reprinted in *Zeszyty Historyczne* 27 (1974): 7.

48. Viscount Hayashi, London, telegraph no. 103 to the foreign minister, Jutaro Komura, March 16, 1904, in Jerzy Lerski, "A Polish Chapter of the Russo-Japanese War," *Transactions of the Asiatic Society of Japan,* ser. 3, vol. 7 (1959): 77; Tadasu Hayashi, March 28, 1904, London, to Jodko-Narkiewicz, Lwów, in *Zeszyty Historyczne* 27 (1974): 27.

49. Pilsudski, Warsaw, letter of March 19, 1904, cited in *Kalendarium,* 1:199.

50. Pilsudski, Warsaw (?), undated, in *Zeszyty Historyczne* 27 (1974): 14. I am grateful to Julian Bussgang for helping me render this sentence in English.

51. Cited in *Zeszyty Historyczne* 27 (1974): 18n35.

52. *Zeszyty Historyczne* 27 (1974): 18; Władysław Pobóg-Malinowski, *Józef Piłsudski, 1867–1914* (1964; repr., Łomianki: Wydawnictwo LTW, 2015), 243–244; Andrzej Garlicki, *Józef Piłsudski* (Warsaw: Czytelnik, 1988), 85.

53. Ziuk [Pilsudski], April 24, 1904, Kraków, to Alexander Malinowski, London, in *Niepodległość* (New York) 12 (1979): 37.

54. Ziuk [Pilsudski], April 24, 1904, Kraków, to Alexander Malinowski, London, in *Niepodległość* (New York) 12 (1979): 38.

55. Ibid., 39.

56. Quotation from Wacław Sieroszewski, *Marszałek Józef Piłsudski* (Warsaw: Dom Książki Polskiej, Spółka Akcyjna, 1935), 18.

57. Ziuk [Pilsudski], May 10, 1904, Kraków, to T. Filipowicz, London, in *Zeszyty Historyczne* 27 (1974): 28.

8. From a Tokyo Mission to the Union of Active Struggle

Epigraph: PZU, 2:213.

1. T. Filipowicz, May 13, 1904, London, to Ziuk [Pilsudski], Kraków, in *Zeszyty Historyczne* 27 (1974): 30; *Kalendarium,* 1:202.

2. Ziuk [Pilsudski], May 26, 1904, to T. Filipowicz and A. Malinowski, London, in *Zeszyty Historyczne* 27 (1974): 32–33.

3. [Pilsudski], June 3, 1904, London, to Bolesław A. Jędrzejowski, Kraków, in *Zeszyty Historyczne* 27 (1974): 34.

4. Hayashi, London, to Foreign Minister Komura, Tokyo, June 9, 1904, in Jerzy Lerski, "A Polish Chapter of the Russo-Japanese War," *Transactions of the Asiatic Society of Japan,* ser. 3, vol. 7 (1959): 76; Pobóg-Malinowski, *Józef Piłsudski, 1901–1908* (Warsaw: Nakład Gebethner i Wolff, 1935), 195.

5. Quotation from *Zeszyty Historyczne* 27 (1974): 38.

6. Ziuk [Pilsudski], June 13, 1904, New York, to A. Malinowski, London, in *Zeszyty Historyczne* 27 (1974): 38.

7. Filipowicz, June 21, 1904, San Francisco, to A. Malinowski, London, in *Zeszyty Historyczne* 27 (1974): 40–41.

8. Ziuk [Pilsudski], enclosed note to Malinowski, London, in ibid., 41.

9. *PZ*, 2:249–250.

10. Ibid., 253 (emphasis in the original), 257.

11. Tytus Filipowicz, Tokyo, diary entry of July 11, 1904, in *Zeszyty Historyczne* 27 (1974): 50.

12. Filipowicz, Tokyo, diary entries of July 15, 1904, in *Zeszyty Historyczne* 27 (1974): 52–53.

13. Roman Dmowski, July 20, 1904, report to the Japanese foreign ministry, in Lerski, "A Polish Chapter," 87–88.

14. Kawakami, July 23, 1904, Tokyo, to Pilsudski, Tokyo, in *Zeszyty Historyczne* 27 (1974): 58.

15. Andrzej Friszke, introduction, in Leon Wasilewski, *Józef Piłsudski jakim go znałem*, ed. A. Friszke (1935; Warsaw: Muzeum Historii Polski, 2013), 26.

16. Ibid.; *Zeszyty Historyczne* 27 (1974): 71–72.

17. Stanisław Wojciechowski, *Moje wspomnienia*, vol. 1 (Lwów: Książnica-Atlas, 1938), 164.

18. *Zeszyty Historyczne* 27 (1974): 83–84. With an exchange rate of $4.87 to £1 in June 1904 (see *New York Times*, June 15, 1904, 12), the Japanese contribution came to $97,400 at a time when the average annual salary for an American worker was $400. See "U.S. Statistics in the Year 1905," Free Republic, http://www.freerepublic.com/focus/f-chat/1425436/posts.

19. Wasilewski, *Józef Piłsudski*, 89–90 (1935 edition).

20. Walery Sławek, "Wspomnienia (1895–1910): Cz. III," *Niepodległość* 18 (1985): 120; Protocols, conference of the Central Committee of the PPS, Kraków, October 17–20, 1904, in *PZU*, 2:189.

21. See Leon Wasilewski, "Kierownictwo P.P.S. zaboru rosyjskiego (1893–1918)," *Niepodległość* 11 (1935): 357; *PZU*, 2:196n1.

22. Jozef Pilsudski, "Wspomnienie o Grzybowie," *Głos Prawdy*, November 9, 1929, in *PZ*, 9:205.

23. Sławek, "Wspomnienia (1895–1910): Cz. III," 121. For a reproduction of the circular, see "Do wszystkich robotników warszawskich," Warsaw Workers' Committee of the Polish Socialist Party, November 11, 1904, reproduced in *Precz caratem! Rok 1905*, ed. Andrzej Stawarz (Warsaw: Muzeum Niepodległości, 2005), 40.

24. "The Russian Reservists," *Times* (London), November 11, 1904, 3.

25. Bronisław Żukowski, "Pamiętniki bojowca," *Niepodległość* 1 (October 1929): 123; Sławek, "Wspomnienia (1895–1910): Cz. III," 122.

26. Robert Blobaum, *Rewolucja: Russian Poland, 1904–1907* (Ithaca, NY: Cornell University Press, 1995), 43; "Warsaw Rioters Slain," *New York Times*, November 14, 1904, 1; "The Disturbances at Warsaw," *Times* (London), November 17, 1904, 3.

27. Alexandra Pilsudska, *Pilsudski: A Biography by His Wife* (New York: Dodd, Mead, 1941), 106.

28. Sławek, "Wspomnienia (1895–1910): Cz. III," 122.

29. "Zbrojna demonstracja P.P.S. w Warszawie," *Naprzód* (Kraków), November 16, 1904, 1; "Desperate Rioting in Russian Poland, Paradors Carried Revolvers," *New York Times,* November 27, 1904, 4. From the French press, see *Le Temps* (Paris), November 15, 1904.

30. Ziuk [Pilsudski], November 17, 1904, Zakopane, to T. Filipowicz, London, in *Zeszyty Historyczne* 27 (1974): 76–77.

31. Abraham Ascher, *The Revolution of 1905: Russia in Disarray* (Stanford: Stanford University Press, 1988), 88–92.

32. "Nasza deklaracja polityczna," Warsaw Committee of the PPS, January 28, 1905, in *PPS-Lewica, 1906–1918: Materiały i dokumenty,* ed. Feliks Tych (Warsaw: Książka i Wiedza, 1961), 1:3–4.

33. Henry Tobias, *The Jewish Bund in Russia* (Stanford, CA: Stanford University Press, 1972), 299; Ascher, *The Revolution of 1905: Russia in Disarray,* 138.

34. Michał Sokolnicki, *Czternaście lat* (Warsaw: Instytut Badania Najnowszej Historii Polski, 1936), 144–147.

35. "VII zjazd Polskiej Partii Socjalistycznej," *Robotnik,* April 14, 1905, 1–2; *Kalendarium,* 1:218; Wasilewski, "Kierownictwo P.P.S. zaboru rosyjskiego," 357–358.

36. Ziuk [Pilsudski], March 29, 1905, Kraków, to S. Wojciechowski, London, in *Zeszyty Historyczne* 27 (1974): 89–90.

37. Wasilewski, *Józef Pilsudski,* 94–95.

38. Pilsudski, addresses to the Party Council of the Central Committee of the PPS, Józefów, June 16, 1905, in *PZU,* 2:202.

39. Wasilewski, *Józef Piłsudski,* 164.

40. Pilsudski, undated letter from 1905, Kraków, to T. Filipowicz, London, in *Zeszyty Historyczne* 27 (1974): 96.

41. Ascher, *The Revolution of 1905: Russia in Disarray,* 218–219; Richard D. Lewis, "The Labor Movement in Russian Poland in the Revolution of 1905–1907" (PhD diss., University of California at Berkeley, 1971), 226.

42. Ziuk [Pilsudski], November 3, 1905, Kraków, to Wojciechowski, London, in *Zeszyty Historyczne* 27 (1974): 94–95.

43. Sokolnicki, *Czternaście lat,* 201–202; Wasilewski, *Józef Piłsudski,* 99–100.

44. Kazimierz Sosnkowski, *Materiały historyczne,* ed. J. Matecki (London: Gryf, 1966), 566–567; *PZU,* 2:210n8; Walery Sławek, "Wspomnienia (1895–1910): Cz. IV," *Niepodległość* 19 (1986): 178; W. Pobóg-Malinowski, *Józef Piłsudski, 1867–1914* (1964; reprint, Łomianki: Wydawnictwo LTW, 2015), 318; *Kalendarium,* 1:225.

45. "VIII Zjazd P.P.S.," *Robotnik* (Warsaw), April 7, 1906, 4; Party convention minutes, in Aleksy Rżewski, *W służbie idei* (Łódź: nakł. Komitetu uczczenia pracy Aleksego Rżewskiego, 1938), 160–162; Sosnkowski, *Materiały historyczne,* 566–567; *PZU,* 2:210n18; Pobóg-Malinowski, *Józef Piłsudski, 1901–1908,* 366.

46. Wasilewski, *Józef Piłsudski,* 102–103.

47. Aleksy Rzewski, *W walce z trójzaborcami o Polskę niepodległą: Wspomnienia* (Łódź: Wydawnictwo Księgarni Łódzkiej "Czytaj," 1931), 22–23.

48. Peter Kenez, *A History of the Soviet Union from the Beginning to Its Legacy*, 3rd ed. (New York: Cambridge University Press, 2016), 9.

49. Pilsudska, *Pilsudski*, 115–116.

50. Ibid.„ 115–117.

51. "Uchwały Rady Partynej," *Robotnik* (Warsaw), July 3, 1906, 1.

52. Protocols of the First Conference of the Polish Socialist Party's Combat Organization, July 5, 1906, Kraków, in *PZU*, 2:213.

53. *Kalendarium*, 1:230; "Two Generals Killed on a Train in Poland," *New York Times*, July 29, 1906, 1.

54. "The Anarchy in Russian Poland," *Times* (London), August 27, 1906, 3; *New York Times*, August 17, 1906, 1; Janusz Wojtasik, *Idea walki zbrojnej o niepodległość Polski, 1864–1907* (Warsaw: Wydawn. Ministerstwa Obrony Narodowej, 1987), 216; Blobaum, *Rewolucja*, 207; *Kalendarium*, 1:231;

55. Pilsudski, *Poprawki historyczne* (Warsaw: Inst. Badania Najnowszej Historii Polski, 1931), in *PZ*, 9:280.

56. T-z. [Pilsudski], "Polityka walki czynnej," *Trybuna*, November 1, 1906, 18–19.

57. Report of the Lwów police department, beginning of 1905, in *Kalendarium*, 1:216.

58. Col. Franz Kanik, Przemyśl, report to the Austro-Hungarian General Staff, Vienna, September 29, 1906, in *Galicyjska działalność wojskowa Piłsudskiego, 1906–1914*, ed. Stefan Arski et al. (Warsaw: Państwowe Wydawnictwo Naukowe, 1967), 443–444.

59. "Tried to Catch a Bomb, Russian Railway Clerk Maimed," *New York Times*, November 10, 1906, 4. On the raid and stolen funds, see Blobaum, *Rewolucja*, 208.

60. For the text of the resolution, see *W sprawie Organizacji Bojowej Polskiej Partii Socjalistycznej* (Warsaw: PPS, 1906), 5–15.

61. Protocols, Ninth Party Congress of the PPS, November 21, 1906, Vienna, in *PZU*, 2:224.

62. *Sprawozdanie z IX zjazdu P.P.S.* (Kraków, 1907), 40–41, in Tych, *PPS-Lewica*, 1:145–146.

63. "Deklaracja delegatów, ustępujących z dziewiątego zjazdu Polskiej Partii Socjalistycznej," November 22, 1906, in *W sprawie Organizacji Bojowej Polskiej Partii Socjalistycznej* (Warsaw: PPS, 1906), 20–22.

64. Sokolnicki, *Czternaście lat*, 235–236.

65. "Program Polskies Partii Socjalistyczney," *Robotnik* (Warsaw), March 22, 1907, 2. For the text of the program, see ibid., 1–2; and Feliks Tych, ed., *Polskie program socjalistyczne, 1878–1918* (Warsaw: Ksiażka i Wiedza, 1975), 458–471.

66. "Referat o taktyce bojowej na X zjeździe Polskiej Partii Socjalistycznej (I zjeździe PPS—Frakcji Rewolucyjnej)," March 9, 1907, Vienna, in *PZU*, 2:240–241.

67. [Pilsudski], resolution of the Combat Organization on tactics, March 11, 1907, in *PZU*, 2:249.

68. Antony Polonsky, *The Jews in Poland and Russia* (London: Littman Library of Jewish Civilisation, 2012), 3:57; Shlomo Lambroza, "The Pogroms of 1903–1906," in *Pogroms: Anti-Jewish Violence in Modern Russian History,* ed. John D. Klier and Shlomo Lambroza (New York: Cambridge University Press, 1992), 228.

69. "Troops Declared That Their Orders Were to Kill Jews," *New York Times,* September 12, 1906, 6.

70. From Pilsudski's 1910 publication on the party's Combat Organization, in *Joseph Pilsudski: The Memories of a Polish Revolutionary and Soldier,* trans. and ed. D. R. Gillie (London: Faber and Faber, 1931), 172–173.

71. Pobóg-Malinowski, *Józef Piłsudski, 1901–1908,* 532–537; Adam Zamoyski, *Poland: A History* (London: Harper Press, 2009), 288.

72. Kazimiera Iłłakowiczówna, *Ścieżka obok drogi,* 2nd ed. (Warsaw: Towarzystwo Wydawnicze "Rój," 1939), 19–20.

73. Wasilewski, *Józef Piłsudski,* 118.

74. Bogusław Miedziński, "Moje wspomnienia: Pierwsze spotkanie ze Sławkiem," *Zeszyty Historyczne* 34, no. 4 (1974): 164.

75. Bronisław Pilsudski, *Materials for the Study of the Ainu Language and Folklore* (Kraków: Imperial Academy of Sciences, 1912). Also see *The Complete Works of Bronisław Pilsudski,* 4 vols. (Berlin: Mouton de Gruyter, 1998–2012). Between 1985 and 2018, Kraków has hosted four international conferences devoted to Bronisław Pilsudski's scholarly legacy.

76. Pilsudska, *Pilsudski,* 149, 181.

77. Wasilewski, *Józef Piłsudski,* 118–119.

78. On the Duma elections, see Ascher, *The Revolution of 1905: Authority Restored* (Stanford, CA: Stanford University Press, 1992). Also see Geoffrey A. Hosking, *The Russian Constructional Experiment: Government and Duma, 1907–1914* (New York: Cambridge University Press, 1973); Alfred Levin, *The Second Duma: A Study of the Social-Democratic Party and the Russian Constitutional Experiment,* 2nd ed. (Hamden, CT: Archon Books, 1966); D. D. B. Lieven, *Russia's Rulers under the Old Regime* (New Haven, CT: Yale University Press, 1989).

79. [Pilsudski], "Jak mamy się gotować do walki zbrojnej," *Robotnik* (Kraków), February 4, 1908, in *PZ*, 2:293, 295.

80. [Pilsudski], December 1, 1907, Zakopane, to W. Jodko-Narkiewicz, Lwów, in *Niepodległość* (New York) 19 (1986): 66; *PZ,* 2:286; Pilsudska, *Pilsudski,* 184; *PZU,* 2:251n6.

81. [Pilsudski], May 25, 1908, Kraków, to W. Jodko-Narkiewicz, Lwów, in *Niepodległość* (New York) 19 (1986): 69.

82. Kazimierz Sosnkowski, interview in *Gazeta Polska* (Warsaw), September 15, 1935, in Sosnkowski, *Materiały historyczne,* 569–570.

83. Andrzej Chwalba, *Legiony Polskie, 1914–1918* (Kraków: Wydawnictwo Literackie, 2018), 11.

84. Ziuk [Piłsudski], Vilna, to Maria Piłsudska, Kraków, March 1908, in *PZU*, 2:250–251. I am grateful to Filip Mazurczak for helping me render parts of these passages in English.

85. Ziuk [Piłsudski], Vilna, to Maria Piłsudska, Kraków, July or early August 1908, in *PZU*, 2:251–252.

86. Ziuk [Piłsudski], Vilna, to Maria Piłsudska, Kraków, September 1908, in *PZU*, 2:256.

87. Daria Nałęcz and Tomasz Nałęcz, *Józef Piłsudski* (Warsaw: Młodzieżowa Agencja Wydawnicza, 1986), 124.

88. Alexandra Piłsudska, London, to Michał Sokolnicki, Ankara (Turkey), July 26, 1962, quoted in Ryszard Świętek, *Ludowa ścian* (Kraków: Platan, 1998), 408n134.

89. Maria Piłsudska, Kraków, undated letter, to Piłsudski, Vilna [?], in *PZU*, 2:257n7.

90. Ibid.

91. Alexandra Piłsudska, London, to Michał Sokolnicki, Ankara (Turkey), July 26, 1962, quotation in Świętek, *Ludowa ściana*, 408n134.

92. Piłsudski, early 1909, to Alexandra Szczerbińska, quotation in Nałęcz and Nałęcz, *Józef Piłsudski*, 122–123; and in *Kalendarium*, 1:262.

9. Building an Armed Force for Independence

Epigraph: Joseph Piłsudski: *The Memories of a Polish Revolutionary and Soldier*, trans. and ed. D. R. Gillie (London: Faber and Faber, 1931), 160.

1. Piłsudski, Vilna, to Feliks Perl, September 1908, in *Joseph Piłsudski: The Memoirs*, 160.

2. Ibid., 160–161.

3. Alexandra Piłsudska, *Piłsudski: A Biography by His Wife* (New York: Dodd, Mead, 1941), 191. For a second account by a participant, see Walery Sławek, "Wspomnienia (1895–1910): Cz. V," *Niepodległość* 22 (1989): 137–142.

4. Wacław Jędrzejewicz, *Piłsudski: A Life for Poland* (New York: Hippocrene Books, 1982), 42.

5. Piłsudska, *Piłsudski*, 191.

6. Pobóg-Malinowski, *Józef Piłsudski, 1901–1908* (Warsaw: Nakład Gebethner i Wolff, 1935), 632; Włodzimierz Suleja, *Józef Piłsudski* (Wrocław: Zakład Narodowy imienia Ossolińskich, 1995), 84; Andrzej Garlicki, *Józef Piłsudski, 1867–1935* (Warsaw: Czytelnik, 1990), 130; *Kalendarium*, 1:254; Piłsudska, *Piłsudski*, 183.

7. "Russian Railway Outrage," *Times* (London), September 30, 1908, 5.

8. Bohdan Urbankowski, *Józef Piłsudski: Marzyciel i strateg* (Poznań: Zysk i S-ka, 2014), 105.

9. Pilsudska, *Pilsudski*, 193.

10. Ibid.

11. Michał Sokolnicki, *Czternaście lat* (Warsaw: Instytut Badania Najnowszej Historii Polski, 1936), 330–331. I am grateful to Professor Hadassah Kosak for helping me render this passage in English.

12. Piłsudski, Kraków, end of 1908, to Alexandra Szczerbińska, in *Kalendarium*, 1:257.

13. Ziuk [Pilsudski], Kraków, to W. Jodko-Narkiewicz, Lwów, January 12, 1909, in *Niepodległość* 19 (1986): 70–71.

14. Walery Sławek, "Wspomnienia (1895–1910): Cz. V," *Niepodległość* 22 (1989): 147; *Kalendarium*, 1:258.

15. Ziuk [Pilsudski], Vienna, to W. Jodko-Narkiewicz, Lwów, February 21, 1909, in *Niepodległość* 19 (1986): 72; Ziuk [Pilsudski], Abbazia, to W. Jodko-Narkiewicz, Lwów, February 27, 1909, in *Niepodległość* 19 (1986): 73.

16. [Pilsudski], "Zadania praktyczne rewolucji w zaborze rosyjskim" (1909), in *PZ*, 3:5–6.

17. Ibid., 14, 17, quotation from 14. The lectures discussed here first appeared in the party newspaper between March and September 1910 as "Nasze zadania rewolucyjne," *Robotnik* (Warsaw), March–September 1910, and were subsequently published together in a 28-page volume as Z. Mieczysław [Pilsudski], *Zadania praktyczne rewolucji w zaborze rosyjskim* (Warsaw: Nakładem wydawnictwa "Życie," 1910).

18. Sławek, "Wspomnienia (1895–1910): Cz. V," 149–150; Józef Rybak, *Pamiętnik Generała Rybaka* (Warsaw: Czytelnik, 1954), 38; "Protokoły przesłuchania generała Rybaka," *Dzieje Najnowsze* 24, no. 4 (1992): 93. On this meeting, see also Jerzy Gaul, *Działalność wywiadowczo-informacyjna obozu niepodległościowego w latch 1914–1918* (Warsaw: Agencja Wydawnicza CB, 2001), 55.

19. Rybak, *Pamiętnik Generała Rybaka*, 39.

20. "Protokoły przesłuchania generała Rybaka," 93.

21. Quotations from Małgorzata Wiśniewska, *Związek Strzelecki, 1910–1939* (Warsaw: Wydawnictwo Neriton, 2010), 33; Gaul, *Działalność wywiadowczo-informacyjna*, 58.

22. Urbankowski, *Józef Piłsudski*, 125.

23. Resolution of the Second Party Congress, Vienna, August 28, 1909, in *PZU*, 2:264.

24. Pilsudska, *Pilsudski*, 180.

25. Pilsudski, Zakopane, to Alexandra Szczerbińska, September 7, [1909?], quotation from Pilsudska, *Pilsudski*, 202.

26. Ibid., 203.

27. Sokolnicki, *Czternaście lat*, 360–361, 364. On Jozef and Maria Pilsudski's move to Szlak Street in 1910, see Janusz Cisek, *Józef Piłsudski w Krakowie* (Kraków: Księgarnia Akademicka, 2003), 24.

28. Sokolnicki, *Czternaście lat*, 364.

29. Ibid., 364, 367. Sokolnicki's book appeared as K. M-cki [Michał Sokolnicki], *Sprawa armii polskiej* (Kraków: W.L. Anczyc, 1910).

30. Piłsudski, Kraków, to Alexandra Szczerbińska, Lwów, May 1, 1910, quoted in *Kalendarium*, I:271–272.

31. Piłsudski, Kraków, to Alexandra Szczerbińska, Summer 1910, quoted in *Kalendarium*, I:274.

32. Andrzej Garlicki, *Geneza legionów* (Warsaw: Książka i Wiedza, 1964), 29.

33. Wiśniewska, *Związek Strzelecki (1910–1939)*, 30, 36; Wacław Lipiński, *Walka zbrojna o niepodległość Polski w latach 1905–1918* (1931; repr., Warsaw: Oficyna Wydawnicza, 1990), 33.

34. Pilsudska, *Pilsudski*, 201.

35. Central Committee report of the PPS Revolutionary Fraction, July 1910, Kraków, in *PZU*, 2:283. I am grateful to Filip Mazurczak for helping to render this passage in English.

36. *Kalendarium*, 1:276. The lectures, presented in July 1910 as "Historia Organizacji Bojowej P.P.S.," first appeared in print as [Pilsudski], "Szkic rozwoju historycznego Organizi Borowej P.P.S, 1904–19010," *Przedświt* (Lwów), no. 4, April 1914, 134–144, and later in *PZ*, 3:23–36, and in English translation in *Joseph Pilsudski: The Memories*, 163–175. The others included Z. Mieczysław [Pilsudski], "Geografia militarna Królestwa Polskiego," and [Pilsudski], "Reform Armii Rosyjskiegj," both in *PZ*, 3:37–50, 55–64; [Pilsudski], "Bunt więzienny w Irkucku: Ze wspomnień," *Kalendarz Robotniczy* (Kraków), January 1911, in *PZ*, 3:65–74, and in English as "Mutiny in Irkutsk Gaon, 1887," in *Joseph Pilsudski: The Memories*, 17–26.

37. Pilsudski, Nervi, to Stanisław Witkiewicz, March 3, 1911, in *PZ*, 3:74–77. Janusz Cisek published the four extant letters Pilsudski wrote from Nervi. See Cisek, "Niepublikowane listy Józefa Piłsudskiego z roku 1911," *Studia Historyczne* 35, no. 4 (1992): 561–565.

38. [Pilsudski], "Kryzysy bojów," *Życie*, May 20, 1911, in *PZ*, 3:77–78.

39. "W przeddzień rewolucji r. 1905," lecture delivered on February 2, 1912, Kraków, in *PZ*, 3:144, 146.

40. [Pilsudski], "O rewolucji 1905 roku," second part of lecture delivered February 2, 1912, Kraków, in *PZ*, 3:152.

41. Pilsudski, Kraków, to Alexandra Szczerbińska, Lwów, January 1912, quotation from *Kalendarium*, 1:284.

42. J. Pilsudski, Kraków, May 7, 1912, to Stanisław Witkiewicz, in *PZ*, 3:147–148.

43. The lectures first appeared in 1929 in a 64-page booklet: Jozef Pilsudski, *Zarys Historii Militarnej Powstania Styczniowej: Wykłady wygłoszone w 1912 w Szkole Nauk Społeczno-Politycznych w Krakowie* (Waraw: Wojskowe Biuro Historyczne, 1929). The publication was reprinted in Pilsudski, *Rok 1863*, ed. Stefan Kieniewicz (Warsaw: Książka i Wiedza, 1989), 14–74.

44. Piłsudski, "Zarys historii militarnej Powstania Styczniowego," in *PZ*, 3:84.

45. Ibid., 118.

46. Ibid., 141. I am grateful to Antony Polonsky for assisting me in rendering this last passage in English. On this lecture series, see Andrzej Chwalba, *Józef Piłsudski: Historyk wojskowości* (Kraków: Universitas, 1993), 13–35.

47. Patrice Dabrowski, *Commemorations and the Shaping of Modern Poland* (Bloomington: Indiana University Press, 2004), 190.

48. The note appears in a report of the Austrian Ministry of Internal Affairs dated March 9, 1912, reprinted in *Galicyjska działalność wojskowa Piłsudskiego, 1906–1914*, ed. Stefan Arski et al. (Warsaw: Państwowe Wydawnictwo Naukowe, 1967), 533; and Austrian Minister of Foreign Affairs, Leopold Berchtold, July 31, 1912, to the Russian ambassador, Vienna, reprinted in Arski et al., *Galicyjska działalność wojskowa*, 564.

49. *Kalendarium*, 1:290.

50. Report of the Seventh Party Council of the PPS Revolutionary Fraction, Kraków, May 31, 1912, in *PZU*, 2:292n1.

51. [Piłsudski], "Organizational Plan for an Uprising in the Kingdom of Poland in the Event of a Russo-Austrian War: Report for the Austro-Hungarian Army," Zakopane, August or September 1912, in *PZU*, 2:309–310; on Capt. Rybak, see 311n2.

52. *PZU*, 2:314n1.

53. Jozef Piłsudski, address at the Conference of Polish Irredentists, Zakopane, August 25, 1912, in *PZU*, 2:313.

54. Ibid., 314.

55. W. Studnicki, *Z przeżyć i walk* (Warsaw: Drukarnia W. Łazarskiego, 1928), 310.

56. "Zjazd niemieckiej socjalnej demokracji w Austrii," *Naprzód* (Kraków), November 5, 1912, 2–3, in *PZ*, 3:160.

57. Resolutions of the Provisional Commission of Confederated Independence Parties, Vienna, November 10, 1912, written in Piłsudski's hand, *PZU*, 2:321–322, quotation on 321; also see Daria Nałęcz and Tomasz Nałęcz, *Józef Piłsudski: Legendy i fakty* (Warsaw: Młodzieżowa Agencja Wydawnicza, 1986), 143; Władysław Pobóg-Malinowski, *Józef Piłsudski, 1867–1914* (1964; repr., Łomianki: Wydawnictwo LTW, 2015), 386–387.

58. *Nowa Reforma* (Kraków), December 2, 1912, quotation from Dabrowski, *Commemorations*, 190. The lecture given on December 8, 1912, in Lwów, appeared in print as "Mobilizacja powstania," *Przedświt* (Lwów), no. 1, January 1914, 6–7, in *PZ*, 3:161–162.

59. Mieczysław Szumański, "Wspomnienia z zaczątków skautingu we Lwowie z lat 1910–1914," *Niepodległość* 10 (1976): 159.

60. Mieczysław [Piłsudski], Commander, order to heads of the Riflemen, the Riflemen's Association and the Polish Rifle Squads, Lwów, February 12, 1913, in *PZU*, 2:329–330; Andrzej Chwalba, *Legiony Polskie, 1914–1918* (Kraków: Wydawnictwo Literackie, 2018), 11–12.

61. Józef Hłasko, interview with Pilsudski, in *Kurjer Litewski* (Vilna), February 25, 1913, in *PZ*, 3:171. Recall from Chapter 8 that Pilsudski acquired two multivolume scholarly histories of the Boer War in 1905.

62. Ibid., 172–173.

63. Testimony of Walery Sławek, September 9, 1936, in *PZ*, 3:173n1.

64. Protocols, Meeting of the Provisional Commission of Confederated Independence Parties, Kraków, May 8, 1913, in *PZU*, 2:334–335.

65. Report, Meeting of the Central Council of the Riflemen's Association, June 29, 1913, in *PZU*, 2:356; Pobóg-Malinowski, *Józef Piłsudski, 1867–1914*, 391–392.

66. J. Pilsudski, Lwów, to H. Śliwiński, July 11, 1913, in *PZ*, 3:183; Ziuk [Pilsudski], Lwów, to Walery Sławek, Kraków, July 15, 1913, in *PZU*, 2:354–355; Commander Mieczysław [Pilsudski], Kraków, to the Polish Falcons of America, Pittsburgh, March 15, 1913, in *PZU*, 2:330–331; Garlicki, *Józef Piłsudski*, 153; Pobóg-Malinowski, *Józef Piłsudski, 1867–1914*, 389.

67. Pilsudski, address to officers of the Union of Active Struggle, Kraków, June 1, 1913, in *PZ*, 3:178.

68. *PZU*, 2:356n1.

69. Report, Meeting of the Provisional Commission of Confederated Independence Parties, Kraków, July 21, 1913, in *PZU*, 2:335.

70. Chief Commander, Mieczysław [Pilsudski], and Chief of Staff, Józef [Kazimierz Sosnkowski], Order to the Riflemen's Association, October 31, 1913, Lwów, in *PZ*, 3:188.

71. Chief Commander, Mieczysław [Pilsudski], and Chief of Staff, Józef [Kazimierz Sosnkowski], Order to the Peasant Organization, December 22, 1913, Lwów, in *PZ*, 3:190–191.

72. Pilsudsk, address to a meeting of the Commission of Confederated Independence Parties, Lwów, December 1, 1913, in *PZU*, 2:377–379.

73. J. Pilsudski, *22 stycznia 1863* (Poznań: Wielkopolska Księgarnia Nakładowa Karola Rzepeckiego, 1913), in *PZ*, 3:192–249. Sokolnicki describes his collaboration on the preparation of this publication in Michael Sokolnicki, *Rok czternasty* (London: Gryf, 1961), 94–95.

74. Dabrowski, *Commemorations*, 186, 188–190.

75. Chief Commander, Mieczysław [Pilsudski], and Chief of Staff, Józef [Kazimierz Sosnkowski], Order to local heads of the Riflemen's Association, January 12, 1914, Lwów, in *PZU*, 2:391–392.

76. Ziuk [Pilsudski], Geneva, to Walery Sławek, Kraków, February 12, 1914, in *PZU*, 2:396–397.

77. Jerzy Śmigielski, "Wizytacja genewskiego oddziału Związku Strzeleckiego przez Komenanta Głównego w lutymn 1914 roku," *Niepodległość* 17 (January–June 1938): 279, 281–282. The author later served in Pilsudski's First Brigade during World War I and subsequently served under the Pilsudski government in the Ministry of Foreign Affairs in the late 1920s and as a diplomat in the early 1930s.

78. "Relacja agenta ochrany o przemówieniu Piłsudskiego w Paryżu 21 lutego 1914 roku," *Niepodległość* 15 (1982): 102–103; *Kalendarium*, 1:324.

79. Pilsudski, "O polskim ruchu strzeleckim," lecture given on February 21, 1914, Paris, in *PZ*, 3:250, 252.

80. Memoirs of Viktor Chernov (1953), cited in *Kalendarium*, 1:327.

81. The eulogy appears in *PZ*, 3:255. After Pilsudski's assumption of power in 1918, he pushed through parliament a law that provided a fixed pension for veterans of the 1863 uprising as well as a network of health care facilities for them, a group that numbered an estimated 4,500 veterans in 1920. In 1933 the Powązki Cemetery in Warsaw created a separate quarter for veterans of the 1863, 1848, and 1830 Polish uprisings, a quarter that remains to this day. I am grateful to Daria Nałęcz for sharing this information with me.

82. Tadeusz Bogalecki, "Polskie Związki Strzeleckie w latach 1910–1914," *Wojskowy Przegląd Historyczny*, no. 2 (1996): 41; Wiśniewska, *Związek Strzelecki (1910–1939)*, 46; Pobóg-Malinowski, *Józef Piłsudski, 1867–1914*, 392.

83. Quotation from Dabrowski, *Commemorations*, 189.

84. Sokolnicki, *Czternaście lat*, 433–434.

85. Leon Wasilewski, *Józef Piłsudski jakim go znałem* (Warsaw: Towarzystwo Wydawnicze Rój, 1935), 89–90.

86. *Naprzód* (Kraków), November 16, 1904; *Le Temps* (Paris), November 15, 1904; *New York Times*, November 27, 1904.

87. Sokolnicki, *Czternaście lat*, 144–147.

88. Pilsudski, *22 stycznia 1863*.

89. Pilsudski, "Z wojny bałkańskiej," *Strzelec* (Lwów), April–July 1914.

10. The Polish Legions and the Beginnings of World War I

Epigraph: Rudolf Starzewski, diary entry of December 24, 1914, in Starzewski, *Dziennik: Listopad 1914—Marzec 1915*, ed. Joanna Jaśkowiec (Kraków: Wydawnictwo Uniwersytetu Jagiellońskiego, 2007), 43–44.

1. Frédéric Chopin's "Revolutionary Étude" (Étude op. 10, no. 12, in C minor), composed in 1831 in Paris, is believed to express anguish at the Russian repression in the 1830 Polish Insurrection. It was sometimes referred to as the "Étude on the Bombardment of Warsaw."

2. Lord Acton, "Nationality," *Home and Foreign Review* (July 1862), quotation from Roma Szporluk, *Communism and Nationalism: Karl Marx versus Friedrich List* (Oxford: Oxford University Press, 1988), 84.

3. Stanisław Wojciechowski, *Moje wspomnienia*, vol. 1 (Lwów: Książnica-Atlas, 1938), 223.

4. "Protokoły przesłuchania generała Rybaka," *Dzieje Najnowsze* 24, no. 4 (1992): 86.

5. Andrzej Garlicki, *Józef Piłsudski, 1867–1935* (Warsaw: Czytelnik, 1990), 163–164.

6. Andrzej Chwalba, *Historia Polski, 1795–1918* (Kraków: Wydawnictwo Literackie, 2000), 571; *Kalendarium*, 1:349–350; Garlicki, *Józef Piłsudski*, 165; Andrzej Nowak, *Niepodległa! 1864–1924: Jak Polacy odzyskali ojczyznę* (Kraków: Biały Kruk Sp., 2018), 43–44.

7. Pilsudski, Kraków, speech to the First Cadre Company, August 3, 1914, in *PZ*, 4:7–8.

8. Alexandra Pilsudska, *Pilsudski: A Biography by His Wife* (New York: Dodd, Mead, 1941), 216.

9. First leaflet: CBW, DU-1458; second leaflet: Jozef Pilsudski, Chief Commander of the Polish Army, Warsaw, August 3, 1914, CBW, DU-1458, emphasis in the original.

10. Alexandra Pilsudska [Szczerbińska], "Odział żeński 'Strzelca' w sierpniu 1914," in *W czterdziestolecie wymarszu Legionów* (London, 1954), cited in *Kalendarium*, 1:350.

11. Tadeusz A. Kasprzycki, "Wymarsz kadrowej," in *W czterdziestolecie wymarszu legionów: Zbiór wspomnień* (London: Pilsudski Institute, 1954), 12.

12. Piotr A. Kalisz, *Oleandry Kolebka niepodległości* (Kraków: Fundacja Centrum Dokumentacji Czynu Niepodległościowego, 2015), 36–37.

13. Quotation from Garlicki, *Józef Piłsudski*, 166.

14. M. Norwid-Neugerbauer, "Wspomnienia z dnia 6-go sierpnia 1914," *Panteon Polski* (Lwów), August 1, 1925, 7–8.

15. J. Pilsudski, Krzeszowice (Austrian Galicia), August 6, 1914, to Capt. Józef Rybak, Kraków, in Pilsudski, *Korespondencja*, 2nd ed., ed. Stanisław Biegański and Andrzej Suchcitz (London: Instytut Józefa Piłsudskiego, 1986), 13–14.

16. Andrzej Chwalba, *Wielka Wojna Polaków, 1914–1918* (Warsaw: PWN, 2018), 162; Garlicki, *Józef Piłsudski*, 166; *Kalendarium*, 1:353.

17. Chief Commander of the Polish Army, Jozef Pilsudski, "Rząd Narodowy do Ogółu Obywaleli Ziemi Kieleckiej," August 10, 1914, in Pilsudski, *Korespondencja*, 13–14.

18. Pilsudski, "My First War Experience: Ulina Mala" (September 1917), in *Joseph Pilsudski: The Memories of a Polish Revolutionary and Soldier*, trans. and ed. D. R. Gillie (London: Faber and Faber, 1931), 234.

19. "Protokoły przesłuchania generała Rybaka," *Dzieje Najnowsze* 24, no. 4 (1992): 106.

20. *Kalendarium*, 1:355–356.

21. "An Appeal to Poles by Grand Duke Nikolai Mikhailovich, Russia's Supreme Commander-in-Chief, August 14, 1914," in *Imperial Russia: A Source Book, 1700–1917*, 3rd ed., ed. Basil Dmytryshyn (Fort Worth, TX: Holt, Rinehart and Winston, 1990), 512.

22. "The Proclamation to Poland," *Times* (London), August 17, 1914, 9.

23. Nowak, *Niepodległa!*, 150; Garlicki, *Jozef Pilsudski*, 171; Jerzy Holzer and Jan Molenda, *Polska w pierwszej wojnie światowej* (Warsaw: Wiedza Powszechna, 1963), 74–75.

24. Alexander Watson, *Ring of Steel: Germany and Austria-Hungary in World War I* (New York: Basic Books, 2014), 96.

25. Polish Parliamentary Circle, Kraków, "Do Narodu Polskiego!," August 16, 1914, in *Legiony Polskie 16 sierpnia 1914–16 sierpnia 1915: Dokumenty* (Piotrków: Nakładem Departamentu Wojskowego Naczelnego Komitetu Narodowego, 1915), 2–6.

26. Resolutions of the Polish Parliamentary Circle, Kraków, August 16, 1914, in *Legiony Polskie*, 8.

27. R. F. Leslie, ed., *The History of Poland since 1863* (Cambridge: Cambridge University Press, 1980), 114; *Kalendarium,* 1:359.

28. W. L. Jaworski, Juliusz Leo, and W. Sikorski, "Do Legionów Polskich!," Kraków, August 21, 1914, in *Legiony Polskie*, 11–12.

29. Michał Sokolnicki, *Rok czternasty* (London: Gryf, 1961), 206, 244.

30. Ibid., 217–218.

31. Jozef Pilsudski, Chief Commander, and Kazimierz Sosnkowski, Chief of Staff, "Żołnierze!," Kielce, August 22, 1914, in *PZ*, 4:9–10; J. Pilsudski, Chief Commander of the Riflemen, to Lt.-Col. Jan Nowak, August 22, 1914, in *Galicyjska działalność wojskowa Piłsudskiego, 1906–1914: Dokumenty,* ed. Stefan Arski et al. (Warsaw: Państwowe Wydawnictwo Naukowe, 1967), 533; Archduke Friedrich, announcement of August 27, 1914, Vienna, in Arski et al., *Galicyjska działalność,* 671–673.

32. Julisz Leo, W. Jaworski, and W. Sikorski, "Do komend organizacji militarnych," Kraków, August 30, 1914, in *Legiony Polskie,* 19.

33. Pilsudski, September 5, 1914, Kielce, to W. Jaworski, Kraków, in *Komisariaty wojskowe Rząd Narodowego w Królestwie Polskim, 6.VII—5.IX 1914,* ed. Tadeusz Pelczarski (Warsaw: Instytut Józefa Piłsudskiego, 1939), 252.

34. Andrzej Chwalba, *Legiony Polskie, 1914–1918* (Kraków: Wydawnictwo Literackie, 2018), 17–18.

35. Pilsudski, September 6, 1914, to W. Jaworski, in Pelczarski, *Komisariaty wojskowe,* 252.

36. [Pilsudski], November 15, 1914, to W. Jaworski, in Pilsudski, *Korespondencja,* 23.

37. Sokolnicki, *Rok czternasty,* 236.

38. PON, circular, September 5, 1914, quotation from Holzer and Molenda, *Polska w pierwszej wojnie światowej,* 82–83; Nowak, *Niepodległa!,* 154.

39. Garlicki, *Jozef Pilsudski,* 174.

40. Regiment Commander [Pilsudski], Kielce, to Gen. Baczyński, Kraków, September 9, 1914, in *PZ*, 4:11–12.

41. Presidium of the Supreme National Committee, Kraków, September 14, 1914, titled "Komendant Józef Piłsudski: I. pułk Legionów polskich," in *Legiony Polskie*, 8. On Pilsudski's actions in Nowy Korczyn, see Sokolnicki, *Rok czternasty*, 232–233; Nowak, *Niepodległa!*, 154; and *Kalendarium*, 1:366.

42. Tomasz Nałęcz, *Polska Organizacja Wojskowa, 1914–1918* (Wrocław: Wydawnictwo Polskiej Akademii Nauk, 1984), 15, 20; Nowak, *Niepodległa!*, 156.

43. Pilsudski, "My First War Experience: Ulina Mala" (September 1917), in *Joseph Pilsudski: The Memories*, 236–237. For the original passage, see *PZ*, 4:305.

44. Pilsudski, "My First War Experience: Ulina Mala," 261.

45. Ibid., 265.

46. *Joseph Pilsudski: The Memories*, 292–293; for the report he drafted, see Jozef Pilsudski, regiment commander, Report on Ulina Mała, Kraków, November 12, 1914, in *PZ*, 4:15–16.

47. Order of Archduke Friedrich, November 15, 1914, in Arski et al., *Galicyjska działalność wojskowa*, 679.

48. [Pilsudski], Freistadt, to W. Jaworski, Kraków, November 15, 1914, in Pilsudski, *Korespondencja*, 25.

49. Sokolnicki, *Rok czternasty*, 283.

50. Ibid., 260.

51. Chwalba, *Legiony Polskie*, 34; Nowak, *Niepodległa!*, 158; Janusz T. Nowak, *Szlak bojowy Legionów Polskich* (Kraków: Wydawnictwo M, 2014), 87; Wacław Lipiński, *Walka zbrojna o niepodległość Polski, 1905–1918* (1935; repr., Warszawa: Volumen, 1990), 59.

52. Holzer and Molenda, *Polska w pierwszej wojnie światowej*, 97; Leslie, *History of Poland*, 112; Nowak, *Niepodległa!*, 158; M. B. Biskupski, *The United States and the Rebirth of Poland, 1914–1918* (Dordrecht: Republic of Letters, 2012), 45n22. I am grateful to Jan Bruski of the Jagiellonian University for his comments on these organizations.

53. Michał Sokolnicki, Vienna, to Pilsudski, November 24, 1914, in Pilsudski, *Korespondencja*, 27.

54. "Brigadier Piłsudski w Wiedniu," *Wiedeński Kurier Polski* (Vienna), December 18, 1914, 1.

55. Diary entry of December 19, 1914, in Rudolf Starzewski, *Dziennik*, 43–44. The original diary is housed at the Jagiellonian University Library Archives, Manuscript Division, no. 9801. I am grateful to Joanna Jaśkowiec of Jagiellonian University for bringing this diary to my attention.

56. Władysław L. Jaworski, diary entry of December 19, 1914, in Jaworski, *Diariusz, 1914–1918*, ed. Michał Czajka (Warsaw: Oficyna Naukowa, 1997), 20.

57. "Uczta na cześć Piłsudskiego," *Wiedeński Kurier Polski* (Vienna), December 22, 1914, 4.

58. Jaworski, diary entry of December 21, 1914, Vienna, in Jaworski, *Diariusz*, 21.

59. Jaworski's speech, December 21, 1914, in Jaworski, *Diariusz*, 22–23; Sokolnicki, *Rok czternasty*, 295.

60. *Kalendarium*, 1:383; Pilsudski, "My First War Experience: Limanowa-Marcinkowice" (September 1917), in *Joseph Pilsudski: The Memories*, 345.

61. Pilsudski, Vienna, dinner banquet speech of December 21, 1914, quotation from "Bankiet w Wiedniu na cześć Pilsudskiego," *Naprzód* (Kraków), December 23, 1914, 1. Also see *PZ*, 4:21.

62. Diary entry of December 21, 1914, Vienna, in Jaworski, *Diariusz*, 21.

63. Rudolf Starzewski, diary entry of December 24, 1914, in Starzewski, *Dziennik*, 43–44. For press coverage of Pilsudski's speech, see "Uczta na cześć Piłsudsskiego," *Wiedeński Kurier Polski* (Vienna), December 22, 1914, 4; "Bankiet w Wiedniu na cześć Piłsudskiego," *Naprzód* (Kraków), December 23, 1914, 1; *Wiadomości Polskie*, December 26, 1914. The speech was subsequently printed in Konstanty Srokowski, *N.K.N.: Zarys historii Naczelnego Komitetu Narodowego* (Kraków: Nakł. Krakowskiej spółki wydawniczej, 1923); and in *PZ*, 4:21–22.

64. Rudolf Starzewski, diary entry of December 24, 1914, in Starzewski, *Dziennik*, 44–45.

65. Nowak, *Niepodległa!*, 161; Pilsudski, "My First War Experience: Limanowa-Marcinkowice," 345; *Kalendarium*, 1:388; Włodzimierz Suleja, *Józef Pilsudski* (Wrocław: Zakład Narodowy imienia Ossolińskich, 1995), 131.

66. J. Pilsudski, Kraków, to Władysław Jaworski, October 6, 1916, in *Joseph Pilsudski: The Memories*, 186–187. For Pilsudski's estimate of losses, see Pilsudski, "Żołnierze!," January 3, 1915, in *PZ*, 4:24.

67. Wacław Sieroszewski, *Józef Pilsudski* (Piortrków: Nakładem Departmamentu Wojskowego Naczelnego Komitetu Narodowego, 1915), 85–86.

68. Pilsudski, January 10, 1915, to the Army Headquarters, Vienna, in Pilsudski, *Korespondencja*, 31–34.

69. "Już blizko . . . ," Warsaw, March 1915, leaflet, CBW, DU-742.

70. Michał Sokolnicki, Kielce, Commissioner of the Polish Army, September 1, 1914, with the entire leaflet reproduced in *Jews, Poles, Legionary, 1914–1920*, ed. Artur Tanikowski (Warsaw: Museum of the History of Polish Jews, 2014), 123.

71. Żydzi-Legioniści, "Do młodzieży żydowskiej!" March 1915, Kingdom of Poland, original reproduced in Tanikowski, *Jews, Poles, Legionary*, 124. For a memoir of a Jewish legionnaire who interacted personally with Pilsudski, see Henryk Gruber, *Wspomnienia i uwagi* (London: Gryf, 1968). Authorship of the circular is confirmed in Marek Gałęzowski, *Na wzór Berka Joselewicza: Żołnierz I oficerowie pochodzenia żydowskiego w Legionach Polskich* (Warsaw: IPMN, 2010), 39, 608; and Rafał Żebrowski, "Jakuba Szackiego żywot paradoksalny," *Kwartalnik Historii Żydów* no. 2 (2002): 174.

72. Diary entry of February 17, 1915, in Jaworski, *Diariusz*, 29.

73. Diary entry of January 28, 1915, in Starzewski, *Dziennik*, 99.

74. Letter of Pilsudski to Sikorski, April 30, 1915, in *Kalendarium*, 1:407; Michał Sokolnicki, Vienna, to Pilsudski, April 22, 1915, in Pilsudski, *Korespondencja*, 54.

75. Ziuk [Pilsudski], to Tytus Filipowicz, Aleksander Dębski, and Marian Malinowski, May 31, 1915, in Pilsudski, *Korespondencja*, 61–62.

76. Pilsudski, May 1915, to Sikorski, in *Kalendarium*, 1:407.

77. I. Boerner, "Z pamiętnika," *Niepodległość* 17 (1938), in *Kalendarium*, 1:408.

78. W. Jaworski, Vienna, to Pilsudski, June 3, 1915, in Pilsudski, *Korespondencja*, 66. Also see Starzewski's diary entry of February 24, 1915, quotation from Starzewski, *Dziennik*, 148.

79. Holger H. Herwig, *The First World War: Germany and Austria-Hungary, 1914–1918*, 2nd ed. (London: Bloomsbury Academic, 2014), 147.

80. Pilsudski, June 3, 1915, to the NKN's military department, in *PZ*, 4:36–37.

81. Diary entry of July 25, 1915, in Jaworski, *Diariusz, 1914–1918*, 49–50.

82. Quotation from P. Samuś, *Walery Sławek: Droga do niepodległej Polski* (Płock: Wydawn. Naukowe Novum, 2002), 421.

83. Pilsudski, address to the Legions, August 6, 1915, in *Joseph Pilsudski: The Memories*, 346–347. The original can be found in *PZ*, 4:40.

84. Jędrzejewicz, *Pilsudski*, 59; *Kalendarium*, 1:426.

85. Herwig, *The First World War*, 147–148.

86. "Polacy!," Warsaw, August 16, 1915, CBW, DU-817.

87. Memoirs of Tadeusz Katelbach, quotation from *Kalendarium*, 1:428.

88. Michał Sokolnicki, Kraków, to Pilsudski, September 18, 1915, in Pilsudski, *Korespondencja*, 97.

89. Diary entry of August 19, 1915, in Jaworski, *Diariusz*, 53.

90. Ziuk [Pilsudski], November 14, 1915, to I. Daszyński, in Pilsudski, *Korespondencja*, 110. I am grateful to Filip Mazurczak for helping to render this phrase in English.

91. Gałęzowski, *Na wzór Berka Joselewicza*, 479–480.

92. For a reproduction of the forty-five plates, including the one of Mansperl, see *History of The Statute of Kalisz Issued by Boleslaus the Pious in 1264 and Its Illustration by Arthur Szyk in the Years 1926–1928*, ed. M. Fuks et al. (Kraków: Jagiellonian University, 2017). For a discussion of this collection, see Steven Luckert, *The Art and Politics of Arthur Szyk* (Washington, DC: United States Holocaust Memorial Museum, 2002), 16–23.

93. On Blauer and Sternschuss, see Gałęzowski, *Na wzór Berka Joselewicza*, 174–176, 600–604; and Tanikowski, *Jews, Poles, Legionary*, 130–131. The obituaries appeared in *Wiadomości Polskie* (Piotrków) on September 15 and 23, 1915, and March 12, 1916.

94. Marian Fuks, *Żydzi w Warszawie: Życie codzienne wydarzenia ludzie* (Poznań: Sorus, 1992), 269; Marian Fuks, "Udział Żydów w orodzieniu się Rzeczypospolitej Polskiej," https://www.jhi.pl/blog/2018-11-13-udzial-zydow-w-odrodzeniu

-sie-rzeczypospolitej-polskiej; Marek Gałęzowski, "Spadkobiercy Berka Josele-wicza: Żydzi w Legionach Polskich," *Biuletyn IPN* 11 (2010): 25–33.

95. Fuks, *Żydzi w Warszawie,* 269.

96. Krzysztof Kawalec, *Roman Dmowski* (Warszawa: Editions Spotkania, 1996), 155–156.

97. Roman Wapiński, *Roman Wapiński* (Lublin: Wydawnictwo Lubelskie, 1988), 219–220; Nowak, *Niepodległa!* 175–176; Jerzy Lukowski and Hubert Zawadzki, *A Concise History of Poland,* 2nd ed. (New York: Cambridge University Press, 2006), 280–281.

11. An Emerging National Leader

Epigraph: Władysław L. Jaworski, diary entry of July 8, 1917, in Władysław L. Jaworski, *Diariusz, 1914–1918,* ed. Michał Czajka (Warsaw: Oficyna Naukowa, 1997), 204.

1. Pilsudski, September 1915, a talk with Polish activists in the Kingdom of Poland, in Pilsudski, *Korespondencja, 1914–1917,* 2nd ed., ed. Stanisław Biegański and Andrzej Suchcitz (London: Instytut Józefa Pilsudskiego, 1986), 91–92.

2. Beseler, Warsaw, report from the fall of 1915, quotation from Rober Blobaum, *A Minor Apocalypse: Warsaw during the First World War* (Ithaca, NY: Cornell University Press, 2017), 13.

3. Pilsudski, Otwock, September 1, 1915, to Władysław L. Jaworski, Kraków, in Pilsudski, *Korespondencja,* quotations on 75, 79. For a discussion of Pilsudski's position at this time, see Michał Sokolnicki, *Rok czternasty* (London: Gryf, 1961), 341.

4. Wacława Milewska, Janusz Nowak, and Maria Zientara, *Legiony Polskie, 1914–1918: Zarys historii militarnej i poitycznej* (Kraków: Księgarnia Akademicka Wydawnictwo Narukowe, 1998), 78; *Kalendarium,* 1:430; Jerzy Holzer and Jan Molenda, *Polska w pierwszej wojnie światowej* (Warsaw: Wiedza Powszechna, 1963), 150.

5. Resolution of the Central National Committee, Warsaw, February 2, 1916, in *Dokumenty Naczelnego Komitetu Narodowego, 1914–1917* (Kraków: Nakładem Naczelnego Komitetu Narodowego, 1917), 210.

6. [J. Pilsudski], May 16, 1916, to Tadeusz Kasprzycki, in Pilsudski, *Korespondencja,* 157.

7. Ziuk [Pilsudski], May 15, 1916, to Walery Sławek, in Pilsudski, *Korespondencja,* 153.

8. Pilsudski, Lwów, March 19, 1916, to Kazimierz Sosnkowski, in Pilsudski, *Korespondencja,* 135.

9. CKN, Warsaw, to the Supreme National Committee, Kraków, March 25, 1916, in *Dokumenty Naczelnego Komitetu Narodowego,* 225–226.

10. Władysław L. Jaworski, diary entries of January 29 and 31 (Krakow) and March 13, 1916, in Jaworski, *Diariusz,* 79, 86.

11. Pilsudski, dinner banquet speech, April 1916, Lublin, in *PZ*, 4:52.

12. Andrzej Garlicki, *Józef Piłsudski, 1867–1935* (Warsaw: Czytelnik, 1990), 187.

13. Pilsudski, dinner banquet speech, March 29, 1916, Kraków, in *PZ*, 4:50.

14. Holger H. Herwig, *The First World War: Germany and Austria-Hungary, 1914–1918*, 2nd ed. (London: Bloomsbury Academic, 2014), 203; Alexander Watson, *Ring of Steel: Germany and Austria-Hungary in World War I* (New York: Basic Books, 2014), 309–310.

15. Andrzej Chwalba, *Legiony Polskie, 1914–1918* (Kraków: Wydawnictwo Literackie, 2018), 90, 214; Michał Klimecki, *Pod rozkazami Piłsudskiego: Bitwa pod Kostiuchnówką, 4–6 lipca 1916 r.* (Warsaw: Instytut Wydawn. Związków Zawodowych, 1990); also Lesław Dudek, "Polish Military Formations in World War I," in *East Central European Society in World War I*, ed. Bela K. Kiraly and N. Dreisziger (New York: Columbia University Press, 1985), 458.

16. J. Pilsudski, "Rozkaz z powodu bitwy pod Kostiuchnówką," Czeremoszno, July 11, 1916, in *PZ*, 4:54–55; Pilsudski, commander of the First Brigade, report on the Battle of Kostiuchnówka for July 4–6, 1916, in *PZ*, 4:80; Ziuk [Pilsudski], July 13, 1916, to Walery Sławek, in Pilsudski, *Korespondencja*, 183.

17. J. Pilsudski, July 29, 1916, to the Polish Legions command headquarters, Kraków, in Pilsudski, *Korespondencja*, 199–200.

18. J. Pilsudski, July 25, 1916, to Ignacy Daszyński, in Daszyński, *Pamiętniki* (Kraków: Nakładem drukarni ludowej, 1926), 2:231.

19. Władysław L. Jaworski, diary entries of August 28, 1916, in Jaworski, *Diariusz*, 119.

20. J. Pilsudski, July 24, 1916, to Władysław L. Jaworski, Kraków, in Pilsudski, *Korespondencja*, 198. I am grateful to Filip Mazurczak for helping me render part of these passages in English.

21. J. Pilsudski, Order of August 6, 1916, in *Joseph Pilsudski: The Memoirs of a Polish Revolutionary and Soldier,* trans. and ed. D. R. Gillie (London: Faber and Faber, 1931), 347–348. For the original, see *PZ*, 4:80–81.

22. "Do Naczelnego Komitetu Narodowego," August 30, 1916, petition of the Council of Colonels, signed by Jozef Pilsudski, Kazimierz Sosnkowski, Józef Haller, and Bolesław Roja, CBW, DU-17.

23. Felicjan Sławoj Składkowski, diary entry of September 2, 1916, in Składkowski, *Moja służba w Brygadzie* (Warsaw: Instytut Badania Najnowszej Historii Polski, 1933), 2:371–372. See also *Kalendarium*, 1:508.

24. Władysław L. Jaworski, Kraków, to J. Pilsudski, October 5, 1916, in *Dokumenty Naczelnego Komitetu Narodowego*, 299–300.

25. J. Pilsudski, Kraków, to Władysław L. Jaworski, October 6, 1916, in *Joseph Pilsudski: The Memories*, 186–187; for the original, see *Dokumenty Naczelnego Komitetu Narodowego*, 301–302; *PZ*, 4:83–84.

26. Centralny Komitet Narodowy, "Komunikat," Warsaw, October 6, 1916, CBW, DU-1948.

27. Jörn Leonhard, *Pandora's Box: A History of the First World War*, trans. Patrick Camiller (Cambridge, MA: Belknap Press of Harvard University Press, 2018), 398, 427–428; Watson, *Ring of Steel*, 300, 324.

28. Watson, *Ring of Steel*, 412; Robert Machray, *Poland, 1914–1931* (London: G. Allen and Unwin, 1932), 74.

29. Quotation from Machray, *Poland, 1914–1931*, 75. For the original memorandum, see *Dokumenty Naczelnego Komitetu Narodowego*, 317–319.

30. J. Pilsudski, Kraków, November 3, 1916, to the Central National Committee, Warsaw, in Pilsudski, *Korespondencja*, 226–227.

31. Nowak, *Niepodległa! 1864–1924: Jak Polacy odzyskali ojczyznę* (Kraków: Biały Kruk Sp., 2018), 188.

32. Adam Zamoyski, *Paderewski* (London: Collins, 1982), 155.

33. Leon Wasilewski, *Józef Piłsudski jakim go znałem* (Warsaw: Towarzystwo Wydawnicze "Rój," 1935), 198.

34. J. Pilsudski, Kraków, to Col. Rydz-Śmigły, November 5, 1916, in *PZ*, 4:86. I am grateful to Filip Mazurczak for helping me render the last sentence of this passage in English.

35. Wacław Jędrzejewicz, *Wspomnienia*, ed. Janusz Cisek (Wrocław: Zakład Narodowy im. Ossolińskich, 1993), 49.

36. Jerzy Pająk, *O rząd i armię Centralny Komitet Narodowy, 1915–1917* (Kielce: Wydawnictwo Akademii Świętokrzyskiej, 2003), 152; *Kalendarium*, 2:19.

37. "Polacy!," Centralny Komitet Narodowy, Warsaw, November 10, 1916, CBW, DU-659. The document is reprinted in Artur Śliwiński, "Rozmowa z Beselerem," *Niepodległość* 5 (November 1931–April 1932): 75–76.

38. J. Pilsudski, Kraków, November 6, 1916, to Józef Brudziński, Warsaw, in *PZ*, 4:88.

39. Quotation from Śliwiński, "Rozmowa z Beselerem," 80.

40. Quotation from the transcript of the exchange between Pilsudski and Beseler, in Pilsudski, *Korespondencja*, 243n2.

41. Quotation from B. Miedziński, "Wspomnienia (4)," *Zeszyty Historyczne* 36 (1976): 149–150. I am grateful to Magdalena Macińska for helping me render the term "tokować jak głuszec" in English.

42. "Archduke Charles to Govern Poland," *New York Times*, December 14, 1916, 6.

43. Timothy Snyder, *The Red Prince: The Secret Lives of a Habsburg Archduke* (New York: Basic Books, 2008), 27, 59–60.

44. [Pilsudski], Warsaw, to the German Governor-General [Beseler], Warsaw, December 26, 1916, in *PZ*, 4:92.

45. [CKN], Warsaw, n.d., "O armię polska," CBW, DU-1946.

46. Pilsudski, interview appearing on January 6, 1917, in *Tygodnik Ilustrowany* (Warsaw), in *PZ*, 4:105.

47. Wasilewski, *Józef Piłsudski,* 199–200. On the history of the Provisional State Council, see Włodzimierz Suleja, *Tymczasowa Rada Stanu* (Warsaw: Wydawn. Sejmowe, 1998).

48. For the official document showing Pilsudski as a member of the Provisional State Council, see AAN, sygn. 1634/6, fol. 25; Pilsudski discussed his nomination in Ziuk [Pilsudski], Warsaw, to Kazimierz Sosnkowski, January 11, 1917, in Pilsudski, *Korespondencja,* 244.

49. *Kalendarium,* 2:43. Also see Marian M. Drozdowski, ed., *Kronika narodzin II Rzeczypospolitej, 1914–1923* (Warsaw: Bellona, 2018), 164; Holzer and Molenda, *Polska,* 196.

50. Interview with Pilsudski, March 3, 1917, in Władysław Baranowski, *Rozmowy z Piłsudskim* (1938; repr., Warsaw: Zebra, 1990), 38.

51. Ibid., 40–41.

52. Quotation from H. H. Fisher, *America and the New Poland* (New York: Macmillan, 1928), 96–97. For the text of the declaration, see Stanislas Filasiewicz, *La question polonaise pendant la guerre mondiale* (Paris: Section d'études et de publications politiques de Comité national polonais, 1920), 151, doc. 75.

53. Tomasz Nałęcz, *Polska Organizacja Wojskowa, 1914–1918* (Wrocław: Wydawnictwo Polskiej Akademii Nauk, 1984), 101–102, 114–115.

54. Ibid., 106.

55. Pilsudski, speech to the 5th session of the Provisional State Council, Warsaw, February 1, 1917, in *PZ,* 4:118; Pilsudski, February 19, 1917, in *PZ,* 4:106.

56. "List Józefa Piłsudskiego do Profesora N . . . w Krakowie," March 15, 1917, circular, CBW, DU-723, reprinted in *PZ,* 4:107–108.

57. [Pilsudski], "O armii narodowej," speech delivered on March 16, 1917, in *PZ,* 4:110.

58. From the summary of Beseler's reply, in *PZ,* 4:143n2.

59. Pilsudski's address at the 12th session of the Provisional State Council, Warsaw, March 31, 1917, in *PZ,* 4:143–144.

60. Minutes of the 13th session of the Provisional State Council, Warsaw, April 13, 1917, in *PZ,* 4:154–155; *Kalendarium,* 2:57; *PZ,* 4:154n2; Fisher, *America and the New Poland,* 99–100.

61. CKN, leaflet dated April 16, 1917, Warsaw, CBW, DU-1938.

62. Minutes of the 20th session of the Provisional State Council, Warsaw, July 2, 1917, in *PZ,* 4:201–202.

63. Quotation from Milewska, Nowak, and Zientara, *Legiony Polskie,*229; *Kalendarium,* 2:71.

64. Nałęcz, *Polska Organizacja Wojskowa,* 141; Drozdowski, *Kronika,* 206; Milewska, Nowak, and Zientara, *Legiony Polskie,* 231–232.

65. "Obywatele," Warsaw, July 17, 1917, on board a military transport train, in CBW, DU-630.

66. Władysław L. Jaworski, diary entry of July 8, 1917, in Jaworski, *Diariusz,* 204.

67. Iza Moszczeńska's, letter to Jaworski, cited in Jaworski's diary entry of January 14, 1917, in Jaworski, *Diariusz,* 154. For Moszczeńska's open letter, see "List otwarty do Brygadiera Piłsudskiego, byłego członka Rady Stanu," Warsaw, July 11, 1917, CBW, DU-1492.

68. Quotation from Alexandra Pilsudska, *Pilsudski: A Biography by His Wife* (New York: Dodd, Mead, 1941), 261.

69. Pilsudski, Warsaw, to Gen. Von Beseler, July 20 (?), 1917, in Pilsudski, *Korespondencja,* 259–268.

70. Quotation from Michał Sokolnicki, "Przed aresztowaniem Komendanta," in *Za kratami więzień i drutami obozów* (Warsaw: Tow. Wydawn. "Polska Zjednoczona," 1928), 2:10–12.

71. Władysław L. Jaworski, diary entry of July 24, 1917, Krakow, in Jaworski, *Diariusz,* 208.

72. "Poles Balk at Oath of Fidelity to Kaisers—Leaders and Council of State Demand Release of General Pilsudski and Others," *New York Times,* July 30, 1917, 2.

73. "Polish Regiments Refuse to Take Oath," *Boston Daily Globe,* July 30, 1917, 7; and *Times* (London), August 3, 1917, 5. For clandestine circulars that appeared, see "Józef Piłsudski został przez Niemców aresztowany," July 1917, CBW, DU-1937; and "Rodacy," September 15, 1917, CBW, DU-1521.

74. Quotation from "Through German Eyes," *Times* (London), August 15, 1917, 5.

75. *PZ,* 4:208n1.

76. Borislav Chernev, *Twilight of Empire: The Brest-Litovsk Conference and the Remaking of East-Central Europe, 1917–1918* (Toronto: University of Toronto Press, 2017), 73.

77. "Rado Regencyjna!," n.d., CBW, DU-658.

78. Austrian government report, July 30, 1917, quotation from Stefan Arski, *My pierwsza brygada* (Warsaw: Czytelnik, 1963), 193–194.

79. "Central Powers to Split Poland, Revoking Pledges," *New York Times,* September 7, 1917, 1.

80. Andrzej Chwalba, *Wielka Wojna Polaków, 1914–1918* (Warsaw: PWN, 2018), 294; Daria and Tomasz Nałęcz, *Józef Piłsudski: Legendy i fakty* (Warsaw: Młodzieżowa Agencja Wydawnicza, 1986), 166.

81. "Oświadczenie," n.d. [December 1917?], Warsaw, signed by the Party of National Independence, the Polish Socialist Party, the Polish Peasant Party, and the Union of Democratic Parties, CBW, DU-1343.

82. "Instrukcja No. 1," Warsaw, February 1918, 1, CBW, DU-687.

83. Pilsudski, "Magdeburg, 1917–1918" (1925), in *Joseph Pilsudski: The Memories,* 354, 360. For the original, see *PZ,* 8:165–171.

84. Pilsudski, Magdeburg, to Alexandra Szczerbińska, Warsaw, February 20, 1918, in *Kalendarium*, 2:87.

85. Pilsudski, Magdeburg, to Alexandra Szczerbińska, Warsaw, April 7, 1918, in Pilsudska, *Pilsudski*, 266. The date of the March 1918 letter is given in "Z listów Józefa Pilsudskiego do Aleksandry Szczerbińskiej," *Tygodnik Powszechny*, November 13, 1988.

86. *Kalendarium*, 2:90.

87. Ignacy Paderewski, *Pamiętniki, 1912–1932*, ed. Mary Lawton (Kraków: Polskie Wydawnictwo Muzyczne, 1992), 48; see also M. B. Biskupski, *The United States and the Rebirth of Poland, 1914–1918* (Dordrecht: Republic of Letters, 2012), 234.

88. Edith Wilson, *My Memoir* (New York: Bobbs-Merrill Co., 1939), 113, quotation from Zamoyski, *Paderewski*, 156.

89. Edward House, letter of January 15, 1931, quotation from Biskupski, *United States and the Rebirth of Poland*, 208; and in Louis L. Gerson, *Woodrow Wilson and the Rebirth of Poland, 1914–1920* (New York: Archon Books, 1872), 70. On House's relations with Wilson, see Godfrey Hodgson, *Woodrow Wilson's Right Hand: The Life of Colonel Edward M. House* (New Haven, CT: Yale University Press, 2006).

90. Woodrow Wilson, "Address to the Senate of the United States," January 22, 1917, in *War Addresses of Woodrow Wilson*, ed. A. R. Leonard (Boston: Ginn and Co., 1918), 8. For a discussion of this speech, see Jan Karski, *The Great Powers and Poland* (1985; New York: Rowman and Littlefield, 2014), 16.

91. Quotation from "Poles Thank Wilson," *New York Times*, February 1, 1917, 3.

92. Pilsudski, Warsaw, March 3, 1917, interview with Władysław Baranowski, published in Baranowski, *Rozmowy z Piłsudskim*, 39, 41.

93. Woodrow Wilson, "Address to Congress, April 2, 1917," in Leonard, *War Addresses of Woodrow Wilson*, 42; for a discussion of this speech, see Leonhard, *Pandora's Box*, 599–600.

94. Paderewski, late August 1917, to Roman Dmowski and Count Maurycy Zamoyski, Paris, in Biskupski, *United States and the Rebirth of Poland*, 302–303.

95. Report of Dmowski Commitee, May 15, 1917, Papers of Roman Debicki, PIA, RG 40 / 17, fol. 2; Roman Dmowski, July 18, 1917, letter to Zydmunt Wasilewski, cited in Arski, *My pierwsza brygada*, 176. On Dmowski's anti-Jewish positions during World War I, see Paul Latawski, "The Dmowski-Namier Feud, 1915–1918," *Polin* 2 (1987): 37–49; and Antony Polonsky, *The Jews in Poland and Russia* (Oxford: Littman Library of Jewish Civilization, 2012), 2:104, 3:27–28.

96. Piotr Wandycz, *The Lands of Partitioned Poland* (Seattle: University of Washington Press, 1974), 360.

97. Report of the Dmowski Commitee, May 15, 1917, Papers of Roman Debicki, PIA, RG 40 / 17, fol. 1.

98. Chernev, *Twilight of Empire*, 73; Oleg S. Pidhaini, *The Ukrainian-Polish Problem in the Dissolution of the Russian Empire, 1914–1917* (Toronto: New Review Books, 1962), 106–107.

99. "Central Powers and the Ukraine Sign Peace," *Atlantic Constitution*, February 10, 1918, 3. For the full text of the treaty, see "Treaty of Peace between Ukraine and the Central Powers, 9 February 1918," in J. W. Wheeler-Bennett, *The Forgotten Peace: Brest-Litovsk, March 1918* (New York: William Morrow, 1939), 392–402.

100. Quotation from R. F. Leslie, ed., *The History of Poland since 1863* (New York: Cambridge University Press, 1980), 124. On the resignation of the Kucharzewski government, see "Germany Faces Crisis in Poland: Treaty of Peace with Ukraine Causes Demonstrations in Lemberg and Cracow—Polish Government Resigns," *Christian Science Monitor*, February 18, 1918, 1.

101. Chernev, *Twilight of Empire*, 215.

102. Woodrow Wilson, "The Program of Peace: Address to Congress, January 8, 1918," in Leonard, *War Addresses of Woodrow Wilson*, 99.

103. "Freedom for Poland Agreed on by Allies," *New York Times*, June 6, 1918, 1; "Allies Demand a Free Poland," *Christian Science Monitor*, June 6, 1918, 2. Also see Jerzy Lukowski and Hubert Zawadzki, *A Concise History of Poland*, 3rd ed. (New York: Cambridge University Press, 2019), 284.

12. The Father of Independent Poland

1. Alexandra Pilsudska, *Pilsudski: A Biography by His Wife* (New York: Dodd, Mead, 1941), 270.

2. Ibid.

3. Prince Lubomirski, 1923 account, in W. Lipiński, "Powrót Józefa Piłsudskiego z Magdeburga," *Niepodległość* 15 (1937): 238.

4. "Relacja Adama Koca z przyjazdu Józefa Piłsudskiego do Warszawy 10 listopada 1918 roku," in *Listopada 1918 we wspomnieniach i relacjach*, ed. Piotr Łossowski and Piotr Stawecki (Warsaw: Wydawnictwo Ministerstwa Obrony Narodowej, 1988), 98.

5. Adam Koc, "Powrót Józefa Piłsudskiego z Magdeburga i Przewrót listopadowy w r. 1918 według relacji Adama Koca, Ks. Zdzisława Lubomirskiego i Kardynała Aleksandra Kakowskiego," *Niepodległość* 15 (1937): 235.

6. Prince Lubomirski, interview, in Lipiński, "Powrót Józefa Piłsudskiego," 236.

7. Col. Adam Koc, account in Lipiński, "Powrót Józefa Piłsudskiego," 235.

8. "Przed mieszkaniem Piłsudskiego," *Kurier Polski*, November 11, 1918, in *Pierwsze dni wolności: Warszawa od 10 do 18 listopada 1918—Wybór materiałów prasowych*, ed. Andrzej Stawarz (Warsaw: Muzeum Niepodległości, 2008), 9.

9. Wacław Jędrzejewicz, *Wspomnienia*, ed. Janusz Cisek (Wrocław: Zakład Narodowy im. Ossolińskich, 1993), 68.

10. Pilsudska, *Pilsudski*, 271.

11. *Kurier Warszawski*, November 11, 1918, 3.

12. Prince Lubomirski, testimony, in Lipiński, "Powrót Józefa Piłsudskiego," 237.

13. Piotr Wróbel, *Listopadowe dni 1918: Kalendarium narodzin II Rzeczypospolitej* (Warsaw: Instytut Wydawniczy Pax, 2018), 74–75.

14. Diary entry of November 10, 1918, in Władysław L. Jaworski, *Diariusz, 1914–1918,* ed. Michał Czajka (Warsaw: Oficyna Naukowa, 1997), 295.

15. Prince Lubomirski, recollections in Lipiński, "Powrót Józefa Piłsudskiego," 237.

16. Pilsudska, *Pilsudski,* 272.

17. Pilsudski, Warsaw, address to the German Military Council, November 11, 1918, in *PZ,* 5:13–14.

18. Prince Lubomirski, testimony, in Lipiński, "Powrót Józefa Piłsudskiego," 238. For the Regency Council's announcement on the independence of Poland, see "Rada Regencyjna do narodu polskiego," *Kurier Warszawski* (Warsaw), November 12, 1918, 1; *Kurier Poranny* (Warsaw), November 12, 1918, 3; "Z Warszawy: Rada Regencyjna przekazuje dyktaturę wojskową Piłsudskiemu," *Naprzód* (Kraków), November 13, 1918, 1–2; "Government for Poland," *Times* (London), November 16, 1918, 6. For the Regency Council's announcement on Pilsudski as army commander, see Aleksander Kakowski, Józef Ostrowski, Zdzisław Lubomirski, and Jozef Pilsudski, "Rada Regencyjna do Narodu Polskiego," November 11, 1918, AAN, sygn. 1634/6, fol. 29; reprinted in *Źródła do dziejów II Rzeczypospolitej,* ed. J. Piłatowicz, D. Sowińska, and A. Zawadzki (Siedlce: Instytut Historii i Stosunków Międzynarodowych, 2014), 1:17.

19. *Kurier Poranny,* November 11, 1918, quotation from Wróbel, *Listopadowe dni 1918,* 86.

20. "Wódz narodu," *Nowa Gazeta,* November 11, 1918, 1, quotation from Wróbel, *Listopadowe dni 1918,* 86.

21. See "Manifesto of the Provisional People's Government of the Polish Republic (November 7, 1918)," reprinted in *For Your Freedom and Ours,* ed. Krystyna Olszer (New York: F. Unger, 1981), 193–195; and Dorota Malczewska-Pawelec, "U źródeł niepodległości: Spory wokół Konwentu," *Res Historica* 8 (1999): 222–232. For Gen. Rydz-Śmigły's quote, see Gen. Edward Rydz-Śmigły, Lublin, November 7, 1918, "Żołnierze polscy! Do broni!," AAN, sygn. 2/290/65, reprinted in *Informator o zasobie Archiwalnym,* ed. Edward Kołodziej (Warsaw: Archiwum Akt Nowych, 2009), 1: between 480 and 481.

22. Ignacy Daszyński, *Pamiętniki* (Kraków: Nakładem Drukarni Ludowej, 1926), 2:327–328.

23. "Przed utworzeniem rządu narodowego," *Kurier Warszawski,* November 13, 1918, 1.

24. Pilsudski, "Uwagi do pamiętników Ignacego Daszyńskiego," in *PZ,* 9:312–313.

25. *Kurier Warszawski,* November 13, 1918, 1; *Kalendarium,* 2:107.

26. "Przed utworzeniem rządu narodowego," *Kurier Warszawski,* November 13, 1918, 1. For the Gruenbaum citation, see Szymon Rudnicki, *Żydzi w parlamencie II Rzeczypospolitej,* 2nd ed. (Warsaw: Wydawn. Sejmowe, 2015), 31.

27. Rudnicki, *Żydzi w parlamencie,* 31.

28. *Kurier Warszawski,* November 12, 1918, 2; *PZ,* 5:15.

29. Jozef Pilsudski, "Żołnierze," Warsaw, November 12, 1918, in *Kurier Warszawski,* November 13, 1918, 2; *Nowa Gazeta,* November 13, 1918, 1; *Kurier Poranny,* November 13, 1918, 2. For a reprint, see *PZ,* 5:16–17. The original document is reproduced in *Polonia restituta: O niepodległość i granice, 1914–1912,* ed. Jolanta Niklewska (Warsaw: Muzeum Niepodległości, 2007), 62.

30. "Z rady miejskiej," *Kurier Warszawski,* November 13, 1918, 4.

31. "Koledzy i Koleżanki!," Warsaw, November 12, 1918, CBW, DU-1334.

32. "Upadek Rady Regencyjnej," *Nowa Gazeta,* November 13, 1918, 1.

33. *Świat* (Warsaw), November 16, 1918, in *Pierwsze dni wolności, Warszawa od 10 do 18 listopada 1918: Wybór materiałów prasowych* ed. Andrzej Stawarz (Warsaw: Muzeum Niepodległości, 2008), 60.

34. Archbishop Aleksander Kakowski, 1923 account, in Lipiński, "Powrót Józefa Piłsudskiego," 241.

35. Diary entry of November 14, 1918, Warsaw, in Maria Dąbrowska, *Dzienniki, 1914–1965 w 13 tomach* (Warsaw: Polska Akademia Nauk, 2009), 1:169.

36. *Kurier Warszawski,* November 14, 1918, 1, in *PZ,* 5:19.

37. Grzegorz Nowik, *Odrodzenie Rzeczpospolitej w myśli politycznej Józefa Piłsudskiego, 1918–1922* (Warsaw: Oficyna Wydawnicza Volumen, 2018), 1:253.

38. Pilsudski, speech delivered in Warsaw at the Hotel Bristol on July 3, 1923, in *Joseph Pilsudski: The Memoirs of a Polish Revolutionary and Soldier,* trans. and ed. D. R. Gillie (London: Faber and Faber, 1931), 366–367. For the original, see *PZ,* 6:24–35.

39. Prince Lubomirski, 1923 account, in Lipiński, "Powrót Józefa Piłsudskiego," 238.

40. Diary entry of November 15, 1918, in Władysław Konopczyński, *Dziennik, 1918–1921* (Warsaw-Kraków: Muzeum Historii Polski, 2016), 1:233.

41. Diary entry of November 15, 1918, in Jaworski, *Diariusz,* 296.

42. Andrzej Nowak, *Niepodległa! 1864–1924: Jak Polacy odzyskali ojczyznę* (Kraków: Biały Kruk Sp., 2018), 233.

43. Pilsudski, Warsaw, to Ignacy Daszyński, November 17, 1918, *Kurier Polski,* November 18, 1918, 2, in *PZ,* 5:25; Antony Polonsky, "The Emergence of an Independent Polish State," in *The History of Poland since 1863,* ed. R. F. Leslie (New York: Cambridge University Press, 1980), 127.

44. Wincenty Witos, *Moje wspomnienia* (Paris: Instytut Literacki, 1964), 2:232.

45. Paweł Skibiński, *Polska 1918* (Warsaw: Muza, 2018), 46; Polonsky, "The Emergence," 127.

46. "Gabinet Moraczewskiego," *Kurier Warszawski,* November 18, 1918, 4.

47. Witos, *Moje wspomnienia,* 2:232.

48. Władysław L. Jaworski, diary entry of November 19, 1918, in Jaworski, *Diariusz,* 296.

49. "Rodacy! Opamiętacie się! Ojczyzna w niebezpieczeństwie," Warsaw, November 19, 1918, AAN, sygn. 56 / 7.

50. Diary entry of November 18, 1918, in Leon Wasilewski, *Wspomnienia 1870–1904, fragment dziennika 1916–1926, diariusz podróży po kresach 1927* (Łomianki: Wydawnictwo LTW, 2014), 298–299.

51. Jędrzej Moraczewski, prime minister, "Odezwa Rządu," *Kurier Polski,* November 20, 1918, 7. For a reprint, see Stawarz, *Pierwsze dni wolności,* 108–110.

52. J. Piłsudski, Warsaw, November 22, 1918, "Dekret o najwyższy władzy reprezentacyjnej Republiki Polskiej," in *Źródła do dziejów II Rzeczypospolitej,* 1:20.

53. J. Piłsudski, Head of State, and J. Moraczewski, Prime Minister, Warsaw, November 23, 1918, "Dekret o 8-godzinnym dniu pracy," *Kurier Warszawski,* November 26, 1918, 3; reprinted in Wróbel, *Listopadowe dni 1918,* 210–211.

54. Electoral Law of November 28, 1918, in *Źródła do dziejów II Rzeczypospolitej,* 1:21–32.

55. Piłsudska, *Piłsudski,* 279. On Piłsudski's support for women's suffrage, see Magdalena Gawin, *Spór o równouprawnienie kobiet, 1864–1919* (Warsaw: Wydawnictwo Neriton, Warszawa, 2015); Małgorzata Fuszara, "Polish Women's Fight for Suffrage," in *The Struggle for Female Suffrage in Europe,* ed. Ruth Rubio-Marín and Blanca Rodriguez-Ruiz (Leiden: Brill, 2012), 150–151.

56. *Monitor Polski* (Warsaw), November 18, 1918, 1; *Kurier Warszawski,* November 18, 1918, 4–5; *PZ,* 5:20–24.

57. J. Piłsudski, Warsaw, to President Wilson, Washington DC, November 16, 1918, in *Papers Relating to the Foreign Relations of the United States, 1919: The Paris Peace Conference,* vol. 2 (Washington, DC: US Government Printing Office, 1942), 410. For commentary on this telegram, see Piotr S. Wandycz, *The United States and Poland* (Cambridge, MA: Harvard University Press, 1980), 126; Piłsudski, Warsaw, to Gen. Ferdinand Foch, Paris, November 16, 1918, *Monitor Polski,* November 18, 1918, 1, in *PZ,* 5:21.

58. "Poland's Resurrection," *New York Tribune,* November 16, 1918, 10.

59. "Poles Control Posen," *New York Times,* November 17, 1918, 4; "Posen, German City, Captured by the Poles," *New York Tribune,* November 17, 1918, 2; "Poles Seize Most of Posen Province," *New York Tribune,* November 22, 1918, 3.

60. Szymon Słomczyński, "'There Are Sick People Everywhere—in Cities, Towns, and Villages': The Course of the Spanish Flu Epidemic in Poland," *Roczniki Dziejów Społecznych i Gospodarczych* 72 (2012): 85. I am grateful to Andrzej Nowak for bringing this article to my attention.

61. "Ukrainians Take Lemberg," *Washington Post,* November 5, 1918, 1; Michał Klimecki, *Wojna polsko-ukraińska: Lwów i Galicja Wschodnia, 1918–1919* (Warsaw: Bellona, 2014), 120; Jochen Böhler, *Civil War in Central Europe, 1918–1921: The Reconstruction of Poland* (Oxford: Oxford University Press, 2018), 78; Christopher Mick, *Lemberg, Lwów, L'viv, 1914–1947: Violence and Ethnicity in a Contested City* (W. Lafayette, IN: Purdue University Press, 2016), 114; Antoni Czubiński, *Walka o*

granice wschodnie polski w latach 1918–1921 (Opole: Instytut Śląski w Opolu, 1993), 58; Maciej Dalecki, *Przemyśl w latach 1918–1939 przestrzeń, ludność, gospodarka* (Przemyśl: Archiwum Państwowe w Przemyślu, 1999), 75; Walerian Kramarz, *Ludność Przemyśla w latach 1521–1921* (Przemyśl: Towarzystwo przyjaciół nauk w Przemyślu, 1930), 108; *Encyclopedia of Ukraine* (1993), 3:842.

62. Damian K. Markowski, *Dwa powstania—bitwa of Lwów, 1918–1919* (Kraków: Wydawnictwo Literackie, 2019), 20; Michał Klimecki, "Lwów: W obronie miasta i południowo-wschodniej granicy 1918–1920 i 1939 r.," *Niepodległość i Pamięć* 13, no. 3 (2006): 41; Michał Klimecki, *Lwów, 1918–1919* (Warsaw: Dom Wydawniczy, 2000), 12.

63. Markowski, *Dwa powstania*, 166.

64. Polish National Committee, Paris, to the American Ambassador in France, William Graves Sharp, November 13, 1918, in *Papers Relating to the Foreign Relations of the United States, 1919: The Paris Peace Conference*, 2:411–412.

65. J. Pilsudski, Warsaw, to Gen. Bolesław Roja, Kraków, November 16, 1918, in *PZ*, 5:23–24; Klimecki, *Wojna polsko-ukraińska*, 139–140; Klimecki, *Lwów, 1918–1919*, 129; Czubiński, *Walka o granice wschodnie*, 64.

66. Gen. Roja, Provisional Army Commander for East Galicia, Lwów, order dated November 22, 1918, in Niklewska, *Polonia Restituta*, 82. Markowski, *Dwa powstania*, 350. On casualty figures, see Klimecki, "Lwów," 44; Klimecki, *Lwów, 1918–1919*, 129; Marian M. Drozdowski, ed., *Kronika narodzin II Rzeczypospolitej, 1914–1923* (Warsaw: Bellona, 2018), 368; Nowak, *Niepodległa!*, 237.

67. Vasyl Kuchabsky, *Western Ukraine in Conflict with Poland and Bolshevism, 1918–1923* (Edmonton: Canadian Institute of Ukrainian Studies Press, 2009), 50 (orig. pub. German, 1934).

68. Text of appeal quoted in "Ukrainians in N.Y. Ask to Free Lemberg: Say Capture by Poles Violates Wilson Principles," *Detroit Free Press*, November 28, 1918, 11.

69. *Sprawozdanie Żydowskiego Komitetu dla niesienia pomocy ofiarom rozruchów i rabunków w listop. 1918 we Lwowie* (Lwów: Żydowski Komitet Ratunkowy, 1919), cited in William W. Hagen, *Anti-Jewish Violence in Poland, 1914–1920* (New York: Cambridge University Press, 2018), 156. For a complete list of the seventy-three murder victims of the Lwów pogrom, see Max Blokzyl, *Poland, Galicia and the Persecution of the Jews at Lemberg* (Amsterdam: n.p., 1919), 58. For a chart of the victims by profession, see Josef Bendow [Joseph Tenenbaum], *Der Lemberger Judenpogrom (November 1918—Jänner 1919)* (Vienna: M. Hickl-Verlag, 1919), 161. For three additional contemporaneous reports on anti-Jewish violence in Poland, including details of the Lwów pogrom, see Leon Chasanowich, *Die polnischen Judenpogrome im November und Dezember 1918: Tatsachen und Dokumente* (Stockholm: Verlag Judaea A.B., 1919); Israel Cohen, *A Report on the Pogroms in Poland* (London: Central Office of the Zionist Organization, 1919); "Mission of the United States to Poland: Henry Morgenthau, Sr.'s Report," October 3, 1919, *New*

York Times, January 19, 1920, 6, reprinted in Henry Morgenthau, *All in a Life-Time* (New York: Doubleday, Page, 1925), 407–420. For scholarly treatments of the Lwów pogrom, see Hagen, *Anti-Jewish Violence,* 151–172; Alexander Victor Prusin, *Nationalizing a Borderland: War, Ethnicity, and Anti-Jewish Violence in East Galicia, 1914–1920* (Tuscaloosa: University of Alabama Press, 2005), chap. 5; and Jerzy Tomaszewski, "Lwów, 22 listopada 1918," *Przegląd Historyczny* 75, no. 2 (1984): 279–285.

70. Hagen, *Anti-Jewish Violence,* 156, 163.

71. Chasanowich, *Die polnischen Judenpogrome,* 33–36; "Mission of the United States to Poland."

72. Hagen, *Anti-Jewish Violence,* 189.

73. "W sprawie zajść z żydami," *Kurier Warszawski,* November 26, 1918, 2.

74. Hagen, *Anti-Jewish Violence,* 123–124; Piotr Wróbel, "Foreshadowing the Holocaust: The Wars of 1918–1921 and Anti-Jewish Violence in Central and Eastern Europe," in *Legacies of Violence: Eastern Europe's First World War,* ed. Jochen Bohler et al. (Munich: Oldenbourg, 2014), 197. The latter figure is derived, in part, from Cohen, *A Report on the Pogroms* (1919), and Cohen, "Pogroms in Poland, 1918–1919," in Israel Cohen, *A Jewish Pilgrimage: The Autobiography of Israel Cohen* (London: Vallentine Mitchell. 1956), 134–148.

75. Joachim Schoenfeld, *Jewish Life in Galicia under the Austro-Hungarian Empire and in Reborn Poland, 1898–1939* (Hoboken, NJ: Ktav, 1985), 201, quoted in Marsha Rozenblit, *Reconstructing a National Identity: The Jews of Habsburg Austria during World War I* (Oxford: Oxford University Press, 2001), 136.

76. Quotation from "German Version of Massacre of Jews by Troops in Lemberg," *New York Times,* November 29, 1918, 20. The story simultaneously appeared in papers across the country: "Poles are Accused of Burning Jews," *St. Louis Post-Dispatch,* November 28, 1918, 13; "Berlin Reports Great Pogrom by Polish Army: Lemberg Ghetto District Sacked and Burned," *New York Tribune,* November 29, 1918, 3; "1100 Jews Slain in Massacre at Lemberg," *San Francisco Chronicle,* November 30, 1918, 1; "The Massacres in Poland," *American Israelite* (Cincinnati), December 5, 1918, 4.

77. Minutes of the meeting between a Jewish delegation and Pilsudski, in I. Grünbaum, ed., *Materijały w sprawie żydowskiej w Polsce* (Warsaw: Biuo Prasowe Organizacji Sjonistycznej w Polsce, 1919), 1:26–33.

78. Dr. Braun, Delegate of the Kielce Jewish Community, memorandum presented to Piłsudski, November 25, 1918, in Grünbaym, *Materijały,* 1:26.

79. "Wobec zajść w Kielcach: Deputacja żydowska u Piłsudskiego i Moraczewskiego," *Kurier Poranny* (Warsaw), November 27, 1918, 2. The same exchange appeared in *Der moment* (Warsaw), November 27, 1918, 3; *Kurier Warszawski,* November 27, 1918, 6; and *Nowy Dziennik* (Kraków), December 1, 1918, 3. For a discussion of this exchange in the scholarly literature, see Isaac Lewin, *A History of Polish Jewry during the Revival of Poland* (New York: Shengold, 1990), 96n22;

Shoshan Ronen, *A Prophet of Consolation on the Threshold of Destruction: Yhoshua Ozjasz Thon, an Intellectual Portrait* (Warsaw: Dom Wydawniczy Elipsa 2015), 228–229.

80. "A delegatsie beym komendant Pilsudski," *Haynt* (Warsaw), November 26, 1918, 3; "Di galitsishe deputatsye bey Pilsudski," *Haynt*, November 27, 1918 (Warsaw), 2; "Di yidishe delegatsie baym komendant Pilsudski un baym premier," *Der moment* (Warsaw), November 27, 1918, 3; "Echa pogromu lwowskiego w Warszawie," *Nowy Dziennik* (Kraków), December 5, 1918, 3; "Wobec zajść w Kielcach: Deputacja żydowska u Piłsudskiego i Moraczewskiego," *Kurier Poranny*, November 27, 1918, 2. For the minutes of the meeting between Thon, Gruenbaum, and Pilsudski, see "Do Pana Naczelnika Państwa Komendanta Józefa Piłsudskiego: Memoriał w sprawie położenia Żydów w Galicji," in Grünbaum, *Materijały*, 1:37–39.

81. Pilsudski, quotation from *Nowy Dziennik*, December 5, 1918, 3; Grünbaum, *Materijały*, 1:40.

82. *Nowy Dziennik*, December 5, 1918, 3; Grünbaum, *Materijały*, 1:40–41.

83. *The Pogroms in Poland and Lithuania* (London: Jewish Socialist Labor Confederation, 1919), 25.

84. Ozjasz Thon, "Z rozmyślań przymusowych wakacyj (wspomnienia i refleksje)," *Nowy Dziennik*, December 7, 1927, 6. On Thon's view of Pilsudski, see Shoshan Ronen, *A Prophet of Consolation*, 228–229.

85. Thon, "Z rozmyślań przymusowych wakacyj," 6.

86. Ibid, 7.

87. Cohen, *A Report on the Pogroms* (1919), 34.

88. Lewin, *A History of Polish Jewry*, 61.

89. "The Polish Outrages," *Jewish Chronicle*, November 29, 1918, 5.

90. "8,000 Here Demand Justice for Jews: Great Meeting Passes Resolution Calling for Action by the Peace Conference," *New York Times*, December 12, 1918, 5.

91. "Polish Problems: Heavy Tasks of New Government: Truth about the Pogroms," *Times* (London), December 23, 1918, 7; "The Polish-Jewish Problem," *Jewish Chronicle*, December 27, 1918, 3.

92. "Gen. Pilsudski Urges Recognition by Allies with Help in the Form of Arms," *New York Times*, December 17, 1918, 13.

13. Statesman and Diplomat

Epigraph: Pilsudski, speech to the Legislative Sejm, February 10, 1919, in *PZ*, 5:55.

1. "Gen. Pilsudski Urges Recognition by Allies with Help in the Form of Arms," *New York Times*, December 17, 1918, 13 (from a December 15 dispatch, Associated Press).

2. Harold H. Fisher, *America and the New Poland* (New York: Macmillan, 1928), 119–120.

3. Robert Machray, *Poland, 1914–1931* (London: G. Allen and Unwin, 1932), 107.

4. "Gen. Pilsudski Urges Recognition."

5. Polish National Committee, Paris, minutes of the 156th session, November 16, 1918, in Marek Jabłonowski and Dorota Cisowska-Hydzik, eds., *O niepodległą i granice*, vol. 6: *Komitet Narodowy Polski: Protokoły posiedzeń, 1917–1921* (Warsaw: Wyd. Uniwersytetu Warszawskiego, 2007), 597–599.

6. Polish National Committee, minutes of the 157th session, Paris, November 22, 1918, in Jabłonowski and Cisowska-Hydzik, *O niepodległą i granice*, 6:604–605.

7. Stanisław Grabski, *Pamiętniki*, ed. Witold Stankiewicz (Warsaw: Czytelnik, 1989), 2:88.

8. Conversation with Stanisław Stroński, December 5, 1918, quotation from *Kalendarium*, 2:133.

9. Grabski, *Pamiętniki*, 2:90.

10. Diary entry of December 8, 1918, in Leon Wasilewski, *Wspomnienia, 1870–1904, fragment dziennika 1916–1926, diariusz podróży po kresach 1927* (Łomianki: Wydawnictwo LTW, 2014), 303–304.

11. Stanisław Grabski, Warsaw, to Roman Dmowski, Paris, December 11, 1918, in *Komitet Narodowy Polski a Ententa i Stany Zjednoczone, 1917–1919*, ed. Marian Leczyk (Warsaw: Państwowe Wydawn. Naukowe, 1966), 304.

12. Maurycy Zamoyski, Paris, to the French government, December 13, 1918, in *Przegląd Wieczorny* (Warsaw), December 13, 1918.

13. Kay Lundgreen-Nielsen, *The Polish Problem at the Paris Peace Conference* (Odense: Odense University Press, 1979), 102.

14. Polish National Committee, Paris, minutes of the meeting held of December 11, 1918, reprinted in Jabłonowski and Cisowska-Hydzik, *O niepodległą i granice*, 6:623, quotation on 622–623.

15. "Prof. Grabski o swej misji," *Kurier Poranny*, December 21, 1918, 3; "Daremne usiłowania," *Dziennik Powszechny*, December 21, 1918; "Spawozdanie prof. Grabskiego," *Kurier Warszawski*, December 21, 1918, 2–3.

16. Major Julian L. Coolidge, Paris, memorandum dated December 11, 1918, in *Papers Relating to the Foreign Relations of the United States, 1919: The Paris Peace Conference* (hereafter cited as *The Paris Peace Conference*), vol. 2 (Washington, DC: US Government Printing Office, 1942), 414.

17. Ibid., 415.

18. Pilsudski, December 9, 1918, to President Woodrow Wilson, Washington, Michał Mościcki Papers, PIA, RG 75/11, fol. 8; on Polish American volunteers in Haller's army, see Joseph Hapak, "Recruiting a Polish Army in the United States, 1917–1919" (PhD diss., University of Kansas, 1985), 171, 195.

19. For Pilsudski's instructions to the delegation, see Pilsudski, Warsaw, to Kazimierz Dłuski, December 19, 1918, in Kazimierz Dłuski, *Wspomnienia z Paryża*

od 4.I do 10.VII 1919 r. (Warsaw: Drukarnia "Dziennika Powszechnego," 1920), 3. On the composition of the delegation, see Michał Sokolnicki, "W służbie Komendanta," *Kultura* (Paris), 12, no. 4 (1953): 85; *Kalendarium,* 2:140; Jabłonowski and Cisowska-Hydzik, *O niepodległą i granice,* 6:637n9; Lundgreen-Nielsen, *The Polish Problem,* 452n31.

20. Pilsudski, Przemyśl, to Roman Dmowski, Paris, December 21, 1918, in *PZ,* 5:45–46. For the quotation of Pilsudski's letter to General Foch, see Pilsudski, Warsaw, to Marshal Ferdinand Foch, Paris, December 18, 1918, in *PZ,* 5:39–40.

21. Jan Karski, *The Great Powers and Poland: From Versailles to Yalta* (1985; repr., Lanham, MD: Rowman and Littlefield, 2014), 36n2; Andrzej Nowak, *Polska i Trzy Rosje,* 3rd ed. (Kraków: Arcana, 2015), 93.

22. French ambassador to the United States, Jean Jules Jusserand, to the US secretary of state, Robert Lansing, Washington, DC, November 26, 1918, in *The Paris Peace Conference,* 2:412.

23. Baranowski, interview with Pilsudski, Warsaw, December 26, 1918, in Baranowski, *Rozmowy z Piłsudskim, 1916–1931* (1938; repr., Warsaw: Zebra, 1990), 48.

24. Sokolnicki, "W służbie Komendanta," 85.

25. *Naprzód* (Kraków), December 20, 1918 (special edition), 1, copy in Michał Mościcki Papers, PIA, RG 75 / 13.

26. "Naczelniku!," *Naprzód* (Kraków), December 20, 1918 (special edition), 2.

27. "O gabinet narodowy," *Czas* (Kraków), December 21, 1918, 1; and on the previous quotation, expressing dissatisfaction with his program, see "Powitanie naczelnika państwa," *Czas* (Kraków), December 20, 1918, 1.

28. Baranowski, interview with Pilsudski, Belvedere Palace (Warsaw), December 26, 1918, in W. Baranowski, *Rozmowy,* 47.

29. Ibid., 49.

30. W. Baranowski, interview with Pilsudski, Belvedere Palace (Warsaw), December 29, 1918, in Baranowski, *Rozmowy,* 52.

31. Text of declaration as quoted in "Poles' Debt to Mr. Wilson: Message of Gratitude," *Times* (London), December 28, 1918, 5.

32. William J. Rose, "My Mission from Silesia," *Polish Review* (London) 2, no. 3 (December 1918): 222.

33. "Forces in the New Poland," *Times* (London), December 31, 1918, 7.

34. [William Rose], "Joseph Pilsudski," *New Europe* (London), December 12, 1918, 200.

35. Ibid., 202.

36. Dłuski, *Wspomnienia,* 5. On the Dłuski Mission's contact with British diplomats in Berne, see Sokolnicki, "W służbie Komendanta," 85–86; "British Mission to Poland," *Times* (London), December 28, 1918, 5.

37. Dłuski, *Wspomnienia,* 4.

38. The original French-language telegram appears in Dłuski, *Wspomnienia,* 5.

39. Sokolnicki, "W służbie Komendanta," 85.

40. Pilsudski's address to soldiers, Warsaw, November 29, 1918, in *PZ*, 5:33.

41. Wacław Jędrzejewicz, *Wspomnienia*, ed. Janusz Cisek (Wrocław: Zakład Narodowy im. Ossolińskich, 1993), 71.

42. "Rozkaz noworoczny," January 1, 1919, in *PZ*, 5:47–48.

43. Jędrzej Moraczewski, *Przewrót w Polsce*, ed. Tomasz Nałęcz (1919; repr., Warsaw: Muzeum Historii Polski, 2015), 61.

44. "Nasz Naczelnik!," n.d., n.p., CBW, DU-572.

45. W. J. Rose, *The Polish Memoirs of William John Rose*, ed. Daniel Stone (Toronto: University of Toronto Press, 1975), 85; Sokolnicki, "W służbie Komendanta," 86; Dłuski, *Wspomnienia*, 6. The date of the Dłuski Mission's arrival is confirmed in the *Times* (London), January 6, 1919, 7.

46. Rose, *Polish Memoirs*, 85.

47. "Need for Polish Unity: A Mission to Paris," *Times* (London), January 5, 1919, 7.

48. Rose, *Polish Memoirs*, 85.

49. Sokolnicki, Paris, diary entry of January 6, 1919, in Sokolnicki, "W służbie Komendanta," 104.

50. Sokolnicki, Paris, journal entries for January 8–9, 1919, in Sokolnicki, "W służbie Komendanta," 91.

51. Polish National Committee, Paris, minutes of the 173rd session, January 6, 1919, in Jabłonowski and Cisowska-Hydzik, *O niepodległą i granice*, 6:639.

52. Sokolnicki, Paris, journal entries for January 8–9, 1919, in Sokolnicki, "W służbie Komendanta," 90.

53. Bliss diary entries for December 29, 1918, and January 1, 1919, quotation from Lundgreen-Nielsen, *The Polish Problem*, 105–106. For Bliss's report to the US secretary of state on the meeting with Dmowski, see Gen. T. Bliss, Paris, to the US secretary of state, Robert Lansing, January 8, 1919, in *The Paris Peace Conference*, 2:426–427.

54. "Working to Unite Polish Factions," *New York Times*, January 14, 1919, 2. From a January 13, 1919, Associated Press wire.

55. R. C. Foster, Warsaw, to Professor A. C. Coolidge, Paris, January 15, 1919, in *The Paris Peace Conference*, 12:369.

56. Diary entry of January 4, 1919, in William R. Grove, *War's Aftermath: Polish Relief in 1919* (New York: House of Field, 1940), 35.

57. *L'Echo de Paris*, quotation from the *Times* (London), January 6, 1919, 7.

58. Polish Army General Staff, Intelligence Report for the Kraków and Warsaw districts, January 8, 1919, in Marek Jabłonowski, Piotr Stawecki, and Tadeusz Wawrzyński, *O niepodległą i granic: Raporty i komunikaty naczelnych władz wojskowych o sytuacji wewnętrznej Polski, 1919–1920* (Warsaw: Wydział Dziennikarstwa i Nauk Politycznych, 2000), 2:27.

59. "Paderewski and Pilsudski: Need of a Coalition Ministry," *Times* (London), January 11, 1919, 8.

60. Paderewski, Warsaw, to Col. Edward House, January 12, 1919, in *The Intimate Papers of Colonel House* (Boston: Houghton Mifflin, 1925), 4:263.

61. R. S. Blake, memorandum on the present situation in Poland, January 13, 1919, cited in Lundgreen-Nielsen, *The Polish Problem,* 106.

62. "Une méthode d'action en Pologne: Nécessité d'une Pologne forte," December 20, 1918, quotation from Janusz Pajewski, *Wokół sprawy polskiej: Paryż-Lozanna-Londyn, 1914–1918* (Poznań: Wydawnictwo Poznańskie, 1970), 230.

63. Rose, *Polish Memoirs,* 78.

64. Quotation from *Kalendarium,* 2:146. For an analysis of Piłsudski's letter, including a reproduction of the handwritten original, see Wacław Jędrzejewicz, "Drogi Panie Romanie!," *Wiadomości* (London), July 22, 1973, 1.

65. Quotation from Marian M. Drozdowski, *O niepodległą i demokratyczną Rzeczpospolitą* (Kraków: Księgarnia Akademicka, 2018), 51.

66. "Urges Immediate Aid for Starving Poles," *New York Times,* December 29, 1918, 4. Also see "Poland's Need for Concord," *Times* (London), December 30, 1918, 8.

67. "Russia To-Day," *Times* (London), December 28, 1918, 5.

68. "Poland's Plight: Industry Wrecked, Country a Prey to Extremists," *Times* (London), January 2, 1919, 6 (dispatch dated December 29, 1918).

69. Polish Army General Staff, Intelligence Report for the Warsaw, Łódź, and Kielce districts, January 15 and 16, 1919, in Jabłonowski, Stawecki, and Wawrzyński, *O niepodległą i granice,* 2:34–37; "Paderewski Puts Down Bolsheviki," *Boston Daily Globe,* January 23, 1919, 1.

70. "Warsaw Coup," *Times* (London), January 7, 1919, 8.

71. Quotation from *Kalendarium,* 2:157.

72. Diary entry of January 5, 1919, Warsaw, in Maria Dąbrowska, *Dzienniki, 1914–1965 w 13 tomach* (Warsaw: Polska Akademia Nauk, 2009), 1:175.

73. Col. William R. Grove, Warsaw, to Gen. Marlborough Churchill, January 9, 1919, in *The Paris Peace Conference,* 2:427–428.

74. "Polacy!," n.d., Warsaw, CBW, DU-1341.

75. Vernon Kellogg, report dated January 7, 1919, Warsaw, enclosed in a letter to Hubert Hoover, January 9, 1919, reprinted in M. B. Biskupski, "The Origins of the Paderewski Government in 1919: A Reconsideration in Light of New Evidence," *Polish Review* 34, no. 1 (1988): 162.

76. W. Baranowski, interview with Piłsudski, Belvedere Palace (Warsaw), January 13, 1919, in Baranowski, *Rozmowy,* 58.

77. Sokolnicki, "W służbie Komendanta," 92.

78. Paderewski, Warsaw, telegram to Roman Dmowski, Paris, January 14, 1914, in Jabłonowski and Cisowska-Hydzik, *O niepodległą i granice,* 6:651–652. For a discussion of this letter, see Lundgreen-Nielsen, *The Polish Problem,* 117–118.

79. Polish National Committee, Paris, minutes of the 185th session, Paris, January 30, 1919, reprinted in Jabłonowski and Cisowska-Hydzik, *O niepodległą i granice,* 6:661.

80. Esmé Howard, *Theatre of Life: Life Seen from the Stalls* (London: Hodder and Stoughton, 1936), 327.

81. J. Moraczewski, January 17, 1919, Warsaw, reprinted in Moraczewski, *Przewrót w Polsce*, 149–152.

82. For the list of cabinet members, see I. Paderewski and J. Pilsudski, January 16, 1919, "Nowy Gabinet," *Dziennik Urzędowy Rozporządzeń*, January 17, 1919, 1–2. On the new cabinet, see Stanisław Wojciechowski, *Moje wspomnienia* (1938; repr., Warsaw: Muzeum Historii Polski, 2017), 2:8; Marian Marek Drozdowski, *Józef Piłsudski: Naczelnik Państwa Polskiego 14 XI 1918–14 XII 1922* (Warsaw: Oficyna Wydawnicza Rytm, 2017), 33–34; and the following press accounts: "Paderewski Heads New Polish Cabinet," *Boston Daily Globe*, January 18, 1919, 2; "Paderewski Forms New Polish Cabinet, Reaches Agreement with Gen. Pilsudski," *New York Times*, January 18, 1919, 3.

83. Pilsudski, Warsaw, to Kazimierz Dłuski, Paris, January 17, 1919, in *Kwartalnik Historyczny* 65, no. 4 (1958): 1151.

84. Ibid., 1154.

85. Quotation from Titus Komarnicki, *Rebirth of the Polish Republic: A Study in the Diplomatic History of Europe, 1914–1920* (London: William Heinemann, 1957), 262.

86. Edward House, Paris, to President Woodrow Wilson, January 21, 1919, in *Intimate Papers of Colonel House*, 4:264.

87. James Headlam-Morley, Paris, memorandum of interview with Mr. Posner, January 22, 1919, in J. Headlam-Morley, *A Memoir of the Paris Peace Conference 1919*, ed. Agnes Headlam-Morley, Russell Bryant, and Anna Cienciala (London: Methuen and Co., 1972), 11.

88. James Headlam-Morley, Paris, to Lewis Namier, January 24, 1919, in Headlam-Morley, *A Memoir*, 13.

89. "Poles Here Demand Complete Freedom, 8,000 at Meeting Ask for Recognition of Paderewski's Government," *New York Times*, January 27, 1919, 7.

90. "Poles Practically United," *New York Times*, January 30, 1919, 2; *Kalendarium*, 2:168; Wacław Jędrzejewicz, *Pilsudski: A Life for Poland* (New York: Hippocrene Books, 1982), 80.

91. [Pilsudski], Warsaw, undated letter to Roman Dmowski, Paris, written between January 22 and January 26, 1919, reprinted in *Niepodległość* 7 (1962): 12.

92. Pilsudski interview in *Il Secolo* (Genoa), February 1, 1919, in *PZ*, 10:179–177.

93. "Piłsudczycy," *Rząd i Wojsko* (Warsaw), January 26, 1919, 1–2.

94. Table 3 in Antony Polonsky, "The Emergence of an Independent Polish State," in *The History of Poland since 1863*, ed. R. F. Leslie (New York: Cambridge University Press, 1980), 132; Andrzej Nowak, *Niepodległa! 1864–1924: Jak Polacy odzyskali ojczyznę* (Kraków: Biały Kruk Sp., 2018), 253; Szymon Rudnicki, *Żydzi w parlamencie II Rzeczpospolitej*, 2nd ed. (Warsaw: Wydawnictwo Sejmowe, 2015), 37;

Przemysław Hauser, *Przedstawiciele mniejszości niemieckiej w parlamencie II Rzec-zypospolitej* (Warsaw: Wydawnictwo Sejmowe, 2014), 29; Winson Chu, *The German Minority in Interwar Poland* (Cambridge: Cambridge University Press, 2012), 123.

95. Alexandra Pilsudska, *Pilsudski: A Biography by His Wife* (New York: Dodd, Mead, 1941), 282.

96. Ibid.

97. Wincentry Witos, *Moje wspomnienia* (Paris: Instytut Literacki, 1964), 2:242.

98. Diary entry of February 10, 1919, Warsaw, in Grove, *War's Aftermath,* 109.

99. Pilsudski, speech to the Legislative Sejm, February 10, 1919, in *PZ,* 5:55.

100. Ibid., 56–57.

101. The chant is recorded in the minutes: *Sprawozdanie stenograficzne z 1. posiedzenia Sejmu Ustawodawczego z dnia 10 lutego 1919* (Warsaw: Sejm, 1919): 3.

102. That boisterous applause is noted in the minutes of the speech: ibid. Also see *PZ,* 5:56.

103. Diary entry of February 10, 1919, Warsaw, in Grove, *War's Aftermath,* 109; Witos, *Moje wspomnienia,* 2:243.

104. Witos, *Moje wspomnienia,* 2:244; Wojciechowski, *Moje wspomnienia,* 2:17–18; "The Armistice and Poland," *Times* (London), February 21, 1919, 9 (Warsaw dispatch dated February 14, 1919).

105. *Le Matin* (Paris), February 19, 1919, in *PZ,* 5:58–59.

106. Dinner toast, Belvedere Palace, Warsaw, February 18, 1919, in *PZ,* 5:57–58.

107. Pilsudski's speech to the Legislative Sejm, February 20, 1919, in *PZ,* 5:60–61; minutes of the Legislative Sejm's 3rd session (*Sprawozdanie stenograficzne z 3. posiedzenia Sejmu Ustawodawczego z dnia 20 lutego 1919* [Warsaw: Sejm, 1919], 4). The speech appeared in print the following day as "Deklaracja Piłsudskiego," *Gazeta Warszawska,* February 21, 1919, 4.

108. Resolution of the Legislative Sejm on the reinstatement of Pilsudski to the position of head of state, February 20, 1919, reprinted in *Źródła do dziejów II Rzec-zypospolitej,* ed. J. Piłatowicz, D. Sowińska, and A. Zawadzki (Siedlce: Instytut His-torii i Stosunków Międzynarodowych, 2014), 1:59; for an English translation, see Bernadette E. Schmitt, ed., *Poland* (Berkeley: University of California Press, 1945), 91–92. The text also appeared in *Gazeta Warszawska,* February 21, 1919, 3–4, as well as in the official minutes of the 3rd session of the Legislative Sejm for February 20, 1919.

109. *Sprawozdanie stenograficzne z 3. posiedzenia Sejmu9,* 5.

110. Pilsudski, address to the Legislative Sejm, February 20, 1919, in *PZ,* 5:62–63.

111. "Pilsudski Returns Power: But Authority as Chief of State Is Re-conferred on Him by Diet's Assembly," *New York Times,* February 22, 1919, 2.

112. Grove, *War's Aftermath,* 197.

113. Piotr Wandycz, *Polish-Soviet Relations, 1917–1921* (Cambridge, MA: Har-vard University Press, 1969), 75.

114. Wojciechowski, *Moje wspomnienia,* 2:19.

14. The State Builder

Epigraph: Pilsudski, interview in *L'Écho de Paris,* February 12, 1920, quotation from M. K. Dziewanowski, *Joseph Pilsudski: A European Federalist* (Stanford, CA: Hoover Institution Press, 1969), 285.

1. Harold H. Fisher, *America and the New Poland* (New York: Macmillan, 1928), xxiii.

2. Roman Debicki, *Foreign Policy of Poland, 1919–1939* (London: Pall Mall Press, 1962), 19; Edward M. House, *The Intimate Papers of Colonel House,* ed. Charles Seymour (Boston: Houghton Mifflin, 1925), 4:264n1.

3. Esmé Howard, *Theatre of Life: Life Seen from the Stalls, 1905–1936* (London: Hodder and Stoughton, 1936), 312.

4. Esmé Howard, diary entry of February 14, 1919, Warsaw, ibid., 321–322.

5. Ibid., 333.

6. Carton de Wiart, *Happy Odyssey: The Memoirs of Lieutenant-General Sir Adrian Carton de Wiart* (London: Jonathan Cape, 1950), 95.

7. Diary entry of July 14, 1919, Warsaw, in Arthur Goodhart, *Poland and the Minority Races* (London: G. Allen and Unwin, 1920), 19–20.

8. Interview with Pilsudski in *Il Secolo* (The Century), February 1, 1919, in *PZ,* 10:177.

9. Ibid., 179.

10. Ibid., 178.

11. Eugène Pralon, Warsaw, report on conversation with Pilsudski, May 31, 1919, in *Documents on British Foreign Policy, 1919–1936,* 1st ser. (London: H.M. Stationery Office, 1949), 3:342–343.

12. Interview with Pilsudski, Belvedere Palace (Warsaw), February 7, 1919, in W. Baranowski, *Rozmowy z Piłsudskim, 1916–1931* (1938; repr., Warsaw: Zebra, 1990), 64.

13. Jerzy Borzęcki, "Piłsudski's Unorthodox Capture of Wilno in Spring 1919: Risk-Taking, Good Fortune, and Myth-Making," *Journal of Slavic Military Studies* 28 (2015): 138; Antoni Czubiński, *Walka o granice wschodnie polski w latach 1918–1921* (Opole: Instytut Śląski w Opolu, 1993), 81; M. B. Biskupski, *The History of Poland,* 2nd ed. (Santa Barbara, CA: Greenwood Press, 2018), 70.

14. Czubiński, *Walka o granice wschodnie polski,* 81.

15. Pilsudski's address in Grodno, June 1, 1919, in *PZ,* 10:179.

16. Pilsudski's talk to military leaders, March 6, 1919, Warsaw, quotation from Bogusław Miedziński, "Wspomnienia," *Zeszyty Historyczne* (Paris) 36 (1976): 201.

17. Pilsudski, Warsaw, to Prime Minister George Clemenceau, Paris, March 7, 1919, in *PZ,* 5:64–65.

18. "La vie, les prisons, les combats du géneral Pilsudski, president de la République polonaise," *Le Petit Parisien* (Paris), March 23, 1919, 1 (interview dated March 19, 1919).

19. Ibid.

20. Pilsudski, Warsaw, to Leon Wasilewski, Paris, April 8, 1919, in *PZ*, 5:73.

21. Borzęcki, "Piłsudski's Unorthodox Capture of Wilno," 147.

22. Michał Romer, notes on meeting with Pilsudski, April 6, 1919, quotation from Andrzej Nowak, "Reborn Poland or Reconstructed Empire? Questions on the Course and Results of Polish Eastern Policy, 1918–1921," *Lithuanian Historical Studies* 13 (2008): 140.

23. Jozef Pilsudski, Vilna, April 22, 1919, in *PZ*, 5:75–76.

24. Pilsudski, lecture presented at the Stefan Baroty University in Vilna, August 16, 1923, in *PZ*, 6:103, quotation from Borzęcki, "Pilsudski's Unorthodox Capture of Wilno," 137n21.

25. Czubiński, *Walka o granice wschodnie*, 82.

26. Pilsudski, Vilna, to Gen. Józef Haller, Leszno, April 21, 1919, in *PZ*, 5:74.

27. *Documents on British Foreign Policy*, 1st ser., 3:327n4.

28. Telegram from British commissioner in Warsaw to Mr. Balfour, London, July 25, 1919, in *Documents on British Foreign Policy*, 1st ser., 1:239–249; Czubiński, *Walka o granice wschodnie*, 107; "Polish Army Joins with Rumanian Line," *Boston Daily Globe*, June 4, 1919, 2.

29. Czubiński, *Walka o granice wschodnie*, 107; Andrzej Chwalba, *1919: Pierwszy Rok Wolności* (Wołomiec: Wydawnictwo Czarne, 2019), 272; Andrzej Chwalba, *Przegrane Zwycięstwo. Wojna polsko-bolszewicka 1918–1920* (Wołoniec: Wydawnictwo Czarne, 2020), 38; *Kalendarium*, 2:218, 224.

30. J. Pilsudski, order to the 5th Polish Rifle Division (Siberian), November 19, 1919, in *PZ*, 5:119; Chwalba, *Przegrane Zwycięstwo*, 38; "Kazimierz Rumsza (1886–1870)," *Polski Słownik Biograficzny* 33 (1991–1992): 95–96; *Kalendarium*, 2:285.

31. William W. Hagen, *Anti-Jewish Violence in Poland, 1914–1920* (Cambridge: Cambridge University Press, 2018), 325–326; Antony Polonsky, *The Jews in Poland and Russia* (Oxford: Littman Library of Jewish Civilization, 2012), 3:45; "Jews Massacred, Robbed by Poles," *New York Times*, May 26, 1919, 1.

32. David Engel, "What's in a Pogrom? European Jews in the Age of Violence," in *Anti-Jewish Violence: Rethinking the Pogrom in East European History*, ed. J. Dekel-Chen, D. Gaunt, N. Meir, and I. Bartal (Bloomington: Indiana University Press), 33.

33. H. N. Brailsford, letter to the editor from Pinsk dated May 21, 1919, in *Times* (London), May 23, 1919, 8.

34. Szymon Rudnicki, "The Vilna Pogrom of 19–12 April 1919," *Polin* 33 (2021): 490; Polonsky, *Jews in Poland and Russia*, 3:46.

35. Minister in Poland, Warsaw, to the Acting US Secretary of State, June 17, 1919, in *Papers Relating to the Foreign Relations of the United States, 1919: The Paris Peace Conference* (Washington, DC: US Government Printing Office, 1942) (hereafter cited as *The Paris Peace Conference*), 2:767–768.

36. H. N. Brailsford, letter to the editor, *Times* (London), May 23, 1919, 8.

37. *New York Times*, March 5, 1919, 6.

38. Israel Cohen, diary entry of January 23, 1919, Warsaw, in Israel Cohen, *Travels in Jewry* (New York: Dutton, 1953), 73.

39. "Further Outbreaks in Galicia and Poland," *Jewish Chronicle* (London), May 23, 1919, 8.

40. Hugh Gibson, Warsaw, to Mr. Lansing [US secretary of state], May 31, 1919, in *The Paris Peace Conference*, 2:752. This telegram also appears in *With Firmness in the Right: American Diplomatic Action Affecting Jews, 1840–1945*, ed. Cyrus Adler and Aaron M. Margalith (New York: American Jewish Committee, 1946), 157.

41. "Poland Promises to Protect Jews: American Minister Assured of Strong Measures to Prevent Persecution," *New York Times*, June 4, 1919, 8.

42. Henry Morgenthau, *All in a Life-Time* (New York: Doubleday, Page, 1925), 360; Polonsky, *Jews in Poland and Russia*, 3:47–48.

43. Morgenthau, *All in a Life-Time*, 375–376.

44. "Declaration of the Polish and Czechoslovak Delegates to the Conference of Spa with regard to the Question of Teschen in Silesia," July 10, 1920, and "Resolution of the Spa Conference on July 11, 1920," both reprinted in *Plebiscites since the World War with a Collection of Official Documents*, ed. Sarah Wambaugh (Washington, DC: Carnegie Endowment for International Peace, 1933), 2:122–125.

45. Hagen, *Anti-Jewish Violence*, 360.

46. "Mission of the United States to Poland: Henry Morgenthau, Sr.'s Report, October 3, 1919," in Morgenthau, *All in a Life-Time*, 415.

47. "Will Outline Plans to Aid Pilsudski, Polish Convention Opens Here Today," *Boston Daily Globe*, July 4, 1919, 8.

48. Jozef Pilsudski, *Year 1920 and Its Climax: Battle of Warsaw during the Polish-Soviet War, 1919–1920* (1924; New York: PIA, 1972), 200–201.

49. Wiart, *Happy Odyssey*, 118–119.

50. Adam Ulam, *Expansion and Coexistence: The History of Soviet Foreign Policy, 1917–1973*, 2nd ed. (New York: Holt, Rinehart and Winston, 1974), 106.

51. Quotation from Andrzej Nowak, *Polska i Trzy Rosje: Studium polityki wschodniej Józefa Piłsudskiego do kwietnia 1920 roku*, 3rd ed. (Kraków: Arcana, 2015), 402.

52. Quotation from Dmitry Merezhkovsky, *Joseph Pilsudski*, trans. Harriet E. Kennedy (London: Sampson Low, 1921), 9–10.

53. Pilsudski, address given in Minsk, September 19, 1919, in *PZ*, 5:107.

54. Pilsudski, speech on the occasion of the opening of Vilna University, Vilna, October 12, 1919, in *PZ*, 5:111–112.

55. Piotr Wandycz, *Soviet-Polish Relations, 1917–1921* (Cambridge, MA: Harvard University Press, 1969), 139–140.

56. For the transcripts of these intercepts, see Grzegorz Nowik, *Zanim złamano "Enigmę": Polski radiowywiad podczas wojny z bolszewicką Rosją, 1918–1920*, vol. 1 (Warsaw: Rytm, 2004).

57. *Kalendarium*, 2:286–287.

58. Jędrzejewicz, *Pilsudski,* 94–95.

59. Andrzej Nowak, *Pierwsza zdrada Zachodu: 1920—Zapomniany appease-ment* (Kraków: Wydawnictwo Literackie, 2015), 150–151; Nowak, "Reborn Poland or Reconstructed Empire?," 141; Alfred Senn, *The Great Powers, Lithuania, and the Vilna Question, 1920–1928* (Leiden: E.J. Brill, 1966), 20.

60. Piotr Łossowski, "Próba przewrotu polskiego w Kownie w sierpniu 1919 r.," *Najnowsze Dzieje Polski, 1914–1939* 8 (1964): 67; Łossowswki, *Konflikt polsko-litewski, 1918–1920* (Warsaw: Kisążka i Wiedza, 1995), 79; Andrzej Nowak, *Niepodległa! 1864–1924: Jak Polacy odzyskali ojczyznę* (Kraków: Biały Kruk Sp., 2018), 274; Marian M. Drozdowski, ed., *Kronika narodzin II Rzeczypospolitej, 1914–1923* (Warsaw: Bellona, 2018), 511; *Kalendarium,* 2:269–270; Dziewanowski, *Joseph Pilsudski,* 167–168.

61. See Pilsudski's statements in "Poland Now Fears Bolshevist Invasion," *New York Times,* August 14, 1919, 3.

62. Report by Boris Shaposhnikov, January 27, 1920, to Leon Trotsky, in Nowak, *Polska i Trzy Rosje,* 502–508; Andrzej Nowak, *History of Geopolitics* (Warsaw: Polish Institute of International Affairs, 2008), 163–164; Nowak, "Rok 1920: Pierwszy plan ofensywy sowieckiej przeciw Polsce," *Niepodległość* 49 (1997): 7–19.

63. Magocsi, *A History of Ukraine: The Land and Its Peoples,* 2nd ed. (Toronto: University of Toronto Press, 2010), 534. For the full text of the two agreements between Petliura and Pilsudski's delegation, see Michael Palij, *The Ukrainian-Polish Defensive Alliance, 1919–1921* (Toronto: Canadian Institute of Ukrainian Studies, 1995), 70–75.

64. Pilsudski, Żytomir, to Prime Minister Skulski, Warsaw, April 26, 1920, *Niepodległość* 7 (1962): 87.

65. Jozef Pilsudski, commander in chief of the Polish Army, proclamation to the inhabitants of Ukraine, April 26, 1920, in *PZ,* 5:156. The proclamation first appeared in Warsaw's official government paper: *Monitor Polski* (Warsaw), April 28, 1920, 2. For an English translation, see Stephan Horak, *Poland's International Affairs, 1919–1960* (Bloomington: Indiana University Press, 1964), 233–234.

66. Diary entry for April 28, 1920, in Kazimierz Sokołowski, *Dziennik 1920* (Toruń: Wydawnictwo Naukowe Uniwersytetu Mikołaja Kopernika, 2018), 194–196.

67. Lt.-Col. Elbert E. Farman, Warsaw, May 17, 1920, in Janusz Cisek, ed., *American Reports on the Polish-Bolshevik War, 1919–1920* (Warsaw: Wojkowe Centrum Edukacji Obywatelskiej, 2010), 128.

68. Dziewanowski, *Joseph Pilsudski,* 284.

69. Pilsudski, interview in *L'Écho de Paris,* February 12, 1920, quotation from Dziewanowski, *Joseph Pilsudski,* 285. For the original text, see *PZ,* 5:145–147.

70. Quotation from Janusz Cisek, "Pilsudski's Federalism," in *Wilsonian East Central Europe,* ed. John Micgiel (New York: PIA, 1995), 48.

71. Polish Ministry of Foreign Affairs, April 26, 1920, reprinted in Horak, *Poland's International Affairs*, 234–235.

72. J. Pilsudski, telegram to Petliua, May 6, 1920, in *PZ*, 5:157.

73. Pilsudski, order of May 8, 1920, quotation from Dziewanowski, *Joseph Pilsudski*, 285.

74. Pilsudski to the prime minister, May 1, 1920, *Niepodległość* 7 (1962): 102.

75. Diary entry of May 9, 1920, in Sokołowski, *Dziennik 1920*, 209.

76. Pilsudski, address dated May 17, 1920, in *PZ*, 5:158–159.

77. Wojciech Trąmpczyński, Warsaw, speech at the parliamentary session, May 18, 1920, quotation from W. F. Reddaway, *Marshal Pilsudski* (London: George Routledge, 1939), 131. For the quotations in the original, see *Kalendarium*, 2:355.

78. *Gazeta Warszawska*, April 27, 1920, quotation from Palij, *Ukrainian-Polish Defensive Alliance*, 77.

79. Jan Moffat, US Legation in Warsaw, to Hugh Gibson, Washington, May 29, 1920, in Cisek, *American Reports*, 143.

80. *Kalendarium*, 2:360–361; "Great Red Drive on Polish Front," *New York Times*, June 4, 1920, 1; "Poles Wipe Out Two Red Divisions," *New York Times*, June 10, 1920, 13.

81. Czubiński, *Walka o granice wschodnie*, 181; *Kalendarium*, 2:362; Lech Wyszczelski, *Wyprawa kijowska Piłsudskiego, 1920* (Warsaw: Bellona, 2015), 213; Adam Zamoyski, *Warsaw 1920: Lenin's Failed Conquest of Europe* (London: Harper Press, 2008), 47; "Kieff Retaken by the Reds, Polish Lines Cut," *Times* (London), June 14, 1920, 14; Serhii Plokhy, *The Gates of Europe: A History of Ukraine* (New York: Basic Books, 2015), 211.

82. *Kalendarium*, 2:368.

83. Quotation from Zamoyski, *Warsaw 1920*, 53.

84. J. Pilsudski, Warsaw, "Obywatele Rzeczypospolitej!," July 3, 1920, CBW, DU-577. On the creation of the ROP, see Nowak, *Niepodległa!*, 296; *Kalendarium*, 2:374; and "Defense Council Formed in Poland," *New York Times*, July 16, 1920, 12.

85. Quotation from *Kalendarium*, 2:379.

86. Jay Moffat, Warsaw, to Hugh Gibson, Washington, July 20, 1920, in Cisek, *American Reports*, 209.

87. *Kalendarium*, 2:382; Nowak, *Niepodległa!*, 304.

88. Maxime Weygand, *Mémoires*, vol. 2 (Paris: Flammerion, 1952), quotation from *Kalendarium*, 2:383.

89. Diary entry of June 29, 1920, Warsaw, in Vincent D'Abernon, *The Eighteenth Decisive Battle of the World: Warsaw, 1920* (London: Hodder and Stoughton, 1931), 38–39.

90. "Aid for Poland: Anglo-French Mission's Proposals," *Times* (London), July 30, 1920, 12.

91. "Fate of Warsaw in the Balance," *New York Times*, August 10, 1920, 1. The figure of six hundred French officers serving in Poland is confirmed in the minutes

of the Anglo-French Conference held in London on August 8–9, 1920. See *Documents on British Foreign Policy,* 1st ser., 8:738.

92. Julian Marchlewski, Manifesto to Polish Workers and Peasants, Białystok, July 30, 1920, in *Polonia restituta: O niepodległość i granice, 1914–1912,* ed. Jolanta Niklewska (Warsaw: Muzeum Niepodległości, 2007), 97.

93. "Red Advance on Warsaw," *Times* (London), August 2, 1920, 8.

94. For the original document, sometimes referred to as the Wieprz Offensive, see Gen. Rozwadowski, Chief of the General Staff, Order no. 8358/III, August 6, 1920, Papers of Gen. Tadeusz Rozwadowski, PIA, RG 701/3/3, folder 40, fols. 382–386. On authorship and cooperation with Pilsudski on the battle plan, see Nowak, *Niepodległa!,* 307; and *Kalendarium,* 2:390.

95. Gen. Weygand, Warsaw, to Marshal Foch, Paris, August 6, 1920, quotation from *Kalendarium,* 2:390.

96. Wincentry Witos, *Moje wspomnienia* (Paris: Instytut Literacki, 1964), 2:289.

97. Alexandra Pilsudska, *Pilsudski: A Biography by His Wife* (New York: Dodd, Mead, 1941), 301.

98. Weygand, *Mémoires,* 2:145.

99. Quotation from "Polish Appeal to the World: Nation Prepared to Die for Freedom," *Times* (London), August 11, 1920, 9.

100. "Movement Begun to Oust Pilsudski," *New York Times,* August 16, 1920, 1 (from an August 14 cable).

101. J. Pilsudski, "Ludu Polski!," August 18, 1920, Warsaw, reprinted in *Bitwa warszawska 13–28 VIII 1920: Dokumenty operacyjne,* ed. Marek Tarczyński (Warsaw: Rytm, 1995), 2:77.

102. "Poles Thrust Reds Back from Warsaw: Pilsudski Leads Brilliant and Successful Counter-Offensive," *Boston Daily Globe,* August 18, 1920, 1.

103. Wincenty Witos, statement dated August 25, 1920, quotation from Wandycz, *Soviet-Polish Relations,* 242. Also see "Poles, Warned by Wilson, Won't Invade," *New York Times,* August 24, 1920, 1; and "American Policy Restrains Poland: Pilsudski to Stop Armies at Russian Boundary," *Boston Daily Globe,* August 24, 1920, 8.

104. Zamoyski, *Warsaw 1920,* 110.

105. Nowak, *Niepodległa!,* 315; Zamoyski, *Warsaw 1920,* 110.

106. Andrzej Garlicki, *Józef Piłsudski* (1990; London: Scolar Press, 1995), 103–104.

107. Theodore R. Weeks, *Vilnius between Nations, 1795–2000* (DeKalb: Northern Illinois University Press, 2016), 97; *Kalendarium,* 3:103.

108. Weeks, *Vilnius between Nations,* 115, 119.

109. Pilsudski, announcement presented in Vilna, April 18, 1922, in *PZ,* 5:236; Pilsudski, address in Vilna, April 20, 1922, in *PZ,* 5:236–240.

110. Jozef Pilsudski, "Rozkaz na Zakończenie Wojny," October 18, 1920, in *PZ,* 5:175–176.

111. Jerzy Borzęcki, *The Soviet-Polish Peace of 1921 and the Creation of Interwar Europe* (New Haven, CT: Yale University Press, 2008), 277.

112. Gen. Kazimierz Sosnkowski, Order of August 16, 1920. I am grateful to Prof. Szymon Rudnicki for providing me with a copy of this order.

113. Jerzy Tomaszewski, "Polski formacje zbrojne wobec Żydów," in *Żydzi w obronie Rzeczypospolitej*, ed. Jerzy Tomaszewski (Warsaw: Cyklady, 1996), 106.

114. Jewish Parliamentary Club, August 16, 1920, to the minister of military affairs, reprinted in *Inwazja bolszewicka a Żydzi: Zbiór dokumentów*, vol. 1 (Warsaw: Narodowy Klub Żydowski Posłów Sejmowych, 1921), 131.

115. Jewish Parliamentary Club, August 19, 1920, to the minister of military affairs, in *Inwazja bolszewicka a Żydzi*, 1:132.

116. Pilsudski, interview on August 26, 1920, *Kurier Poranny*, August 29, 1920, in *PZ*, 5:167.

117. "Zagadka Jabłonny," *Naród*, September 1, 1920, 4–5.

118. "W sprawie obozu w Jabłonnie," *Kurier Poranny*, September 10, 1920, 3.

119. Minutes of the 180th session of the Polish parliament, Warsaw, October 29, 1920 ("Sprawozdanie stenograficzne z 180 posiedzenia Sejmu Ustawodawczego z dnia 29 października 1920 r" [Warsaw: Sejm], 18).

120. Lord D'Abernon, interview in *Gazeta Polska* (Warsaw), August 17, 1930, quotation from Robert Machray, *Poland, 1914–1931* (London: G. Allen and Unwin, 1932), 165.

121. Norman Davies, *White Eagle, Red Star: The Polish-Soviet War, 1919–1920* (New York: St Martin's Press, 1972), 265.

122. "Warsaw 1920," in Simon Goodenough, *Tactical Genius in Battle* (Oxford: Phaidon Press, 1979), 61–66.

123. General Weygand, interview in *L'Information* (Paris), August 21, 1920, quotation from Piotr Wandycz, *France and Her Eastern Allies, 1919–1926* (Minneapolis: University of Minnesota Press, 1962), 173. The interview was reprinted in English translation in *The Illustrated London News*, August 28, 1920, 319; Quotation of memoirs from Weygand, *Mémoires*, 2:166.

15. From the First Years of Peace to the 1926 Coup

Epigraph: Pilsudski, luncheon address, Paris, February 3, 1921, in *PZ*, 5:186.

1. "Pilsudski pierwszym marszałkiem Polski: Lwów, 19 marca," *Kurier Lwowski*, March 21, 1920, 2; M. B. Biskupski, *Independence Day: Myth, Symbol and the Creation of Modern Poland* (Oxford: Oxford University Press, 2012), 39.

2. *PZ*, 5:180.

3. Text of decree as reprinted in "Dekret Wodza Naczelnego o organizacji Naczelnych Władz Wojskowych," January 7, 1921, in *PZ*, vol. 8 supplement, iii–ix.

4. *Kalendarium*, 3:11–12.

5. Ibid., 12; "Marshal Pilsudski in Paris," *Times* (London), February 4, 1921, 9.

6. W. Baranowski, Paris, conversations with Pilsudski, February 3–6, 1921, in Baranowski, *Rozmowy z Pilsudskim, 1916–1931* (1938; repr., Warsaw: Zebra, 1990), 83.

7. Pilsudski, Paris, luncheon address, February 3, 1921, in *PZ*, 5:186.

8. Pilsudski, speech at Paris City Hall, February 5, 1921, in *PZ*, 5:188–189.

9. "Political Agreement between France and Poland on February 19, 1921," in *Poland's International Affairs, 1919–1960*, ed. Stephan Horak (Bloomington: Indiana University Press, 1964), 149–150; "Franco-Polish Accord Signed Feb. 19," *New York Times*, February 22, 1921, 13; *Kalendarium*, 3:21–22.

10. For the text of Pilsudski's addresses at these ceremonies, see *PZ*, 5:189–190; and "French-Polish Entente," *Times* (London), February 7, 1921, 9.

11. *Kalendarium*, 3:25.

12. Joseph Rothschild, "The Ideological, Political, and Economic Background of Pilsudski's Coup d'État of 1926," *Political Science Quarterly* 78, no. 2 (June 1963): 228; Joseph Rothschild, *Pilsudski's Coup d'État* (New York: Columbia University Press, 1926): 7.

13. *Polish Constitution of 1921*, sec. III, art. 43, http://libr.sejm.gov.pl/teko1/txt/kpol/e1921.html. For the full text, see H. Lee McBain and L. Rogers, *The New Constitutions of Europe* (New York: Doubleday, 1922), 405–425.

14. Wincenty Witos, *Moje wspomnienia* (Paris: Instytut Literacki, 1964), 2:410.

15. *The Treaty of Versailles and After: Annotations of the Text of the Treaty* ed. Denys P. Myers (Washington, D.C.: United States Government Printing Office, 1947), 213. Also see Andrzej Nowak, *Niepodległa! 1864–1924: Jak Polacy odzyskali ojczyznę* (Kraków: Biały Kruk Sp., 2018), 326; M. B. Biskupski, *The History of Poland*, 2nd ed. (Santa Barbara, CA: Greenwood Press, 2018), 76n6.

16. "Marshal Pilsudski's Regrets," *Times* (London), May 16, 1921, 8.

17. Pilsudski, speech at the Jagiellonian University, April 29, 1921, in *PZ*, 5:199.

18. J. Pilsudski, Commander in Chief and First Marshall of Poland, address on the occasion of the 100th anniversary of Napoleon's death, April 29, 1921, in *PZ*, 5:207–208.

19. *Kalendarium*, 3:43–44.

20. Pilsudski, speech in Toruń, June 5, 1921, quotation from Alexandra Pilsudska, *Pilsudski: A Biography by His Wife* (New York: Dodd, Mead, 1941), 306.

21. On Skirmunt's foreign policy circulars, see Piotr Wandycz, "The Foreign Policy of the Second Republic, 1921–1932," in *Reflections on Polish Foreign Policy*, ed. John Micgiel (New York: Columbia University Press, 2007), 27–28.

22. Włodzimierz Suleja, *Józef Piłsudski* (Wrocław: Zakład Narodowy im. Ossolińskch, 1995), 255–256; "New Polish Cabinet," *Times* (London), September 22, 1921, 9.

23. "Tries to Assassinate President Pilsudski," *New York Times*, September 27, 1921, 18.

24. "Polish Cabinet Crisis: The Chief of State's Powers Defined," *Times* (London), June 19, 1922, 7.

25. *Kalendarium*, 3:115–116.

26. Pilsudski, Warsaw, to Sejm speaker, July 14, 1922, in *PZ*, 5:258; "Pilsudski Offers Resignation to Diet: Korfanty insists on Forming Polish Government despite President's Stand," *New York Times*, July 16, 1922, 19; "Pilsudski Rejects New Cabinet," *New York Times*, July 21, 1922, 27.

27. *Kalendarium*, 3:114–117; Robert Machray, *Poland, 1914–1931* (London: G. Allen and Unwin, 1932), 158.

28. Stanisław Wojciechowski, *Moje wspomnienia* (1938; repr., Warsaw: Muzeum Historii Polski, 2017), 2:207; *Kalendarium*, 3:115–116; Antony Polonsky, *Politics in Independent Poland, 1921–1939* (Oxford: Oxford University Press, 1972), 105.

29. Szymon Rudnicki, *Żydzi w parlamencie II Rzeczypospolitej*, 2nd ed. (Warsaw: Wydawn. Sejmowe, 2015), 193.

30. Garlicki, *Józef Piłsudski, 1867–1935* (Warsaw: Czytelnik, 1990), 243–244; *Kalendarium*, 3:119–120.

31. Garlicki, *Józef Piłsudski*, 246–247.

32. Pilsudski, Kraków, speech to the convention of the Union of Polish Legionnaires, August 5, 1922, in *PZ*, 5:273.

33. Pilsudski, September 16, 1922, conversation with W. Baranowski, Ploieşti (Romania), in Baranowski, *Rozmowy*, 89–90.

34. Antony Polonsky, "The Emergence of an Independent Polish State," in *The History of Poland since 1863*, ed. R. F. Leslie (Cambridge: Cambridge University Press, 1980), 150–153; Garlicki, *Józef Piłsudski*, 247. For a list of Jewish members of the new Sejm, see Rudnicki, *Żydzi w parlamenciej*, 493–495.

35. *Pierwszy Powszechny Spis Rzeczypospolitej Polskiej z dnia 30 września 1921 roku* (Warsaw: Nakładem Głównego Urzędu Statystycznego Skład Główny, 1927).

36. Pilsudski, address to the Sejm, November 28, 1922, in *PZ*, 5:283–284.

37. Pilsudski, address to the Council of Ministers, Warsaw, December 4, 1922, in *PZ*, 5:295–296.

38. August Zaleski unpublished memoirs (n.d.), August Zaleski Papers, box 14, folder 1, pp. 169–170, Hoover Institution Archives, Stanford. The memoir, written in English, was published in an abridged Polish translation that does not include the passages quoted here. See August Zaleski, *Wspomnienia*, trans. Elżbieta Gołębiowska (Warsaw: Polski Instytut Spraw Międzynarodowych, 2017).

39. *Kalendarium*, 3:154–155.

40. Pilsudska, *Pilsudski*, 310.

41. Quotation from ibid., 311.

42. Pilsudski, "Wspomnienia o Gabrielu Narutowiczu," July 1923, in *PZ*, 6:58.

43. Rudnicki, *Żydzi w parlamencie*, 193; Stefan Arski, *My pierwsza brygada* (Warsaw: Czytelnik, 1963), 349.

44. On this press campaign, see Paul Brykczynski, *Primed for Violence: Murder, Antisemitism, and Democratic Politics in Interwar Poland* (Madison: University of Wisconsin Press, 2016), 83; Richard M. Watt, *Bitter Glory: Poland and Its Fate, 1918–1939* (New York: Simon and Schuster, 1979), 192; and Piotr Wandycz, "Śmierć prezydenta," *Tygodnik Powszechny,* November 4, 1990, 2.

45. *Gazeta Poranna* (Warsaw), December 10, 1922, quotation from Polonsky, *Politics in Independent Poland,* 105.

46. *Gazeta Warszawska,* December 10, 1922, quotation from Polonsky, *Politics in Independent Poland,* 105. For an extended discussion of the anti-Jewish motif in the campaign against Narutowicz, see Brykczynski, *Primed for Violence,* 18–28.

47. M. Rataj, *Pamiętniki* (Warsaw: Ludowa Spółdzielnia Wydawnictwa, 1965), quotation from Polonsky, *Politics in Independent Poland,* 111.

48. Quotation from Watt, *Bitter Glory,* 192.

49. Quotation from Brykczynski, *Primed for Violence,* 115.

50. Quotation from ibid., 119.

51. Pilsudski, interview with *Kurier Polski,* December 31, 1922, in *PZ,* 6:7.

52. "Prawda i dykteryjki," *Gazeta Warszawska,* January 4, 1923, quotation from Brykczynski, *Primed for Violence,* 123. The Warsaw daily of the National Democrats, as well as the party's regional organs, printed the entire speech. See "Sprawa E. Niewiadomskiego," *Gazeta Warszawska,* 1 January 1923, 1–3; "Proces Eligiusza Niewiadomskiego," *Kurjer Poznański,* 3 January 1923, 2–5.

53. Adolf Nowaczyński, "Testament," *Myśl Narodowa,* January 6, 1923, quotation from Brykczynski, *Primed for Violence,* 123–124.

54. Quotation from Watt, *Bitter Glory,* 195; and Brykczynski, *Primed for Violence,* 125. On the assassin's family, including a twenty-two-year-old son and a twenty-year-old daughter, see "Niewiadomski Eligiusz," *Polski Słownik Biograficzny* 23 (1978).

55. Zygmunt Wasilewski, "Ś.p. Eligiusz Niewiadomski," *Gazeta Warszawska,* January 30, 1923, quotation from Brykczynski, *Primed for Violence,* 126.

56. "Na grobie ś.p. E. Niewiadomskiego," *Gazeta Warszawska,* February 6, 1923, quotation from Brykczynski, *Primed for Violence,* 127; "Niewiadomski Eligiusz," *Polski Słownik Biograficzny* 23 (1978).

57. "Niewiadomski Eligiusz," *Polski Słownik Biograficzny* 23 (1978).

58. Poznań district court prosecutor, February 21, 1923, motion against bookshop owner; and police report dated February 13, 1923, on church activities in honor of Niewiadomski. From the collection of Dr. Maciej Moszyński, provided with permission to the author. I am grateful to Izabela Wagner for providing these documents.

59. Izabela Wagner, *Bauman: A Biography* (Cambridge: Polity Press, 2020), 411n10.

60. W. F. Reddaway, *Marshal Pilsudski* (London: George Routledge and Sons, 1939), 171.

61. Jędrzejewicz, *Pilsudski,* 170.

62. Watt, *Bitter Glory,* 195.

63. Polonsky, *Politics in Independent Poland,* 115–116.

64. "Decision of the Conference of Ambassadors, March 15, 1923," in Horak, *Poland's International Affairs,* 238–240; J. Lukowski and H. Zawadzki, *A Concise History of Poland,* 3rd ed. (Cambridge: Cambridge University Press, 2018), 297.

65. Pilsudska, *Pilsudski,* 318.

66. Pilsudski, address, June 13, 1923, in *PZ,* 6:19.

67. Pilsudski, interview with Romanian paper *Adverul,* mid-June 1923, in *PZ,* 6:21–22.

68. Pilsudski, banquet speech, Bristol Hotel (Warsaw), July 3, 1923, in *PZ,* 6:24–35, from the English translation in Andrzej Garlicki, *Józef Pilsudski 1867–1935,* trans. John Coutouvidis (London: Scolar Press, 1995), 114.

69. Pilsudski, "Wspomnienia o Gabrielu Narutowiczu," July 1923, in *PZ,* 6:36. On Narutowicz's origins, see Janusz Pajewski, *Gabriel Narutowicz: Pierwszy prezydent Rzeczypospolitej* (Warsaw: Książka i Wiedza, 1993).

70. Pilsudski, "Wspomnienia o Gabrielu Narutowiczu," July 1923, in *PZ,* 6:51, 56, 59.

71. Lukowski and Zawadzki, *Concise History of Poland,* 304.

72. Polonsky, "The Emergence," 156.

73. S. Baranowski, conversation with Pilsudski, Sulejówek, September 1924, in Baranowski, *Rozmowy,* 98.

74. Pilsudski, *Rok 1863* (Warsaw: Towarzystwo Wydawnicze "Ignis," 1924), in *PZ,* 6:165, 167.

75. M. Tukhachevsky, "The March before the Vistula," lecture to the Moscow Military Academy, February 7, 1923, reprinted in Jozef Pilsudski, *Year 1920 and Its Climax: Battle of Warsaw during the Polish-Soviet War, 1919–1920* (1924; New York: PIA, 1972), 263–264.

76. Pilsudski, *Year 1920,* 220.

77. Ibid., 222.

78. W. Jędrzejewicz, *Wspomnienia* (Wrocław: Ossolińskich, 1993), 117.

79. Preface to T. Kutrzeba (1924), *Naczelni Wodzowie,* in *PZ,* 6:181.

80. Pilsudski, "Demokracja a Wojsko," June 20, 1924, in *PZ,* 8:15–16.

81. Pilsudski, "W dziesiątą rocznicę powstania Legionów," August 10, 1924, in *PZ,* 8:30.

82. J. Wielmożny, Polish Consul General in Chicago, to Marshal Jozef Pilsudski, Sulejówek, October 1, 1924, Jozef and Alexandra Pilsudski Collection, AAN, II / 96, fol. 97.

83. "Odezwa Komitetu Obchodu dnia 6 Sierpnia," [n.d., ca. October 1924], AAN, 232, leaflet collection, Jozef Pilsudski (1918–1937).

84. Gustav Stresemann, *His Diaries, Letters and Papers*, ed. E. Sutton (London: Macmillan, 1937), 2:503.

85. "Treaty of Mutual Guarantee between France and Poland of October 16, 1925," in Horak, *Poland's International Affairs*, 154–155; Polonsky, "The Emergence," 158.

86. Quotation from Piotr Wandycz, *France and Her Eastern Allies, 1919–1925* (Minneapolis: University of Minnesota Press, 1962), 364.

87. Quotation from Jan Karski, *The Great Powers and Poland* (New York: Rowman and Littlefield, 2014), 87.

88. Quotation from Polonsky, *Politics in Independent Poland*, 139.

89. Pilsudski, "Deklaracja złożona prezydentowi Rzeczypospolitej Stanisławowi Wojciechowskiemu," Sulejówek, November 13, 1925, in *PZ*, 8:247–248. Also see *Kalendarium*, 3:363–364.

90. Mariusz Wołos, *O Piłsudskim, Dmowskim i zamachu majowym: Dyplomacja sowiecka wobec Polski w okresie kryzysu politycznego, 1925–1926* (Kraków: Wydawnictwo Literackie, 2013), 74.

91. Ibid., 77. On the crowd size, also see *Kalendarium*, 3:304.

92. Quotation from Pilsudska, *Pilsudski*, 328.

93. "Obywatele!," n.d. (late 1925), leaflet of the PSL-Liberation, CBW, DU-825.

94. Z. Landau and J. Tomaszewski, *Zarys historii gospodarczej Polski, 1918–1939* (Warsaw: Książka i Wiedza, 1971), 98; Wojciech Roszkowski, *Historia Polski, 1914–2015* (Warsaw: PWN, 2017), 56; Czesław Witkowski, *Majowy zamach stanu: Wojskowy rokosz Piłsudskiego* (Warsaw: Bellona, 2016), 101; Joseph Rothschild, *East Central Europe between the Two World Wars* (Seattle: University of Washington Press, 1974), 52.

95. Sir Max Muller, Warsaw, to British Foreign Office, January 20, 1926, in Peter D. Stachura, *Poland, 1918–1945: An International and Documentary History of the Second Republic* (London: Routledge, 2004), 71.

96. Witkowski, *Majowy zamach stanu*, 311.

97. "Rząd większości parlamentarnej," *Kurier Warszawski*, May 11, 1926, 1; Roszkowski, *Historia Polski*, 57.

98. Pilsudski, interview in *Kurier Poranny*, May 11, 1926, quotation from Polonsky, *Politics in Independent Poland*, 157.

99. Garlicki, *Józef Piłsudski*, 357–358; Rafał Ziemkiewicz, *Złowrogi cień Marszałka* (Lublin: Fabryka słów, 2017), 369; Stachura, *Poland, 1918–1945*, 65.

100. Polonsky, *Politics in Independent Poland*, 155.

101. Roszkowski, *Historia Polski*, 56; Andrzej Garlicki, *Przewrót Majowy* (Warsaw: Czytelnik, 1979), 262.

102. Andrzej Skrzypek, *Zamachy stanu w Polsce XX wieku: Działania spiskowców i bezpardonowa walka o władzę* (Warsaw: Bellona, 2014), 53; Witkowski, *Majowy zamach stanu*, 313; Norman Davies, *God's Playground* (New York: Columbia University Press, 2005), 2:422.

103. Witkowski, *Majowy zamach stanu*, 194–200; Garlicki, *Przewrót Majowy*, 269; Włodzimierz Suleja, *Mundur na nim szary . . . Rzecz o Józefie Piłsudskim* (Warsaw: IPN, 2018), 291; Roszkowski, *Historia Polski*, 58–59.

104. Pilsudska, *Pilsudski*, 331.

105. Rothschild, *East Central Europe*, 55.

106. Recent studies of the coup include Z. Cieślikowski, *Materiały źródłowe do przewrotu majowego* (Warsaw, 2002); M. Sioma, ed., *Zamach stanu Józefa Piłsudskiego 1926 roku* (Lublin: Wydawn. Uniwersytetu Marii Curie-Skłodowskiej, 2007); *Zamach stanu Józefa Piłsudskiego i jego konsekwencje w interpretacjach polskiej myśli politycznej XX wieku*, ed. Z Karpus et al. (Toruń: Wydawnictwo Naukowe Uniwersytetu Mikołaja Kopernika, 2008).

16. The Path to Authoritarian Rule

Epigraph: "Do społeczeństwa!," *Robotnik*, September 11, 1930, 1.

1. Andrzej Garlicki, *Józef Piłsudski, 1867–1935* (Warsaw: Czytelnik, 1990), 366.

2. J. D. Gregory, Warsaw, May 21, 1926, in Peter D. Stachura, *Poland, 1918–1945: An International and Documentary History of the Second Republic* (London: Routledge, 2004), 72.

3. Pilsudski, Minister of War and First Marshall, Order to Soldiers, May 22, 1926, Papers of Gen. Józef Jaklicz, PIA, RG 109 / 115, fol. 297.

4. Pilsudski, interview with *Le Matin* (Paris), May 25, 1926, in *PZ*, 9:21.

5. Ibid., 22.

6. Ibid.

7. Pilsudski, Order-of-the-Day to Soldiers, May 22, 1926, PIA, RG 109 / 115.

8. Pilsudski, May 29, 1926, in *PZ*, 9:31.

9. "Poland: Pilsudski Touted," *Time*, June 7, 1926, 13; "Government Upset," *Time*, May 24, 1926, 15.

10. Przemysław Hauser, *Przedstawiciele mniejszości niemieckiej w parlamencie II Rzeczypospolitej* (Warsaw: Wydawnictwo Sejmowe, 2014), 109; Szymon Rudnicki, *Żydzi w parlamencie II Rzeczypospolitej*, 2nd ed. (Warsaw: Wydawn. Sejmowe, 2015), 272.

11. Rudnicki, *Żydzi w parlamencie*, 272; Hauser, *Przedstawiciele mniejszości niemieckiej*, 109; Garlicki, *Józef Piłsudski*, 386.

12. "Enuncjacja prasowa o prof. Ignacy Mościckim," *Kurier Poranny*, June 2, 1926, in *PZ*, 9:35–36.

13. Bolesław Barczyński, "List otwarty do Józefa Piłsudskiego," Kielce, May 27, 1926, CBW, DU-1771 (2); Stanisław Biernacki, "Były piłsudczyk do Marszałka Piłsudskiego: List Otwarty," June 2, 1926, CBW, DU-1771 (1).

14. [Jerzy Sochacki], *Przeciw dyktatorze Piłsudskiego (przemówienie posła komunistycznego w Sejmie 8 VII 1926* (Lwow, 1926); Jan Młot [Edward Ligocki], *Ryzykanci* (Poznań, 1926).

15. Antoni Anusz, *Pierwszy marszałek Polski, Józef Piłsudski: Budowniczy i wskrzesiciel Państwa Polskiego* (Warsaw: Wojskowy Insytut Naukowo-Wydawniczy, 1927), 18–19.

16. Interview with Pilsudski, Warsaw, June 1926, in W. Baranowski, *Rozmowy z Piłsudskim, 1916–1931* (1938; repr., Warsaw: Zebra, 1990), 111; diary entry, second half of May 1926, in Kazimierz Świtalski, *Diariusz, 1919–1935* (Warsaw: Czytelnik, 1992), 144.

17. Wojciech Roszkowski, *Historia Polski, 1914–2015* (Warsaw: PWN, 2017), 60.

18. "Ustawa zmieniająca i uzupełniająca Konstytucję Rzeczypospolitej dnia 17 marca 1926 r.," August 2, 1926, in *Źródła do dziejów II Rzeczypospolitej,* ed. J. Piłatowicz, D. Sowińska, and A. Zawadzki (Siedlce: Instytut Historii i Stosunków Międzynarodowych, 2014), 2:254–257. For analysis of the decree, see Włodzimierz Suleja, *Józef Piłsudski* (Wrocław: Zakład Narodowy imienia Ossolińskich, 2009), 317–318.

19. W. Baranowski, interview with Pilsudski, Druskienniki (then in northeastern Poland), August 26, 1926, in Baranowski, *Rozmowy,* 116–117.

20. "Rząd marsz. Piłsudskiego," *Chwila* (Lwów), October 3, 1926, 1.

21. Pilsudski, address in Nieśwież, October 25, 1926, in *PZ,* 9:47–48. For Potocki's quote, see Jerzy Potocki, Nieśwież, October 27, 1926, quotation from *Kalendarium,* 3:410.

22. Quotation from Jan Tomicki, *Polska Partia Socjalistyczna, 1892–1948* (Warsaw: Książka i Wiedza, 1983), 290; see also Hans Roos, *A History of Modern Poland,* trans. from the German by J. R. Foster (1961; New York: Knopf, 1966), 116.

23. Pilsudski, radio address on the 8th anniversary of independence, November 11, 1926, in *PZ,* 9:47–48.

24. Pilsudski, speech at the convention of Legionnaires, Kielce, August 7, 1927, in *PZ,* 9:87–88.

25. Speech of Marshal Pilsudski at Wawel Castle, Kraków, June 27, 1927, in *Monitor Polski* (Warsaw), June 30, 1927, 4, and in *PZ,* 9:72.

26. M. B. Biskupski, *Independence Day: Myth, Symbol and the Creation of Modern Poland* (Oxford: Oxford University Press, 2012), 59–60.

27. Hauser, *Przedstawiciele mniejszości niemieckiej,* 14; Winson Chu, *The German Minority in Interwar Poland* (Cambridge: Cambridge University Press, 2012), 93; Richard Blanke, *Orphans of Versailles: The Germans in Western Prussia, 1918–1939* (Lexington: University Press of Kentucky, 1993), 90. On the national composition of Poland in 1931, see P. Magocsi, *Historical Atlas of Central Europe* (Seattle: University of Washington Press, 2002), 131.

28. Rudnicki, *Żydzi w parlamencie,* 271.

29. Ibid., 271–272.

30. "Żydzi wobec przedłożeń rządowych," *Nasz Przegląd* (Warsaw), June 19, 1926, quotation from Rudnicki, *Żydzi w parlamencie*, 272.

31. Rudnicki, *Żydzi w parlamencie,,* 269.

32. Quotation from Apolinary Hartglas, *Na pograniczu dwóch światów*, ed. Jolanta Żyndyl (Warsaw: Oficyna Wydawnicza, 1996), 229.

33. Hartglas, interview in *Nasz Przegląd* (Warsaw), February 5, 1928, cited in Szymon Rudnicki, *Równi, ale niezupełnie* (Warsaw: Biblioteka Midrasza, 2008), 145n4.

34. Quotation from Giuseppe Motta, *The Great War against Eastern European Jewry, 1914–1920* (Newcastle upon Tyne, UK: Cambridge Scholars Publishing, 2017), 174.

35. Quotation from Antony Polonsky, *The Jews in Poland and Russia* (Oxford: Littman Library of Jewish Civilization, 2012), 3:73.

36. Resolution on national minorities, session of the Polish cabinet, August 18, 1926, reprinted in Marek Jabłonowski and Dorota Cisowska-Hydzik, eds., *O niepodległą i granice* (Warsaw: Wyd. Uniwersytetu Warszawskiego, 2004), 5:469.

37. On Bartel's attitude toward the Jews, see Sławomir Kalbarczyk, *Kazimierz Bartel (1882–1941): Uczony w świecie polityki* (Warsaw: Instytut Pamięci Narodowej, 2015), 343; Shoshan Ronen, *A Prophet of Consolation on the Threshold of Destruction: Yehoshua Ozjasz Thon, an Intellectual Portrait* (Warsaw: Dom Wydawniczy Elipsa 2015), 247; Polonsky, *Jews in Poland and Russia*, 3:74.

38. Gustaw Dobrucki, address on October 18, 1927, quotation from Rudnicki, *Równi, ale niezupełnie*, 145; Polonsky, *Jews in Poland and Russia*, 3:73.

39. Rudnicki, *Równi, ale niezupełnie*, 130.

40. Quotation from Felicjan Składkowski, *Kwiatuszki administracyjne i inne* (London: B. Swiderski, 1959), 275.

41. Polonsky, *Jews in Poland and Russia*, 3:74–75.

42. Hartglas, *Na pograniczu dwóch światów*, 229.

43. Quotation from Blanke, *Orphans of Versailles*, 91.

44. Pilsudski, interview with *Głos Prawdy*, December 24, 1926, in *PZ*, 9:64–65.

45. Diary entry, December 18, 1926, in Świtalski, *Diariusz*, 203.

46. Roszkowski, *Historia Polski*, 62.

47. Campaign circular, untitled, March 1928, CBW, DU-48; "Co o rządu marszałka Piłsudskiego mówią najwyżsi dostojnicy kościoła?," ca. February 1928, CBW, DU-827; Andrzej Chojnowski, *Piłsudczycy u władzy: Dzieje Bezpartyjnego Bloku Współpracy z Rządem* (Wrocław: Ossolineum, 1986), 82.

48. Chojnowski, *Piłsudczycy u władzy*, 61–62; Roszkowski, *Historia Polski*, 64.

49. Roszkowski, *Historia Polski*, 64; Chojnowski, *Piłsudczycy u władzy*, 61–62; Antony Polonsky, "The Emergence of an Independent Polish State," in *The History of Poland since 1863*, ed. R. F. Leslie (New York: Cambridge University Press, 1980), tables 7 and 8, at 154, 168.

50. Świtalski, diary entry, March 24, 1928, in Świtalski, *Diariusz*, 347–348.

51. F. Słowoj Składkowski, *Strzępy meldunków* (Warsaw: Instytut Badania Najnowszej Historii, 1936), 77.

52. "Polish Parliament Opened," *Times* (London), March 28, 1928, 15; Składkowski, *Strzępy meldunków*, 78.

53. Summary of Pilsudski comments in a meeting with advisors, diary entry, March 13, 1928, in Świtalski, *Diariusz*, 339–340.

54. Paweł Duber, *Działalność polityczna Kazimierza Bartla w latach 1926–1930* (Warsaw: Wydawnictwo Sejmowe, 2014), 200–201; "Zmiana rządu. Nowy gabinetu prof. Bartla," *Robotnik*, June 28, 1928, 1; "Wobec zmiany gabinetowej," *Kurier Warszawski*, June 28, 1928, 1; "Rekonstrukcja gabinetu," *Rzeczpospolita* (Warsaw), June 28, 1928, 1.

55. Diary entry of June 18, 1928, in Świtalski, *Diariusz*, 352.

56. Pilsudski, "Wywiad z redaktorem 'Głosu Prawdy,'" July 1, 1928, in *PZ*, 9:112–113, 116. On coverage of this interview in the Western press, see "A Pilsudski Outburst: Candid Views on Parliament," *Times* (London), July 2, 1928, 16.

57. "P.P.S. wobec wywiadu marsz. Piłsudskiego: Uchwały, powzięte na wczorajszym posiedzeniu plenarnym," *Robotnik* (Warsaw), July 3, 1928, 1.

58. Diary entry of July 17, 1928, in Świtalski, *Diariusz*, 354, 357.

59. Piłsudski, address at a convention of Legionaries in Vilna, August 12, 1928, in *PZ*, 9:128.

60. "The New Poland: Celebration of Tenth Anniversary," *Times* (London), November 12, 1928, 15.

61. Paul Super, *Twenty-Five Years with the Poles* (Trenton, NJ: Paul Super Memorial Fund, n.d.), 98, quotation from Biskupski, *Independence Day*, 62–63. The event is also described in real time in "Poles Hail Pilsudski," *New York Times*, November 11, 1928, 27.

62. Biskupski, *Independence Day*, 63.

63. Ibid.

64. "The New Poland: Celebration of the Tenth Anniversary (from Our Own Correspondent)," *Times* (London), November 12, 1928, 15; Piotr Wandycz, *The Twilight of French Eastern Alliances, 1926–1936* (Princeton, NJ: Princeton University Press, 1988), 129.

65. *Times* (London), November 12, 1928, 15; Biskupski, *Independence Day*, 66.

66. "Żydzi wobed święto niepodległości," *Ilustrowany Kurier Codzienny*, November 11, 1928, 8, quotation from Biskupski, *Independence Day*, 66; "Poles Hail Pilsudski," *New York Times*, November 11, 1928, 27; "The New Poland: Celebration."

67. Pilsudski, "Dno Oka, czyli wrażenia człowieka chorego z sesji budżetowej w Sejmie," *Głos Prawdy* (Warsaw), April 7, 1929, in *PZ*, 9:145–153, quotation from 153, as quoted in Polonsky, "The Emergence," 171.

68. Diary entry, May 3, 1929, in Świtalski, *Diariusz*, 423.

69. Chojnowski, *Piłsudczycy u władzy*, 96; Garlicki, *Józef Piłsudski*, 541.

70. "Oświadczenie na rozprawie Trybunału Stanu," June 23, 1929, in *PZ*, 9:180–181.

71. W. Pobóg-Malinowski, *Najnowsza historia polityczna Polski* (London: B. Swiderski, 1967), 2:707–708.

72. Pilsudski, "Gasnącemu światu," *Głos Prawdy*, September 22, 1929, in *PZ*, 9:185–192.

73. *Gazeta Chłopska*, October 10, 1929, quotation from Polonsky, *Politics in Independent Poland*, 294.

74. Polonsky, *Politics in Independent Poland*, 294n4.

75. Mieczysław Niedziałkowski, "Nasz stosunek do Józefa Piłsudskiego," *Robotnik* (Warsaw), October 1, 1929, 1.

76. Garlicki, *Józef Piłsudski*, 563.

77. "Rozmowa Marszałka Piłsudskiego z marszałka sejmu," *Gazeta Polska* (Warsaw), November 1, 1929, 1; this exchange also appears in *PZ*, 9:193–1943, and in Słowoj Składkowski, *Strzępy meldunków*, 153–155.

78. "Wspomnienie o Grzybowskie," November 9, 1929, in *PZ*, 9:206.

79. "Charges Pilsudski Fears to Face Diet," *New York Times*, November 7, 1929, 11.

80. *Robotnik*, December 30, 1929, 1; *Kalendarium*, 4:169.

81. "Uchwały Rady Naczelnej P.P.S.," *Robotnik*, February 4, 1930, 1. This sentence appeared in all-caps.

82. In A. Czubiński, *Centrolew* (Poznań, 1963), 203, quotation from Polonsky, *Politics in Independent Poland*, 308. Also see "From Anti-Pilsudski Bloc," *New York Times*, June 21, 1930, 8.

83. Witos, *Moje wspomnienia*, 3:184–185.

84. Garlicki, *Józef Piłsudski*, 579–580.

85. Centrolew resolution, June 29, 1930, reprinted in Witos, *Moje wspomnienia*, 3:181.

86. Text of Centrolew resolution, June 29, 1930, Kraków, in *For Your Freedom and Ours*, ed. Krystyna Olszer (New York: F. Unger, 1981), 218.

87. *Robotnik* (Warsaw), July 1, 1930, quotation from Polonsky, *Politics in Independent Poland*, 311.

88. Witos, *Moje wspomnienia*, 3:181.

89. Ibid., 185.

90. *Kalendarium*, 4:185; Polonsky, *Politics in Independent Poland*, 311.

91. Quoted in "Poland to Prosecute 33 Opposition Members for Cracow Resolution against Dictatorship," *New York Times*, July 4, 1930, 6.

92. *Robotnik* (Warsaw), August 24, 1930, quotation from Polonsky, *Politics in Independent Poland*, 314.

93. "Zmiana rządu," *Gazeta Polska* (Warsaw), August 24, 1930, 1; Słowoj Składkowski, *Strzępy meldunków*, 205–206; *Kalendarium*, 4:185.

94. *Gazeta Polska* (Warsaw), August 27, 1930, in *PZ*, 9:221.

95. Interview with Pilsudski, Warsaw, June 1926, in Baranowski, *Rozmowy,* 111–112.

96. Polonsky, *Politics in Independent Poland,* 314.

97. Słowoj Składkowski, *Strzępy meldunków,* 223.

98. "Do społeczeństwa!," *Robotnik,* September 11, 1930, 1.

99. Marian Leczyk, *Sprawa Brzeska: Dokumenty i materiały* (Warsaw: Książka i Wiedza, 1987), 32–33; "Aresztowani b. posłowie socjalistyczni," *Robotnik,* September 12, 1930, 1.

100. Quotation from Daria Nałęcz and Tomasz Nałęcz, *Józef Piłsudski: Legendy i fakty* (Warsaw: Młodzieżowa Agencja Wydawnicza, 1986), 281.

101. Pilsudski, interview in *Gazeta Polska,* September 13, 1930, in *PZ,* 9:231–233.

102. Roszkowski, *Historia Polski,* 71; Polonsky, *Politics in Independent Poland,* 314–315.

103. Garlicki, *Józef Piłsudski,* 586.

104. Lidia Ciołkosz, *Spojrzenie wstecz: Rozmowy przeprowadził Andrzej Friszke* (Paris: Éditions du Dialogue, 1995), 62.

105. Garlicki, *Józef Piłsudski,* 585–586; Suleja, *Józef Piłsudski* (Wrocław: Ossolineum, 1995), 343.

106. Polonsky, *Politics in Independent Poland,* 320; Garlicki, *Józef Piłsudski,* 585–586; Włodzimierz Suleja, *Józef Piłsudski* (Wrocław: Ossolineum, 1995), 343.

107. *Kalendarium,* 4:215; Bohdan Urbankowski, *Józef Pilsudski: Marzyciel i strateg* (Poznań: Zysk i S-ka, 2014), 425.

108. On Pilsudski's affair with Eugenia Lewicka, see Nałęcz and Nałęcz, *Józef Piłsudski,* 284; Ludwik Malinowski, *Miłości Marszałka Piłsudskiego* (Warsaw: Kisiążka i Wiedza, 1997), 132–133; Iwona Kienzler, *Kobiety w życiu marszałka Piłsudskiego* (Warsaw: Bellona, 2012), 288–289; Urbankowski, *Józef Piłsudski,* 425.

109. Piotr Wandycz, "Polish Diplomacy 1914–1945: Aims and Achievements," in *Polish Diplomacy, 1914–1945* (London: Orbis, 1988), 21.

110. Piotr Wandycz, "The Foreign Policy of the Second Republic, 1921–1932," in *Reflections on Polish Foreign Policy,* ed. John Micgiel (New York: Columbia University Press, 2007), 39.

111. Wandycz, *The Twilight, 1926–1936,* 122.

112. Ibid., 135–136.

113. Ibid., 123.

114. Ibid., 123–124.

115. Quotation from W. Jędrzejewicz, "Rozmowa Marszałka Piłsudskiego ze Stresemanem w Genewie w 1927 roku," *Niepodległość* 10 (1976): 142.

116. Paul Schmidt, *Statist auf diplomatischer Bühne* (Bonn: Athenäum-Verlag, 1949), quotation from Alfred Erich Senn, *The Great Powers, Lithuania, and the Vilna Question, 1920–1928* (Leiden: E. J. Brill, 1966), 197; on this exchange, also see *Kalendarium,* 4:62–63.

117. Senn, *The Great Powers,* 197–198.

118. *Le Temps,* January 19, 1928, quotation from Senn, *The Great Powers,* 205.

119. Senn, *The Great Powers,* 206–207.

120. "The Polish-Lithuanian Negotiations," *Times* (London), June 14, 1928, 15.

121. Wandycz, *The Twilight,* 122.

122. "Protocol between Estonia, Latvia, Poland, Rumania and the USSR of February 9, 1929," in Stephan Horak, *Poland's International Affairs, 1919–1960* (Bloomington: Indiana University Press, 1964), 158–160.

123. Quotation fromy Wacław Jędrzejewicz, *Pilsudski: A Life for Poland* (New York: Hippocrene Books, 1982), 281.

17. Poland in a Changing World

Epigraph: Quotation from *Papers Relating to the Foreign Relations of the United States, 1931* (Washington, DC: United States Government Printing Office, 1946), 1:600.

1. Eva Plach, *The Clash of Moral Nations: Cultural Politics in Pilsudski's Poland, 1926–1935* (Athens, OH: Ohio University Press, 2014), 73.

2. Marjan Porczak, *Dyktator Józefa Piłsudskiego i "piłsudczycy"* (Kraków: self-pub., 1930), 14.

3. Ibid., 27, 88. One year later Porczak characterized Pilsudski as a mafia boss. See Marjan Porczak, *Piatiletka sanacyjna w piątą rocznicę zamachu majowego 1926 r.* (Kraków: Nakładem Tow. Uniwersytetu Robotniczego, 1931), 14, quotation in Plach, *Clash of Moral Nations,*189–190n108.

4. H. N. Brailsford, letter to the editor, *Times* (London), May 23, 1919, 8.

5. H. N. Brailsford, "Pilsudski Turning Poland to Fascism," *Sun* (Baltimore), October 3, 1930, 13.

6. Roman Debicki, *Foreign Policy of Poland, 1919–1939* (London: Pall Mall Press, 1962), 67.

7. "Daughter, 11, Boss of Polish Dictator: Pilsudski's Attention to Jadwiga and Wanda, 13, Belies Iron Man Role," *Washington Post,* November 23, 1930, A5.

8. "Poland Welcomes Pilsudski at Home: Two Daughters First to Greet Him," *Washington Post,* March 30, 1931, 7.

9. Ivan T. Berend, *Decades of Crisis: Central and Eastern Europe before World War II* (Berkeley: University of California Press, 1998), 253; François Crouzet, *A History of the European Economy, 1000–2000* (Charlottesville: University of Virginia Press, 2001), 179; Wojciech Roszkowski, *Historia Polski, 1914–2015* (Warsaw: PWN, 2017), 73.

10. Ignacy Mościcki, "Autobiografia," *Niepodległość* 14 (1981): 108.

11. Kazimierz Świtalski, diary entry of April 29, 1931, Warsaw, in Kazimierz Świtalski, *Diariusz 1919–1935* (Warsaw: Czytelnik, 1992), 606.

12. "Nowy rząd," *Gazeta Polska* (Warsaw), May 28, 1931, 1; "P. Prystor utworzył nowy rząd," *Robotnik,* May 28, 1931, 1.

13. Resolution of the 22nd Convention of the PPS, in *Robotnik,* May 28, 1931, 3.

14. "Zamordowanie posła Tadeusza Hołówki," *Gazeta Polska,* August 30, 1931, 1; "Polish Deputy Slain; Ukrainian Suspected," *New York Times,* August 30, 1931, 7.

15. Jerzy Holzer, "Tadeusz Ludwik Hołówko (1889–1931)," *Polski Słownik Biograficzny* 9 (1960–1961): 600–602.

16. Pilsudski, Warsaw, letter to Tadeusz Hołówko's mother, September 3, 1931, in *PZ,* 9:323.

17. F. Słowoj Składkowski, *Strzępy meldunków* (Warsaw: Instytut Badania Najnowszej Historii, 1936), 321.

18. "Pilsudski Ill in Rumania," *New York Times,* October 21, 1931, 6.

19. "Relacja płka R. Michałowskiego o pobycie Marszałka Piłsudskiego w Rumunii jesienią 1931 r.," March 20, 1973, Papers of Roman Michałowski, PIA, RG 72 / 1.

20. "Pilsudski Attends First Public Event since Illness," *New York Times,* November 30, 1931, 8; *Kalendarium,* 4:239.

21. Artur Śliwiński, interview with Pilsudski on November 9, 1931, in "Marszałek Piłsudski o sobie," *Niepodległość* 43 (1937): 367–368.

22. Artur Śliwiński, interview with Pilsudski on November 3, 1931, in "Marszałek Piłsudski o sobie," *Niepodległość* 47 (January–June 1938): 345–347.

23. "Wniosek o 'numerus clauses' w Komisji Oświatowej sejmu," *Nasz Przegląd,* March 4, 1932, 3; *"Numerus Clausus* w Komisji Oświatowej Sejmu," *Robotnik,* March 4, 1932, 3; "Bans Curb on Jews in Polish Colleges," *New York Times,* March 5, 1932, 4; Szymon Rudnicki, *Żydzi w parlamencie II Rzeczpospolitej,* 2nd ed. (Warsaw: Wydawnictwo Sejmowe, 2015), 429. For a transcript of speeches in the Sejm on this matter, see *Nasz Przegląd,* March 5, 1932, 3–4.

24. "Joseph Beck: Polish Minister of Foreign Affairs," Jozef Beck Papers, PIA, RG 34 / 1.

25. John N. Willys, US Ambassador, Warsaw, to Henry L. Stimson, US Secretary of State, October 15, 1931, in *Papers Relating to the Foreign Relations of the United States, 1931* (Washington, DC: US Government Printing Office, 1946), 1:597.

26. US Secretary of State Henry L. Stimson, London, to President Hoover, Washington, July 24, 1931, in *Papers Relating to the Foreign Relations of the United States, 1931,* 1:549.

27. Neal Pease, *Poland, the United States and the Stabilization of Europe, 1919–1933* (Oxford: Oxford University Press, 1986), 146.

28. Memorandum by the Undersecretary of State, W. R. Castle Jr., of a conversation with the Polish ambassador (Filipowicz), October 22, 1931, in *Papers Relating to the Foreign Relations of the United States, 1931,* 1:600.

29. John Wiley, chargé d'affaires in Poland, Warsaw, to the Secretary of State, Washington, December 2, 1931, in *Papers Relating to the Foreign Relations of the United States, 1931,* 1:603–604.

30. William Borah, press conference of October 22, 1931, quotation from *Herbert Hoover and Poland: A Documentary History of a Friendship,* ed. George J. Lerski, (Stanford, CA: Hoover Institution Press, 1977), 38.

31. White House press release, October 25, 1931, in *Papers Relating to the Foreign Relations of the United States, 1931,* 1:603.

32. Quotation from *Kalendarium,* 4:240. I am grateful to Filip Mazurczak for helping me render this passage in English.

33. "M. Zaleski's Visit to London," *Manchester Guardian,* December 14, 1931, 12; Maria Nowak-Kiełbikowa, "Wizyta Augusta Zaleskiego w Londynie w grudnia 1931 r.," *Dzieje Najnowsze* 6 (1974): 29–30; Piotr Wandycz, *Twilight of French Eastern Alliances, 1926–1936* (Princeton, NJ: Princeton University Press, 1988), 219–220.

34. P. Wandycz, "The Place of the French Alliance in Poland's' Foreign Policy," in *Bâtir une nouvelle sécurité: La coopération militaire entre la France et les états d'Europe centrale et orientale de 1919 à 1929* (Vincennes: Centre d'études d'histoire de la défense, Service historique de l'armée de terre, 2001), 189.

35. Wandycz, *Twilight,* 236.

36. "British Naval Visit to Danzig," *Times* (London), June 16, 1832, 13; "Danzig Is Aroused by Polish Warship," *Washington Post,* June 16, 1932, 11.

37. Wandycz, *Twilight,* 237.

38. "Non-Aggression Pact between Poland and the USSR of July 25, 1932," in *Poland's International Affairs, 1919–1960,* ed. Stephan Horak (Bloomington: Indiana University Press, 1964), 163.

39. Pilsudski, Pikieliszki, letter to the convention of legionnaires, Gdynia, August 12, 1932, in *PZ,* 9:330. I am grateful to Filip Mazurczak for helping me render this passage in English.

40. Douglas MacArthur, *Reminiscences* (Annapolis, MD: Bluejacket Books, 1964), 99.

41. Richard J. Evans, *The Coming of the Third Reich* (New York: Penguin, 2003), 293.

42. *Sunday Express* (London), February 12, 1933, 1.

43. "Polish Troops in Danzig Harbor," *Times* (London), March 9, 1933, 11; Włodzimierz Suleja, *Józef Piłsudski* (Wrocław: Ossolineum, 2009), 350; Gerhard L. Weinberg, *Hitler's Foreign Policy, 1933–1939* (New York: Enigma, 2005), 50; Richard M. Watt, *Bitter Glory: Poland and Its Fate, 1918–1939* (New York: Simon and Schuster, 1979), 315.

44. Weinberg, *Hitler's Foreign Policy,* 50.

45. Quotation from Martin J. Kozon, "Sanacja's Foreign Policy and the Second Polish Republic, 1926–1935" (MA thesis, University of Wisconsin–Milwaukee, 2015), 100.

46. R. J. B. Bosworth, *Mussolini* (London: Arnold, 2002), 273–276.

47. Draft of the Four Powers Pact, dated March 4, 1933, in *Documents on German Foreign Policy, 1918–1945* (Washington, DC: US Government Printing Office, 1957), series C, 1:162.

48. Memorandum of the German Foreign Minister, Berlin, March 14, 1933, in *Documents on German Foreign Policy, 1918–1945,* series C, 1:160.

49. *Gazeta Polska* (Warsaw), quoted in "Poland and the Four Powers Pact," *Manchester Guardian*, March 28, 1933, 18.

50. Hans von Moltke, Warsaw, to the German foreign minister, Berlin, April 23, 1933, in *Documents on German Foreign Policy, 1918–1945*, series C, 1:329.

51. Alan Palme, *The Penguin Dictionary of Modern History, 1789–1945* (New York: Penguin, 1962), 257.

52. Robert Vansittart, *The Mist Procession: The Autobiography of Lord Vansittart* (London: Hutchinson, 1958), 468.

53. For a recent discussion of this subject, see Paweł Duber, "Józef Piłsudski a zagadnienie tzw. Wojny Prewencyjnej w latach 1933–1934," *Niepodległość* 69 (2014): 51–68. For two early articles with opposite conclusions, see Wacław Jędrzejewicz, "The Polish Plan for a 'Preventive War' against Germany in 1933," *Polish Review* 11, no. 1 (1966): 62–91; and Zygmunt Gasiorowski, "Did Pilsudski Attempt to Initiate a Preventive War in 1933?," *Journal of Modern History* 27, no. 2 (1955): 135–151. Also see, more recently, Leszek Moczulski, *Wojna prewencyjna: Czy Piłsudski planował najazd na Niemcy?* (Warsaw: Bellona, 2017).

54. Beck, *Dernier rapport: Politique polonaise, 1926–1939* (Neuchâtel [Switzerland]: Éditions de la Baconnière, 1951), 66.

55. Jan Karski, *The Great Powers and Poland* (1985; New York: Rowman and Littlefield, 2014), 127; Watt, *Bitter Glory*, 318–319.

56. Józef Beck, Warsaw, instructions to Alfred Wysocki, Berlin, April 18, 1933, reprinted in Józef Lipski, *Diplomat in Berlin, 1933–1939: Papers and Memoirs of Józef Lipski* (New York: Columbia University Press, 1968), 74–75.

57. M. B. Lepecki, diary entry of April 18, 1933, published as "Marszałek Piłsudski i przewidywana w roku 1933 wojna z Niemcami," *Wiadomości* (London), no. 169 (June 26, 1949): 1.

58. Zygmunt Gasiorowski, in his "Did Pilsudski Attempt to Initiate a Preventive War in 1933?," 151n103, claimed the document was likely a fiction. But Paweł Duber convincingly demonstrates that the document is reliable. See Duber, "Czy mógł powstać polski rząd obrony narodowej?," *Wiadomości Historyczne* 4 (2014): 41.

59. Kazimierz Świtalski, diary entry of July 6, 1932, in Świtalski, *Diariusz: Uzupełnienie z lat 1919–1932*, ed. Paweł Duber and Włodzimierz Suleja (Warsaw: Wydawnictwo Sejmowe, 2012), 196.

60. Sir H. Rumbold, Berlin, to Sir J. Simon, April 4, 1933 (received April 24), in *Documents on British Foreign Policy, 1919–1939* (London: Her Majesty's Stationery Office, 1956), 2nd ser., 5:27.

61. Minutes of the Conference of Ministers held at the Reich Chancellery, Berlin, April 7, 1933, in *Documents on German Foreign Policy, 1918–1945*, series C, 1:259.

62. Hans von Moltke, Warsaw, to the German foreign minister, Berlin, April 25, 1933, in *Documents on German Foreign Policy, 1918–1945*, series C, 1:342–343.

63. Hans von Moltke, Warsaw, to the German foreign minister, Berlin, April 23, 1933, in *Documents on German Foreign Policy, 1918–1945*, series C, 1:331.

64. Heinrich Brüning, article from July 1947, quotation from Jędrzejewicz, "The Polish Plan," 68.

65. Heinrich Brüning, letter to Stanisław Sopicki, November 5, 1949, in Józef Lipski Papers, PIA, file 3, as quoted in Jędrzejewicz, "The Polish Plan," 9–10.

66. Anatol Muhlstein, Chantilly, to Józef Beck, April 17, 1933, reprinted in Jan Szembek, *Diariusz i teki Jana Szembeka*, ed. Tytus Komarnicki (London: Orbis, 1964), 1:12. The letter was also reprinted in Robert Jarocki, *Żyd Piłsudskiego: Opowieść o Anatolu Muhlsteinie* (Warsaw: ARS Print Production, 1997), 62–64.

67. Paweł Duber, "Józef Piłsudski a zagadnienie tzw Wojny Prewencyjnej w latach 1933–1934," *Niepodległość* 69 (2014): 62.

68. Ibid., 67.

69. Piotr Wandycz, "Jeszcze o misji Jerzego Potockiego w 1933 roku," *Zeszyty Historyczne* 18 (1970): 81–83; Jędrzejewicz, "The Polish Plan," 81.

70. Report of meeting, April 13, 1933, reprinted in Szembek, *Diariusz i teki*, 1:14.

71. Hans von Moltke, Warsaw, to the German foreign minister, Berlin, February 22, 1933, in *Documents on German Foreign Policy, 1918–1945*, series C, 1:73–74.

72. Kazimierz Glabisz, account preserved in PIA, as quoted in Jędrzejewicz, "The Polish Plan," 83.

73. Robert Machray, *The Poland of Pilsudski* (London: George Allen and Unwin, 1936), 324.

74. "German Outlook Abroad: Herr von Papen's Declaration," *Times* (London), April 28, 1933, 14.

75. Wysocki, Berlin, to Foreign Minister Beck, dated May 2, 1933, in *Official Documents concerning Polish-German and Polish-Soviet Relations, 1933–1939* (New York: Roy, 1940), 11.

76. Communiqué issued by the Wolff Agency on an interview between Chancellor Hitler and M. Wysocki, May 3, 1933, in *Official Documents*, 13.

77. Extracts from Chancellor Hitler's Speech to the Reichstag, May 17, 1933, in *Official Documents*, 13–15; for the full text in English translation, see "Hitler's Address in Full," *New York Herald Tribune*, May 18, 1933, 1.

78. Gen. Max Schindler, Warsaw, to the Reichswehr Minister and Foreign Minister, Berlin, May 10, 1933, in *Documents on German Foreign Policy, 1918–1945*, series C, 1:401–402.

79. Ibid., 403.

80. Wysocki, Berlin, to Beck, July 13, 1933, in *Official Documents*, 15–16.

81. A. Wysocki, *Tajemnice dyplomatycznego sejfu* (Warsaw: Książka i Wiedza, 1974), 175.

82. Pilsudski as quoted in *Kalendarium*, 4:324.

83. Pilsudski, Pikieliszki, address to the Legionnaires Convention in Warsaw, August 12, 1933, in *PZ*, 9:330.

84. Juliusz Słowacki, "Beniowski," canto 5, stanzas 50–51, in *Poland's Angry Romantic: Two Poems and a Play by Juliusz Słowacki*, ed. Peter Cochran (Newcastle upon Tyne: Cambridge Scholars, 2009), 298.

85. "List Marszałka Piłsudskiego do Legionistów," *Gazeta Polska*, August 7, 1933, 1. The letter also appears in *PZ*, 9:330–331.

86. Otto Meissner memoirs (1950), cited in Karski, *Great Powers and Poland*, 117.

87. Heinrich Brüning, letter to Stanisław Sopicki, November 5, 1949, quotation from Jędrzejewicz, "The Polish Plan," 10.

88. Notes of Minister Szembek on his meeting with Marshal Pilsudski, October 21, 1933, reprinted in Szembek, *Diariusz i teki*, 1:80–81.

89. Jędrzejewicz, "The Polish Plan," 85–86.

90. Beck, *Dernier rapport*, 66, quotation from Wandycz, *Twilight*, 270.

91. Lipski, report on a meeting with Pilsudski, November 5, 1933, in Lipski, *Diplomat in Berlin*, 95–96, 98.

92. Lipski, report on talks with Hitler, November 15, 1933, in *Official Documents*, 17.

93. Communiqué issued by the Wolff Agency on an interview between Chancellor Hitler and M. Lipski, November 15, 1933, in *Official Documents*, 19.

94. German Foreign Minister, Berlin, to the German minister in Poland, Warsaw, November 24, 1933, in *Documents on German Foreign Policy, 1918–1945*, series C, 2:148–149.

95. *Documents on German Foreign Policy, 1918–1945*, series C, 2:157.

96. German minister in Poland, Warsaw, to the German Foreign Minister, Berlin, November 27, 1933, in *Documents on German Foreign Policy, 1918–1945*, series C, 2:156.

97. Memorandum by the German Foreign Minister, Baron von Neurath, January 9, 1934, in *Documents on German Foreign Policy, 1918–1945*, series C, 2:312.

98. "Polish-German Declaration on January 26, 1934," in Horak, *Poland's International Affairs*, 166–167. For a complete English translation of the Declaration, see *Documents on German Foreign Policy, 1918–1945*, series C, 2:421–422; also in *Official Documents*, 20–21.

99. Alexandra Pilsudska, *Pilsudski: A Biography by His Wife* (New York: Dodd, Mead, 1941), 341.

100. Kazimierz Świtalski, diary entry of March 7, 1934, Warsaw, in Świtalski, *Diariusz*, 660–661.

101. "Pilsudski and Nobel Peace Prize," *Irish Times*, January 29, 1934, 8.

102. M. Beck to all Polish diplomatic missions abroad, January 26, 1943, in *Official Documents*, 21.

103. Extracts from Chancellor Hitler's Speech to the Reichstag, January 30, 1934, in *Official Documents*, 22–23.

104. Quotation from Jean-Baptiste Duroselle, *France and the Nazi Threat: The Collapse of French Diplomacy, 1932–1939*, trans. Catherine E. Dop and Robert L. Miller (1979; New York: Enigma Books, 2004), 66.

105. M. Laroche, French ambassador in Warsaw, to the French foreign ministry, Paris, January 29, 1934, in *Documents Diplomatiques Français, 1932–1939*, 1st ser., vol. 5 (Paris: Imprimerie Nationale, 1972), 553–554.

106. "L'Allemagne et la Pologne," *Le Temps* (Paris), January 28, 1934, 3.

107. Soviet government statement, as quoted in "Russians Distrust Polish-Reich Pact," *New York Times*, January 30, 1934, 7.

108. Marek Kornat, *Polityka równowagi, 1934–1939: Polska między wschodem a zachodem* (Kraków: Wydawnictwo Arcana, 2007), 213–214.

109. Jan Szembek, report of a conference with Piłsudski, April 12, 1934, in Szembek, *Diariusz i teki*, 1:155, as quoted in Wandycz, *Twilight*, 326.

110. Kazimierz Świtalski, diary entry of March 7, 1934, Warsaw, in Świtalski, *Diariusz*, 659–660.

111. Ibid., 660.

112. Piotr Wandycz, "Wypowiedzi Marszałka Piłsudskiego na konferencji byłych premierów 7 marca 1934 roku," *Niepodległość* 9 (London, 1974): 345. For a recent discussion of this document, see Małgorzata Gmurczyk-Wrońska, "Jozef Pilsudski and the Polish-French Alliance (1926–1935)," *Studia z dziejów Rosji i Europy Środkowo-Wschodniej* 54 (special issue) (2019): 75–77.

18. Pilsudski's Last Year

Epigraph: Irena Protassewicz, *A Polish Woman's Experience in World War II: Conflict, Deportation and Exile* (London: Bloomsbury Academic, 2019), 73.

1. Jan Szembek, Warsaw, report of conversation between Marshal Pilsudski and France's foreign minister, Bartheau, April 23, 1933, in Jan Szembek, *Diariusz i teki Jana Szembeka*, ed. Tytus Komarnicki (London: Orbis, 1964), 1:156–157.

2. M. Laroche, French ambassador in Warsaw, to the French foreign ministry, Paris, April 24, 1934, in *Documents diplomatiques français, 1932–1939*, 1st ser., vol. 6 (Paris: Imprimerie Nationale, 1972), 333–334.

3. Ibid., 324.

4. Jan Szembek, Warsaw, report of conversation between Marshal Pilsudski and France's foreign minister, Bartheau, April 23, 1933, in Szembek, *Diariusz i teki*, 1:157–158; Józef Beck, *Final Report* (New York: Robert Speller and Sons, 1967), 54.

5. Szembek, *Diariusz i teki*, 1:159.

6. "M. Barthou in Warsaw: Talk with Marshal Pilsudski," *Times* (Warsaw), April 24, 1934, 13.

7. Quotation from "Pobyt ministra Ludwika Barthou w Warszawie," *Gazeta Polska*, April 24, 1934, 2.

8. "Minister Barthou o stosunkach polsko-francuskick," *Gazeta Polska* (Warsaw), April 24, 1934, 1–2. For a more cautious but nonetheless positive report, see the right-wing opposition press's account: "Minister Barthou w Warszawie," *Kurier Warszawski,* April 23, 1934, 1.

9. "La Visite de M. Barthou a Varsovie," *Le Temps* (Paris), April 24, 1934, 1.

10. "Déclaration de M. Barthou à la presse," *Le Temps* (Paris), January 28, 1934, 1; "Przemówienie min. Barthou," *Kurier Poranny* (Warsaw), April 23, 1934, 3.

11. "Sojusz francusko-polski jest trwały i niezachwiany," *Gazeta Polska* (Warsaw), April 23, 1934, 1.

12. "L'impression en U.R.S.S.," *Le Temps* (Paris), January 28, 1934, 3.

13. Quotation from Małgorzata Gmurczyk-Wrońska, "Józef Piłsudski and the Polish-French Alliance (1926–1935)," *Studia z dziejów Rosji i Europy Środkowo-Wschodniej* 54 (special issue) (2019): 78.

14. "Protocol Renewing the Pact of Non-Aggression of July 25, 1932, of May 5, 1934, with the USSR," in Stephan Horak, *Poland's International Affairs, 1919–1960* (Bloomington: Indiana University Press, 1964), 168. For the original, see "Zado-wolenie opinii Z.S.R.R. z przedłużenia paktu nieagresji," *Gazeta Polska* (Warsaw), May 7, 1934, 1.

15. "Minister propagandy Rzeszy Goebbels w Warszawie," *Gazeta Polska,* June 14, 1934, 1.

16. "Goebbels' 'Warm' Welcome: A Fiasco," *Jewish Chronicle* (London), June 22, 1934, 35.

17. See von Moltke's report on the meeting, in Hans von Moltke, German minister in Warsaw, to the German foreign minister, Berlin, June 15, 1934, in *Documents on German Foreign Policy, 1918–1945* (Washington, DC: US Government Printing Office, 1957), series C, 4:1226–1227.

18. "Deklaracja programowa Obozu Narodowo-Radykalnego," Warsaw, April 14, 1934, printed the following day in *ABC* (Warsaw), April 15, 1934, 3. For a reprint of this program, see *Programy partii i stronnictw politycznych w Poslce w latach 1918–1939,* ed. E. Orlof and A. Pasternak (Rzeszów: Wyższa Szkoła Pedagogiczna w Rzeszowie, 1993), 49–50.

19. "Polish Nazis Are Banned," *New York Times,* June 15, 1934, 5.

20. Quotation from Szymon Rudnicki, *Obóz Narodowo-Radykalny: Geneza i działalność* (Warsaw: Czytelnik, 1985), 252. The contents of Mosdorf's words to the interior ministry secretary were reported on in the Polish and foreign press. See *New York Times,* June 19, 1934, 7.

21. "Polish Minister Slain," *New York Times,* June 16, 1934, 6; "Zamordowanie ministra spraw wewnętrznych Bronisława Pierackiego," *Gazeta Polska,* June 16, 1934, 1.

22. "Plot against Polish Cabinet," *Irish Times,* June 19, 1934, 8.

23. Mieczysław Lepecki, *Pamiętnik adiutanta Marszałka Piłsudskiego* (Warsaw: Państwowe Wydawnictwo Naukowe, 1987), 218; *Kalendarium,* 4:367–368. Note

that Pilsudski died less than one year later, in May 1935, but his successors kept the camp operational until the outbreak of World War II in September 1939.

24. Kazimierz Świtalski, diary entry of July 2, 1934, in Świtalski, *Diariusz 1919–1935* (Warsaw: Czytelnik, 1992), 660–663.

25. Rudnicki, *Obóz Narodowo-Radykalny*, 253; "Rozwiązanie O. N. R.," *Robotnik*, July 11, 1934, 1; "Poland Acts to Smother Drive against Jews," *Chicago Daily Tribune*, July 12, 1934, 10.

26. "Sprawa 16 bojowców ukraińskich," *Gazeta Polska*, July 11, 1934, 6; *Robotnik*, July 11, 1934, l.

27. *Times* (London), July 11, 1934, 13.

28. Grzegorz Rossolinski-Liebe, *Stepan Bandera: The Life and Afterlife of a Ukrainian Nationalist* (Stuttgart: Ibidem-Verlag, 2014), 117, 119.

29. Kazimierz Fabrycy, "Komórka specjalna," *Niepodległość* 5 (1955): 217.

30. Ibid., 218.

31. K. Glabisz, "Laboratorium," *Niepodległość* 6 (1958): 155–156.

32. Kazimierz Fabrycy, "Komórka specjalna," *Niepodległość* 5 (1955): 217, 219. On the Laboratory of Fabrycy and its significance, also see Szembek's reoprt of April 12, 1934, in Szembek, *Diariusz i teki*, 1:153–156; Antoni Szymański, *Zły sąsiad: Niemcy 1932–1939 w oświetleniu polskiego attaché wojskowego w Berlinie* (London: Veritas, 1959); Bohdan Urbankowski, *Józef Piłsudski: Marzyciel i strateg* (Poznań: Zysk i S-ka, 2014), 882; Włodzimierz Suleja, *Mundur na nim szary . . . Rzecz o Józefie Piłsudskim* (Warsaw: IPN, 2018), 350; Andrzej Garlicki, *Józef Piłsudski, 1867–1935* (Warsaw: Czytelnik, 1990), 687.

33. Beck, *Final Report*, 77.

34. "Infringements Not Expected, Minister Says," *Jewish Telegraph Agency*, September 17, 1934; "Polish Minorities: M. Beck's Reassurance," *Scotsman*, September 17, 1934, 10.

35. "Poland Repudiates Minorities' Pact; League Is Shocked," *New York Times*, September 14, 1934, 1; "Three Powers Arraign Poland," *Jewish Daily Bulletin* (New York), September 16, 1934, 1. For an English translation of the speech, see "M. Beck's Speech to the League: Uniformity Demanded," *Manchester Guardian*, September 14, 1934, 13.

36. "Another 'Bombshell' at Geneva: Poland and Protection of Minorities," *Scotsman*, September 14, 1934, 9.

37. Dr. J. Thon, "To nie jest afera żydowska, a jednak . . . ," *Nowy Dziennik* (Kraków), September 15, 1934, 1. Thon's article was quoted at length the following day in New York's *Jewish Daily Bulletin*, September 16, 1934, 12. Also see Shoshan Ronen, *A Prophet of Consolation on the Threshold of Destruction: Yehoshua Ozjasz Thon, an Intellectual Portrait* (Warsaw: Dom Wydawniczy Elipsa, 2015), 249–250.

38. "Le roi Alexandre et M. Barthou assassinés à Marseille," *L'Écho de Paris*, October 10, 1934, 1; "Le roi Alexandre I de Yougoslavie et M. Louis Barthou sont

assassinés à Marseille," *Le Temps,* October 11, 1934, 1; "Zamordowanie króla Aleksandra w Marsylji, Minister zabici," *Gazeta Polska,* October 10, 1934, 1; "King Alexander, Barthou Slain," *Washington Post,* October 10, 1934, 1.

39. On Barthou's project to form an Eastern Pact, see Frédéric Dessberg, *Le triangle impossible: Les relations franco-soviétiques et le facteur polonaise dans les questions de sécurité en Europe, 1924–1935* (Brussels: Peter Lang, 2009), 333–350; Henry Rollet, *La Pologne au XX siècle* (Paris: Éditions A. Pedone, 1984), 281–282.

40. F. Słowoj Składkowski, *Strzępy meldunków* (Warsaw: Instytut Badania Najnowszej Hisotii, 1936), 533–534.

41. Kazimierz Świtalski, diary entry of January 31, 1934, in Świtalski, *Diariusz,* 653.

42. Antony Polonsky, *Politics in Independent Poland, 1921–1939* (Oxford: Oxford University Press, 1972), 387.

43. Pilsudska, *Pilsudski,* 342.

44. K. Glabisz, "'Laboratorium': Studia polityczno-wojskowe nad Rosją i Niemcami," *Niepodległość* 6 (1958), quoted in *Kalendarium,* 4:394–395. On Hitler's decrees regarding the German Army, see John W. Wheeler-Bennett, *The Nemesis of Power: The Germany Army in Politics, 1918–1945* (London: Macmillan, 1954), 338; and "Hitler Scraps Versailles Pact, Arms 480,000 Men," *Washington Post,* March 17, 1935, 1.

45. Diary entry, April 2, 1935, in Aleksander Hrynkiewicz, "Dziennik adiutanta Marszałka Józefa Piłsudskiego," *Zeszyty Historyczne* 85 (1988): 104.

46. Beck, *Final Report,* 83–85.

47. Anthony Eden, *The Memoirs of Anthony Eden, Earl of Avon: Facing the Dictators, 1923–1938* (Boston: Houghton Mifflin, 1962), 187–188.

48. Anthony Eden, April 3, 1935, report enclosed in Sir H. Kennard, Warsaw, to Sir J. Simon, April 3, 1935, in *Documents on British Foreign Policy, 1919–1939* (London: Her Majesty's Stationery Office, 1972), ser. 2, vol. 12, reference C, 799.

49. Diary entry of April 2, 1935, in Lepecki, *Pamiętnik,* 288.

50. *New York Times,* April 4, 1935, 17.

51. Pilsudska, *Pilsudski,* 342.

52. Kazimierz Świtalski, diary entry of March 7, 1934, Warsaw, in Świtalski, *Diariusz,* 661.

53. "Marshal Pilsudski: Increase of Salary Refused," *Times of India* (Mumbai), March 29, 1934, 20.

54. Polonsky, *Politics in Independent Poland,* 389–390.

55. "Le Maréchal Pilsudski et mort," *Le Temps* (Paris), May 14, 1935, 1.

56. "Marshal Pilsudski," *Times* (London), May 13, 1935, 17.

57. "Marshal Jozef Pilsudski, Death Late Last Night, the Maker of Modern Poland," *Times* (London), May 13, 1935, 18.

58. President Mościcki, address to the nation, May 12, 1935, in Eric J. Patterson, *Pilsudski: Marshal of Poland* (London: Arrowsmith, 1935), 139–140. Orig. pub. *Gazeta Polska,* May 13, 1935, 2.

59. "500,000 See Pilsudski's Cortege Move to Cathedral," *Chicago Daily Tribune,* May 16, 1935, 10; *Kalendarium,* 4:426.

60. "A Nation in Mourning," *Observer,* May 19, 1935, 17.

61. "Lithuania to Give Poland Body of Pilsudski's Mother," *Chicago Daily Tribune,* May 23, 1935, 16; "Pilsudski's Heart Goes to Birthplace for Honor," *New York Herald Tribune,* May 31, 1935, 13.

62. Mr. Sadowski, "Joseph Pilsudski: The Father of the Polish Republic," address delivered to the US House of Representatives, May 24, 1935, reprinted in *Congressional Record: Proceedings and Debates of the First Session of the Seventy-Fourth Congress of the United States of America,* vol. 79, pt. 8 (Washington: US Government Printing Office, 1935), 8167.

63. Ibid.

64. Antony Polonsky, *The Jews in Poland and Russia* (Oxford: Littman Library of Jewish Civilization, 2012), 3:79.

65. "Two Grodno Stories," April 2007, *L'chaim* (Minsk), https://lechaim.ru/ARHIV/180/karp.htm.

66. "Book of Kielce: History of the Jewish Community of Kielce," 54, JewishGen, https://www.jewishgen.org/Yizkor/kielce/Kie047.html.

67. Memorial Book of Dąbrowa Tarnowska, JewishGen KehilaLinks, https://kehilalinks.jewishgen.org/dabrowa_tarnowska/.

68. USC Shoah Foundation, University of Southern California, oral testimony of Sam Kudewitz (b. 1910), July 11, 1991, West Bloomfield, MI.

69. USC Shoah Foundation, University of Southern California, oral testimony of Stella Faiek (b. 1914), March 6, 1997, Chicago.

70. USC Shoah Foundation, University of Southern California, oral testimony of Hershel Binstock (b. 1911), October 27, 1996, Mayfield Heights, Ohio.

71. Garlicki, *Józef Piłsudski,* 704.

72. M. B. Biskupski, *The History of Poland,* 2nd ed. (Santa Barbara, CA: Greenwood Press, 2018), 82.

73. "Pogrom in a Polish Town: One Jew Killed, Many Wounded," *Manchester Guardian,* June 11, 1935, 9.

74. "Anti-Jewish Riots Spread over Poland; 80 Injured in Week," *Chicago Daily Tribune,* June 13, 1935, 1. The Grodno pogrom has recently received scholarly attention. See Adrei Zamoiski, "Pogrom w Grodnie 7 czerwca 1935," in *Pogromy Żydów na ziemiach polskich w XIX i XX wieku,* ed. Kamil Kijek, Artur Markowski, and Konrad Zieliński (Warsaw: Instytut Historii im. Tadeusza Manteuffla Polskej Akademii Nauk, 2019), 2:371–390; and Jeffrey Koerber, *Borderland Generation: Soviet and Polish Jews under Hitler* (Syracuse, NY: Syracuse University Press, 2020), 85–90.

75. Ilya Karpanko, "Two Grodno Stories," *Lechaim* (April 2007), https://lechaim.ruK/ARHIV/180/karp.htm. Jews commonly referred to Pilsudski as "grandfather."

76. Jolanta Żyndul, *Zajścia antyżydowskie w Polsce w latach 1915–1937* (Warsaw: Fundacja im. K. Kelles-Krauz, 1994), 54–55; Anna Cichopek-Gajraj and Glenn Dynner, "Pogroms in Modern Poland, 1918–1946," in *Pogroms: A Documentary History,* ed. Eugene Avrutin and Elissa Bemporad (Oxford: Oxford University Press, 2021), 193.

77. Józef Beck, speech to the Polish Ministry of Internal Affairs, Warsaw, June 5, 1935, reprinted in Marek Kornat, "Józef Beck o stosunkach polsko-niemieckich," *Zeszyty Historyczne* 137 (2001): 121–125.

78. Polonsky, *Politics in Independent Poland,* 473.

79. Report of June 12, 1935, in Szembek, *Diariusz i teki,* 1:316.

80. Diary entry of March 7, 1938, in Galeazzo Ciao, *Diary, 1937–1943* (New York: Enigma, 2002), 67.

81. Zara Steiner, *The Triumph of the Dark: European International History, 1933–1939* (Oxford: Oxford University Press, 2011), 366; Gerhard L. Weinberg, *Hitler's Foreign Policy, 1933–1939* (New York: Enigma, 2005), 444.

82. Louis Fischer, *Men and Politics: Europe Between the Two World Wars* (New York: Harper Colophon Books, 1946), 290.

83. Wacław Jędrzejewicz, *Wspomnienia* (Wrocław: Ossolineum, 1993), 275.

84. Quotation from Weinberg, *Hitler's Foreign Policy,* 444n63.

85. Diary entry of March 7, 1938, in Ciao, *Diary, 1937–1943,* 67.

86. *Kalendarium,* 4:240.

Epilogue

1. Grade Humphrey, *Poland, the Unexplored* (Indianapolis: Bobbs-Merrill, 1931), 217.

2. Galeazzo Ciano, diary entry of February 28, 1939, Warsaw, in *The Ciano Diaries, 1939–1943,* ed. Hugh Gibson (New York: Doubleday, 1946), 35.

3. Robert M. McBride, *Towns and People of Modern Poland* (New York: R.M. McBridge, 1938), 46.

4. Diary entry from November 1978, in Kazimierz Brandys, *A Warsaw Diary, 1978–1981* (New York: Vintage Books, 1983), 24.

5. Danusza Goska, recollections published in *Front Page Magazine,* July 19, 2019, https://www.frontpagemag.com/fpm/2019/07/banned-facebook-mentioning-t-r-danusha-v-goska/.

6. "Poland Rehabilitates a Date, Celebrating Its 1918 Rebirth," *New York Times,* November 12, 1981, 1.

7. "East Europeans Break Political Taboos," *Christian Science Monitor,* September 12, 1988, 1.

8. "Polish Strongman Haunts Campaign: Political Ads Dwell Fondly on Pilsudski, a Marshal Who Imposed Order in '20s," *New York Times,* November 26, 1990, 9.

9. Ibid.

10. Adam Michnik, *In Search of Lost Meaning: The New Eastern Europe* (Berkeley: University of California Press, 2011), 43.

11. Mikołaj Mirowski and Jan Rojewski, "Podkulturowe odcienie Piłsudskiego," *Tygodnik Powszechny* no. 9 (2018), reprinted in *Piłsudski [nie] znany: Historia i popkultura,* ed. Mikołaj Mirowski (Warsaw: Muzeum Historii Polski, 2018), 256.

12. "Speech by President Donald Tusk," November 10, 2018, https://www .consilium.europa.eu/en/press/press-releases/2018/11/10/speech-by-president -donald-tusk-november-11-2018-poland-and-europe-two-anniversaries-two -lessons/.

13. Dr. Iwona Korga, New York, August 13, 2020, letter to the author.

14. Quotation from Roman Wolczuk, *Ukraine's Foreign and Security Policy, 1991– 2000* (London: Routladge, 2003), 73; Karol Kujawa and Monika Byrska, "Poland and Ukraine," in *2014 Crisis in Ukraine: Perspectives, Reflections, International Reverberations,* ed. K. Kujawa and V. Morkva (Gliwice, Poland: Aslan, 2015), 4.

15. Piotr Wandycz, "Śmierć prezydenta," *Tygodnik Powszechny* (Kraków), November 4, 1990, 2.

16. Adolf Nowaczyński, "Testament," *Myśl Narodowa,* January 6, 1923, quotation from Paul Brykczynski, *Primed for Violence: Murder, Antisemitism, and Democratic Politics in Interwar Poland* (Madison: University of Wisconsin Press, 2016), 123–124.

17. Quotation in Michnik, *In Search of Lost Meaning,* 43.

18. Władysław Pobóg-Malinowski, *Najnowsza Historia Polityczna Polski, 1864– 1945,* vol. 2: *1914–1939* (London, 1963; repr., Warsaw: Wydawnictwo Antyk Marcin Dybowski, 2000), 761, quoted in Michnik, *In Search of Lost Meaning,* 43.

19. Joseph Rothschild, *Piłsudski's Coup d'État* (New York: Columbia University Press, 1966), 370–371.

20. Anatol Muhlstein, *Le Maréchal Pilsudski* (Paris : Librairie Plon, 1939), 340.

Acknowledgments

After many years conducting research in archives and libraries, as well as discussing the topic of Pilsudski with a host of individuals, I would like to take this opportunity to express my gratitude. Scholars, writers, and museum curators who generously answered queries during the course of my research and writing include Ivan Berend, Winson Chu, Andrzej Chwalba, the late Janusz Cisek, Isabella Davioin, Frédéric Dessberg, Paweł Duber, Glenn Dynner, James Felak, Tomek Frydel, Konstanty Gebert, Jack Jacobs, Nicole Jordan, Martyna Rusiniak-Karwat, Valérié Drechster-Kayser, Mario Kessler, Audrey Kichelewski, Marek Kornat, Roman Koropeckyj, Dominic Lieven, Magdalena Macińska, Margaret MacMillan, Paul Robert Magocsi, Artur Markowski, Małgorzata Mazurek, Daria Nałęcz, Andrzej Nowak, Piotr Nowak, Grzegorz Nowik, Andrzej Paczkowski, Brian Porter-Szucs, Moshe Rosman, Szymon Rudnicki, Artur Tanikowski, Theodore Weeks, Mariusz Wołos, and Konrad Zielinski. I am also grateful to Antony Polonsky, Piotr Wróbel, my late mother, Lorraine Zimmerman, and my wife, Anna Gross, for reading various chapters and giving valuable comments.

A special thanks to Andrzej Kaminski for inviting me to the manuscript workshop at the Jagiellonian University in Kraków in the summers of 2018 and 2020. Both in the setting of Kraków and later in a virtual meeting, a panel of experts analyzed my manuscript and provided detailed, invaluable feedback. A huge thank you to those participants: Jan Jacek Bruski, Yaroslav Hrytsak, Adam Kożuchowski, Daria Nałęcz, Andrzej Nowak, and Marek Wierzbicki. The initiator for my participation in the Kraków manuscript workshop was my editor at Harvard University Press, Kathleen McDermott. From conceptualization to completion, Kathleen supported my project wholeheartedly while applying her extraordinary literary talents not only to strengthening the ideas laid out in the biography but in sharpening and tightening the prose.

Many librarians and archivists helped me find rare materials. These include Shuli Berber, Hallie Cantor, Zvi Erenyi, Paul Glassman, Shulamit Hes, Edith Lubetski, and John Moryl of Yeshiva University Library; Ettie Goldwasser, Leo Greenbaum, Marek Web, and Vital Zajka of the Yivo Institute Library; Iwona Korga, president of the Jozef Pilsudski Institute of America; Irena Czernichowska and Chad E. Noyes of the Hoover Institution Archives at Stanford University; Joanna Jaśkowiec of the Jagiellonian University archives in Kraków; Magdalena Święch and Piotr Wilkosz, photo archivists at the National Museum in Kraków; and Ian Beilin of Columbia University Library. I would also like to thank the art director at Yeshiva University, Emily Scherer Steinberg, for her generous help with some of the images. Others deserving mention include Grzegorz Krzywiec, Maciej Moszyński, and Izabela Wagner, who provided me with some archival documents on the 1922 Narutowicz assassination; and Joanna and Janusz Onyszkiewicz, who allowed me access to their Solidarity-era clandestine publications on Pilsudski and also helped me construct the Pilsudski family tree.

As I went through and analyzed thousands of documents in foreign languages, mostly in Polish, several individuals helped me render words and phrases in English. They include Bruce Alderman, Julian Bussgang, Jeffrey Freedman, Inna Kapilevich, Hadassah Kosak, and Filip Mazurczak, and I thank them all.

These acknowledgments would not be complete without thanking my wife, Anna, for lovingly caring for our children during the endless hours I was tucked away in libraries and archives and at conferences abroad, researching and writing. Without her support, the publication of this book would not have been possible.

Illustration Credits

24 Reproduced from *Wilno i ziemia wileńska* (Vilna: Wydawnictwo Wojewódzkiego Komitetu Regionalnego, 1930), I:44.

27 From the archives of the Jozef Pilsudski Institute of America, Brooklyn, NY, Record Group 151—photographic collection.

36 Reproduced from Aleksandra and Andrzej Garlicki, *Józef Piłsudski* (Warsaw: Kancelaria Sejmu, 1993).

37 Geneanet.org.

47 Reproduced from Aleksandra and Andrzej Garlicki, *Józef Piłsudski* (1993).

54 Reproduced from W. Suleja, *Marszałek Piłsudski* (Wrocław: Wydawnictwo Dolnoslaskie, 2001).

56 Reproduced from Aleksandra and Andrzej Garlicki, *Józef Piłsudski* (1993).

62 Reproduced from Joanna Wieliczka-Szarkowa, *Józef Piłsudski, 1867–1935* (Kraków: Wydawnictwo AA s.c., 2015), 37.

78 *Ilustrowany Tygodnik Polski* / Wikimedia.

111 Reproduced from Aleksandra and Andrzej Garlicki, *Józef Piłsudski* (1993).

139 Reproduced from Aleksandra and Andrzej Garlicki, *Józef Piłsudski* (1993).

146 Reproduced from S. Svistun, ed., *Sankt-Peterburgskaia psikhiatricheskaia bol'nitsa sv. Nikolaia Chudotvortsa: k 140-letiiu* (St. Petersburg: IPK Kosta, 2012), I:6.

188 Fundacja Rodziny Józefa Piłsudskiego / Muzeum Józefa Piłsudskiego.

194 Reproduced from W. Jędrzejewicz and J. Cisek, *Kalendarium życia Józefa Piłsudskiego, 1867–1935* 3rd ed. (2006), I:89.

198 Reproduced from Aleksandra and Andrzej Garlicki, *Józef Piłsudski* (1993).

214 Reproduced from Aleksandra and Andrzej Garlicki, *Józef Piłsudski* (1993).

225 Reproduced from *Jew, Pole, Legionary, 1914–1920*, ed. Artur Tanikowski (Warsaw: Museum of the History of Polish Jews, 2014), 130.

236 Reproduced from Filip Żelewski, *Piłsudczana w zbiorach Muzeum Niepodległości w Warszawie* (Warsaw: Muzeum Niepodległości, 2018).

248 Reproduced from *History of the Statute of Kalisz Issued by Boleslaus the Pious in 1264 and Its Illustration by Arthur Szyk in the Years 1926–1928*, ed. M. Fuks (Kraków: Jagiellonian University, 2017), 32.

254 Reproduced from *Sztuka Legionów Polskich,* ed. Alina Jurkiewicz-Zejdowska and Piotr Wilkosz (Kraków: National Museum in Kraków, 2017), 8–9. Photograph by Stanisław Starzewski.

Index